Based on

NIELIT 'O' Level Revised Syllabus of year 2020 for M1-R5
'O' Level *made simple* MODULE -1

IT TOOLS and Network Basics

(Also covers syllabus for A1-R5 paper of NIELIT 'A' Level Examination)

by
Satish Jain

B.Sc., B.E.(IISc), M.E.(IISc), M.Tech.(IIT Kanpur),
Wing Commander (Retd.)
Ex-Professor of Information Technology,
Institute of Information Technology & Management
GGS Indraprastha University, Delhi.

M.Geetha

B.Com. Dipl. Computer Science

Dedicated to

Sri Raja Rajeshwari and Sri Sai Baba
Whose blessings overcome all hurdles in life

PREFACE

The objective of 'O' Level made simple Module-1 (M1-R5) is to meet the growing need of students learning the Information Technology and basic networks. It is observed that most of the books available in the market do not cater to the specific needs of beginners who wish to undergo professional courses in this emerging field. `O' Level Module-1 (M1-R5) course is quite comprehensive. It needs a thorough study of both commerce and computer science. For this reason, we have used all our teaching experience and theoretical knowledge in Information Technology and basic network in bringing out this book to meet the requirements of the students appearing in this examination.

The book is divided into nine chapters. Each chapter covers specific topic as per the syllabus outlined by NIELIT. Each chapter contains diagrams and screens are used to explain each concept clearly. It is hoped, that a person with some understanding of elementary English language would be able to use this book and work on a personal computer (PC) for Internet access, word processing using Word, Spreadsheet, and create presentations using PowerPoint. This book will be able to generate interest in using PC for letter writing, sending e-mails, and send instant messaging via WhatsApp, Facebook Messenger, and Telegram. It also discusses the latest trends of e-governance services such as railway reservation, passport, and e-hospital.

The last two chapter contains Application of Digital Financial Services. This chapter talks in particular on, how to use Internet for digital financial services such as saving, banking service, Bank on mobile, and wallets, and the final chapter contains Future Skills and Cyber Security.

A set of solved and Uusolved papers are also included to enable you to get a feel of thequestions likely to be asked in the examinations.

We shall feel obliged if you send us your critical opinion regarding the presentations,readability, and coverage in this book.We request you to mail their your suggestions, if any, toimprove the subject matter. The suggestions may be e-mailed to Sales@bpbonline.com.

Date: 25th February 2020 **Authors**

Table of Contents

CHAPTER 1

Introduction to Computer

Structure

- What is a computer?
- Computer and latest IT gadgets Intelligence in our daily lives
- Evolution of computers and its applications
- Basics of hardware and software
- Central Processing Unit
- Input output devices
- Computer memory and storage
- Mobile Apps

Objectives

After completing this chapter, the readers will be able to:

- Identify computers IT gadgets, and explain their evolution and applications.
- Get familiar with various input, output and hardware components of a computer along with storage devices.
- Get familiar with various types of software and utilities used for computer and mobile apps.

Now-a-days, computers have become an integral part of our lives. Ever since its invention, the power of the computer is growing rapidly. Strangely enough, the cost of hardware has been declining by the year. A large number of application software packages are now available that make computers highly productive, versatile and easy to use.

What is Computer?

The word *computer* comes from the word compute, which means to calculate. So, a computer is normally considered to be a calculating device that can perform arithmetic operations at an enormous speed. But more accurately, the computer may be defined as a device that operates upon data.

A computer is an electronic device which processes given data to derive the required and useful information. During the process, the computer has to perform various functions, like accepting data from the input, processing it into useful information and storing it away for safekeeping or late use. The concept of generating output information from the input four data is also referred to as input-process-output concept, as shown in *Figure 1.1*:

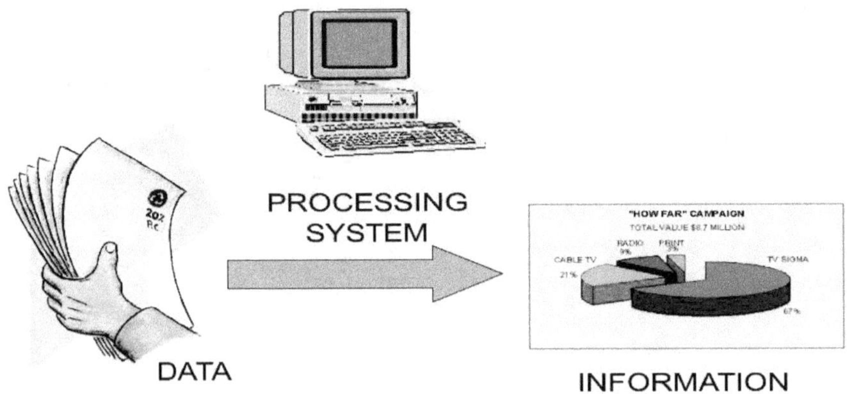

Figure 1.1: *Input-Output-Process of computer*

A computer performs five major operations or functions, irrespective of its size and make. These are:

- It accepts data or instructions as input.
- It stores data and instruction.
- It processes data as per the instructions.
- It controls all the operations taking place inside a computer.
- It gives results in form of output.

Computers work through an interaction of hardware and software. Now, before proceeding further, there are few terms that we need to understand:

- **Data:** Raw facts or figures that need to be processed.
- **Information:** Meaningful data which is processed, organized and presented in an understandable form.
- **Instruction:** Command that tells the computer what to do.
- **Processing:** Sequence of action taken on data to convert it into information.
- **Hardware:** The physical components of a computer.
- **Program:** The instructions that tell the computer what to do, either in sequential or non-sequential manner.
- **Software:** A collection of related instructions organized for a common purpose is referred to as software.

An electronic device designed to accept data, perform mathematical and logical operations at a high speed, and display the results of these operations.

The two basic types of computers are as follows:

- Analog Computers
- Digital Computers

Analog Computers

Analog computer is that computer which is used to process change continuously varying data. This changeable continuous data is called analog data. It can be used in scientific and industrial applications such as measuring the electrical current, frequency and resistance of capacitor, and so on. Examples of analog computer are temperature, pressure, frequency of signal, voltage, and so on.

Digital Computers

A computer that represents discrete information by numerical digits is called a digital computer. It uses a binary number system and thus it can understand *only 0 and 1*. Examples of a digital computer are IBM PC, the Apple Macintosh as well as modern smartphones.

Advantages of Using Computers

The advantages of using computers have the following reasons:

- **Speed:** Computers have the ability to perform routine tasks at a greater speed than human beings. It can perform millions of calculations in seconds.
- **Accuracy:** It is used to perform tasks in a way that ensures accuracy.
- **Storage:** It can store large amount of information. Any item of data or any

instruction stored in the memory can be retrieved by the computer at any time it is needed.

- **Automation:** It can be instructed to perform complex tasks automatically (which increases the productivity).
- **Diligence:** It can perform the same task repeatedly and with the same accuracy without getting tired.
- **Versatility:** They are flexible to perform both simple and complex tasks.
- **Cost effectiveness:** It reduces the amount of paper work and human effort, thereby reducing costs.

Limitations of Computers

The limitations of using computers have the following reasons:

- **Lack of common sense:** A computer cannot think for itself. It has no self-intelligence.
- **Memory without brain:** Computer can store data in its memory. However, if a wrong instruction is provided, it does not have a brain to correct the wrong instructions.
- **Slavery:** A computer is a slave; it cannot execute the program by itself. It requires instructions to execute the program and generate information.

Computer and Latest IT Gadgets

The computer is an electronic device, operating under the control of instructions stored in its own memory, that can accept data, process the data according to specified rules, produce results, and store the results for future use. Similarly, smartphones and tablets are indeed considered computers. Typically, with a smartphone and tablet, input is provided using a touch screen interface and the output is seen on a screen.

Desktop computers, laptops, smartphones, and tablets have a lot in common. They all contain a CPU, memory and display functionality, and use an operating system that runs programs (apps) to perform different functions.

Evolution of Computer and its Applications

The evolution of computer started from the 16th century and resulted in the form that we see today.

The present-day computer, however, has also undergone rapid change during the last 50 years. The period during which the evolution of computer took place can be divided into *five phases*, based on the major technological development that basically changed the way computers operate. These phases are known as *Generations of Computer*.

First Generation (1940-1956)

The period of the first generation was 1940-1956 and the main features are:

- **Hardware Technology:** It used *vacuum tubes* as the basic components for memory and circuitry for CPU. Input was based on punched cards and paper tapes, and output was displayed on printouts, as shown in *Figure 1.2:*

Figure 1.2: *Vacuum Tube*

- **Software Technology:** The instructions were written in machine language, and it used 0s and 1s for coding.
- **Examples:** *Universal Automatic Computer (UNIVAC), Electronic Numerical Integrator and Computer (ENIAC), and Electronic Discrete Variable Automatic Computer (EDVAC).*

The main characteristics are as follows:

- Used vacuum tubes for circuitry
- Electron emitting metal in vacuum tubes burned out easily
- Size of machines was big
- Very expensive
- Generated lot of heat so it needed air conditioning
- Consumed lot of electricity
- Required large amounts of energy for processing
- Not reliable

- Used mostly for scientific applications
- Used magnetic tapes
- Used Machine language and had limited primary memory

Second Generation (1956-1963)

The period of the second generation was 1956-1962 and the main features are:

- **Hardware Technology: Transistors** replaced vacuum tubes. They allowed computers to become smaller, faster, cheaper, more energy efficient and reliable. Magnetic cores were used as the primary memory and magnetic tape and disks as secondary storage devices, as shown in *Figure 1.3:*

Figure 1.3: *Transistor*

- **Software Technology:** High-level programming languages like **FORTRAN** and **COBAL** were used.
- **Examples:** IBM 7094, CDC 1604 and UNIVAC LARC, Honeywell 400 and Mark III.

The main characteristics are as follows:

- Used transistors
- Faster and more reliable than first generation systems
- Smaller and cheaper
- Less expensive compared to G1 computer
- Needed lower power consumption
- Portable
- Required less maintenance than the first-generation computer
- Introduced assembly language and operating system software
- Used for scientific and commercial purposes

Third Generation (1964-1971)

The period of third generation was 1964-1971 and the main features are:

- **Hardware Technology: Integrated Circuits (ICs)** were used in place of transistors. A single IC has many transistors, registers and capacitors on a single silicon chip. The use of IC chip increased the speed and the efficiency of the computer and manifold, as shown in *Figure 1.4:*

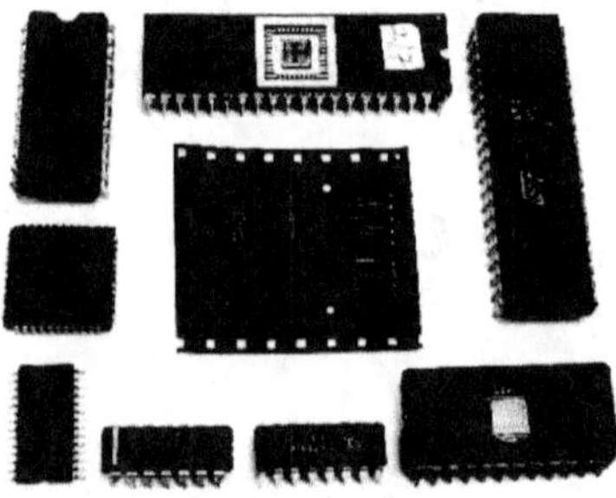

Figure 1.4: *Integrated Circuit*

- **Software Technology:** Multi-programming operating systems were used. High-level programming languages such as **FORTRAN, COBOL, Pascal** and **BASIC** were used.
- **Examples:** IBM System 360/370, PDP-8/11 (Personal Data Processor) and CDC 6600.

The main characteristics are as follows:

- Used ICs and parallel processing
- Smaller in size and faster
- Lower power consumption and generated less heat
- Easy to operate
- Supported high-level language
- Input device introduced, which made it easier for the user to interact with the computer
- Used for scientific, commercial and interactive online applications

Fourth Generation (1972-2010)

The period of fourth generation was 1972-2010 and the main features are:

- **Hardware Technology:** They used the **Large Scale Integration (LSI)** and the **Very Large Scale Integration (VLSI)** technology. Thousands of transistors are on a small silicon chip using the LSI technology. VLSI allows hundreds of thousands of components to be integrated in a small chip. Microcomputers came into existence and gave rise to personal computers in this generation. In this generation, time sharing, real-time networks and distributed operating systems were used. You can also find the development of pointing devices and handheld devices, as shown in *Figure 1.5:*

Figure 1.5: *Microprocessor*

- **Software Technology:** Operating Systems like *MS-DOS* and *MS-Windows* were developed during this time. It also supported the Graphical User Interface. It is a user-friendly interface that allows users to interact with the computer through menus and icons. Programs are written in high-level programming languages, such as **C**, **C++** and **DBASE**.
- **Examples:** VAX 9000, PDP 11, CRAY-1, 2 (Super computer) and CRAY-X-MP.

The main characteristics are as follows:
- Used CPUs which contained thousands of transistors
- Much smaller and fitted on a desk, palms and laps
- Very high speed of processing, accurate, reliable, diligent and versatile
- Great developments in the field of networks
- For general purpose
- More external storage mediums were introduced like CD-ROM and DVD-ROM
- Used for commercial and network applications

Fifth Generation (2010- Present)

The period of fifth generation was 2010 and the main features are:

- **Hardware Technology:** Fifth generation uses **Ultra Large Scale Integration (ULSI)** chips. Millions of transistors are placed in a single IC in ULSI chips. The use of parallel processing and super conductors is helping to make artificial intelligence a reality.
- **Software Technology:** Programming is done in high-level programming languages such as **Java**, **Python** and **C#**.
- Examples: IBM notebook, Pentium PCs, SUN Workstations and PARAM 10000.

The main characteristics are as follows:
- Portable computers, powerful, cheaper, reliable and easier to use desktop machines
- Development of true artificial intelligence
- Development of natural parallel processing
- More user-friendly interfaces with multimedia features
- Used for commercial, interactive online multimedia (that is, graphics, audio, video) and network applications

IT Gadgets and their Applications

Gadget is a device or an application for information technology. It is a term that covers all available devices, such as television sets, cell phones, personal computers and tablets. The devices are used in business, education, communication, healthcare and entertainment to communicate with each other in the digital world through specially-designed applications. You can use a computer for different applications by changing various kinds of software packages.

The following are some of the IT devices:
- Laptops and Notebooks
- Personal Digital Assistants (PDAs)
- Tablet Personal Computer (PC)

Laptops and Notebooks

A laptop computer is a portable, personal computer often designed to fit on your lap and hence the name is given to it. It can operate on batteries or a power supply or both. It can be carried in your suitcase easily. *Figure 1.6* depicts a laptop model.

Figure 1.6: *A Laptop Model*

A notebook is a smaller and lighter version of the laptop model.

PDAs (Personal Digital Assistants)

Personal Digital Assistant (PDA) is a handheld computer and popularly known as a **palmtop**. It has a touch screen and a memory card for storage of data, as shown in *Figure 1.7*. It provides personal information management functions, such as a calendar, an appointment book, an address book, a calculator and a notepad.

Figure 1.7: *PDA*

Tablet PC

Tablet Computers are commonly shortened as Tablet PCs and are defined as flat, thin mobile computers that come fitted with a touchscreen display. Tablets come installed with applications that perform all kind of tasks. The **two operating systems** used with tablets are **Apple iOS** which is used with iPads and Google Android which is used with Android tablets. *Figure 1.8* depicts a Tablet PC.

Figure 1.7: *PDA*

Uses of Computer

The use of computers on a daily basis in our life is very important. Technically, in daily life, a computer is used to convert raw facts and data into meaningful information. From the government to the private sector, everyone is using the computer. Users of the computer are constantly growing, as shown in *Figure 1.9*:

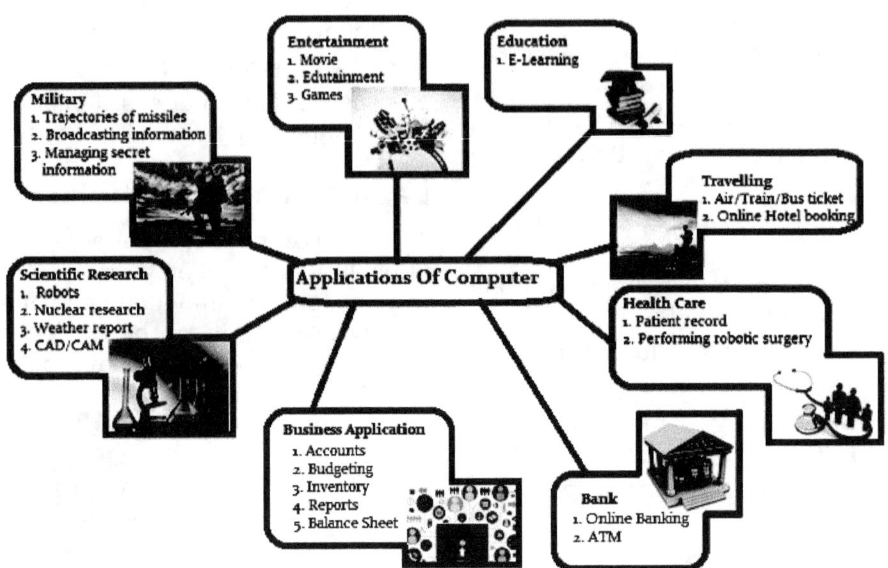

Figure 1.9: *Picture Showing Different fields where Computer can be employed*

The uses of computer are discussed below:

- **Scientific Research:** There are various computer applications used in scientific research such as data storage, data analysis, instrumentation control and knowledge sharing. The speed and the accuracy of computer is enabled in scientific analysis has to be carried out very fast. Computers are now an integral part of teaching techniques in Universities and research institutes. Without computers, researchers find themselves in a very difficult situation to carry out their studies.

- **Office Management:** Almost every organization (business or non-business) is moving towards making paperless office, so computers are widely used today.

- **Internet:** It is a network of computers in the world. You can browse through much more information than you could do in a library. That is because computers can store enormous amounts of information. You can also have very fast and convenient access to information. Through e-mail, you can communicate with a person sitting thousands of miles away in seconds.

- **Books Publishing:** With desktop publishing, you can create page layouts for a multitude of books on your personal computer. Now-a-days, newspapers and magazines/books are designed using DTP and are printed at one place and distributed so that you can get them every morning.

- **Computers in Medicine:** You can diagnose diseases. You can learn the cures. Software is used in magnetic resonance imaging to examine the internal organs of the human body. It is used for performing surgery. Computers are used to store patients' data.

- **Mathematical Calculations:** Thanks to computers, which have computing speeds of over a million calculations per second, you can perform the biggest of mathematical calculations.

- **Banks:** All financial transactions are done by computer software programs. They provide **security**, **speed** and **convenience**. The use of a computer has allowed the banks to improve many of the facilities offered by them. One can use the Automated Teller Machines (ATM) to deposit and withdraw cash **24 hours** a day, throughout the year.

- **Travel:** One can book air tickets or railway tickets and make hotel reservations online. It reduces the time wastage and travel time for everyone.

- **Telecommunications:** All mobile phones have software embedded in them for maintaining customer details, and also sending messages, audio and video. Now-a-days, Internet is available in the mobile phone itself.

- **Defense:** There is software embedded in almost every weapon. Software is used for controlling the flight and targeting in ballistic missiles. It is used to control access to atomic bombs.

- **E-learning:** Instead of a book, it is easier to learn from an e-learning software. It not only contains text, but also images and animations. So, it is very easy to understand everything.

- **Examinations:** You can give online exams and get instant results. You can check your examination results online.

- **Computers in Business:** Shops and supermarkets use software, which calculates the bills. Taxes can be calculated and paid online. Accounting is done using computers. Software is used in major stock markets. One can do trading online.

- **Entertainment:** Movies, animation films, advertisement in newspapers, TVs, and so on use computers extensively. The entertainment industry uses computer even to plan the production of movies as well as to create various special effects.

- **Communication:** Use of e-mail or electronic mail to send long messages, reports, and so on to many persons all over the world for a very low price.

- **Accounting:** Specialized programs, such as Tally.ERP 9, are available to handle company financial accounts and inventory management.

Basics of Hardware and Software

Let's discuss the concept of hardware and software in brief.

Hardware

The physical parts of a computer are called hardware. There are many different kinds of hardware components that can be installed inside and connected to the outside of a computer. Examples of hardware components are motherboard, microprocessors, ICs, hard disks, floppy disks, optical disks, monitors, keyboard, printer, and computer projector.

Figure 1.10 shows the five major building blocks or functional units of a digital computer system. These five units correspond to the *five basic operations*, namely *input unit, storage unit, central processing unit, output unit,* which further includes Arithmetic unit, and control unit carried out by all computer systems.

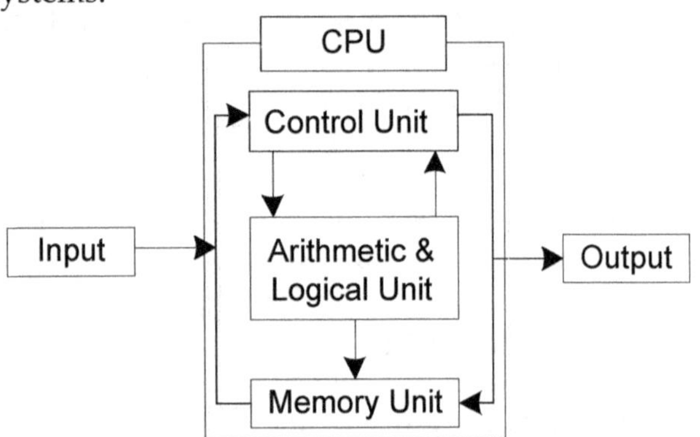

Figure 1.10: *Block diagram of computer system*

The four operations are:

- **Input:** Sending the data to the computer is known as input.
- **Storage:** A place to save a result inside or outside the computer is known as storage.
- **Output:** The result displayed by the computer is known as output.
- **Processing:** The task of processing operations like arithmetic and logical operations is called processing. The CPU takes data and instructions from the storage unit and makes all sorts of calculations based on the instructions given and the type of provided. It is then sent back to storage unit. CPU includes ALU and CU.

Central Processing Unit (CPU)

The central processing unit (CPU), also known as a **microprocessor**, acts as the brain of the computer. It controls most of the machine's operations and carries out commands. Instructions are sent to the CPU by pressing a key, clicking the mouse, or starting an application or file.

A microprocessor contains a **Control Unit** and an **Arithmetic and Logic Unit (ALU)**. When main memory is added to a microprocessor, it becomes the CPU.

The major sections of the CPU are:
- Primary Storage Unit
- ALU
- Control Unit

Primary Memory

This is also called as **Main Memory**. Before the actual processing starts, the data and the instructions fed to the computer through the input units are stored in this primary storage unit. Similarly, the data which is to be output from the computer system is also temporarily stored in the primary memory. It is also the area where intermediate results of calculations are stored. The main memory has the storage section that holds the computer programs during execution. Thus, the primary unit:

- Stores data and programs during actual processing.
- Stores temporary results of intermediate processing.
- Stores results of execution temporarily.

Arithmetic Logic Unit (ALU)

Arithmetic and logic unit is the part of the CPU, where all the processing jobs are performed. The two types of operations are performed inside the ALU, namely, **arithmetic operation** and **logical operation**. Arithmetic operations mean calculations like addition, subtraction, multiplication and division on data. Similarly, logical operations mean comparison of data like equal to, greater than, less than and not equal.

All the operations are by ALU under directions of the control unit. Once the data enters into memory, the data necessary for processing is transferred into the ALU. When processing completes, the data is again transferred back into the memory unit. This transfer of data from the memory unit to the ALU is done under the directions of control unit. After the completion of processing, the final results, which are stored in the memory unit, are released to an output device.

Control Unit (CU)

This unit is responsible for controlling the entire working of the computer. The timing and control signals are generated by this unit and sent to other units for execution of the program for proper control. It also controls the transfer of data between memory and input/output devices.

Input Devices

Input device is a hardware device that sends data and instructions to the computer. These devices are discussed below.

Mouse

A mouse is a **pointing device**. It is held in one hand and is moved across a flat surface. *Figure 1.11* shows a latest type of mouse.

Figure 1.11: *Mouse*

The mouse can be used to select text, icons, files and folders and to draw diagrams, etc., on the monitor screen. Once you have moved the pointer to an icon, folder, or other object, clicking or double clicking that object opens the document or executes the program.

One type of mouse uses a rolling ball, while others use optical sensing techniques. They are linked to the PC by using a cable or by using infrared light. A typical mouse has **two** or **three buttons**. What the mouse buttons do depend on the application program running in your PC. In some systems, it is also possible to specify independent functions to the buttons.

Techniques for Using a Mouse

Five essential techniques for using a mouse are discussed below:

- **Pointing:** It means to move the cursor to the icon or a menu item.
- **Clicking:** It means to press and release the left mouse button once.
- **Double clicking:** It means to press and release the left mouse button twice in rapid succession.
- **Dragging:** It means to hold the left mouse button as you move the pointer.
- **Right clicking:** It means to press and release the right mouse button.

Advantages of a Mouse

The following are some of the advantages of a mouse:

- It can be installed without any installation software.
- The mouse gives the computer user the freedom to move cursors in any direction.
- It performs various tasks, such as opening a file or moving a folder.

Disadvantages of a Mouse

The following are some of the disadvantages of a mouse:

- Unlike the arrows on a keyboard, which force the user to a limited set of directions, they move the pointer in all directions.
- They need a flat surface or else they won't function.
- A mouse cannot easily be used with a laptop or a note book or palmtop computers.

A mouse can be connected to a computer system in one of the following ways:

- Using a serial port
- A bus connection
- PS/2 mouse port
- USB port
- Wireless

Let us read these different types of mouse connections in detail.

- **Serial Mouse:** A serial port is the most common method of connecting a mouse. A serial mouse is connected to either a **COM1** or **COM2 port**, i.e. to any one of the available serial ports on the computer. Connecting a serial mouse is very easy as one needs to just plug in the connector attached to the mouse wire to the vacant serial port on the PC.
- **Bus Mouse:** Difference between a bus mouse and a serial mouse is this. A serial mouse is connected to a serial port, whereas the bus mouse is connected to a special board made just for the mouse.
- **PS/2 Port Mouse:** This method is similar to the bus mouse approach, except that the mouse control circuitry is directly built into the motherboard of the PC and not connected to a separate card.

- **USB Mouse:** The USB port can be used to connect a mouse. As the mouse is not required during power on/bootup process, no special BIOS is required for handling USB mouse.
- **Wireless Mouse:** In this type of mouse, everything is similar to the conventional mouse, except that no cable is used to connect the mouse to the computer system.

Keyboard

The keyboard is a device through which you can enter data or instructions in a computer and it is known as an input device. It looks like a **typewriter**. It contains multiple keys. When a key is pressed, an electronic signal is produced, which is detected by an electronic circuit called keyboard encoder *(See Figure 1.12)*.

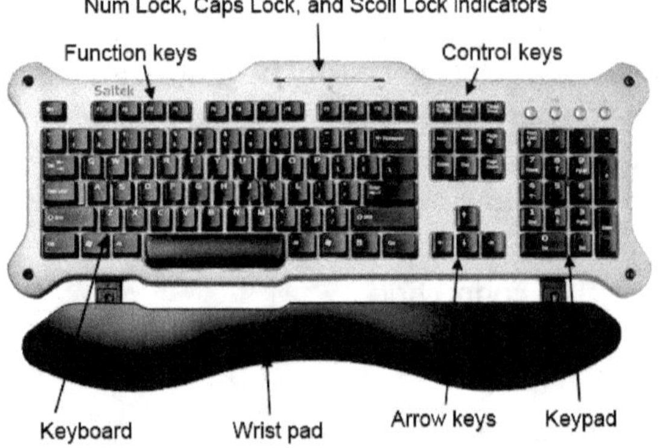

Figure 1.12: *Keyboard Depicting Different Keys*

At the top of the keyboard are function keys (F1 to F2). Their functions depend upon the program being run. F1 key is used to get help from the program

Advantages of a Keyboard

The following are some of the advantages of a keyboard:
- Keyboards have special keys that perform specific functions.
- Instead of using the mouse to move the cursor, you can use the arrow key situated on the keyboard to move the cursor on the monitor.
- Keyboard is less expensive.
- Available in variety of formats

Disadvantages of a Keyboard

The following are some of the disadvantages of a keyboard:
- Very slow while moving windows or other objects.

- Not much useful for enlarging or changing sizes of windows on screen.
- Not entering some specific type of data, for example, pictures, games, and so on.

Joystick

A Joystick is an input device that is used to control the movement of the cursor or other graphic elements of video games. It has a spherical ball at its lower end as well as at its upper end, as shown in *Figure 1.13*. The lower spherical ball moves in a socket. The joystick can be moved **right** or **left**, **forward** or **backward**. The electronic circuitry inside the joystick detects and measures the displacement of the joystick from its central position. This information is sent to the processor.

Figure 1.13: *Joystick*

Advantages of a Joystick

The following are some of the advantages of a joystick:
- It gives the user the feeling of a more realistic action.
- It moves an object in any direction.
- It is easier to hold than a mouse.

Disadvantages of a Joystick

The following are some of the disadvantages of a joystick:
- It is limited to certain appliances.
- A mouse is better and easier in controlling on-screen pointers.

Light Pen

A light pen is a computer input device. It is a light-sensitive computer input that completely looks like a writing pen. It is used to select text, draw images, and interacts with user interface elements on a monitor, as shown in *Figure 1.14*:

Figure 1.14: *Light Pen*

Advantages of a Light Pen

The following are some of the advantages of a light pen:

- The light pen allows you to select any object on the display screen directly.
- It does not need any screen coating.
- It is very useful for fine selection and drawing.
- It is more reliable than a touch screen.
- It is small in size.

Disadvantages of a Light Pen

The following are some of the disadvantages of a light pen:

- The light pen requires picking it to use.
- It does not work with LDC screens.
- It works only with CRT based screens.
- It works on detecting the brightness.
- It is not very accurate while drawing.
- It is sensitive to dust that can interfere with IR beams.

Touch Screen

A touch screen is a computer display screen that is sensitive to human touch, allowing a user to interact with the computer by touching pictures or words on the screen. Touch screens are used with information kiosks, computer-based training devices, and systems designed to help individuals who have difficulty in manipulating a mouse or keyboard, as shown in *Figure 1.15*:

Figure 1.15: *Touch Screen*

Advantages of a Touch Screen

The following are some of the advantages of a touch screen:

- Easy to use — intuitive, don't need much training.
- No extra peripherals, such as a mouse.
- It is the main interface on smart phones and tablet computers.
- The use of finger gestures to make sophisticated actions such as zooming and selecting.
- Selecting and controlling apps that have been designed with a touch screen.

Disadvantages of a Touch Screen

The following are some of the disadvantages of a touch screen:

- Not suitable for inputting large amount of data.
- Not very accurate; selecting objects can be difficult with fingers.
- Tiring to use for long time.
- Screen can get very dirty with constant touching.

Graphics Tablet

A graphics tablet is a graphic input device that functions like a drawing tablet. The user makes contact with the graphic tablet with a device called a **cursor**, which is a pen-like instrument that is connected to the tablet by a wire or without wires, as shown in *Figure 1.16*. For sketching, the user draws with the tablet cursor, and the screen cursor "draws" a corresponding image. For tracing an existing image, the screen cursor is often not required.

Figure 1.16: *Graphics Tablet*

Advantages of Graphics Tablet

The following are some of the advantages of graphics tablet:

- It is much more natural to draw a diagram with a pencil type implement (the stylus) rather than with a mouse.
- A great level of accuracy can be achieved.
- It can work on an LCD screen on the tablet face.
- It quickly attaches to the computer through the USB cable.

Disadvantages of Graphics Tablet

The following are some of the disadvantages of graphics tablet:

- Not really suitable for general selection work, such as pointing and clicking on menu items.
- Graphics tablets are much more expensive than a mouse.

Microphone

A Microphone is an example of a transducer, a device which converts energy from one form to another. It converts acoustical energy (sound waves) into electrical energy (the audio signal). There are plenty of types of microphones, all representing different ways of converting sound into signal. Each type of microphone has its own sound when compared to the other types. The thin piece of material contains aluminum or plastic which vibrates when it is struck by sound waves. These vibrations are converted into an electrical current which becomes the audio signal. A sample image of a microphone is shown as follows:

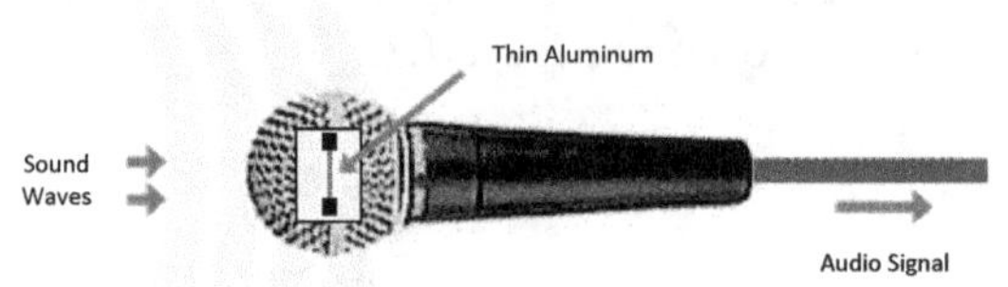

Figure 1.17: *Microphone*

Advantages of a Microphone

The following are some of the advantages of a microphone:

- Moving coil microphone is the rugged construction of these microphones for rough use.
- Inexpensive to manufacture.
- Tolerates extremely high sound pressure levels.
- Requires no power supply.

Disadvantages of a Microphone

The following are some of the disadvantages of a microphone

- Reduced high frequency performance.
- Needs amplification.

Scanner

Scanner is an input device that optically scans images, printed text, handwriting, or an object, and converts it into a digital file. A scanner is connected to a computer through a USB, as shown in the following *Figure 1.18*:

Figure 1.18: *Scanner*

It has three types. They are as follows:

- **Flatbed Scanner:** A Flatbed scanner is also known as a **desktop scanner** and it works just like a photocopier. This scanner allows the user to place a full piece of paper, book, magazine, photo or any other object onto the glass surface of the scanner. It has the capability to scan that object and convert it into digital form.

- **Sheetfed Scanner:** A Sheetfed scanner is also known as a **rollerfed scanner**. It works like a fax machine. The image is passed over a roller where it is captured. A Sheetfed scanner is very versatile in scanning loose sheets of paper.
- **Handheld Scanner:** A handheld or **portable scanner** is an optical scanner which is designed to be moved by hand across the object or document being scanned. It is used for reading an image or data optically from a document. It is operated by hand.

Advantages of a Scanner

The following are some of the advantages of a scanner:

- Flatbed scanners are very accurate and can produce high quality images.
- Any image which is digitized by the scanner can be included on electronic documents.
- Images once digitized can be enhanced with a graphics application.
- Captures image accurately, but the original source may be more important than the scanned image.

Disadvantages of a Scanner

The following are some of the disadvantages of a scanner:

- Images produced by the scanner can take up a lot of memory space.
- Images lose some quality in the scanning and digitizing process.
- The quality of the final image is dependent on the quality of the original image

Voice or Speech Recognition System

It is one of the most interactive systems to communicate with the computer. The user can instruct the computer with the help of a microphone to perform a task. It is the technology by which sounds, words spoken by human are converted into digital signals, and these signals are transformed into computer generated text or commands. Most speech recognition systems are speaker-dependent, so they must be separately trained for each individual user. The user has to train the words to recognize their voice so that it can more accurately convert the speech to text.

Advantages of a Speech Recognition System

The use of these systems reduces fatigue as manual key stroking is replaced with verbal instructions. Higher accuracy is also gained when data is entered using voice instead of a keyboard. The operator enjoys freedom of movement with a voice recognition system as compared to a keyboard device. With voice recognition, the operator is free to stand up and move around, entering data with a conveniently located microphone. Training of operators is an easy task in the case of a voice recognition system.

Optical Mark Reader (OMR)

Optical Mark Recognition is also called **mark sensing device**. These devices use light beam to read data. The data is converted into digital signals. The signals are then sent to the computer for further processing. OMT technology scans a printed form and reads predefined positions and records where marks are made on the form. This technology is useful for applications in which large numbers of hand-filled forms need to be processed quickly and accurately.

The OMR enables a high-speed reading, big quantities of data and transferring these data to the computer without using a keyboard. This technology is used to read answer sheets. Its special printed forms/documents are printed with boxes, which can be marked with a dark pencil or ink.

OMR focuses light on the page being examined, and the light pattern reflected from the dark marks is then detected. *Figure 1.19* shows the OMR characters.

Figure 1.19: *Optical Marks in an Answer Sheet*

Advantages of OMR

The following are some of the advantages of OMR:

- A fast method of inputting large amounts of data – up to 10,000 forms can be read per hour, depending on the quality of the machine used.

- Only one computer is needed to collect and process the data.
- OMR is much more accurate than data.

Disadvantages of OMR

The following are some of the disadvantages of OMR:

- If the marks do not fill the space completely, or are not in a dark enough pencil, they may not be read correctly.
- Only suitable for recording one out of a selection of answers, not suitable for text input.
- The OMR reader needs the answers to be on the prepared forms, which will all be identical to one another. You can't just pick up a blank sheet of paper and mark your answers on it.

Barcode Reader

Barcode is a machine-readable code in the form of a pattern of vertical lines of varying widths. It is commonly used for labelling goods that are available in the supermarket. This code is sensed and read by a barcode reader using a lens and a light sensor translating for optical impulses into electrical signals. These are primarily used for identification of goods, such as books, postal packages and badges, as shown in *Figure 1.20*:

Figure 1.20: *Barcodes*

Advantages of a Barcode Reader

The following are some of the advantages of a barcode reader:

- This is a fast method of data entry.
- This method eliminates possible human error.

Disadvantage of a Barcode Reader

The following are some of the disadvantages of a barcode reader:

- Scratched or crumpled barcodes may cause problems in accurate data entry.
- Barcode reader works with computers or POS terminals.
- It does not have read/write capabilities.
- It requires optical line of sight scanning.

Magnetic Ink Character Recognition (MICR)

MICR code is a code printed on cheques using Magnetic Ink Character Recognition technology. This enables identification of the cheques which in turn means faster processing. It is a **9-digit code** that identifies the bank branch and speeds up the electronic clearing system process. The first three digits in the MICR code represents the **city code** that is the city in which the bank branch is located. The next three digits stand for the **bank code**, while the last digits represent the bank branch code. *Figure 1.21* shows a bank cheque which will be processed using an MICR device.

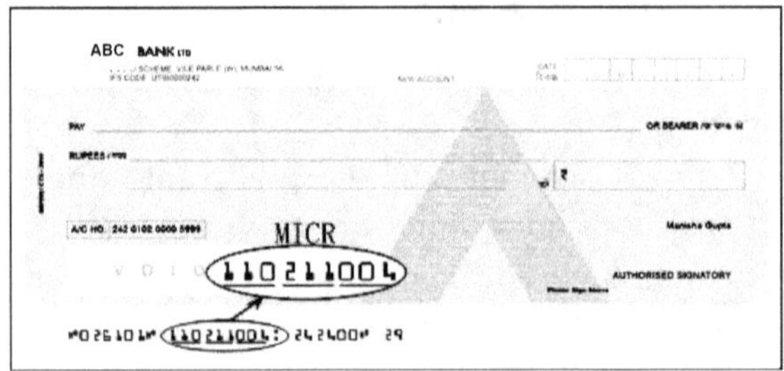

Figure 1.21: *A Bank Cheque Processed using an MICR Device*

Advantages of MICR

The following are some of the advantages of MICR:

- It offers greater security than OCR since the printed characters cannot be altered.
- There is no manual input, thus errors are reduced.
- Characters can still be read even when somebody writes on them.

Disadvantages of MICR

The following are some of the disadvantages of MICR:

- Only certain characters can be read.
- It is a more expensive method of data entry.

Trackball

Trackball is an input device. It looks like an upside-down mouse. The onscreen pointer is moved by the trackball with a thumb or finger. It requires less arm and wrist motion than a regular mouse and makes it less stressful for the user. Two buttons are also embedded with trackball socket for selecting any object or text. Now-a-days, it is mainly used in a notebook or laptop computer, instead of a mouse. An image of trackball is shown as follows:

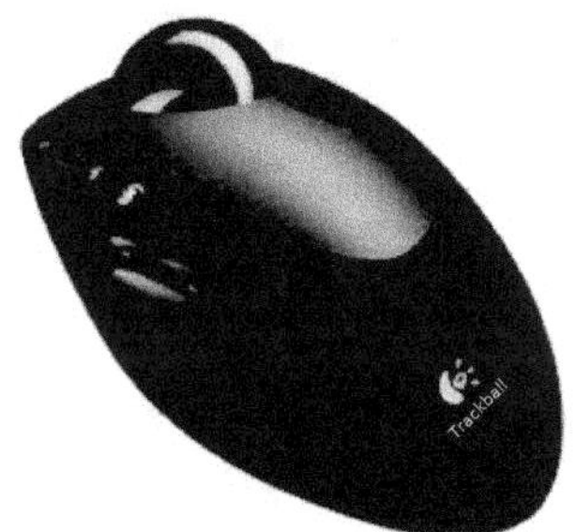

Figure 1.22: *Trackball*

Advantages of Trackball

The following are some of the advantages of trackball:

- It does not need the same fine control as a mouse.
- User uses with limited hand/wrist movement and finds it easier to use than a mouse.
- Pointer can be positioned more accurately on the screen than with a mouse.
- It takes less desk space than a mouse.

Disadvantages of Trackball

The following are some of the disadvantages of trackball:

- They need a flat space close to the computer.
- It requires fine control of the ball with just one finger or thumb.

Web Cameras

Web camera is a computer digital camera which works the same way as a digital camera but is designed to interact with the web pages and other internet pages. It captures the real-time images through a tiny grid of light detectors known as **Charge-Coupled Device (CCD)**. The CCD converts the image into a digital format so that the computer can access this data. Today, most webcams are embedded into the display with laptop computers or connected to the USB port on the computer.

The image of the object can be seen on the monitor of the distant computer connected through a network or through Internet. Voice can also be transmitted over the network. Thus, two or more persons can talk and see one another in this way. This method is used in video conferencing, as shown in *Figure 1.23*:

Figure 1.23: *Web Camera*

Advantages of Web Cameras

The following are some of the advantages of a web camera:

- Can be left on constantly on the computer rather than using a digital camera.
- Allows face-to-face video chat.
- Many webcams can also be used as a still camera.
- To interact with people with international communication.

Disadvantages of Web Cameras

The following are some of the disadvantages of a web camera:

- They need to be connected to the computer.
- Limited features and poor quality.
- It is not secure and can create security issues.
- It consumes a lot of battery power.

Biometric Sensor

The word biometrics is derived from the Greek words where bio means life and metric means to measure. It is used to identify the physical and behavioral characteristics of a person. Based on the designing, this system can be used as an identification system. These systems are divided into various types, which include vein pattern, fingerprints, DNA, voice pattern, iris pattern, signature dynamics and face detection. A biometric sensor is a transducer that changes into an electrical signal. They are used for security purposes to identify the persons who are permitted to enter the organization (*see Figure 1.24*).

Figure 1.24: *Biometric Sensor*

Advantages of a Biometric Sensor

The following are some of the advantages of a biometric sensor:

- Fingerprints are unique.
- Fingerprint sensors are cheap.
- The pattern in iris, retina or fingerprint remain the same throughout life.
- No duplication of individual's identity.

Disadvantages of a Biometric Sensor

The following are some of the disadvantages of a biometric sensor:

- Most fingerprint readers do not work when wet or dirty.
- Many people do not like to use fingerprint technology.

Output Devices

Output device is any peripheral device that receives output from the computer and displays it. Some examples of different types of output devices commonly found on a computer are as follows:

Monitor

A computer monitor, technically termed as a **VDU**, can be plainly described as an electronic device that transmits information from the computer onto a screen, thereby acting as an interface and connecting the user with the computer.

A monitor is an output device that displays video, images and text. It is made up of circuitry, a screen, a power supply button, to adjust screen settings. The following image is a sample monitor:

Figure 1.25: *Monitor*

There are two main types of computer monitors, one is CRT and the other one is LCD.

Cathode Ray Tube (CRT): This monitor utilizes a cathode ray tube to display images. It is a technology used in computer monitors and televisions. The image on CTR is displayed by using electrons from the back of the tube of phosphorus located to the front of the screen. When the electron heats the phosphorus, they light up, and they are projected on a screen. The color you view on the screen is red, blue and green.

There are several advantages and disadvantage of using CRT monitors, which are as follows:

Advantages of CRT Monitor

- These monitors are highly reliable and efficient, and are capable of generating a resolution of up to 2048 x 1536 pixels, thereby providing a clear picture quality. Also, CRT monitors that are now available are capable of producing thousands of different colors.
- Secondly, CRT monitors are affordable and cost effective.
- Maintenance is easy; if damaged, it can be serviced.

Disadvantages of CRT Monitor

- The Gaussian beam produces images with softer edges that are not as sharp as an LCD at its resolution.
- They are large, heavy and bulky. They consume a lot of electricity and produce a lot of heat.
- CRT monitor emits radiation that is greater than the LCD. This radiation has a negative impact on the eye so that the eye gets tired.

Liquid Crystal Display (LCD): A liquid crystal display is a thin, flat display screen that is generally used in laptop computer screen, cell phones and video games. LCD is composed of several layers which includes two polarized panel filters and electrodes. This technology is used for displaying the image in electronic devices. Light is projected from a lens on a layer of liquid crystal. This combination of colored light with the grayscale image of the crystal forms the colored image. LCD displays screen works on the principle of blocking light rather than emitting light. It requires backlight as they do not emit light by them.

Some major advantages and disadvantages of using an LCD monitor include the following:

Advantages of LCD

- Produces very bright image due to high peak intensity. It is suitable for environments that are brightly lit.
- It produces low electric, magnetic and electromagnetic fields than CRTs.
- It consumes less than one third the power of a CRT.
- LCDs are thinner and lighter when compared to CRT and LED.

Disadvantage of LCD

- The aspect ratio and resolution is fixed.
- In a high temperature environment, there is loss of contrast.
- It is relatively bright but not suitable for very brightly environments.
- It consumes a lot of electricity which produce a lot of heat.
- It has individual liquid crystals which cannot complete all block of the backlight.

Light-Emitting Diodes (LED): It is a light-emitting diode monitor; an LED display is a flat screen, flat panel computer monitor or television. The LED monitor has many panels, and each panel has several LEDs to backlight the display, whereas the LCD monitors use cold cathode fluorescent light to backlight the display.

Some advantages of LED monitors are as follows:

- Lower Power Consumption.
- Longer lifespan and less environmental impact.
- The device does not need any heating and warm up time.
- Better Picture quality (true black picture).
- Brighter and sharper images.

Some disadvantages of LED monitors are as follows:

- LED are more expensive than conventional lighting technologies.
- LED is a lot thinner than the LCD.
- Very High Price.
- LED performance largely depends on the ambient temperature of the operating environment.

Other Output devices are those devices of computer system that supply information or results either in the form of hardcopy (printer) or softcopy (monitor). Some of the common output devices are as follows:

- Printers
- Plotters
- Multimedia Projector
- Speech Synthesizer

Printers

A printer is an output device that takes data from a computer and generates output in the form of text on the paper. There are two types of printers:

- IMPACT PRINTERS:

  The impact printer uses a hammer or print head to print the character on the paper. The hammer or print head strikes an ink ribbon against the paper to print characters and images. Impact printers are further divided into two types:

  - o Line Printers:

    A line printer prints one line of the text at a time. Printing speed may vary from 300*3000 lines per minute. Different types of line printers are Drum printer and Chain printer.

    - ■ Drum Printer:

      A drum printer consists of a cylindrical drum on which characters are embossed. The printer receives all characters to be printed in one line of the text from the processor. The hammers hit the ribbon and paper against the desired character on the drum when it comes in the printing position. Its noise level is high and speed varies from 200 to 2000 lines per minute. They are expensive also.

    - ■ Chain Printer:

      A chain printer uses a rapidly rotating chain which is called print chain. To print a line, the characters in the line are transmitted from the memory to printer buffer. The band is rotated at a high speed. The noise level of the printer is high, and its speed lies in the range of 400-2400 lines per minute.

o Dot Matrix Printer:

A dot matrix printer is the most popular serial printer (see Figure 1.26). The printhead contains a vertical array of pins. As the printhead moves across the paper, selected pins fire against the ribbon to form a pattern of dots on the paper.

The dot matrix printer is faster than the letter quality printer. These printers operate at two or three speeds. The lower the speed, the better is the printing quality. Higher speed is for draft printing, and lower speed is for Near-Letter Quality (NLQ) printing.

o Letter Quality Printers:

These printers print full characters, which means that a character is not made up of dots. The most popular printer of this type is a daisy-wheel printer. In a daisy-wheel printer, the printhead resembles a daisy flower, with its print arms appearing like the petals of the flower. The daisy-wheel printer has a speed up to 90 characters per second. These are no longer used.

Figure 1.26: *Dot Matrix Printer*

- Non-Impact Printers:

Non-Impact printer does not touch the paper when making lines and images. They use shower ink and other uses warm, heat and pressure for producing lines and graphics. They do not make any noise and produce better quality printouts. They are cheap and much speedier than impact printers. These printers are categorized as:

o Electromagnetic Printer: This printer uses magnetic recording techniques. By using this technique, the required output is written on a drum surface. Then this surface is passed through a magnetic powder, which adheres to the charged areas. The powder is then pressed onto the paper.

o Thermal Printer: This type of printer uses a special heat-sensitive paper. These papers have a special heat-sensitive coating. When a spot on the paper is heated, it becomes dark. A character is printed with a matrix of dots. These printers have a speed of 200 characters per second.

o Inkjet Printer: Inkjet printers are more efficient than dot matrix printers. The print quality is good because the character is formed by dozens of tiny ink dots. These printers produce better quality of text and graphics and are faster. Almost all inkjets offer a color option as standard, in varying degrees of resolution. Inkjet printers are capable of producing high quality print, which almost matches the quality of a laser printer. A standard ink jet printer has a resolution of 300 dots per inch, although newer models have improved on that, as shown in *Figure 1.27*:

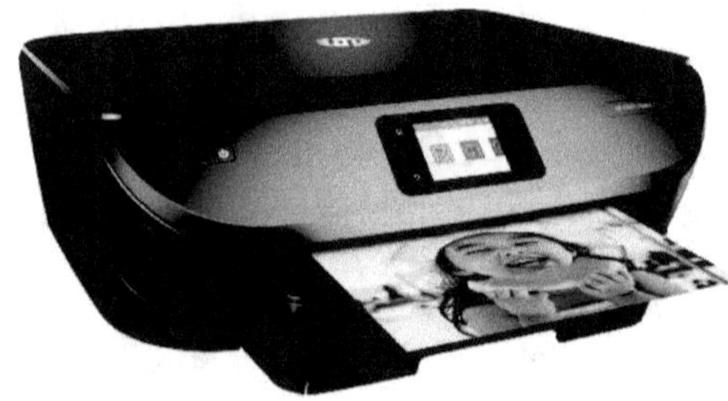

Figure 1.27: *Inkjet Printer*

o Laser Printer: Laser printers are non-impact type printers. These printers are expensive and require periodic maintenance. Low-speed laser printers produce 10 pages or more per minute and are used with microcomputers. High-speed laser printers produce up to 300 pages per minute, and they are used with mini and large computers. Laser printers have become popular for voluminous printing work. They are mainly used for desktop publishing work. *Figure 1.28* illustrates a laser printer.

Figure 1.28: *Laser Printer*

- Advantages:
- The following are some of the advantages of a laser printer:
  - It is a very fast printer and its efficiency is very high.
  - The printing cost of a laser printer is less than an inkjet printer.
  - It has the ability to print high-resolution images that are 1200 dpi, consuming less time.
  - It makes no noise during the printing process.
  - Can print overhead transparencies.

- Disadvantages:
  The following are some of the disadvantages of a laser printer:
  - It is a very fast printer and its efficiency is very high.
  - It is very expensive.
  - The maintenance cost is high.
  - Very bulky and difficult to repair.
  - Also emits Ultraviolet radiation that can cause eye damage.
  - Does not normally take paper size larger than A4.

3D Printer

3D printing is a form of additive manufacturing technology where a three-dimensional object is created by laying down successive layers of material. It is also known as **rapid prototyping**. It is a mechanized method whereby 3D objects are quickly made on a reasonably sized machine connected to a computer containing blueprints for the object. This method for creating 3D models with the use of inkjet technology saves time and cost by eliminating the need to design; print and glue together separate model parts. Now, you can create a complete model in a single process using 3D printing. The basic principles include materials like cartridges, flexibility of output, and translation of code into a visible pattern.

3D Printers are machines that produce physical 3D models from digital data by printing it layer-by-layer. It can make physical models of objects either designed with a CAD program or scanned with a 3D Scanner. It is used in a variety of industries including jewellery, footwear, industrial design, architecture, engineering and construction, automotive, aerospace, dental and medical industries, education and consumer products.

Plotter

A plotter is a larger printer that is used to print vector graphics and continuous lines. It is most used for **Computer-Aided Design (CAD)** and **Computer-Aided Engineering (CAE)**. It prints more precisely than a traditional printer and was one of the first types of printers that could print in color and render full-sized engineering drawings such as mechanical drawings, building plans, circuit diagrams, and so on. *Figure 1.29* shows a plotter.

Advantages

The following are some of the advantages of a plotter:
- Can produce huge printouts
- Print quality is extremely high
- Good for map and blueprints

Disadvantages

The following are some of the disadvantages of a plotter:
- Slow in operation
- Expensive to buy and maintain
- Takes space

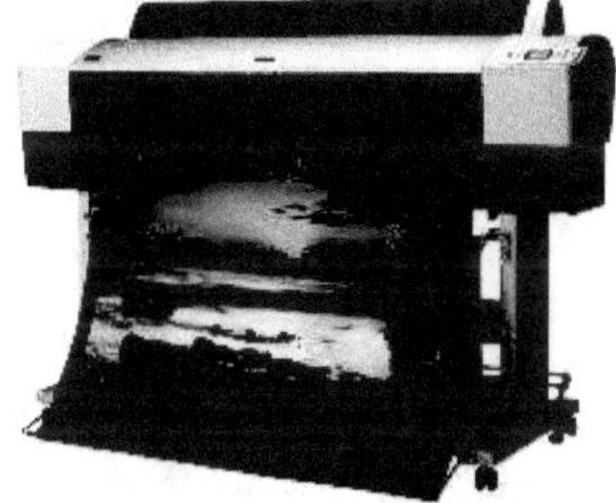

Figure 1.29: *Plotter*

Multimedia Projector

Projector is used to project information from a computer on to a large screen so that it can be viewed by a large group of people. It is an optical device that projects an image on a projection screen. It creates an image by shining a light through a small transparent lens, but newer types of projectors can project the image directly by using lasers. Projectors are used for classroom trainings or conference rooms or for a multimedia presentation with the audience. *(See Figure 1.30).*

Figure 1.30: *Projector*

Advantages

The following are some of the advantages of a projector:

- Enables many people to see a presentation rather than crowding around a small computer.
- Avoids the need of connecting several computers together.
- Allows you to prepare all your slides in advance.
- Can build up information point-by-point through the use of overlays.

Disadvantages

The following are some of the disadvantages of a projector:

- Images can sometimes be fuzzy.
- Is expensive.
- A blown bulb or power failure can spoil all your work.

Speech Synthesizer

Speech Synthesizer is an output device that converts textual data into spoken sentences. To produce the speech, basic sound units called phonemes are combined. The sequence of words in a text is combined into phonemes, is amplified and outputted through a speaker attached to a computer, as shown in *Figure 1.31:*

Figure 1.31: *Speech Synthesizer*

Advantages

The following are some of the advantages of a speech synthesizer:

- Listens to any text or topic at any time.
- Adjusts the reading speed.
- Correct pronunciation of words.

Disadvantages

The following are some of the disadvantages of a speech synthesizer:

- Text to speech is not 100% accurate.

Speakers

Speakers are hardware devices connected to a computer sound card that outputs the sounds generated by the card. The speaker makes a sound by being fed on electrical signals which is changed or modulated, corresponding to the sound that is to be made. The speaker converts the changes or waves in the electrical signal to matching sound waves, which you hear.

Figure 1.32: *Speakers*

There is no volume control in the PC, since it was not intended to produce sophisticated sounds. Speakers are further attached to the system to enhance the sound quality. *(See Figure 1.32.)*

Advantages

The following are some of the advantages of a speaker:

- They are provided with the computer.

- They are very simple to operate.
- They help blind people to use the computer because text can be converted into sound.

Disadvantages

The following are some of the disadvantages of a speaker:

- The output from speakers can disturb others who are trying to work.
- High quality external speakers can be expensive.

Computer Memory and Storage

A computer needs memory to store data. It also needs memory to perform arithmetical operations and storing programs and pictures. Computer memory is of two types:

- Primary Memory/Main Memory
- Secondary Memory/Auxiliary Memory

Primary Memory

Primary memory is a part of the CPU, whereas the secondary memory is external to the CPU. The secondary memory stores the data and keeps it even when the electricity to the PC is cut off, whereas the primary memory loses its contents immediately after the power supply is cut off.

Primary memory is made up of electronic circuits and keeps data as long as the voltage supply is on. When power supply to a PC is switched off, the data is lost.

Primary memory can be divided into the following two types:

Random Access Memory (RAM)

RAM is a hardware device located on the motherboard of a computer and acts as an internal memory of the CPU. It is much faster to read from and write to than the other kinds of storage in the computer like the hard disk or floppy disk. RAM is a volatile memory, which means it does not store data permanently. However, the data and instruction in RAM stays there only as long as the computer is switched on. When the computer is turned off, RAM loses all its contents. When the computer is rebooted, the operating system and the program is started, the computer loads it into RAM and does all the processing there. It allows the computer to run the application faster. Any new information that is created is kept in RAM, and it needs to continuously save the information to the hard disk.

Advantages of RAM

The following are some of the advantages of RAM:

- RAM is used to store the data for processing on CPU.
- More RAM is a factor to increase the speed of a computer.
- If a CPU wants to read the data from the RAM, then it is fast as compared to data access from hard disk, CD, DVD, floppy and USB.

Disadvantages of RAM

The following are some of the disadvantages of RAM:

- Less RAM is a factor to decrease the speed of a computer.
- If a CPU wants to read the data from the RAM, then it is slow as compared to data access from registers and cache.

Static and Dynamic RAM

Static RAM and dynamic RAM are both different from each other in many contexts such as speed, capacity, and so on. These are difference in the technique which is used to hold data. DRAM makes use of single transistor and capacitor for each memory cell, whereas each memory cell of SRAM makes use of an array of 6 transistors. DRAM needs refreshing, whereas SRAM does not require refreshing of the memory cell.

DRAM stands for **Dynamic Random Access Memory** that is widely used as the main memory for a computer system. DRAM takes 1 transistor and 1 capacitor to store 1 bit. Means, each memory cell in a DRAM chip holds one bit of data and is composed of a transistor and a capacitor. The transistor functions as a switch that allows the control circuitry on the memory chip to read the capacitor or change its state, while the capacitor is responsible for holding the bit of data in the form of a 1 or 0.

SRAM stands for **Static Random Access Memory**; it is normally used to build very fast memory, known as cache memory. SRAM takes 6 transistors to store 1 bit and it's much faster compared to DRAM. Static RAM uses a completely different technology compared to DRAM. In static RAM, a form of flip-flop holds each bit of memory. A flip-flop for a memory cell takes 4 or 6 transistors along with some wiring but never has to be refreshed. This makes static RAM significantly faster than dynamic RAM. Unlike dynamic RAM (DRAM), which stores bits in cells consisting of a capacitor and a transistor, SRAM does not have to be periodically refreshed.

Read Only Memory (ROM)

ROM is Read Only Memory. In this type of memory, the data is permanently stored. The information can only be read and new data cannot be written onto this memory. However, the contents of the ROM are not lost, even when the power is turned off, that is, this memory is non-volatile. Such memories are also called as **field stores** or **permanent stores.**

There are a number of high-level functions which are required to be performed by the computer system. Such functions are performed by writing special programs called **micro programs**. Micro programs generally execute the low-level machine functions. These programs are mainly used as a substitute for hardware. Such programs can be stored on ROMs and be used again and again. This results in reducing the hardware of the system. ROM helps to increase the efficiency of the CPU as it can perform specialized tasks. ROM comes in the form of a chip. Once information is stored on a ROM chip, it cannot be changed or altered.

Advantages of ROM

The following are some of the advantages of ROM:

- The chip has to be taken out of the system for erasing and programming.

- Selective erasing is not possible.

Disadvantages of ROM

The following are some of the disadvantages of ROM:

- EPROMs are more flexible than ROMs and PROMs due to its reprogrammablity feature.

Types of Read Only Memory

ROM is differentiated on the basis of methods used to write data on ROM chips and the number of times they can be written. It can be classified into the following types:

- **Mask Read Only Memory:** The very first ROMs were hard-wired devices that contained a pre-programmed set of data or instructions.

- **Programmable Read Only Memory:** It is read-only memory that can be modified only once by a user. The user buys a blank PROM and enters the desired contents using a PROM programmer. It is a one-time programmable device.

- **Erasable and Programmable Read Only Memory:** The EPROM can be erased by exposing it to ultra violet light for a duration

of up to 30 minutes. After exposing, the chip returns to its initial state and can be reprogrammed. It is a non-volatile memory, that is, it can retain data even if the power supply is cut off. The basic limitation being encountered in PROM is that once it is programmed, it cannot be changed or altered.

- **Electrically Erasable and Programmable Read Only Memory:** The EEPROM is programmed and erased electrically. It can be erased and reprogrammed about ten thousand times. It uses electrical signals instead of ultra violet rays. In EEPROM, both erasing and programming take about 3 to 10 minutes. In any location, it can be selectively erased and programmed. EEPROMs can be erased one byte at a time, rather than erasing the entire chip. Hence, the process of re-programming is flexible but slow.

- **Flash Read Only Memory:** It is a universal flash programming non-volatile utility, used in computer as a storage medium. It can be electrically erased and reprogrammed.

Difference between RAM and ROM

The following table shows the difference of RAM and ROM:

S.No.	RAM	ROM
1.	Temporary storage	Permanent storage
2.	Stores data in MBs	Stores data in GBs
3.	Volatile	Non-volatile
4.	Used in normal operations	Used for startup process of computer
5.	Writing data is faster	Writing data is slower

Table 1.1

Secondary Memory

Secondary memory is where programs and data are kept on a long-term basis. Common secondary devices are the hard disk and optical disk. Secondary memory is not accessed directly by the CPU. Instead, data accessed from a secondary memory is first loaded into RAM and is then sent to the processing unit.

Secondary memory is also termed as **external memory** and refers to the various storage media on which a computer can store data and programs. The storage media can be fixed or removable.

Fixed storage media is an internal storage medium like hard disk that is fixed inside the computer. Removable storage media can be taken outside the computer such as external hard disk.

Data is stored now-a-days in hard disk, **Compact Disk Read Only Memory (CD-ROM), Digital Video/Versatile Disk (DVD)**, pendrive and portable hard drive. Data stored on hard disk and CD-ROM, and so on can be accessed directly. Thus, these storage devices are faster.

Random access devices are direct access devices. In such devices, the information is available at random, i.e., it is available in any order.

> An access storage device is one in which any location in the device may be accessed at random and retrieval of information stored is direct.

Magnetic disks and magnetic drums are typical direct access storage devices.

Magnetic Tape

Magnetic tape is one of the most popular storage mediums for large volumes of data that are needed to be serially accessed and processed. The tape is a plastic ribbon usually **1/2-inch-wide** that is coated on one side with an iron-oxide material which can be magnetized. The tape ribbon itself is stored in reels of **50** to **2400** feet. It is similar to the tape used on a tape-recorder except that it is of higher quality and more durable. The magnetic tape can be erased and reused again and again *(see Figure 1.33)*.

Figure 1.33: *Magnetic Tape*

Advantages of Magnetic Tape

The following are some of the advantages of a Magnetic tape:

- Virtually unlimited storage capacity
- Low cost
- Easy to handle and store
- Easy to port

Disadvantages of Magnetic Tape

The following are some of the disadvantages of a Magnetic tape:

- Serial access so can be quite slow to access data
- These are not suitable for frequent data access
- Must be operated in a dustless environment
- Less robust than other media as the tape can easily break

Hard Disk

A hard disk is a device used for mass storage of data needed for direct access. It is more stable, rigid and is contained in a dust-free environment. It stores more information. The data and instructions that are entered into the computer system through input units must be stored inside the computer before the actual processing can start. Similarly, the results produced by the computer after processing must also be kept somewhere inside the computer system before those can be passed onto the output units. Moreover, the intermediate results produced by the computer must also be preserved for ongoing processing, as shown in *Figure 1.34*:

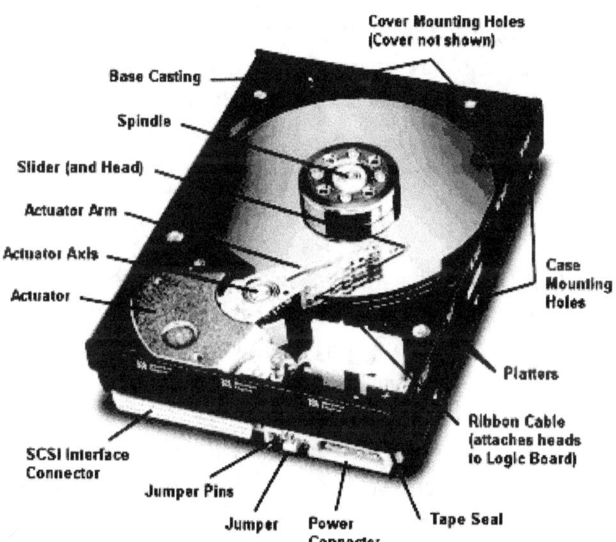

Figure 1.34: *Hard Disk*

The specific function of the storage unit is to store the following:

- All data and instructions to be processed.
- Intermediate results of processing.
- Final results before sending them to output devices.

                                                      IT Tools & Basics of Networks

> Computers also provide the facility of dividing the main memory into words or bytes. A byte usually consists of 8 bits of information.

Advantages

The following are some of the advantages of a hard disk:

- Large storage capacity.
- Stores and retrieves data much faster than a floppy disk or CD/DVD.
- Stored items are not lost when you switch off the computer.
- Cheap on a cost per megabyte compared to other storage devices.
- Have two hard disks in a machine, one can act as a mirror of the other and create a backup copy.

Disadvantages

The following are some of the disadvantages of a hard disk:

- Slower to access data than ROM or RAM chips.
- Hard disks can crash, which stops the computer from working.
- Regular crashes can damage the surface of the disk, leading to loss of data in that sector.
- The disk is fixed inside the computer and cannot easily be transferred to another computer.
- Heavy power consumption.

Compact Disc (CD)

The CD-Drive is a mechanism used to read/write digital information on a CD. It is easily available in different formats. CD-Drive is for reading purpose only (CD/R), whereas (CD/RW) is for the purpose of both reading and writing.

CD-Drive is an optical disc drive that uses Laser light or Electromagnetic waves of suitable wavelength as part of the process of reading or writing data to CD. The drives are commonly both readers and recorders, also called **burners** or **writers**. **Compact Disc (CD)**, **Digital Versatile Disc (DVD)** and **Blue-ray Disc (BD)** are common types of optical media. A typical CD can store around 600 MB to 700 MB of data that is equivalent to 80 minutes of uncompressed audio files. The following image shows CD:

Figure 1.35: *Compact Disc*

Following are the types of CD ROM drives:

- CD Read Only Memory (CD-ROM):

  Given below are the features of CD-ROM:
    o Contents of CD cannot be erased by the user.
    o Computer users can only read data and music from the discs, but they cannot burn their own information onto the discs from their personal computers.

- CD Recordable (CD-R):

  Given below are the features of CD-R:
    o It is known as compact disc recordable and WORM (write Once Read Many). It is a blank disc that users can put into a CD-ROM drive to burn or make a copy of their personal data such as music, videos and information.
    o Contents can be written only once.
    o After that, they can be read several times but cannot be written or erased.

- CD Rewritable (CD-RW):

  Given below are the features of CD-RW:
    o Contents on the CD can be written on, read and erased several times
    o Made up of alloys of silver, indium, antimony and tellurium

Advantages

The following are some of the advantages of a compact disc:

- Small and portable
- Useful for archiving files securely
- It is read-only and cannot be updated
- Fast to access the data compared to a floppy disk or magnetic tape

Disadvantages

The following are some of the disadvantages of a compact disc:

- Easy to snap or scratch
- Smaller storage capacity than a hard drive or DVD
- Slower to access than the hard disk

Digital Video Disc (DVD)

Digital Video Disc (DVD) was introduced by **Philips** and **Sony** in **1995**. A circular optical disc made up of thin platted glass and plastic polycarbonate material. It is an optical storage device that looks the same as a CD. The DVD has the same dimensions as the standard CD but cannot be read by a CD player, although a DVD player can read standard CDs. A single-sided DVD can store up to 4.7 GB of data. DVDs which store data on both sides can hold over 9 GB of data.

Following are the types of DVD:

DVD-ROM

Given below are the features of DVD-ROM:
- Contents of DVD cannot be written on or erased by the user.
- It is used to distribute large amounts of databases and applications.

DVD-R/DVD+R

Given below are the features of DVD-R/DVD+R:
- Write once recordable format.
- DVD-R (DVD minus R) and DVR+R (DVD plus R) are two different kinds of disc.
- There is no difference between them and both the DVDs are supported by modern devices.

DVD-RW/DVD+RW

Given below are the features of DVD-RW/DVD+RW:
- Rewritable disc allowing up to 1,000 rewrites before it is used. And there is not much difference in -RW and +RW.

DVD-RAM

Given below are the features of DVD-RAM:
- DVD - Random Access Memory (DVD-RAM) has higher data security and storage capacities.
- It supports up to 1,00,000 rewrites.
- DVD-RAMs are accessed just like a hard disk.

Comparison Chart of CD and DVD

Following table shows differentiation of CD and DVD:

Basic for	CD	DVD
Stands for	Compact disk	Digital Versatile disk
Size	700 MB	4.7 to 17 GB
Usage	Less as compared to DVDs	Middle of the Disk
Metal layer position of the disk	Top	Middle of the disk
Layers of the pits purpose	CDs are made with the purpose of holding audio files as well as program files	DVDs are made with the purpose of holding video files, movies, and so on
Write mechanism	1200 Kib/s	10.5 Mbit/s
Developed by	Philips, Sony	Sony, Toshiba and Panasonic

Table 1.2: *Comparison between CD and DVD*

Advantages

The following are some of the advantages of a DVD:
- Very large storage capacity.
- Sound and picture quality is excellent to store videos and sound files.
- DVDs are now mass produced so they are relatively cheap.
- DVD players can read CDs.

Disadvantages

The following are some of the disadvantages of a DVD:
- DVDs do not work in CD-Drives.
- There is no single standard of DVD.
- They can be easily damaged by breaking or scratching.

Thumb Drive

A thumb drive, also known as a **flash drive**, **pen drive** or **USB drive**, is a small portable device in the shape of the thumb, which can be connected to the USB port of a computer. The main component of the thumb drive is flash memory. Flash memory is a special type of memory which can retain data even when there is no current passing through it. It is somewhat like an external hard drive, as shown in *Figure 1.36*:

Figure 1.36: *Pen Drive*

Advantages

The following are some of the advantages of a pen drive:
- They are more compact and portable than CDs or DVDs.
- They hold more data than a CD.
- They are reliable as they have no moving parts.
- They are not affected by magnetic fields.

Disadvantages

The following are some of the disadvantages of a pen drive:
- More expensive than CD or DVD.
- They can be easily lost.
- The metal part, which is inserted into the USB port, can be snapped off or damaged if they are handled roughly.

Memory Cards

A memory card is a device offering an easy, fast and reliable way for storing and transferring digital files. It works like a portable hard disk drive but comes with some superior advantages, since almost every memory card is based on flash memory technology of having much smaller form factor and being non-volatile and solid state. This makes flash memory cards much more durable and reliable than hard disk drives. Memory cards are made by a variety of manufacturers and can be available with different storage capacities and transfer speeds.

MicroSD Memory Card

The MicroSD card is even smaller than the MiniSD card. It is designed for use in cellular phones, small mobile devices and GPS devices. It can be accessed in an SD card slot via an adapter. It contains 8 pins and maximum transfer rate is **200 MBPS** (*see Figure 1.37*).

Figure 1.37: *SD Card*

Portable Hard Drive

Portable hard disk drive is plugged into an external port on a computer, such as USB or FireWire used for backup. For laptops, the PC Card slot may be used to connect a cable to a full-sized drive, or the hard disk may be contained entirely inside the PC Card (*see Figure 1.38*). The portable hard drives available in the market are of different sizes of 320 GB, 500 GB and 1 Tetra GB.

This hard drive allows the user to back up or store important information separate from the main internal hard drive, which could be compromised by online or offline activities. Documents such as music files, DVD images, movies, disk images, and even a backup of the contents of your main internal hard drive can all be kept securely and safely on an external hard drive.

Figure 1.38 : *Portable Hard Drive*

Advantages

The following are some of the advantages of a portable hard drive:
- Portable transfer files between computers.
- High storage capacity compared to optical disks.

Disadvantages

The following are some of the disadvantages of a portable hard drive:

- More prone to errors than fixed hard drive.
- Could be damaged if incorrectly ejected from computer.

Software

Software, also called a **program**, consists of a series of related instructions, organized for a common purpose, that tells the computer what tasks to perform and how to perform them. You interact with a program through its user interface. The user interface controls how you enter data and instructions and how information is displayed on the screen. The software programs are classified into the following categories:

- Application Software
- System Software

The classification of software packages is shown in *Figure 1.39*.

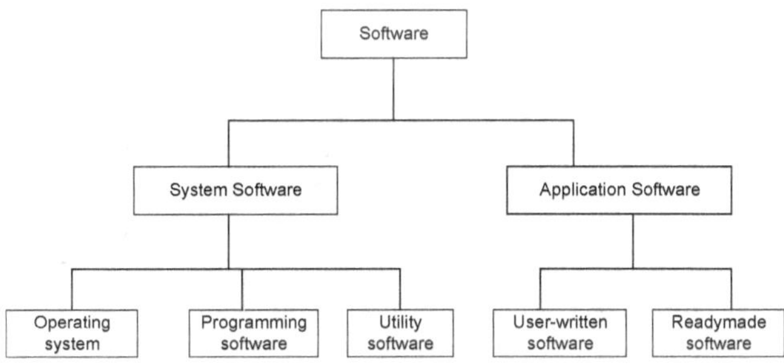

Figure 1.39: *Categories of Software*

Application Software

An application is any program, or group of programs, that is designed for the end user. Application software can be divided into two general classes: system software and application software. Application software (also **called end-user programs**) includes database programs, word processors, Web browsers and spreadsheets, while system software consists of low-level programs that interact with computers at a basic level.

Typical software applications that you might use are:

- **Word Processors:** For example, Microsoft Word or the free OpenOffice Writer.
- **Spreadsheet Software:** For example, Microsoft Excel or OpenOffice Calc.
- **Graphics Software:** For example, Microsoft Paint, Adobe Photoshop or Corel Paintshop Pro.
- **Web Design Software:** For example, Adobe Dreamweaver.

Differences between System and Application Software

System software is general-purpose software which is used to operate computer hardware. It provides a platform to run application software. Application software is a specific-purpose software which is used by the user for performing a specific task. Following table shows the difference between system software and application software:

System Software	Application Software
It is used for hardware.	It is used by user to perform specific task.
It is installed on the computer when operating system is installed.	It is installed according to user's requirements.
The user does not interact with system software because it works in the background.	The user interacts with application software.
It can run independently. It provides platform for running application software.	It cannot run independently. They cannot run without the presence of system software.
The workgroup support of network operating systems.	It supports electronic mail, group scheduling, shared work.
Examples of system software are compiler, assembler, debugger, driver, etc.	Examples of application software are word processor, web browser, media player, etc.

Table 1.3: *Difference between System and Application software*

System Software Application Software

Application software can be classified into different categories:

- **Readymade Software:** Readymade software is the software that is developed not for any specific user but for the users in general. Since the readymade software is for a general user, it is not necessary that all the modules of such software are of use for every user. One of the readymade software is Tally.

- **User-written Software:** End-user development is used to meet specific needs such as spreadsheet templates, word processor macros, scientific simulations, and scripts for graphics and animations. It depends on how competently the user-written software has been integrated into purchased application packages.

System Software

System software can be designed as the software in such a way so that it can control and work with computer hardware. It acts as an interface between the device and the end user. Generally, the system software performs the following functions:

- It communicates with hardware devices, controls and monitors the proper use of various hardware like CPU, memory, peripheral devices like monitor, printer, and so on.
- It supports the execution and development of other application software.

Few example of system software are:

- Operating system
- Programming language translators
- Communication software
- Compiler and Interpreters

Operating Systems

An operating system is a master control program that runs the computer and acts as a scheduler. It controls the flow of signals from CPU to various parts of the computer. It is the first program loaded (copied) into the computer memory after the computer is switched on. Popular operating systems include **MS-DOS, Linux, Windows** and **UNIX**.

The operating system is an important component of the computer system because it sets the standards for the application programs that run on it. All programs must be written to "talk to" the operating system.

The operating system performs the following functions:

- **Job Management:** In small computers, the operating system responds to commands from the user and loads the desired application program into the memory for execution. In a large-sized computer, the operating system carries out its Job Control Instruction (JCI), which can be described as the mix of programs that must be run for an entire shift.

- **Task Management:** In single tasking computers, the operating system has virtually no task management to do, but in multitasking computers, it is responsible for the concurrent operation of one or more programs (jobs). Advanced operating systems have more fine-tuning capabilities so that a specific job can be speeded up or slowed down by commands from the computer operator. Multitasking is accomplished by designing the computer in such a way to allow instructions to be executed during the time data is coming into the computer or being displayed by it.

- **Data Management:** One of the major functions of an operating system is to keep track of the data on the disk. The application program does not know where the data is actually stored or how to get it. That knowledge is contained in the operating system access method or device driver routines. When a program is ready to accept data, it signals the operating system with the coded message. The operating system finds the data and delivers it to the program. Conversely, when the program is ready to produce output, the operating system transfers data from the program onto the next available space on the disk.

- **Security:** Multiuser operating systems maintain a list of authorized users and provide password protection against unauthorized users who may try to gain access to the computer system. They also provide backup and recovery routines to start all over again in the event of a system failure.

- **Bootstrap Program:** Boot means start or make the computer system ready so that it can take our instructions. The word "boot" comes from "bootstrap". Since bootstrapping helps you to get your boots on, likewise booting the computer helps it to get its ROM instructions loaded in its main memory.

Programming Software

This type of software offers the user several tools for writing computer programs of different languages. Some basic tools used in the programming software are:

- **Assemblers:** An assembler translates a program written in assembly language into machine language and is effectively a compiler for the assembly language, but can also be used interactively like an interpreter. It is a low-level programming language. It helps in understanding the programming language to machine code. In computer, there is an assembler that helps in converting the assembly code into machine code executable. It is designed to understand the instruction and provide to machine language for further processing. It mainly depends on the architecture of the system whether it is the operating or computer architecture. It produces with the help of compiling the high-level language source code like C, C++.

- **Compiler:** A compiler is a computer program which helps you transform source code written in a high-level language into low-level machine language. It translates the code written in one programming language to some other language without changing the meaning of the code. The compiler also makes the end code efficient which is optimized for execution time.

- **Interpreters:** An interpreter is a computer program, which converts each high-level program statement into the machine code. This includes source code, pre-compiled code, and scripts. Both compiler and interpreters do the same job, which is converting high-level programming language to machine code. However, a compiler will convert the code into machine code (create an exe) before program run. Interpreters convert code into machine code when the program is run.

Utility Software

Utility Software is a kind of system software designed to help, analyze, configure, optimize and maintain the computer. A single piece of utility software is usually called a **utility** or **tool**. If any problem related to system arises, then we can solve it through utility software, for example, Antivirus.

Open Source and Proprietary Software

The term **open source software** refers to the software that is developed and tested through open collaboration, i.e., anyone can access the source code, modify it, and distribute his own version of the updated code. It is a certification mark owned by the **Open Source Initiative (OSI)**. Any software under the open source license is meant to be shared openly among users and redistributed by others. Examples of such software are Linux, Mozilla Firefox, OpenOffice.org, and Python.

Proprietary Software means the software is owned by the company which developed it. No one may duplicate it or distribute it without permission. The owner or publisher of the software holds intellectual property rights of the source code exclusively. You call this type of software "proprietary software" because the proprietor of the software will be able to make modifications to the software as well as add or remove features from the software. The software can be run on the computer of a person who purchases the software under a license agreement. Examples of such software are Microsoft Office, Adobe Photoshop, CorelDRAW, Windows 7 and macOS.

	Open Source	**Proprietary**
Licensing	They have the right to copy, modify and share the product.	They cannot copy, modify or share the product.
Cost of product	Free.	Not free (unless it is freeware).
Examples software	Python Mozilla Firefox, Google Chrome, Linux.	Internet Explorer, Photoshop, Windows, iOS, iTunes.
Vendor lock-in	Users can switch to other alternative open source products or modify the software.	Users rely on the vendor to support and update the product.
Updates and improvements	A community of contributors with a range of expertise can contribute to the continuous improvement of the product.	The vendor is in complete charge of the update cycle and developing new features.

Table 1.4: *Difference between open source and proprietary software*

Mobile Apps

In modern age, mobile application uses and development is a new and rapidly growing sector.

Mobile application (also known as mobile app) is a type of application software designed to run on a mobile device, such as a smartphone or tablet computer.

Mobile applications frequently serve to provide users with similar services to those accessed on PCs. Apps are generally small, individual software units with limited function. This use of app software was originally popularized by Apple Inc. and its App Store, which offers thousands of applications for the iPhone, iPad and iPod Touch.

Using mobile application, developing countries are upgrading themselves, thereby making it easy to use and accessible from anywhere and any place. Nowadays, many people are using mobile application to contact friends, browse Internet, file content management, entertainment, etc. From everywhere, users can get facility of mobile application and can do many things of his daily life and business.

Mobile application is a fast-developing segment of the global information and communication technology. It has wide uses for its vast functioning areas like calling, messaging, browsing, chatting, social network communication, audio, video, game, and so on. Some mobile applications are pre-installed in the phone, while others can be downloaded from the Internet and installed in the mobile phone.

According to usage, there are different categories of mobile applications.

- **Communications:** Internet browsing, email, and so on.
- **Multimedia:** Graphics, image viewer, presentations viewer, and so on.
- **Games:** Candy Crash Saga, Angry Birds, and so on.
- **Productivity:** Calendars, Calculators, Notepad.
- **Travel:** City Guide, GPS/maps, Weather, and so on.
- **Utilities:** Profile manager, File Manager, Call manager, Flash light, Speed Test, and so on.

Finding and Installing Mobile Apps

The three major players in the mobile apps space are:

- **Google Play:** For Android devices
- **Apple's App Store:** For iPads and iPhones
- **Amazon App Store:** For Amazon Fire devices

Many websites also offer corresponding apps and provide download links. Installation is fast and easy. Simply navigate to the appropriate store, find the app you want, and download it. Your device will install it automatically once the download completes.

Types of Mobile Applications

Mobile applications are of three types:

- **Native Application:** Native app can be installed from application store like Android's Google Play and Apple's App Store.
- **Web Application:** Web applications run from mobile web browsers like Chrome, Firefox, Opera and Safari.
- **Hybrid Application:** Hybrid apps are combinations of native apps and web apps.

Present Uses of Mobile Application

From the last few years, every mobile company is making the smartphone and feature phone. By increasing the computing power of mobile phone, they rapidly increase the smart mobile application. Every standard mobile has Facebook application.

Users can share information, videos, audio and so on, with friends and family from anywhere and any place like in car or in train. You can call in any corner of the world with low cost using VoIP application and Internet.

Road navigation apps use the GPS system, which searches current position of the user with the help of a map. For example, Google Maps helps us find out any place. Using mobile commerce, you can select a product and order for it. People can do business work using mobile applications. Mobile banking and e-Ticketing are other features of mobile application.

Conclusion

Computer is a very powerful tool man has ever created for calculations and making decisions. Computers have made a great impact on our everyday life. It is basically a programmable computing machine and operates on binary digits 0 and 1. Then, in this chapter, you learnt about various computer generations which are based on major technological changes in computer. you also understood the major components of digital computer, which are Central Processing Unit (CPU), Memory, input device and output device. Thus, the input and output devices are also known as peripherals. You learnt about the computer memory, which is the storage space where data is to be processed, and instructions needed for processing are stored. Two types of memories are primary and secondary memory. Then you covered the basics of hardware and software along with few examples. Hardware means physical components of a computer system which we can see and touch. The term software refers to a set of computer programs. Lastly, you discussed mobile apps. Thus, in this chapter, you tried to get familiar with various types of computers along with its various parameters and features.

In the next chapter, you will learn Windows 10 operating system for personal computers.

REVIEW QUESTIONS WITH ANSWERS

A. Multiple Choice Questions.

1. Find out the Proprietary software.
   a. Auto CAD
   b. Adobe Photoshop
   c. CorelDRAW
   d. All of the above

2. Which of the following holds the ROM, CPU, RAM and expansion cards?.
   a. Hard disk
   b. Floppy disk
   c. Motherboard
   d. None of the above

3. Which of the following memory provides back-up storage for instructions and data?
   a. Internal processor memory
   b. Primary memory
   c. Secondary memory
   d. None of these

4. CD-ROM is a:
   a. Temporary memory
   b. Permanent storage
   c. Magnetic memory
   d. None of the above

5. Information retrieval is fastest from:
   a. Pen drive
   b. CD
   c. Hard disk
   d. All of the above

6. RAM means:
   a. Random Access Memory
   b. Read Also Memory
   c. Read Access Memory
   d. Random Also Memory

7. Which one of the following is a secondary storage device?
   a. CD-ROM
   b. RAM
   c. Both a and b
   d. None of the above

8. The language that the computer can understand and execute is called:
   a. Machine language
   b. Application software
   c. System program
   d. None of the above

9. Which one of the following is not an input device?
   a. Microphone
   b. Mouse
   c. Scanner
   d. None of the above

10. What is the function of control unit in the CPU?
    a. To transfer data to primary storage
    b. To store program instructions
    c. To perform logic functions
    d. To decode program instruction

B. State whether the following statements are True or False.

1. Computers cannot help in decision making process.

2. ALU is a part of CPU.

3. Using mobile application, developing countries are upgrading themselves, thereby making a new type of IT infrastructure.

4. Users have to pay to the software company if they want to use the software.

5. You cannot modify the software which is open source software.

6. Transistors are smaller than vacuum tubes.

7. Access to data stored on magnetic tape is random.

8. Computer software is normally classified as system software and application software.

9. The group of 8 bits is used to represent a byte.

10. An SC card is an output device.

C. Match the following:

1. Printer:	a. Compiler
2. RAM:	b. Laser beam
3. Software:	c. Output device
4. A program which translates a high-level language program into a machine language program is called a:	d. Speech synthesizers
5. The device that converts text information into speech sentences:	e. A type of memory
6. They can operate on batteries and hence are very popular with travelers:	f. A set of computer programs that enables hardware to perform different tasks
7. The technology used in optical disks is:	g. Primary and Secondary
8. Full form of TTS:	h. Typographic Text Speech
9. Two basic types of memory in a computer are:	i. Laptop
10. Transforming data into informationt:	j. Text to speech
	k. Processing

D. Fill in the blanks.

> Brain   IC   Input, processing, output and storage
> Hardware   Secondary   Handheld   CPU
> Software   Barcode   Application   Storage
> Arithmetic Unit

1. The third-generation computer was made with ___________.
2. Personal digital assistant (PDAs) are also known as _________ computers.
3. The four basic functions of a computer are _______________.
4. The CPU is the _____________ of a computer system.
5. Hard disk is an example of ___________ memory.

6. The control unit and the arithmetic logic unit are located in the ___________.
7. ___________ is any part of the computer that you can physically touch.
8. _________ identifies the product to the supermarket computer which has the latest description and price.
9. System software is the set of programs that enables your computer hardware devices and _________ software to work together.
10. Hard disk drives and CD-Drives are examples of _________ devices.

SHORT ANSWER QUESTIONS.

1. **Distinguish between analog and digital computers.**

   Answers: Analog Computer: Analog computers handle or process information which is of a physical nature, as for example, measuring temperature, pressure, and so on.

   Digital Computer: Digital computers process data which is essentially in a binary or two-state form, namely, zero and one. Presently, we use PCs which are digital computers.

2. **How can you say that the CPU is the brain of the computer system?**

   Answers: A CPU is the brain of a computer because its primary function is to execute programs. Besides executing programs, the CPU also controls the operation of all other components such as memory, input and output devices. Under its control, programs and data are stored in the memory and outputs are displayed on the monitor screen or printed on paper, once processing has taken place.

3. **Explain any two fields where computer can be used.**

   Answers: (a) Banks: Almost every bank uses computers to keep the records of money transactions and financial documents. It is also used in this sector because of speed, convenience and security that it provides.

   (b) Business: Computer has now become

an integral part of corporate life. Today, computers can be found in every store, supermarkets, restaurants, offices, etc. One can buy and sell things online, bills and taxes can be paid online and even the future of business can be predicated using artificial intelligence software.

4. **Differentiate between RAM and ROM.**
   Answers:
   RAM: It is the main memory and allows you to temporarily store data. The CPU reads data from RAM to perform specific tasks. RAM is volatile, which means it is available only while the computer is turned on. The contents of RAM must be copied to a storage device if you want to save the data in the RAM.

   ROM: It is the memory that retains its contents even after the computer is turned off. Almost every computer with a small amount of ROM contains the boot firmware. This consists of a few kilobytes of code that tells the computer what to do when it starts up, e.g., running hardware diagnostics and loading the operating system into RAM.

5. **Differentiate System Software and Application Software.**
   Answers:
   a. System software gets installed when the operating system is installed on the computer while application software is installed according to the requirements of the user.
   b. System software includes programs such as compilers, debuggers, drivers, assemblers while application software includes media players, word processors, and spreadsheet programs.
   c. Generally, users do not interact with system software as it works in the background, whereas users interact with application software while doing different activities.
   d. A computer may not require more than one type of system software while there may be a number of application software

programs installed on the computer at the same time.
   e. System software can run independently of the application software while application software cannot run without the presence of the system software.

6. **List various sub units of the CPU and give the function of each of the units.**
   Answers: Central Processing Unit (CPU) is the brain of any computer system. All major calculations, manipulations and comparisons are made by the CPU. The CPU is also responsible for activating and controlling the operations performed by all other units of the computer system.

   The major parts of a CPU are:
   a. Arithmetic and Logic unit (ALU)
   b. Control unit (CU)
   c. Main Memory or Primary Memory

   Arithmetic Logic Unit (ALU): All calculations, including comparisons, are made by the ALU. The data and instructions, stored in the primary memory prior to processing, are transferred to the ALU where processing takes place. Results generated in the ALU are transferred to the primary memory. After completion of processing, the final results available in the primary memory are sent to an output device, such as printer.

   ALUs are designed to perform the four basic arithmetic operations (add, subtract, multiply, divide) and logic operations (comparison between numbers, letter and or special characters) and conditions (less than, equal to, or greater than).

   Control Unit: Control Unit obtains instructions from the program stored in the main memory, interprets the instructions, and issues electrical signals that cause other units of the system to perform their functions. The control unit acts as the central nervous system for all other components of the computer. It coordinates the entire jobs done by the computer system.

   Memory: The function of the memory is to store information. The main memory (primary memory) is a fast memory. It stores programs along with data, which are to be executed. It also stores necessary programs of system software, which are required to execute the user's program. The main memory is directly addressed by the CPU. Semiconductor memories, RAMs are used as main memory.

Input and Output Devices: Input devices are those through which we enter data and instructions. An input device converts input data and instructions into a suitable binary form which is stored in the memory of a computer. The most commonly used input devices are keyboard and mouse. Other input devices are MICR, Light pen, OCR, Joystick, and OMR, etc.

Output devices are those devices of computer system that supplies information or results either in the form of hardcopy (printer) or softcopy (monitor). Some of the common output devices are Monitor, Printer, Plotter, Multimedia Projector, and speech synthesizer. Devices which works both.

DESCRIPTIVE TYPE QUESTIONS

1. What is a computer? What are the advantages and disadvantages of a computer?
2. What are the main components of a PC system? Explain each component.
3. What is the role of input and output devices in a computer system?
4. Name some of the input and output devices used with computers.
5. What are the five basic operations performed by any computer system? Explain each one of them.
6. How many types of memory does a computer have? Justify the need for each type.
7. List different types of Memory in the Computer System. Explain their uses.
8. Explain the functions of Compiler, Interpreter and Assembler.
9. Differentiate between hardware and software.
10. Write a short note on MICR.

Answers

A.	1. D	2. c	3. c	4. b	5. c
	6. a	7. a	8. a	9. d	10. d

B.	1. F	2. T	3. T	4. T	5. F
	6. T	7. F	8. T	9. T	10. d

C.	1. C	2. e	3. f	4. a	5. d
	6. i	7. b	8. j	9. g	10. k

D.	1. b	2. f	3. c	4. a	5. e
	6. g	7. d	8. i	9. j	10. k

■■

CHAPTER 2

Introduction to Operating System Windows

Structure

In this chapter, we will discuss the following topics:

- Operating System
- OS for desktop, laptop, mobile phone and laptop
- UI for desktop and laptop
- Simple settings of OS
- File and folder management
- Types of file extensions
- Keyboard shortcuts

Objectives

The reader will be able to understand the following

- Operating System and its applications for both desktop and mobile devices.
- Identify various desktop screen components and modify various properties, date, time, etc.
- Add and remove new program and features, manage files and folders.
- Adding, removing and sharing printers.
- How to manage File and Folder.

Operating system (OS), is a collection of software that manages computer hardware resources and provides common services for computer programs. It is an essential component of the system software in a computer system. Application programs usually require an operating system to function. In other words, Operating System can be defined as a program that acts as an intermediary between a user of a computer and the computer hardware. The objectives of operating system are as follows:

- It executes user programs and makes solving of user problems easier.
- It makes the computer system convenient to use.
- It uses the computer hardware in an efficient manner.

Operating System

An Operating System (OS) is a set of system software programs in a computer that regulates the ways in which application software programs use the computer hardware and the ways in which users control the computer. For hardware functions, such as input/output and memory space allocation, operating system acts as an intermediary between application programs and the computer hardware. Although application programs are usually executed directly by the hardware, Operating System is also a field of study within Applied Computer Science.

Basics of Operating System

Operating system works as an interface between the user and the computer and all other programs need an OS to get started. It is a software that controls the internal activities of the computer hardware and provides user interface. It is the first program loaded into the computer memory and starts the computer authentically when the power is turned on. Popular operating systems are Windows XP, Windows 10, LINUX and UNIX.

The operating system:

- Controls and coordinates the operation of computer.
- Controls input and output devices.
- Controls execution of computer programs.
- Does all the interaction between user and the computer.
- Helps you manage and manipulate files and use main memory of the computer.

An operating system performs the following functions:

An OS is an interface between a computer user and hardware. It is a software which performs all the basic tasks like file management, memory, process management, handling input and output, and controlling peripheral devices such as disk drives and printer and a file system. The following image shows important functions of an operating system:

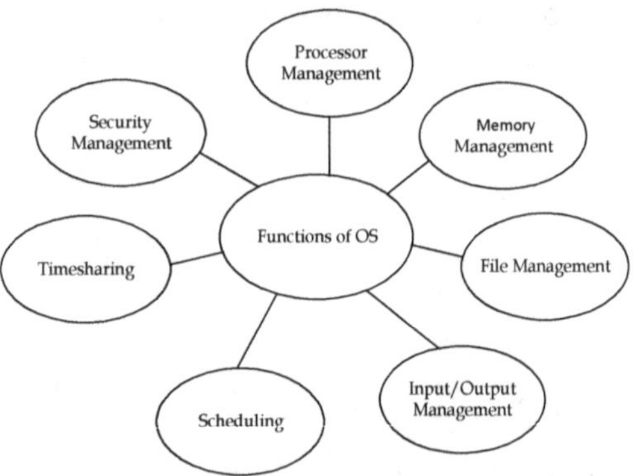

Figure 2.1: *Functions of OS*

Let us understand each function:

- **Processor Management:** It assigns processors (if a computer has more than one processor) to the different tasks that must be performed by the computer system. It keeps track of the processor and status of the process. The program responsible for this task is known as traffic controller.
- **Memory Management:** It allocates the main memory and secondary memory to the system programs, user programs and data. It keeps track of primary memory, that is, which bytes of memory are used by which user program. In multiprogramming, the OS decides the order in which process has access to memory, and for how long.

- **Input/output Management:** It carries out the input/output management, co-ordinates and assigns tasks to different input and output devices. It keeps track of all devices connected to the system, and designates a program responsible for every device known as the input/output controller. It decides which process gets access to a certain device and for how long.
- **File Management:** It manages files on various storage devices and transfers these files from one storage device to another. It keeps track of information, location uses, statuses, and so on. The collective facilities are often known as file system.
- **Scheduling:** It establishes and enforces the job priority. It is a task of operating system to schedule the process of different states like ready, running, and waiting. This task is very useful in maintaining the computer system. It allocates the time interval of each process in which the process is to be executed by the CPU.
- **Timesharing:** It co-ordinates and assigns compilers, assemblers, utility programs, and other software packages to various users working on the computer system. In a transaction processing, the processor executes each user program in a short or quantum of computation. That is, if n users are present, then each user can get a time quantum. When the user submits the command, the response time is in few seconds at most.
- **Security Management:** It establishes data security and integrity. It protects the data and information of a computer system against malware threat.

All operating systems can be classified into following categories:

- **Single User Operating System:** It allows only one user to work on a computer at a time, for example, Windows XP.
- **Multiuser Operating System:** It allows a number of users to work together on a single computer by providing a terminal connected to a single computer, for example, Unix.
- **Single Tasking Operating System:** It executes a single job/program at a time, for example, MS-DOS.
- **Multitasking Operating System:** It supports the execution of more than one task at a time, for example, Windows 2012.
- **Multiprogramming Operating System:** In this, several programs can be run at the same

time through a time-sharing mechanism, for example, Linux.

- **Real-Time Operating System:** It responds to an event within a pre-determined time, for example, Windows CE.
- **Batch Processing Operating System:** Similar types of task are grouped under one batch and then these tasks are executed without any user interruption, for example, MS-DOS.
- **Multiprocessing Operating System:** It uses more than two CPUs within a single computer system, for example, LINUX and UNIX.

Operating Systems for Desktop and Laptop

All computers and computer-like devices require operating systems, including your laptop, tablet, desktop and smartphone. Some examples include versions of Microsoft Windows' latest Windows 10 and Apple's MacOS. A desktop computer is a personal computer that is placed at a fixed location. On the other hand, a laptop is a compact version of a desktop computer. Generally, the desktop is larger than the laptop.

The laptop is a single unit with all components, such as keyboard, mouse, monitor, webcam and speakers built in it. Therefore, users do not need to connect and disconnect such components every time when there is a need to change locations. Unlike the portable laptop computers, most of the desktop computers are heavy, which makes them stationary. Many components, such as the monitor, keyboard, mouse, speakers and webcam, which make up a desktop computer, get separated, and the user must connect all the components correctly for the computer to be functional. Users must also disconnect all the components and pack them well before moving from one place to another while changing locations. In case the user misplaces some components like the power cable, the computer cannot function. Most components in the desktop are easily removable, making it easier to upgrade. Since desktop cases are usually much bigger, they are easier to work on while doing any upgrading. Repairing the desktop computer is much easier than the laptop.

Memory and hard drive components can be upgraded in a laptop. The remaining components are built-in and not designed to work with an upgraded version of the component. A need to upgrade anything other than the hard drive and memory usually requires a new laptop.

Operating Systems for Mobile Phone and Tablets

A mobile operating system (or Mobile OS) is an operating system for phones, tablets, smart watches, or other mobile devices. It is specifically designed for mobile devices such as mobile phones, smartphones, PDAs, tablet computers and other handheld devices. Mobile-based tablets run on mobile apps to perform a function. Examples of mobile operating system are **Apple's iOS** and **Google Android**. This system features a core kernel along with middleware that supports databases, multimedia and graphics.

Two operating systems currently dominate mobile computing: Apple iOS and Google Android. iOS is a proprietary OS that runs on the iPhone, iPad and iPod Touch devices originally known as the iPhone OS.

Apple iOS is based on the Mac OS X operating system. It uses a multi-touch interface in which simple gestures operate the device, such as swiping your finger across the screen to move to the next page or pinching your fingers to zoom out. iOS is different from most other operating systems, in that, it puts each app in its own protective shell, which keeps other apps from tampering with them, which makes it impossible for a virus to infect apps on the mobile operating system. The protective shell around apps also poses limitations as it keeps apps from directly communicating with one another.

Apple iOS includes the following features:

- Wi-Fi, Bluetooth and cellular connectivity along with VPN support.
- Gesture recognition supports shaking the device to undo the recent action.
- Integrated front and rear facing cameras with video capabilities.
- Direct access to the Apple App store and the iTunes catalog of music, podcasts and television shows.
- Compatibility with Apple's cloud service.
- Cross-platform communication between Apple devices through AirDrop and through Apple Pay, which stores a user's credit card data to pay for goods and services directly with an iOS device.

Android is a **Linux based operating system**. It is designed for touch screen mobile devices such as smartphones and tablet computers. It supports a large number of applications in smartphones. These applications are more convenient for users. The hardware that supports the Android software is based on an ARM architecture platform. It is an open source operating system, which means that it is free and any one can use it.

Android includes the following features:

- Storage
- Connectivity as CDMA, Bluetooth, Wi-Fi, LTE, GPS and EDGE
- Messaging as SMS, MMS, **C2DM (cloud to device message) GCM (Google could messaging)**
- Multilanguage support
- Multi-touch
- Video calling
- Screen capture
- Optimized graphics
- Streaming media support
- External storage

Microsoft Tablet PC introduced a specific edition of Windows XP called the Windows XP, Tablet PC edition. It allowed handwritten recognition and voice recognition functionality and gesture support. Windows 10 introduces Metro-style apps; these apps are designed to run across multiple Microsoft product families such as tablets, smartphones and embedded systems. The comparison between Android and iOS is shown in *Table 2.1*:

	Android	**iOS**
OS family	Linux	OS X, UNIX
Developer	Google	Apple Inc.
Available language(s)	100+ languages. Coding languages used are Java and C/C++.	34 languages. Coding languages used are C/C++.
File transfer	Easier than iOS. Using USB port and Android transferred File Transfer desktop app. Photos can be Transferred via USB without apps.	More difficult. Media files can be transferred using iTunes desktop app. Photos can be transferred via USB without apps.
Available on	Many phones and tablets. Major manufactures are Samsung, Motorola, LG, HTC and Sony.	iPod Touch, iPhone, iPad
Calls and messaging	Third-party apps such as Facebook, Messenger, WhatsApp, Google Duo and Skype could be used.	iMessage, FaceTime (with other Apple devices only). Third-party apps like Google Hangouts, Facebook Messenger, WhatsApp, Google Duo and Skype could be used.
Internet browsing	Google Chrome and other browsers are available.	Mobile Safari and other browsers are available
App Store and Interface	Google Play apps and Amazon.	Apple App store
Video chat	Google Duo	FaceTime
Voice commands	Voice-operated assistant still being developed.	Siri
Maps	Google Maps	Apple Maps and Google Maps
Battery life and Management	Many Android phones and devices are equipped with large batteries with a longer life.	Apple batteries are not larger than Android batteries. However, it is able to squeeze decent battery life via hardware/ software optimizations.
File manager	File manager included in this device.	Not available

Photos and video back-up	Apps available for automatic backup of photos and videos.	Up to 5 GB of photos and videos can be automatically backed up with iCloud.
Security	Android devices are not running updated, fully patched software.	They never encounter a problem with malware because they do not go outside the Play Store for apps.
Cloud Services	Integration with Google cloud storage. 15 GB up to 1TB available for Amazon photos, OneDrive and Dropbox.	Integration with iCloud. 5GB to 1TB available for Google Drive and Google, Amazon Photos, OneDrive and Dropbox.
Interface	Touch Screen	Touch Screen
Supported Version	Android 5.0 & later	iOS & later

Table 2.1: *The comparison between Android and iOS*

User Interface for Desktop and Laptop

Windows 10 is one of the best operating systems, which is simple, easy-to-use and better than the older Windows OS. Windows UI is much more improved and combines the features of both Windows 7 and 8 operating systems. It is very user-friendly and has easy-to-learn new features. It is mainly designed for **touch** as well as **non-touch devices**.

Lock Screen with Log in

When you turn on your computer or laptop power button, after the booting, you can see the first user interface of Windows 10, that is **Lock Screen**. The bottom-left portion shows the time, day and date information, and the bottom-right shows the `connect to internet' and battery life, as shown in *Figure 2.2:*

Figure 2.2: *Lock Screen*

The center shows your Photo (if added to your account), name of your computer and password entering portion. The bottom-right side contains the **connect to Internet, ease of access** and **Power button**, as shown in *Figure 2.2.*

Connect to Internet: It helps to connect your PC with internet via Wi-Fi or modem. This option is also available in your Windows 10 desktop.

From the lock screen, you log into your Windows 10 system desktop. To get the login screen, if you just click anywhere or press the **Enter** key on your keyboard, you will go to the User Accounts screen, as shown in *Figure 2.3:*

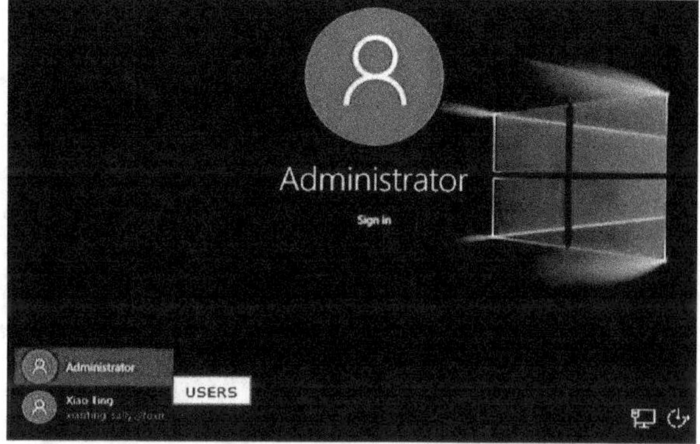

Figure 2.3: *User Accounts Screen*

Ease of Access: It is a very helpful option for people having some eyesight problem. It contains the Narrator, Magnifier, On-board screen keyboard, High contrast (ON/OFF), Sticky key (ON/OFF) and Filter key (ON/OFF). On-board keyboard is mainly for touch screen device to enter the password in the specified location. Click on the **side arrow** button to get into the Windows 10 desktop/laptop interface.

Windows 10 Desktop Area

This is the main UI of Windows 10 called **Desktop**. It contains the shortcut icons of My Computer and several other Windows 10 programs installed in your PC. The **My Computer** or **This PC** helps to explore the different locations of your stored files in the hard disk. You can also store the files, folders, videos, pictures, and so on, in the desktop area, as shown in *Figure 2.4*:

Figure 2.4: *Desktop Screen of Windows 10*

Desktop

Desktop areas is where your Desktop icons such as program and application icons appear. Here, you can open the program and folders by double-clicking on their icons. To minimize all program/app windows and display desktop, press **Windows key + D** on your keyboard. By default, the desktop shows only the Recycle bin icon. You can drag any program icon from the Start menu. To add shortcuts to files or folders, **right-click** an empty area of desktop, choose **New** and **shortcut**.

Start Button

Although Windows 8 replaced the old Start Menu with the Start Screen, the Start Menu is back and better than before in Windows 10. The Start button provides access to the apps on your Windows 10 PC and also to the enhanced Start Menu. When you click on the Start button, the Start menu is displayed, as shown in *Figure 2.5*:

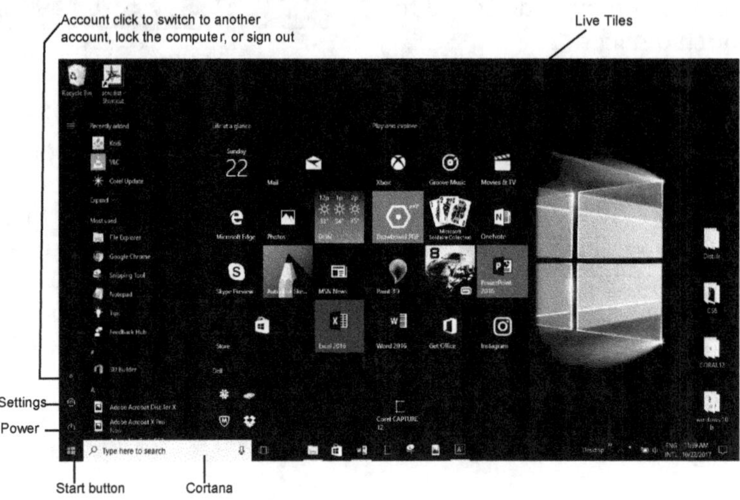

Figure 2.5: *Start Menu of Windows 10*

The left-hand side of the Start menu contains links to frequently used apps, a list of quick links to items such as the Power button, and the alphabetic list of all the apps on the computer. The right-hand side of the Start menu is where apps can be pinned so that they are always available. This is displayed as a collection of large-colored tiles (square and rectangular-colored blocks called Tiles). When you click or tap on it, it starts an app. The app will then perform a specific task such as sending and receiving e-mail, viewing web pages, editing photographs or playing a game.

Some apps can be displayed as Live Tiles, which can show information from that app. For example, Mail messages will be summarized in the Mail app's tile, while the Weather app's tile will show you the weather forecast.

These tiles can be moved and dragged to different places by holding the mouse button. You can also configure them by right-clicking on them to get several options, such as resize them or **unpin** them (remove them) from the Menu.

Search Box/Cortana

The Windows 10 search bar is pretty simple, but there are ways to find things faster. The Search tool allows you to search specific types of items, such as apps, documents, e-mail, photos, folders, and so on. For example, to search for a specific file, simply type your keyword in the search field. Depending on you search item, the results may point to documents, apps, web pages, and other type of content.

In *Figure 2.6*, Cortana helps you find information, both on your computer and on the Internet. For example, type a few words from one of your files into the box, and Cortana should find the file and list its name, ready for you to open it with a click. Cortana does the same if you type the name of a setting or a program. It also understands speech commands. Click the little microphone in the box and say your command:

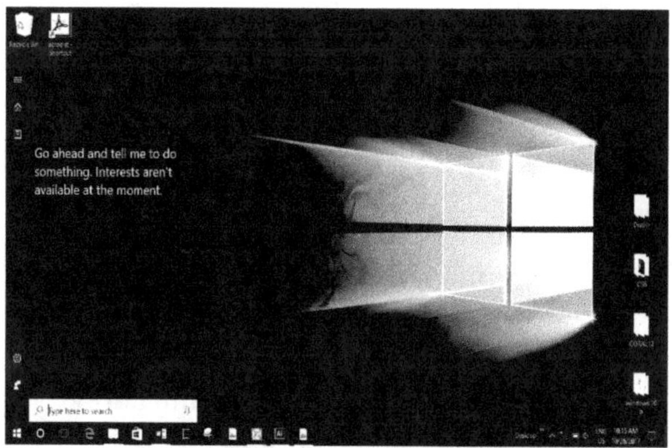

Figure 2.6: *Cortana in Windows 10*

Task View

Another new feature in Windows 10 is Task View, which lets you have several desktops open. This allows you to have multiple desktop screens where you can keep open windows organized. A desktop is a set of apps that is saved on the same page. If you have a lot of apps that you're switching between, you can group them into a few different desktops and then switch between desktops instead of constantly minimizing one window.

1. Click **Task View** on the Taskbar.
2. Click the **New desktop** option on the lower-right corner. You can access or delete the new desktop by clicking Task View again.

Whether you are running Windows on a PC, laptop, or tablet, you can bring any missing app to the forefront by following these two quick steps:

1. Click or tap the Task View button. The screen clears, and Windows displays miniature views of your open apps and programs, as shown in *Figure 2.7*:

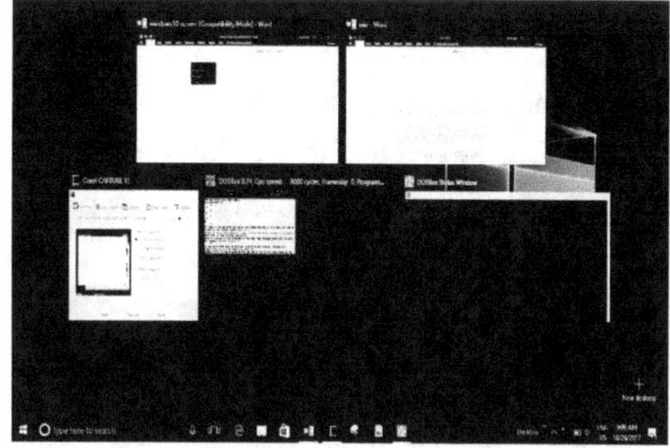

Figure 2.7: *Taskview of Windows 10*

2. Tap or click any thumbnail to return the app or program to its full size. Currently running apps and programs also appear as icons on the taskbar (the narrow strip along the bottom of the screen).

   - To close an unwanted app shown in thumbnail view, click or tap the X in its upper-right corner (shown in the title bar). With a mouse, you can also right-click the app's thumbnail and choose Close from the pop-up menu.

   - After you close an app, the miniature views of the other running apps remain onscreen, letting you either switch to them or close them. To leave the Task View mode, click or tap the desktop.

Microsoft Edge

Microsoft Edge is the new Windows 10 web browser, as shown in *Figure 2.8*. By default, Edge can be accessed by clicking on the icon placed on the taskbar. When Edge opens, it presents a window similar to most browsers.

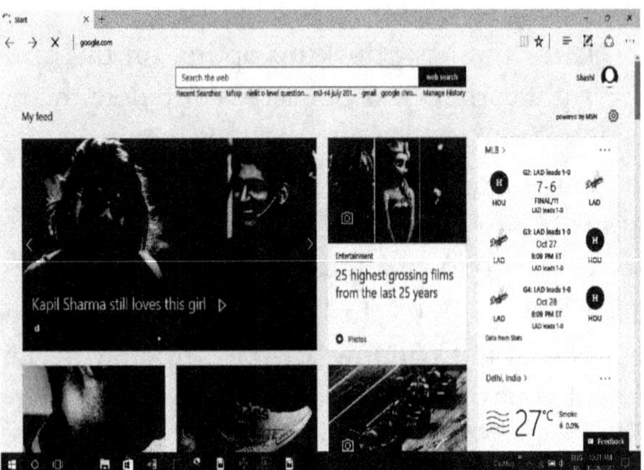

Figure 2.8: *Microsoft Edge*

It features the following buttons:

- **Back:** Takes you to the previous web page.
- **Forward:** Takes you to the next web page.
- **Refresh:** Reloads the web page.
- **New tab:** Adds another tab to see a different web page.
- **Hub (Favourites and History):** Shows the list of favorite web pages and history of visited web pages.

- **Web Notes:** Makes Web Notes on the web page.
- **Share:** Shares the web page via e-mail or other methods.
- **More options:** Helps configure the browser.

File Explorer

The Documents folder icon helps to quick access your saved files. By clicking the Folder icon on the taskbar, you can access the file and folder documents.

Notification Area

Click the Notification icon on the right side of the Taskbar. It shows different types of notifications from your computer, like your Internet connection or the volume level *(See Figure 2.8)*.

Opening the Action Center

The Action Center is a united place for all system notifications, such as incoming e-mails and quick access to various system settings. The right edge of the taskbar contains different icons. To open the Action Center, click the Action Center icon, and then the Action Center pane appears, as shown in *Figure 2.9*:

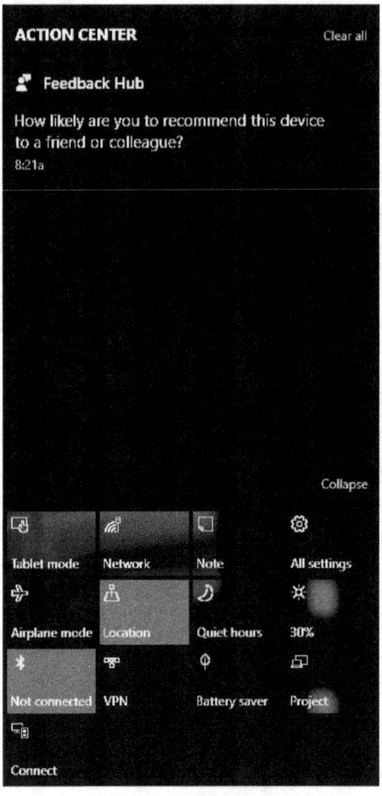

Figure 2.9: *The Action Center Pane*

The Action Center lists information about your latest e-mails, upcoming appointments, and other notifications. It also provides a list of four handy buttons along the bottom:

- **Tablet mode:** Click or tap this button to toggle Tablet mode. When it is colored, you're in Tablet mode, which works well only on touchscreens.
- **Connect:** This tells Windows to start searching for something you've connected, often wirelessly. Choose this after you turn on a wireless monitor or Bluetooth speaker.
- **All Settings:** This brings up the new Windows 10 Settings app, a huge panel of organized switches, which replaces most of the Control Panel found in older Windows versions. You can also open the Settings app by clicking the Start button and clicking the option Settings.

Your Action Center may contain different buttons based on your computer's configuration.

- **Tablet Mode:** Toggles between tablet and desktop mode.
- **Quiet Hours:** Temporarily disables notifications.
- **Battery Saver:** Turns on battery-saving features at the cost of performance.
- **All Settings:** Opens the All Settings screen.
- **Connect:** Connects to a Bluetooth device.
- **VPN:** Connects to a Virtual Private Network.
- **Bluetooth:** Manages Bluetooth devices.
- **Brightness:** Adjusts your screen brightness.
- **Note:** Creates a note in Microsoft OneNote.
- **Wi-Fi:** Toggles Wi-Fi.
- **Location:** Toggles location services on and off.
- **Airplane Mode:** Turns off Wi-Fi and Bluetooth.

Navigation Pane

Windows gathers your PC's most frequently used items and places them in the Navigation Pane. Along the left edge of every folder, the Navigation Pane contains several main sections: Quick Access, OneDrive, and This PC. The detailed description of each part of the Navigation Pane is as follows:

- **Quick Access:** Formerly called Favourites, these locations serve as clickable shortcuts to your most frequently accessed locations in Windows.

- **Desktop:** Your Windows desktop is actually a folder which is always open across your screen. Clicking Desktop quickly shows you the content.
- **Downloads:** Click this shortcut to find the files which you have downloaded with Explorer while browsing the Internet.
- **Documents:** This folder stores most of your work: spreadsheets, reports, letters, and other things you have created.
- **Pictures:** This takes you to photos you shot yourself or saved from the Internet.
- **OneDrive:** This free online storage space was handed over to you by Microsoft when you created a Microsoft account. Since it's password-protected and online, it's tempting to fill it with favorite files for access from any PC.
- **This PC:** This section lets you browse through your PC's folders and hard drives.

Dismiss a Notification

You can also ignore notifications without opening them.

1. Click the **Action Center** button on the taskbar.
2. Click a **notification's Close** button in the upper-right corner.
3. You can also click the **Clear All button** to clear all of your notifications at once.

Taskbar

The bottom dark portion is called taskbar. It contains the Windows 10 Start menu, Cortana Search box, Task View, Quick Access pinned icons of Microsoft Edge, Windows store, Documents, battery life, sound, Internet notifications and other icons, as shown in *Figure 2.10*. It also helps you see the currently active or open Windows program in your computer.

Figure 2.10: *Windows 10 Taskbar*

Configure the Taskbar

The simplest way to configure your taskbar is by pinning various apps and shortcuts to it so that you can access them quickly. You can manage some of its features from the shortcut menu that appears when the app's icon appears on the taskbar to indicate it is running, right-click the icon and select the **Pin to taskbar** option from the context menu. It will immediately add a new shortcut for the app to the taskbar.

To prevent changes from the taskbar, right-click on the taskbar and select **Lock** the taskbar. A check mark indicates that an option on the shortcut menu is active.

OR

To prevent or allow changes to the taskbar:

1. Open the Taskbar and Start Menu Properties dialog box.

2. On the **Taskbar** tab, select or clear the **Lock the taskbar** check box, accordingly.

3. Click **Apply** and **OK** to implement the change and close the dialog box.

4. Move the Taskbar.

To move the taskbar:

1. Drag the taskbar to any edge of the screen.

2. Right-click the taskbar, and then click **Properties.** On the Taskbar tab of the Properties dialog box, in the Taskbar location on screen list, click Left, Right, or Top (or click Bottom to return the taskbar to its default location).

To change the taskbar height:

1. Click on the inside edge of the taskbar.

2. When the pointer changes to a double-headed arrow, drag the inside edge of the taskbar to change its height (or width, when vertical) to the size you want. The height or width can be up to 50 percent of the screen height or width.

To attach or pin the application icon to your Windows taskbar:

1. Search for the application you want to pin in the Start Menu.

2. Right-click on the application.

3. Select the **More** option at the top of the menu.

4. Select the **Pin to taskbar** option.

Unpin an Application from the taskbar:

1. Just right-click its icon in the taskbar.

2. Select Unpin from taskbar.

3. You can pin it back again any time you want.

Icons and Shortcuts

All Windows versions feature different icons on the desktop background. An icon is a graphical representation of an application or a file.

To add desktop Apps:

1. Select the Window button to open the Start menu, as shown in the following image:

Figure 2.11: *Start button*

2. Select **All Apps**, as shown in the image given below:

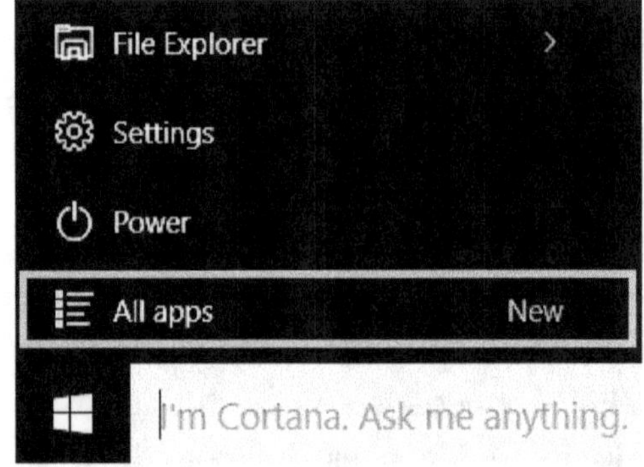

Figure 2.12: *Apps*

3. Right-click on the app for which you want to create a desktop shortcut. Here, we are selecting Google Chrome:

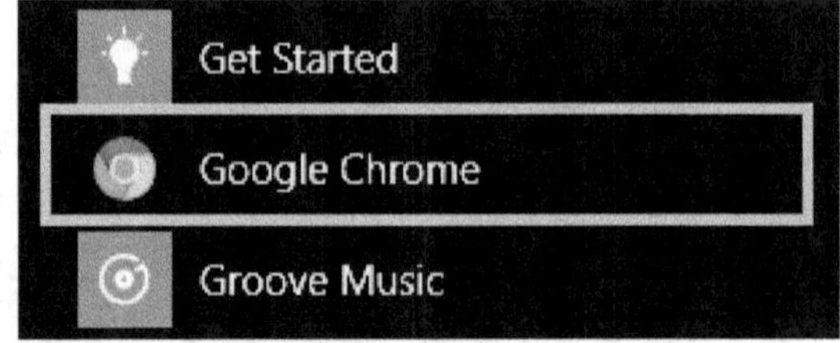

Figure 2.13: *Right clicking on the App*

4. Click the **More option**, as shown in the following screenshot. The sub-options appear:

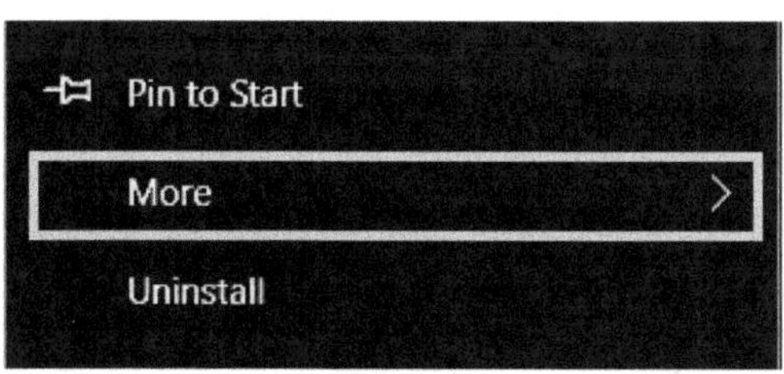

Figure 2.14: *The More option*

5. Select **Open file location**. The application file window opens.

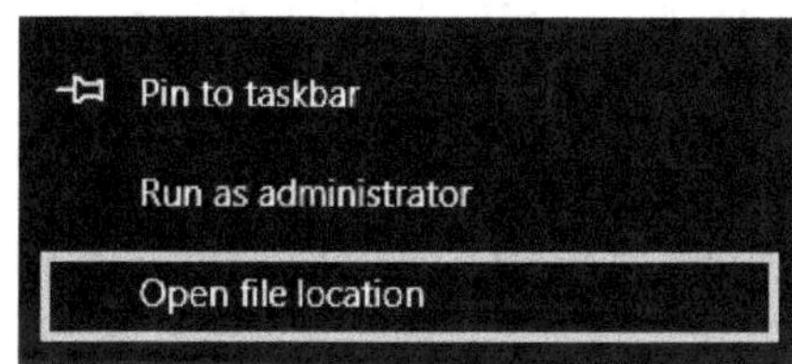

Figure 2.15: *Open file location option*

6. Right-click on the selected apps icon:

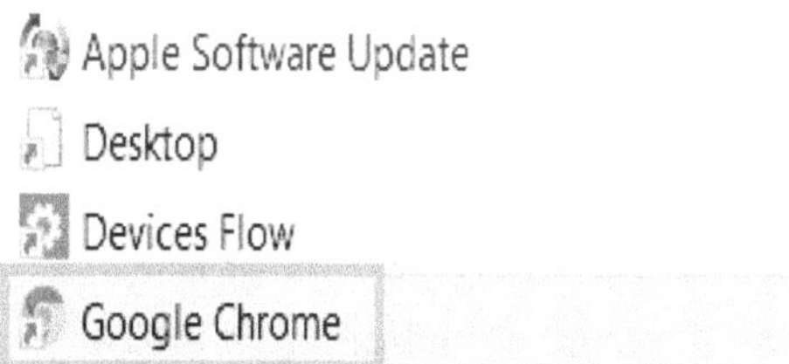

Figure 2.16: *Selecting the app*

7. Select **Create shortcut**, as shown in following image:

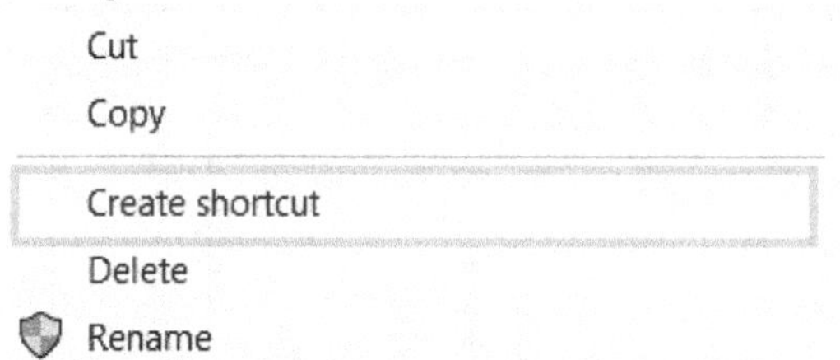

Figure 2.17: *Selecting Create shortcut option*

8. Select **Yes**. You have a desktop shortcut of your Desktop program:

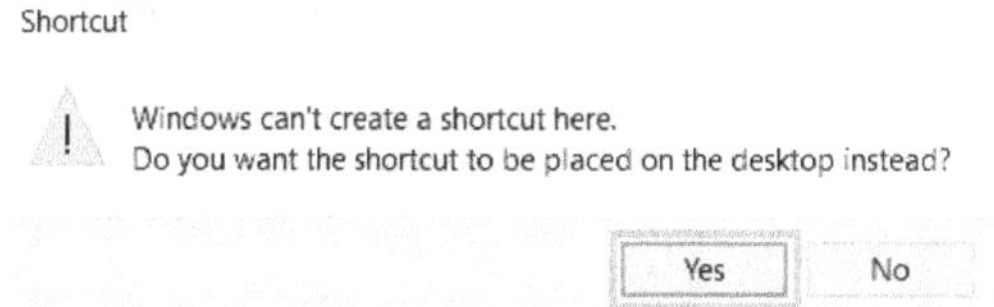

Figure 2.18: *Select Yes*

To create program shortcut on desktop by dragging and dropping, perform the following steps:

1. Minimize all running programs.
2. Click the Start button on the taskbar to see the Start menu.

Figure 2.19: *Dragging an App icon to Create Shortcut*

3. Click the apps, and then look for the program that you would like to see on the desktop as shortcut. Click on the program and then drag and drop it to the desktop to create a shortcut of the program on the desktop, as shown in *Figure 2.19*.
4. The shortcut will appear on the desktop.

> **Tips:** If you cannot see any icons on the desktop, right-click on desktop, then click View menu, and then click the Show Desktop icons option

A shortcut is a small file that is linked to a program, document, folder or an Internet address. The file is represented by an icon with an arrow in its lower-left corner.

Shortcut is linked to a file or folder, which can be located anywhere on a local hard disk or CD-ROM drive or on a floppy disk.

To create a shortcut using the create shortcut wizard:

1. Right-click the desktop; from the Context menu, choose New, and then choose **Shortcut**, as seen in *Figure 2.20*:

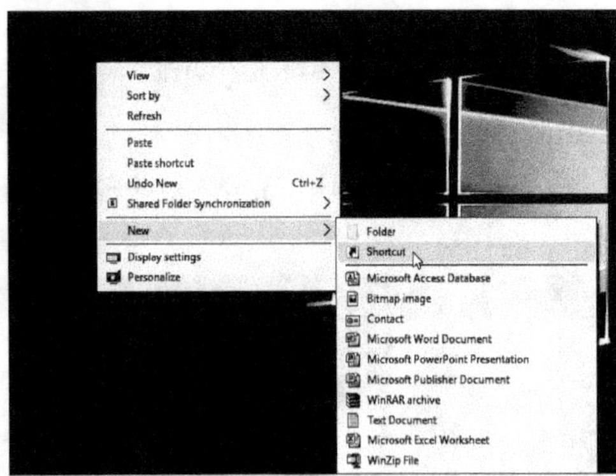

Figure 2.20: *Creating Shortcut*

2. The wizard for Create Shortcut appears, as shown in *Figure 2.21*.
3. Click the Browse... button. In the Browse for Folder dialog box, locate the item for which you want to create a shortcut.
4. Click **Next > type** a name for your shortcut, click Finish, and your shortcut will appear on the desktop, as shown in *Figure 2.21*:

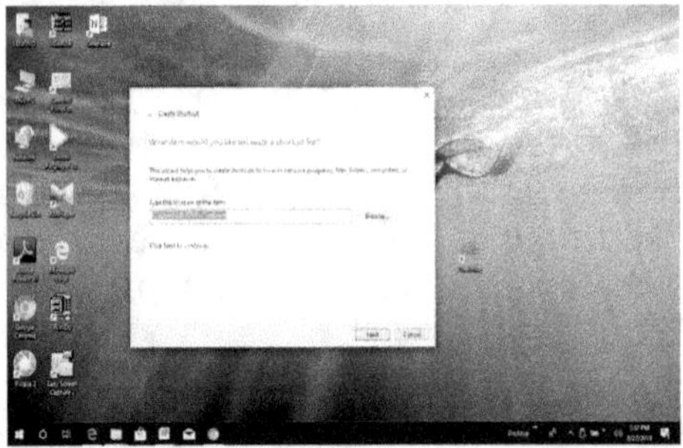

Figure 2.21: *Using the Create Shortcut Wizard*

Renaming a Shortcut

When you create a shortcut, Windows gives it a default name based on the underlying object.

To change the shortcut name:
1. Right-click the shortcut.
2. From the context menu, choose **Rename**.
3. Type the name that you want to use.

Deleting a Shortcut

To delete a shortcut:

1. Select the icon and press the * **key**. Alternatively, right-click the shortcut to be deleted and choose **Delete** from the context menu.

2. Windows prompts you for confirmation before deletion.

Desktop Icons

In Windows 10, by default, the Recycle Bin is added to the desktop. Double-clicking the Recycle Bin icon opens a window where you can view files and folders that you have marked for deletion. Other common desktop icons you can add to the desktop are as follows:

- **Computer:** Double-clicking the Computer icon opens a window where you can access hard disk drives and devices with removable storage. Right-click the Computer icon and choose **Manage** to open the Computer Management window. Also, clicking on Map Network Drive enables you to connect to shared network folders. Selecting Disconnect Network Drive enables you to remove a connection from a shared network folder.

- **Control Panel:** Double-clicking the Control Panel icon opens Control Panel, which provides access to system configuration and management tools.

- **Network:** Double-clicking the Network icon opens a window where you can access the computers and devices on your network.

- **User's Files:** Double-clicking the User's Files icon opens your personal folder.

To choose the icons which you want to appear:

1. Enter Desktop icons into the Control Panel Search box and click on the Show or hide common icons on the desktop link. See *Figure 2.22*:

Figure 2.22: *Desktop Icon Setting Dialog Box*

2. Select the checkbox for each of the five system folders (Computer, User's Files, Network, Recycle Bin and Control Panel) that you want to add to the desktop. Clear the checkbox for

each icon that you want to remove from the desktop. If the check mark appears, it means option is **ON**, otherwise option is **OFF**.

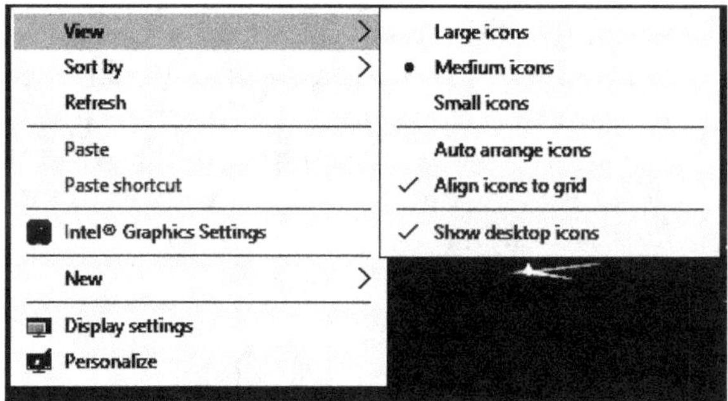

Figure 2.23: *View Menu*

To control the display of icons on the Desktop:

1. To resize the icons, bring out the View menu and click **Large icon**s, **Medium icons** or **Small icons**.

2. To hide all the icons, bring out the View menu and click Show desktop icons again.

Running an Application Window

Application Window contains a program which you are running and working with, namely, the Window that shows **MS Word**, **Excel**, **PowerPoint**, and so on. Most of the work that you do will be in the application window.

To open an application window:

1. Click the Start button. The Start menu appears.

2. The **All Apps** (that is, the menu named All Programs or just program) items on the Start menu that displays the list of programs comes up. The option that has a pointer to the right of its name is a Program group. A Program group is a collection of programs and related document files. When you choose a Program group, it opens a menu listing the items in the program group, as shown in the *Figure 2.24*:

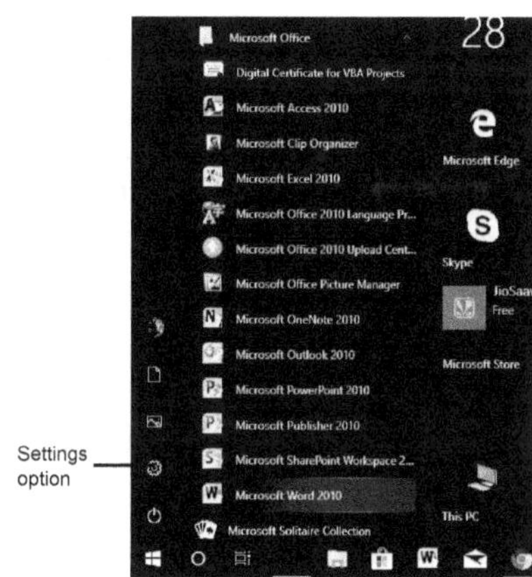

Figure 2.24: *Apps Item List and the Selected Application*

3. From the Apps item list, click the desired application, such as Word, Access and PowerPoint. For example, an application window (MS-Word) opens, as shown in *Figure 2.25*:

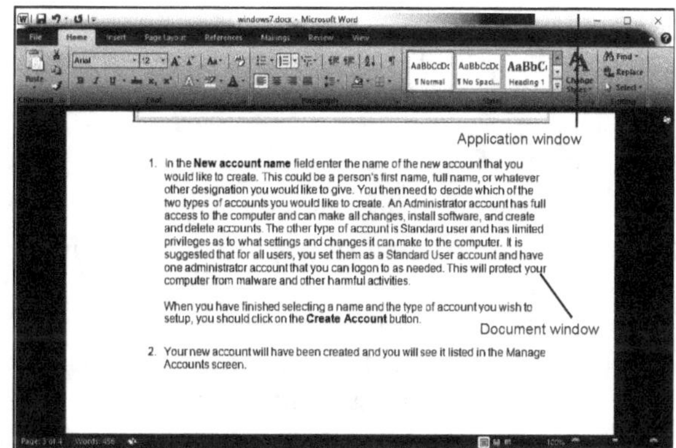

Figure 2.25: *Application Window (Document opened in MS-Word)*

Here, you have opened the Word application Window.

Closing Apps

There are several ways to close a Windows Apps; these are discussed below:

1. Click on the **Close button**. Or,

2. Select **File** menu and choose Exit. Or,

3. Press **Alt+F4** keys. Or,

4. Right-click on the icon on the Taskbar and select Close **Window**.

If you have not saved your document, a warning message to save your associated file will be displayed.

Simple Setting of Operating System

Most of the operating system settings on a computer are managed through Control Panel. The following examples are from the Settings of the Windows 10 operating system, which can be accessed by clicking Start, followed by Settings. This will display a Window that allows you to change the necessary settings.

Using Mouse and Changing its Properties

If you use a laptop or a desktop PC, you can customize your mouse in a variety of ways in Windows. For instance, you can swap the functions of your mouse buttons; make the mouse pointer more visible; and alter the scroll speed of the mouse wheel.

The following list describes basic mouse functions:
- Points to and selects objects on the screen.
- Selects or moves the files by dragging and dropping.
- Scrolls app Windows or web pages by clicking and holding a scroll bar, or by moving the mouse wheel.

Let us understand the functioning of the mouse in detail.

Mouse Pointer

A mouse pointer is a visible indicator displayed on a computer screen. By moving the mouse, the user can move the mouse pointer around the screen. Where the mouse pointer is located on the screen can determine how and where the user can press a button on the mouse to input text or execute a command. By default, it looks like a pointed arrow. When positioned over selectable text, it appears as an I-beam cursor. When hovering over a link, it appears as a pointing hand.

The following list describes the types of mouse clicks:

1. **Click:** Single press on the left mouse button. It selects data and performs commands.
2. **Double-click:** Double press the left mouse button. It opens files or folders and shortcuts.
3. **Right-click:** Pressing the right mouse button displays shortcut menus and drop-down menus. In some applications, right-clicking a menu item can access contextual information for that item.
4. **Center-click:** Some mouse support clicking the scroll wheel or a center mouse button while using some software applications and Internet browsers. Clicking the scroll wheel once opens a scroll graphic, allowing

you to scroll up or down, depending on the placement of the mouse pointer.

5. **Drag-and-drop or select:** Press and hold the left mouse button. While using the select feature within text, the text is selected or highlighted. Drag-and-drop can be used to rearrange tiles on the Windows 10 Start screen, or to close open apps. On the Windows desktop, you can use drag-and-drop to move files or folders:
   - From one folder to another
   - To the desktop
   - From the desktop to a folder
   - From any location to the Recycle Bin

To change the basic settings of mouse:

1. Open the **Start Menu** by clicking the **Start** button on the bottom-left corner of your desktop. Then, click **Settings** to open the app, as shown in *Figure 2.24*.
2. In the **Settings** app, click on **Devices**, as shown in *Figure 2.25*:

Figure 2.25: *Selecting Devices from Windows Settings*

3. On the left pane of the Window, select **Mouse** to access the mouse configuration settings, as shown in *Figure 2.26*:

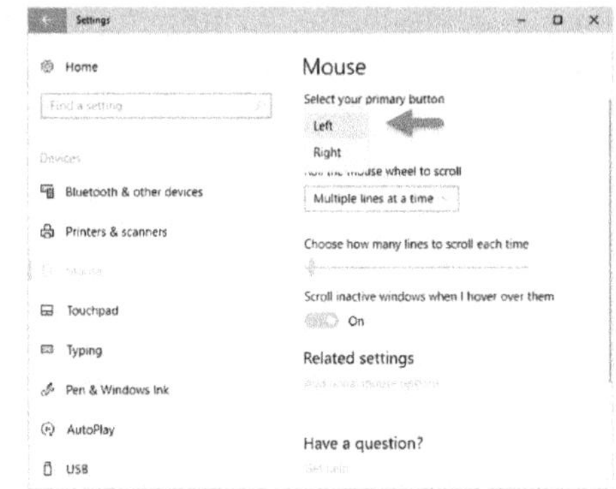

Figure 2.26: *Selecting Mouse from the Left Pane*

4. Under Select your primary button, click the down arrow to open the list of options and choose between your left or right mouse button to set as primary. The default setting is left, as shown in *Figure 2.26*.

5. From Roll the mouse wheel to scroll selection choose one of the available options:
   - **Multiple lines at a time:** The first is the default setting. If you choose to scroll multiple lines at a time, you can use the scrollbar below the setting to set how many lines to scroll each time. Click and drag the cursor to the left or to the right to decrease or increase the number of lines respectively. The default setting position is 3 when you click the on slider, as shown in *Figure 2.26*.
   - **One screen at a time:** Selecting the second option makes the mouse wheel scroll a whole screen of content at a time. The easiest way to see how these scrolling options work is to open a website.

6. If Scroll inactive Windows when I hover over them is set to **On**, when you move the mouse cursor over an inactive Window, you can scroll it without having to focus on it. If it is turned Off, you first have to click on the inactive windows before scrolling their contents. The default setting is **On**, as shown in *Figure 2.26*.

7. If you want to explore additional mouse settings, click the Additional mouse options under the Related settings section.

8. The Mouse Properties dialog box appears as shown in *Figure 2.27*:

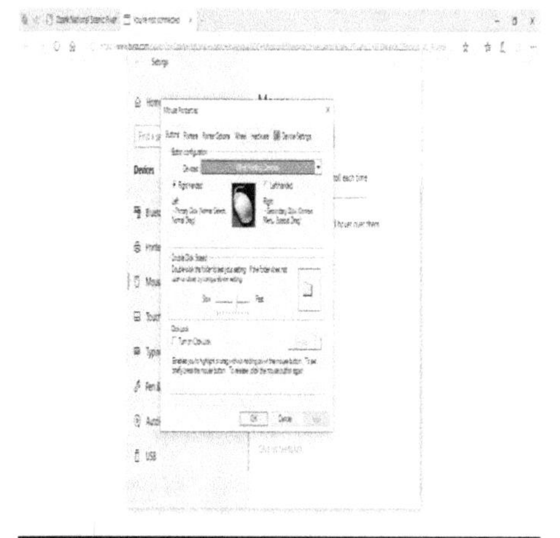

Figure 2.27: *Mouse Properties Dialog Box*

Button Tab of the Mouse

To configure the behavior of the mouse:

1. Click the **Buttons** tab in the Mouse properties dialog box, as shown in the above *Figure 2.27*.

2. To swap the functions of the right-handed and left-handed mouse buttons, under Button configuration, select the **Switch primary** and **secondary** buttons check box.

3. To change how quickly you must click the mouse buttons to perform a double-click, under Double-click speed section, move the Speed slider toward Slow or Fast.

4. To turn on **ClickLock**, which enables you to highlight or drag items without holding down the mouse button, under ClickLock, select the Turn on ClickLock checkbox.

Pointers Tab of the Mouse

To configure the behavior of the mouse, click the Pointers tab in the Mouse properties dialog box, as shown in *Figure 2.28*:

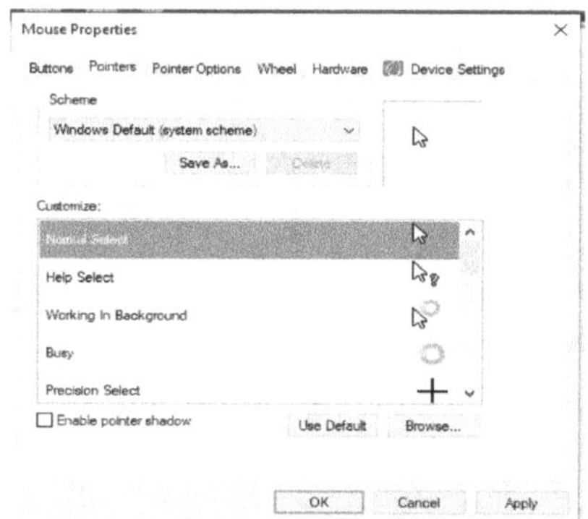

Figure 2.28: *Mouse Properties Dialog Box of Pointers Tab*

To change the appearance of your mouse pointer, select the **Pointers** tab and use one of the following options:
- To change all of your pointers at one time, select a new scheme under Scheme.
- To change a particular pointer, select it in the Customize list. Click the **Browse...** button. A list of selected cursor files appears. Select the name of the new pointer file you want to use for that task.

Pointer Options Tab of the Mouse

To configure the behavior of the mouse, click the **Pointer Options** tab in the Mouse properties dialog box, as shown in *Figure 2.29*:

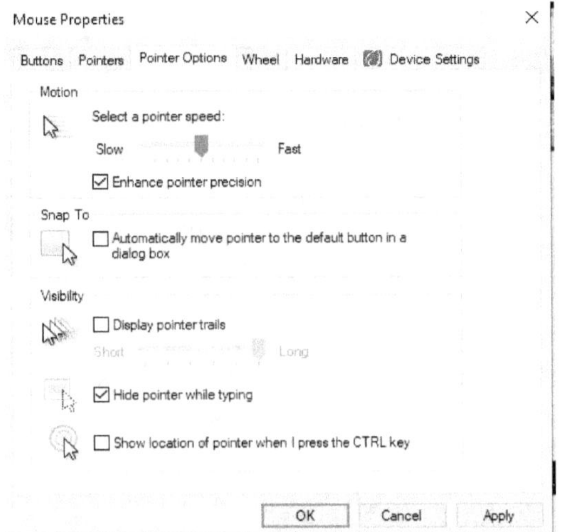

Figure 2.29: *Selecting Pointers Options*

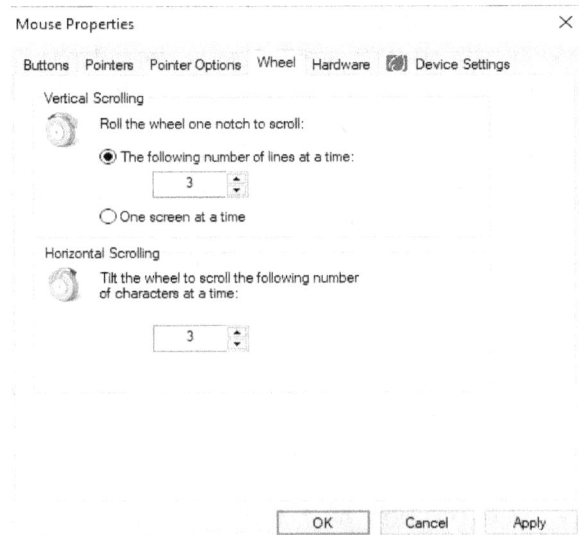

Figure 2.30: *Selecting Wheel Tab*

In the Motion section:

1. Drag the slider to adjust the speed of your mouse. It causes the pointer to respond more quickly or slowly to the movements of the mouse.

Or

Select the Enhance pointer precision checkbox to provide finer control of your pointer at short distances without closing the ability to move the point quickly across the screen. Clear the checkbox to turn off this feature.

2. In the Snap To section, you can get the mouse snap to default buttons (such as OK or Apply) in dialog boxes by selecting Automatically move pointer to the default button in a dialog box.

In the Visibility section:

1. If you select the Display pointer trails checkbox, you can adjust the length of the pointer trail by moving the slider below the checkbox.

2. To make the pointer invisible while typing, select the Hide pointer while typing checkbox. The pointer disappears when you type and reappears when you move the mouse.

3. Select the Show location of pointer when I, press the * key checkbox to find the pointer more easily when it is not in motion.

Wheel Tab of the Mouse

To configure the behavior of the mouse, click the Wheel tab in the Mouse properties dialog box, as shown in *Figure 2.30*:

In the Scrolling section:

1. Select the number of lines to scroll with each notch on the wheel.

   Or, click one screen at a time option. It means it is equivalent to using the page up or page down keys on your keyboard.

2. If your mouse does not have a mouse wheel, the Wheel tab may not appear.

The second method is to open the mouse's basic settings:

1. Right-click on the Windows 10 **desktop** and select **Personalize** from the context menu, as shown below in *Figure 2.31*:

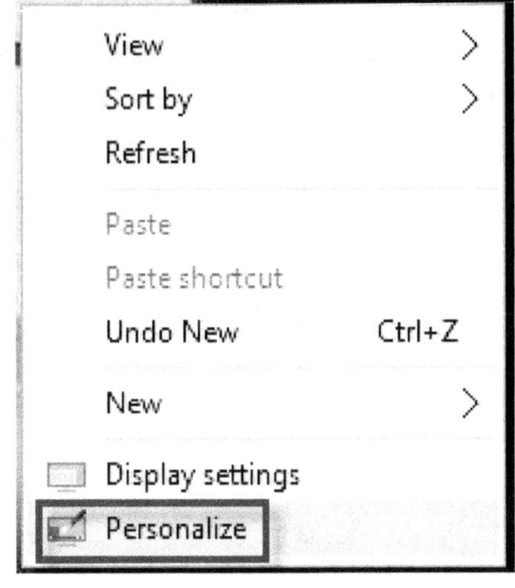

Figure 2.31: *Selecting Personalize*

2. In the Personalization page of the Settings app, click the **Themes** option at the left side and click **Mouse Cursor**. The Mouse Properties

dialog box will open, as shown in *Figure 2.27*.

Changing System Date and Time

You can change the Date and Time of your system by clicking the Settings options in Control Panel or by typing date and time in the Start menu search box.

To change the Date and Time:

1. Click the Start menu and choose Settings. The Windows Settings page opens. Click the **Time & Language** button on the left side of the screen to display time and language settings, as shown in *Figure 2.32*:

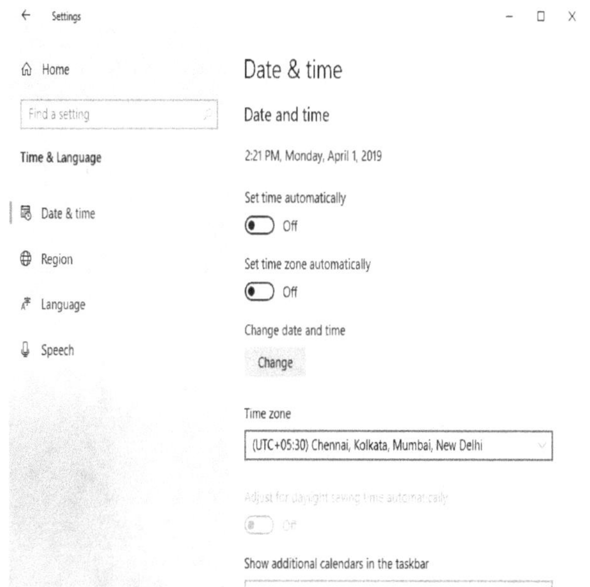

Figure 2.32: *Data & Time Page in Settings Window*

2. Click on the **Date & Time** category on the left side of this window to view the date and time settings in the area to the right.

> Tips: Both set automatically. Set time zone automatically must be off to make this change.

3. Under Change date and time, click the **Change** button. The Change date and time dialog box appears as shown in following *Figure 2.33*. Enter the Date and Time and press the Change button:

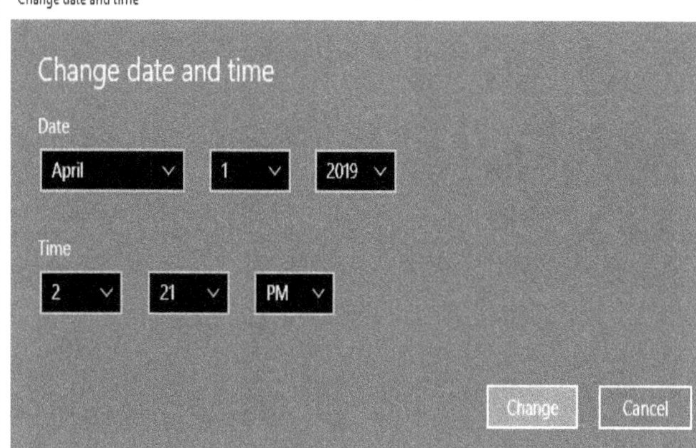

Figure 2.33: *Change Date and Time Dialog Box*

To change date and time formats in Control Panel:

1. In the Search box, type *control panel*. The Control Panel dialog box appears. Select the Clock and Region link as shown in *Figure 2.34*:

Figure 2.34: *Selecting Clock and Region in Control Panel*

2. Click the Date and Time link as shown in *Figure 2.35*:

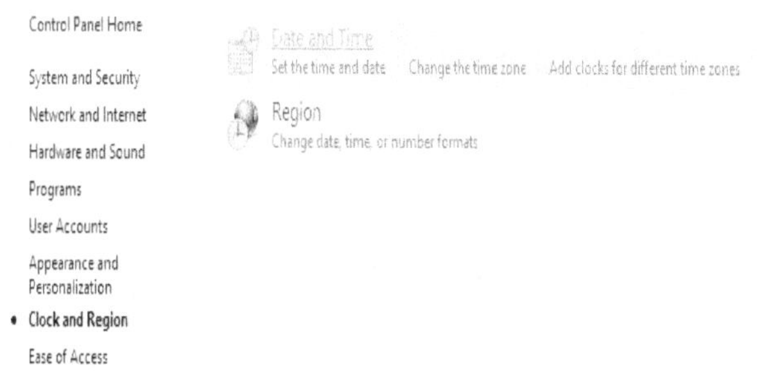

Figure 2.35: *Selecting Date and Time*

3. The Date and Time dialog box appears with the Date and Time tab, as shown in *Figure 2.36*:

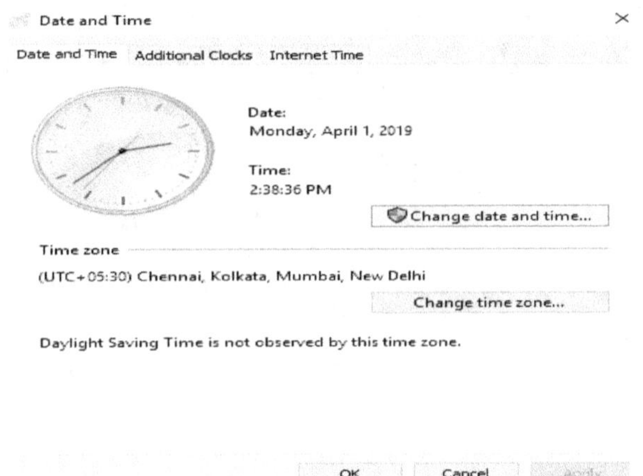

Figure 2.36: *Date and Time dialog box*

4. Select the Change date and time button in the Date and Time tab. It opens the Date and Time Settings dialog box, as shown in *Figure 2.37*:

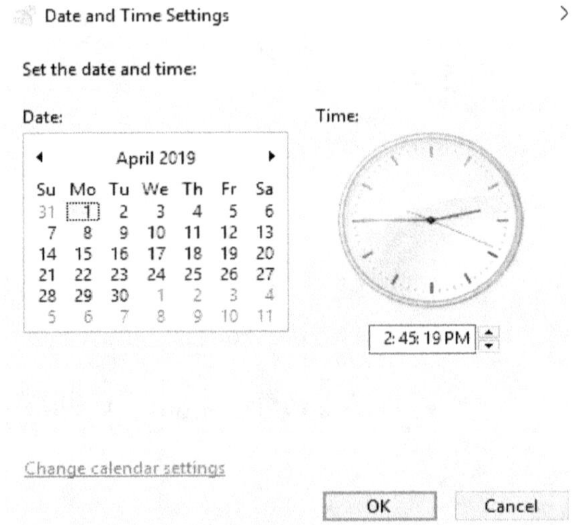

Figure 2.37: *Date and Time Settings Dialog Box*

5. To change the Date, click the arrow in the month list until you get the current month. Select the current date.
6. To change the Time, click the up and down arrow until you get the correct time.
7. Select the Change time zone button from the Date and Time dialog box to open Time Zone settings.
8. Click the drop-down arrow to select the Time zone and then click the **OK** button.

9. Again, come to the Date and Time dialog box and click the **OK** button.

Changing System Display Properties

The display properties window is accessible from the Windows Control Panel or by simply right-clicking on your desktop. The display properties window allows access to several settings, such as Windows color scheme and background themes, resolution and monitor system drivers. After you have accessed the window, you can set each tab configuration to settings that make it more comfortable to work.

Display

On the Display page, you will find a number of options to change the DPI scaling settings, which makes the size of text, apps, and other visual elements bigger. You can also change the orientation of the screen, brightness level and for a multiple display setup. Advanced display settings allow you to identify and connect to a new display to your PC. The display page looks as follows:

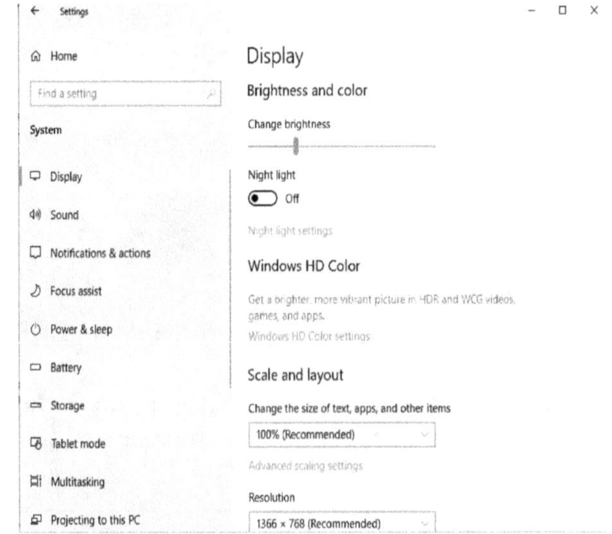

Figure 2.38: *Display Settings*

The related settings include:

- **Color calibration:** It helps you improve the color on your display and makes sure that the color you select appears accurately.
- **ClearType text:** Adjust the settings to improve the readability on your PC by making the words look sharper and clearer.
- **Advanced sizing of text and other items:** This setting allows you to change the size of apps and text on your PC if you want.
- **Display adapter properties:** This tab takes you to the Intel HD Graphics Control Panel.

Apps and Features

This page lists all the apps installed on your PC and is sorted by name. You can select any app to uninstall.

Default Apps

You can select which app Windows 10 should launch by default when opening a link or a file type. It allows a quick way to change the default app for mail, maps, music payer, video player, photo viewer, and web browser. However, you can use the link at the bottom of the page to choose default apps by file type and protocol. To change a default app, simply click the app, and choose a different app as default.

Notifications and Actions

The notification area is located on the far-right side of the Windows taskbar. It includes many of the options to customize action center. Here, you can rearrange the quick action buttons, or you can also add or remove quick actions that appear at the bottom of the action center. Simply click the app to open its settings, and use the toggle switch to turn on or off the different options, including to disable notifications, show banner, and play sound when a notification arrives.

Power and Sleep

This page, you can control when the screen should turn off or the computer should go to sleep if it is running on battery or plugged into the electrical outlet.

Storage

This page, you can manage a number of storage settings. You can see a list of all storage devices connected to your computer with capacity information. For example, you can click This PC to see the storage usage of the main drive and find out which files are taking the most space. If you click on System & reserved, you will get information about the space used by system files, virtual memory, hibernation and system restore.

Tablet Mode

This page, you can change various aspects when detaching the keyboard from a 2-in-1 device. This setting is for tablet users. You can make your Windows 10 more touch-friendly by turning the button On and can also adjust your system settings when you are operating Windows 10 on a touch-friendly device.

Multitasking

You can arrange two or more Windows side-by-side just by dragging them to the sides or corners of the screen. You can change a number of settings for the snap feature, such as Snap Assist, automatically size to fit Windows, and the ability to two resize two snapped apps simultaneously.

Project to this PC

This page, you will find the options that allow another PC or phone screen to project to your device, including using the mouse and keyboard.

Apps for Websites

This page, you can allow or prevent certain websites to open using its apps if they are installed on your computer. For example, if you have the Facebook app installed on your PC, but you are using Microsoft Edge, then browsing to Facebook will open the app instead of loading the website.

About

This page, you will find information about the hardware and operating system on your computer, including edition, version, processor, memory and system type.

To Add or Remove Program and Features

Each edition of Windows comes with a pre-defined set of programs, features and apps installed. You can customize Windows by removing the features that you do not need and by adding those which you need but are not installed by default. And if you remove unwanted features, programs or apps, you can save quite a bit of space on your hard disk.

If you are new to Windows 10, you may not know how to uninstall programs or apps. In older versions of Windows, uninstalling a program was not an easy task. You had to go through the Programs and Features menu in the Control Panel. But in Windows 10, uninstalling programs (either a desktop program or an app) is much simpler.

There are three different ways to uninstall a software in Windows 10.

To add or remove programs and apps:

1. Click the **Start** menu and choose **All Apps**. Find the application or program you want to remove. For example, in *Figure 2.39*, select the Spyder program to get uninstalled:

Figure 2.39: *Select the Program and Choose Uninstall*

2. Right-click on it and choose **Uninstall** from the drop-down menu, as shown in *Figure 2.39*.

3. If you are uninstalling an application, you will

see a pop-up window open, which reads This app and its related info will be uninstalled. You need to click Uninstall to complete the process, as shown in *Figure 2.40*:

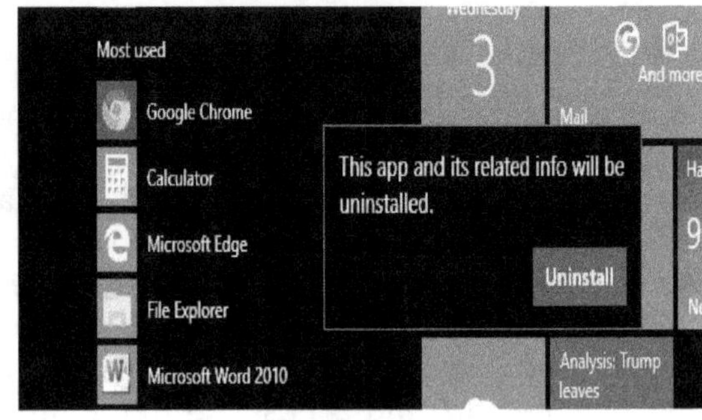

Figure 2.40: *Pop-up Window*

4. If you are uninstalling a desktop program, you will see the Programs and Features window open up, as shown in *Figure 2.41*:

Control Panel › Programs › Programs and Features   ∨ ↻   Search Programs and Features

Uninstall or change a program

To uninstall a program, select it from the list and then click Uninstall, Change, or Repair.

Organize ▼   Uninstall   Change

Name	Publisher	Installed On	Size	Version
Microsoft OneDrive	Microsoft Corporation	4/3/2019	116 MB	19.033.0218.0011
Microsoft Visual C++ 2010 x64 Redistributable - 10.0....	Microsoft Corporation	8/29/2018	13.8 MB	10.0.40219
Microsoft Visual C++ 2010 x86 Redistributable - 10.0....	Microsoft Corporation	8/29/2018	11.1 MB	10.0.40219
Microsoft Visual C++ 2013 Redistributable (x64) - 12.0...	Microsoft Corporation	12/15/2018	20.5 MB	12.0.30501.0
Microsoft Visual C++ 2013 Redistributable (x86) - 12.0...	Microsoft Corporation	12/15/2018	17.1 MB	12.0.30501.0
Microsoft Visual Studio 2010 Tools for Office Runtime...	Microsoft Corporation	12/15/2018		10.0.50903
Microsoft Visual Studio Code	Microsoft Corporation	9/25/2018	190 MB	1.27.2
Mobile Broadband HL Service	Huawei Technologies Co.,Ltd	12/15/2018		22.001.29.01.284
Picasa 3	Google, Inc.	3/16/2019		3.9
Potplayer-64 Bits	Daum Kakao Corp.	3/16/2019		
Python 3.7.0 (32-bit)	Python Software Foundation	4/3/2019	89.7 MB	3.7.150.0
Python 3.7.0 (Anaconda3 5.3.0 64-bit)	Anaconda, Inc.	12/15/2018		5.3.0
Python Launcher	Python Software Foundation	10/1/2018	1.77 MB	3.7.6386.0
Realtek Card Reader	Realtek Semiconductor Corp.	12/15/2018	14.6 MB	10.0.14393.31231
Realtek High Definition Audio Driver	Realtek Semiconductor Corp.	12/15/2018	46.2 MB	6.0.1.7910
The KMPlayer (remove only)	PandoraTV	3/16/2019		3.8.0.123
Update for Windows 10 for x64-based Systems (KB40...	Microsoft Corporation	12/7/2018	1.01 MB	2.52.0.0
Windows 10 Update Assistant	Microsoft Corporation	12/15/2018	5.00 MB	1.4.9200.22589

Python Software Foundation   Product version: 3.7.150.0   Support link: http://www.python.org/   Help link: http://www.python.or...   Size: 89.7 MB

Figure 2.41: *Programs and Features Window*

5. Find the program you want to uninstall, select it, and click **Uninstall**. Then, a pop-up Window will appear asking you if you are sure to uninstall the program. Click **Yes** and the program will be uninstalled.

To Remove Apps and Programs from the Settings Menu:

1. Click the **Start menu** and choose **Settings**.

2. From the Windows Settings, choose **Apps** and then click **Apps & Features**. You will see a full list of applications and programs on your computer, sorted by size. You can search for apps with the help of a search box at the top of the screen, as shown in *Figure 2.42*:

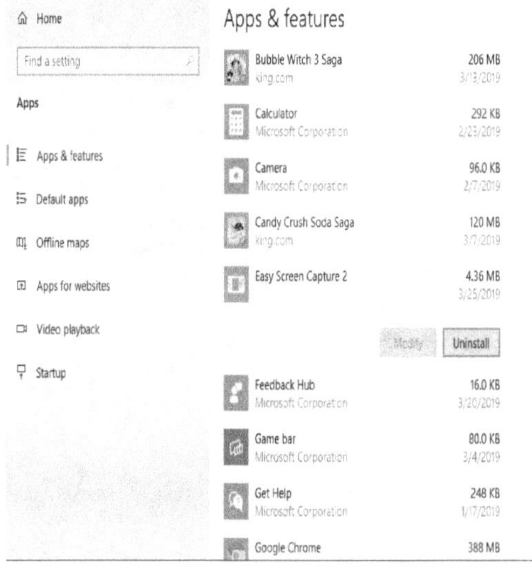

Figure 2.42: *Apps & Features Window*

3. Find the app you want to **uninstall**, select it, and click **Uninstall**. A pop-up Window will appear informing you that the app will be uninstalled, as shown in the preceding image.

4. Click Uninstall to complete the process.

From the Control Panel, you can only uninstall the desktop programs, not apps. To add or remove desktop Programs from Control Panel:

1. In the Search box, type Control Panel and select Control Panel, as shown in *Figure 2.43*:

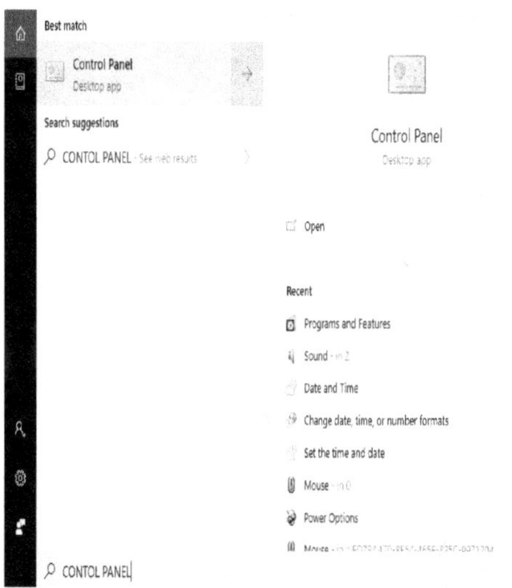

Figure 2.43: *Typing Control Panel in the Search Box*

2. The **Control Panel** dialog box appears; select **Programs**.

3. The Programs Window appears. From the right side, select the Programs and Features link, as shown in *Figure 2.44*:

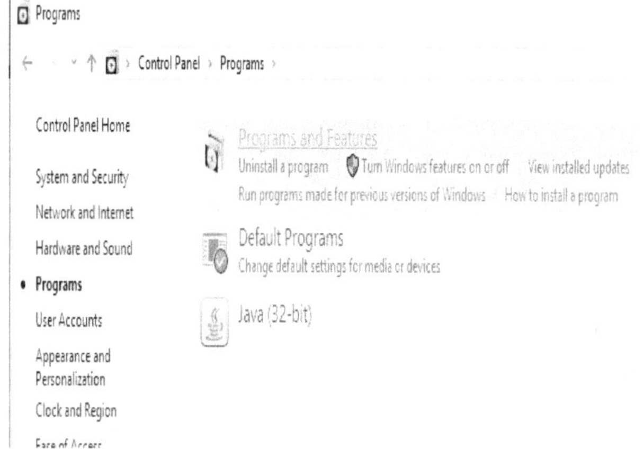

Figure 2.44: *Selecting Programs and Features from Programs Window*

4. Scroll down the list of installed programs to find the one you want to remove.

5. Click on the program, and then click the **Uninstall button** that appears below it, as shown in *Figure 2.45*:

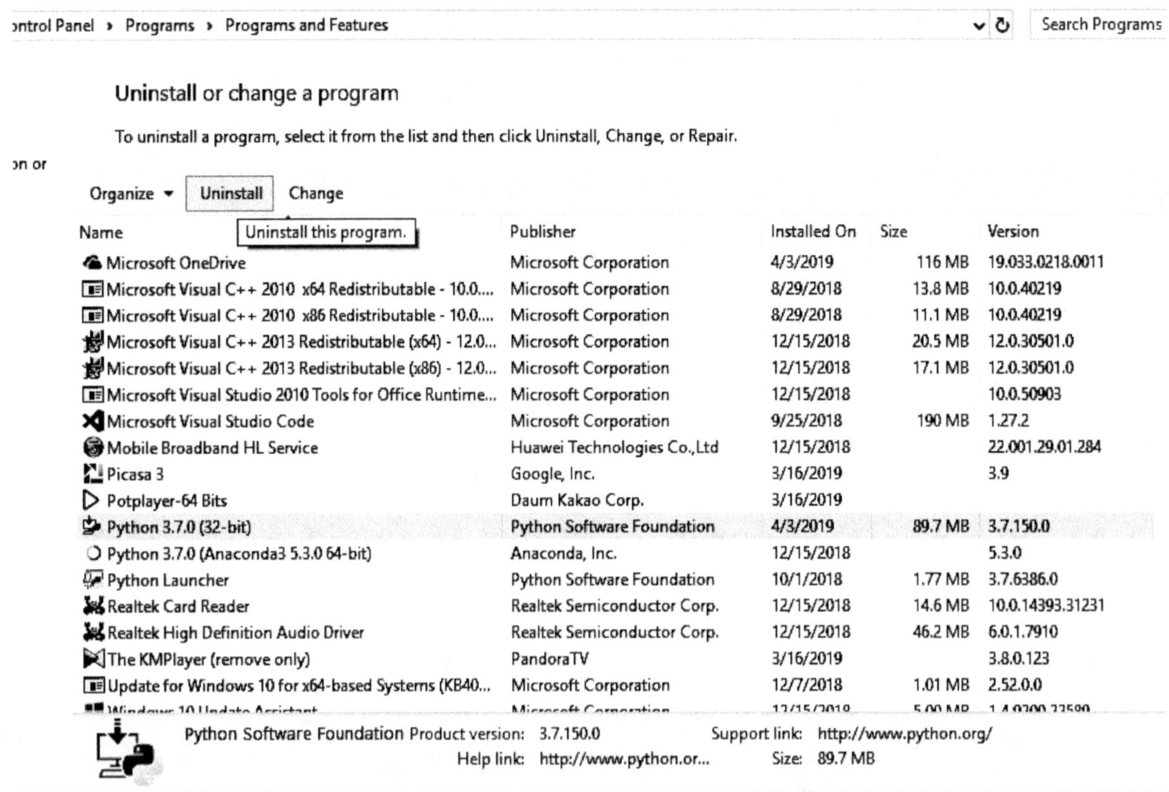

Name	Publisher	Installed On	Size	Version
Microsoft OneDrive	Microsoft Corporation	4/3/2019	116 MB	19.033.0218.0011
Microsoft Visual C++ 2010 x64 Redistributable - 10.0....	Microsoft Corporation	8/29/2018	13.8 MB	10.0.40219
Microsoft Visual C++ 2010 x86 Redistributable - 10.0....	Microsoft Corporation	8/29/2018	11.1 MB	10.0.40219
Microsoft Visual C++ 2013 Redistributable (x64) - 12.0...	Microsoft Corporation	12/15/2018	20.5 MB	12.0.30501.0
Microsoft Visual C++ 2013 Redistributable (x86) - 12.0...	Microsoft Corporation	12/15/2018	17.1 MB	12.0.30501.0
Microsoft Visual Studio 2010 Tools for Office Runtime...	Microsoft Corporation	12/15/2018		10.0.50903
Microsoft Visual Studio Code	Microsoft Corporation	9/25/2018	190 MB	1.27.2
Mobile Broadband HL Service	Huawei Technologies Co.,Ltd	12/15/2018		22.001.29.01.284
Picasa 3	Google, Inc.	3/16/2019		3.9
Potplayer-64 Bits	Daum Kakao Corp.	3/16/2019		
Python 3.7.0 (32-bit)	Python Software Foundation	4/3/2019	89.7 MB	3.7.150.0
Python 3.7.0 (Anaconda3 5.3.0 64-bit)	Anaconda, Inc.	12/15/2018		5.3.0
Python Launcher	Python Software Foundation	10/1/2018	1.77 MB	3.7.6386.0
Realtek Card Reader	Realtek Semiconductor Corp.	12/15/2018	14.6 MB	10.0.14393.31231
Realtek High Definition Audio Driver	Realtek Semiconductor Corp.	12/15/2018	46.2 MB	6.0.1.7910
The KMPlayer (remove only)	PandoraTV	3/16/2019		3.8.0.123
Update for Windows 10 for x64-based Systems (KB40...	Microsoft Corporation	12/7/2018	1.01 MB	2.52.0.0
Windows 10 Update Assistant	Microsoft Corporation	12/15/2018	5.00 MB	1.4.9200.22590

Figure 2.45: *Selecting Uninstall from the Programs and Features*

6. Confirm that you want to uninstall the app by clicking **Uninstall** in the pop-up.

7. Click **Yes** when User Account Control asks if you want the program to make changes to your device; the program will be uninstalled.

Adding, Removing and Sharing Printers

Windows 10 provides the feature of adding a printer to simplify installing printers. The most common way to connect a printer to your PC/laptop is by USB cable, which makes it a local printer.

To add a printer:

1. Click the **Start menu**. Select the Settings apps, and then choose **Devices**, as shown in *Figure 2.46*:

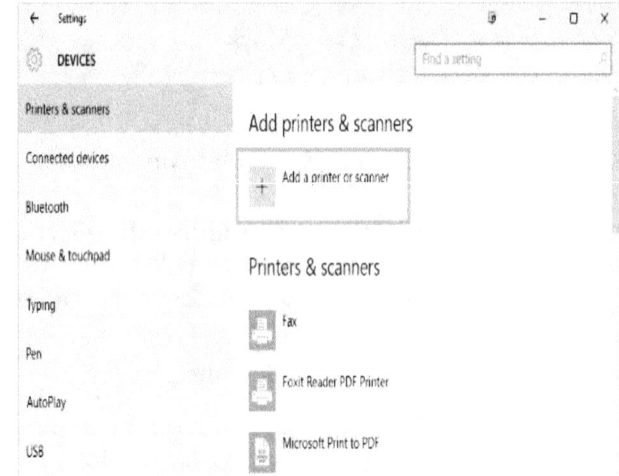

Figure 2.46: *Selecting Add a printer or scanner in Device Page*

2. Click **Printers & scanners** on the left side of the Devices page. Select Add a printer or scanner on the right side of the page, as shown in the previous figure.

3. If Windows detects your printer, click on the **name of the printer** and follow the on screen instructions to finish the installation.

Or

If you want to share a printer with your local network, click on the printer that you want isn't listed link on the right side of the page, as shown in *Figure 2.47*:

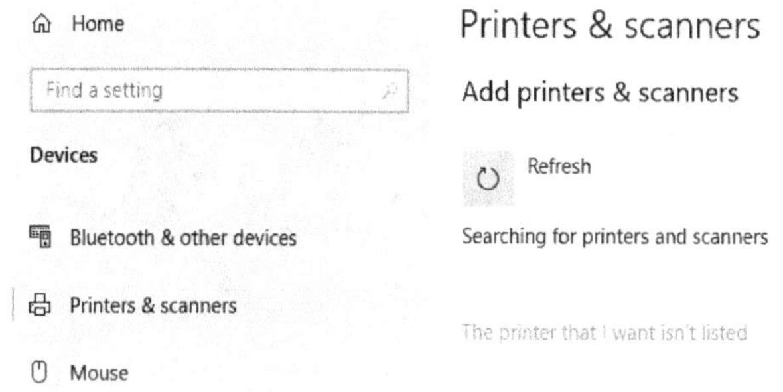

Figure 2.47: *Selecting the printer that I want isn't listed*

4. In the Add printer dialog box, click the Select a shared printer by name radio button option. Type in the network path of the shared printer.

   Click **Next**.

You can also use the IP address or computer name of the PC the shared printer is connected to.

For example: `\\Computer name\Share name of the shared printer` or `\\IP Address\Share name of shared printer`, as shown in *Figure 2.48*:

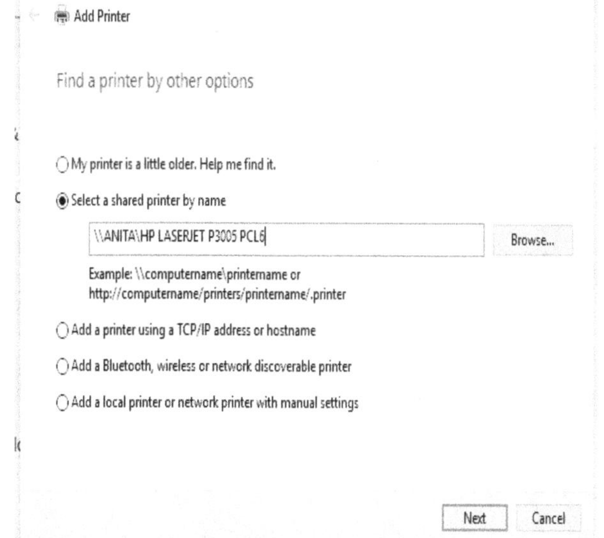

Figure 2.48: *Adding a path to Share the Printer*

5. Now, your PC will try to locate the shared printer. Then, download and install the driver from the computer the shared printer is connected to, and finally the selected printer driver will be installed, as shown in *Figure 2.49*.

You've successfully added HP Color LaserJet Pro MFP M477 PLC 6 on Brink-Desktop

Printer name: HP Color LaserJet Pro MFP M477 PLC 6 on Brink-Desktop

This printer has been installed with the HP Color LaserJet Pro MFP M477 PCL 6 driver.

Figure 2.49: *Installed Printer Driver*

6. Click **Next** if the shared printer has been successfully added.
7. The shared printer will now be available on your PC, as shown in *Figure 2.50*:

Printers & scanners
Add printers & scanners
  + Add a printer or scanner
Printers & scanners
  Fax
  HP Color LaserJet Pro MFP M477 PLC 6 on Brink-Desktop

Figure 2.50: *The Selected Printer Available in the Printer & Scanners*

8. After it gets installed, now you can **close** Settings.

To remove a printer:

1. If you will not be using a printer any more, you can remove it from the Printers & scanners page.
2. Click **Installed** Printer Devices and select **Remove device**.
3. Pop-up message appears Are you sure you want to remove the device. Click the **Yes** button to remove the printer device.

> **Tips:** If you cannot delete the printer, right-click it again. Click Run as administrator. Then click Remove device, and then click Yes.

File and Folder Management

File management is organizing and keeping track of files and folders. A folder is a container for storing programs and files. Windows allows you to organize folders and files in a file hierarchy, copying the way you store documents in a folder. The Windows file hierarchy allows you to organize the files in folders, and then place folders in other folders. Windows 10 comes with four libraries:

- Documents
- Pictures
- Music
- Video

Using the file management tools, you can save files in folders with appropriate names for easy identification. You can also search for a file when you cannot remember where you stored it. A folder can hold different types of files, such as text, spreadsheet.

File Explorer

Everything on your computer is saved in the form of files on your hard disk. The File Explorer Window is a powerful, easy-to-use tool for working with files in the desktop in Windows 10. The File Explorer program displays the entire computer system graphically, including all its files, in a tree structure form. It includes a ribbon in place of the command bar. With Explorer, you can access every data inside the computer's hard disk.

To start File Explorer:

1. Click the **File Explorer** icon on the taskbar (that is, it looks like a folder). *See Figure 2.51:*

Figure 2.51: *File Explorer icon on Taskbar*

2. When you launch File Explorer in Windows 10, you can see the Quick Access Window. You can see your most frequently accessed folders and files created, as shown in *Figure 2.52:*

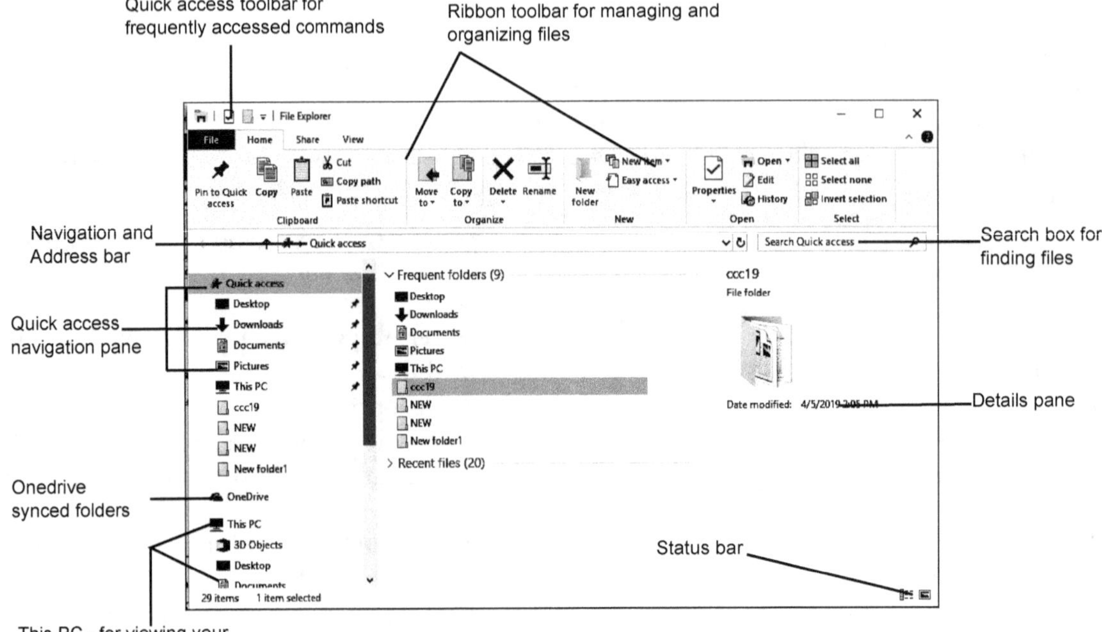

Figure 2.52: *File Explorer Window*

3. You can use File Explorer for a variety of tasks. The various elements of this window are designed to help you navigate around Windows or work with files, folders, and libraries more easily. Each Explorer includes the following elements:

- **Address bar:** It is located at the top of File Explore. As shown in Figure 2.52, it displays the path of the currently selected folder.

- **Navigation pane:** In this pane, you can access recent files from the Quick Access area, and also navigate folders you use regularly.
- **Ribbon toolbar:** It enables you to manage files quickly, such as copy, move, delete, and rename.
- **Forward and Back button:** If you go to a different folder, you can choose the back button to return to the last folder you accessed.
- **Search box:** You can search for subfolders, documents, images, programs, in the current folder.
- **Preview/Details pane:** It enables you to quickly preview an item such as an image, without opening the file.
- **Status bar:** It display information about a selected folder and its contents, such as number of items in the folder. You can quickly switch between thumbnail and detail views for the items displayed.
- **OneDrive synced folders:** You can also store files in the online storage service and have those synced to your computer.

To change the Open File Explorer:

1. Open **File Explorer**.
2. Select the **View** tab on the Ribbon and click **Options** under Show/hide group. Click Change folder and search options, as shown in *Figure 2.53*:

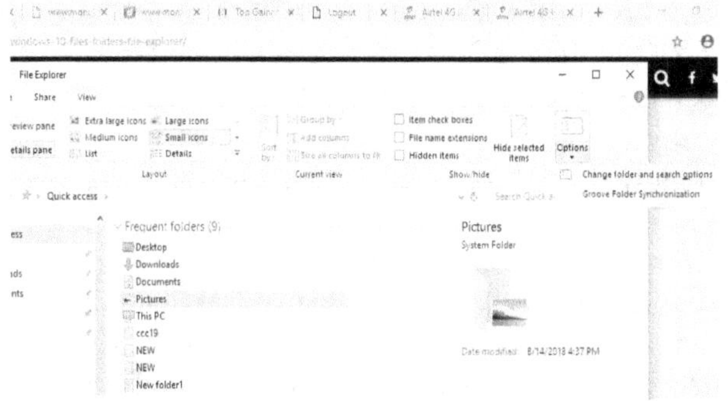

Figure 2.53: *Selecting Change folder and search options*

3. The Folder Options dialog box appears with the **General** tab, as shown in *Figure 2.54*:

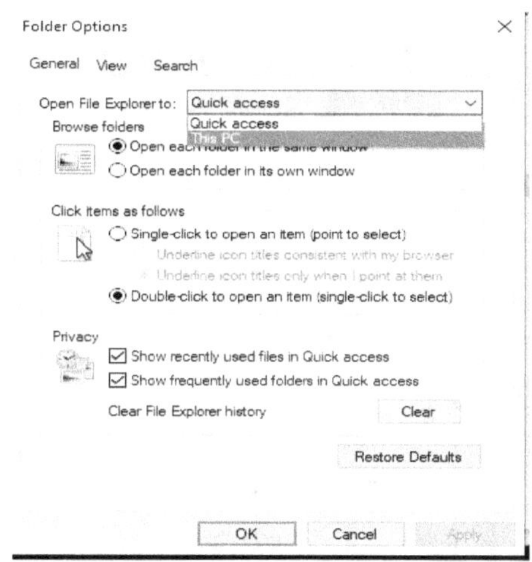

Figure 2.54: *Folder Options Dialog Box*

4. Click on **Open File Explorer** to list the box and choose **This PC**. Then, click Apply and **OK**, as shown above.
5. Suppose, you do not want to use frequently accessed folders and recently accessed files, you can adjust those settings. Under **Privacy**, uncheck the following:
   - Show recently used files in Quick access.
   - Show frequently used folders in Quick access.
6. You can choose to erase all traces by clicking the **Clear** button.

Displaying Subfolders

If a folder contains subfolders, that folder name will have a small right-pointing triangle next to it. To display the subfolders, just click on the folder name.

If the folder name has no triangle next to it, it means the folder has no subfolders.

If the folder name contains a right-pointing triangle next to it, it means that the folder has subfolders.

If the folder name contains a down-pointing triangle next to it, it means that subfolders are currently displayed for that folder.

To view subfolders of a folder, click the right-pointing. It will change into a down-point triangle, and the subfolders will be displayed, as shown in *Figure 2.55*:

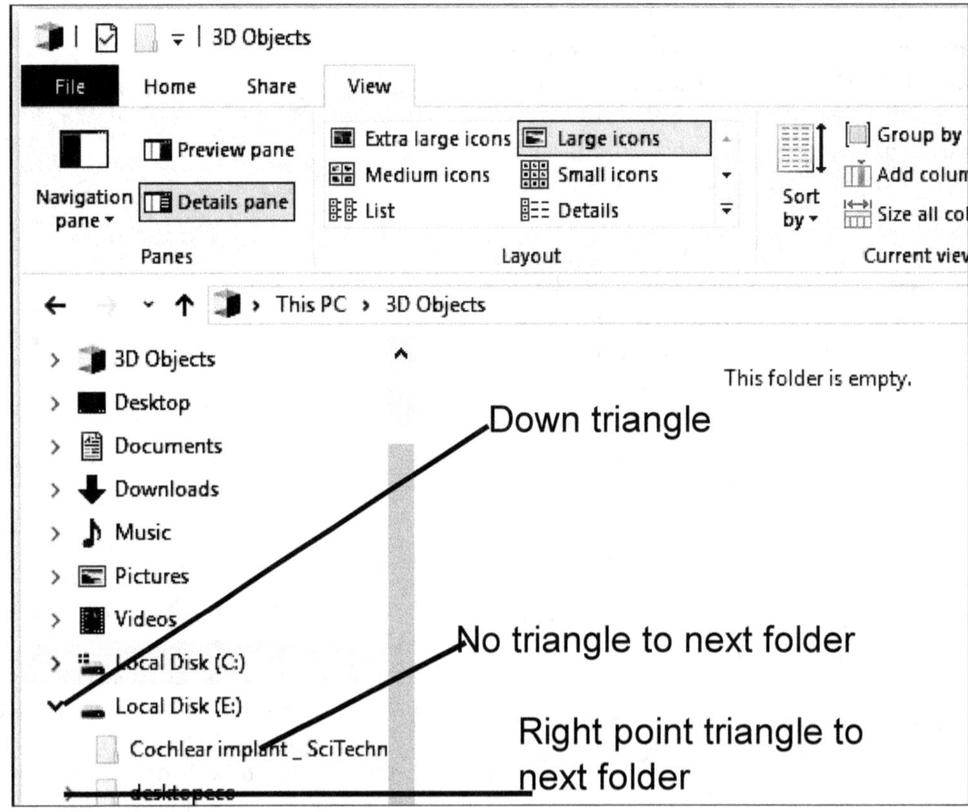

Figure 2.55: *Viewing Subfolders in the Navigation Pane*

To hide the subfolders, click on the down-pointing triangle of that folder.

Accessing Your Files and Folders

There are a number of ways you can navigate to your files and folders in File Explorer. These are:

- Using the Address bar which shows the full path of your current location.
- Forward and Backward buttons.
- From the Folders pane.
- Using the Search function.
- Using the Address Bar.

The Address bar, which is located at the top of the File Explorer, as shown in *Figure 2.56*, displays the path of the currently selected folder:

You can access or view files and subfolders in the File Explorer drop-down menus in the Address bar. You can easily go backward or forward in the folder path by clicking on the right-pointing arrow next to the folder and selecting a subfolder from the drop-down menu.

Viewing Folders at the Same Level as Your Current Folder.

To view the folders at the same level as the current folder, click on the right-pointing arrow to the left of that folder listing in the Address bar. The new breadcrumb trail feature is used to help you in navigating to the address bar. To use this feature, click any folder name to move straight to that location or click the down arrow next to the folder to display other subfolders at the same level, as shown in *Figure 2.57*:

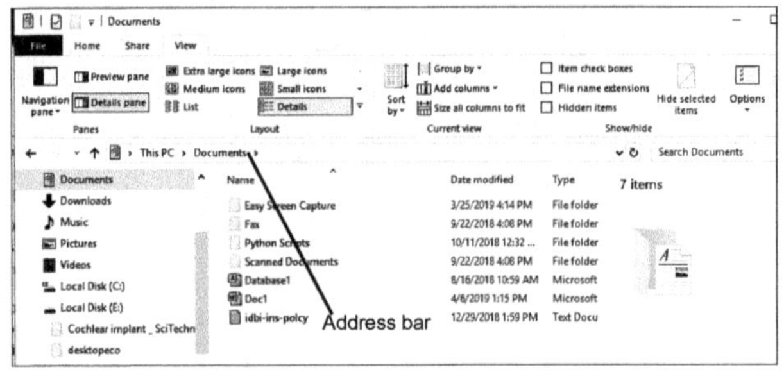

Figure 2.56: *Address Bar*

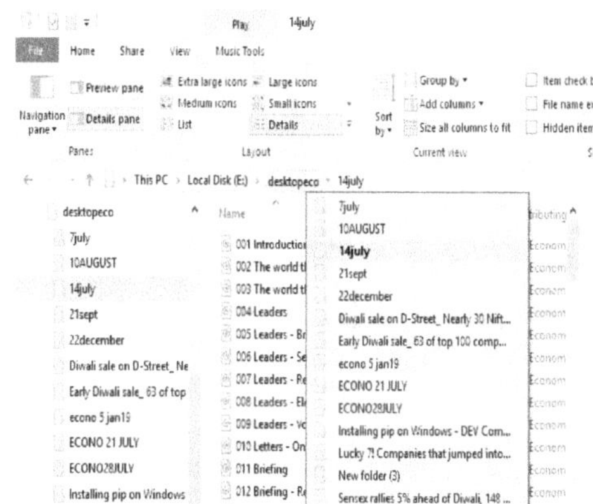

Figure 2.57: *Viewing Folders at the Current Folder*

The current folder (in this example, the 14July folder) is shown in boldface type.

Viewing Previously Visited Folders in the Address Bar

To view previous folders:

1. Click on the **forward** or **back** buttons shown in the following image. (These buttons work just like the forward and back buttons on a Web browser.)

Back button   Forward button

Figure 2.58: *Forward or Back buttons*

2. Click on a folder name in the Address bar:

Click here

Figure 2.59: *Folder name in Address bar*

Changing How Your Files and Folders are displayed

You can change how your folder and file icons appear, as well as different information displayed by them.

> **Tips:** Changes you make will apply to the contents of the current folder only.

1. Navigate to the folder whose display you want to change.

2. Click on the View tab to display the Ribbon, shown as follows:

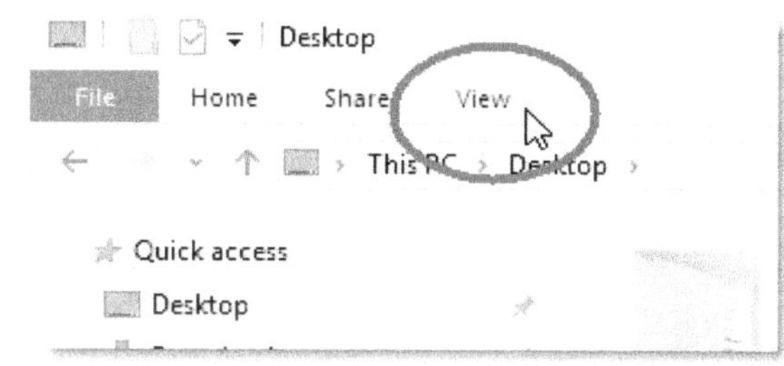

Figure 2.60: *View tab*

3. In the View tab, you can see the following available display options:

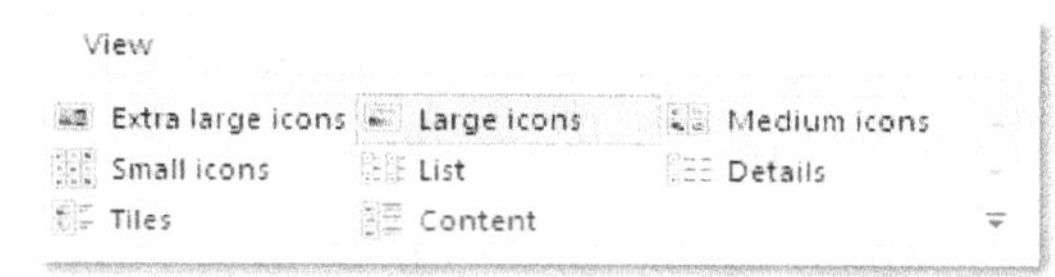

Figure 2.61: *Options in View tab*

4. Move your mouse over each option to see a quick preview of that option in the area where your files and folders are displayed. To choose an option, just click on it.

5. The following Table 2.2 lists and briefly describes each display option:

File/Folder view	Description
Extra-large icons	Shows the largest available view of file and folder icons. Only the name of the file or folder is displayed.
Small icons	Virtually the same as the List view.
Tiles	Shows icons of each item. It shows file type and size.
Large icons	Shows a larger view of file and folder icons. Only the name of the file or folder is displayed. Windows displays a thumbnail of images.
List	It shows you the file and folder name and its associated icon.
Content	It displays listing of files, folders, and program shortcuts and their associated icons.

M e d i u m icons	Virtually the same as the Tiles view, except that only the file or folder name is displayed. Windows displays a thumbnail of images.
Details	It shows information about your files and folders such as date last modified, file type, size and date created.

Table 2.2: *Various Types of Display Options*

Adding a Column Heading

You can add a column heading to display additional information about your files and folders.

To add column heading:

1. Navigate to the folder which you want to add a column heading.

2. Right-click on any column heading.

3. From the drop-down menu, click on the heading you want to add so that a check mark appears, as shown in *Figure 2.62*:

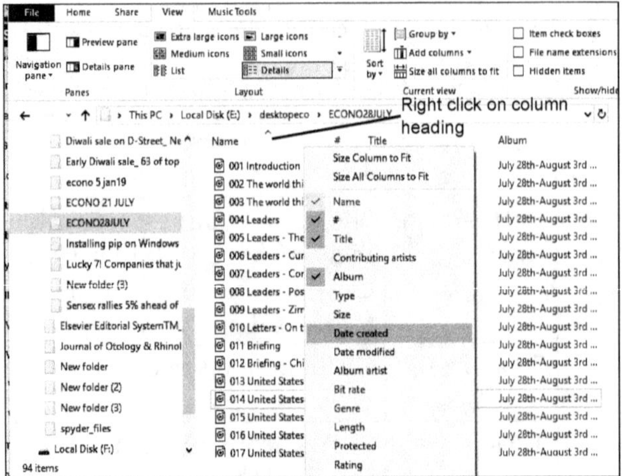

Figure 2.62: *Selecting Column Heading*

4. The column heading is added and will be displayed in the middle of the pane, as shown in *Figure 2.63*:

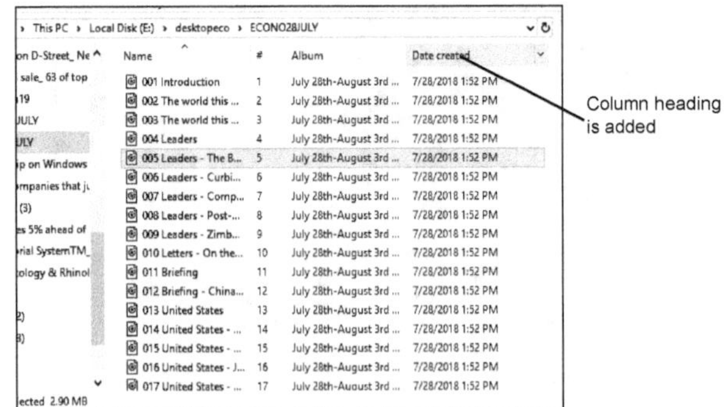

Figure 2.63: *Adding Column Heading*

5. Repeat *steps* 2 and 3 until you have added all the desired column headings.

Removing a Column Heading

To remove a column heading, perform the following steps:

1. Navigate to the folder from which you want to remove column headings.

2. Right-click on any column heading to display a drop-down menu of column headings. The headings that are currently displayed have check marks next to them, as shown in *Figure 2.64*:

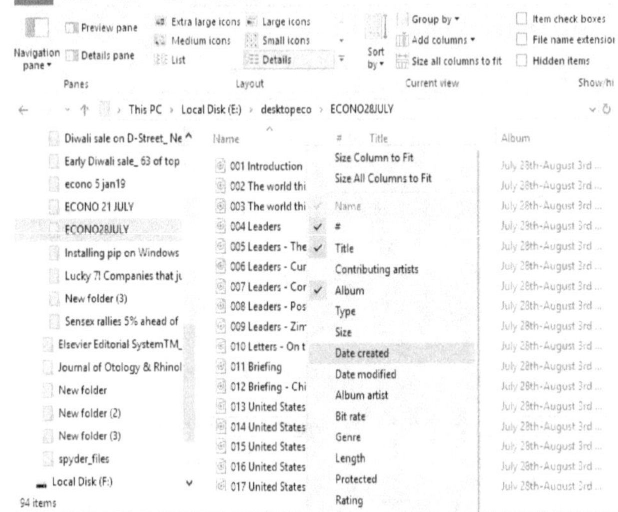

Figure 2.64: *Removing Column Heading*

3. Click on the column heading you want to remove so that the check mark no longer appears for that heading. The column heading will no longer be displayed for the current folder contents.

4. Repeat *steps* 2 and 3 until you have removed all the desired column headings.

Selecting Files and Folders in Windows 10

To select a single file:
1. Open the folder or Windows Explorer window containing the file.
2. Click the **file**.

To select multiple files:
1. Open the **folder** or Windows Explorer window containing the file.
2. Click the first file.
3. Then press and hold down * **key**, and then click the other files you want to select, as shown in *Figure 2.65*:

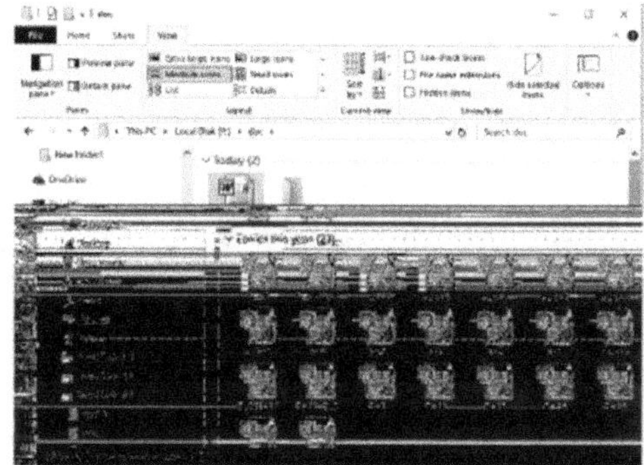

Figure 2.65: Selecting Multiple Files

To select a group of files:
1. Open the folder or Windows Explorer window containing the file.
2. Move and position the mouse to the left of the first file you want to select.
3. Then click and drag the mouse to the right until all the files you want are selected, as shown in *Figure 2.66*:

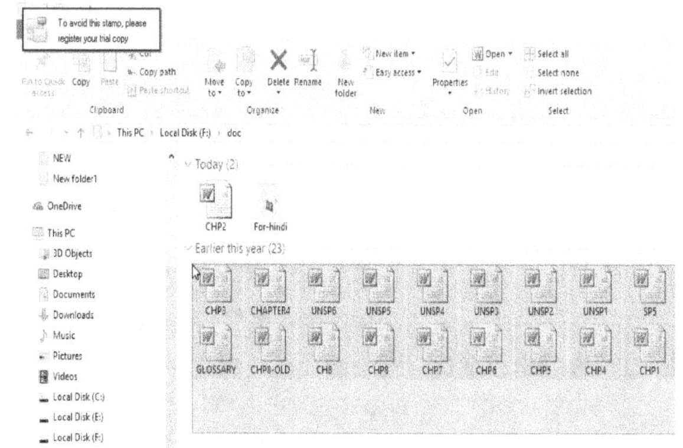

Figure 2.66: Selecting Group of Files

To select all the items in a folder:
1. Open the folder or Windows Explorer Window containing the files.

2. Click the **Home** tab and choose Select all in the Select group. Or press the **Ctrl + A** keys together.
3. Windows Explorer selects all the files in the folder.

Creating a New File and Folder in Windows 10

To create a new file/folder:

1. Navigate to the location where you want to add folder/file.

2. In the File Explorer, click the **Home** tab and choose **New folder** in the New group, as shown in *Figure 2.67*. Or right-click an empty area of folder window and choose New.

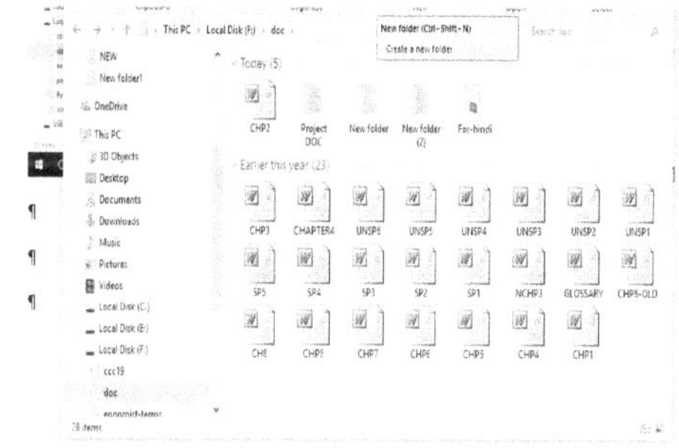

Figure 2.67: Creating New File or Folder

3. A submenu shows you types of files such as create folders and shortcuts, as shown above.

4. A default new folder appears, as shown in *Figure 2.67*. Enter the name of your new folder.

5. After you enter the name, click anywhere outside the text area to complete creation of the folder name.

Renaming Files and Folders in Windows 10

To rename a file or folder:

1. Select the file/folder you want to rename.

2. Click the Home tab and choose Rename in the Organize group. Or press the *F2* key, as shown in *Figure 2.68*. Or, alternatively, right-click the file/folder and choose Rename from the context menu.

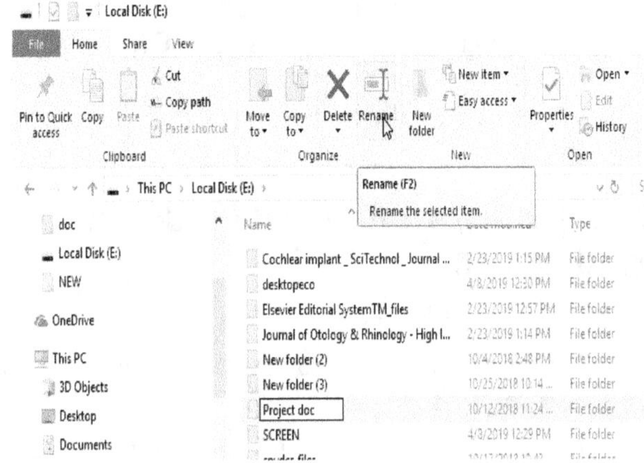

Figure 2.68: *Renaming a Folder*

3. A box appears around the current name with its details selected. Type the new name in the box and press the **Enter** key, as shown above.

Opening File and Folder in Windows 10

To open a file or folder:

1. You have to double-click a file or folder in this pane to open it, as shown in *Figure 2.68*.

Or

If you want to open a folder, select the folder and then click the **Open folder icon** that appears in the **Open** group.

3. If you want to open a file, select the file and then click Open file with the selected application icon that appears in the Open group, as shown in *Figure 2.69*:

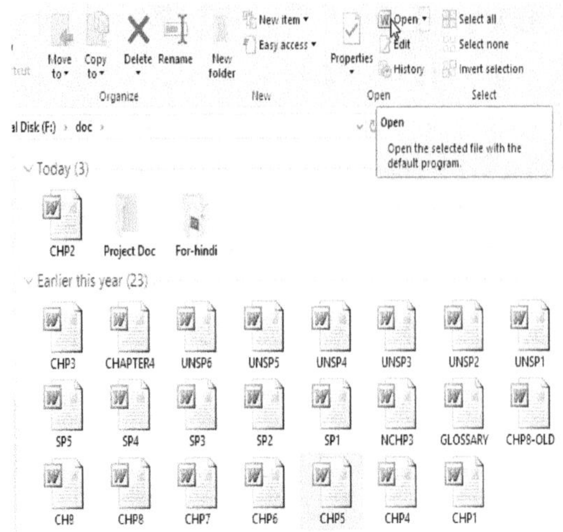

Figure 2.69: *Opening a File*

Moving or Copying Folder and File

Moving/copying a file or folder to another drive or folder is easy. Just drag a file/folder from the right pane to another disk drive (or a folder on another drive) to copy/move it there.

To move a file or folder to another drive or folder:

1. Click the **File Explorer** button in the Taskbar.
2. Select the file or folder you want to move.
3. Point to the selected file or folder, and then press and hold down the left mouse button.
4. Drag the file/folder from the right pane to the left pane and drop it into the selected folder or drive where you want, as shown in *Figure 2.70*:

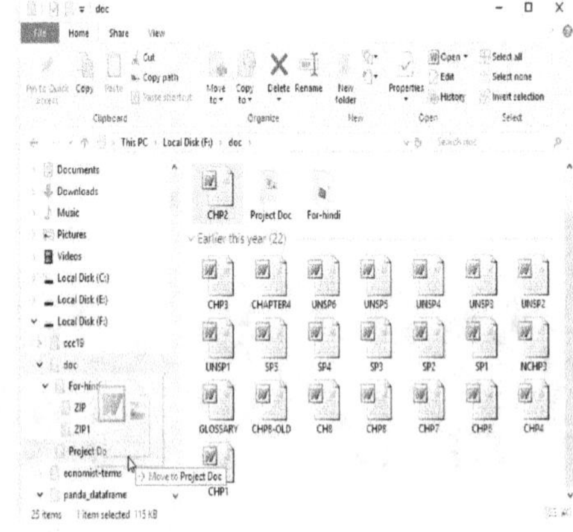

Figure 2.70: *Moving a File or Folder from one location to another*

5. A **Move** button, as shown in Figure 2.70, indicates where the file or folder will be moved.
6. Release the mouse button to move the file/folder into desired place. Or,

   Select the file, and click **Move** to drop-down arrow in the **Organize** group of **Home** tab.
7. Choose the folder where you want to move the file.

To copy a file or folder to another drive or folder:

1. Click the **File Explorer** button in the Taskbar.
2. Select the file or folder which you want to copy.
3. Point to the selected file or folder, and then press and hold down the left mouse button.
4. Press the **Ctrl** key while dragging the file/folder from the right pane to the left pane and drop it into the selected folder or drive where you want, as shown in *Figure 2.71*:

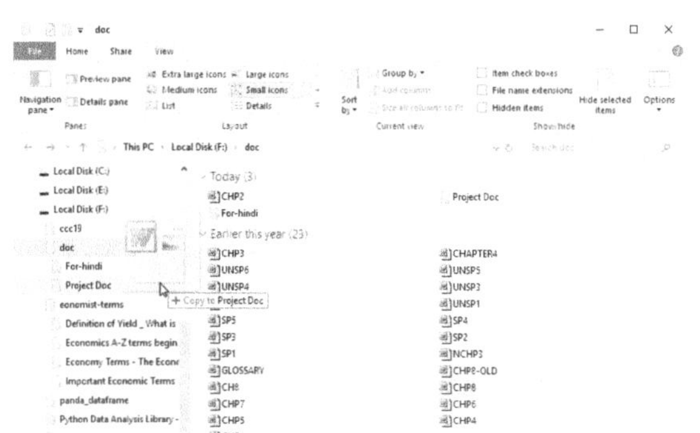

Figure 2.71: *Copying a File or Folder*

5. A **Copy** button, as shown in the Figure 2.71, indicates where the file or folder will be copied.
6. Release the mouse button to copy the file/ folder into desired place.

Or

Select the file, and click **Copy** to drop-down arrow in the **Organize** group of **Home** tab.

7. Choose the folder where you want to copy the file, as shown in *Figure 2.72*:

Figure 2.72: *Selecting Copy to drop-down arrow*

Deleting Files and Folders in Windows 10

To delete file(s) and folder(s):

1. Select the file or folder that you want to delete.
2. Click the **Home** tab. In the Organize group, choose **Delete**, as shown in *Figure 2.73*. Or alternatively, right-click the file/folder and choose Delete from the context menu.

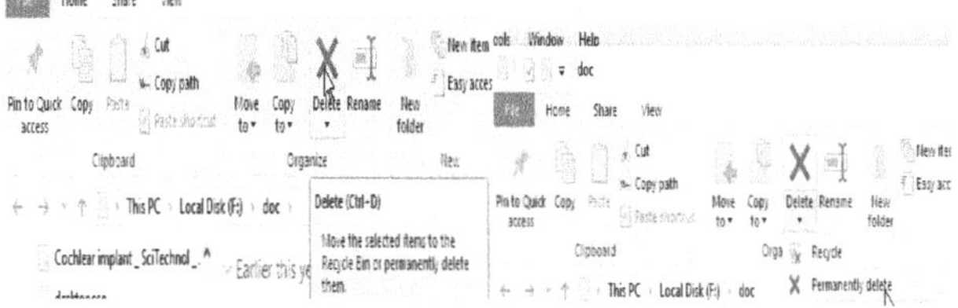

Figure 2.73: *Selecting Delete*

3. The **Delete** File/Folder dialog box appears. Click **Yes** in this dialog box.
4. The selected file is deleted from the folder.
5. When you delete your file/folder, it goes to **Recycle bin**. However, if you want to delete it permanently, click the Delete drop-down arrow in the Organize group. Select Permanently delete, as shown in *Figure 2.73*.

> **Tips:** Objects deleted from your computer are sent to the Recycle Bin. You can recover them by double-clicking the Recycle Bin folder, if desired.

Types of File Extensions

The main function of a computer is to manage data and information. The stored data and information on your computer can be considered as file. File includes text, photos, and videos. Each file has its specific icon that makes you understand the type of file.

A file extension (or simply "extension") is the suffix at the end of a filename that indicates what type of file it is. For example, in the filename **BPB.docx**, the .docx is the file extension shown as follows. It indicates the file is a document. Some other examples include .txt, which is used for Notepad files, and **.PSD**, which is the standard file extension for **Photoshop documents**.

Figure 2.74: *Example of file extension*

By having file extensions, you can quickly identify the type of file and have a better idea of how that file may be opened.

You can turn file extensions on or off easily. In File Explorer click on the View tab at the top to display the View ribbon. You will find an option called **File name extensions**. Click on the box next to it to turn on the check mark and show the extensions. Click to uncheck the box to remove the check mark and hide the extensions.

Keyboard Shortcuts of Windows 10

The Following table shows various shortcut keys:

Shortcut key	Description
Windows logo key	Open or close Start
Windows logo key + A	Open Action Center
Windows logo key + B	Set focus in the notification area
Windows logo key + D	Display and hide the desktop
Windows logo key + Alt + D	Display and hide the date and time on the desktop
Windows logo key + L	Lock the computer
Windows logo key + E	Open File Explorer
Windows logo key + I	Open Settings
Windows logo key + M	Minimize all windows
Windows logo key + S	Open search
Windows logo key + Tab	Open Task view
Windows logo key + up arrow	Maximize the window
Ctrl + Tab	Move forward through tabs
Ctrl + Shift + Tab	Move back through tabs
Alt + D	Select the address bar
Ctrl + E or Ctrl + F	Select the search bar
Ctrl + N	Open a new window
Ctrl + W	Close the active window
Ctrl + Shift + E	Display all folders above the selected folder
Ctrl + Shift + N	Create a new folder
Num Lock + asterisk (*)	Display all subfolders under the selected folder
Num Lock + plus (+)	Display the contents of the selected folder
Num Lock + minus (-)	Collapse the selected folder
Shift + click	Open an app or quickly open another instance of an app
Ctrl + Shift + click	Open an app as an administrator
Backspace	Go back to the settings home page

Table 2.3: *Keyboard Shortcuts*

Conclusion

Thus, an operating system is software that runs on a computer system. It manages the computer memory and process as well as its software and hardware. It has three main functions: it manages the computer resources, such as central processing unit, memory, disk drives and printers; it establishes a user interface; and it executes and provides services for applications software. Then, you learnt about the basics of OS. You also saw OS for desktop, laptop, mobile phone and tablet. Similarly, you saw User Interface for desktop and laptop. You covered simple settings of OS, such as changing mouse properties, changing date and time, display properties, adding and removing programs and features and printers. Further, you learnt about file and folder management and types of file extensions. Lastly, we studied various keyboard shortcuts used in Windows 10.

In the next chapter, you will learn Word processing using MS-Word. It is used to manipulate a text document, such as editing, formatting and printing a document.

REVIEW QUESTIONS WITH ANSWERS

A. Multiple Choice Questions.

1. When you click the Start menu and then press the Up arrow, what is displayed?
   a. The Shutdown menu
   b. Microsoft Edge
   c. The File Explorer
   d. The All Apps menu

2. The term Operating System means __________.
   a. A set of programs which controls the working of a computer
   b. The way a computer operator works
   c. Conversion of high-level language into machine-level language
   d. The way a floppy disk drive operates

3. The operating system of a computer serves as a software interface between the user and the _________.
   a. Memory
   b. Peripheral
   c. Hardware
   d. Screen

4. By default, Windows 10 automatically turns the battery saver feature on when the battery charge of a laptop falls below _________.
   a. 15 percent
   b. 20 percent
   c. 5 percent
   d. 10 percent

5. _____________ is the screen background and main area of Window where you can open and manage programs.
   a. Windows Settings
   b. Desktop
   c. Application window
   d. All Apps

6. An application can be opened through a shortcut on desktop by _____________.
   a. Double clicking on its shortcut
   b. Right-clicking and choosing the Open option
   c. Selecting the icon and pressing the Enter key
   d. All of the above

7. Which of the following statements is incorrect in context of shortcut icon?
   a. Shortcuts can be created by dragging and dropping
   b. Shortcuts can be created using cut and paste methods
   c. Shortcuts can be created by using the Shortcut wizard
   d. None of the above

8. A new printer can be added by the Printers and scanners option in.
   a. Control Panel
   b. File Manager
   c. Dynamic Data Exchange
   d. None of these

9. GUI is used as an interface between _____________.
   a. Hardware and software
   b. Man and machine
   c. Software and user
   d. None of the above

10. From the Start menu, you can access _________.
    a. Lock your computer
    b. Search for apps, settings and files
    c. Shut down your computer
    d. All of the above

11. You can navigate to your files and folders in File Explorer by using. _____________.
    a. Address bar
    b. Forward and Backward buttons
    c. Search function
    d. All of the above

12. What is the meaning of "Sleep" in Windows 10?
    a. Restart the computer in safe mode
    b. Restart the computer in sleep mode
    c. Shutdown the computer, terminating all the running applications
    d. Shutdown the computer without closing the running applications

13. Windows ____ is the newest version of the Windows operating system.
    a. 6
    b. 7
    c. 8.1
    d. 10

14. _________ is the shortcut to snap app to right.
    a. Windows icon + right arrow
    b. Windows icon + left arrow
    c. Windows icon + up arrow
    d. Windows icon + down arrow

15. The ____ list contains programs that accomplish a variety of tasks commonly required on a computer. Most of these programs are installed with the Windows 10 operating system, such as Notepad, Snipping Tool, Quick Assist and WordPad.
    a. Helper Programs
    b. Necessities
    c. Utilities
    d. Windows Accessories

16. What is the function of an operating system?
    a. Manages computer's resources very efficiently
    b. Takes care of scheduling jobs for execution
    c. Manages the flow of data and instructions
    d. All of the above
17. Right-click a tile to display a menu for performing other actions with that tile, which may include __________.
    a. Unpin from Start
    b. Pin to taskbar
    c. Uninstall
    d. All of the above

B. State whether the following statements are True or False.

1. Printers can be classified by the method of their printing.
2. Light pen and joystick are both pointing devices.
3. An optical disk is a secondary storage device of the computer system.
4. Title bar is at the top-most line of a Window.
5. A folder cannot contain files as well as subfolders.
6. Recycle Bin does not allow you to easily recover deleted files and folders in Windows.
7. The icon for hidden items is dimmed to differentiate them from items that are not hidden.
8. Microsoft Edge in Windows 10 is the Web browser that is intended to replace Internet Explorer.
9. Cortana is the name of the new built-in browser included in Windows 10.
10. Windows key + PrtScr is the shortcut key to take a screenshot of entire display and save.

C. Match the following:

1. It gives you access to all of your computer settings and enables you to install and remove programs:	a. Windows apps
2. A small program available for free or for purchase in the Windows Store that can run on Windows desktops, laptops and phones is:	b. Start menu
3. A small rectangle you can click in order to issue a command to an application program is:	c. Control Panel
4. Which family of Windows does Windows 10 belong to:	d. Windows key + D
5. Which desktop feature has been included in Windows 10 that was omitted from Windows 8:	e. File management
6. To minimize all open windows and displays in the screen:	f. Tile
7. It manages files on various storage devices and transfers these files from one storage device to another:	g. Windows NT
8. It establishes data security and integrity:	h. File Explorer

9. By clicking the Folder icon on the taskbar, you can access the file and folder documents:	i. Security Management
10. Access to system configuration and management tools:	j. Windows Explorer
	k. Control panel

D. Fill in the blanks:

Shift + Delete   Start menu   Taskbar   Continuum
Interface   Hardware   Tablet PC   Windows
key + PrtScr   Cortana   Folder   Software   Alt + F4

1. ___________ features allow Windows 10 to adapt to different device type.
2. The __________ contains start button, Search box and Notification area.
3. A _________ is a set of files and folders.
4. The left side of the ________ contains a list of frequently used folders, including documents, pictures, music and games.
5. ___________ key combination is used to permanently delete a file or folder.
6. A common boundary between two computer systems is known as ________.
7. A ________ is another type of portable PC, but it can accept handwritten input when the user touches the screen with a special pen.
8. The operating system is the intermediary between programs and _________.
9. __________ is the shortcut key to take a screenshot of the entire display and save.

SHORT ANSWER QUESTIONS

1. **What is GUI?**

   Answers: GUI is short for Graphical User Interface. It provides users with an interface wherein actions can be performed by interacting with icons and graphical symbols. A user finds it easier to interact with the computer when in a GUI, especially when using the mouse. Instead of having to remember and type commands, users click on buttons to perform a process.

2. **Explain the main purpose of an operating system?**

   Answers: Operating systems exist for two main purposes. One is that it is designed to make sure a computer system performs well by managing its computational activities. Another is that it provides an environment for the development and execution of programs.

3. **How to change the icon of a folder in Windows?**

   Answers: Operating systems exist for two main purposes. One is that it is designed to make sure a computer system performs well by managing its computational activities. Another is that it provides an environment for the development and execution of programs.

   a. Browse the location of the folder whose icon you would like to change, or create a new one.

   b. Right-click the folder, and select Properties from the bottom of the drop-down menu that appears.

   c. In the folder properties menu, select the Customize tab and then the Change Icon button.

   d. In the Change Icon window, make your selection and then click OK.

   e. Now, back on the Properties window, click Apply and then OK.

   f. Your folder should now display its new icon.

4. **How to change or rename a file or folder in Windows?**

   Answers: Method one:

a. Highlight the file or folder.

b. Right-click the file and click Rename from the menu that appears.

Method two:

a. Highlight the file or folder.

b. Press the F2 key on the keyboard.

Method three:

a. Highlight the file or folder.

b. Click File at the top of the Window and select Rename from the list of available options. Or

c. Highlight the file or folder you want to rename by single-clicking the file.

d. Once highlighted, wait a few seconds and click the file again. A box should appear surrounding the file or folder name, and you should be able to rename the file or folder.

5. **What is a file?**

   Answers: A file is an object on a computer to store data, information, and commands used with a computer program. In a GUI such as MS Windows, files display as icons that relate to the program to open the file. For example, the picture is an icon associated with an Adobe Acrobat pdf file. If this file was on your computer, double-clicking the icon in Windows would open that file in the PDF reader installed on the computer.

6. **What are the different operations performed by an operating system in the computer system?**

   Answers: The following are some of the tasks performed by file management of operating system of any computer system:

   a. It helps to create new files in computer system and place them at the specific locations.

   b. It helps in easily and quickly locating these files in the computer system.

c. It makes the process of sharing in separate folder known as directories. These directories help users search files according to their types or uses.

d. It helps the user to modify the data of files or to modify the name of the file in the directories.

7. **How to copy a file or folder in Windows?**

   Answers: a. Go the files or folders you want to copy.

   b. Highlight the file or folder you want to copy by clicking them once with the mouse. If you need to highlight more than one file, you can hold down the *Ctrl* or *Shift* keys on your keyboard or drag a box around the files you want to copy.

   c. Once highlighted, right-click the file or folder and select copy. Alternatively, you can press the *Ctrl + C* shortcut key, or in Windows Explorer, click the Home tab at the top of the window and choose Copy.

   d. Open the destination folder, right-click and empty space in the folder, and choose paste in the Clipboard group.

8. **Discuss the five different parts of Window 10 desktop screens.**

   Answers: The different parts of Windows 10 Desktop screens are:

   a. Start menu

   b. Search box

   c. Pinned Apps

   d. Action Center

   e. Desktop Icons

DESCRIPTIVE TYPE QUESTIONS.

1. What is the purpose of Windows 10 File Explorer?
2. Discuss the various functions of Operating System.
3. Explain the need of Operating System in a computer.
4. What are the three types of user interface?
5. Differentiate between copying a file and moving a file.
6. Give the procedure to create a new folder in Windows 10.
7. What do you mean by types of file extensions?

———— Answers ————

A.	1. d	2. a	3. c	4. b	5. c	6. d
	7. d	8. a	9. c	10. d	11. d	12. d
	13. d	14. a	15. d	16. d	17. d	

B.	1. T	2. T	3. T	4. T	5. F
	6. F	7. T	8. T	9. F	10. T

C.	1. c	2. a	3. f	4. g	5. b
	6. d	7. e	8. I	9. h	10. k

D.	1. d	2. c	3. j	4. b	5. a
	6. e	7. g	8. f	9. h	10. j

■■

CHAPTER 3

Word Processing Using MS-Word

Structure

In this chapter, we will discuss the following topics:

- Word processing basics
- Opening and closing document
- Text creation and manipulation
- Formatting the text
- Table manipulation
- Mail merging
- Table of contents
- Adding and deleting comments
- Tracking and revising changes

Objectives

The reader will be able to understand the following:

- Word Processing and their usage, details of word processing screen.
- Opening, saving and printing a document including pdf files.
- Document creation, formatting of text, paragraph and whole document.
- Inserting Header and Footer in the document.
- Finding text in a word document and correcting spellings.
- Inserting and manipulating tables, enhancing table using borders and shading features.
- Preparing copies of a document labels, and so on, for sending various recipients using Mail Merge.

MS-Word is the most popular word processing software used today. A Word processor is essentially a computerized version of the standard typewriter. However, it has several features like spell check, the ability to save and store documents, copy and paste functions, and the ability to add images and shapes to documents and much more. When attached to an electronic mail, documents created by MS-Word can be delivered in seconds. The benefit is that it helps the user to type faster and more accurately.

The main advantage of word processing software over a typewriter is that you can make changes without retyping the entire document. If you make a typing mistake, you can simply take the cursor there and correct your mistake. If you want to delete a paragraph, you can simply remove it, without leaving a trace. It is equally easy to insert a word, sentence, or paragraph in the middle of a document. Word processor also makes it easy to move sections of text from one place to another within a document, or between documents. When you have made all the changes you want, you can send the file to a printer to get a hardcopy. You can also mail it electronically to the addressee.

Word Processing Basics

Word processing package, such as Word 2013, helps enter text and manipulate words and phrases. You can change a typed letter, document and report easily and store them for future use. You can even print these documents as and when desired. Thus, documents created on a word processor can be made accurately, thereby giving a better look; they can be printed for use.

> **Tips:** A word processor allows you to work more effectively and efficiently with minimum effort.

Opening Word Processing Package (MS Word 2013)

To start Word 2013, perform the following steps:

1. Click the **Start** button. Highlight **All Programs** and click the **Microsoft Office 2013** folder. Select **Word 2013**, as shown in *Figure 3.1*:

Figure 3.1: Starting MS Word 2013

Word opens the screen with recent documents that were created in the left pane. At the right side, you can see the Blank document and templates, as shown in *Figure 3.2*:

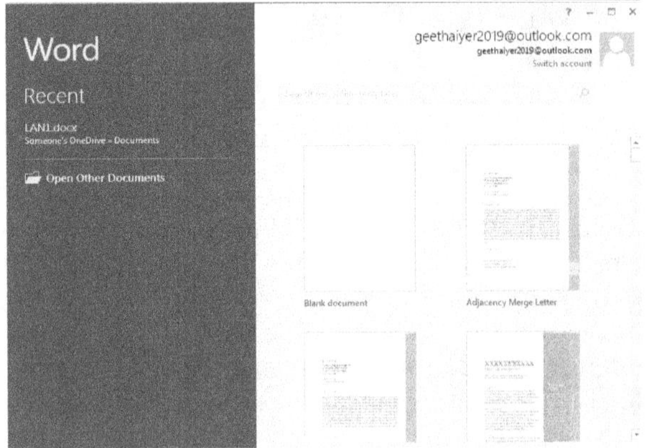

Figure 3.2: Recent Document

The Application Window

When you start an Office application such as Word, Excel, or PowerPoint, the program window is displayed with a blank document with

a default name such as (`Document1`, `Book1`, `Presentation1`) respectively. For example, using Word, the application window screen is explained in detail, as shown in *Figure 3.3*:

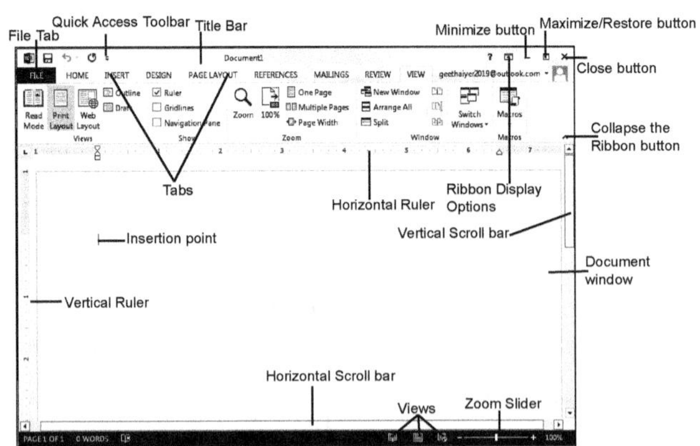

Figure 3.3: Application Window

Menu/Ribbon and & Tabs

The new user interface replaces menus, toolbars, and most of the task panes from previous versions of MS-Word. These have been replaced by the File tab and Ribbon. The interface is designed to help you to be more productive. You can find the right features of various tasks more easily, discover new functionality and be more efficient. *Figure 3.3* shows the elements of Word 2013 application window and an open Word 2013 document in detail.

- **File tab:** This button is located in the upper-left corner of the Word 2013 Window. The commands related to managing Word 2013 and its documents are put together on a menu.
- **Quick Access Toolbar:** This toolbar is located by default at the top of the Word 2013 Window. This toolbar displays the set of commonly used commands, including New, Open, Save, Quick Print, E-mail, Touchscreen device, Undo and Redo, and so on.
- **Dialog box Launchers:** The dialog box launchers are small icons that appear in some groups. Clicking a Dialog Box Launcher opens a related dialog box or task pane, providing more options related to that group.
- **Document Window:** You create a document in the document Window. When more than one document is opened, each document has its own Window.
- **Title bar:** It is displayed at the top of the application Window. It displays the name of the active file, identifies the app, and provides tools for managing the app window, ribbon, and content.

- **Minimize button:** It is represented by an underscore (_) at the right of the title bar, which stores an application programme at the bottom of the screen.
- **Maximize button:** It is represented by a box at the right of the title bar that fills available space within the document or application.
- **Close button:** It is represented by a cross at the right of a title bar (X) that closes the Window or dialog box.
- **Restore button:** It is represented by a double box at the right of the title bar that restores an application or document into a sizeable window.
- **Status bar:** At the bottom of the window, the status bar gives you information about the current document. You can turn off the display of an item of information by right-clicking the status bar and then clicking that item.
- **Views:** The right end of the status bar gives you options of viewing your document in five different ways.
- **Mouse pointer:** On-screen arrow, I-beam, or drawing button indicates the current location of the screen.
- **Ruler:** A bar containing a scale that indicates tabs, paragraph indents, and margins in the paragraph to align objects in a document.
- **ScreenTips:** ScreenTips show the name of the command button displayed in ribbon. They appear as soon as you position the mouse pointer on the toolbar button.
- **Ribbon:** Ribbon is displayed just below the title bar. In Ribbon, the Commands are organized in logical groups, which are collected together under tabs. You can hide the Ribbon by double-clicking the active tab. Different types of Tabs are available in Word 2013, as shown in *Figure 3.4*.

Figure 3.4: *Ribbon*

At the bottom-right-hand corner of some groups, there is a diagonal arrow called a Dialog Box Launcher, as shown in *Figure 3.5*. Clicking this button opens a dialog box for that group containing further options for the group.

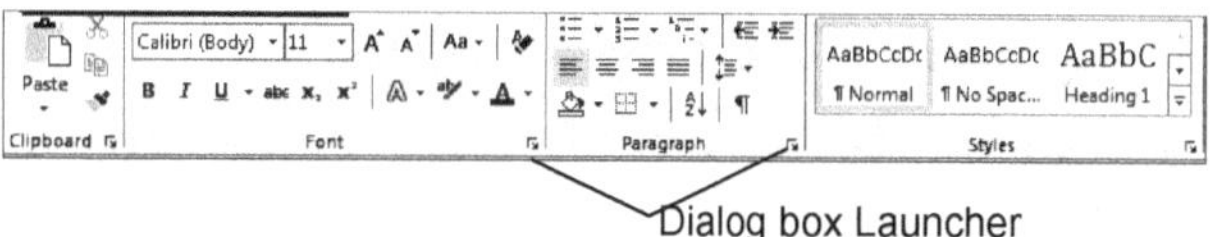

Figure 3.5: *Dialog Box Launcher*

To customize the Quick Access toolbar, perform the following steps:

1. Click the drop-down arrow in the Quick Access Toolbar, as shown in *Figure 3.6*:

Figure 3.6: *Customize Quick Access Toolbar*

2. In the **Customize Quick Access Toolbar** drop-down menu, click the command(s) you wish to add or remove from your Quick Access Toolbar.

3. Click **More Commands...**, as shown above.

4. In the Customize Quick Access Toolbar Window, select a command from the list given on the left under Choose **commands** from to add to your Quick Access Toolbar, as shown in *Figure 3.7*:

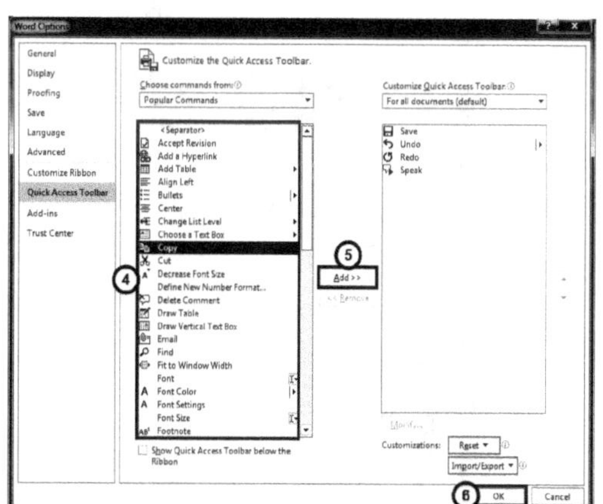

Figure 3.7: *Word Options Dialog Box*

5. Click the **Add>>** button.
6. Click the **OK** button.

Using Quick Access Toolbar

You can add buttons to the Quick Access Toolbar which expands to accommodate them. If you add many buttons, it might become difficult to view the text in the title bar, or all the buttons might not be visible. To resolve this problem, you can move the Quick Access Toolbar below the Ribbon by clicking option from Customize Quick Access Toolbar drop-down menu.

At the right end of the Quick Access Toolbar, click the Customize Quick Access Toolbar button. By default, the Save, Undo, and Repeat buttons appear on the Quick Access Toolbar, as show in *Figure 3.6*.

Using Quick Access Icons by Ribbon Command

If you click the Save icon in the Quick Access toolbar, Word 2013 saves your current file. If you are saving a new file, a dialog box pops up, asking you to choose a name for your file. If you click the Print icon, it immediately prints your entire file through the default printer.

The Redo icon reverses the last Undo command you choose. For example, if you delete a paragraph, it disappears. Then, if you immediately click the Undo icon, the paragraph reappears. If you immediately click the Redo icon, the Redo command reverses the Undo command and deletes the paragraph once more.

The Undo icon is unique. It offers two ways to use it. Firstly, you can click the Undo icon to undo the last action you chose. Secondly, you can click the downward-pointing arrow that appears to the right of the Undo icon to display a list of one or more of your previous actions, as shown in *Figure 3.8*:

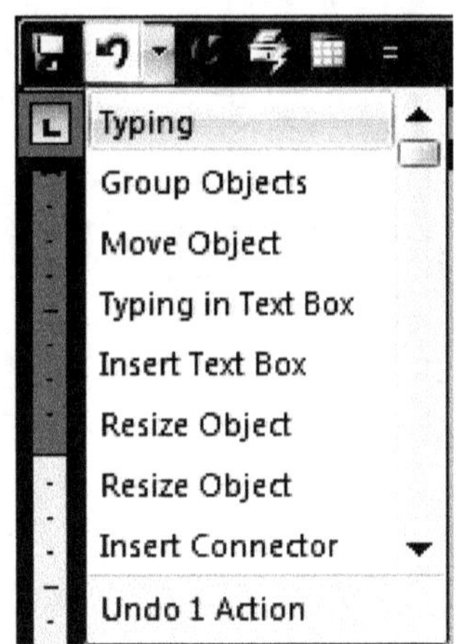

Figure 3.8: *The Undo icon Displays a List of Actions*

Rulers

The ruler helps you to control the margins, paragraph indentation, and tab settings for a document.

Displaying or Hiding Rulers

Word 2013 gives you the flexibility to hide or display ruler according to your working needs.

> **Tips:** The horizontal ruler is always displayed at the top of the document window. The vertical ruler is displayed only in the Page Layout view or in Print Preview.

To display the ruler, perform the following steps:

1. On the **VIEW** tab, in the **Show** group, select the **Ruler check box**, as shown in *Figure 3.9*:

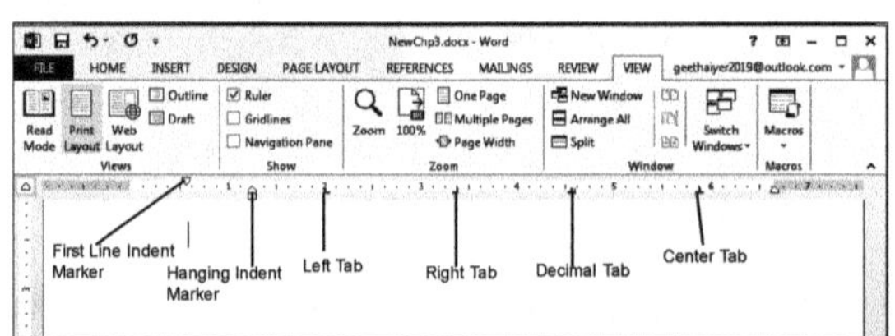

Figure 3.9: *Word 2013 Horizontal Ruler including Tabs Marking*

2. Horizontal and vertical rulers appear above and to the left of the page.

Reading the Horizontal Ruler

Margin settings are managed by the upward facing pointers at the bottom edge of the ruler. Dragging these pointers adjusts the position of the right or left margin. Word 2013 also displays a vertical line showing the position of the margin in the document.

> **Tips:** The indent markers and the tab stops on the horizontal ruler reflect the settings for the paragraph that contains the insertion point.

The paragraph indentation setting is managed by the downward-facing pointer at the top edge of the ruler. Dragging this pointer adjusts the indentation of the first line of a paragraph. Word 2013 also shows a vertical line so that you can see the exact position of the new indentation setting.

Note that you can adjust tab settings by double-clicking on the ruler. There are four types of tabs; their details are given in *Table 3.1*:

Tab	Function
Left-aligned	Characters appear to the right of the tab as you type; it is indicated by an L-shaped angle in the box.
Centre-aligned	Characters are centred at the tab position; it is indicated by an angle with the vertical bar centred over the base line.
Right-aligned	Characters extend to the left of the tab as you type; it is indicated by a reverse L-shaped angle.
Decimal	The decimal point aligns with the tab position; it is indicated by the symbol for a centre-aligned tab with a decimal point to the right of the vertical member.

Table 3.1: *Different Types of Tabs*

The Status Bar

The Status bar, which appears at the bottom of the Word 2013 Window, shows information about the active document or the work you are performing.

Displaying Status Bar

The location of the insertion point is displayed on the status bar. By default, status bar tells you which page the insertion point is on, but you can also display its location by section, line, and column and in inches from the top of the page. Simply right-click the status bar, and then click the option you want to display. After selecting the options, the screen appears as shown in *Figure 3.10*.

Figure 3.10: *Word 2013 Status Bar Elements*

To hide the items on the status bar, right-click on the Status Bar. Customize Status Bar pop menu appears; select the options that you want to hide in the Status bar.

Reading the Status Bar

The status bar shows the information about the text visible on the screen. Table 3.2 explains the message appearing in the Status bar:

Message	Explanation
Page 3	You are on page 3 of the document.
Sec 1	You are in section 1 of the document.
3/11	On page 3 of 11 pages document. This page number is based on the actual number of pages in the document, not on the printed page number. If you have started numbering pages from a number other than 1, this will not match the printed page number.
At 1.3″	A line of text that is in this vertical position from the top of the page.
Ln 19	The nineteen line of the text on this page.
Word count	Number of words in the document.
Col 32	Beginning of the line character position within the line of the text.
Over/Insert	Indicates whether overtype mode is on or off.
View tabs	Different views of the document.
Zoom	Click the Zoom slider. If you do Zoom In, + icon moves to increase. If you do Zoom Out - icon it moves to decrease.

Table 3.2: *Message in the Status Bar*

Using the Help

The Help button in Word is found at the top-right corner of the window. The button looks like a question mark surrounded by a circle. Or, you can see the shortcut key F1 to enable the Help window.

To get help, perform the following steps:

1. Click the **Help** icon, that is, question mark (?) in the upper-right corner of the Ribbon, as shown in *Figure 3.11*:

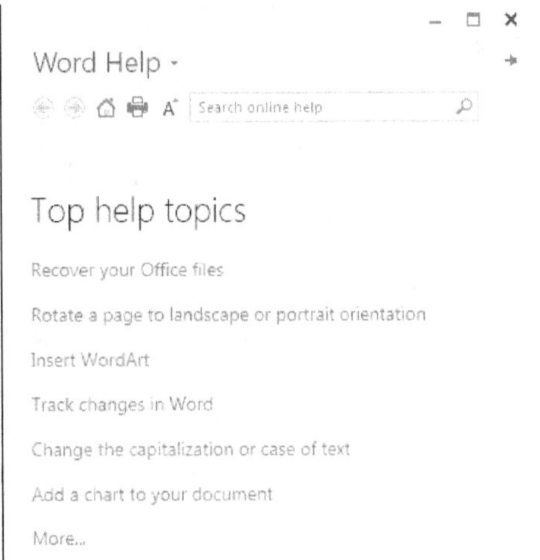

Figure 3.11: *Word Help dialog box*

2. To find help on a specific topic, type a word or phrase related to the topic in the Search box, and then press the **Enter** key. For example, you have type the word such as SmartArt graphics in the Search box, as shown in *Figure 3.12*:

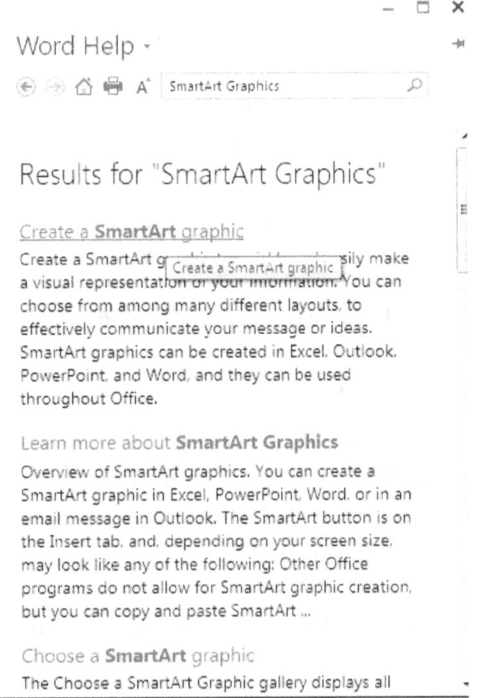

Figure 3.12: *Displayed Search Result*

3. It displays a list of search results, click the link to find the corresponding information, as shown in *Figure 3.11*.

4. To navigate between help topics, click the **Back** and **Forward** button or **Home** button on the toolbar.

5. Click the **Close** button to close the Help Window in the upper-right corner of the Window.

Opening and Closing Documents

To create or work in the document, you need to open the Word application.

Opening Documents

In addition to creating new documents, you will often need to open a document that was previously saved.

To open a document, perform the following steps:

1. Click the **File** tab, backstage view will appear, select **Open**. List of Recent Documents appears, as shown in *Figure 3.13*:

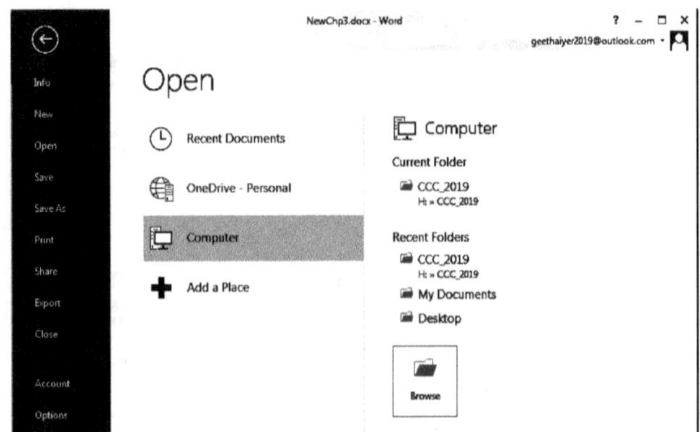

Figure 3.13: *Open Backstage view*

2. Select Computer, then click **Browse**. Alternatively, you can choose **OneDrive** to open files stored on OneDrive.

3. Navigate the file storage folder by clicking the right pane, and then click the recent folder. Then, click any subfolder until you reach the folder you want. Or, in the left pane, click **Browse** to open the **Open dialog box**, as shown in *Figure 3.14*:

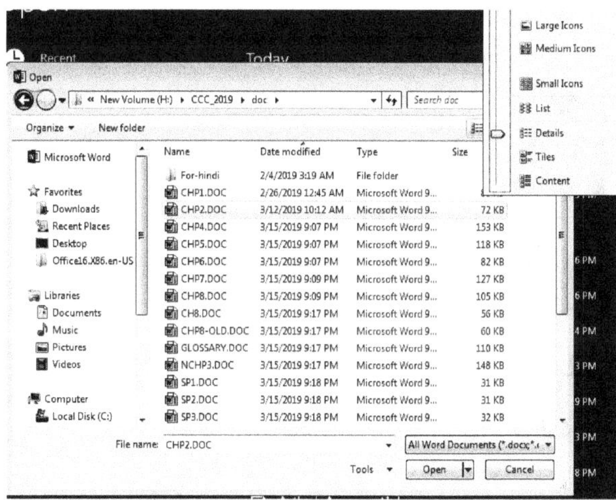

Figure 3.14: *Open Dialog Box*

4. Click the More Options drop-down arrow to change the views of folder or file. Different views of a document are given in the following table:

Button	**Function**
Large Icons	It displays icons in large size. It gives you a better view of graphics and video files.
Medium Icons	It displays icons in medium size.
Small Icons	It displays icons that are only representative of the contents (word document, pdf, executable, graphic file, and so on).
List	Displays icons of files and folders with an identifying icon.
Details	Displays the details, including the size type, last modified, and so on.
Tiles	It displays a medium-sized icon representing each file and folder, along with information about their types and sizes.
Content	It displays each file and folder on a separate row, on which you will see their detailed information

Table 3.3: *Different views of document*

5. Select the document from the list, and then click the **Open** button.

6. The selected **Word 2013** document is opened.

If you frequently work with the same document, you can pin it to backstage view for quick access. To pin a document, perform the following steps:

1. Click the **File** tab to open backstage view, then click **Open**. Your recently edited documents will appear.

2. Hover the mouse over the document you want to pin. A pushpin icon will appear next to the document. Click the pushpin icon, as shown in *Figure 3.15*:

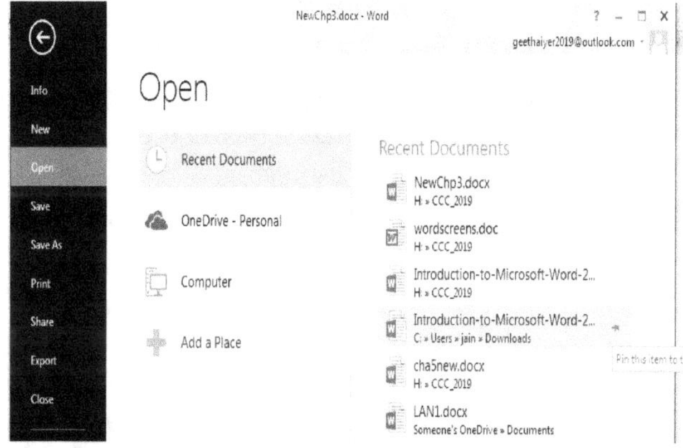

Figure 3.15: *Pin a Document*

3. The document will stay in Recent Documents. To unpin a document, click the pushpin icon again, as shown in *Figure 3.16*:

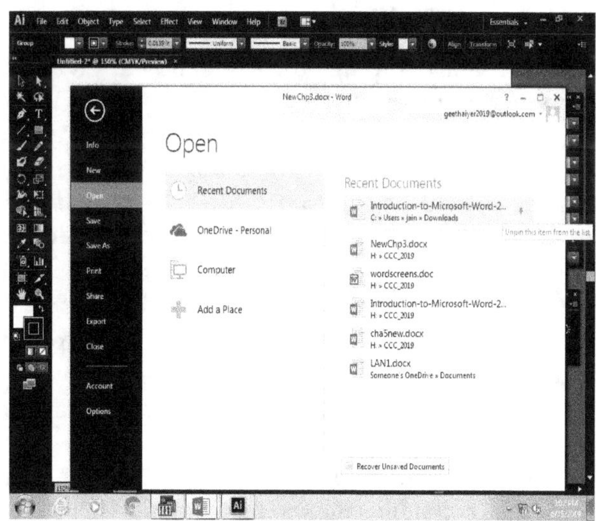

Figure 3.16: *Unpin a Document*

4. You can also pin folders to backstage view for quick access. From backstage view, click Open and locate the folder you want to pin, then click the **pushpin** icon.

Scroll through a document

You can scroll through a document by using the mouse or the keyboard. If you split the document Window, you can display two different parts of a document.

The following table explains scrolling through a document using the mouse:

To	Do this
Scroll up one line	Click the up scroll arrow.
Scroll down one line	Click the down scroll arrow.
Scroll up one screen	Click above the scroll box.
Scroll down one screen	Click below the scroll box.
Scroll to a specific page	Drag the scroll box.
Scroll left	Click the left scroll arrow.
Scroll right	Click the right scroll arrow.
Scroll left, beyond the margin, in normal view	Hold down Shift key and click the left scroll arrow.

Table 3.4: *Scrolling using the mouse*

Typing and Editing a Document

You can start typing in a document without worrying about the end of the right margin. Word will automatically wrap text to the next line at the end of the line. You may correct the text by pressing Backspace key. The editing of documents is based on the Windows principle, that is, select and do.

Save and Save As

The first time you save a file, you need to specify three items:

- The drive and folder in which you want to store your file.
- The name of the file.
- The format to save the file.

To save document, perform the following steps:

1. Click the **File** tab and then select the **Save** option. Alternatively, choose the save button on the Quick Access toolbar.

2. Save As Backstage view appears, as shown in *Figure 3.17*:

Figure 3.17: *Save Backstage View*

3. In the left pane of the backstage view, click Save As.

4. Select **Browse**, Computer or OneDrive desired option to save the document.

5. The **Save As dialog box** appears, as shown in *Figure 3.18*. Select the location where you want to save the document in the Address bar.

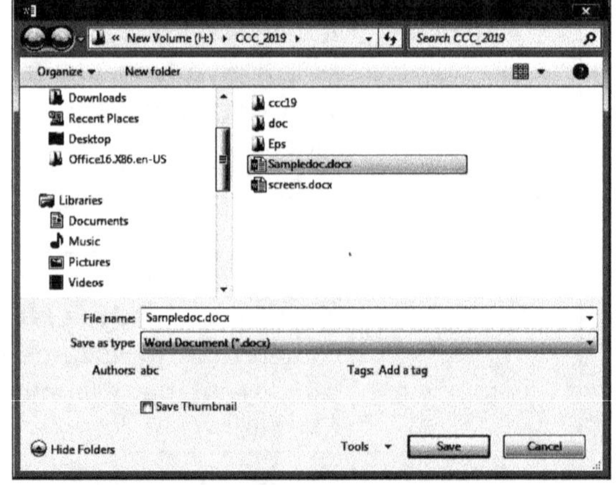

Figure 3.18: *Save As Dialog Box*

6. In the File name: textbox, type a name for your file.

7. Choose the file format in which you want to save from the Save as type drop-down list.

8. Click the **Save** button.

The document gets saved. You can click the save command again to save your changes as you modify the document.

Naming a Document

In Windows, a filename can be from one to 255 characters long, followed by a period and up to three characters' filename extension. (In most cases, it is best to let Word supply the default extension for Word documents, which is .docx). You can use any characters except the following characters for naming the files: ? : [] + = \ / : / <>

An alert box appears if you give the name of character as shown below; the file name is not valid.

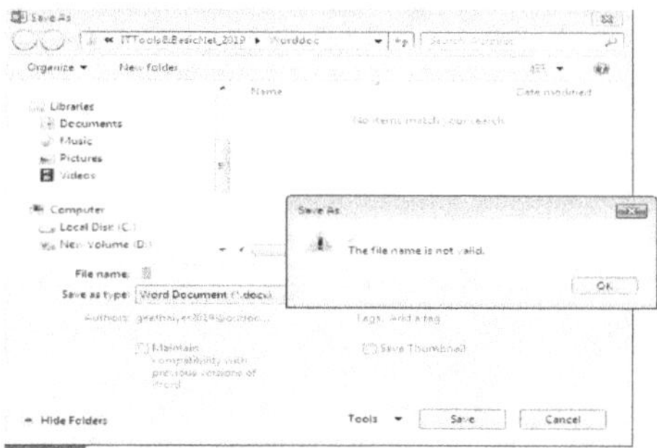

Figure 3.19: *Alert box*

You also cannot use a period except to separate the filename from the extension.

Page Setup Options

In Word 2013, default margins are 1 inch at the top and bottom each and 1 inch on the left and right each. You can change the margins for the entire document or for different parts of the document (if you divide the document into sections).

Note that in Draft and Outline view, you do not see the margins. However, you can see the space between them in Print Layout view, and you can see the page as it will print. Always select the Print Layout view if you want to see headers, footers, page numbers, footnotes, and so on.

You can also select one of the two types of page orientations, namely, **portrait (vertical) and landscape (horizontal)**. You can change the paper size and page orientation for a section or for the entire document.

A page can have only one user-defined left margin setting and only one user-defined right margin setting, but each paragraph on the page can have different left and right indentation.

Page Orientation

Page orientation defines the direction for printing or displaying the document in Word. You can print text on page horizontal wise or vertical wise by setting the page in the required orientation. There are two common page orientations: Portrait (vertical) orientation and Landscape (horizontal) orientation. When you change the page orientation, the values that you set for the top and bottom page margins are automatically applied to the left and right margins.

To change page orientation, perform the following

steps:

1. Open the document that you want to switch to Landscape or Portrait orientation.

2. On the **Page Layout tab**, in the Page Setup group, click the **Orientation drop-down arrow**.

3. Click either Portrait or Landscape to change the page orientation, as shown in *Figure 3.20*:

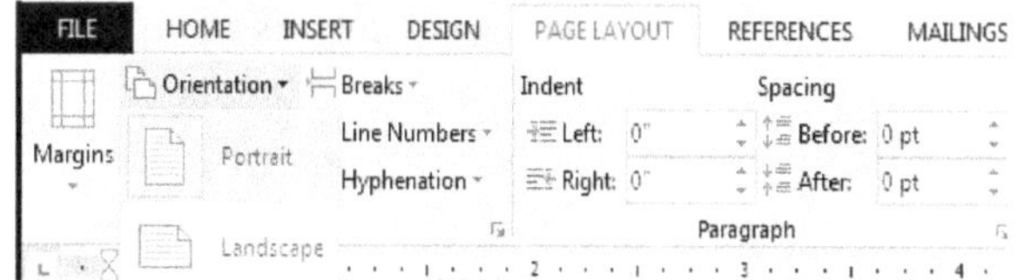

Figure 3.20: *Selecting Page Orientation*

4. The page orientation of the document will be changed.

Page Margins

To set margins with page setup command, perform the following:

1. Select the sections for which you want to change margins. Alternatively, position the insertion point in the section whose margins you want to change.

2. Click **Layout** tab, and then click the right-corner arrow of Page setup. The **Page Setup** dialog box appears. Click the **Margins** tab Margins property sheet as shown in *Figure 3.21* appears.

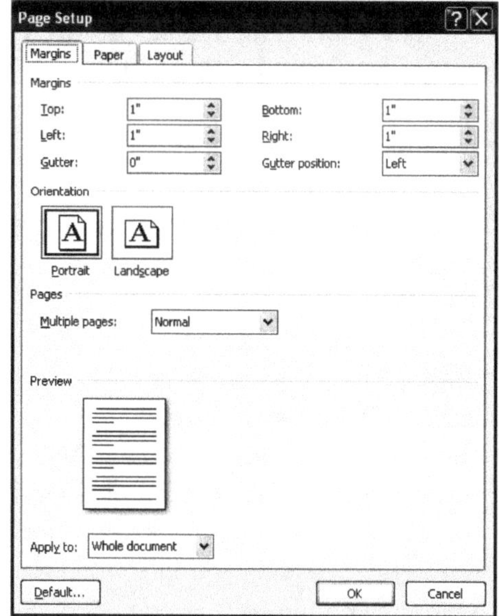

Figure 3.21: *Page Setup Dialog Box*

3. Margins Property sheet has the following options:

Option	Description
Top:	Select or type out the desired margin from the top of the page.
Bottom:	Select or type out the desired margins from the bottom of the page.
Left:	Select or type out the desired margin from the left edge of the page.
Right:	Select or type out the desired margin from the right edge of the page.
Gutter:	Select or type out the gutter space as required. Gutter is the extra space added to the margins to leave the space for binding the documents.
Orientation	Select between Portrait (vertical) and Landscape (horizontal) page setting.

Table 3.5: *Margins Property*

4. In the Pages area, select the Multiple pages: drop-down list.
   - **Mirror margins:** This option adjusts left and right margins so that when you print on both sides of the page, the inside and outside margins of the facing pages are of the same width.
   - The Preview box displays the effect of the settings you select.
5. In the Apply to: choose the portion of the document where you want to apply the new settings.
6. Click **OK**.

To set the margins using the ruler, perform the following steps:

1. Switch to **Print Layout view**.
2. If the ruler is not displayed, click **View** tab. In the Show group, click the **Ruler checkbox**.
3. Point to the transition area on the ruler, that is, where gray becomes white.
4. The mouse pointer will become a two-headed arrow.

5. Drag the margin to the desired position with a mouse. The ruler's dimensions change as you drag, as shown in *Figure 3.22*:

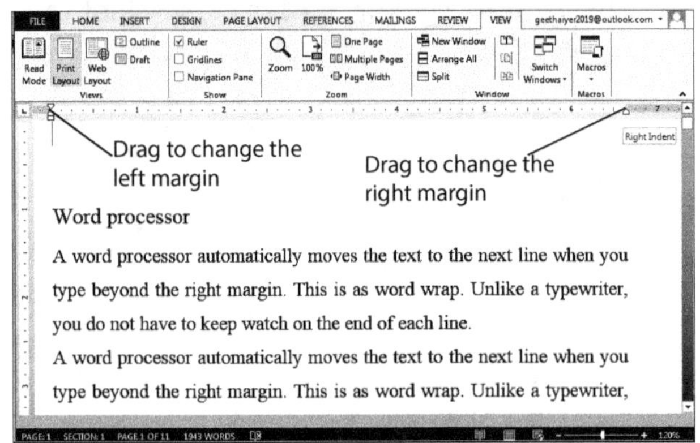

Figure 3.22: *Drag Ruler Ends in Print Layout to Change the Margins*

Paper Size

By default, the page size of a new document is 8.5 inches by **11 inches**. Depending on your project, you may need to adjust your document page size. There is a variety of pre-defined page sizes in Word.

To change the page size, perform the following steps:

1. Select the **Layout tab**, and then click the Size command.
2. A drop-down menu will appear. The current page size is highlighted. Click the desired pre-defined page size, as shown in *Figure 3.23*:

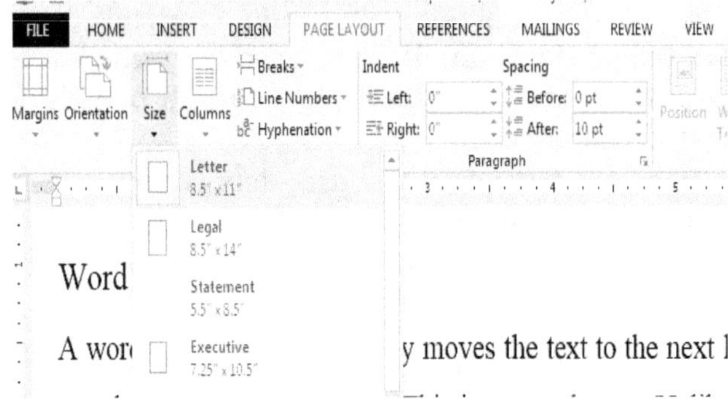

Figure 3.23: *Selecting Page Size*

3. The page size of the document will be changed.

To use a custom page size, perform the following steps:

1. From the **Layout tab**, click Size. Select **More Paper Sizes...** from the drop-down menu, as shown in *Figure 3.24*:

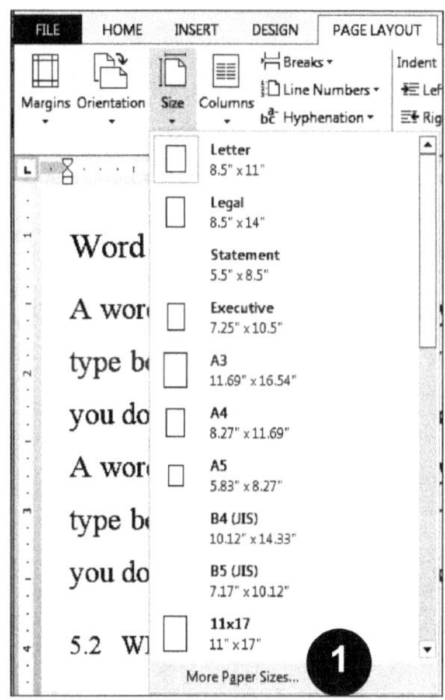

Figure 3.24: *Selecting More Paper Sizes*

2. The Page Setup dialog box will appear, as shown in *Figure 3.25*:

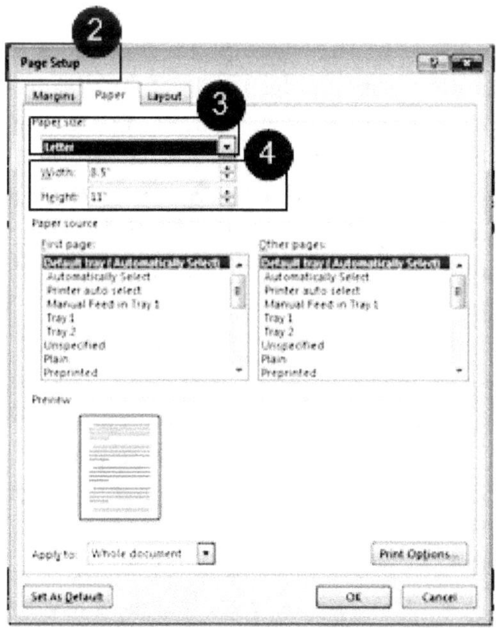

Figure 3.25: *Page Setup Dialog Box*

3. Select the **Paper tab** under the Paper size: drop-down list.
4. Adjust the values for Width: and Height: and then click **OK**.
5. The page size of the document will be changed.
6. In the Apply to: section, select the portion of the document you want to print on the selected paper size.

7. Click the Set As Default button if you want to save these settings as default settings, so that they can apply to all pages printed hereafter.
8. Click **OK**.

Page Margins

A margin is the distance from the text from the edge of the paper. It helps to define where a line of text begins and ends. When page is justified, the text is spread out with the left and right margins automatically. You can set the page margins from the page setup dialog box.

To format page margins, perform the following steps:

1. Select the **Layout tab**, and then click the **Margins** command.
2. A drop-down menu will appear, as shown in *Figure 3.26*. Click the pre-defined margin size you want.

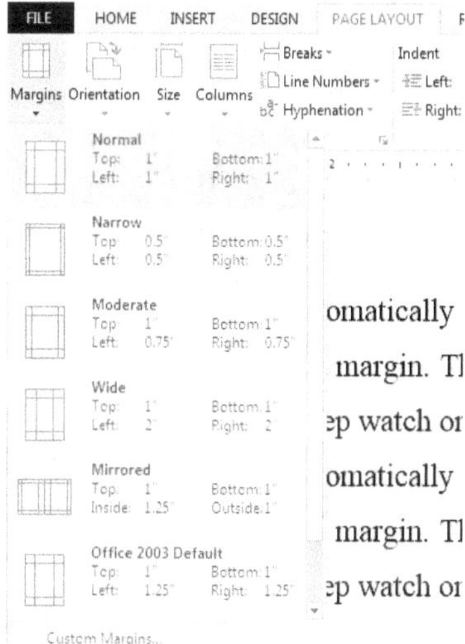

Figure 3.26: *Selecting Pre-defined Margin Size*

3. The margins of the document will be changed.

To use custom margins, perform the following steps:

1. From the **Layout** tab, click **Margins**. Select Custom Margins from the drop-down menu, as shown in *Figure 3.26*.
2. The Page Setup dialog box will appear, as shown in *Figure 3.27*:

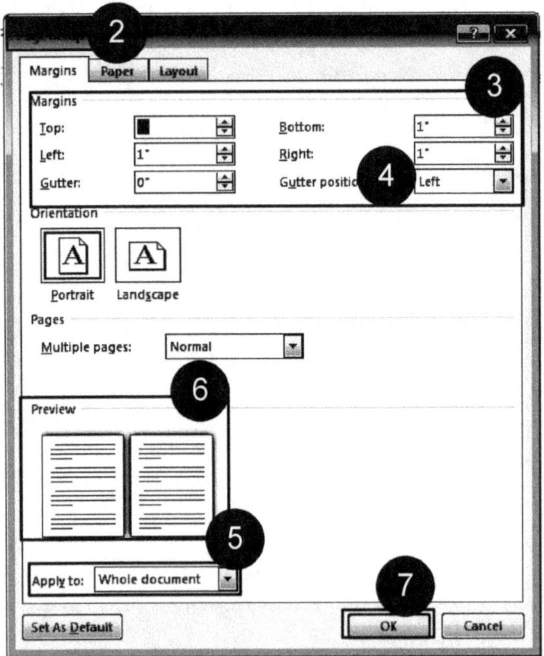

Figure 3.27: *Page Setup with Margins tab Selected*

3. Click the **Margins** tab, and select or type out the desired margin height from the Top: or Bottom: of the page edge.
4. Select or type out the desired margin width from the Left: and Right: of the page edge.
5. In the Apply to:, choose the portion of the document where you want to apply the new settings.
6. The Preview box displays the effect of the settings you select.
7. Click **OK**.

Print Preview

Previewing a document allows you to visualize the document in its printable format before actually executing the Print command. In other words, the preview of a document displays the document in a printable format and shows how the document will appear after taking a printout.

To preview the document, perform the following steps:

1. Open the document whose print preview you want to view.
2. Click the **File** tab, and then choose **Print** option from the **File** tab. The Print options are visible in the backstage view, as shown in *Figure 3.28*:

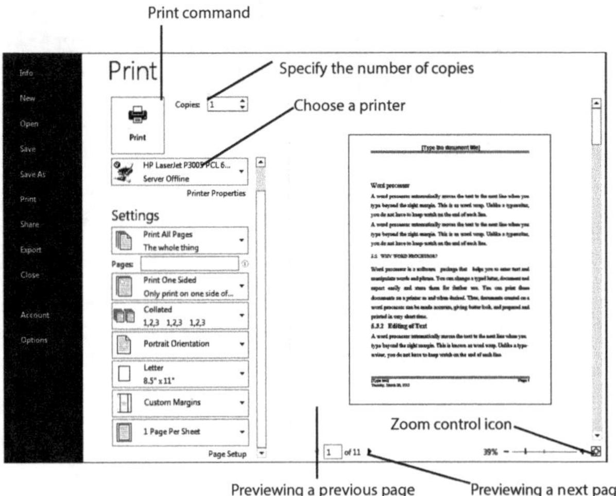

Figure 3.28: *Print Preview in the Backstage View*

3. The Backstage view consists of three panes. The left pane contains several options, such as Save, Save As, Open, Close, Info, and Recent. In the middle pane, print options and its related printer settings are shown. In the right pane, the preview of the document is shown. In the bottom of the right pane, the Zoom control button is available. The **+ (plus)** button is used to increase the size of the document and the **– (minus)** button is used to decrease the size of the preview document. The Next button is used to go to the next page of document, and the previous button to move to the pervious page of document.

To preview a document as it will appear when printed:

1. Display the Print page of the backstage view. The page navigator below the preview pane indicates the number of pages the document will print on.
2. Do any of the following:
   - To move between pages, click the Next **Page** or **Previous Page button**; or enter the number of the pages you want to display in the page navigator box.
   - To preview multiple pages, reduce the magnification until two or more pages fit in the preview pane.
   - To display a single page at the largest size that fits in the preview pane, click the **Zoom** to Page button in the lower-right corner.

Printing of Documents

When you are ready to print a document, you can click the **File** tab to print. The Backstage view appears; then click **Print** icon. Word then uses your computer default printer and the settings specified in the Print Backstage view. You can also use a different printer or change the printer settings on the File tab backstage view. You can then specify which printer to use, what to print, and how many copies to print. You can also make other changes to the settings.

> **Tips:** Before you print a document, you may want to check how it will look on paper by previewing it. Previewing is essential for multi-page documents but is helpful even for one-page documents.

Printing the Current Document

The simplest way to print is to open a document, and click **File** tab. Then choose **Print** tab. The backstage view appears. Choose the **Print** icon. Alternately, click the Print button on the Quick Access toolbar. By default, Word 2013 prints one copy of all pages of the currently open document on the selected printer without printing hidden text.

1. Click the **File** tab to go back to Print Backstage view.
2. From **Print**, you can choose the following options:
   a. Printer–Select a printer as shown in *Figure 3.29*:

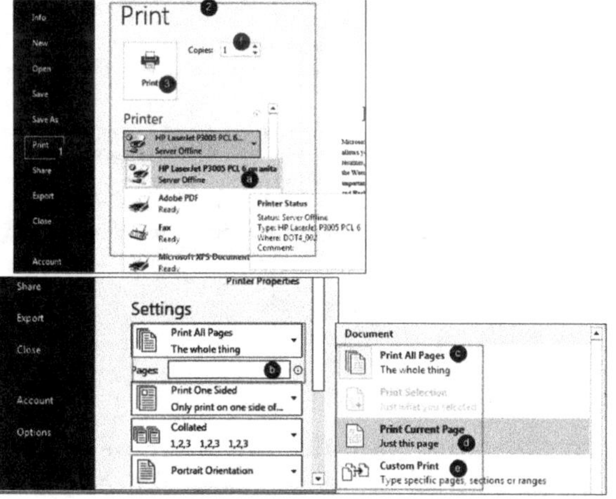

Figure 3.29: *Print Backstage View*

> **Note:** Your list of available printers will be determined by the printers you have installed on your computer.

b. **Settings:** Select the desired setting in which you want to print a document.

c. To print the entire document, select **Print All** pages.

d. To print just one page in your document currently containing the insertion point, click on the Print Current Page button.

e. If you choose Custom print, enter specific pages to print. For example, if it says 1-4 in a document, type the first page number and the last desired page number in the Pages: textbox. Separate the numbers with the hyphen like 1-4.

f. **Copies:** Set the number of copies you want to print.

3. Click the **Print** button.

PDF File and Saving a Document as PDF File

PDFs are one of the most commonly used file types today because files are primarily meant for viewing, not editing. One reason they are so popular is that PDFs can preserve document formatting, which makes them more shareable and helps them to look the same on any device.

Opening and viewing a PDF file is simple. Most web browsers will open PDF files directly in your browser window instead of downloading them to your computer.

There are two ways to create PDFs within Word.

Method 1:

1. Open the file to create a **.pdf** format.
2. Click the **File** tab to go to the backstage view, and select the Save As option.
3. Click the Browse folder to open the Save As dialog box. Choose the location to save the file.
4. Select the PDF file type from the Save as type: drop-down menu, as shown in *Figure 3.30*.

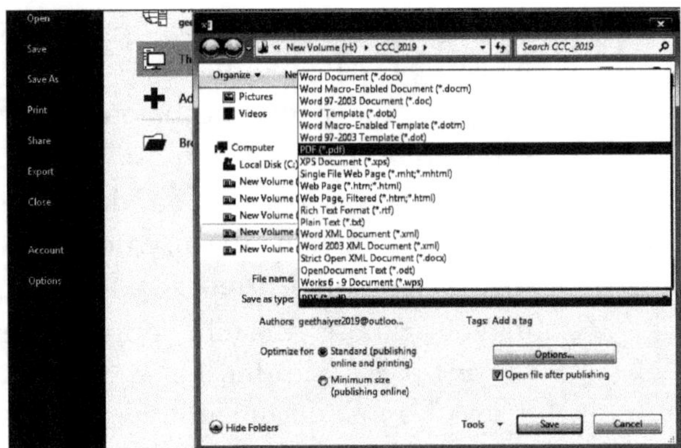

Figure 3.30: *Select the PDF File Format from Save As Dialog Box*

5. Give the name of the file in the File name: drop-down menu.

6. Click the Save button.

Method 2:

1. Click the **File** tab to go to the backstage view.

2. Click the **Export** tab with the Create PDF/ XPS Document option selected. Click the corresponding box on the right side of your screen, as shown in *Figure 3.31*:

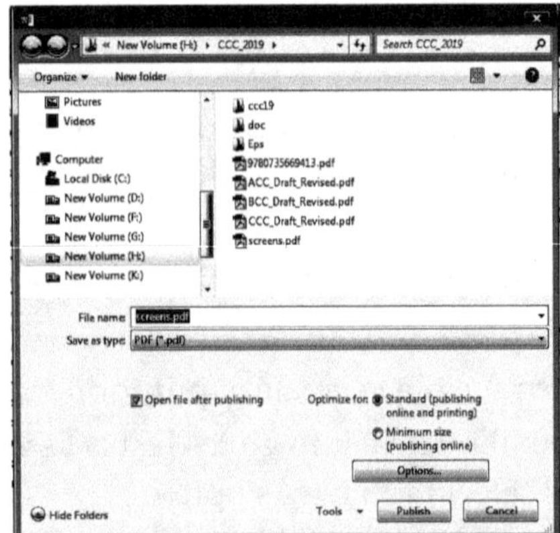

Figure 3.31: *Selecting Publish*

3. A dialog box appears with Publish as PDF or **XPS**. Navigate to the location where you want to save the new PDF file.

4. Click the **Publish** button to create and save the PDF file, as shown in the previous image.

Closing Word 2013

After finishing a document, you should close the Window to remove it from the screen and to free the computer's main memory.

To close a document and exit Word 2013:

1. Click the **File** tab, and then choose the Close tab.

2. The Window closes if no changes have been made to the document since the last saved. However, if you made changes since the last time you saved the document, Word 2013 displays an Alert dialog box, asking whether you want to save your work before closing, as shown in *Figure 3.32*:

Figure 3.32: *Alert Dialog Box*

After you have saved the contents of the document, the Window is closed.

Text Creation and Manipulation

When you open a new document in Word 2013, the insertion point is at the top-left corner of the screen. You can start typing in this document. You can make changes at any time by editing the document.

You can click the **Show/Hide** button on the Paragraph group to display or hide all non-printing characters, such as paragraph marks, tab characters, and spaces. These characters are not printed, even if they are shown on the screen, as shown in *Figure 3.33*:

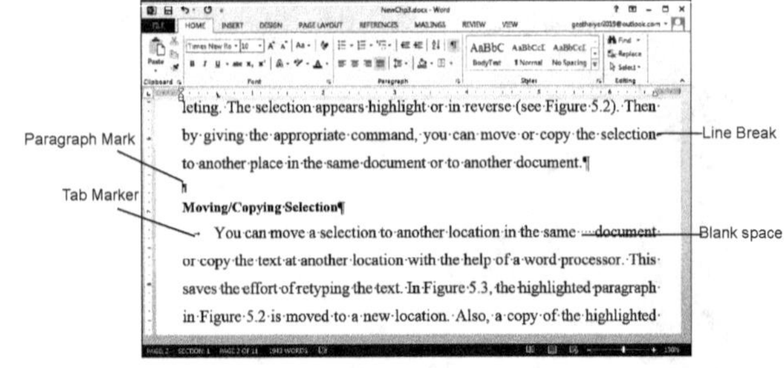

Figure 3.33: *A Screen Displaying Non-printing Characters*

Document Creation

Word files are called **documents**. Whenever you start a new project in Word, you will need to create a new document, which can either be blank or from a template. You will also need to know how to open a close document.

To create a new document, perform the following steps:

1. Click **File** tab; a backstage view appears. Click the New tab in the backstage view, as shown in *Figure 3.34*:

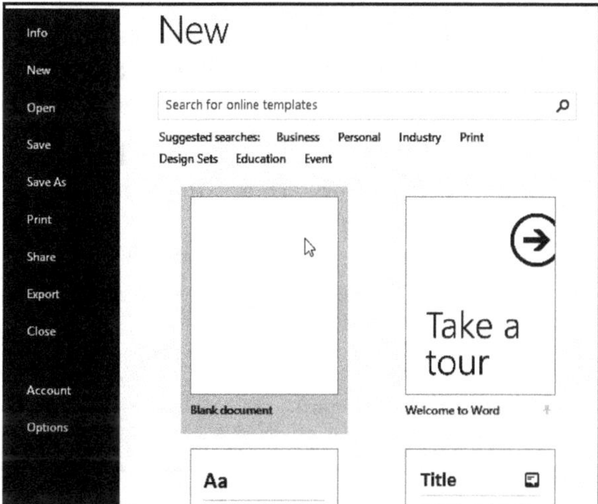

Figure 3.34: *New Backstage View*

2. In the left pane of the backstage view, click New to display the new backstage page.
3. In the right pane, click the Blank document thumbnail, as shown in *Figure 3.34*.
4. A new blank document will appear, as shown in *Figure 3.35*.

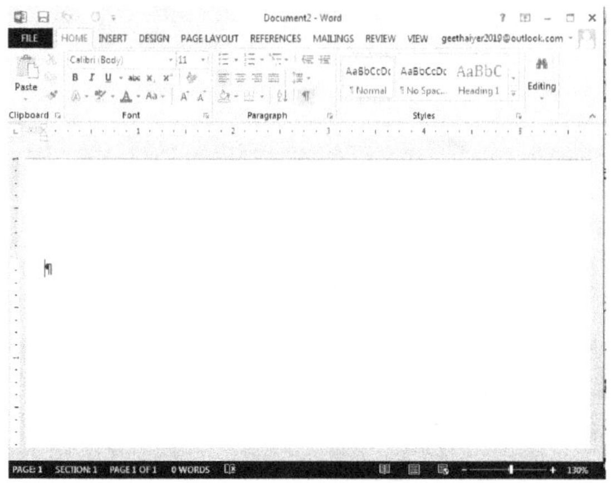

Figure 3.35: *Word Blank Document*

Starting a New Paragraph

In Word 2013, a paragraph is any amount of text or graphics followed by a paragraph mark. A paragraph ends whenever you press the Enter key. Even if you have not typed any text but pressed a key, Word 2013 inserts a paragraph mark ( ). In Word 2013, many types of formatting styles (for example, justification and line spacing) are applied to paragraphs as a whole.

To start a new paragraph, perform the following steps:

1. Position the insertion point where you want to start the new paragraph, and press the **Enter** key.
2. When you press the **Enter** key, Word 2013 inserts a paragraph mark and moves the insertion point to the first line of the new paragraph.

Starting a New Line

Word 2013 automatically wraps text to the next line when the typed text reaches the end of the right margin.

To start a new line within the same paragraph, perform the following steps:

1. Position the insertion point where you want to start the new line, and then press the *Shift + Enter* keys together.
2. Word inserts a line break character and moves the insertion point to the beginning of the next line.
3. To see the line breaks, click the **Show/Hide** command in the Paragraph group of the Home tab.

Editing Text

On a typewriter, when you miss a word or a line, you need to type the whole letter again. But using Word 2013, you can insert new words, new sentences or paragraphs anywhere in the text typed earlier. The new text will get adjusted automatically. Similarly, you can delete any portion of the text, and the remaining part of the matter will get adjusted automatically.

In *Figure 3.36*, you can see the highlighted text is newly inserted, and rest of the text gets deleted.

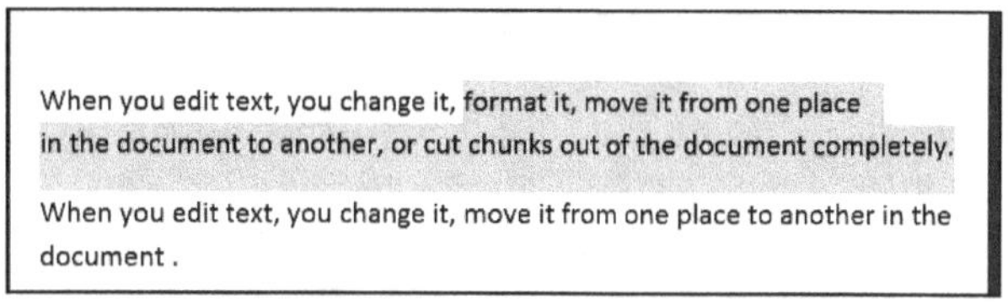

When you edit text, you change it, format it, move it from one place in the document to another, or cut chunks out of the document completely.

When you edit text, you change it, move it from one place to another in the document .

Figure 3.36: *Editing Text in a Document*

Inserting Text

If you notice that some text has been left out of the document, you can move the Insertion pointer to that position and type it in. This method is called **Inserting**.

Typing over the Existing Text

By default, Word moves the existing text to the right as you insert new characters. If you want the new text to replace the existing text, character by character, switch to overtype mode. Again, clicking the overtype mode in the status bar will automatically replace the insert mode.

To type over the existing text, perform the following steps:

1. Click the **File** tab, and then choose **Options**.

2. In the Word Options dialog box, click the **Advanced** tab in the left pane and then under the Editing options, select the Insert key to control overtype mode checkbox.

3. Click **OK**.

Applying Corrections in the Typed Tex

To correct simple typing mistakes, press Backspace or **Delete** keys. To delete more characters, first select the text you want to delete and then press the Backspace or **Delete** key. *Table 3.4* lists different methods for deleting texts and graphics:

Key combination	To delete
Selected text	Press Backspace or Delete
Characters before the insertion point	Press Backspace key
Characters after the insertion point	Press Delete key
A word before the insertion point	Ctrl + Backspace
A word after the insertion point	Ctrl + Del

Table 3.4: Key Combinations for deleting Text or Graphics

To restore the deleted text, perform the following steps:

1. On the Quick Access toolbar, click the Undo button. Alternatively, click the **Ctrl + Z** keys together.

To replace a selection with a new text:

1. Select the text you want to replace.
2. Type the new text.

The text you type replaces the entire selection.

Text Selection

Before you can move, format, delete, or otherwise change text or a graphic picture, you must select the items. You can select the item using a mouse or keyboard. Note that the selected text or graphics are highlighted. To cancel the selection, click outside the selection, or use the arrow keys to move the insertion point.

To select text, perform the following steps:

1. Place the insertion point next to the text you wish to select.

2. Click the mouse, and while holding it down, drag your mouse over the text to select it, shown as follows:

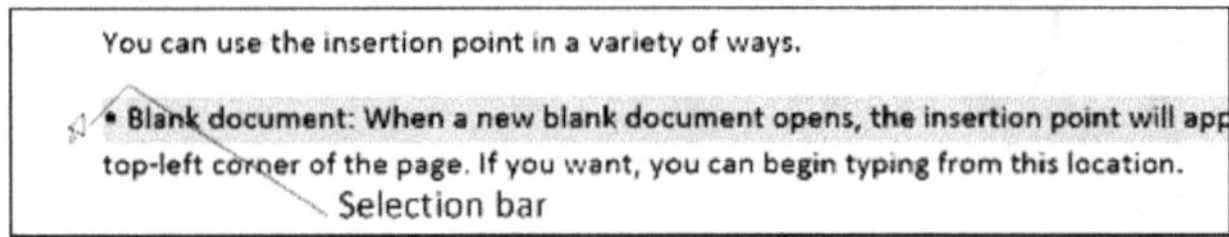

Figure 3.37: Using Selection Bar to Select Text

3. Release the mouse button. You have selected the text. A highlighted box will appear over the selected text, as shown in *Figure 3.37*.

To select multiple lines of text, perform the following steps:

1. Move the mouse pointer to the left of any line so it becomes a right slanted arrow. Click the mouse. The line will be selected.

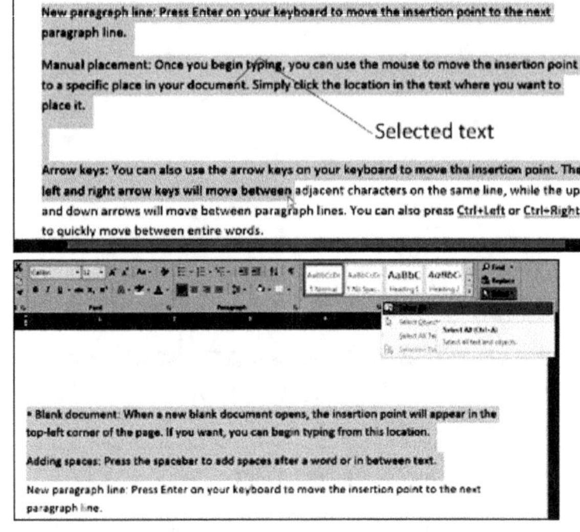

Figure 3.38: Select Multiple Lines of Text

2. To select all of the text in your document, choose the Select command on the Home tab,

and then click Select All. Alternatively, you can press **Ctrl + A** on your keyboard.

3. To select a sentence, hold down the **Ctrl** key and click anywhere in the sentence.

4. To select adjacent words, lines, or paragraphs, drag through the text.

To release a selection, perform the following steps:

1. Click anywhere in the Window other than the selection area.

Selecting Text with a Mouse

You can select a piece of text, a single character, or an entire document. You can also combine mouse and keyboard selection techniques.

To select a small amount of text with the mouse, perform the following steps:

1. Click and hold the mouse button at the beginning of the text you want to select.

2. Drag the pointer in any direction across the text you want to select.

Tips: If the pointer touches the edge of the window as you are dragging, the window scrolls in that direction if more text exists.

Text to select	Mouse Action
A word	Double-click the word.
A line	Click selection bar (blank margin to the left of a line of text).
Multiple lines	Click selection bar and drag up or down till the end of lines.
A paragraph	Double-click selection bar.
Document	Press Ctrl key and click in selection bar.
Rectangular block or column (not within a table)	Click the top left of the column to be selected and then hold Alt key while you drag to select the text.

Table 3.5: *Method for Selecting Text*

Selecting Text with a Keyboard

The method for selecting text is to hold down the Shift key as you move the insertion point. You can select text by using Shift in combination with any move key. Some of these key combinations are listed in *Table 3.6*:

To Select	Press
A Word	Shift + Ctrl + ← or → arrow key
To the beginning of a line	Shift + Home
To the end of a line	Shift + End
To the end of a paragraph	Ctrl + Shift + ↓
To the beginning of a paragraph	Ctrl + Shift + ↑
One line at a time	Shift + ↑ or Shift + ↓
To the beginning of a document	Shit + Ctrl + Home
To the end of a document	Shift + ctrl + End

Table 3.6: *Key Combination for Selecting Text*

To select from the insertion point to a distant location, perform the following steps:

1. Move the insertion point to the beginning of the text you want to select.

2. Press **F8** (Extend Selection).

Tips: While you are in Extend Selection mode, the word appears on the status bar at the bottom of the screen.

3. Press one of the keys listed in the *Table 3.7*. And finally, press the **Esc** key.

To Select	Press
Next or previous character	← or → arrow key
The end of a line	End key
The beginning of a line	Home key
The top of the previous screen	PgUp key
The bottom of the next screen	PgDn key
The beginning of a document	Ctrl + Home keys
The end of a document	Ctrl + End keys

Table 3.7: *Selecting Text from the Insertion Point*

Deleting Text

To delete characters to the right of insertion point, press Delete key, but to delete characters to left of insertion point, use Backspace key. However, when you have to delete a number of lines, deleting one letter at a time becomes a lengthy process. It would be better if you select or highlight all the lines to be deleted as a block.

To delete text, perform the following steps:

1. Select the text to be deleted by pressing the left mouse button.
2. Now, press the **Delete** key from the keyboard.

Cut, Copy and Paste

To remove text from one place in the document and put it in another place, you cut and paste the text. You can also copy and paste text if you want to add copies of your selection elsewhere in your document.

Moving means to remove (cut) the selected text or graphic from one location and insert it in another location in the same document.

Copying means to make a copy of the selected text or graphic and insert it in another location, leaving the original document unchanged.

To Copy and Paste text, perform the following steps:

1. Select the text you want to copy.
2. On the Home tab, in the Clipboard group, click the copy button. You can also right-click your document and select Copy, as shown in *Figure 3.39*:

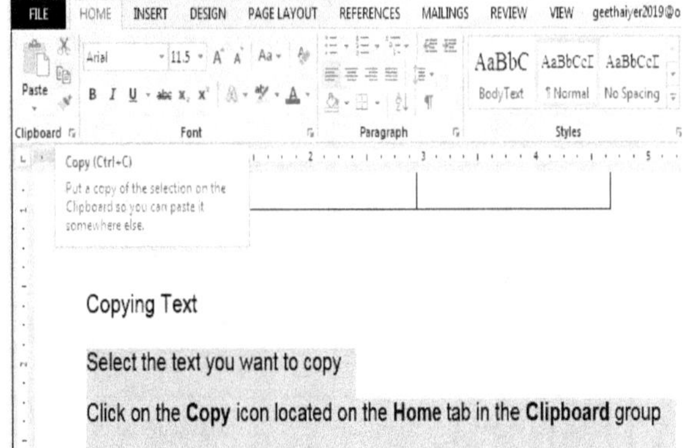

Figure 3.39: *Select the Text to be Copied*

3. Now, position the insertion point at the location you want to place the text.
4. Click the Paste option from the Clipboard group, as shown in *Figure 3.40*. The selected text will be pasted.

Figure 3.40: *Selected Text has been Pasted*

Moving Text

Moving means to remove (cut) the selected text or graphic from one location and insert it in another location in the same document.

To move text, perform the following steps:

1. Do either of the following:

   a. Cut the text from the original location, and then paste it into the new location.
   Or
   Drag the text from the original location to the new location.

2. Select the text you want to move as shown in *Figure 3.41*:

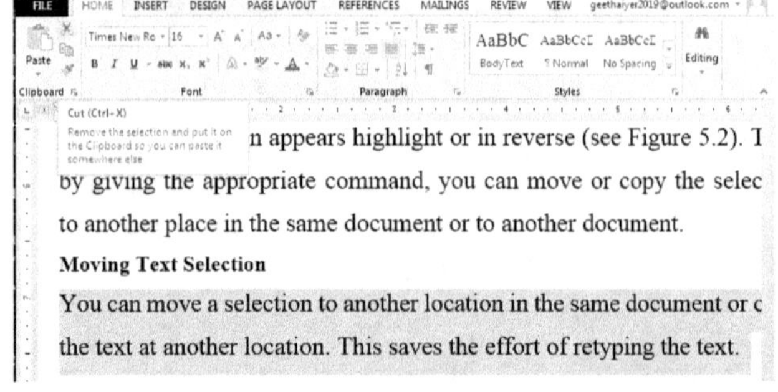

Figure 3.41: *Highlight the Text to Move*

3. Click the Cut option from the Clipboard group. The selected text will disappear from the screen and will be placed on the Clipboard.
4. Now, position the insertion point at the location you want to paste the text.
5. Click the Paste option from the Clipboard group. The sel ected text will be moved to a new location, as shown in *Figure 3.42*:

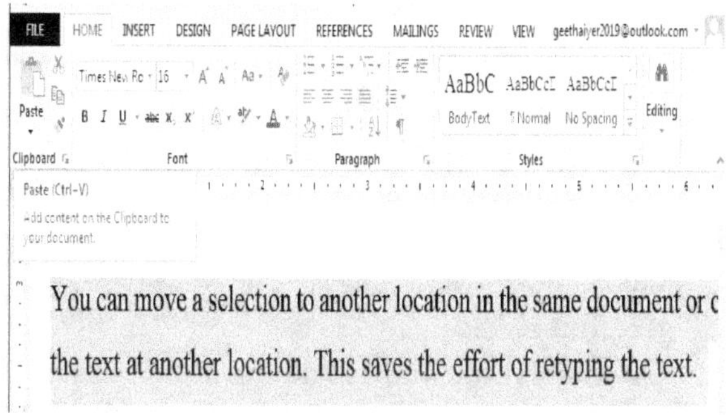

Figure 3.42: *Move the Text and Paste in the New Location*

Moving and Copying using Drag and Drop Technique

Drag-and-drop editing is an easy way to move or copy a selection within a short distance of a document. You can drag and drop items between documents. However, to move or copy a selection to a longer distance in a document or to a different document, you should use the Cut, Copy, and Paste commands.

To move text using drag-and-drop editing, perform the following steps:

1. Select the text or the graphics you want to move.
2. Point to the selected text or graphics, and then press and hold down the left mouse button. When the drag-and-drop pointer appears, as shown in *Figure 3.43*, drag the dotted insertion point to the new location.

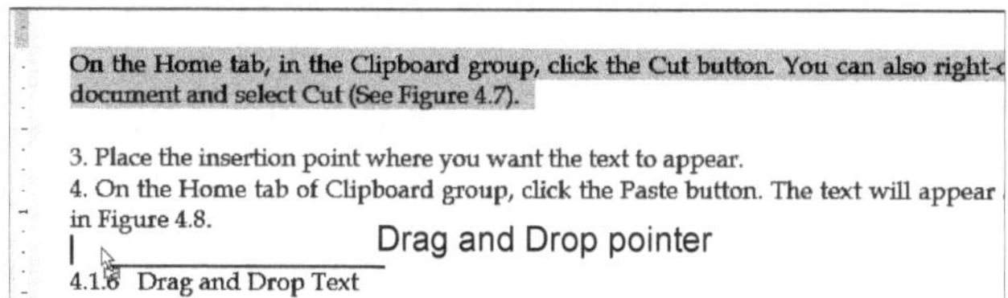

Figure 3.43: *Drag and Drop Mouse Pointer*

3. Release the mouse button to drop the text into desired place.

To copy text/graphics using drag-and-drop editing, perform the following steps:

1. Select the text or the graphics you want to copy.
2. Press and hold down **Ctrl** key. Point to the selected text or the graphics, and then press and hold down the left mouse button while you drag the dotted insertion point to the new location.

To move or copy the text/graphics using the toolbar, perform the following steps:

1. Select the text or the graphics you want to move or copy.
2. Do one of the following:
   a. To move the selection, click the Cut button on the Home tab of Clipboard group.
   b. To copy the selection, click the Copy button on the Home tab of Clipboard group.
   c. Word places the selected text to the Clipboard.
3. Position the insertion point in the new location, where you want to insert the new text or the graphics. Now, click the Paste command on the Home tab of Clipboard group.

Using Keyboard Shortcuts for Moving and Copying

Word 2013 has many keyboard shortcuts, that is, combination of keys for moving and copying text and graphics. *Table 3.9* lists different methods for cutting, copying and moving text or graphics using the keyboard shortcuts.

Action	Key combination
To copy the selected text or the graphics to the Clipboard	Ctrl+ C keys pressed together.
To move the selected text or the graphics to the Clipboard	Ctrl +X or Shift+ Delete keys pressed together.
To paste Clipboard contents into a document	Ctrl + V or Shift + Ins keys pressed together.
To move a paragraph up	Alt + Shift + ↑ arrow keys pressed together.
To move a paragraph down	Alt + Shift + ↓ arrow keys pressed together.

Table 3.9: *Shortcuts for Moving and Copying Text or Graphics*

Font, Color, Style and Size Selection

Character formatting enhances the appearance of text, and includes changing font, font size, and font color and font styles as per the requirement. It can be applied using the commands in the Font group the Home tab and mini toolbar.

By default, the font of each new document is set to **Calibri**. However, Word provides many other fonts you can use to customize text.

To change the font using Ribbon, perform the following steps:

1. Select the text of which you want to change the font.

2. On the Home tab, click the drop-down list that shows all the available fonts. Use the scroll arrow on the right of the drop-down list to scroll through the list. When you move the cursor over the font, you can see the changes in the appearance of text. Alternatively, use the **Ctrl + Shift + F** keys, as shown in *Figure 3.44*:

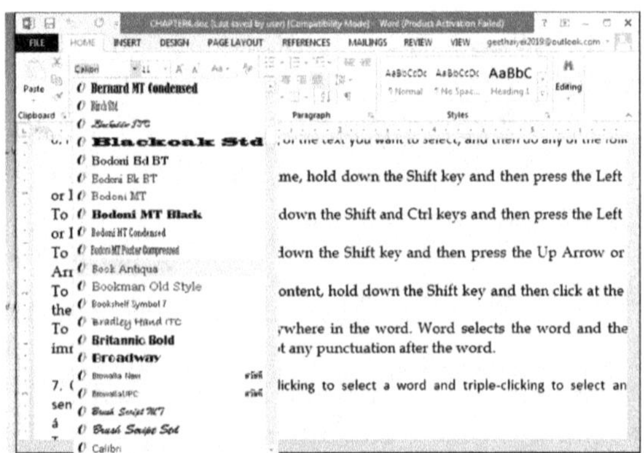

Figure 3.44: *Font Drop-down List*

3. The selected font will to be applied in the document.

To change the font color, perform the following steps:

1. Select the text for which you want to change the font color.

2. On the **Home** tab, click the **Font** Color drop-down arrow. The Font Color menu appears, as shown in *Figure 3.45*:

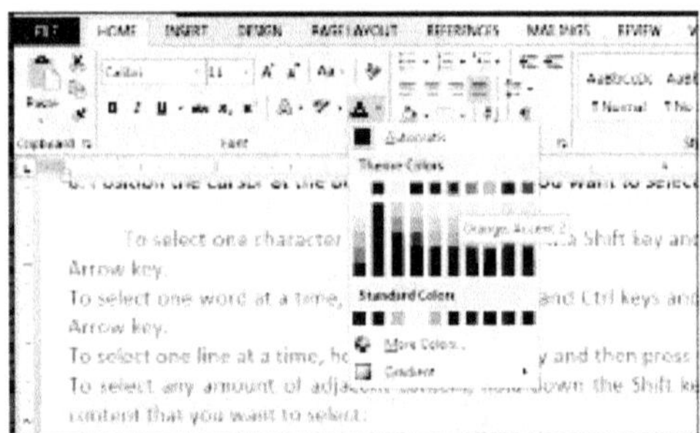

Figure 3.45: *Selecting Font Color*

3. Select the font color you want to use.

4. The font color will change in the document, as shown in *Figure 3.45*.

5. Select More Colors at the bottom of the menu to access the Colors dialog box. Choose the color you want and then click OK.

To change the font size, perform the following steps:

1. Select the text of which you want to change the font size.

2. On the **Home** tab, click the Font size drop-down arrow. Select a font size from the menu, as shown in *Figure 3.46*. If the font size is not available in the menu, you can click the Font size box and type the desired font size; then press *Enter*. Or, you can also select from the mini toolbar.

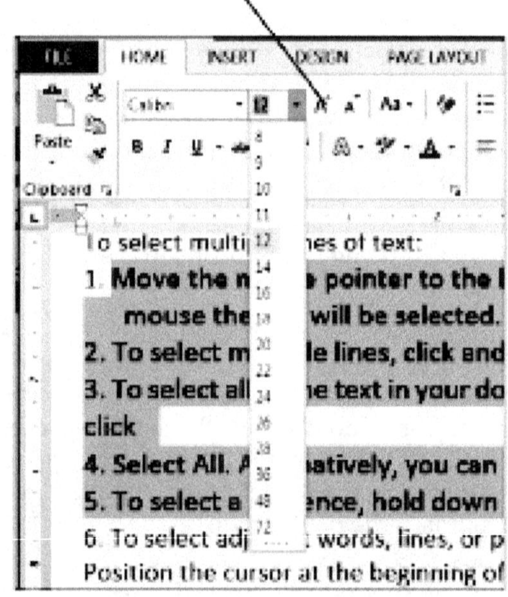

Figure 3.46: *Selected Font Size Applied in the Document*

3. The font size will change in the document, as shown in *Figure 3.44*.

4. You can also use the Grow Font and Shrink Font commands to change the font size.

   a. To increase the font size, click the Increase Font Size button, or press **Ctrl + >**.

   b. To decrease the font size, click the Decrease Font Size button, or press **Ctrl + <**.

To change the font style:

1. Select the text of which you want to change the font style.

2. To make a character Regular, Bold or Italic, click the corresponding button on the mini toolbar, as shown in *Figure 3.47*:

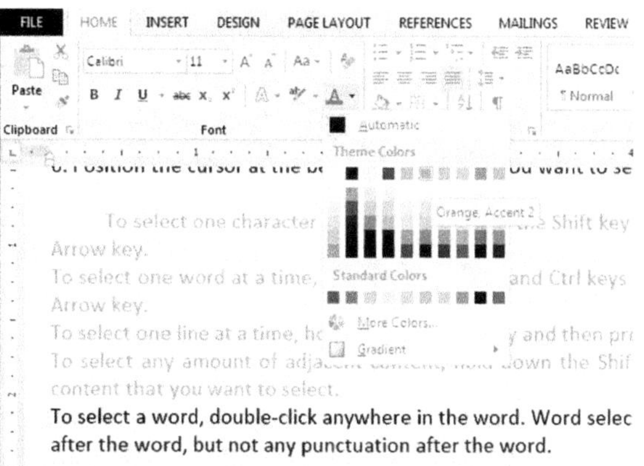

Figure 3.47: *Selected Font Style Applied in the Document*

These are toggle buttons, i.e., clicking them once switches on the option and clicking them the second time switches off the option. Or,

3. On the **Home** tab in the **Font** group, click the button for the desired font style such as **bold**, *italic* or <u>underline</u>.

Applying Character Formatting using Keyboard.

Most of the character formatting can also be applied using the keyboard shortcut, as discussed in the following sections:

To format using shortcut keys:

1. Select the text you want to format and use the shortcut key combinations for the desired formatting effect from the following table:

Format	Shortcut
Bold	Ctrl + B
Italic	Ctrl + I
Single underline	Ctrl + U
Word underline	Ctrl + Shift + W
Double underline	Ctrl + Shift + D
SMALL CAPS	Ctrl + Shift + K
ALL CAPS	Ctrl + Shift + A
Hidden text	Ctrl + Shift + H
Superscript	Ctrl + Shift + =
Subscript	Ctrl + =
Copy formatting	Ctrl + Shift + C
Paste formatting	Ctrl + Shift + V
Remove formatting	Ctrl + Spacebar

Change case of letter	Shift + F3
Font	Ctrl + Shift + F. This command activates the Font dialog box. Type a new font name or use the arrow keys to highlight the desired font.
Symbol font	Ctrl + Shift + Q
Next larger point size available for selected fonts	Ctrl + Shift + >
Next smaller point size available for selected fonts	Ctrl + Shift + <
Up one point size	Ctrl +]
Down one point size	Ctrl + [

Table 3.8: *Character Formatting using Keyboard*

Addition of Regional Language Font

You can add an additional language to Office programs for editing your documents. It consists of the keyboard layout and proofing tools for that language. The proofing tools include language-specific features, such as dictionaries for spelling and grammar checking.

To add a language font, perform the following steps:

1. Click **File** tab, and choose **Options**. The Word Options dialog box appears, as shown in *Figure 3.48*:

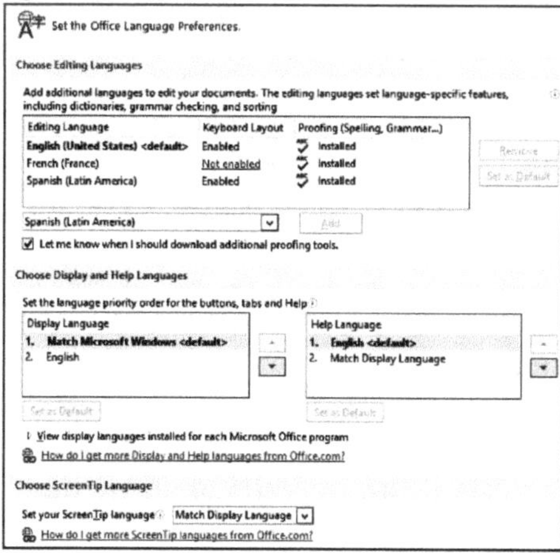

Figure 3.48: *Selected Font style applied in the document*

2. From the left side options, select the Language option.
3. In the Set the Office Language Preferences dialog box, under **Choose Editing Languages**, select the **editing language** that you want to add from the Add additional languages list, and then click Add.
4. The added language appears in the list of editing languages.

If Not enabled appears in the Keyboard Layout column, do the following:

1. Click the Not enabled link.
2. In the Add Languages dialog box, click **Add a language**, select your language in the list, and then click **Add**.
3. Close the Add Languages dialog box. Your language should display as Enabled under Keyboard Layout in the Choose Editing Languages section.

If Not Installed appears in the Proofing column, then go online and get the language pack you need. Click the Not installed link.

Alignment of Text

By default, Word aligns text to the left margin in new documents. The alignment settings control the horizontal position of the paragraph text between the page margins. There are four alignment options (*see Figure 3.49*):

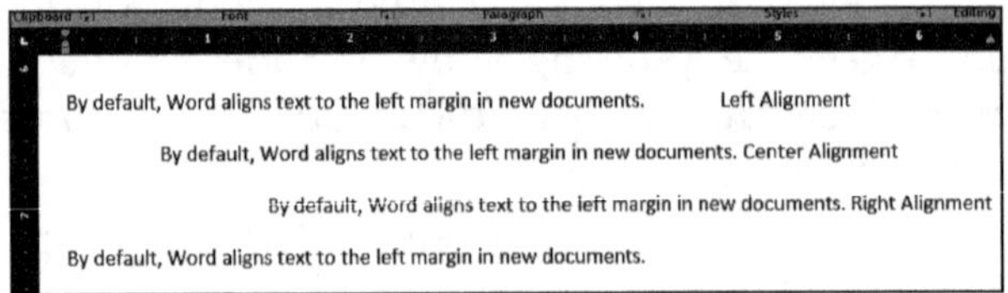

Figure 3.49: *Different Alignment Options*

- **Align Left:** This is the default paragraph alignment. It aligns the left end of the text with the tab stop. It results in a straight left edge and a ragged right edge.
- **Align Right:** It aligns the right end of the text with the tab stop. It results in a straight right edge and a ragged left edge.
- **Center:** It aligns the center of the text with the tab stop. It results in ragged left and right edges.
- **Decimal Tab:** It aligns the decimal point in the text with the tab stop.
- **Bar Tab:** It draw a vertical line at the position of the tab stop.

To change text alignment, perform the following steps:

- Select the text which you want to change.
- On the Home tab, select one of the four alignment options from the Paragraph group. In our example, we have selected Left Alignment, as shown in *Figure 3.50*.

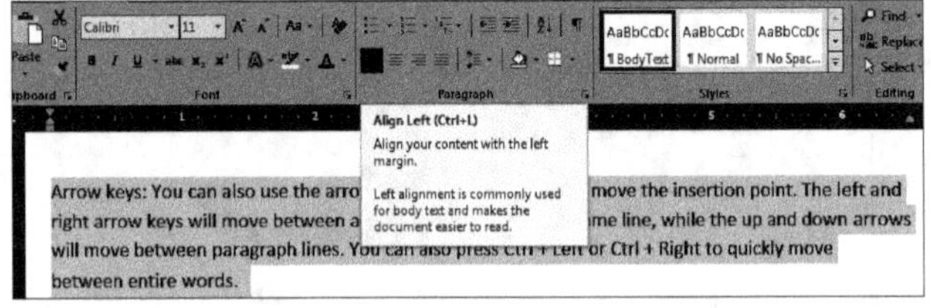

Figure 3.50: *Select Align Left Command*

- The text is re-aligned in the document if it shows straight left edge and a ragged right edge.

Undo and Redo

While working in a document, you accidentally delete some text. Fortunately, you would not have to retype the text you just deleted. Word allows you to undo your most recent action when you make a mistake.

To undo the action, perform the following steps:

1. Select the Undo command on the Quick Access Toolbar (*see Figure 3.51*). Alternatively, you can press *Ctrl + Z* on your keyboard.

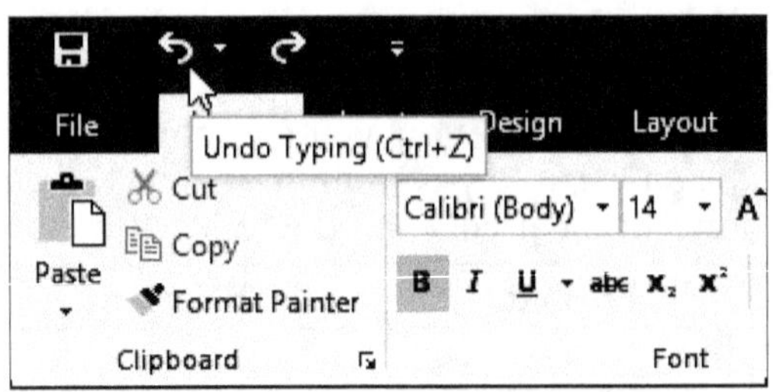

Figure 3.51: *Selecting Undo command*

You can continue using this command to undo multiple changes in a row.

2. By contrast, the Redo command allows you to reverse the last undo. You can also access this command by pressing **Ctrl + Y** on your keyboard (*see Figure 3.52*).

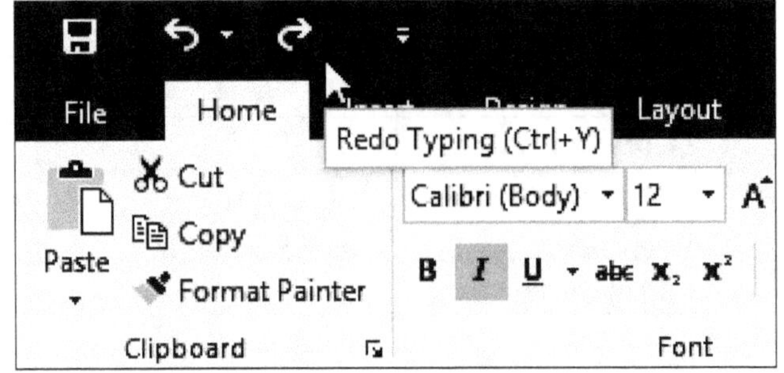

Figure 3.52: *Selecting Redo Command*

- **Align Left:** This is the default paragraph alignment. It aligns the left end of the text with the tab stop. It results in a straight left edge and a ragged right edge.
- **Align Right:** It aligns the right end of the text with the tab stop. It results in a straight right edge and a ragged left edge.
- **Center:** It aligns the center of the text with the tab stop. It results in ragged left and right edges.
- **Decimal Tab:** It aligns the decimal point in the text with the tab stop.
- **Bar Tab:** It draw a vertical line at the position of the tab stop.

Automatic Spelling and Grammar Checking

By default, Word automatically checks your document for spelling and grammar errors, so you may not even need to run a separate check. These errors are indicated by **colored wavy lines**. The red line indicates a misspelled word and the **blue** line indicates a **grammatical** error, including misused words.

To correct spelling errors, perform the following steps:

1. Right-click the underlined word, and then select the correct spelling from the list of suggestions, as shown in *Figure 3.53*.

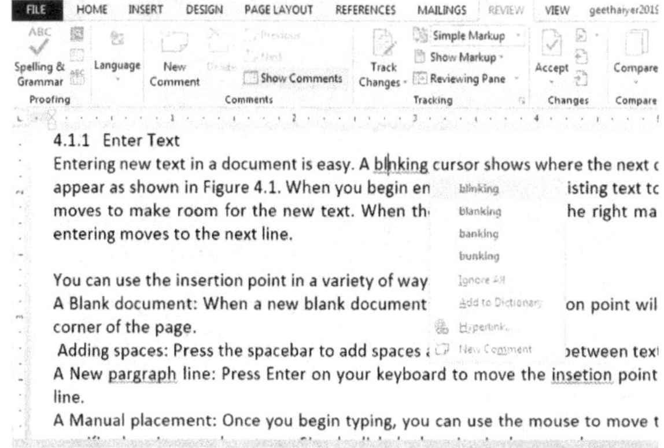

Figure 3.53: *Spelling Error in the Document*

2. The corrected word will appear in the document.

3. You can also choose to **Ignore All** instances of an underlined word or add it to the dictionary.

To correct grammatical errors:

1. Right-click the underlined word or phrase, and then select the correct spelling or phrase from the list of suggestions, as shown in *Figure 3.54*.

2. The corrected phrase will appear in the document.

Hide Spelling and Grammatical Errors in a document

If you are sharing a document like a resume with someone, you might not want that person to see the **red** and **blue** lines. Turning off the automatic spelling and grammar checks only applies to your computer, so the lines may still show up when someone else views your document. Fortunately, Word allows you to hide **spelling and grammatical errors**, so the lines will not show up on any computer.

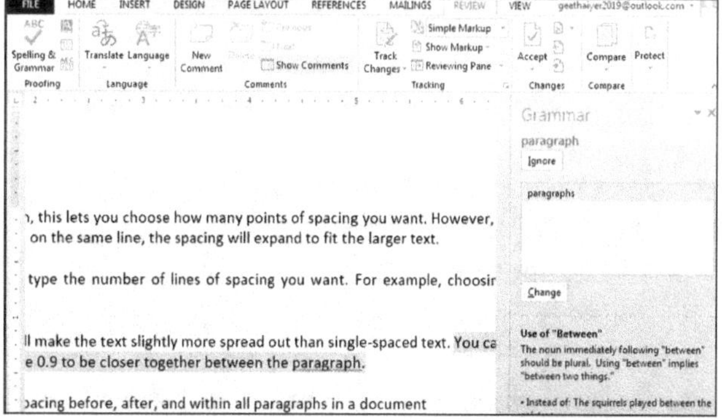

Figure 3.54: *Grammar Navigation Pane*

To hide spelling and grammatical errors in a document, perform the following steps:

1. Click the **File** tab to go to backstage view, and then click **Options**.

2. A dialog box will appear. Select **Proofing**; then check the box next to Hide spelling errors in this document only and Hide grammar errors in this document only. Then click **OK** (see following image).

3. The lines in the document will be hidden.

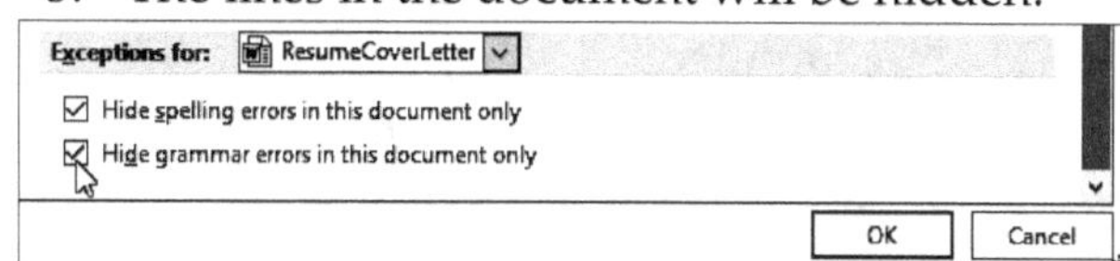

Figure 3.55: *Dialog box*

Correct Proofing Errors

To check the spelling or grammar of the entire document, click the **Spelling & Grammar** button in the Proofing group on the **Review** tab. Word then works its way through the selection or the document and displays the Spelling pane or Grammar pane if it encounters a potential error.

To correct proofing errors, perform the following steps:

1. If you want to begin checking errors from the beginning of the document, press the **Ctrl + Home** keys together.

2. On the **Review** tab, in the **Proofing** group, click the **Spelling & Grammar** button to begin the review. The Spelling pane opens and displays the first possible error. The corresponding location in the document is highlighted. See *Figure 3.56*:

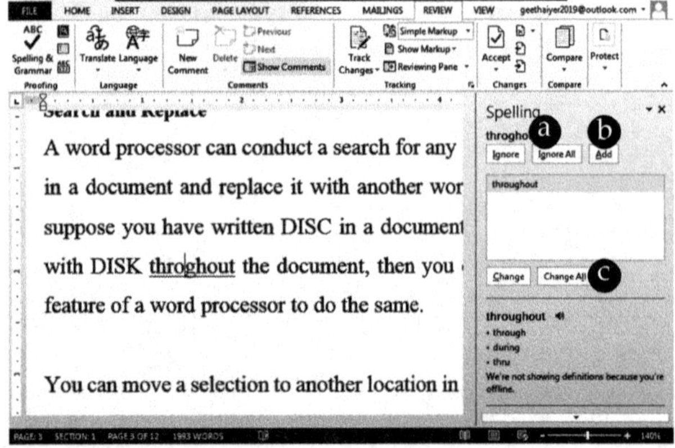

Figure 3.56: *Spelling Navigation Pane*

3. If the selection is identified as a possible spelling error, do any of the following:

   a. Click Ignore to continue the review without changing the highlighted word or Ignore All to continue while ignoring other instances also of the word in the current document.

   b. Click Add to add the word to the Spelling Checker dictionary on your computer.

   c. Select the correct spelling of the word in the suggestions list, and then click

Change to change only this instance of the word or Change All to change all other instances also of this word in the document.

4. Select the desired options to change the correct spelling word in the suggestion list.

Using Autocorrect Feature

The AutoCorrect feature in Word 2013 recognizes typing mistakes and automatically corrects them. It can also be used to type long words from an abbreviation automatically. For example, to automatically type the phrase not applicable, you can type the abbreviation na.

Creating AutoCorrect Entries

To add an autocorrect entry with the commands, perform the following steps:

1. Click the **File** tab on the button. The backstage view appears. Click **Options**. (*Figure 3.54*)

2. The Word Options dialog box appears. From the left pane, select Proofing, as shown in *Figure 3.57*:

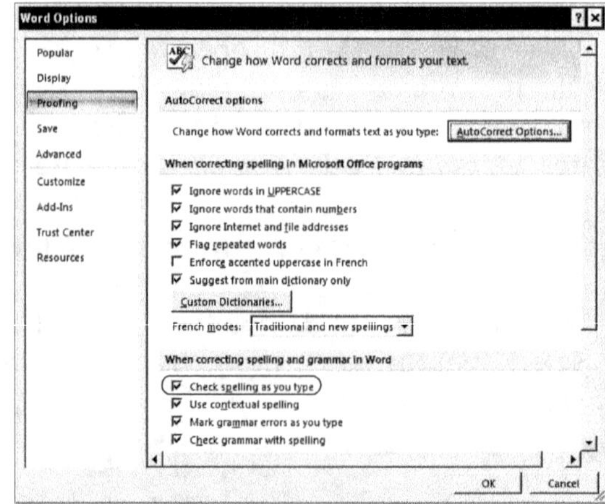

Figure 3.57: *Word Options displaying Proofing Options*

3. In the **Proofing** page under AutoCorrect options, click **AutoCorrect Options**....

4. The AutoCorrect dialog box opens, displaying with the AutoCorrect tab, as shown in *Figure 3.58*:

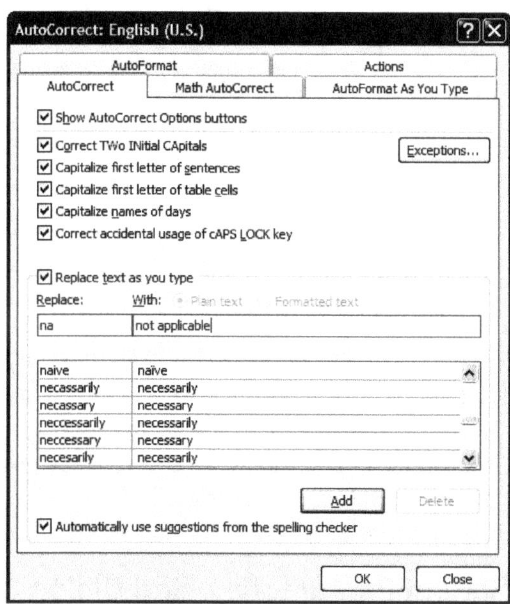

Figure 3.58: *The AutoCorrect Dialog Box*

5. In the Replace: text box, type misspelled words or abbreviations that you wish to get corrected by Word 2013 automatically.

6. In the With: text box, type the correct spelling of the word or phrase.

7. Click Add to add these selected entries to the AutoCorrect list.

8. Click **OK**.

Word 2013 will insert the phrase and then return to the With text box.

Find and Replace

When you are working with longer documents, it can be difficult and time-consuming to locate a specific word or phrase. Word can automatically search your document using the Find feature, and it even allows you to change words or phrases using Replace.

Finding Text

To find text, perform the following steps:

1. On the **Home** tab, click the Find command. Alternatively, you can press **Ctrl + F** on your keyboard.

2. The navigation pane will appear on the left side of the screen, as shown in *Figure 3.59*:

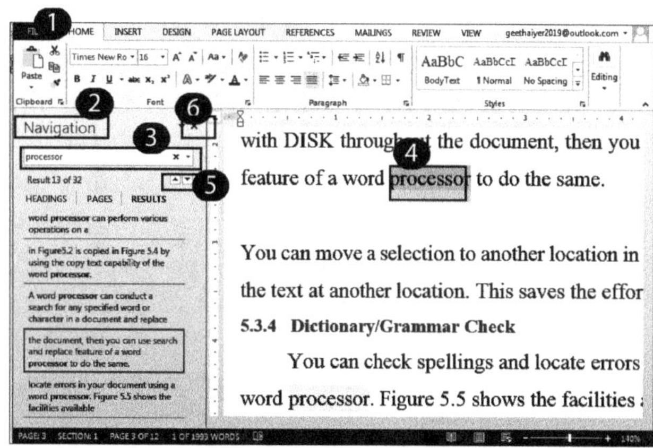

Figure 3.59: *Navigation Pane Screen*

3. Type the text you want to find in the field at the top of the navigation pane. In our example, we have typed the word, insertion.

4. If the text is found in the document, it will be highlighted in yellow, and a preview of the results will appear in the navigation pane.

5. If the text appears more than once, you can click the arrows on the Navigation pane to go through the results. You can also click the result previews on the Navigation pane to jump to the location of a result in your document.

6. When you are finished, click the **X** to close the navigation pane. The highlight will disappear.

Replacing Text

To replace text, perform the following steps:

1. On the **Home** tab, click the **Replace** command. Alternatively, you can press **Ctrl + H** on your keyboard.

2. The Find and Replace dialog box will appear, as shown in *Figure 3.60*:

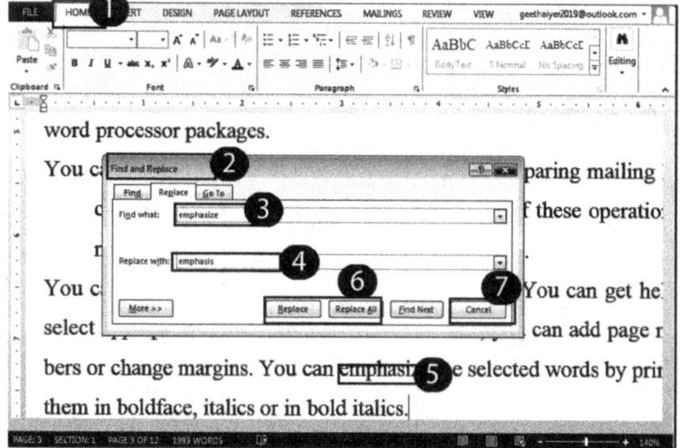

Figure 3.60: *Find and Replace Dialog Box*

3. Type the text you want to search in the Find what: field.

4. Type the text you want to replace it with in the Replace with: field. Then, click Find **Next**.

5. Word will find the first instance of the text and highlight it in gray.

6. If you want to replace it, you can click Replace to change individual instances of text. Alternatively, you can click Replace All to replace every instance of the text throughout the document.

7. The text will be replaced. When you are done, click **Close** or **Cancel** to close the dialog box.

Formatting the Text

The Paragraph formatting involves controlling the appearance of text in a paragraph as a whole. The Paragraph formatting options are text alignment, paragraph indentation, line spacing, spacing before and after the paragraph, border and shading, and so on.

Paragraph Indenting

Indents are the white spaces added to the margins, and thus decreasing the text area for paragraphs. So, when you have a **right margin and you want to add a right indent of 1.0**, your text will be printed 2.0" from the right edge of the paper.

> **Tips:** The first line of each paragraph can be indented differently from other lines in the paragraph. The first line can be shorter than the others, creating a regular indent, or longer than the others, creating a hanging indent.

Once you change the indent, each new paragraph you start by pressing the **Enter** key will maintain the same indentation setting until you change it.

Line Spacing

Line spacing in a paragraph means the amount of space between the lines. Word 2013 offers the following line spacing options, as given in *Table 3.10*:

Description	Option
Single spacing	No blank line space appears between the lines of text.
Double spacing	A blank line space appears between the lines of text.
11/2/1.5 spacing	Half the height of one line space appears between the lines of text.
Exact line height	Specify the space you want between the lines.

Table 3.10: *Different Options for Line Spacing*

Space before and after Paragraphs

There is a spacing box in the Paragraph dialog box which lets you define the amount of white space that Word 2013 must place before and after paragraphs. Space settings can be entered in **points (pts)**, **inches (in)**, **centimetres (cm)**, or **lines (li)**. Thus, 12 points would be entered as **12 pt**.

Formatting Paragraphs using Dialog Box Launcher

To format paragraphs, perform the following steps:

1. Position the insertion point anywhere in the paragraph to be formatted or select multiple paragraphs.

2. Click the dialog box launcher arrow in the Home tab in the Paragraph group. The Paragraph dialog box, as shown in *Figure 3.60*, appears.

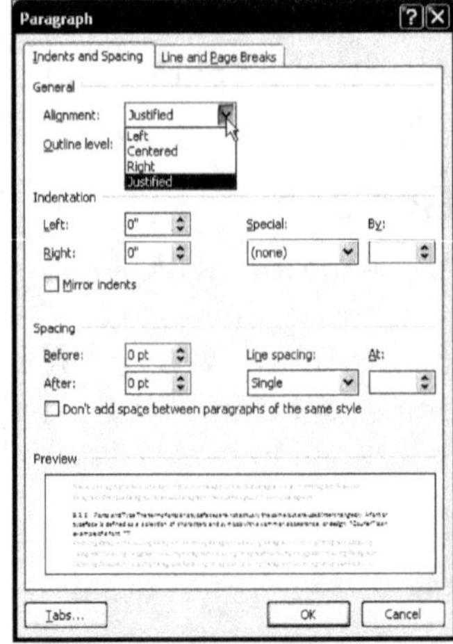

Figure 3.60: *Paragraph dialog box with Indents and Spacing Property sheet*

3. Click the Indents and Spacing tab. The property sheet, as shown in *Figure 3.61*, appears:

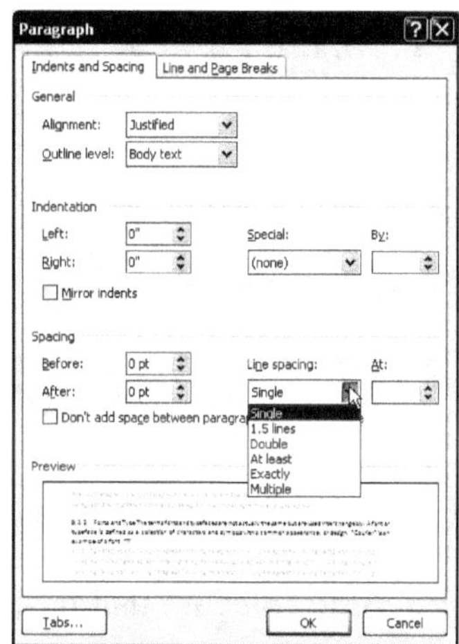

Figure 3.6: *Indents and Spacing Tab with Line Spacing Options*

General Options:

1. The Alignment list box shows the current alignment.
2. Change the current alignment, if need be. For this, click the down arrow next to the list box. The list gets displayed from the list; click alignment option as required.

Paragraph Indent Options:

1. The Left textbox shows the current left indentation. Enter the new value for indentation or use the up and down arrow keys to change the indentation.
2. The Right textbox displays the current right indentation. Enter the new value for indentation or use the up and down arrow keys to change the indentation.
3. To apply the first line indent or the hanging indent, use the Special: list box. Click the down arrow key of the Special: list box to display the options. These are given below:

Option	Effect
First line	This indents only the first line of the paragraph.
Hanging indent	This indents all except the first line of the paragraph.

Table 3.10: *Special: list box*

Click the option as needed to select it.

4. In the By: textbox, enter the indention or use the up and down arrow to give the required

indentation. The Preview box displays the effect of the selected indentation.

Line Spacing Options:

1. Line spacing textbox has the options for controlling the line spacing. Click the down arrow in the spacing box. The options are given below:

Option	Explanation
Single	Default value.
Double	Places a blank line between successive lines.
1.5 Lines	Leaves half the line space between the lines.
At Least	Indicates the minimum space between lines.
Exactly	Gives the exact space between lines.

Table 3.11: *Line spacing options*

Space Before/After Paragraphs Options:

1. Type the space or select the space required in the Before: textbox for adding space before the paragraph.
2. Type the space or select the space required in the After: textbox for adding space after the paragraph.
3. Click OK or press the **Enter** key to close the paragraph dialog box.

Formatting Paragraphs using Ruler

To format paragraphs using ruler, perform the following steps:

1. Position the insertion point anywhere in the paragraph you want to format or select multiple paragraphs to align.
2. Click the appropriate alignment button, that is, **left**, **centre**, **right**, and **justified** alignment on the **Home** tab of **Paragraph** group.

To indent paragraphs using mouse, perform the following steps:

1. Position the insertion point in the paragraph to be indented or select as many paragraphs as you want to indent.
2. On the **Home** tab of **Paragraph** group, click the indentation button.
3. The increase Indent button moves the indent marker to the right by one tab stop, and the decrease indent moves it back by one tab stop.

To indent paragraphs using the ruler, perform the following steps:

1. Position the insertion point in a paragraph or select multiple paragraphs that you want to indent.
2. Indent markers appear on the ruler.
3. Drag the appropriate triangular indent markers to the desired location.
4. As you drag the marker, the rulers scale shows the position of the indent mark in relation to its respective margin (*see Figure 3.62*).

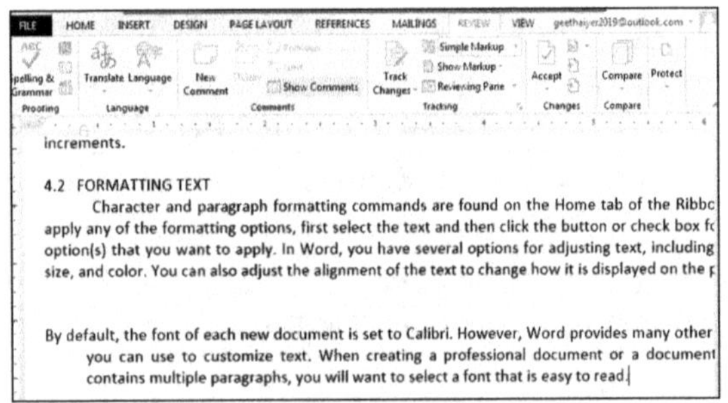

Figure 3.62: *Indentation Buttons on the Paragraph Group*

5. When you release the mouse button after positioning it, the text in selected paragraphs moves accordingly.

Formatting Paragraphs using Shortcut Keys

To format paragraphs using the shortcut keys, perform the following steps:

1. Position the insertion point anywhere in the paragraph to be aligned or select multiple paragraphs.
2. Use one of the keyboard shortcuts given below:

Alignment	Key combinations
Left	Ctrl + L keys together
Right	Ctrl + R keys together
Centre	Ctrl +E keys together
Justify	Ctrl + J keys together

Table 3.12: *Keyboard shortcuts for alignment*

To indent paragraphs using the keyboard shortcuts, perform the following steps:

1. Position the insertion point in a paragraph or select multiple paragraphs to be indented.
2. Use the shortcut key combination explained below:

Key combination	Effect
Ctrl + M	Create a left indent
Ctrl + Shift + M	Reduce left indent
Ctrl + T	Create hanging indent
Ctrl + Shift + T	Reduce hanging indent
Ctrl + Q	Remove paragraphs formatting

Table 3.12: *Shortcut keys for paragraph indentation*

To change the line spacing using the keyboard shortcuts, perform the following steps:

1. Position the insertion point in a paragraph or select the multiple paragraphs for which you want to change the line spacing.
2. Use one of the keyboard shortcuts given below:

Key combination	Effect
Ctrl + 1	Creates single space lines
Ctrl + 2	Creates double space lines
Ctrl + 3	Creates one and half spaced lines
Ctrl + 4	Add or remove one line space preceding a paragraph
Ctrl + Q	Remove paragraphs formatting

Table 3.13

To add a single line of space before a paragraph, perform the following steps:

1. Position the insertion point in a paragraph or select the paragraph before which you want to add single line of space.
2. Press the **Ctrl + 0** (zero) keys together.
3. To remove the single line of space added before the paragraph, press **Ctrl + 0** (zero) a second time.

Bullets and Numbering

Bulleted and numbered lists can be used in the documents to outline, arrange, and emphasize text. You can also learn how to insert new bulleted and numbered lists, select symbols as bullets, and format multilevel lists. The style of each list type can be changed and different bullets can be used.

To create a bulleted list, perform the following steps:

1. Select the text to be bulleted or click at the location where the new list is to be created.
2. On the Home tab, click the drop-down arrow next to the Bullets command. A menu of bullet styles will appear, as shown in *Figure 3.63*:

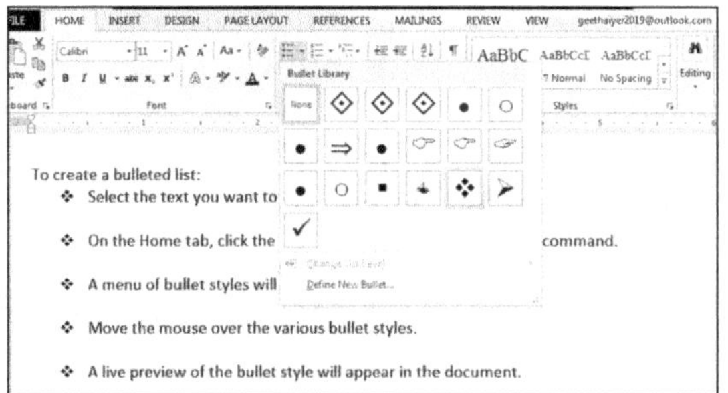

Figure 3.63: *Selecting Bullet Style*

3. Move the mouse over the various bullet styles. A live preview of the bullet style will appear in the document. Select the bullet style you want to use.

> **Tips:** The bullet or number appears at the beginning of a line of text when the Enter key is pressed at the end of the preceding line of text.

4. The selected bullet style appears in the text, as shown in *Figure 3.63*.

Create Numbered Lists

When you need to organize text into a numbered list, Word offers several numbering options. You can format your list with numbers, letters, or Roman numerals.

1. Select the text which you want to format as a list.
2. On the Home tab, click the drop-down arrow next to the Numbering command. A menu of numbering styles will appear, as shown in *Figure 3.64*.

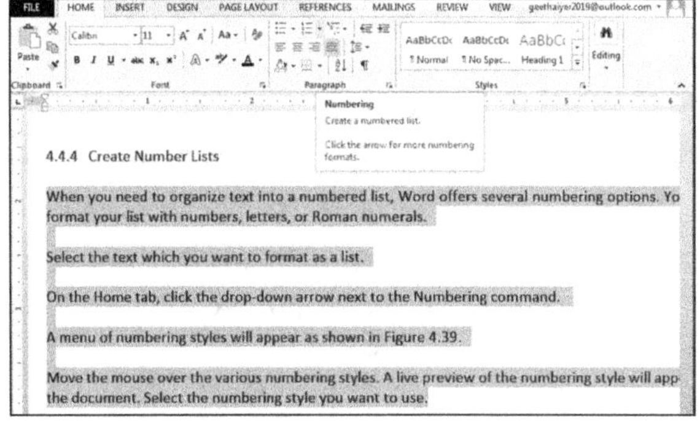

Figure 3.64: *Selecting Number Style*

3. Move the mouse over the various numbering styles. A live preview of the numbering style will appear in the document. Select the numbering style you want to use.
4. The text will be formatted as a numbered list (*see Figure 3.65*).

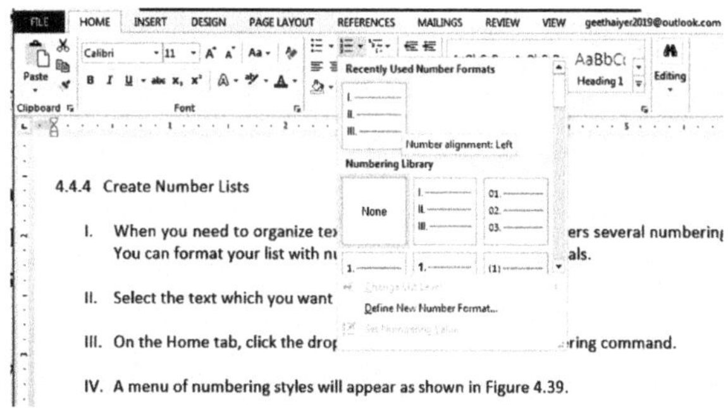

Figure 3.65: *Applied Number Style in the Document*

To start a list or part of a list at a pre-defined number:

1. Place the cursor within an existing list, next to the list item whose number you want to set.
2. Right-click the list item, and then click Set Numbering Value. The **Set Numbering Value** dialog box appears, as shown in *Figure 3.66*.

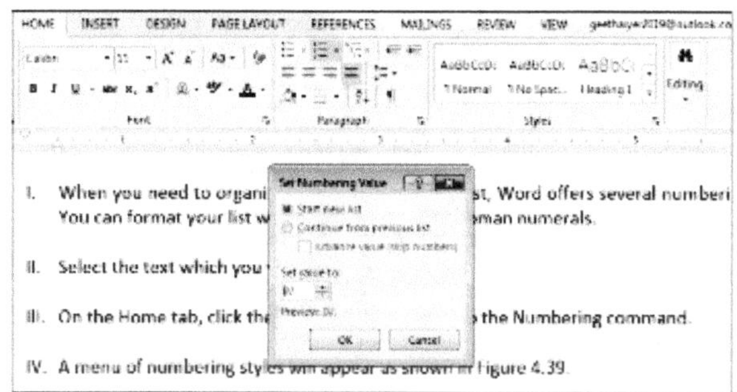

Figure 3.66: *Set Numbering Value Dialog Box*

3. Do either of the following to choose custom numbering:
   a. Click **Start** new list.
   b. Click Continue from previous list, and then select the **Advance value** (skip numbers) checkbox.
4. In Set value to box, enter the number you want to assign to the list item. Then click **OK**.

Customizing Bullets

Customizing the look of the bullets in the list can help you emphasize certain list items and personalize the design of your list. Word allows you to format bullets in a variety of ways. You can use symbols as a bullet.

To use a symbol as a bullet, perform the following steps:

1. Select an existing list you want to format.
2. On the **Home** tab, click the drop-down arrow next to the Bullets command. Select **Define New** Bullet from the drop-down menu, as shown in *Figure 3.67*:

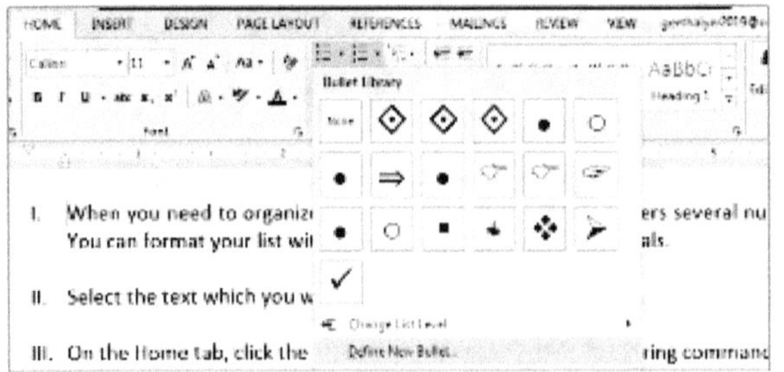

Figure 3.67: *Selecting Define New Bullet*

3. The Define New Bullet dialog box will appear, as shown in *Figure 3.68*. Click the Symbol button.

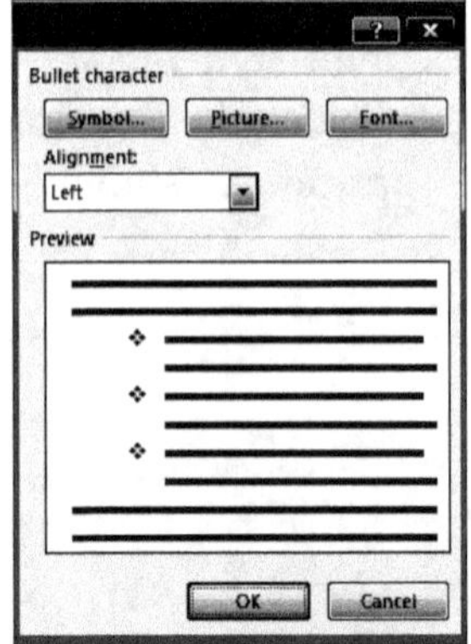

Figure 3.68: *Define New Bullet Dialog Box*

The Symbol dialog box will appear, as shown in *Figure 3.69*:

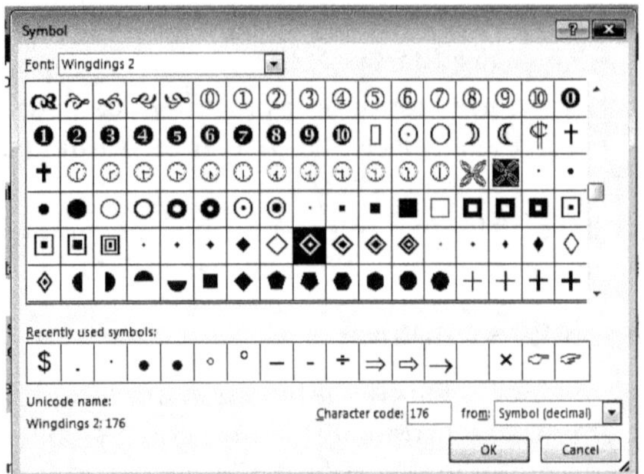

Figure 3.69: *Symbol Dialog Box*

4. Click the Font: drop-down box, and select a font. The Wingdings and Symbol fonts are good choices because they have many useful symbols.
5. Select the desired symbol, and then click **OK**.
6. The symbol will appear in the Preview section of the **Define New Bullet** dialog box. Click OK.
7. The selected symbol style appears in the text document, as shown in *Figure 3.70*, and also appears in the bullet list.

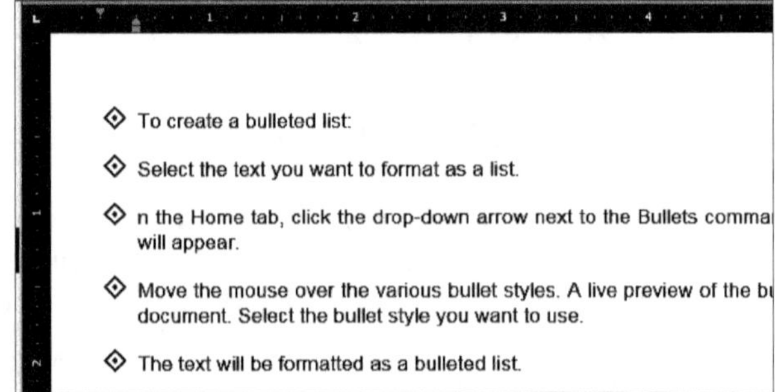

Figure 3.70: *The Selected Symbol Style in the Document*

Multilevel lists

Multilevel lists allow you to create an outline with multiple levels. Any bulleted or numbered list can be turned into a multilevel list by using the *Tab* key. To create a multilevel list, perform the following steps:

1. Place the insertion point at the beginning of the line you want to move.

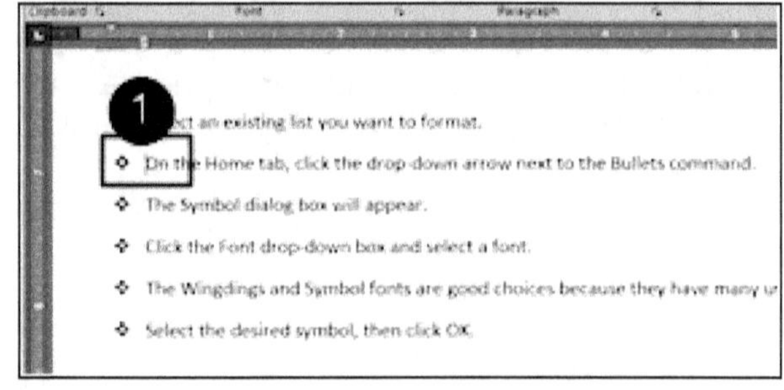

Figure 3.71

2. Press the Tab key to increase the indent level of the line. The line will move to the right and insert default bullet.

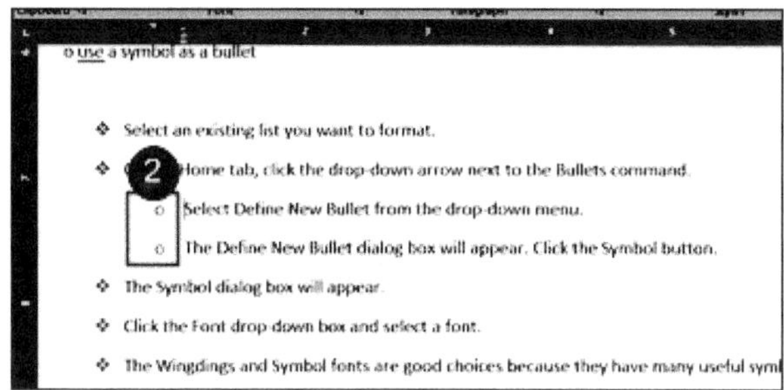

Figure 3.72

Increase or Decrease an indent level

You can make adjustments to the organization of a multilevel list by increasing or decreasing the indent levels. There are several ways to change the indent level.

To increase the indent by more than one level, place the insertion point at the beginning of the line. Then press the **Tab** key until the desired level is reached.

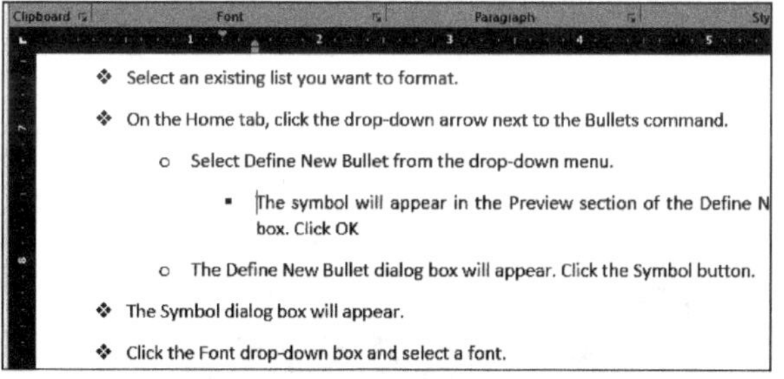

Figure 3.73

To decrease the indent level, place the insertion point at the beginning of the line. Then hold the **Shift** key and press the **Tab** key.

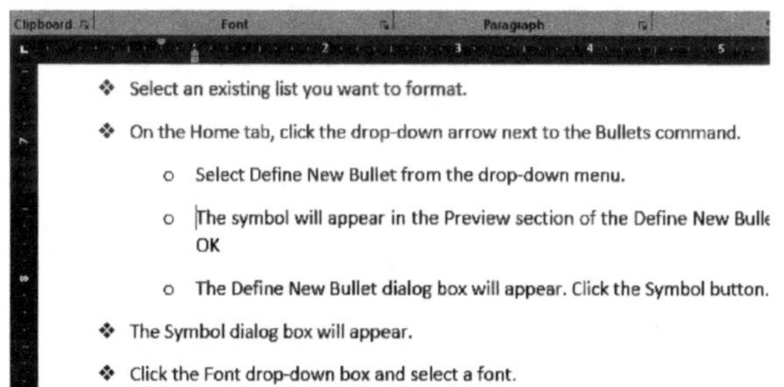

Figure 3.74

You can also **increase** or **decrease** the levels of text by placing the insertion point anywhere in the line and clicking the **Increase Indent** or **Decrease Indent** commands.

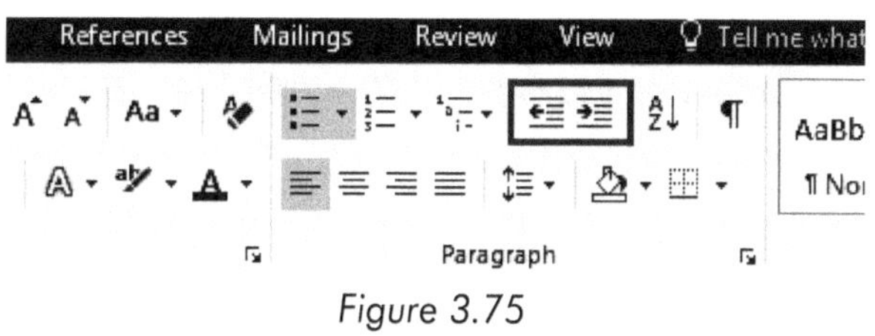

Figure 3.75

Change Case

Word provides facilities to change the case of letters of any text by using the Change Case command.

To apply capitalization, perform the following steps:

1. Select the text for which you want to change case.
2. On the Home tab, in the Font group, click Change Case command (*Figure 3.76*).

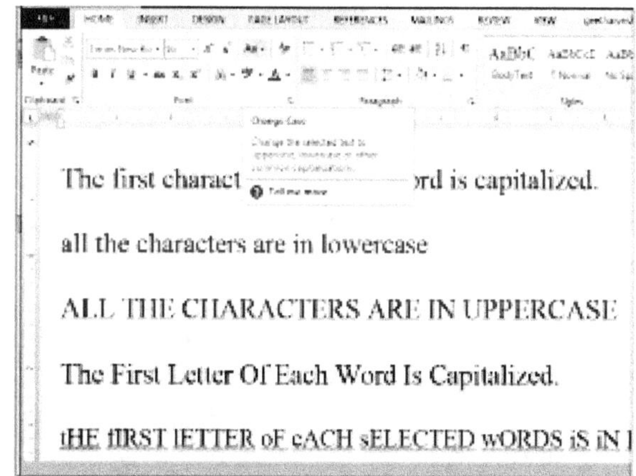

Figure 3.76: *Changed Case Options*

3. The options offered by the Change Case dialog box are as follows:

Option	Description
Sentence case	Only the first character of the first word is capitalized.
lower case	All the characters are in lowercase.
UPPER CASE	All the characters are in uppercase.
Capitalize Each Word	The first letter of each word is capitalized.
tOGGLE cASE	The first letter of each selected word is in lowercase, and the rest are in uppercase.

Table 3.14

4. The above options are applied in the text and are shown in *Figure 3.76*.

Table Manipulation

You should use tables to create documents, such as forms, financial reports, catalogs and biodata. Word tables consist of horizontal rows and vertical columns. You type in the areas called cells formed by intersection of rows and columns. Cells can contain text, numbers, or graphics.

You can even control the size, shape, and appearance of the cells, and use border and shading features. You can insert and delete rows and columns in a table.

> **Tips:** A new feature called the Table Wizard helps you automate table creation.

Concept of Table

A table is made of cells that you can fill with text and graphics. You can use tables to align numbers in columns, and then sort and perform calculation on them. You can also use tables to create page layouts and arrange text and graphics.

- **Rows:** A row is a horizontal block of cells that runs through the entire width of the table.
- **Column:** A column is a vertical block of cells that runs through the entire height of the table.
- **Cell:** A cell is the intersection of a row and a column.

Insert and Draw Table

Word 2013 allows you to draw a table by selecting the Insert Table grid on the **Insert tab** or **Insert table**... using the Table options in the Table groups.

To draw a table using the mouse, perform the following steps:

1. Position the insertion point where you want to insert a table.
2. On the Insert tab, in the Tables group, click the down arrow and choose Insert Table. The Insert Table grid, as shown in *Figure 3.77*, appears. Drag the mouse pointer to highlight the desired number of rows and columns.

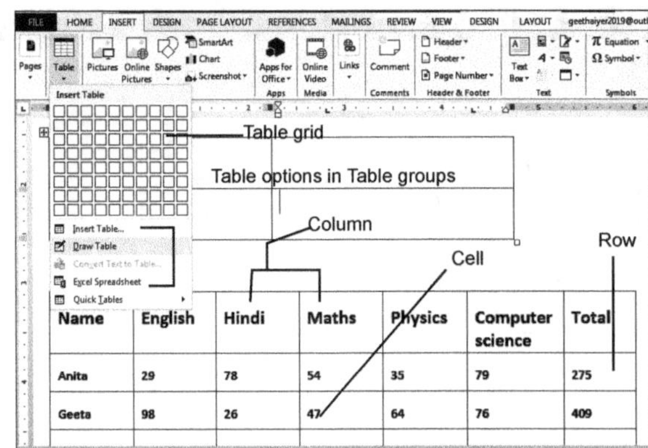

Name	English	Hindi	Maths	Physics	Computer science	Total
Anita	29	78	54	35	79	275
Geeta	98	26	47	64	76	409

Figure 3.77: *Table Grid*

The displayed grid represents the required number of rows and columns. Click the mouse button after getting the right number in the grid.

Word inserts an empty table when you release the mouse button (*see Figure 3.78*).

To create a table using the table option, perform the following steps:

1. Position the insertion point where you want to insert the table.
2. On the Insert tab, in the Tables group, click the Table down arrow. Highlight the Insert Table... option. The Insert Table dialog box appears, as shown in *Figure 3.78*:

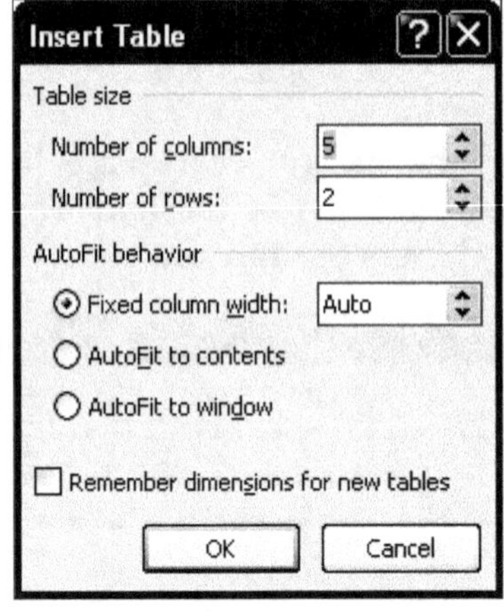

Figure 3.78: *Insert Table Dialog Box*

3. Enter the desired number of rows and columns as required in the table.
4. Click **OK**.

Entering and Editing Text in a Table

You can move, enter and edit text in a table just as you do with other types of text matter. Use mouse or arrow keys to position the insertion point, and then type the text. The cell borders work as margins. Word 2013 automatically wraps text within the cell as you reach the right edge.

To move within a table using the mouse, perform the following steps:

1. Position the pointer in the cell where you want to enter text and click.

To move within a table using the keyboard, perform the following steps:

1. The insertion point will move down and towards left the next row when you press the **Tab** key in the last column on the right side of a table.

2. It will move up one row and towards right when you press *Shift + Tab* in the first column on the left.

You can apply all of Word 2013 paragraph and character formats to the text in cells. Cells can contain multiple paragraphs as well as multiple paragraph formats.

Changing Cell Width and Height
Changing Row Heights

Word 2013 sets the height of each row automatically in order to accommodate the cell containing the tallest entry. For example, if one cell in a row needs 2 to accommodate the text or graphics, then all the cells in that particular row will be 2 high.

To adjust the height of a row, perform the following steps:

1. Click anywhere in the row where you want to change its height.

2. Move the pointer to the vertical ruler at the left edge of the screen or to the top of the row. The pointer changes to an up-and-down arrow. Use it to drag the row to the desired height (*see Figure 3.79*).

Changing the height of row

Name	English	Hindi	Maths	Physics	Computer science	Total
Anita	29	78	54	35	79	275
Geeta	98	26	47	64	76	409
Vineeta	68	46	59	89	76	338
Shashi	57	68	76	56	90	347
Sunita	55	60	50	79	87	331
Bindya	49	52	73	84	92	350

Figure 3.79: *Changing Table Height*

3. Release the mouse button. Or,

   On the **Layout tab**, in the Table Tools contextual tab, select the cell size group. Click the Table Row Height scroll box to change the height of row.

Changing Column Width

To change the width of column using mouse, perform the following steps:

1. Point to a column boundary.

2. The pointer will change shape to a double arrow (see Figure 3.80). Drag the column width marker. Notice the dotted line as well as the ruler settings. Then release the mouse button when it reaches the desired width. Or, Click the Table Column Width scroll box to change the column width in the cell size group.

If you hold down the Shift key while dragging, the column to the right, it does not change size, while the table's overall width increases.

If you hold down the **Ctrl** key while dragging the mouse, all columns to the right change size, but the table's overall width does not change. Thus, the width of the columns on the right will only change.

Changing Column Width

Name	English	Hindi	Maths	Physics	Computer science	Total
Anita	29	78	54	35	79	275
Geeta	98	26	47	64	76	409
Vineeta	68	46	59	89	76	338
Shashi	57	68	76	56	90	347
Sunita	55	60	50	79	87	331
Bindya	49	52	73	84	92	350

Figure 3.80: *Adjusting Column Width*

Alignment of Text in Cell

You can align text in a table cell in nine different ways: Top Left (the default alignment), Top Center, Top Right, Centre Left, Centre, Centre Right, Bottom Left, Bottom Centre, and Bottom Right, as shown in *Figure 3.81*:

Name	English	Hindi	Maths	Physics	Computer science	Total
Anita	29	78	54	35	79	275
Geeta	98	26	47	64	76	409
Vineeta	68	46	59	89	76	338
Shashi	57	68	76	56	90	347
Sunita	55	60	50	79	87	331
Bindya	49	52	73	84	92	350

Figure 3.81: *Tables can Align Text Within Cells in Nine Different Ways*

Deletion/Insertion/Merging of Row, Column and Cell & Cell Splitting

Inserting Rows

To add a new row at the end of an existing table, position the insertion point anywhere in the last cell and press the **Enter key**. Word 2013 inserts a new row using the styles of the cells that are immediately above it.

To insert a single row in the middle of a table perform the following steps:

1. Position the insertion point below the row where you want the new row to be inserted.
2. Click the **Layout contextual** tab. Click **Insert Above** or **Insert Below** in the **Rows & Columns** group. The new row is inserted below the selected row.

Alternatively, right-click and select Insert. Click the small triangle. A sub-menu option appears, as shown in *Figure 3.82*. Select the Insert Row Above or Insert Row Below option:

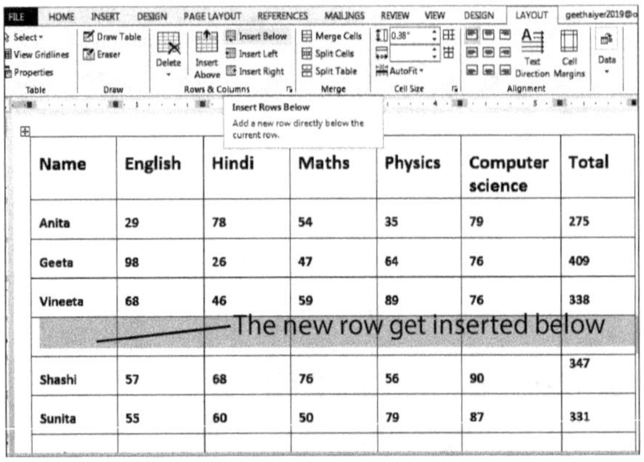

Figure 3.82: *Inserting Rows*

3. To add multiple rows, either repeat the Insert Rows command by clicking the right mouse button or select as many existing rows as you want to insert. Word 2013 inserts as many rows as you have selected.

Inserting Columns

To insert a single column in the middle of a table, perform the following steps:

1. Select the column to the right of which you wish the new column to appear.
2. Click the Layout contextual tab. Click Insert Left or Right in the Rows & Columns group. The new column is inserted to the right of the selected column.

   Alternatively, right-click and select Insert option. Click the small triangle. A sub-menu appears. Select the Insert Columns to Left or Right option from the sub menu list.

3. Word 2013 will add a new column, but it will not change the width of the earlier columns to accommodate this new inserted column. In order to make the enlarged table fit on your page, you will have to adjust margins, column widths or change page orientation.

> **Tips:** New column retains the format of the column adjacent to which it is inserted, but borders will not change.

To insert multiple columns, select as many existing columns as you want to insert new ones to the right of the desired location. If you want to add three columns, select the three existing columns to the right of the desired insertion point. Then click on the Insert columns to the Left button.

To insert a column, perform the following steps:

1. Point to the top of the table where you want to insert a column. A gray insertion indicator with a plus sign appears (*see Figure 3.83*).
2. Right-click and select **Insert**. Click the small triangle. A sub-menu option appears. Select Insert Columns to Right option. Or,

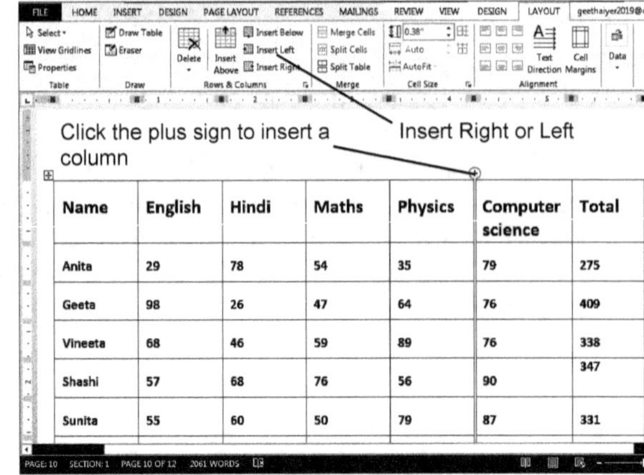

Figure 3.83: *To Insert a Column*

Point to the **plus sign**. When it turns blue, click it to insert a column where indicated.

Deleting Rows

To delete a row or rows of cells, perform the following steps:

1. Select the row(s) to be deleted.
2. Click the **Layout** contextual tab. Click Rows & **Columns group**. Click the down arrow and choose **Delete Rows**. This will delete the rows and their contents.

3. To delete the contents of cells only, leave the cells intact. Select text or graphic and press the **Delete key**.

Deleting Columns

To delete columns, perform the following steps:

1. Select the column(s) to be deleted.
2. Click the **Layout** contextual tab. Click **Rows & Columns** group. Click the Table down arrow and choose **Delete Columns**.
3. Click **OK**.

Merging and Splitting Cells

Cells can be merged by combining two or more cells into one cell. Splitting cells means to divide a cell into two or more cells.

To merge the cells in a table, perform the following steps:

1. Select the cells that you want to merge in the table. A Table Tools contextual tab appears, as shown in *Figure 3.84*.

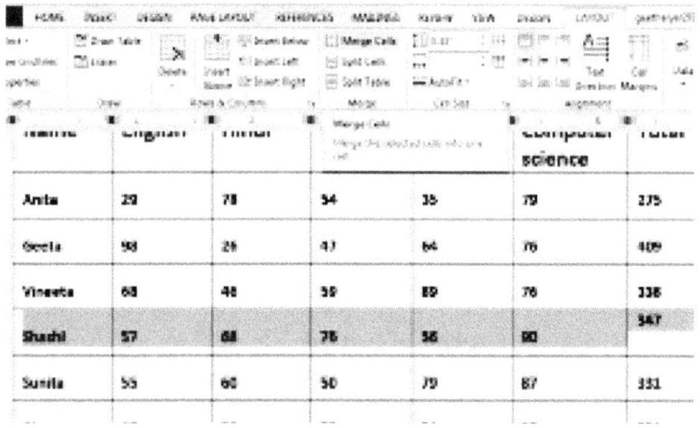

Figure 3.84: *Selecting Merge cells*

2. Click the **Layout** tab on the Ribbon.
3. Click the **Merge Cells** button under the Merge group, as shown in *Figure 3.85*.
4. The selected cells of the table get merged, as shown in *Figure 3.85*.

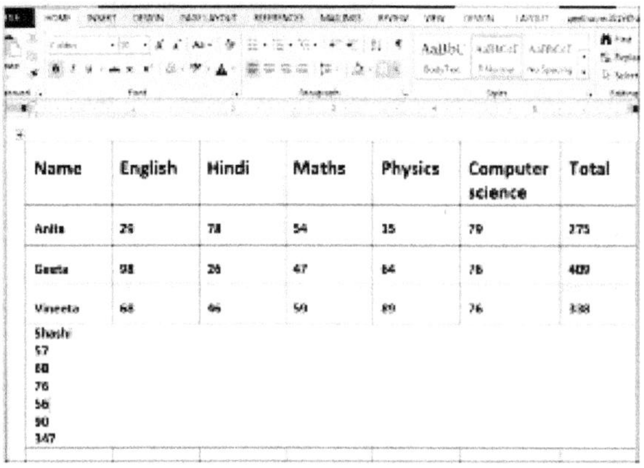

Figure 3.85: *The Selected Cells get Merged*

To split a cell in a table, perform the following steps:

1. Select the cell that you want to split in the table. A Table Tools contextual tab appears.
2. Click the **Layout** tab on the Ribbon.
3. Click the Split Cells button under the **Merge group**, as shown in *Figure 3.86*.

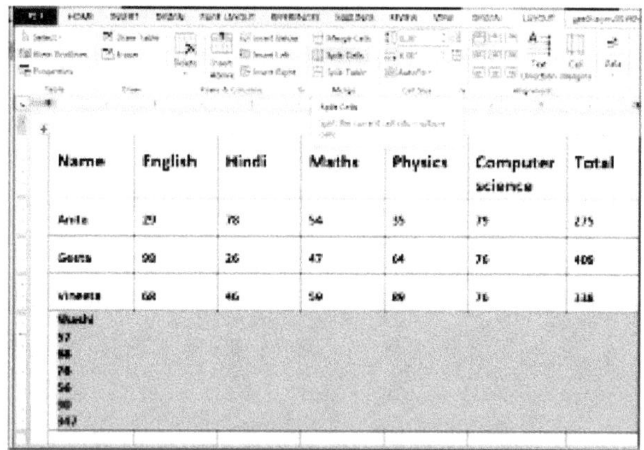

Figure 3.86: *Selecting Split Cells in Layout Tab*

4. The Split Cells dialog box appears, as shown in *Figure 3.87*. You can set the number of rows and columns in the Split Cells dialog box.

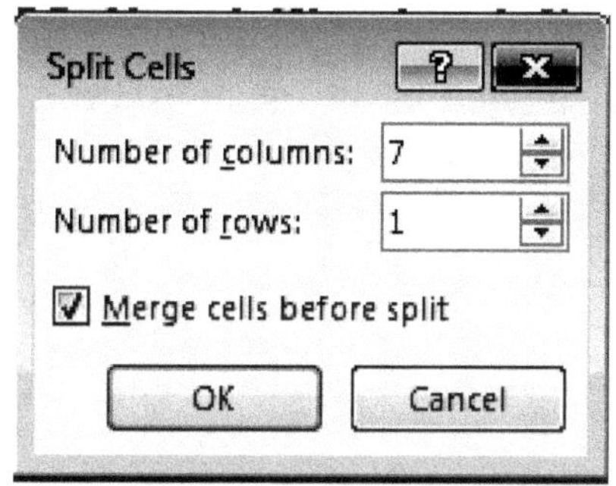

Figure 3.87: *Split Cells Dialog Box*

5. Specify the number of columns in the Number of columns: **spinner box**. For example, we have selected 7, as shown in *Figure 3.87*.
6. Specify the number of rows in the Number of rows: spinner box. For example, we have selected 1, as shown in *Figure 3.87*.
7. Click the OK button in the Split Cells dialog box, as shown in *Figure 3.87*.
8. The selected cell is split according to the number set in the number of columns and rows boxes in the Split Cells dialog box. After this, you can rearrange the column's width equally.

Splitting a Table

Splitting a table means dividing the rows and columns into separate tables so that they could be arranged with ease and comfort.

To split a table, perform the following steps:

1. Select the table which you want to split.
2. Select a row in the table. A Table Tools **contextual tab** appears, as shown in *Figure 3.88*.

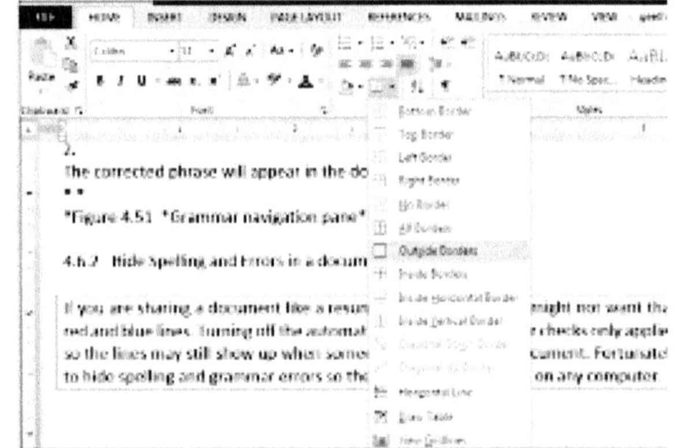

Figure 3.88: *Selecting Row to Split Table*

3. Click the **Layout tab** on the Ribbon.
4. Click the Split Table button under the **Merge** group, as shown in *Figure 3.88*.
5. The selected table is split into two tables, as shown in *Figure 3.89*.

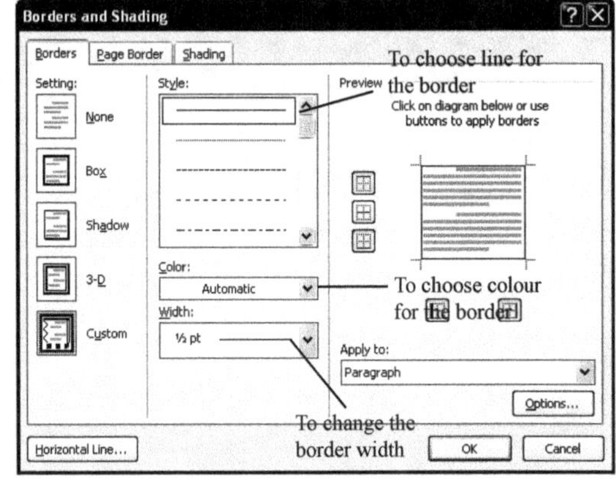

Name	English	Hindi	Maths	Physics	Computer science	Total
Anita	29	78	54	35	79	275
Geeta	98	26	47	64	76	409
Vineeta	58	46	59	89	76	338
Shashi	57	68	76	56	90	347
Sunita	55	60	50	79	87	331
Bindya	49	52	73	84	92	350

Figure 3.89: *The Table Split into Two*

Border and Shading

A border may be a box around a paragraph (or paragraphs) from all sides. It could be a line that sets a paragraph off on one or more sides. A border can include shading, which fills a paragraph with a pattern. Boxes and lines can be solid black, while shading can be **gray** in colour.

If a group of paragraphs is formatted with a box around them and you press Enter key at the end of the last paragraph, your new paragraph falls within the box. However, if you want to create a new paragraph outside the border, then move the insertion point outside the border before you press Enter key.

Applying Borders

To apply borders to a paragraph or group of paragraphs, perform the following steps:

1. Position the insertion point anywhere in the paragraph to be enclosed in a border, or select multiple paragraphs, or select the text to be enclosed (*see Figure 3.90*).

Figure 3.90: *Paragraphs Enclosed in Border*

2. In the **Paragraph group**, click the Borders and **Shading** button. A drop-down menu appears. Choose the border you want to apply for the paragraph, as shown in *Figure 3.90*.

3. Or, in the **Paragraph** group, click the **Borders and Shading** button. A drop-down menu appears. Select the Borders and Shading option. The **Borders and Shading** dialog box appears, as shown in *Figure 3.91*.

Figure 3.91: *Border and Shading Dialog Box*

4. Choose Setting from the options given below:

Option	Effect
None	No box
Box	A box with identical lines on all four sides of the selected text or paragraphs.
Shadow	A box with a drop shadow on the bottom right corner.
3-D	A "Picture frame" box.
Custom	Custom design borders on one or more sides of the selected paragraph(s).

Table 3.14

5. After selecting the setting, choose the Style: from the style scroll list. Style determines the type of line used for border.
6. In the Color: drop-down list, choose the colour you want the border to be in. If you choose Auto option, the colour of text is used by default.
7. In the Width: drop-down list, specify the width for the border.
8. The Preview box shows how the borders are applied to the selected text.
9. In Apply to: choose selected text or paragraph to which you want to apply border.
10. Click **Options**... to specify the gap between the border and the text if need be, as shown in *Figure 3.92*:
11. Click OK or press **Enter**.

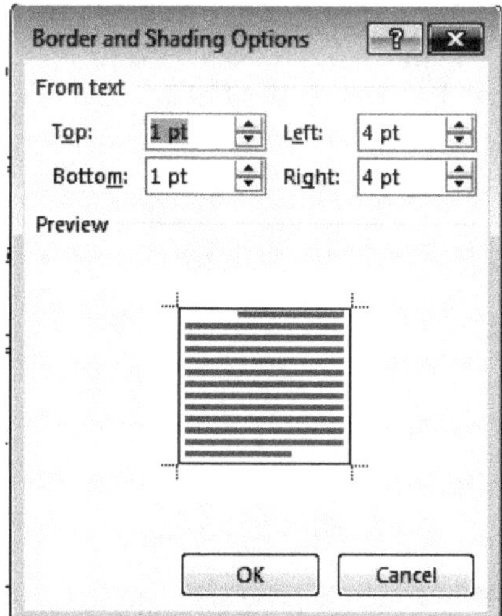

Figure 3.92: *Border and Shading Options*

When paragraphs extend exactly to the margins of your page (as they always do if you do not indent the paragraphs), borders extend slightly outside the margins. If you want borders to fall within or exactly on the margins, you must indent the paragraph. To make borders fall on the margins, indent the paragraph by the width of the border.

To remove or change a box or line from the dialog box launcher command, perform the following steps:

1. Select the paragraph or paragraphs for which you want to remove or change boxes or lines.
2. In the Paragraph group, select the Borders and Shading option.
3. The Border and Shading dialog box appears. Select the Borders tab, as shown *Figure 3.86*.
4. Select the None option in the Setting: group to remove all borders.
5. Select the line to choose a different option from the Style: box. You can also select a different line colour from the Color: list box.
6. Select Box, Shadow, 3-D, or Custom to change the setting of border style.
7. Click OK.

To remove or change a line or box, perform the following steps:

1. Select the paragraph(s) for which you want to remove or change boxes or lines.
2. Click the **Borders and Shading** option on the **Home** tab of the **Paragraph group**. A list of options appears.
3. Select the **No Border** option to remove all borders.

Applying Shading

Shading can be applied in different percentages of black or the selected colour, and in patterns (*see Figure 3.93*). Percentages of black appear as grays of various intensities. For each shade or pattern, you can select a foreground or background colour.

Colours are converted to shades of gray or patterns on a black-and-white printer.

To shade paragraph with the mouse, perform the following steps:

1. Select the text or paragraph/paragraphs to which you want to apply shading.
2. In **Paragraph** group, click the **Border down arrow** and choose Borders and Shading. In the Borders and Shading dialog box, click the **Shading** tab. The property sheet, as shown in *Figure 3.88*, appears.

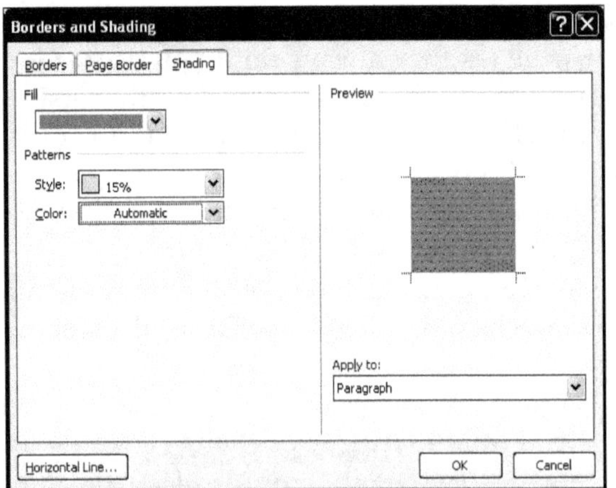

Figure 3.93: *Shading Tab of Borders and Shading Dialog Box*

3. **Fill:** In this box, click the fill colour you want for the shading or click None to remove shading colour.
4. **Style:** In this drop-down list, click the shading style you want to apply "over" this fill colour.
5. **Color:** In this drop-down list, click a colour for the line and dots in the selected shading pattern. The Color: box is not visible if you click colour in the Style: box.
6. **In the Apply to:** section, select paragraph from the drop-down list, and then click the OK button.
7. The selected shading style is applied in the paragraph, as shown in *Figure 3.94*.

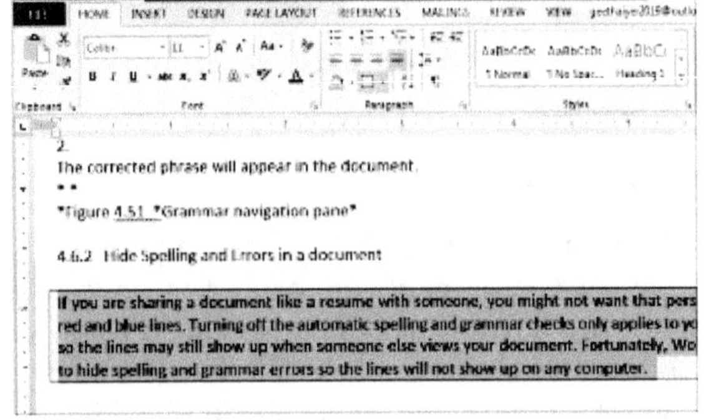

Figure 3.94: *Paragraph with Shading Effects*

To remove shading using mouse, perform the following steps:

1. Select the paragraph or paragraphs from which you want to remove shading.
2. In the **Borders and Shading** dialog box, select the **Shading** tab.
3. Choose **No** fill from the **Fill** group and also clear Style from the patterns group.
4. Click **OK**.

Mail Merge

Mail Merge is a useful tool that allows you to produce multiple letters, labels, envelopes, name tags, and more by using information stored in a list, database, or spreadsheet. The process of creating a mail merge document is quite straightforward and logical. All the tools for performing mail merge operations are available from the Mailings tab. From this tab, you can run the wizard or perform individual steps of the mail merge process on your own.

Creating a Mail Merge Letter

The best way to learn how to create and print a merged document is to consider a practical example. This is described in the following sections.

Creating a Document for Mail-Merge

For mail-merge, you need to do the following:

1. Create a data source.
2. Create main document.
3. Insert fields into the main document.
4. Check for design and data entry errors.
5. Merge the data source document and the main document.
6. Finally, print merged documents.

Starting Mail Merge

Word 2013 has a step-by-step Mail Merge Wizard that guides you through the steps for creating merged documents.

To use the mail merge, perform the following steps:

1. Open an existing Word document, or create a new one.
2. Click the **Mailings** tab. In the Start Mail Merge group, click on the down pointing arrow and select Step-by-Step Mail Merge Wizard..., as shown in *Figure 3.95*.

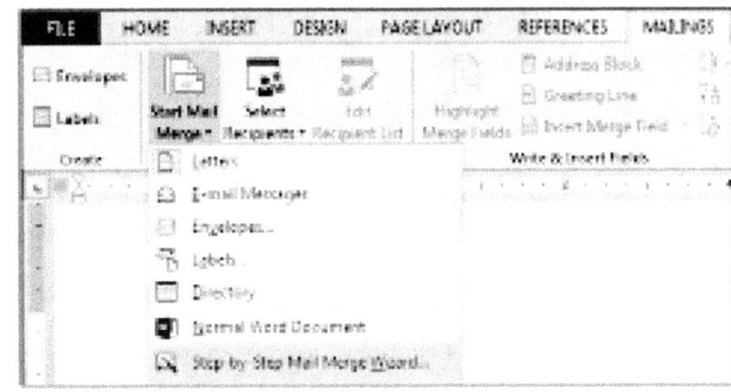

Figure 3.95: *Select Step-by-step Mail Merge Wizard*

3. On the right-hand side, the Mail Merge task pane box appears, as shown in *Figure 3.91*, showing **Step 1** of the Wizard six steps.

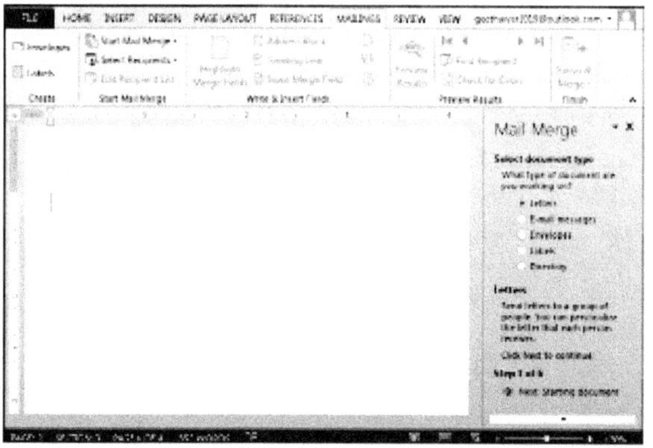

Figure 3.96: *Step 1 of Mail Merge Task Pane*

The following example demonstrates how to create a form letter and merge the letter with a recipient list.

4. Under the Select document type, click **Letters** radio button.
5. Click the Next: Starting document.

The wizard guides you through the rest of the mail process.

There are three options under Select starting document. Click use the current document radio button, which specifies how do you want to set up your letters? (*See Figure 3.97*).

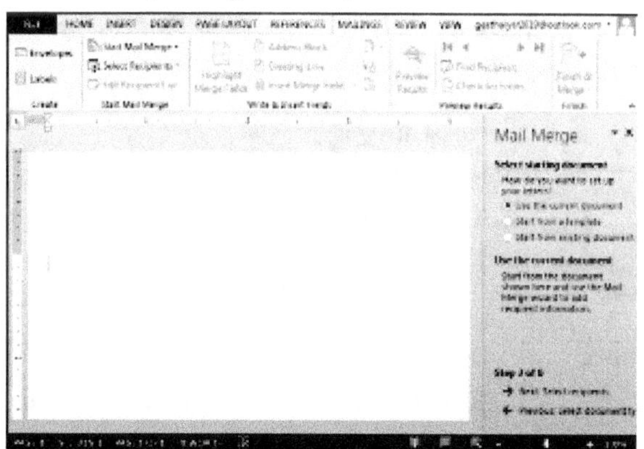

Figure 3.97: *Step 2 of Mail Merge Task Pane*

6. Click Next: Select recipients.

   Under Select recipients, click the Type a new list radio button (*Figure 3.98*).

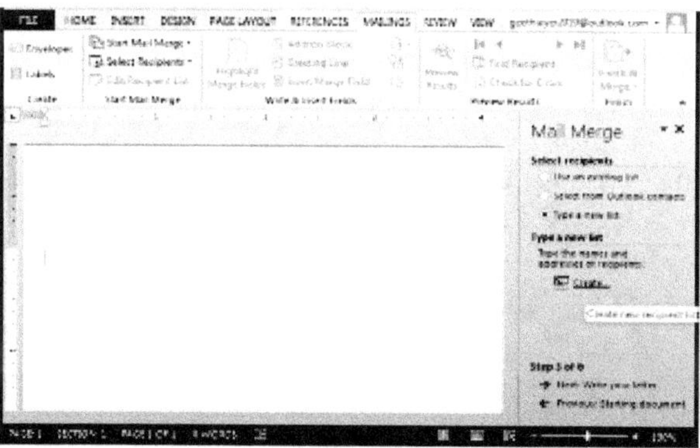

Figure 3.98: *Step 3 of Mail Merge task pane*

Click Create... under the Type a new list section.

7. A New Address List dialog box appears, as shown in *Figure 3.99*. Type the information you want to include for the data source.

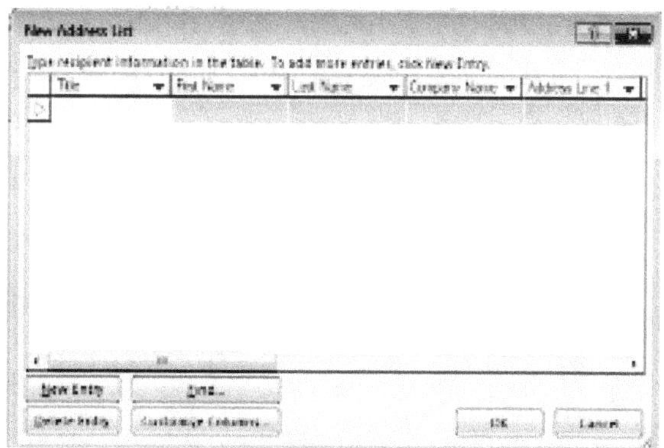

Figure 3.99: *New Address List Dialog Box*

You may not require all the field names in the New Address List dialog box. So, for each field name, first select the field and then click the Customize Columns... button. The Customize Address List dialog box appears, as shown in *Figure 3.100*.

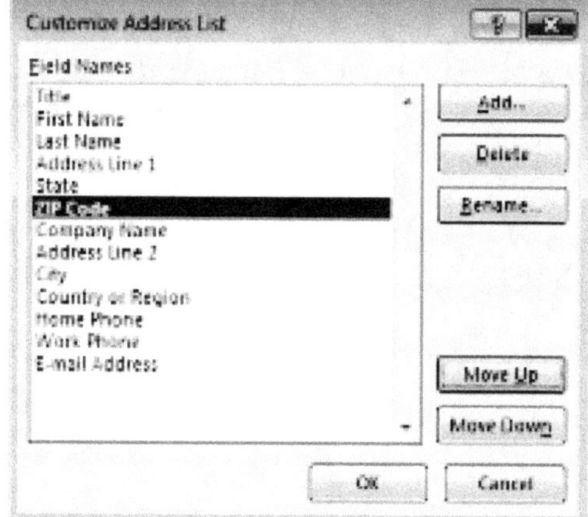

Figure 3.100: *Customize Address List Dialog Box*

8. Field Names appear in the Customize Address list dialog box. If you don't want any field, select the field and then click the Delete button.

9. The selected Field Names are Title, First Name, Last Name, Address Line 1, City, Zip Code.

10. Under Field names, type (use Tab key to go to next field):

    - Title: Mr.
    - First Name: Sanjay
    - Last Name: Sharma
    - Address Line 1: 120-A, Vikaspuri
    - City: New Delhi
    - Zip Code: 110 018

After completing the first entry, click New Entry to enter another data records.

When you have finished adding fields, click OK to save your data source in the New Address List dialog box, as shown in *Figure 3.101*.

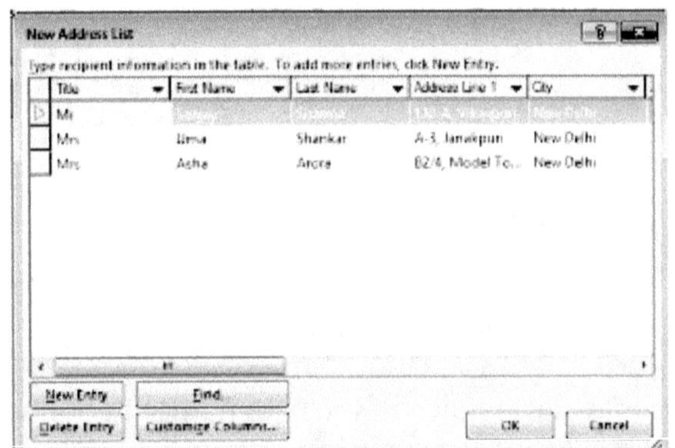

Figure 3.101: *Adding fields in the Address List Dialog Box*

11. The Save Address List dialog box appears, as shown in *Figure 3.102*. Navigate to the folder where you want to save your file. Enter a name for your data source file, say, Data.doc, and click the Save button to save the file.

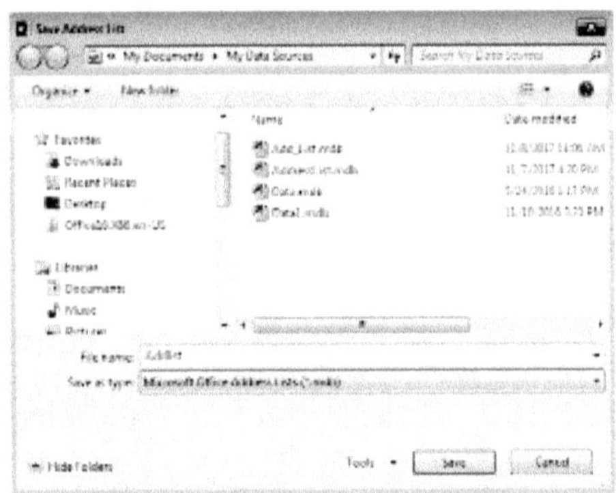

Figure 3.102: *Save Address List Dialog Box*

12. The Mail Merge Recipients dialog box appears, as shown in *Figure 3.103*. Select the recipients that will be used in your merge process.

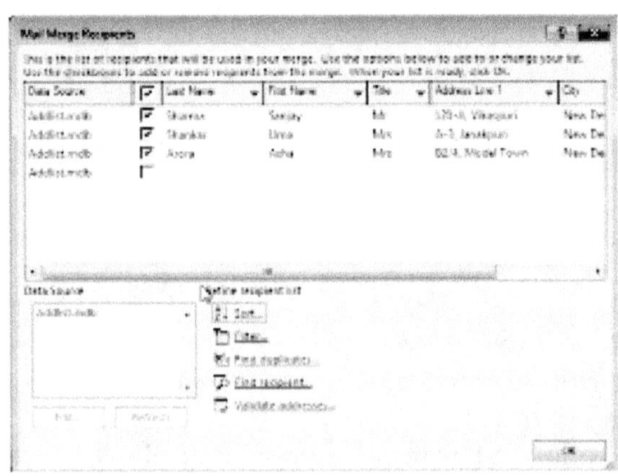

Figure 3.103: *Mail Merge Recipients Dialog Box*

13. Click **OK**.

14. Click **Next**: Write your letter.

    Now, type the following letter:

    Rohini

    New Delhi-110 056

    Ref.Rahul/Comm/20

    Dated: 3rd May, 2019

    To

    <<Title>> <<First_Name>>

    <<Last_Name>>

    <<Address_Line_1>>

    <<City>>-<<ZIP_Code>>

    Dear <<Title>> <<Last_Name>>

I have to inform you that the meeting of the club committee will be held at the *Subroto Park Auditorium* on Tuesday, *25th June, 2019* at 8.00 A.M. I hope you will make it convenient to attend the conference.

The agenda for the conference is as under:

- Confirmation of the minutes of the last meeting (enclosed).
- Accounts and Internal Auditors Report for the months of Feb and March 2019 (enclosed).
- Election of new members.
- List of outstanding results.
- Any other matter with the permission of the Chairman.

Yours faithfully,
P.K. Verma

(Secretary)

To insert a field, perform the followings steps:

1. In the Mailings tab, click Insert Merge Field in the Write & Insert Fields group. Click the down pointing arrow and choose the field names that you can insert in your master document (*see Figure 3.104*).

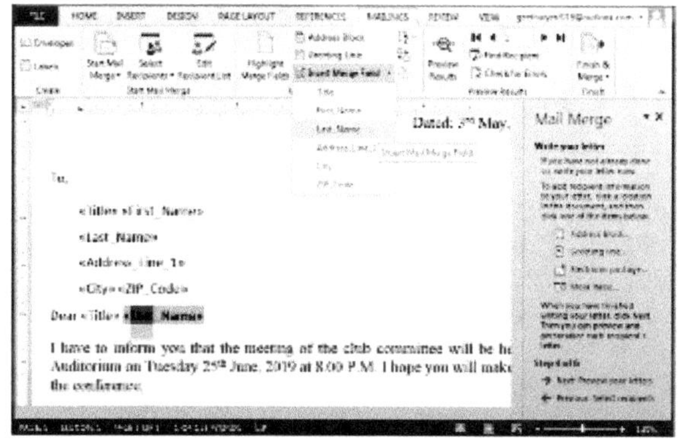

Figure 3.104: *Step 4 of Mail Merge Task Pane*

2. Click Title from merge field name to insert it into the document.
3. Press the spacebar key to insert a blank space between Title and First_Name.
4. Click the Insert Merge Field button to insert the next field name and select First_Name.
5. Press the spacebar key to insert a blank space between the fields First_Name and Last_Name.
6. Click the Insert Merge Field button and select Last_Name.
7. Press the **Enter** key to move to the next line.
8. Place the cursor below <<Title>>. Click the Insert Merge Field button. Select <<Address1>> and press the *Enter* key.
9. Again, place the cursor below <<Address1>>. Click the Insert Merge Field button. Select <<City>>, type a hyphen, and select <<Pin>> from the Merge Field button.
10. Press the **Enter** key twice to leave a blank line.
11. Type Dear and press the Spacebar key.
12. Click the Insert Merge Field button and select <<Title>>.
13. Press the Spacebar to leave a space between the Title and the LastName.
14. Click the Insert Merge Field button and select <<LastName>>.

15. Type a comma, and then press the Enter key twice to leave a blank line.
16. After completing the above steps, your screen will be displayed, as shown in *Figure 3.105*.
17. Now, type the remaining part of the letter.

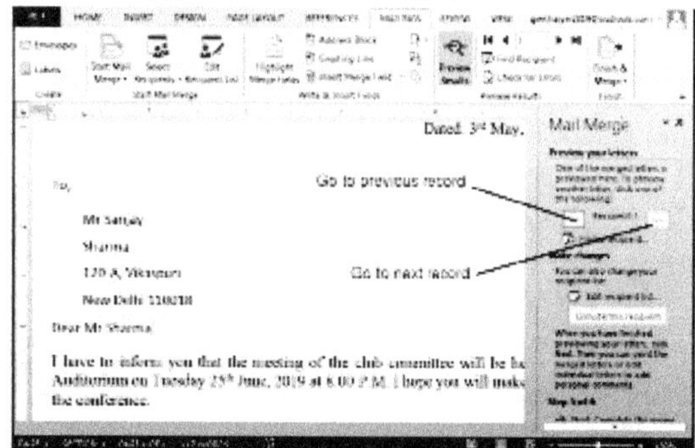

Figure 3.105: *Step 5 of Partially Completed Screen*

Saving the Master Document

18. After you have completed the main document and inserted all of the merge fields, click **Save As** on the File tab.
19. Give the name of the document, and then click the **Save** button.
20. Click Next: Preview your letters.
21. In the Preview your letters, click the arrow button, that is, (<<) to show the first record, and to go to the second record, click the (>>) arrow button (*see Figure 3.106*).
22. Click Next: Complete the merge (*see Figure 3.106*).

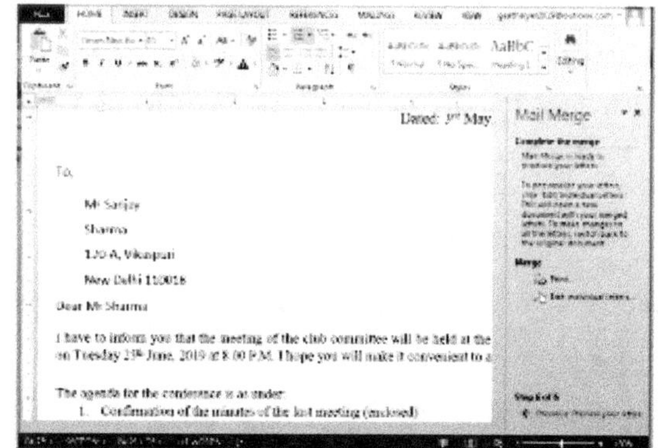

Figure 3.106: *Step 6 of Partially Completed Screen*

23. To personalize individual documents, you complete the merge and then edit the information you want in the resulting merged document.

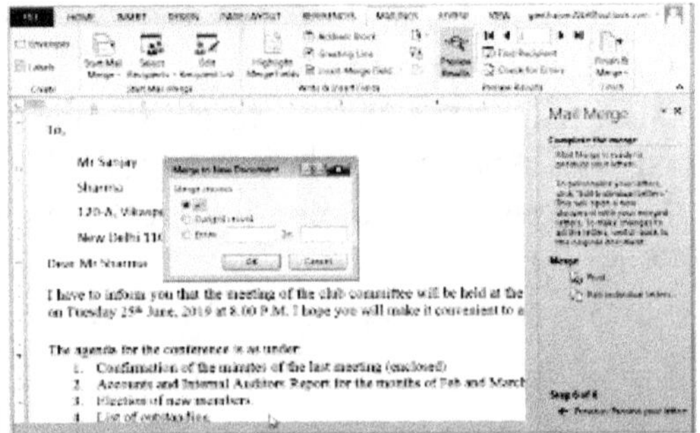

Figure 3.107: *Merge to New Document Dialog Box*

24. Click Edit individual letters...., under the Merge section. The Merge to New Document dialog box appears, as shown in *Figure 3.107*.

25. In the Merge records area, select the records you want to merge.

26. Click the All radio button and then click **OK**.

Word 2013 creates and opens a new merged document. Your main document also remains open. You can switch back to it if you want to make a change to all the documents and then save all the merged documents. Click the Office button and Save the file.

Printing the Merged Letters

If you want to print the letters, make sure that the printer is switched on and is ready to print. Then, **click Finish & Merge** in **Finish** group. Click the down pointing arrow and choose **Print Documents**.... The Merge to Printer dialog box appears. Select the records and click **OK**.

Merging for sending emails using outlook

27. In the Finish group on the **Mailings** tab, you will see a button called **Finish & Merge**. Click on it, and then click **Send Email Messages**..., as shown in *Figure 3.108*).

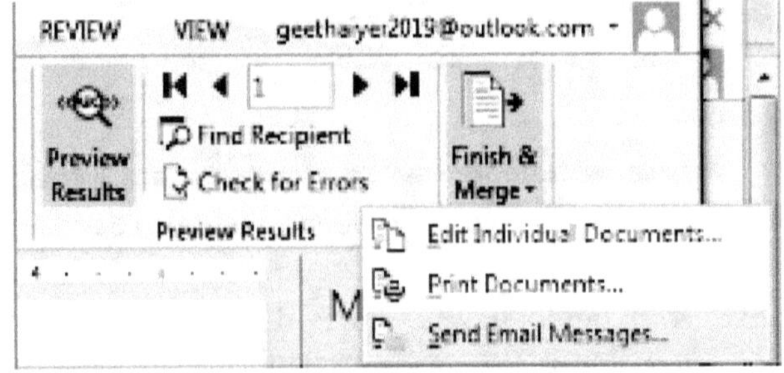

Figure 3.108: *Selecting Send E-mail Messages*

28. **Merge to E-mail** dialog box appears, as shown in *Figure 3.109*. You will be asked to give your message a Subject line: and then you can click on OK to send the messages.

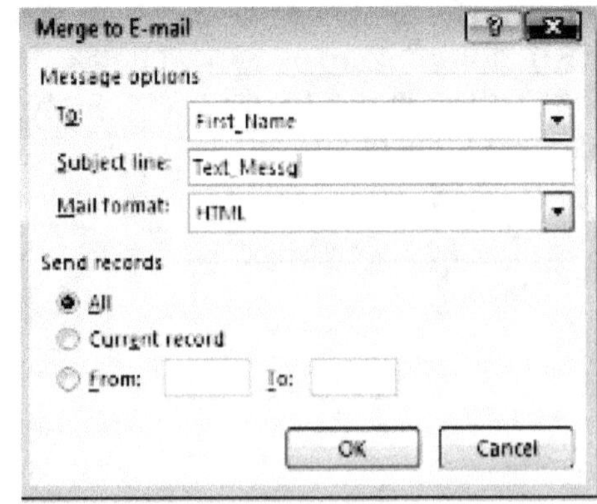

Figure 3.109: *Merge to E-mail Dialog Box*

29. Now, Word 2013 automatically generates all the individual emails and sends them to your Outlook 2013 outbox (or your default email client). Your email merges will be recorded in your sent items folder.

> **Tips:** Attachments are not an option in an email merge. Entire data must be within the body of the email message.

Watermark

A watermark is a faded, background image that displays behind the text in a document. It can be used to indicate a document's status (confidential, draft, and so on) or also to add a company logo.

To add custom watermark in the document, perform the following steps:

1. Click **Design** tab of Page Background group. Click the Watermark drop-down arrow.

2. A list of different Watermark options appears. Select the desired option from the list. Or

3. Click the **Custom Watermark**... option from the list, as shown in Figure 3.110.

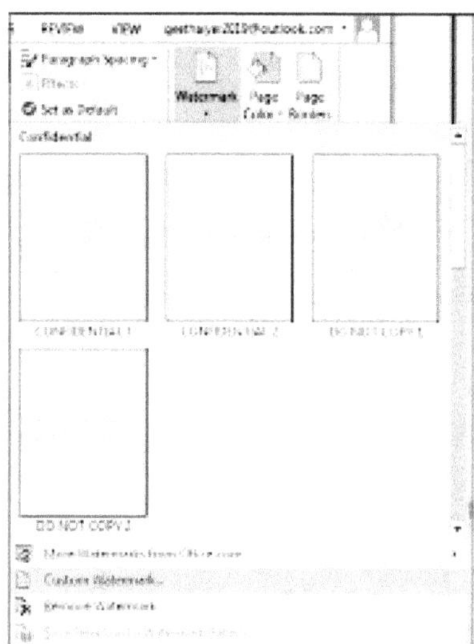

Figure 3.110: *Selecting Custom Watermark*

4. The **Printed Watermark** dialog box appears, as shown in *Figure 3.111*, from where you can choose either to create or add a text watermark or a picture watermark.

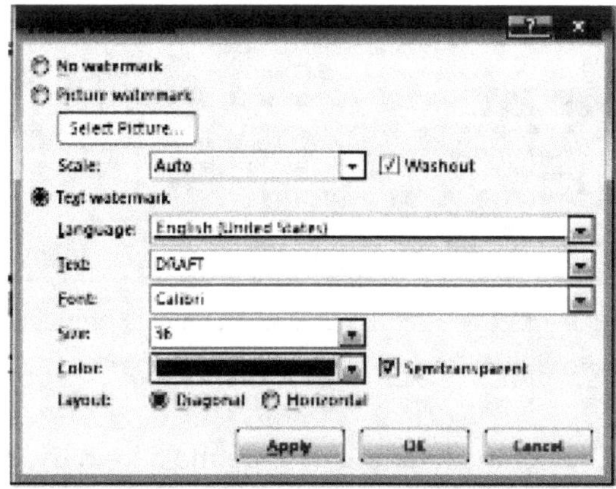

Figure 3.111: *Printed Watermark dialog box*

5. Click the **Text Watermark** radio button to insert a Text watermark.
6. Select Language, Text, Font, Size, Color and the Layout of the watermark and click on Apply.
7. Click the **OK** button. You can see the custom text Watermark on the background of every page in the document.

Table of Contents

Word 2013 builds your table of contents based on headings to identify with heading styles. A style is a predefined combination of font attributes, including color and size that can be applied to any text in your document. To apply a heading style, highlight the text you want to be your heading. Then choose the desired heading option in the Styles group of the Home tab. Heading 1 is usually for your main title, and heading 2 and 3 are for your sub-headings.

Inserting a Table of Contents Based on Headings.

To insert a table of contents, perform the following steps:

1. Insert a blank page at the top of your document.
2. Select the **References** tab on the ribbon.
3. In the **Table of Contents** group, click the Table of Contents button drop-down arrow.
4. Select **Custom Table of Contents…**
5. Choose the style of Table of Contents you wish to insert. Automatic Table 1 creates a ToC titled Contents, as shown in *Figure 3.112*.

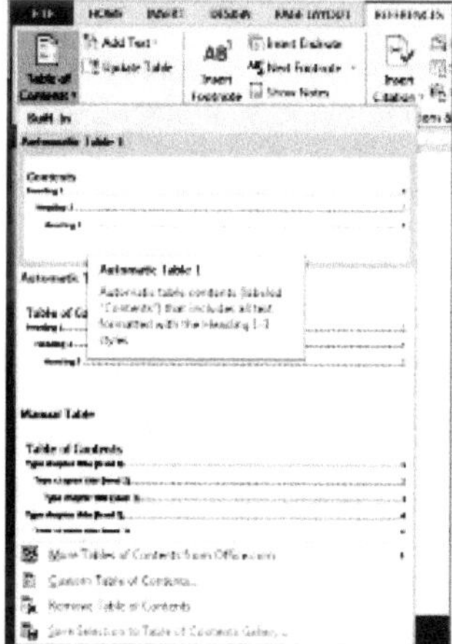

Figure 3.112: *Select Built-In styles of Table of Contents*

Or,

Select Custom **Table of Contents**…. The Table of Contents dialog box appears, as shown in *Figure 113*:

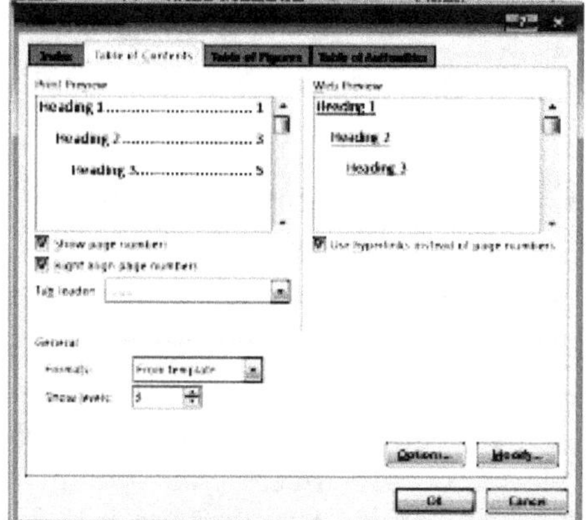

Figure 3.113: *Table of Contents dialog box*

6. To include page numbers, click show page number check box.
7. Click the Tab leader: drop-down arrow to choose a leader style.
8. Choose the number of levels in the Show levels: list box.
9. When finished, click **OK**. A Table of Contents will now appear, as shown in *Figure 3.114*.

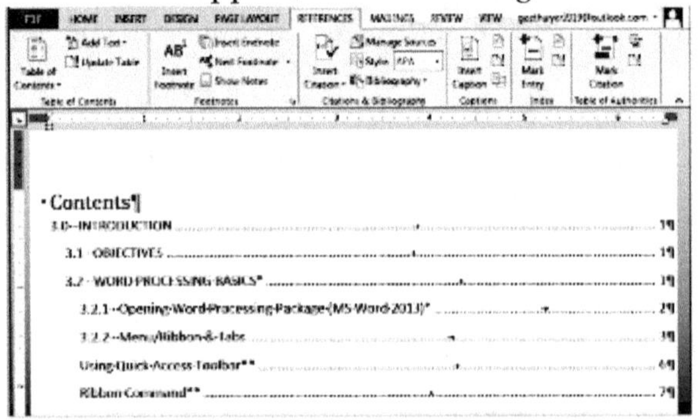

Figure 3.114: *Table of contents is inserted*

Update a Table of Contents

If you added or removed headings or other table of contents entries in your document, you can quickly update the table of contents.

1. Click the **References** tab, in the Tables of Contents group. Click **Update Table**.
2. Update Table of Contents dialog box appears, as shown in *Figure 3.115*.

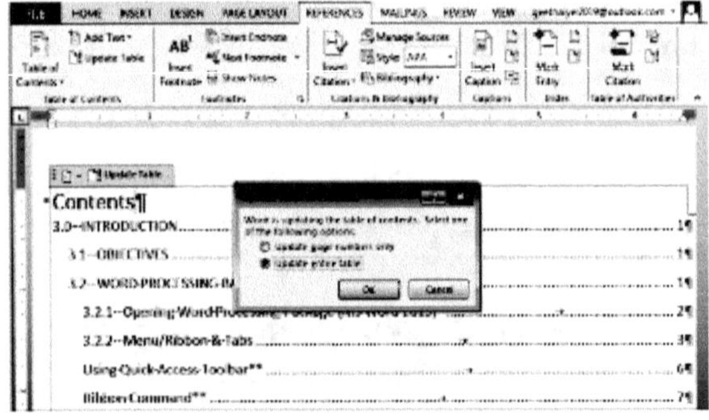

3.115: *Update Table of contents*

3. Choose one of the following options:
   - Update page numbers only
   - Update entire table
4. Select the desired options and click **OK**. Or just select the table of contents, click **Update** Table, and choose **Update Entire Table** in the dialog box that appears, as shown in *Figure 3.115*. The table of contents will then update to reflect any changes.

Mark Indexes Entries

Word 2013 can automatically create an index based on the text you select.

1. Select the text you want to use as an index entry, or click the location to which you want an index entry to refer.
2. Click the **References** tab, in the Index group. Click **Mark Index Entry**, as shown in *Figure 3.116*.

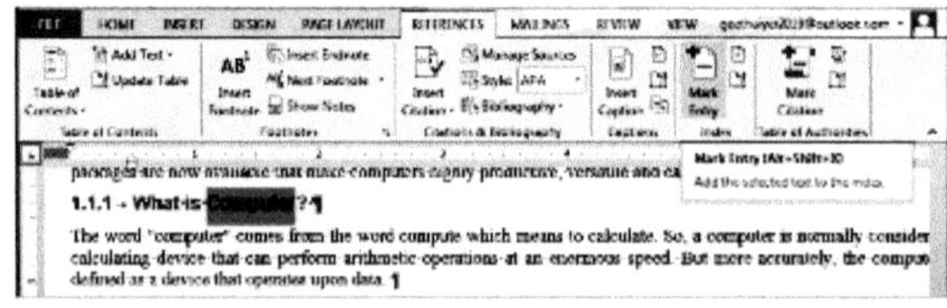

Figure 3.116: *Selecting Mark Entry option in the References tab*

3. Mark **Index Entry dialog box** appears, as shown in *Figure 3.117*.

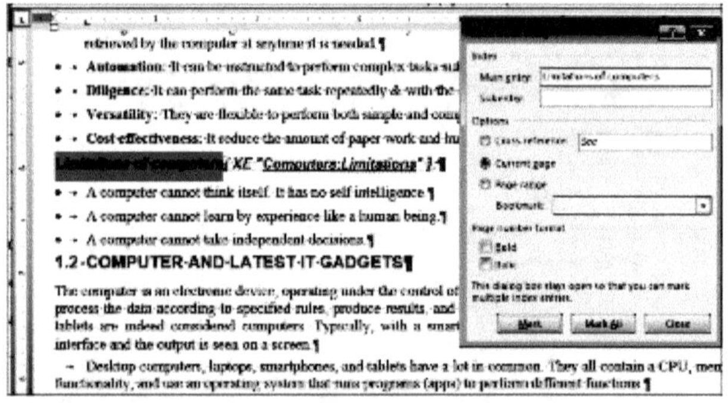

Figure 3.116: *Selecting the text and mark index as entry*

4. Select the heading or type the text in the Main entry: text box.
5. If desired, add a Subentry: text box.
6. Click the desired index option:
   - Cross-reference to refer to another index entry (type the entry in the text box).
   - Current page to refer to the current page only.
   - Page range Bookmark to list a range defined by a bookmark.
8. Click the Mark button to mark all instances of the selected text in the document, as shown in *Figure 3.117*.

Inserting Index Entries

1. Click the **References** tab in the Index group.
2. Click Insert index where you want to begin the index into the document.

3. The **Index** dialog box appears, as shown in *Figure 3.118*.

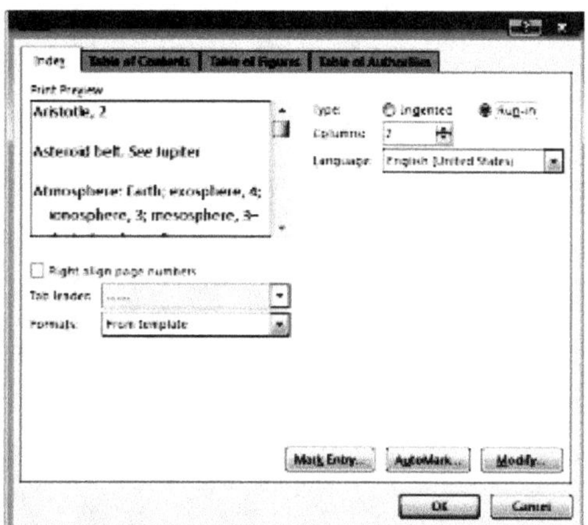

Figure 3.118: *Index dialog box*

4. Select **Index** tab to bring it to the front.
5. Select the desired radio button, that is, Indented or Run-in index type you want to display.
6. The selected style appears in the Print Preview drop-down list.
7. Click or type the Columns: in the list box.
8. Click **OK**. The index entries appears in the document, as shown in *Figure 3.119*.

Figure 3.119: *Selected index entries appears in the document*

Adding Comments

Comments are an important component of document review. When you are working on a document, editing can quickly make changes to the document without documenting them. This can create confusion, and ultimately prevent everyone from working in a cohesive manner that creates the best work possible.

How to Add a Comment in a Word 2013 Document

You can add a comment in Word 2013 so that others viewing the document can see it. Note that any comment you add to the document will include your name so that others can identify who left the comment.

1. Open the document to which you would like to add a comment.
2. Use your mouse to highlight the word, sentence, or part of the document on which you would like to comment.
3. Right-click the selected text, then choose the New Comment option at the bottom of the menu. Or, click the **Insert** tab in the Ribbon and choose the **Comment** button in the **Comments** button group.

Alternatively, click the **Review** tab in the Ribbon and then click the **New Comment** button in the **Comments** button group.

4. Type your comment into the field. It will appear underneath a line with your name, as shown in *Figure 3.120*:

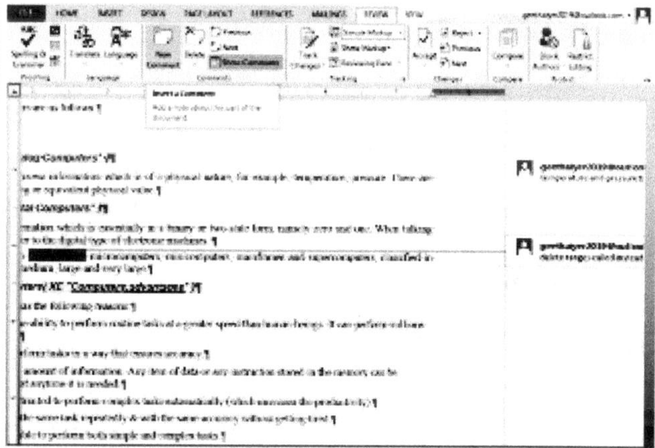

Figure 3.120: *Insert comments in the document*

5. Click anywhere inside the body of the document to complete the comment. It will now be displayed in the Markup Area to the right of the document, with a dotted line drawn from the comment to the part of the document that the comment concerns.
6. To navigate through your comments, use the **Previous** or **Next** buttons on the **Review** tab in the **Comments** button group.
7. To show or hide the comments, click the **Show Comments** toggle button in the same **Comments** button group.
8. When hidden, comments appear as small word balloon icons at the right side of the document window.
9. To temporarily show the comment in a small pop-up window, click this icon.
10. You can edit the comment in the pop-up Window, if needed.

To delete comments, perform the following steps:

1. To delete a single comment, select the comment to delete.
2. Click the **Delete** button in the **Comments** group of the **Review** tab, as shown in *Figure 3.117*. Alternatively, click the drop-down portion of the **Delete** button and choose the **Delete** command.

Figure 3.121: *Delete comment*

3. To delete multiple comments, click the drop-down portion of the **Comments** button.
4. Then choose either the **Delete All Comments Shown** or **Delete All Comments in Document** command.

Tracking Changes

Track changes feature in Word is used for editing or suggesting changes to a document. MS-Word keep track every change you make to a document will appear as a colored markup. If you delete text, the edited text appears with coloured revision marks, such as underlining or strikethrough. This allows you to see edits before making the changes permanent.

To Turn on Track Changes, perform the following steps:

1. Click the **Review** tab, then click the **Track Changes** command:

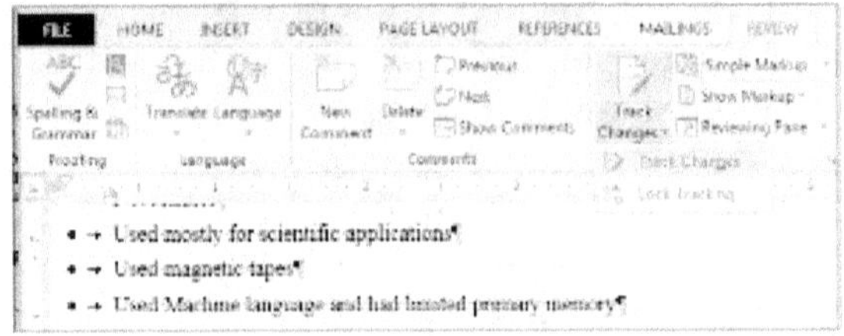

Figure 3.122

2. Track Changes will be turned on. Any changes you make to the document will appears as colored markups, as shown in *Figure 3.123*:

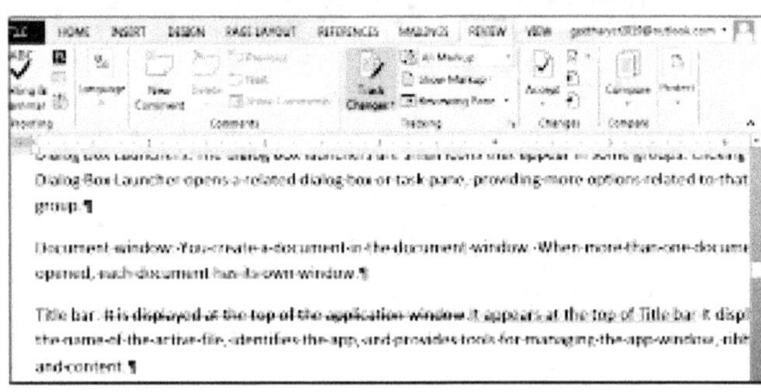

Figure 3.123: *Track Changes applied in the document*

Review Changes

Track changes will mark all the edits made in the document. You can make these edits permanent by selecting accepting or rejecting the changes.

To accept or reject changes:

1. Select the changes you want to **Accept** or **Reject**.

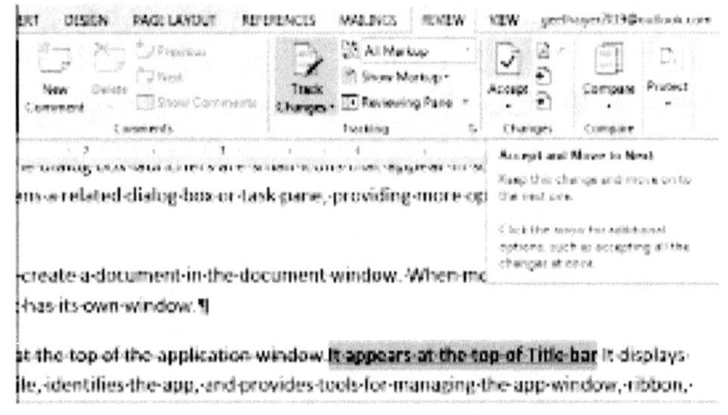

Figure 3.124: *Selecting Accept option to accept the changes*

2. Click the **Review** tab, select the **Accept** or **Reject** command option. For example, here we have selected the Accept option to accept the changes in the document, as shown in *Figure 3.124*.
3. The markup will disappear, and Word will go to the next change. You can continue accepting each change until you have reviewed all of them.
4. After you have finished, click the Track Changes command to turn off.

To hide tracked changes, perform the following steps:

1. Click the **Review** tab, select the Display for Review Command. The Display for Review

command option is located to the right of the Track Changes command, as shown below:

Figure 3.125

2. In the drop-down menu, there are four options:
   - **Simple Markup:** This shows the final version without inline markups. Red marks will appear in the left margin to indicate where a change has been made.
   - **All Markup:** This shows the final version with inline markups.
   - **No Markup:** This shows the final version and hides all markups.
   - **Original:** This shows the original version and hides all markups.

3. For example, we have selected Simple Markup. The red marks in the left margin indicate the change has been made, as shown in *Figure 3.126*:

Figure 3.126: *Selecting simple Markup to indicate the changes made*

4. You can hide and show tracked changes in the document when you click the marker in the left margin and also need to accept or reject the changes before sending to the final document.

Keyboard Shortcuts

The list of keyboard shortcuts built into Word 2013 are as follows:

Create, view, and save documents.

Action	Keyboard Shortcut
Ctrl + N	Create a new document
Ctrl + O	Open a document
Ctrl + W	Close a document
Alt + Ctrl + S	Split the document window
Alt + Shift + C	Remove the document window split
Ctrl + S	Save a document

Perform common tasks:

Action	Keyboard Shortcut
Ctrl + B	To make letters bold
Ctrl + I	To make letters italic
Ctrl + U	To make letters underlined
Ctrl + Shift + <	Decrease font size
Ctrl + Shift + >	Increase font size
Ctrl + [	Decrease font size 1 point
Ctrl +]	Increase font size 1 point
Ctrl + Spacebar	Remove paragraph or character formatting
Ctrl + C	Copy the selected text or object
Ctrl + X	Cut the selected text or object
Ctrl + V	Paste text or an object
Ctrl + Shift + V	Paste formatting only
Ctrl + Z	Undo the last action
Ctrl + Y	Redo the last action

Delete text and graphics:

Action	Keyboard Shortcut
Backspace	Delete one character to the left
Ctrl + Backspace	Delete one word to the left
Delete	Delete one character to the right
Ctrl + Delete	Delete one word to the right
Ctrl + X	Cut the selected content
Ctrl + Z	Undo the last action

Ctrl + F3	Cut selected content to the Spike

Select text and graphics in a table:

Action	Keyboard Shortcut
Select the next cell contents	Tab
Select the preceding cell contents	Shift + Tab
Select a column	Use the Arrow keys to move to the column top or cell, and then do either of the following: • Use the Arrow keys to move to the column top or bottom. • Press Shift + Alt + Page Down to select the column from top to bottom. • Press Shift + Alt + Page Up to select the column from bottom to top.
Select an entire table	Press Alt + 5 on the numeric keypad (with Num Lock off).

Move around in a table:

Action	Keyboard Shortcut
Tab	To the next cell in a row
Shift + Tab	To the previous cell in a row
Alt + Home	To the first cell in a row
Alt + End	To the last cell in a row
Alt + Page Up	To the first cell in a column
Alt + Page Down	To the last cell in a column
Up Arrow	To the previous row
Down Arrow	To the next row

Insert characters and move content in tables:

Action	Keyboard Shortcut
Enter	New paragraphs in a cell
Ctrl + Tab	Tab characters in a cell
Alt + Shift + Up Arrow	Move content up one row
Alt + Shift + Down Arrow	Move content down one row

Apply character and paragraph formatting:

Action	Keyboard Shortcut
Ctrl + Shift + C	Copy formatting from text
Ctrl + Shift + V	Apply copied formatting to text

Apply character formats:

Action	Keyboard Shortcut
Open the Font dialog box to change the formatting of characters	Ctrl + D
Change the case of letters	Shift + F3
Format all letters as capitals	Ctrl + Shift + A
Apply bold formatting	Ctrl + B
Apply an underline	Ctrl + U
Underline words but not spaces	Ctrl + Shift + W
Double-underline text	Double-underline text
Apply hidden text formatting	Ctrl + Shift + H
Apply italic formatting	Ctrl + I
Format letters as small capitals	Ctrl + Shift + K
Apply subscript formatting	Ctrl + Equal sign
Apply superscript formatting	Ctrl + Shift + Plus sign
Remove manual character formatting	Ctrl + Spacebar
Change the selection to the Symbol font	Ctrl + Shift + Q

View and copy text formats:

Action	Keyboard Shortcut
Display non-printing characters	Ctrl + Shift + 8
Review text formatting	Shift + F1 (then click the text with the formatting you want to review)
Copy formats	Ctrl + Shift + C
Paste formats	Ctrl + Shift + V

Align paragraphs:

Action	Keyboard Shortcut
Switch a paragraph between centered and left-aligned	Ctrl + E
Switch a paragraph between justified and left-aligned	Ctrl + J
Switch a paragraph between right-aligned and left-aligned	Ctrl + R
Left align a paragraph	Ctrl + L
Indent a paragraph from the left	Ctrl + M
Remove a paragraph indent from the left	Ctrl + Shift + M
Create a hanging indent	Ctrl + T
Reduce a hanging indent	Ctrl +Shift + T

Work with mail merge and fields:

Action	Keyboard Shortcut
Preview a mail merge	Alt + Shift + K
Merge a document	Alt + Shift + N
Print the merged document	Alt + Shift + M
Edit a mail-merge data document	Alt + Shift + E
Insert a merge field	Alt + Shift + F

Perform function key tasks:

Select a column Use the Arrow keys to move to the column top or cell, and then do either of the following:

Action	Keyboard Shortcut
Get Help	F1
Move text or graphics	F2
Repeat the last action	F4
Choose the GoTo command (Home tab)	F5
Go to the next pane or frame	F6
Choose the Spelling command (Review tab)	F7
Extend a selection	F8
Update the selected fields	F9
Show KeyTips	F10
Go to the next field	F11
Choose the Save As command	F12

Use the Backstage View:

Action	Keyboard Shortcut
Display the Open page of the Backstage view	Ctrl + O
Display the Save As page of the Backstage view (while saving a file for the first time)	Ctrl + S
Display the Save As page of the Backstage view (after initially saving of a file)	Alt + F + S
Close the Backstage view	Esc

Conclusion

A word processor allows you to work more effectively with minimum effort. In this chapter, you learn the basics of Word Processing by opening Word Processing Package (Word 2013). In this, we learnt about Menu/Ribbon and & tabs. Yo saw how to use the option help in word. Then we studied about all the important and most common parameters used in word which are save, save as, page set up, PDF file and saving it. Then we learnt about text creation and manipulation which includes cut, copy, paste options. You also looked at font, color, style and size selection, language selection, alignment of text and options like undo and redo. You learnt how to format the text by indenting the paragraphs, adding bullets and changing cases. Then you learnt the concept of table and its manipulation by inserting or drawing a table, changing the width and height of cell and so on, followed by borders and shading. Further, you learnt mail merging, creating a document for it, and saving a master document. We also saw table of contents points which included inserting of ToC, updating it, and marking and inserting indexes entities. Lastly, you saw how to add or delete a comment in a document, track changes and revise changes.

In the next chapter you will be seeing Spreadsheet Using MS-Excel.

REVIEW QUESTIONS WITH ANSWERS

A. Multiple Choice Questions.

1. When Word gets loaded, the opening screen displays a document named:
   a. Document1
   b. Document
   c. Doc1
   d. No document name is displayed

2. You specify the save details of your file in the:
   a. Save As... dialog box
   b. Save the File As... dialog box
   c. File Save dialog box
   d. None of the above

3. Word offers certain ways by which you can move around in a document:
   a. By scrolling
   b. By moving to a specific page
   c. Both a and b above
   d. None of the above

4. The contents of the Clipboard remain the same until:
   a. You cut other text
   b. You shut down your computer
   c. You copy other text
   d. All of the above

5. Word text can be made Italic by:
   a. Ctrl + I
   b. Ctrl + U
   c. Ctrl + B
   d. None of the above

6. In Word, you can align the selected paragraph to its right by pressing:
   a. Ctrl + E
   b. Ctrl + L
   c. Ctrl + L
   d. None of the above

7. Word automatically places a default left-aligned tab stop at every:
   a. 0.2"
   b. 0.4"
   c. 0.3"
   d. 0.5"

8. What is the term used for the word processing programs that show you directly on the PC screen the appearance of your final document as you might expect when the document is printed on the paper?
   a. Search & Replace
   b. Pagination
   c. Soft Copy
   d. WYSIWYG

9. When you insert a table in a document
   a. Word outlines each cell with continuous lines so that you see the cells when you work in a table
   b. Word outlines each cell with dotted gridlines so that you see the cells when you work in a table
   c. No line is drawn
   d. None of the above

10. After a table has been created, which of the following operations cannot be performed?
    a. Insert rows in a table
    b. Delete and insert columns
    c. Split the table into two tables
    d. None of the above

11. How many scroll bars are visible in the text area if your document is over 200%?
    a. Four
    b. Two
    c. One
    d. Three

12. Which tab will you use to add a chart?

a. View
b. Reference
c. Insert
d. Page Layout

13. Which tab will you use to change margins?
    a. Page Layout
    b. View
    c. Insert
    d. Home

14. What is displayed shown on the Status bar?
    a. Name of document, insert button, and spell check
    b. Number of spellings errors, page number, and document name
    c. Size of Margins, word count, web layout
    d. Number of pages in the document, word count, spelling/grammar check

15. Which tab shows different fonts that are available for use?
    a. View
    b. Page Layout
    c. Reference
    d. Home

16. Which tab shows different document views that are available??
    a. Insert
    b. View
    c. Page Layout
    d. Home

17. Which page view can you use to see what the document will look like when printed?
    a. Outline view
    b. Draft view
    c. Reading view
    d. Print view

18. Which of the following is NOT a new feature in Word 2013?
    a. Ribbon
    b. Button
    c. Charts
    d. Drop-down menu

19. What is the name of the small toolbar at the top that shows the save disk option?
    a. My Documents
    b. Quick Access
    c. Title bar
    d. Find Me

20. Which is NOT on the Insert Ribbon command?
    a. Shapes
    b. Clip Art
    c. Page Numbers
    d. Thesaurus

B. State whether the following Statements are True or False.

1. To highlight the paragraph, double-click the selection bar next to the paragraph.

2. To select an entire document, you will double-click the mouse in the selection bar.

3. Right justification makes the ends of lines uneven.

4. Italic characters are slanted than regular characters.

5. Margins are the distances between the text and the edges of the paper.

6. MS-Word operating system was developed by Microsoft to overcome the limitations of its own MS-DOS operating system.

7. In order to save a file, on the Standard toolbar, click on the Save button.

8. A blank line is also called as a paragraph. It is called as an empty paragraph.

9. You cannot undo certain operations like saving, printing, opening and creating documents.

10. The Print button on the Quick Access toolbar will print the entire document using the default settings.

11. Using the Home tab, you can perform editing functions such as cut, copy, paste, find and replace.

12. Using the Insert menu, you can insert various objects such as page numbers, headers and footers, and pictures.

13. Using the Review tab, you can access various utilities of word such as spell check, macros and mail merge.

14. In MS-Word, every command is available in Ribbon.

15. Formula bar is available in MS-Word 2013

C. Match the following.

1.	By default on which page the header and footer is printed on:	a.	Font Effects
2.	Superscript, subscripts, outline, emboss, Engrave are known as:	b.	To increase left indent
3.	Word automatically moves the text to the Next line when it reaches the right edge of the screen and is called:	c.	Every Page
4.	Word will respond in repeated word as:	d.	Word Wrap
5.	Ctrl + M:	e.	Ctrl + Shift + F8
6.	Backspace:	f.	A red wavy line under the repeated word
7.	It activates the rectangular selection cursor:	g.	Deletes the character to the left of the
8.	The use of All Caps features in Word:	h.	Ctrl + left arrow
9.	Moves to cursor one word left:	i.	Mail Merge
10.	It enables us to send the same letter to different persons:	j.	It changes all selected text into Capital Letter
		k.	Ctrl + Spacebar

D. Fill in the blanks:

> Style   Non-printing characters   Find and Replace   Paragraph   Title barReview   Hanging indent   Alt   Data SourcePage Orientation   Alt + Enter

1. __________ shows the name of the application and the name of the file.
2. __________ tab consists of spelling and grammar, thesaurus, etc.
3. When entering text within a document, the Enter key is normally pressed at the end of every __________.
4. A collection of character and paragraph formatting command is called __________.
5. The special characters Word inserts into your document are called __________.
6. Press the Ctrl + H keys to display the __________ dialog box.
7. The __________ marks all the lines of a paragraph except first line.
8. In Word, the mailing list is known as the __________.
9. To use keyboard instead of the mouse to select tools on the ribbon, you display the key Tips by pressing the __________ key.
10. Change the __________ to create a document in wide format.

Short Questions with Answers.

1. **What is MS-Word?**

   Answers: MS-Word is a widely used commercial word processor designed by Microsoft. It is a component of the MS Office Suite. It is used to create, edit, and organize an attractive and flawless document.

2. **List the important features of a word processor**

   Answers: A word processor has many unique features as discussed under:

   a. **Easy Typing:** Typing in Word is so easy because, each time we need not press thr Enter key after the end of a line as in case of typewriter. Word itself takes the matter to the next line of the document. This facility is called word wrapping.

   b. **Easy:** The document you saved for future use and the method of storing it is called saving.

   c. **Adding, removing and coping:** The text or paragraph you type will automatically be adjusted in the place of deleted or modified text.

   d. **Spell check or words:** Word checks the spellings automatically.

   e. **Change the Style and Shape of Characters and Paragraphs:** In Word, you can make a document attractive and appealing because the shape and style of characters in the documents can be changed according to our requirements.

   f. **Bullets and Numbering:** Bullets and numbering are special symbols which can emphasize a lists or items in a document.

   g. **Headers and Footers:** A Header is the text appearing top of the document and Footer is the text appears below the document.

   h. **Creation of Tables:** To make Tables specify number of rows and columns are required in the document.

3. **What are the advantages of word processing?**

   Answers: Quality: The spelling and grammar check in Word makes the document error free.

   Storage of Text: We can take print any number of copies with word processor. But also, if we need the same document to make some changes, we need not type the same letter again.

   Time saving: We can take a number of copies of a document and can print the document on any printer.

   Security: By giving passwords, we can protect the documents.

   Dynamic exchange of data: We can embed the objects and pictures from other documents into word processing documents, which can be linked to each other.

4. **What do you mean by text alignment?**

   Answers: While adding text in a document, the text of each line appears uniformly at an equal distance from the left margin of the page by default. Such a uniform setting of the text with respect to page margins is called alignment.

5. **Define formatting.**

   Answers: The process of arranging text in a document in a particular way by changing text alignments, font and size is called formatting.

6. **What is Character formatting?**

   Answers: The character formatting plays a significant role in document formatting by determining the appearance of individual characters in the document.

7. **How can you restrict editing for someone in Word 2013?**

   Answers: To restrict editing, do the following:

   a. Go to the review tab and click on Restrict Editing.

   b. A pop-up window appears on the right side of the document.

   In the pop-up window, go to **editing restriction**, select the drop down for which we want to put restriction for, like only comment, track changes, filling in the form, or ready only.

   At the end, we will be asked to set a password for the document to keep access limited to you.

8. **What is the shortcut to move the insertion point to the beginning of the document?**

   Answers: To move the insertion point to the beginning of the document, the shortcut key used is Ctrl + Home.

9. **In what ways you can see the difference between two similar documents?**

   Answers: To see the difference between two similar documents, click the compare buttons and select compare from the review tab in the compare group in the Ribbon.

10. **How can you accept or reject track changes in Word 2013?**

    Answers: To accept or reject changes in Word:

    Select the track changes made in the document.

From the review tab, click the Accept or Reject command; the mark-up will disappear and Word will automatically jump to the next change.

Descriptive Type Questions.

1. You want to underline a sentence. Your insertion point is within the sentence. However, when you click the Underline button, only one word is underlined. Why? How do you correct the problem?
2. Suppose you have just deleted paragraphs from pages 1, 2 and 3. You then realize that the paragraph on the second page should not have been deleted. What can you do to bring back this paragraph?
3. Suppose you are doing grammar check and Word offers a suggestion that you do not understand. What is the best thing to do?
4. On clicking the bullets button, you get a bullet type different from what you want to use. How do you get Word to use the bullet type you want?
5. Put down the procedure of saving a newly typed document on word.
6. What do the red and green wavy lines under some words stands for?
7. What is the procedure of checking the spellings in MS-Word?
8. Differentiate between copying and moving a block of text.
9. Define the Find and Replace feature of Word.
10. What is line spacing? How many types of line spacing are available in the Word?

Answers

A.	1. a	2. a	3. c	4. d	5. a
	6. c	7. d	8. d	9. b	10. d
	11. b	12. c	13. a	14. d	15. b
	16. d	17. d	18. d	19. b	20. b

B.	1. T	2. F	3. F	4. T	5. T
	6. T	7. T	8. T	9. T	10. T
	11. T	12. T	13. F	14. T	15. F

C.	1. c	2. a	3. d	4. f	5. b
	6. g	7. e	8. k	9. h	10. i

D.	1. e	2. f	3. d	4. A	5. B
	6. c	7. g	8. i	9. h	10. j

■■

CHAPTER 4

Spreadsheet Using MS-Excel

Structure

In this chapter, we will discuss the following topics:

- Elements of spreadsheet
- Manipulation of cells and worksheet
- Formatting cell
- Sorting and filtering
- Freezing panes
- Formulas, functions and charts
- Charts (Bar, Pie, Line)
- Pivot Table

Objectives

The reader will be able to understand the following:

- Basic Knowledge of Spreadsheet Processing, their usage, and details of Spreadsheet screen.
- Opening, saving and printing a Spreadsheet.
- Spreadsheet creation, inserting and editing data in cells, sorting and filtering of data.
- Inserting and deleting rows/columns.
- Applying basic formulas and Functions.
- Preparing chart to represent the information in a pictorial form.

MS-Excel is a spreadsheet program that is used to analyze numerical data. It includes many powerful tools that can be used to organize and manipulate large amounts of data, perform basic calculations, create charts and visualize data in a spreadsheet

Introducing Spreadsheet

Spreadsheet applications (sometimes referred to simply as **spreadsheets**) are computer programs that let you create and manipulate spreadsheets electronically. In a spreadsheet application, each value sits in a cell. You can define what type of data is in each cell and how different cells depend on one another. The relationships between cells are called **formulas**, and the names of the cells are called **labels**.

S-Excel is a spreadsheet program that is used to analyze numerical data. It includes many powerful tools that can be used to organize and manipulate large amounts of data, perform basic calculations, create charts and visualize data in a spreadsheet.

Values in the cells are arranged in rows and columns. Each value can have a predefined relationship with the other values. If you change one value, you may need to change other values as well, or they will change automatically.

Once you have defined the cells and the formulas for linking them together, you can enter your data. You can then modify selected values to see how all the other values change accordingly. This enables you to study various what-if scenarios.

Excel 2013 is a popular spreadsheet program, where you design worksheets. It uses a workbook-style presentation which is made up of several worksheets, like pages in a notebook.

Elements of Spreadsheet

When you are working with a spreadsheet package, such as MS-Excel 2013, you have to know some spreadsheet terminologies. Some such terms are given in the following paragraphs.

Workbook: A workbook is a collection of worksheets. In a single file, the user can store information in an organized manner. By default, a workbook contains **three worksheets**, and it has a maximum of **255 worksheets**. The workbook stores all the data that you have entered and allows you to sort or calculate the results. The workbook that is available to be viewed and edited by multiple users on a network is known as a **Shared Workbook**.

Worksheet: A worksheet is a sheet made up of rows and columns. It begins with row number one and column A. Each cell can contain a number, text or formula. It can also reference another cell in the same worksheet, the same workbook or a different workbook. The worksheet is always stored in a workbook.

Chartsheet: Chartsheet is a separate sheet in a workbook that contains only graphs or charts. It is useful when you want to see a chart or tabular data separated from other type of data.

Row: It is a horizontal block of cells that runs through the entire width of the worksheet. The row is identified by the number that is on the left edge of the worksheet. The name of the first row is 1, 2, and so on. Maximum rows numbers range from **1,048,576** in an Excel 2013 worksheet.

Column: Columns in Excel worksheet run vertically. It contains **16,384 (A to XFD)** columns. The column is identified by letters *A B* and final letter *Z*. After the letter *Z*, the next column is *AA, AB, AC, …AZ* and then incrementing to *BA, BB*, and so on, to the last column *XFD*.

Cell: Cell is the intersection between a row and a column is called a Cell. It is identified by row number and column header so the cell is labeled as A1. For example, cell A9 is the intersection of column A and row 9. When you select a cell by clicking it with the mouse, it becomes the active cell.

Formula: In Excel, formulas are used to calculate/manipulate the numbers or text. It is a combination of values, operators (+, -, /,), and cell addresses (for example, A8, C2, and so on). While using formulas, it always beings with the (=) sign, you can refer to either cells or cell ranges or names or labels which represent those cells or cell range.

Function: Functions are pre-defined formulas or programs that perform calculations in Excel on specific values, called **arguments**. Each function takes specific types of arguments, such as numbers, references, text, or logical values.

Creating a Spreadsheet

MS-Excel 2013 needs Windows 8 and 10 operating systems to run on a PC. However, Excel 2013 can also run on a Windows 7 operating system if service pack 3 is installed on Windows 7.

To start Excel 2013, perform the following steps:

1. Click the **Start** button on the taskbar, highlight **All Programs**, and then click **Microsoft Excel 2013**, as shown in *Figure 4.1*:

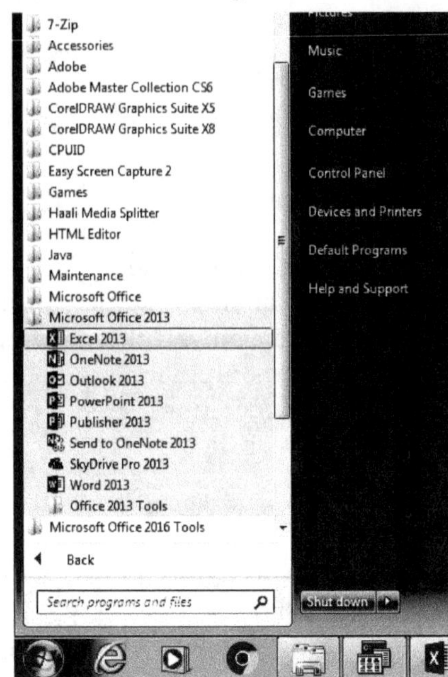

Figure 4.1: *Starting Excel 2013 in Windows 7*

Excel 2013 Interface

Excel 2013 includes the MS-Office Fluent interface, which consists of a customizable visual system of tools and commands. *Figure 4.2* shows the elements of Excel 2013 application window.

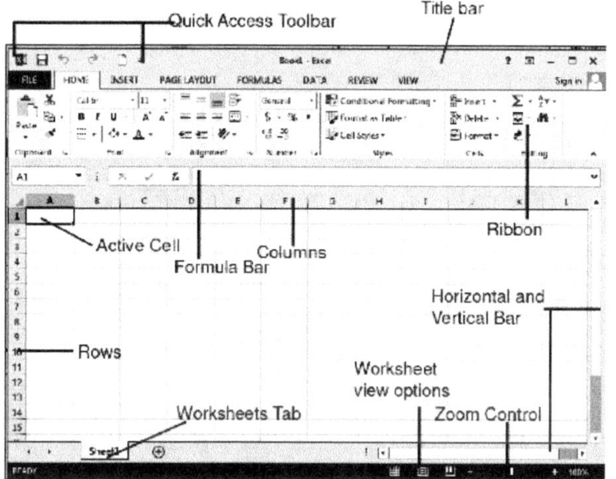

Figure 4.2: *Elements of Excel 2013 window*

Title Bar: At the top of an Excel 2013 window, there is the Title bar. The left edge of this bar has the Office button next to which the name of the open document is displayed. On the right edge of the Title bar, the Minimize, Restore/Maximize and Close buttons are placed, as seen in *Figure 4.2*.

- **Application Window:** The window within which Excel 2013 runs.
- **Quick Access Toolbar:** The Quick Access Toolbar lets you access common commands, no matter which tab is selected. You can customize the commands depending on your preference. This toolbar is located by default at the top of the Excel 2013 window. It provides tools that you use frequently, such as the Save, Undo and Repeat buttons, as seen in *Figure 4.2*. You can customize the Quick Access Toolbar by adding commands to it.
- **Workbook Window:** A window within the Excel 2013 application window in which a worksheet, chart, or dialog box is shown.
- **File Tab:** File tab is the coloured tab which is located in the upper-left corner of Microsoft Office 2016 programs and below the Quick Access Toolbar, as seen in *Figure 4.2*. When you click the File tab, you can see the Backstage view.
- **Ribbon:** Ribbon is displayed just below the Title bar, as seen in *Figure 4.2*. In Ribbon,

Commands are organized in logical groups, which are collected together under tabs. You can hide the Ribbon by double-clicking the active tab. Different types of tabs are described here, which are available in the Ribbon of Excel 2013.

- **Worksheets Tab:** The tab is at the bottom of a workbook window that displays the name of a sheet. Click the sheet tab to move to the next sheet. To display the shortcut menu, right-click the sheet tab. To scroll through the sheet tabs, use the tab scrolling button.
- **Name Box:** The name box is on the left side of the Formula bar, as seen in *Figure 4.2*. It displays the location or name of a selected cell.
- **Formula Bar:** The formula bar displays the constant value or formula used in the active cell. It is also used for editing the cell contents, as seen in *Figure 4.2*.
- **Status Bar:** Status bar appears at the bottom of the Excel 2013 window. It displays information regarding a selected command or an operation in progress. Note that the right side of the status bar shows zoom slider, and different views tool such as Normal, Page Layout, and Page Break view.
- **Tell me:** The Tell me box works like a search bar to help you quickly find tools or commands you want to use.
- **Cell:** An active cell in a rectangular box in a workbook is called a cell. A cell is an intersection of a row and column. The border around the selected cell is called the cell pointer.
- **Worksheet View Options:** It offers three types of views in the Status bar. Click to select the desired view to see differently.
- **Zoom Control:** You can drag the slider to use the zoom control and the number to the right side of the slider displays the zoom percentage.
- **Vertical and Horizontal Scroll bars:** Vertical scroll bars allow you to move up and down whereas horizontal scroll bars move up left to right.

Creating a New Workbook

To create a new workbook, there are many ways to start working with a workbook in Excel. You can choose to create a new workbook or either with a blank workbook, a predesigned template or open an existing workbook.

To create a new workbook:

1. Click the File tab. Here, select New. Under Available Templates, click Blank Workbook. Alternatively, press the **Ctrl + N** keys together, as shown in *Figure 4.3*:

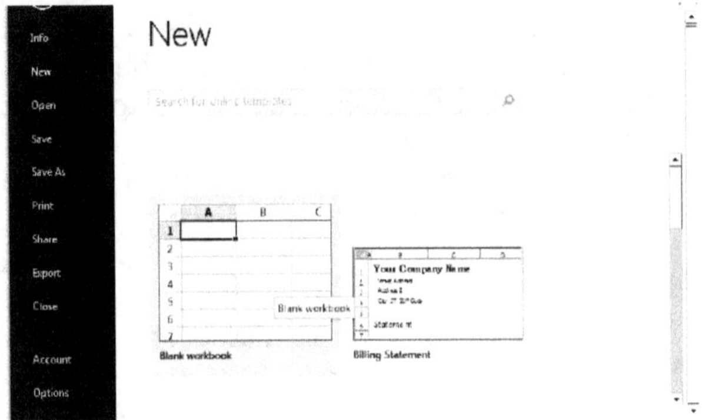

Figure 4.3: *Selecting Blank Workbook*

1. A new blank workbook will appear, as shown in *Figure 4.2*.

Opening and Closing a Workbook

In addition to creating new workbooks, you will often need to open a workbook that was previously saved.

To open an existing workbook, perform the following steps:

1. Click the **File** tab to open Backstage view, and then click **Open**.
2. Click Computer icon; a list of Current Folder and Recent Folders appears. You can open from that folder or click the Browse button, as shown in *Figure 4.4*:

Figure 4.4: *Selecting Open backstage view*

3. The Open dialog box will appear, as shown in *Figure 4.5*. Locate the file or folder in the Address bar:

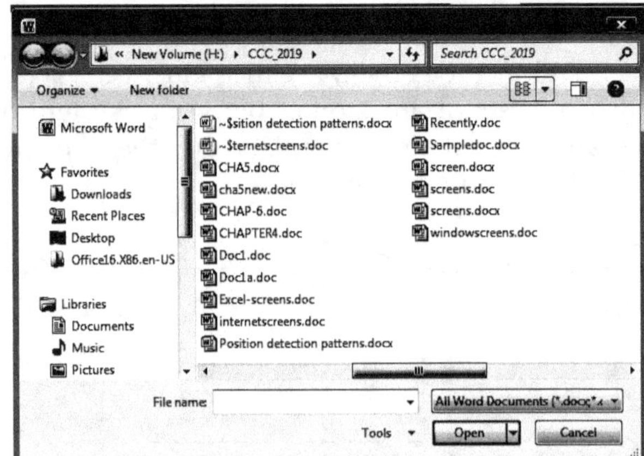

Figure 4.5: *Open Dialog Box*

4. Select the file in the contents pane.
5. Then click the **Open** button.

If you have opened the desired workbook recently, you can browse your Recent Workbooks rather than search for the file.

To pin a workbook:

1. You can pin it to Backstage view to access the file if you often work with Excel workbooks
2. Click the File menu and choose Open to Backstage view. You can see the recently edited workbooks appear, as shown in *Figure 4.6*.

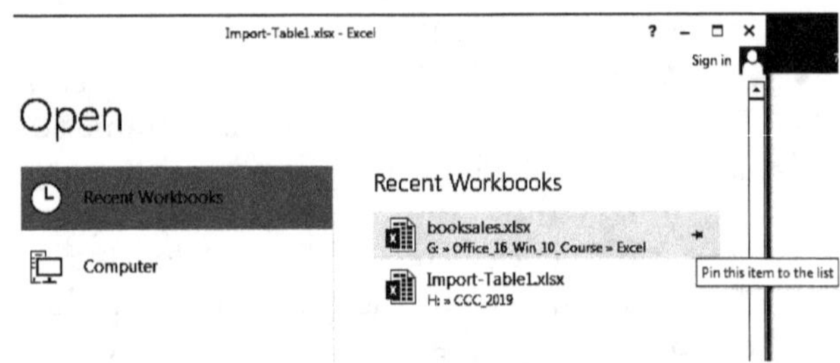

Figure 4.6: Recent files in Open Backstage View

3. Move the mouse pointer to select the workbook you want to pin. A pushpin icon will appear next to the workbook. Click the **pushpin** icon.
4. The workbook will appear in Recent Workbooks. To unpin a workbook, click the pushpin icon again, as shown in *Figure 4.7*:

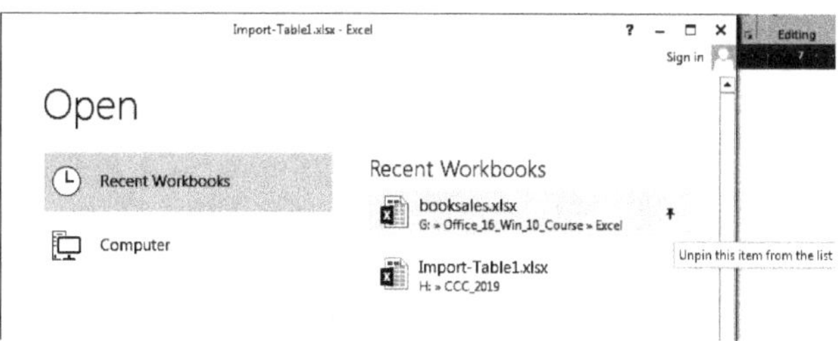

Figure 4.7: *Unpin a Workbook*

When you finish using worksheet or chart, you **close** its Window. If you have made any changes since the last time you saved the workbook, Excel 2013 displays an alert dialog box, as shown in *Figure 4.8*, asking whether you want to save your work before closing:

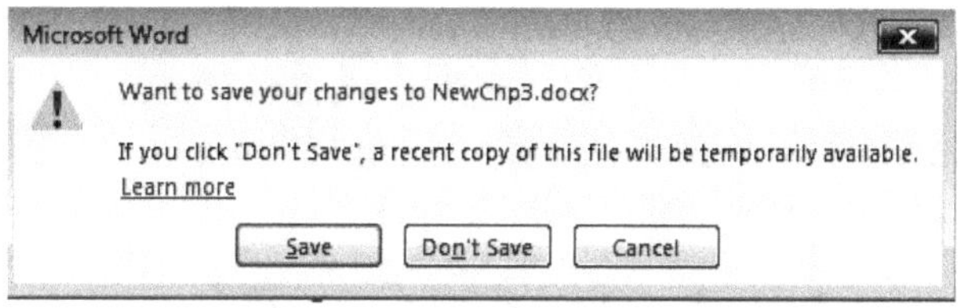

Figure 4.8: *Alert Dialog Box*

To close a file in a workbook, perform the following steps:

1. Click on the **File** tab and choose **Close**. The window closes provided no change has been made to the workbook since it was saved last. Alternatively, press the **Ctrl + W** keys together to close the workbook.

2. If you have made changes to the workbook since the last save, the Alert dialog box appears. In the dialog box, choose Don't Save if you do not want to save a changed version of the file, or choose Save if you want to save the changes. Type a new file name and choose the Save button.

Saving Workbook

Saving your workbook is important if you want to use later or view the file again to open later. **Save** command use to save an existing file, whereas **Save As** command to use for the first time and you can save the file as a new name.

To save the workbook, perform the following steps:

1. If you are saving the file for the first time, click the **File** tab to open the Backstage view.

2. Click **Save As**. The Save As pane will appear in Backstage view, as shown in *Figure 4.9*. You can also access the save command by pressing

Ctrl + S on the keyboard.

Figure 4.9: *Save As Backstage view*

3. Click **Browse**. The **Save As** dialog box will appear as shown in *Figure 4.10*:

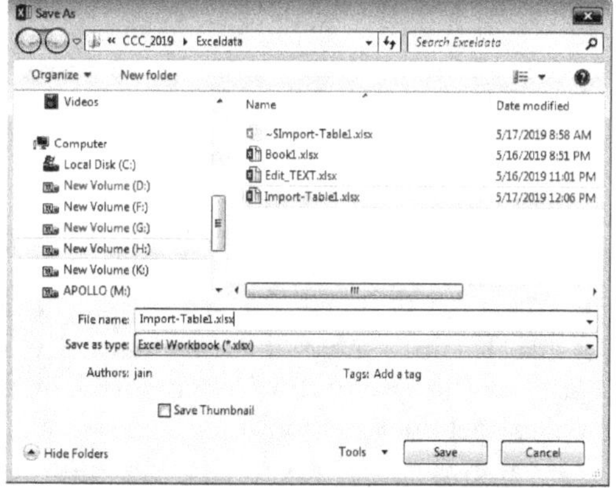

Figure 4.10: *Save As dialog box*

4. Select the location where you want to save the workbook in the Address bar.

5. In the File name: box, give the name of the file.

6. In the Save as type: box, give the type of file.

7. Click the **Save** button.

Excel 2013 worksheet is saved with an **.xlsx** extension, indicating that it uses the XML-based file format.

Concept of Cell Address [Row and Column] and Selecting a Cell

A spreadsheet consists of rows and columns which combine to form cells. A cell is a box where you can enter data. Columns form the vertical lines of cells, while rows form the horizontal lines of cells. The Cell is an intersection of rows and columns. To describe the location or address of a cell, we have to write the names of the column and the row whose intersection has created this cell. In *Figure 4.11*, the intersection of the Column C and the Row 3 is C3.

Here, C3 is called a cell and C3 is its address.

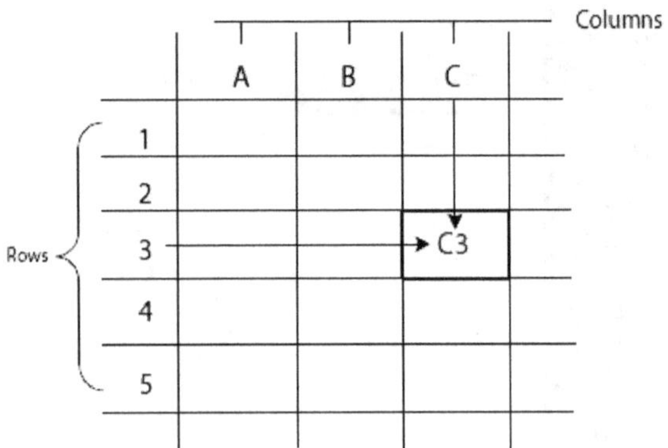

Figure 4.11: *Address of Cells*

Cells can have two types of data in a worksheet:

- **Constant value:** A constant value is data that you type directly into a cell. It can be a number, a date, time, currency, percentage, fraction or text. Constant values do not change unless we edit them.
- **Formula:** A formula is a sequence of values, cell references, names, functions or operators that produce a new value from the existing values. It always starts with the **equal sign** (=). The value that is produced as the result of the formula changes automatically when other values involved in the formula in the worksheet change.

MS-Excel helps you perform calculations on numerical data. For example, if you need to find the sum of some data or calculate through a complex set of formulas, Excel can quickly provide the answer. By using formulas, you can efficiently keep track of your business or personal finances.

To find the sum of numbers from cell address *A1* to *A10*, the formula would be as follows:

$$= +A1+A2+A3+A4+A5+A6+A7+A8+A9+A10$$

A function is a shortcut for a formula. For example, to calculate the sum of numbers from cell address *A1* to *A10*, the function used would be as follows:

$$= Sum(A1:A10)$$

Colon (:) symbol indicates a group of cell addresses. It is easier to write a function as compared to a formula.

Formulas Using Cell Addresses

A formula can also contain cell addresses instead of values or numbers. In that case, the formula is applied on the contents of cell address included in it. Cell addresses could be included in a formula by typing or highlighting them. In a formula, the cell addresses can be used along with numbers, mathematical operators and functions. For example, if the contents of cell address *B20* have to be added to that of cell address *D13*, then type the following formula:

$$= B20+D13$$

If a formula contains various operators, then Excel performs calculations in a preset order, i.e., multiplication is done before addition. For example, in the formula 2x3+4, it will multiply 2 and 3 first. And then, 4 will be added to their product. So, the result will be 10 and not 14.

Selecting a Cell

To select a cell, perform the following steps:

1. To edit cell content, first you need to select the cell.

2. Click on a cell to select it. For example, we have selected cell D25. A rectangular border will appear around the selected cell, under the column heading and row heading until you click another cell in the worksheet, as shown in *Figure 4.12*.

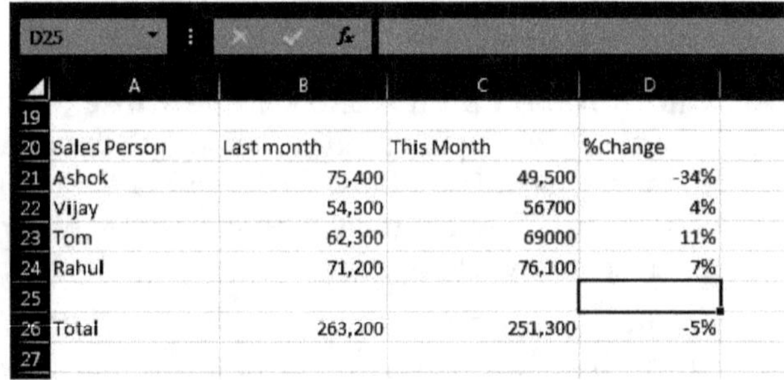

Figure 4.12 *Selecting the Cell*

3. By using the arrow key on the keyboard, you can select the cells.

To select a cell range, perform the following steps:

1. Occasionally, you may want to select a group of cells, or a cell range.

2. Click and drag the mouse until all of the adjacent cells you want get highlighted. In our example, we have selected the cell range B21:C24, as shown in *Figure 4.13*.

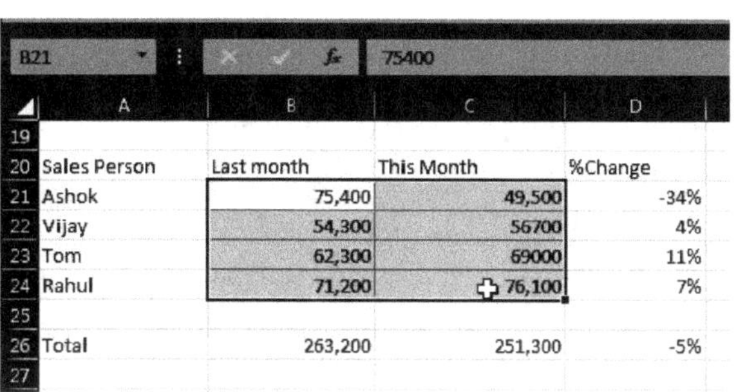

Figure 4.13: *Selecting the Cell Range*

3. Release the mouse button after you select the desired cell range. The selected cell remains highlighted until you select another cell in the worksheet.

Entering Data [text, number, date] in Cells

When you see the message Ready, as shown in *Figure 4.2*, in the Status bar, then you can enter data items in a worksheet. Entering data in Excel 2013 worksheet actually includes three steps:

1. Activate the cell in which you want to enter data.
2. Type the data you want to enter.
3. Finalize the data entry by pressing **Enter** key, or any one of the **arrow keys**.

Example 1: How do you enter data item in a cell?
Solution: To enter data:

1. Click on the desired cell where you want to enter data, just to make it active. The active cell appears with a dark border and its row and column headings appear to be raised to easily identify the cell address.

2. Type your data in the active cell. Two buttons appear in the Formula bar: Enter button and Cancel button. The Status bar shows a cursor to indicate that you are in the process of entering data, as shown in *Figure 4.14*:

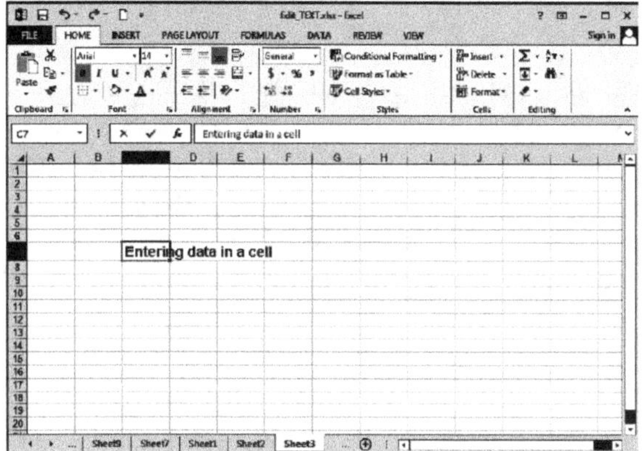

Figure 4.14: *Entering Data in a Cell*

3. Click the **Enter** button to indicate that you have completed the data typing. You can also press Tab key or any one of the arrow keys to complete the data entry.

4. If you make a mistake before finalizing your data entry, press the **key** to delete the character to the left of the insertion point. To erase everything that you have typed, click the cancel button or press **Esc** key.

5. Repeat the above steps to complete the data entry.

Excel provides you with the following two options to enter and edit data:

You can enter data in the Formula bar.

You can also enter and edit data directly in the cell.

To enter and edit data directly in the cell, you need to turn on the in-cell editing option, if not done already.

If the Edit directly in-cell feature is turned off, the entry you type appears in the cell, but the cursor appears in the Formula bar.

To turn on in-cell editing option:

1. Click the **File** Tab; the Info backstage view appears. Click **Options**. **Excel Options** dialog box appears. In this dialog box, click on the **Advanced** button on the left side. Excel Options dialog box appears with Advanced options, as shown in *Figure 4.15*.

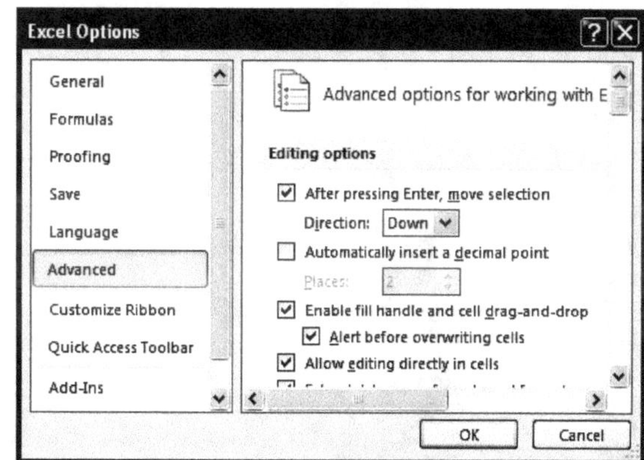

Figure 4.15: *Excel Options with Advanced Properties*

2. Click on the checkbox, that is, **Allow editing directly** in cells under the **Editing options group**, as shown in *Figure 4.15*. The option is on when a checkmark appears.

3. Click **OK** to accept the settings you changed.

Entering Text

Text entries can include alphabetical characters, numbers and symbols.

To enter text in a cell, perform the following steps:

1. Select the cell to type the text entry, and then enter the text by clicking the Enter button in the Formula bar or by pressing the **Enter** key.

2. To enter numbers as text, type an apostrophe (') followed by the number, for example, `'45,000`. Alternatively, place an equal to sign in front of the numbers and enclose the number in quotation marks. For example, to enter the number 45,000 as text, type `="45,000"`.

3. Notice that in a cell with the General format, numbers entered as text will align on the left just like text. Even if you enter a number as text, you can still use the number if it is needed in a numerical formula.

Example 2: How do you quickly format a range of numbers as text in your worksheet by using the Text numeric format?

Solution: To quickly format a range of numbers:

1. Select the range of cells containing the numbers.

2. Select the Text option from the drop-down list of the Number group from the Home Tab, as shown in *Figure 4.16*:

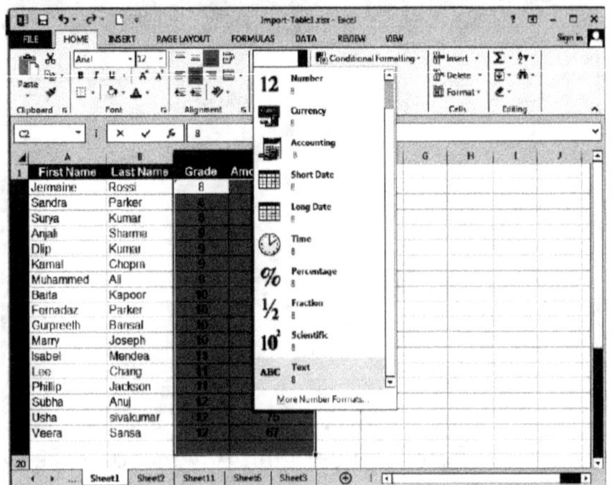

Figure 4.16: *Selecting Text option from drop-down list*

Alternatively, press the *Ctrl + 1* keys or click on the Home tab and then in the Number group, click the Dialog Box Launcher. In this dialog box, click on the Number tab, and select the Text from the Category list: and click OK.

Entering Numbers

Numbers have constant values and contain the characters, which are given in *Table 4.1*.

Character	Function
0 through 9	Any combination of numerals
+	Indicates exponents when used in conjunction with E, such as 3E+3 means 3x103
( )	Indicates negative number
, (comma)	Indicates negative number
/	Thousands marker
$	Currency indicator
%	Percentage indicator
. (period)	Decimal indicator
E or e	Exponent indicator
:	Time separator
(single space)	Separators of compound fractions (for example, 4 1/2); and date time entries (for example, 1/2/94 5:00)

Table 4.1: *Special Characters for Numeric Entries*

To enter a number, perform the following steps:

1. Select the cell, type the number, and then press **Enter** key. Or, click the **Enter** button in the **Formula bar**.

2. You can enter integers, such as 145; decimal fractions, such as *145.437*; integer fractions, such as 1 1/2; or scientific notation, such as *1.45437E+2*.

Entering a number as text enables the number display to exceed the cell's width. If you enter a number in the normal way and the cell is not wide enough to display it, the cell fills with # signs or in some cases it may display the number in scientific notation.

Excel 2013 stores the numbers typed into a cell, as well as the format or appearance in which the numbers should be shown. When you enter a number into a cell, Excel tries to establish how the number should be formatted. For example, it accepts and displays the entries listed in *Table 4.1* with the formats indicated.

Typed Entry	Chosen Format	Result
978	Number, General	978
7555 Mg Rd.	Text, left aligned	7555 Mg Rd
350.09	Number, dollar format	$350.09
44.6%	Number, percent format	4460.00%
(878)	Number, negative	-878
2 ¾	Number, fraction	2 ¾
25600	Number, comma format	25,600.00
-378	Number, comma format	-378.00
1/5/19	Date, m/d/yyyy	01/05/2019
4/4	Date, m/d/yy (current year assumed)	04-Apr

Table 4.2: *Excel Automatic Formats*

The entries of the *Table 4.2* are displayed in *Figure 4.17*, as they would appear in an Excel 2013 worksheet.

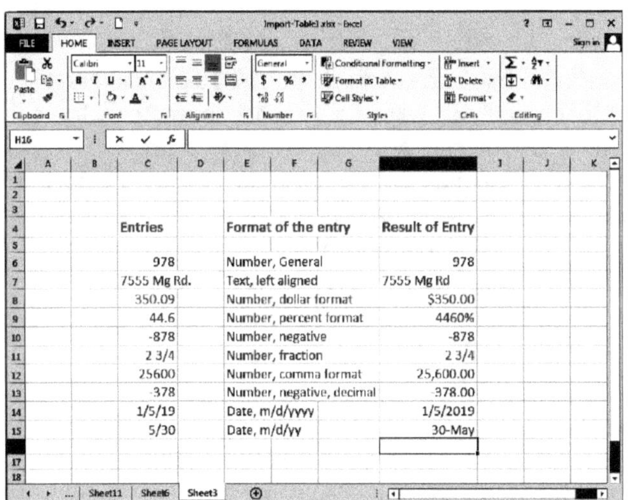

Figure 4.17: *Formats done for data given in Table 4.2*

To control fixed decimal option, do this:

1. Click the **File** Tab and then click **Options**. **Excel Options dialog box** appears. In this dialog box, click on the Advanced button on the left side. Excel Options dialog box appears with **Advanced** properties, as shown in *Figure 4.18*.

2. Click the **Automatically insert decimal point**: checkbox under the **Editing** options group so that the check mark does not appear (*see Figure 4.18*).

3. Click **OK**.

Using the fixed decimal representation feature of Excel 2013, you can automatically add decimals to every value entered in a worksheet.

Entering Date and Time in a Worksheet

Dates and times are two of the most common data types in Excel. It stores dates and time as a number known as the date serial number, or date-time number. When you enter a date, you will need to use a specific format your spreadsheet understands, such as month/day/year (or day/Month/Year, depending on which country you are in). When you enter time, you follow a time format of at least h:mm, that is, the hour and minutes are separated by a colon with no spaces.

For example, if you type **6 June 19** in a cell formatted to show numbers with a comma and two decimal places (#,##0.00), you will see that date as **43,622.00**.

If Excel does not recognize the entry as a valid date or time format and you type a text date such as **Apr 5 19**, Excel treats the entry as text. It aligns it to the left in the cell.

Example 3: Explain the steps to be followed to enter date in different formats.

Solution:

1. Select the cell in which you want to enter the date.

2. Type the date into the cell with any of the following formats. For example, to enter 7th June 2019, type:

   o 6/7/12

   o 6-Jun-12

   o 7-Jun (the year from the system date is used)

   o Jun-19 (only the month and year are shown)

   o 6/7/19 0:00

You can also enter the dates as 6/7, 06/07/19, Jun-19, or June 7, 2019 (*see Figure 4.18*). In any of these date formats, you can use either /, -, or space to separate different elements:

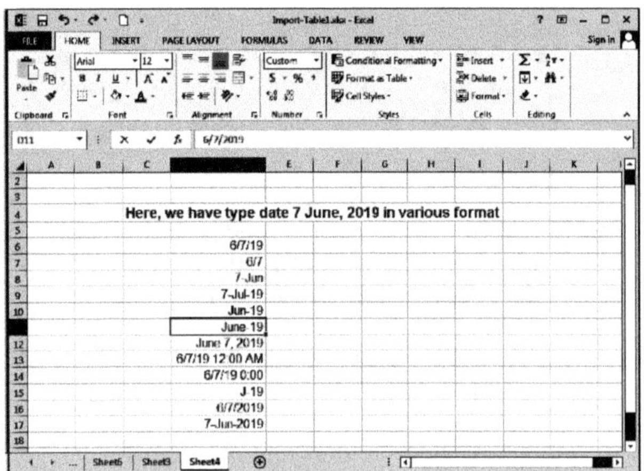

Figure 4.18: *Various Ways to Enter Date in a Work-sheet*

Example 4: How do you enter time in an Excel 2013 worksheet?

Solution:

1. Select the cell in which you want to enter the time.

2. Type the time in any of the following formats. For example, to enter 1:32 PM, type:
   - o   13:32
   - o   13:32:45
   - o   1:32 PM
   - o   1:32:45 PM
   - o   6/7/19 12:00

The first two examples are from a **24-hour clock**. If you use a **12-hour clock**, follow the time with a space and AM or PM (in either upper or lowercase letters).

Leave a space before the AM or PM. Do not mix a **24-hour clock** time with an **AM** or **PM**. As the last format shows, you can combine the date or time during entry.

To enter the current date/time in a cell:

1. To enter the current date, select the cell and press the **Ctrl + ;** keys together.

2. To enter the current time, select the cell and press the **Ctrl + Shift + :** keys together.

To format a date in the default date format, press the **Ctrl + #** keys together. To format a time in the default time format, press the **Ctrl +@** keys together.

Creating Text

To create text in a cell, position the cell-pointer at the desired cell address and then type the entry from the keyboard. For example, to enter text in cell address *A1*, perform the following steps:

1. Move the mouse-pointer to cell address Al and click the left mouse button just once. Instantly, the cell pointer changes like (into, a rectangle shape) at cell address *Al* (*see Figure 4.17*).

2. Now, type Entering text in a cell.

3. Then, press the **Enter** key from the keyboard. Your workbook will look like as shown in *Figure 4.19*:

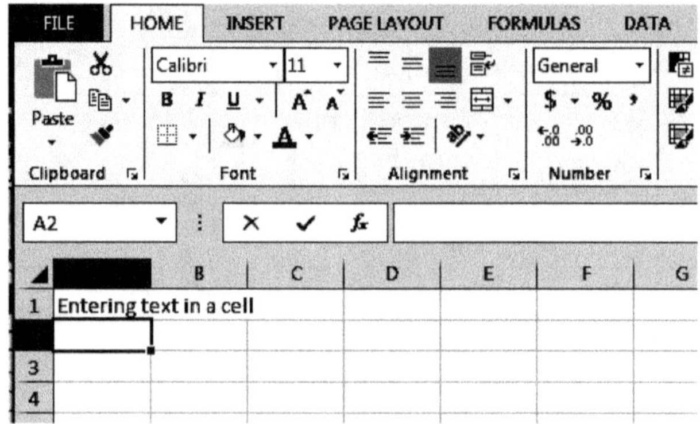

Figure 4.19: *Creating Text in a Cell*

4. Text entries are normally used as row and column headings for entering phone numbers, addresses, and so on. All texts are left-aligned. And a formula cannot be applied over text entries.

Each cell has a default width of 9-10 characters, that is, each cell can hold up to 9-10 characters. In case the entry of cell address is more than its default width, its display gets extended to the next cell. This does not mean that it has occupied the space of the next cell. It has just got displayed over it.

For example, while entering text in a cell at cell address A1, you will observe that the typed text gets extended to the next cell B1 (*see Figure 4.17*).

Although the label is occupying the two cell addresses, that is, *Al* and *B1*, it is normally in cell address *A1*. To find out the cell in which the text is actually displayed

Click the left mouse button over the cell address *B1*. You will see that the Formula bar does not display the text entry.

Now, click the left mouse button over the cell address *A1*. You will see that the Formula bar displays the text Entering text in a cell.

Page Setup

Before you print worksheet, it is better that you change the page setup as per the printer and paper you are going to use for printing a worksheet. Page Setup feature in Excel 2013 involves four options, namely, **Page**, **Margins**, **Header/Footer** and **Sheet**.

To set the Page Setup options, perform the following steps:

1. Under **Page Layout** tab, in **Page Setup** group, click on the Dialog box Launcher button to display the Page Setup dialog box with Page tab, as shown in *Figure 4.20*:

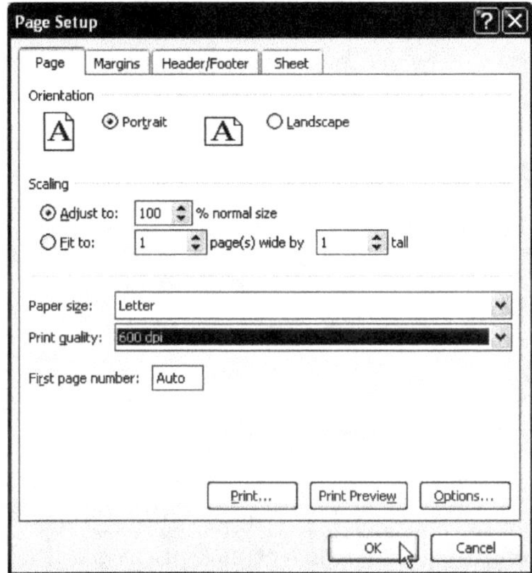

Figure 4.20 : *Page Setup dialog box with Page Tab property sheet*

2. The options available on the Page tab are given in *Table 4.3*:

Option	How to Set from Ribbon	Function
Orientation	Under the Page Layout tab, in the Page Setup group, click arrow next to Orientation and select Portrait or Landscape.	Portrait means page length is more than the page width. Landscape means page width is more than the page length).
Scaling Adjust to	Under the Page Layout tab, in the Scale to Fit group, move Scale: spinner to set the value.	Allows you to enlarge or reduce the printed worksheet. You can reduce it to 10% to fit more of the worksheet on a page. You can also enlarge it to 400% to enhance details.
Fit to	Under the Page Layout tab, in the Scale to Fit group, Fits a worksheet onto a specific number of pages	Fits a worksheet onto a specific number of pages.
	click Width: and Height: drop down list to set the height and width.	
Paper size	Under the Page Layout tab, in the Page Setup group, click arrow next to the Size and then select size from the drop-down list.	Selects paper size from drop-down list.
Print quality	It can be set only through Page Setup dialog box.	Selects resolution (dpi) from list.
First page number	It can be set only through Page Setup dialog box.	Begins numbering at the specified page number.

Table 4.3: *Options of Page Tab property sheet of Page Setup Dialog box*

When you choose the Fit To: option, Excel 2013 ignores any page breaks you have set, and fits the entire worksheet or print area to the specified number of pages.

To set the margins in a worksheet, perform the following steps:

1. Under the **Page Layout** tab, in the **Page Setup** group, click the arrow next to the **Margins**. It will display the predefined margins. Select from here or if you want to set the margins manually, then select the option **Custom Margins...** (*see Figure 4.21*) or click the margins tab of the Page Setup dialog box.

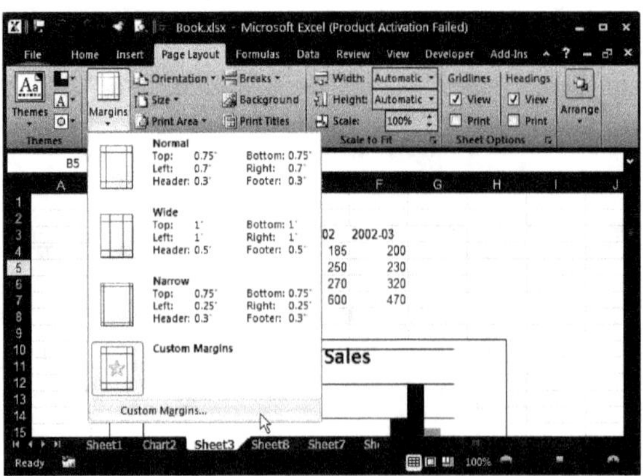

Figure 4.21: *Predefined Margins*

The property sheet, as shown in *Figure 4.22*, appears.

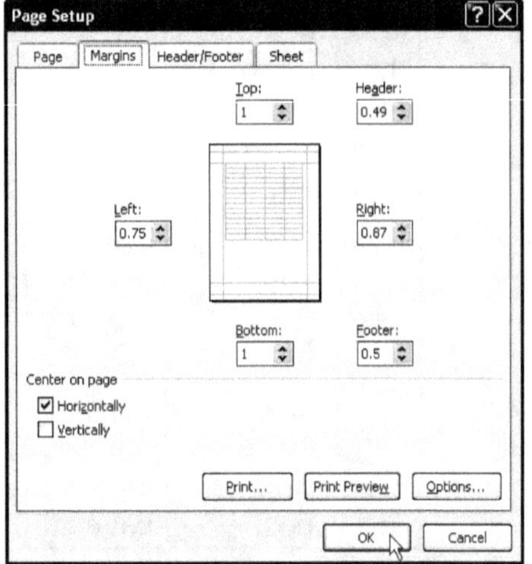

Figure 4.22: *Page Setup dialog box with Margins Tab property sheet*

Set the margins and select the position of headers, footers and print area from the Margins tab in the Page Setup dialog box.

The following options are available:

Option	Function
Top	Gives the distance between the top edge of the page and the data printed on the page.
Left	Gives the distance between the left edge of the page and the data printed on the page.
Right	Gives the distance between the right edge of the page and the data printed on the page.
Bottom	Gives the distance between the bottom edge of the page and the data printed on the page.
Header	Gives the distance between the top of the page and the header.
Footer	Gives the distance between the footer and the bottom of the page.
Center on page	Use this option to center the print area vertically or horizontally between margins.
Horizontally	Choose this option to horizontally center the page.
Vertically	Choose this option to vertically center the page.

Table 4.4: *Available options*

You can preview the worksheet in an area on the dialog box, showing how the margins are set.

Printing a Worksheet

The simplest way to print any opened worksheet is to choose **Print** option from the Backstage view. Alternately, click the **Print Preview** and **Print** button from the **Quick Access toolbar**. In Excel 2013, you can print entire or partial worksheets and workbooks, one at a time or several at once. And if the data that you want to print is in a Microsoft Excel table, you can also print just the Excel table by setting the print area.

You can also print a workbook to a file instead of a printer. This is useful when you need to print the workbook on a different type of printer from the one that you originally used to print it.

To print a spreadsheet, perform the following steps:

1. Open the worksheet that you want to print.

2. Click the **File** tab and then choose the Print

command (*see Figure 4.23*). Alternatively, press the **Ctrl + Shift + F12** keys together.

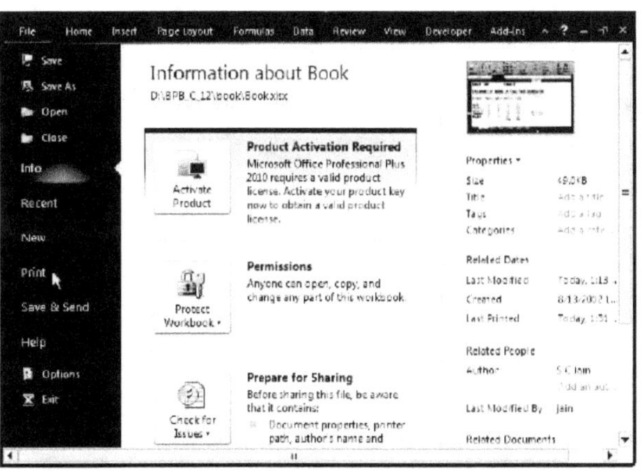

Figure 4.23: *Print command in Backstage view*

3. The Print Backstage view appears. Here, click the **Print** icon.

4. The Print Backstage view closes and in the Status bar, the process of the print job is displayed.

Backstage Print Options are shown in *Figure 4.24*.

Figure 4.24: *Print Options*

The same are described in *Table 4.5* given below:

Option	Function
Print Section: Copies	Specifies the number of copies to be printed.

Printer Section:	This section shows selected printer from a drop-down list, print queue status, type, printer port being used, and whether the printer is busy or idle is also shown below the printer section. Select the desired printer from the Printer drop-down list.
Print to File	Select this option to create a disk file for the selected printer.
Settings	This section shows the Page Setup options, such as page orientation, paper size, and page margins. These options are described below:
• Print what option • Print Active Sheets	Prints only selected worksheet.
• Print Entire Workbook	Prints currently open workbook.
• Print Selection	Prints selected cells.
• Ignore Print Area	Select this option if you want to ignore the print area you have selected.
• Page(s) From:/ To	Select this option to print pages you wish to print.
• Collated	Select this option to collate multiple copies.
Page Orientation	Allows you to change the page orientation, i.e., portrait (vertically) or landscape (horizontally).
Page Size	Allows you to select the paper size.
Margin	Allows you to set the margin of the pages.
Scaling	Allows you to adjust the size of the worksheet.

Table 4.5: *Backstage Print Options*

Printing Sections of a Worksheet or Multiple Worksheets

Suppose you have a year's worth of data accumulated in a given worksheet, but you want to print just one month's worksheet data, then you use this method.

To print a section of a worksheet, perform the following steps:

1. Select the range of cells to print.
2. In the Print Backstage Window, under the Setting section, in the Print what drop-down list, select Print Selection to print the selected cells (*see Figure 4.24*). Excel 2013 ignores any Print Area that has been set and prints the selected range.

To print several worksheets with one command:

1. Select all the sheets (the worksheets must be within the same workbook) you want to print.
2. In the Print Backstage window, under the Setting section, in the Print what drop-down list, select Print Active Sheets.

Manipulation of Cells and Worksheet

The power of Excel lies in storing, manipulating, and displaying data items. Before you can manipulate and display data, you must enter it correctly.

Modifying/Editing Cell Content

While modifying/editing a cell entry, you can edit the text either in the Formula bar or in the cell itself.

Editing Cell Entry in the Formula Bar

To edit cell entry in the formula bar, perform the following steps:

1. Select the cell containing the data you want to edit.
2. Position the pointer in the text where you want to edit, and then click in the formula bar. A flashing insertion point indicates where typing and editing takes place.
3. Edit the cell entry or type new text.

Editing Directly in a Cell

To edit an entry directly in a cell, perform the following steps:

1. Double-click the selected cell or press the *F2* key.
2. Press the arrow keys to move the I-beam that marks the insertion point where you want to edit.

3. Make the desired changes to the cell entry.
4. Press the Enter key to change the text. Alternatively, press the **Esc** key to leave the contents unchanged.

Insert, delete or replace cell contents

To insert characters, click in the cell where you want to insert them, and then type the new characters.

To delete character, click in the cell where you want to delete them, and then press Backspace. Or, select the characters and then press **Delete**.

To replace specific characters, select them and then type the new characters.

To turn on Overtype mode so that existing characters are replaced by new characters while you type, press **Insert**.

To start a new line of text at a specific point in a cell, click in the place where you want to break the line, and then press **Alt + Enter**.

Moving and Copying Cell Contents by Dragging and Dropping

The easiest and most intuitive way to move or copy a cell or range of cells is to drag the cell or the range of cells to the new location and drop it.

How do you move range of cells using drag and drop?

1. Select the cell or range of cells you want to move.
2. Move the mouse pointer over the selection border. The pointer changes to an arrow.
3. Drag the pointer and the gray outline of the selection to the new location. Drag past the edge of a window to make the window scroll. *Figure 4.25* shows the wide gray border that encloses the area to be moved:

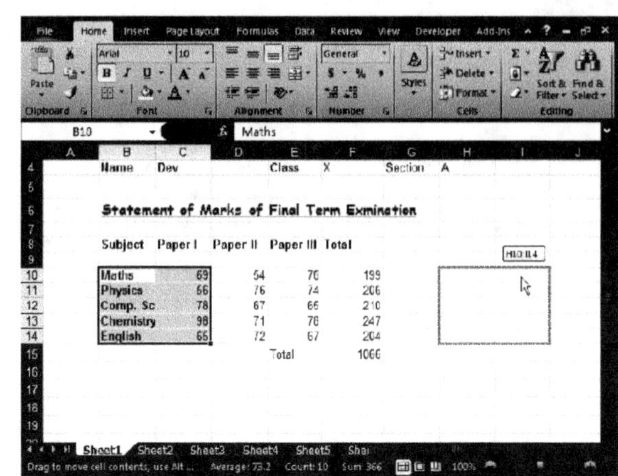

Figure 4.25: *Wide Gray Border Enclosing the area to be moved*

Notice that as you move, you see the range reference where the selection will be pasted.

4. Release the mouse button when the gray outline is placed where you want to place the selected range.

How do you copy range of cells using drag-and-drop?

1. Select the range of cells you want to copy.
2. Hold down the **Ctrl** key and move the pointer over an edge of the selection. The pointer becomes an arrow with a + (plus) sign.
3. Continue holding down the **Ctrl** key as you drag the edge of the selection to the place where you want to copy. The copy location appears to be enclosed by a wide gray border, as shown in *Figure 4.26*:

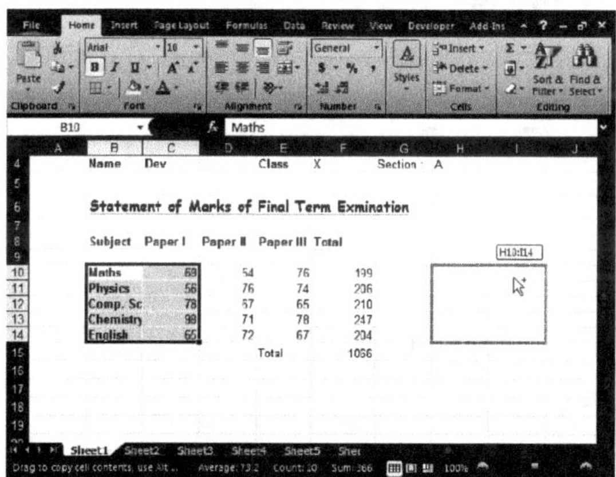

Figure 4.26: *Wide gray Border enclosing the copy location*

Using the drag-and-drop method, you can make only a single copy. You cannot copy to multiple locations.

If you release the **Ctrl** key before you release the mouse button, the copy operation becomes a move operation. The plus sign next to the arrow disappears. You can press the **Ctrl** key again to switch back to copy operation.

Moving and Copying Cells with Ribbon

You can use drag-and-drop technique only when you want to move or copy data between different worksheets, or between panes in a split worksheet.

To move cell contents using the Ribbon command, perform the following steps:

1. Select the cell or range of cells you want to move.
2. Click on the Home Tab and then click the Cut button under the Clipboard group, or press the

Ctrl + X keys together. The cells you selected appear surrounded by a marquee, a moving dashed line. The Office Clipboard can store up to 24 objects from any Office applications as well as from other Windows applications.

3. Select the cell at the upper-left corner, where you want to paste the selected cells.
4. Click the Paste button under the Clipboard group, or press the **Ctrl + V** keys together to paste and retain the copy in memory. Press the **Enter** key to paste only one once.

To copy cell contents using the Ribbon command, perform the following steps:

1. Select the cell or range of cells you want to copy.
2. Click on the Home Tab and then click the Copy button under the Clipboard group, or press the **Ctrl + C** keys together. The cells to copy are surrounded by a marquee, a moving dashed line.
3. Select the cell at the top-left corner, where you want the duplicate to appear. Check to see whether other cell contents will be overwritten.
4. Click the Paste button under the Clipboard group, or press the **Ctrl + V** keys together to paste and retain the copy in memory. Press the **Enter** key to paste only one time.

To copy a picture of the selected cell(s) instead of actual contents, click the down arrow of Copy button and then select Copy as Picture... option as shown below:

Figure 4.27

Filling or Copying Cell Contents with Fill Handle

You can save a great deal of data-entry time with Excel 2013 Copy and Fill commands and the many other shortcuts that copy or fill. Rather than typing each formula in a worksheet, you can type a few formulas and copy or fill them into other cells. You can also copy the formulas and format at the same time.

Using the Fill Handle

If you use a mouse and need to fill data or formulas into adjacent cells, then use the fill handle which is a black square at the lower-right corner of the selected cell or a range of cells. Dragging the fill handle across cells can fill the cells with copies or a series of data items.

To fill adjacent cells, perform the following steps:

1. Select the cell or range of cells that contains the data or formulas.

2. Drag the fill handle so that the wide gray border encloses all cells to fill (*see Figure 4.28*).

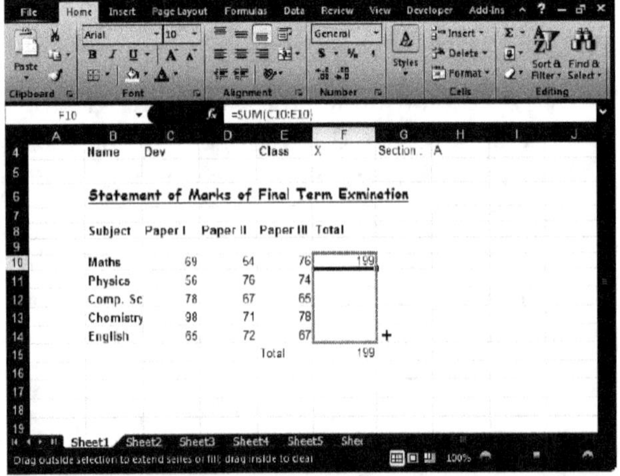

Figure 4.28: *Using Fill Handle*

3. Release the mouse button.

   Filling formulas into an area produces the same result as copying and pasting. Relative reference formulas adjust as though they were copied. Even if the formula references other spreadsheets, appropriate adjustments will automatically be made by Excel 2013.

Formatting Cell (Font, Alignment, Style)

Basic formatting can customize the look and feel of your workbook, allowing you to draw attention to specific sections and making your content easier to view and understand.

Change Font and Font Size

To change the font size, perform the following steps:

1. Select the cell(s) of which you want to change the font size.

2. On the Home tab, click the drop-down arrow next to the Font Size command; then select the desired font size. In our example, we have selected 22 to make the text larger. Hover the mouse pointer over the font size to see the text font size change, as shown in *Figure 4.29*:

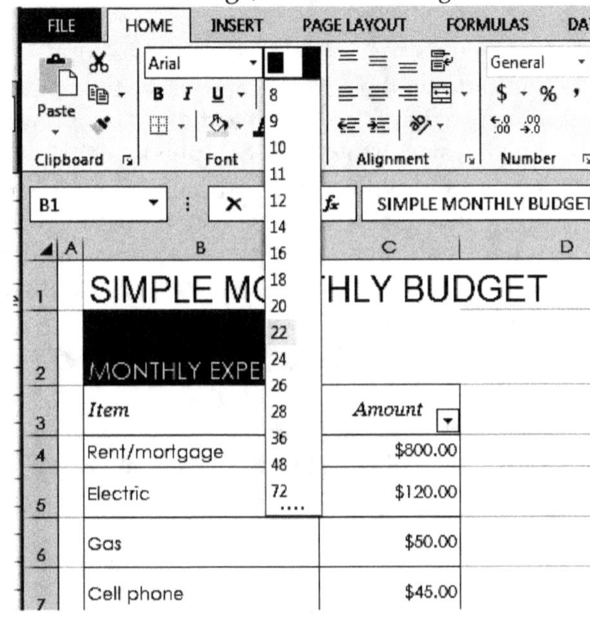

Figure 4.29: *Selecting Font Size*

3. The text will change to the selected font size.

4. You can also use the Increase Font Size and Decrease Font Size commands or enter a custom font size using your keyboard.

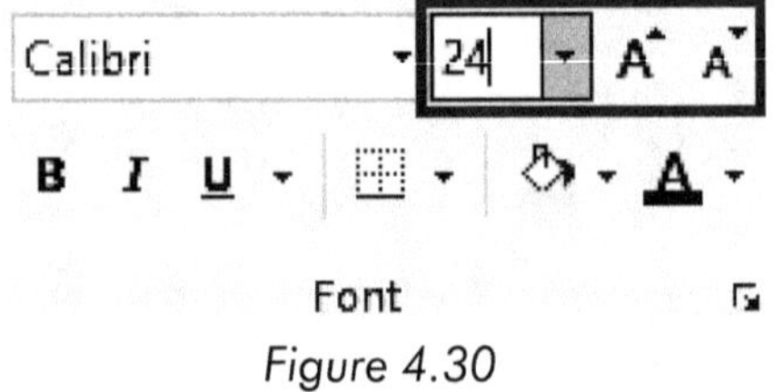

Figure 4.30

To change the font, perform the following steps:

By default, the font of each new workbook is set to Calibri. However, Excel provides many other fonts you can use to customize your cell text.

1. Select the cell(s) of which you want to change the font.

2. On the Home tab, click the drop-down arrow next to the Font command; then select the desired font. In our example, we have chosen Arial font type, as shown in *Figure 4.31*:

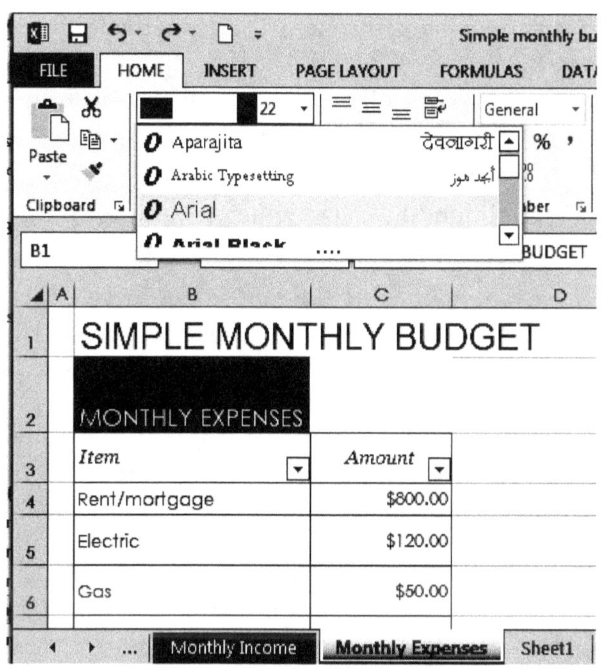

Figure 4.31: *Selecting Font Type*

3. The text will change to the selected font.

Cell Styles

Instead of formatting cells manually, you can use Excel's predesigned cell styles. Cell styles are a quick way to include professional formatting for different parts of your workbook, such as titles and headers. To apply a cell style, perform the following steps:

1. Select the cell(s) of which you want to apply cell style.

2. Click the Cell Styles command on the Home tab in the Styles group; then choose the desired style from the drop-down menu, as shown in *Figure 4.32*:

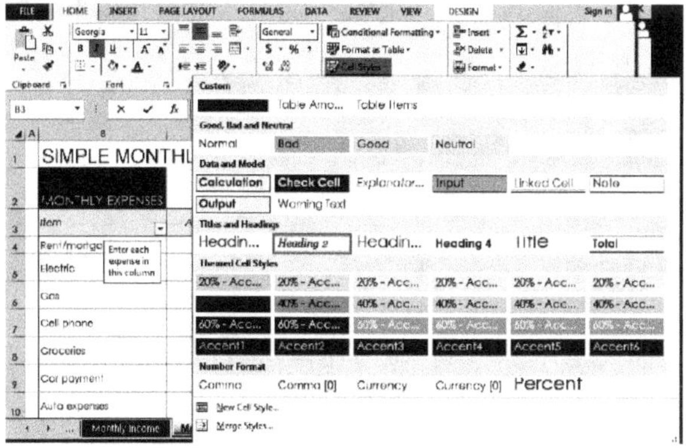

Figure 4.32: *Selecting in-built style in the Styles group*

3. The selected cell style will appear.

4. Applying a cell style will replace any existing cell formatting except for text alignment.

Text Alignment

By default, any text entered into your worksheet will be aligned to the bottom-left of a cell, while any numbers will be aligned to the bottom-right. Changing the alignment of your cell content allows you to choose how the content is displayed in any cell, which can make your cell content easier to read.

To align text using the Ribbon Command, perform the following steps:

1. Select the cell or range of cells containing the contents you want to align.

2. To make horizontal alignment, click the Left, Centre, or Right Align button from the Alignment group under the Home Tab. In our example, we have selected Centre horizontal alignment, as shown in *Figure 4.33*.

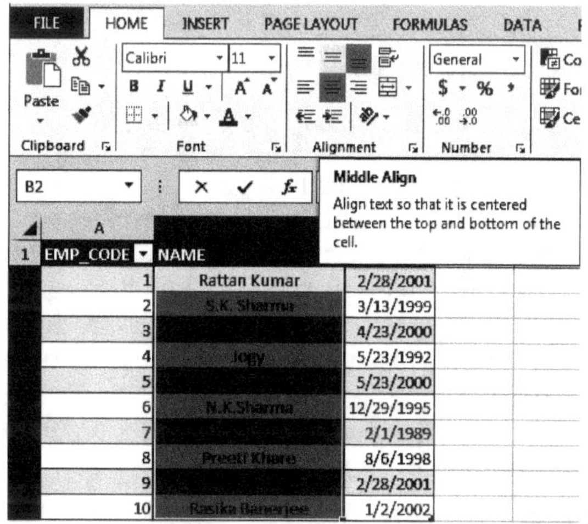

Figure 4.33: *The selected cell aligned Horizontally and Vertically using Ribbon command*

3. To make vertical alignment, click the Top align, Middle align or Bottom align button from the Alignment group under the **Home** Tab. In our example, we have selected the Bottom vertical alignment.

4. To indent the cell contents, click the Increase Indent button. To decrease indent, click **Decrease Indent button**.

Cut, Copy and Paste and Paste Special

You can copy the text content and paste that text content to other cells in a spreadsheet, which can save you time and effort.

To copy and paste cell content, perform the following steps:

1. Highlight the cell(s) you want to copy. In our example, we have selected D4:D6.

2. On the **Home** tab of **Clipboard** group, click the Copy command, or press **Ctrl + C** on the keyboard, as shown in *Figure 4.34*:

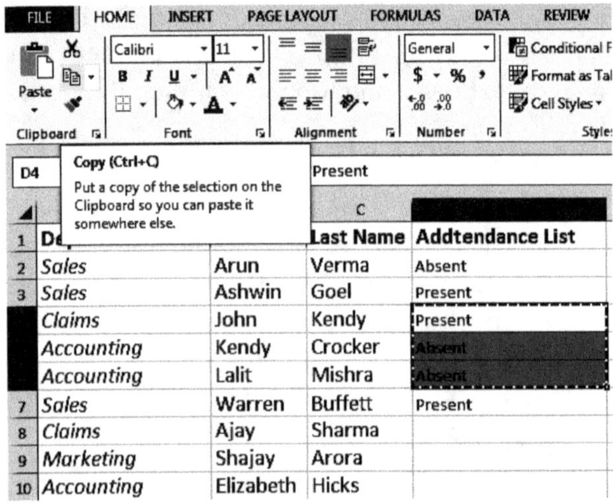

Figure 4.34: *Selecting the Content to Copy*

3. Highlight the cell(s) where you want to paste the content. In our example, we have selected D8:D10. The copied cell(s) will have a rectangular box around them.

4. On the **Home** tab of **Clipboard** group, click the **Paste** command, or press **Ctrl + V** on your keyboard.

5. The selected content will be pasted in the cells, as shown in *Figure 4.35*:

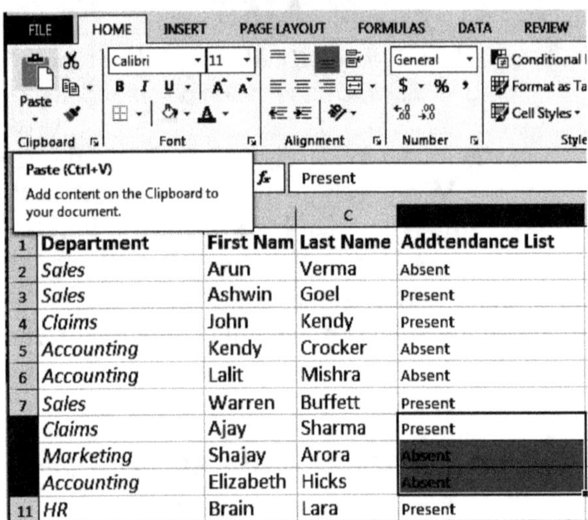

Figure 4.35: *Selected content gets pasted*

To cut and paste cell content, perform the following steps:

Any content of a cell or range of cells in worksheet, you can cut or copy to another cell or to another Worksheet and workbooks by using **Clipboard**.

1. Highlight the cell(s) which you want to cut. In our example, we have selected D9:D10.

2. By right-clicking the mouse on the cell, select the Cut command. Alternatively, press **Ctrl + X** on your keyboard, as shown in *Figure 4.36*:

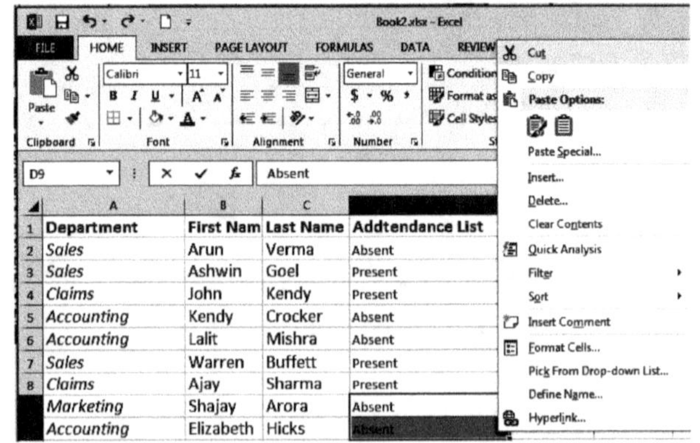

Figure 4.36: *Selecting the content to Cut*

3. Select the destination cells where you want to paste the content. In our example, we have selected **E9:E10**. The cut cells will now have a dashed box around them.

4. The cut portion gets removed from the original cells and pasted into the selected cells, as shown in *Figure 4.37*:

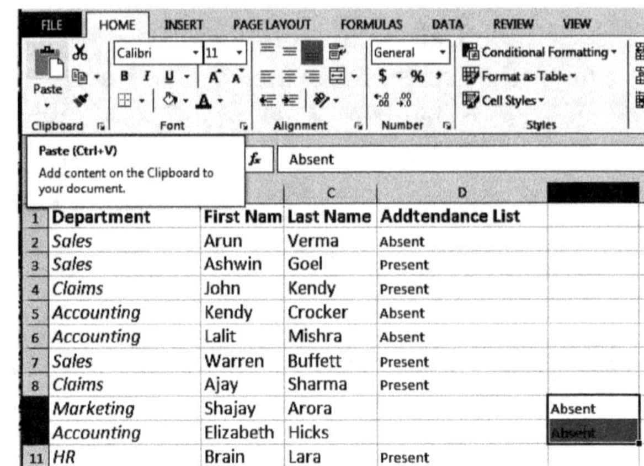

Figure 4.37: *Cut and Paste the content to new selected cell*

Using Paste Special

Paste Special is very useful tool to copy and paste part of a cell's attribute, such as the format or value, but not both. With this command, you can reorient database layouts into worksheet layouts and vice-versa. This command also enables you to combine the attributes of cells by pasting them together.

Tips

Paste button of the **Clipboard** group places the contents of the clipboard where the cursor is. The drop-down arrow of the Paste button is called **Paste Preview** (shown below). It describes various ways to paste data. Point to an option for a description and click to select it:

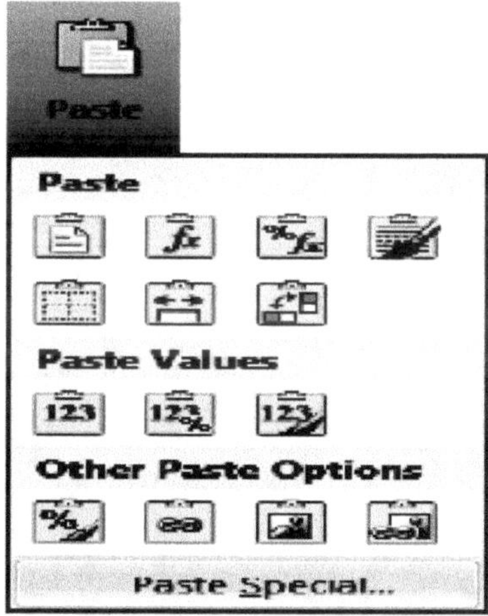

Figure 4.38

To use Paste Special, perform the following steps:

1. Select the cell or range of cells.
2. Click on the **Home** Tab and then click the **Copy** button under the **Clipboard** group, or press the **Ctrl + C** keys together.
3. Select the upper-left corner of the worksheet where you want to paste. While transporting (flipping) rows and columns, be sure to consider which cells are covered when the pasted area is rotated **90** degrees.
4. Click the arrow next to the **Paste** button under the **Clipboard** group, and then select **Paste Special**... to display the Paste Special dialog box (*see Figure 4.39*).

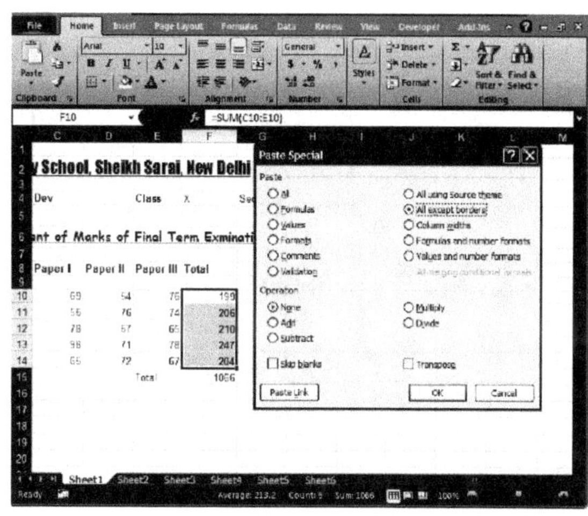

Figure 4.39: Paste Special dialog box

5. Select the ways in which you want data to be transferred, as explained in the *Table 4.6*:

Option	Function
All	Paste all the original contents and characteristics.
Formulas	Paste only the formulas.
Values	Paste only the values and formula results.
Formats	Paste only the cell formats.
Comments	Paste only note contents.
Validation	Paste data validation rules.
All using Source theme	Paste all cell contents and formatting using the theme.
All except borders	Paste everything except any borders applied to the selected range.
Column widths	Paste the width of one column to another.
Formulas and number formats	Paste formulas but not values with their number format.
Values and number formats	Paste only values with their number format.

Table 4.6: Paste Special options and their functions

6. Select from the dialog box how you want the transferred characteristics or information combined with the cells being pasted into.

Table 4.7 gives the different Paste Special Operations:

Option	Function
None	Replaces the receiving cell.
Add	Adds to the receiving cell into which they are being pasted.
Subtract	Subtracts from the receiving cell into which they are being pasted.
Multiply	Multiplies by the receiving cell into which they are being pasted.

Table 4.7: *Different Paste Special Operations*

7. Select the Skip blanks checkbox if you do not want to paste blank cells which you have selected when you copy a range.

8. Select the Transpose checkbox to change rows to columns or to change columns to rows.

9. Click **OK**.

Inserting and Deleting Rows, Columns

With Excel 2013, you can delete or insert entire rows or columns. You can also easily delete or insert cells, leaving the surrounding rows and columns unaffected. This technique enables you to add or remove cells without having to change entire rows or columns.

Inserting Cells, Rows, or Columns

If you need to add new data within the existing worksheet, you can insert cells, rows, or columns in the worksheet. You can insert blank cells above or below, left or right of the selected cell on a worksheet.

To insert cells, perform the following steps:

1. Highlight a cell or range of cells where you want to insert a new blank cells.

2. Click the drop-down arrow to Insert Cells... option from Cells group of the Home tab. Alternatively, press the **Ctrl + +** (plus) keys together, or by right-clicking the mouse button, select Insert.... The Insert dialog box appears, as shown in *Figure 4.40*:

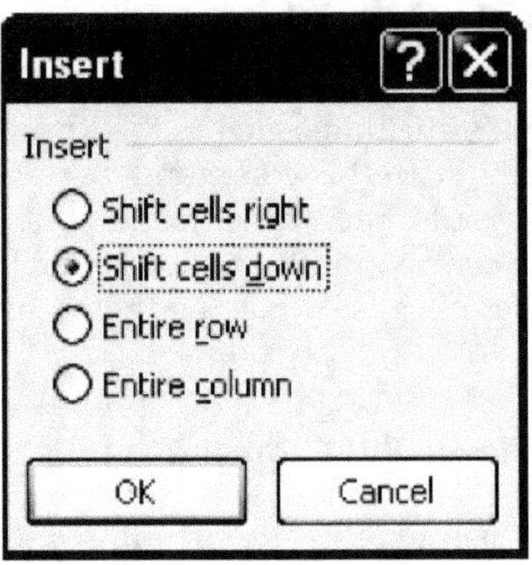

Figure 4.40: *Insert dialog box*

3. To insert cells, select the direction in which you want selected cells to be inserted.

The various options to insert cells are summarized in the table given below:

Option	Function
Shift cells right	Selected cells move right.
Shift cells down	Selected cells move down.
Entire row	Insert a row at each selected cell.
Entire column	Insert a column at each selected cell.

Table 4.8

4. Click **OK**.

To insert rows or columns, perform the following steps:

1. Highlight the cells where you want to insert new sheet rows or columns.

2. To insert new sheet rows, click **Insert Sheet Rows** from **Insert** drop-down list from the Cells group of the **Home** tab.

3. To insert new columns, click **Insert Sheet Columns** from the Insert drop-down list of the Cells group of the **Home** tab.

Deleting Cells, Rows or Columns

The **Delete** command removes cells, rows, or columns from the worksheet. It is different from the Clear command in the **Editing** group. The Clear command removes a cell's contents, formatting, or comments, but it leaves the cell intact.

To delete cells, rows or coumns, perform the following steps:

1. Highlight the cells or range of cells to be deleted, or select cells in the rows and columns to be deleted.

2. On the **Home** Tab, click the Delete drop-down in the **Cells** group. Then select Delete Cells..., as shown in *Figure 4.41*, or press the **Ctrl + –** (minus) keys together, or by right-clicking the mouse button to select the **Delete...** option.

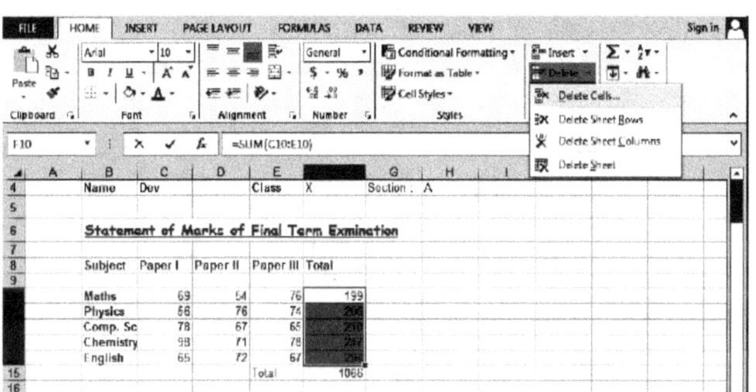

Figure 4.41: Selected Group of Cells

The Delete dialog box appears (*see Figure 4.42*):

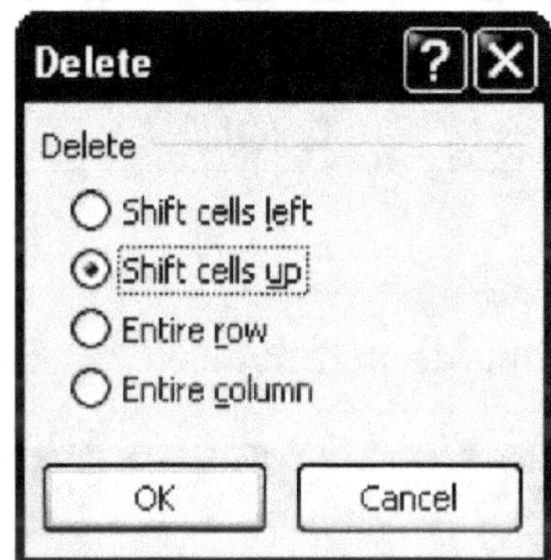

Figure 4.42: Delete dialog box

3. To delete cells, select the direction in which you want remaining cells to move. The following table explains every option:

Option	Description
Shift cells left	Cells to the right of the deleted cells move left.
Shift cells up	Cells below the deleted cells move up.
Entire row	Deletes entire row containing the selected cell.
Entire column	Deletes entire column containing the selected cell.

Table 4.9

4. Click **OK**.

Clearing, Inserting or Deleting Cells in a Worksheet

After you have drafted and tested the worksheet, you may find that you need to reorganize or restructure the layout of the worksheet. When you restructure, you may need to insert or delete cells, rows or columns.

Shortcut keys that are very helpful in reorganizing the worksheet layout are given in *Table 4.10*:

key(s)	Action
Del	Clears selected formulas or contents; same as the Home Tab > Editing Group > Clear Contents.
Backspace	Clears the Formula bar; activates and clears the Formula bar contents.
Ctrl + C	Copies the selection so that it can be pasted; same as the Home Tab > Clipboard Group > Copy Command.
Ctrl + X	Cuts the selection so it can be pasted; same as the Home Tab > Clipboard Group > Cut Command.
Ctrl + V	Paste at the selected cell; same as the Home Tab > Clipboard Group > Paste Command.
Ctrl + Z	Undoes the last command.
Ctrl + Backspace	Repositions the worksheet so that the active cell is in view.

Table 4.10: Shortcut Keys for Changing the Worksheet Layout

Changing Cell Height and Width

In order to improve the appearance of a worksheet or table in it, you can adjust columns width and row height. Thus, you can fit more data on a page. If need be, you can even hide confidential data.

How to Adjust Column Width?

You can adjust the width of one or more columns to improve the appearance of a worksheet. If a column is not wide enough to display a number, date, or time, Excel 2013 displays it using # characters in the cell. Therefore, you may need to adjust column width to show complete information.

Example 5: Describe the ways by which you can adjust column width.

Solution: To adjust column width with mouse, perform the following steps:

1. Select the columns of which you need to change the width.

2. Move the pointer onto the column separator to the right of the column heading (*see Figure 4.43*). Pointer changes to a two-headed, horizontal arrow.

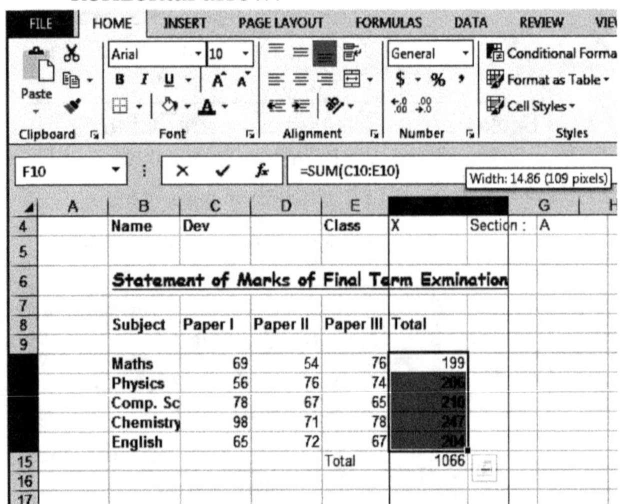

Figure 4.43: *Changing Column Width with Mouse*

3. Drag the column left or right until the column is of the required width. Then release the mouse button. The Width box appears as you drag the column, displaying the numeric value for the column width.

To adjust column width using Ribbon, perform the following steps:

1. Select the columns of which you want to change the width.

2. Under **Home** tab, click **Cells** group, and then click the arrow next to Format. It pops up the menu (*see Figure 4.44*):

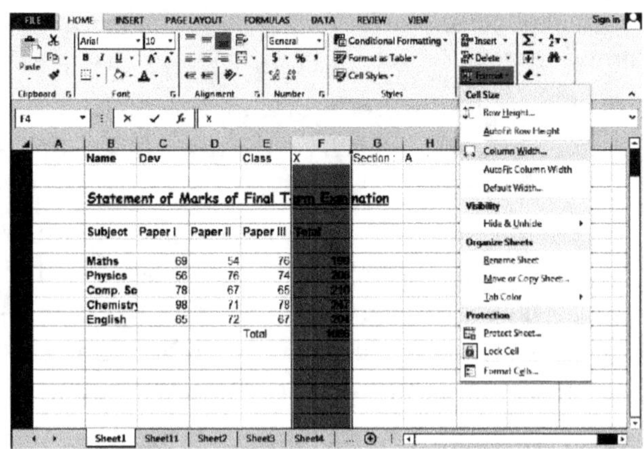

Figure 4.44: *Format Column option*

3. Use one of the following options to adjust column width:

Option	Description
Column Width...	The Column Width dialog box appears (See Figure 4.45). Type the width, and then click OK.
AutoFit Selection	This option adjusts the column width automatically.
Default Width...	This option would the default column width for all the selected columns.

Table 4.11

4. Enter the desired number and click the **OK** button.

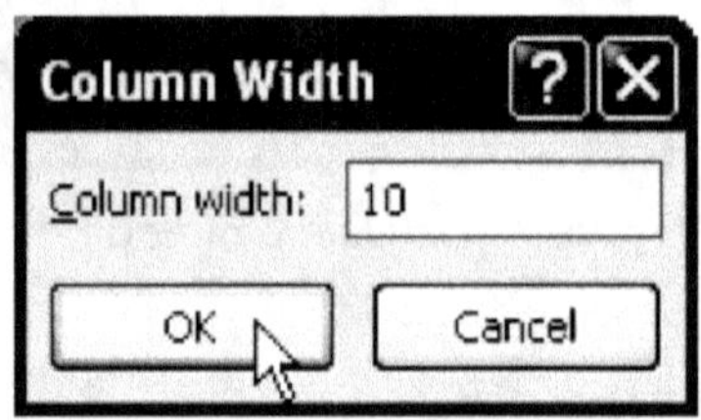

Figure 4.45: *Column Width dialog box*

How to Adjust Row Height?

You can adjust row height in a worksheet to create enough space for titles, subtotals, grand totals, and so on.

Example 6: How would you adjust row height?

a) Using mouse

b) Ribbon

Solution: a.

1. Select the rows of which you want to change the height.

2. Move the mouse pointer to the line directly under the header of the row you want to change. The mouse pointer changes to a two-headed vertical arrow (*see Figure 4.46*).

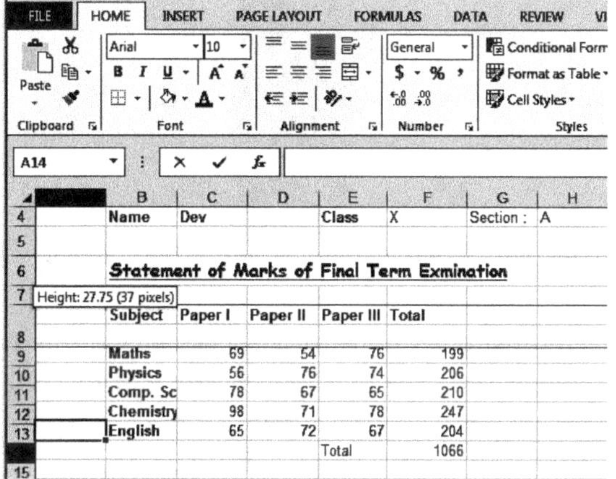

Figure 4.46: *Changing Row Height with Mouse*

3. Drag the two-headed arrow pointer up or down until the row is of the required height. Then release the mouse button. The screen tip displays the numeric value for the row height.

Solution: b.

1. Select the cell in each row of which you want to change the height.

2. Under Home tab, click Cells group, and then click the arrow next to Format. It appears with a list of options (*see Figure 4.44*).

3. Click one of the following options:

Option	Description
Row Height...	Displays the Row Height dialog box. Here, type the row height, and click OK (See Figure 4.47).
AutoFit Row Height	This option adjusts row height automatically.

Table 4.12

4. Click on **OK**.

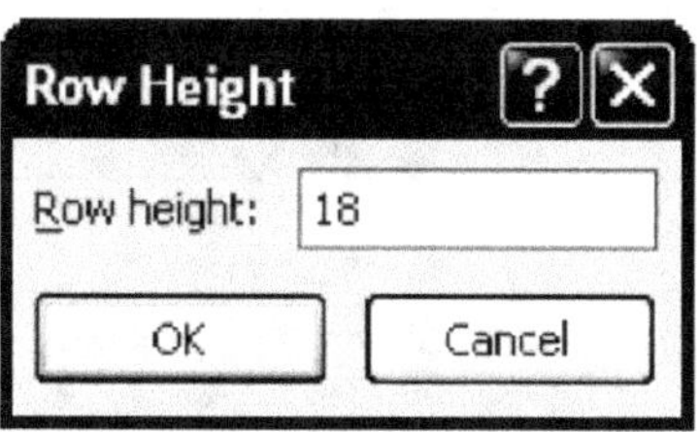

Figure 4.47: *Row Height dialog box*

4.3.6 AutoFill

Excel 2013 makes it very easy to enter a series of dates, number or text. For example, you can insert a column heading like Jan, Feb, Mar, and so on, or enter a number at equal intervals, such as 2, 4, 6, 8, and so on, very easily.

You can enter the above type of series in two ways:

1. Using the mouse to drag the fill handle.

2. Using a command that gives you the capability to create many types of series.

Example 7: Create a number series with the help of *Fill Series* dialog box.

Solution:

1. Enter the two numbers in the starting cells.

2. For a series like 2,2,2,2.., drag the fill handle as shown in *Figure 4.48*.

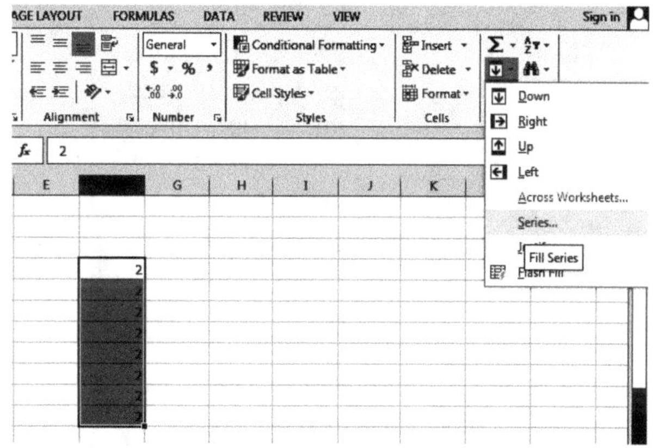

Figure 4.48: *Enter the number in a cell*

To fill series through the Series dialog box, perform the following steps:

1. Click on **Home** tab. In the **Editing** group, click on the **Fill drop-down** list, and then choose **Series...** to display the Series dialog box (*see Figure 4.49*):

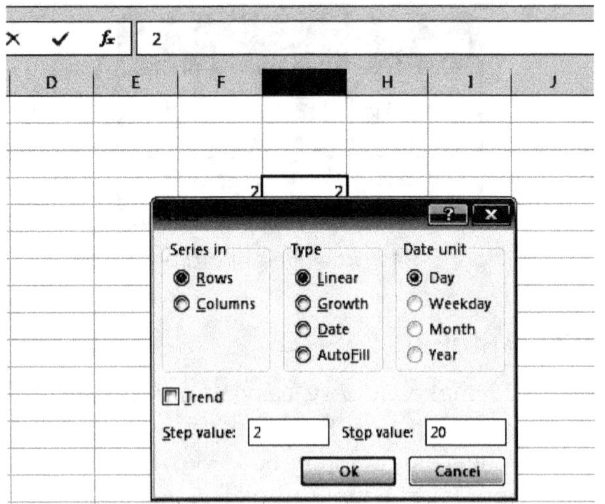

Figure 4.49: *Series dialog box*

2. Select one of the following Type options:

Option	Description
Linear	Adds the Step Value to the preceding number in the series.
Growth	Multiplies the Step Value by the preceding number in the series.
Date	Enables the Date Unit group so that the increment applies to a Day, Weekday, Month, or Year.
AutoFill	Creates automatic series that may include text, dates and labels.

Table 4.13

3. In the Step value: box enter the step value. This number is the constant amount by which the series changes from cell to cell. The Step Value may be positive or negative.
4. In the Stop value: box enter a value at which you want to stop the fill. This is required only if you think that you highlighted too many cells when you selected the range to fill.
5. Click **OK**. The series gets filled automatically, as shown in *Figure 4.50*:

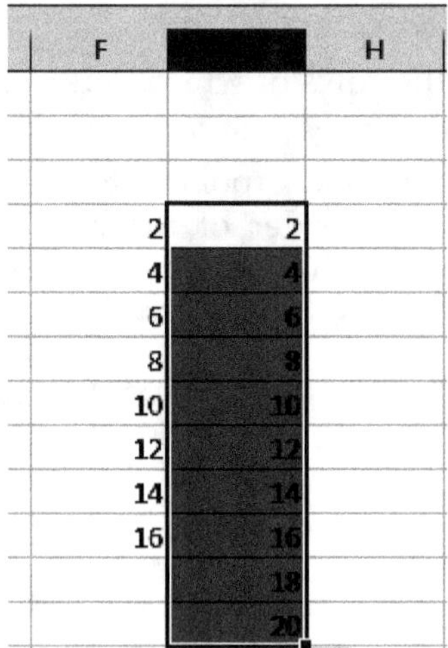

Figure 4.50: *The series filled automatically*

To create Date Series, perform the following steps:

1. Enter the starting date and format the cell.
2. Hover the mouse over the lower-right corner of the cell until you see the **Fill handle**.
3. With the Right mouse button pressed, drag to select the cells to use autofill options, as shown in *Figure 4.51*:

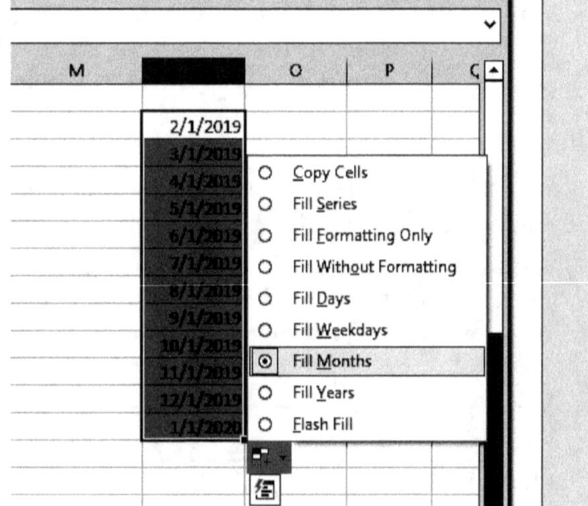

Figure 4.48: *Using the AutoFill options to select the Fill Months*

4. Release the mouse button and select Fill Months from the menu that is displayed, as shown in *Figure 4.51*.

Sorting and Filtering

In Excel, you can perform sorting data alphabetically from smallest to largest or largest to smallest.

1. Select a cell or column by which you want to sort data. For example, we have selected column as First Name, as shown in *Figure 4.52*.

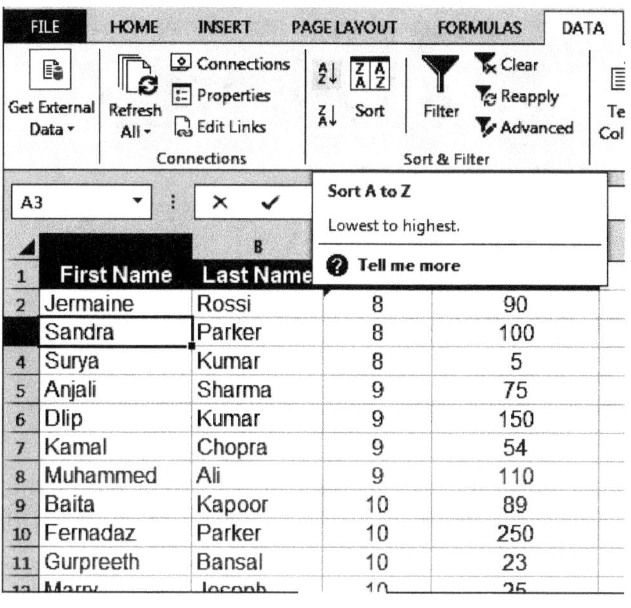

Figure 4.52: *Selecting Sort command*

2. Click on the **Data** tab in the **Sort & Filter** group, then choose the desired option, that is, **A-Z** command or the Z-A command. We have selected **A to Z**.

3. The worksheet gets sorted alphabetically by the selected column, that is, First Name in ascending order, as shown in *Figure 4.53*:

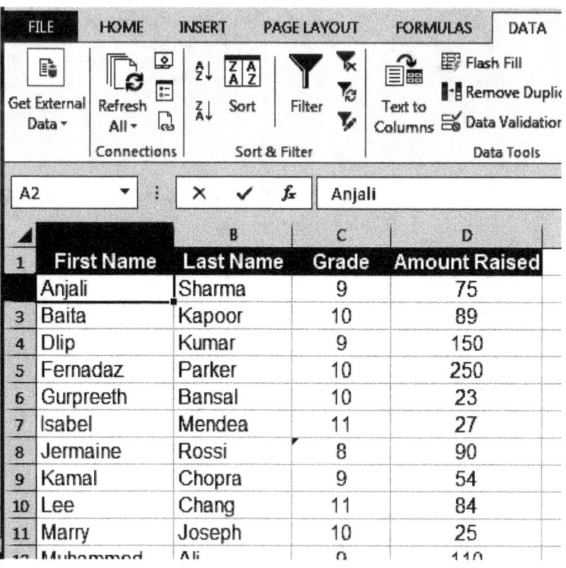

Figure 4.53: *The selected column gets sorted*

alphabetically

If you click a single cell, Excel will select all the surrounding data and sort the rows of continuous data into the required order.

4. If want to sort data additionally more than one more columns, click the Sort command to open Sort dialog box. The Sort dialog box appears as shown in *Figure 4.54*:

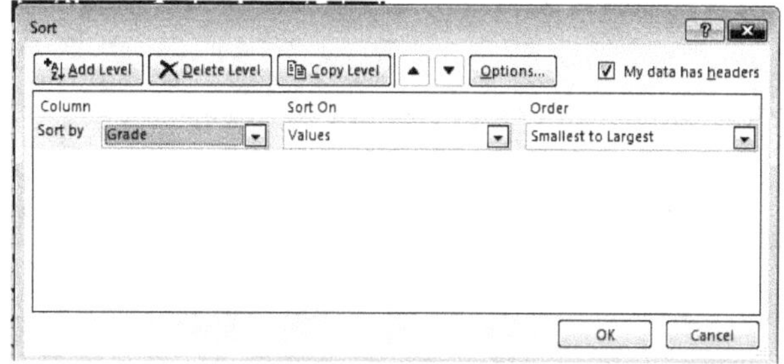

Figure 4.54: *Sort dialog box*

5. Under the Column section, click the **Sort** by drop-down list and choose the column you want to **Sort** by. In our example, we chose the Grade option.

6. Under the Order drop-down list, select Smallest to Largest.

7. Once you are satisfied with the selection, click the **OK** button.

8. The selected Grade column is sorted in Smallest to Largest order, as shown in *Figure 4.55*:

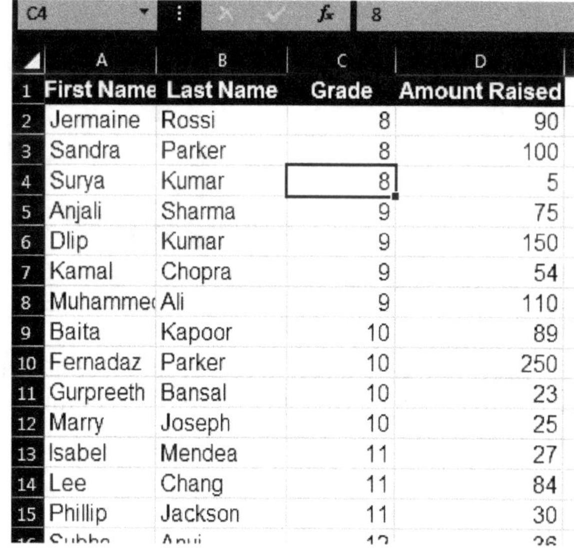

Figure 4.55: *Grade column sorted smallest to largest*

Filters

You can filter the data to hide entries that are not of immediate interest.

1. Click a cell; select the **Data** tab, and click the **Filter** command in the **Sort & Filter** group, as shown in *Figure 4.56*:

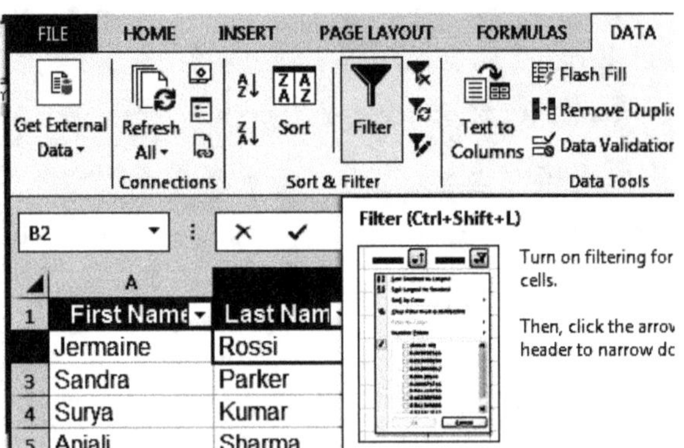

Figure 4.56: *Selecting the Filter command*

2. Click a filter icon, for example, "Last Name", to display its **AutoFilter**.

3. Uncheck the Select All box to deselect all entries, then select the specific entry you want, for example, check "Kumar", as shown in *Figure 4.57*:

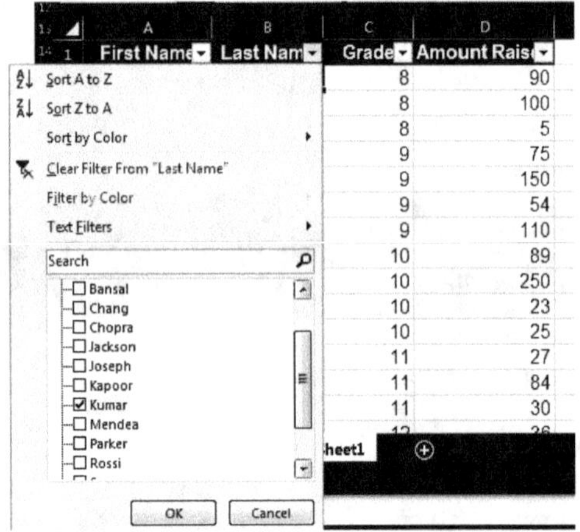

Figure 4.57: *Selecting the Filter by Last Name*

4. Click **OK** to apply the filter. Filter is displayed by Last Name, as shown in the following image:

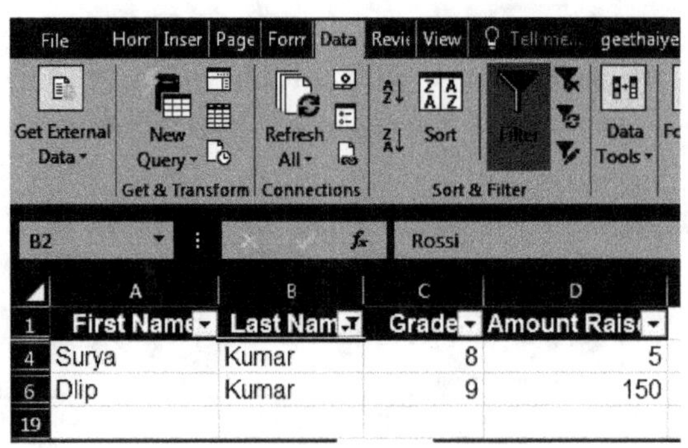

Figure 4.58

Number Filters

You can apply number filters to columns which contain values to hide unwanted value temporarily.

1. On the **Data** tab, click the **Filter** command in the **Sort & Filter** group. A drop-down arrow will appear in the header cell, as shown in *Figure 4.59*:

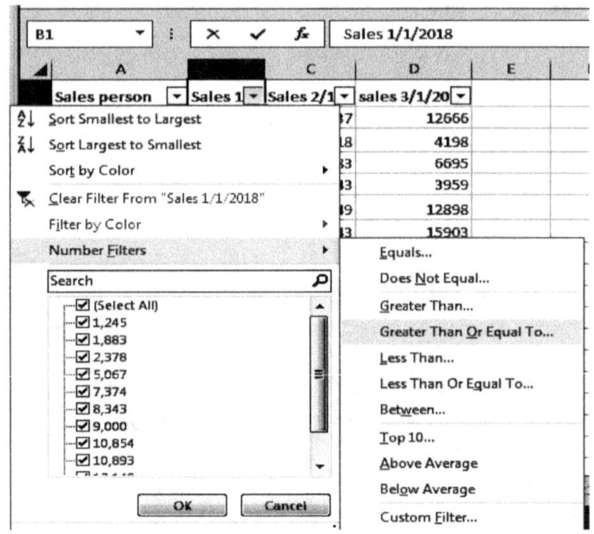

Figure 4.59: *Selecting Number filters from Filter drop-down menu*

2. Select the desired column you want to filter. In our example, we have selected column B.

3. Point to choose the Number Filters, and then select the desired number filter from the drop-down menu. In our example, we have chosen the Greater Than Or Equal To option to view sales of Jan-18 between a specific number range, as shown in *Figure 4.59*.

4. The Custom AutoFilter dialog box appears as shown in *Figure 4.60*. Enter the desired number(s) to the right of each filter, and then click **OK**. In our example, we want to filter the

sales of *Jan-18*, that is, number(s) greater than or equal to 10,000 range.

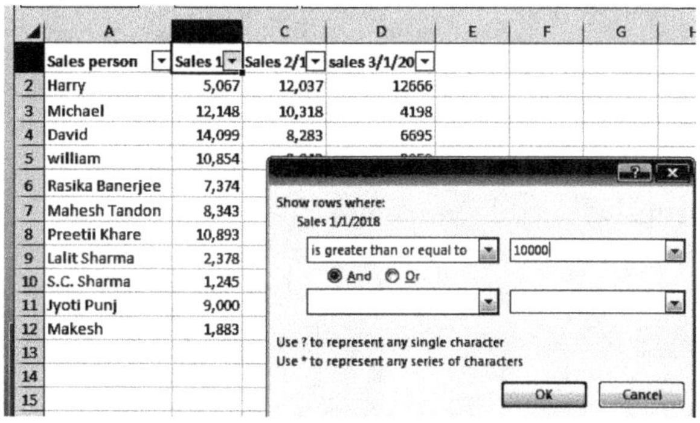

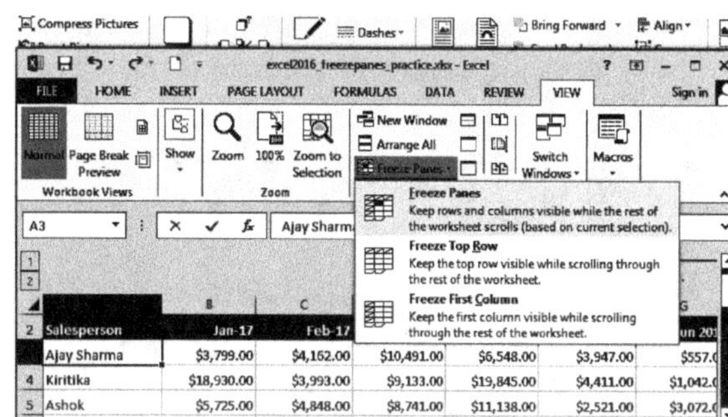

Figure 4.60: *Custom AutoFilter dialog box*

5. The data will be filtered by the selected number filter, as shown in *Figure 4.61*:

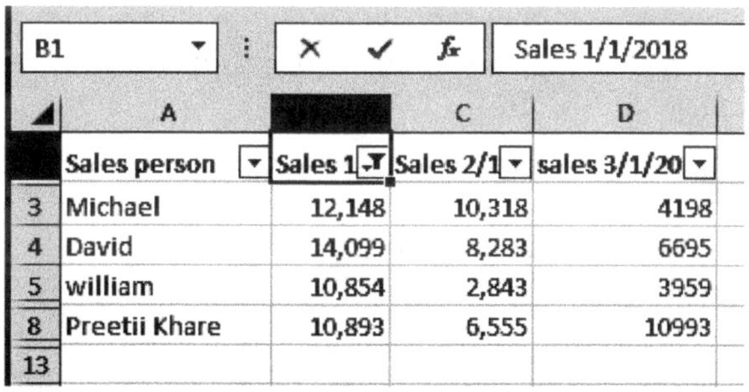

Figure 4.61: *Displaying the Selected Records*

Freezing Panes

When you are working in Excel, you have huge amounts of data on your worksheet; it can be difficult to compare one or more rows with others that are towards the bottom of the workbook. Excel's freeze panes feature solves this problem by letting you lock certain rows so that you can see all the rows when you scroll.

To freeze rows, perform the following steps:

1. Select the row right below the row or rows you want to freeze. In our example, we want to freeze rows 1 and 2, so we have selected row 3.

2. Click the **View** tab, select the **Freeze Panes** option in the **Window** group. Then choose Freeze Panes from the drop-down menu, as shown in *Figure 4.62*:

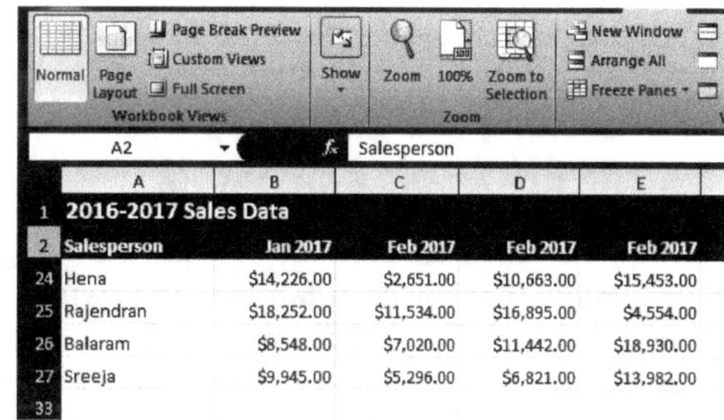

Figure 4.62: *Selecting Freeze Panes*

3. Select Freeze Top Row to keep the top row visible while scrolling through the rest of the worksheet.

4. The rows will be frozen in place as indicated by the gray line. You can scroll down the worksheet while continuing to view the frozen rows at the top. In our example, we have scrolled down to row 27, as shown in *Figure 4.63*:

Figure 4.63: *Freezing Top Row and scrolling down to row 27*

To freeze columns, perform the following steps:

1. Click the column to the right of the column or columns you want to freeze. In our example, we want to freeze column *A*, so we have selected column *B*.

2. Click the **View** tab, select the **Freeze Panes** option in the **Window** group. Then choose Freeze First Column from the drop-down menu, as shown in *Figure 4.64*:

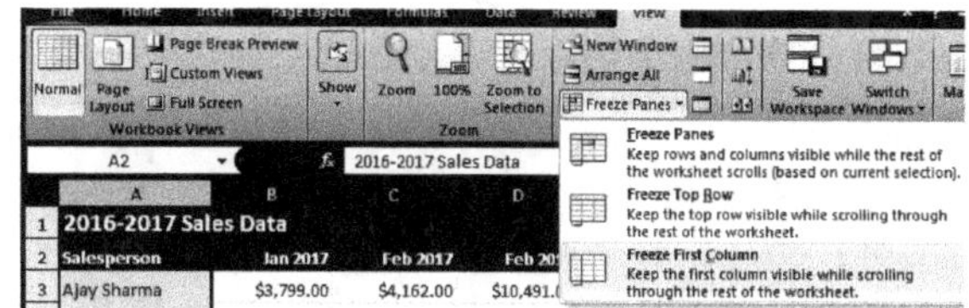

Figure 4.64: *Selecting Freeze First Column*

3. The selected column gets frozen in place as showed by the gray line. You can scroll across the worksheet while continuing to view the

frozen column on the left. In our example, we have scrolled across to column K, as shown in *Figure 4.65*:

Figure 4.65: *The First column gets frozen and the worksheet scrolled across to column K*

To unfreeze panes, perform the following steps:
1. To **unfreeze rows** or **columns**, click the **Freeze Panes** command, and then select **Unfreeze Panes** from the drop-down menu.

Formulas, Functions and Charts

In Excel, you can enter formula and functions and perform mathematical calculations. You will also be able to create charts and graphics using the data. You can specify mathematical relationships between the numbers using the formula. Formulas are used for simple addition, subtraction, multiplication and division, as well as for complex calculations. Functions are inbuilt in formulas. The users have to provide cell references and addresses only. These are called arguments of the functions and are given in parentheses, that is, () after the function name.

Using Formulas for Numbers (Addition, Subtraction, Multiplication and Division)

Creating Formula

A formula is entered into a cell. It performs calculations of some type or returns a result, which is displayed in the cell. It always begins with an equal to sign (=) and can include the following types of data items:
- Bumeric and text values (constants).
- Arithmetic operator, comparison operators (<,=>) text operators (&), functions (SUM), parentheses.

- Cell references and names.

By combining these components, you can calculate the result you want by using the information in the worksheet. Excel also gives you the option to display formulas on worksheet, or the results of the formulas.

In Excel, 2013 the formulas are available in the **Formulas** tab. If you click the Formulas tab, you can see the corresponding ribbon displaying the available formulas, as shown in *Figure 4.66*:

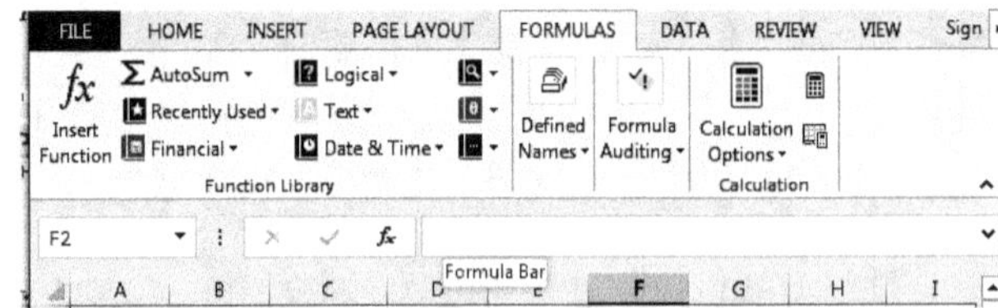

Figure 4.66: *Showing Formulas tab and Formula bar*

In the following example, we use simple addition to display the solution:

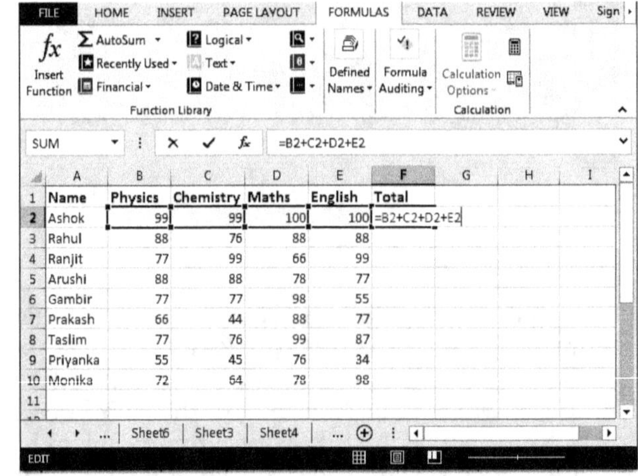

Figure 4.67

Here, for addition, we have typed = B2+C2+D2+E2 in the cell *F2*. It will return sum of the marks in Physics, Chemistry, Maths and English, that is, total marks of one individual person.

Copying a formula

In the above example, just drag the handle column down to cover the remaining cells in the Total column. This will automatically copy the formula and calculate the corresponding sum of the respective rows of the other students, as shown in *Figure 4.68*:

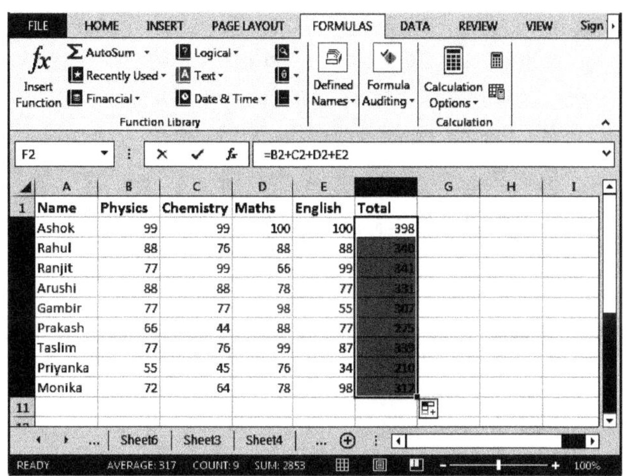

Figure 4.68: *Dragging the handle to copy a formula*

Examples of formulas such as Addition, Multiplication, Subtraction and Division are shown in *Figure 4.69*:

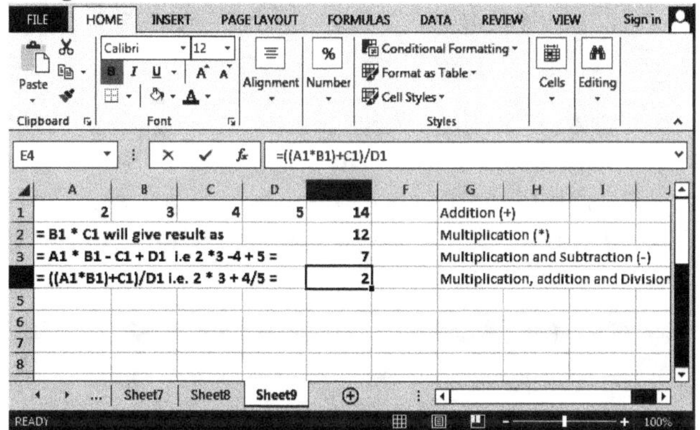

Figure 4.69: *Showing different formulas Addition, Multiplication, Subtraction and Division*

Display the use of arithmetic operators shown in the *Table 4.8.*

Operator	Formula	Result	Type of Operation
+	=5+2	7	Addition of 5 with 2
–	=5-2	3	Subtraction of 2 from 5
–	–5	5	Negation (negative of the umber)
	=52	10	Multiplication of 5 with 2
/	=5/2	2.5	Division of 5 by 2
%	5%	.05	Percentage

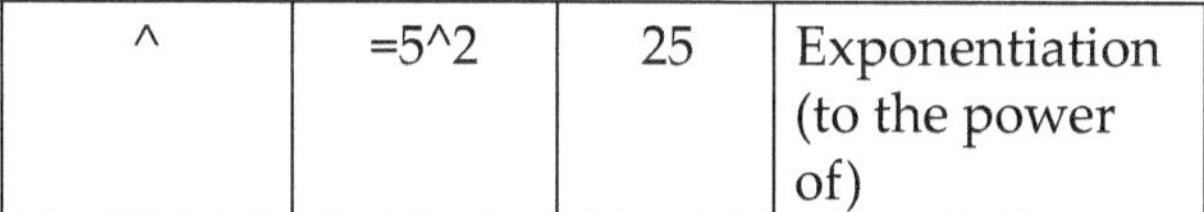

^	=5^2	25	Exponentiation (to the power of)

Table 4.14: *Arithmetic Operator*

For example, if A1 = 2, B1 = 3, C1 = 4, and D1 = 5 then

   (i)   = A1 + B1 + C1 + D1 = 14

   (ii)   = A1 B1 will give result as 2 3 = 6

   (iii)   = A1 B1 - C1 + D1 will give result as 2 3 - 4 + 5 = 7

   (iv)   = ((A1 B1) + C1)/D1 will give result as ((2 3) + 4)/5

        = (6 + 4)/5 = 10/5 = 2

AutoSum Feature

The AutoSum feature makes it very easy to total rows and columns using the SUM worksheet function. There is a special command button on the standard toolbar.

To use AutoSum in Excel, perform the following steps:

1. Select a cell in which you want the sum.

2. Click the **Formulas** tab to select the **AutoSum** button. In the **Function Library** group, click the **AutoSum** drop-down arrow to select the Sum option, as shown in *Figure 4.70*. Alternatively, press the **Atl + =** sign keys together.

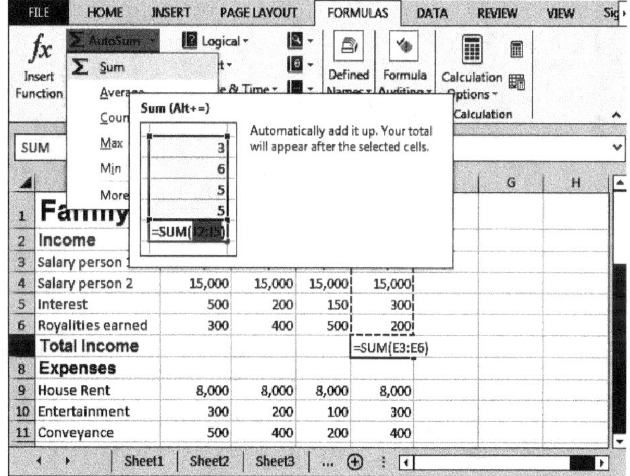

Figure 4.70: *Selecting Sum in the Formulas Tab*

3. Excel will automatically find the range of data in the column where you clicked and create a SUM formula that will add up those cells.

4. Press Enter. Alternatively, you can write = SUM(E3:E6) in the cell *E7*.

Functions (Sum, Count, MAX, MIN, AVERAGE)

SUM()

To add several ranges, simply refer to each of them, separated by a comma, using the SUM function. It adds all the numbers in a range of cells.

Syntax:

SUM(number1,number2,...)

To add several ranges, perform the following steps:

1. In cells **A20:A26**, enter prices from Re. 1 to Rs. 100.
2. Select cells **B20:B26** and type the formula = A208% to calculate the tax amount.
3. Press the **Ctrl + Enter** keys together.
4. In cells **C20:C26**, type some discount values from -1 to -3.
5. In cell **C28**, add all three columns with the following function (*see Figure 4.66*):

   =SUM(A20:A26, B20:B26,C20:C26)

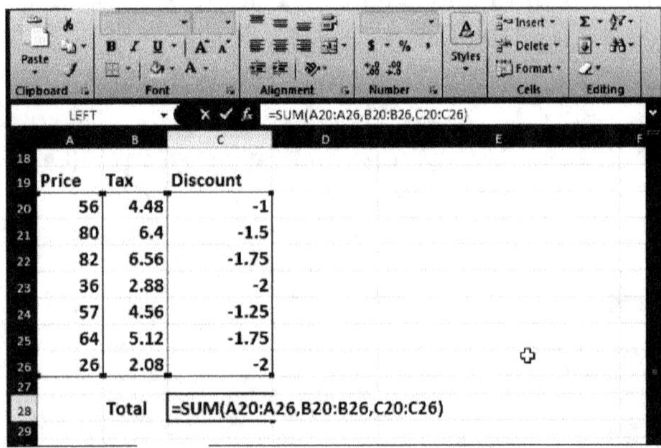

Figure 4.71: *Entering Sum function for several ranges*

6. Press the **Enter** key.

Count()

Count function counts the number of cells that contain numbers within the list of arguments. In other words, it returns the count of values that are numbers, generally cells that contain numbers. Values can be supplied as constants, cell references, or ranges. The syntax is COUNT(value1, value2,....).

To use the COUNT function, perform the following steps:

1. Select the cell that contains the function. In our example, we have selected cell *A12,* as shown in *Figure 4.67.*
2. Click the **Formulas** tab on the **Ribbon** to access the Function Library.

3. Click the Recently Used drop-down arrow to select the COUNT function, which will count the number of cells in the column that contain numbers, as shown in *Figure 4.72*.

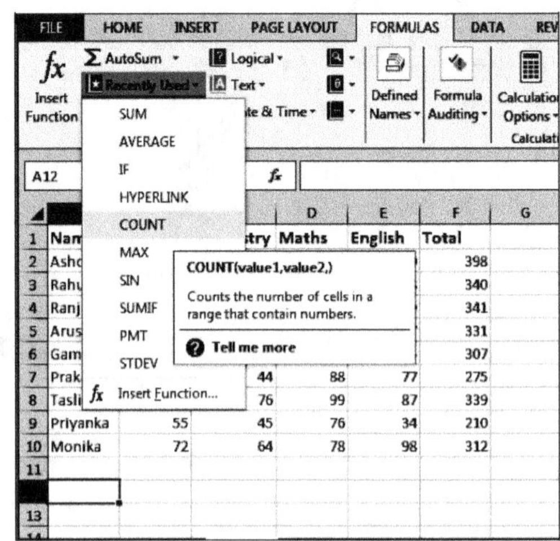

Figure 4.72: *Select the COUNT function in the Formulas tab*

4. The Function Arguments dialog box will appear as shown in *Figure 4.73*. Select the Value1 field, and then enter or select the desired cells. In our example, we have entered the cell range *A3:E3*.

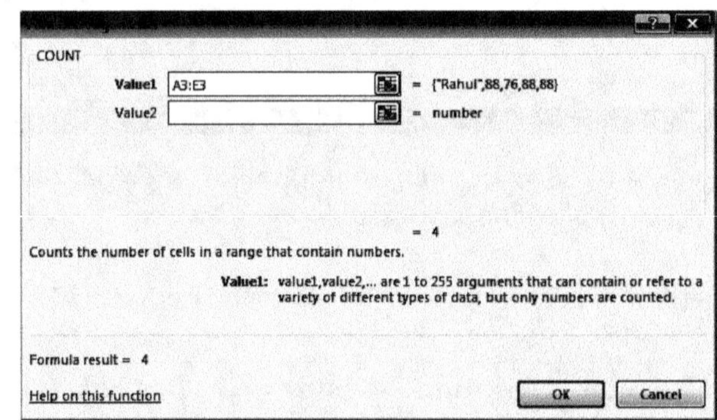

Figure 4.73: *Function Arguments dialog box*

5. Click **OK**.
6. The function will be performed, and the result will appear in the cell. In our example, the result shows a total of 4.

MAX()

Max function returns the largest value in a set of values stored in a cell. The syntax MAX(number1,number2,...). Maximum number of argument can be 255 that is, number1, number2,... number255.

To use the MAX function, perform the following steps:

1. Select the cell that contains the function. In our example, we have selected cell *G2*, as shown in *Figure 4.74*:

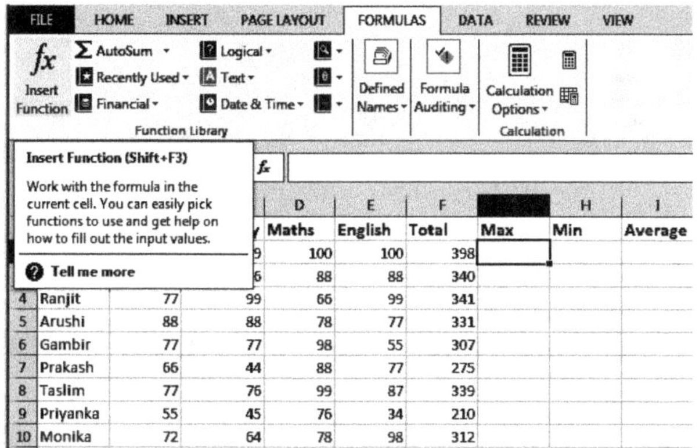

Figure 4.74: *Selecting Insert Function from the Formulas tab*

2. Click the **Formulas** tab on the Ribbon to access the Function Library.
3. Click Insert Function. Alternatively, press the *Shift + F3* keys together.
4. The Insert Function dialog box appears. Type the function in the Search for a function: box, or you can select the function from the Select a function: list box, as shown in *Figure 4.75*:

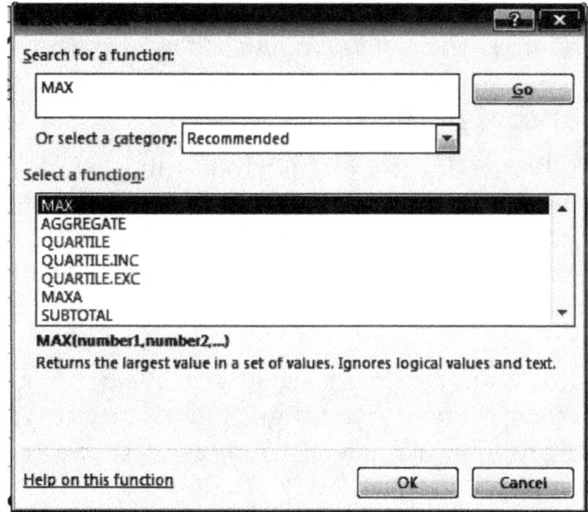

Figure 4.75: *Insert Function dialog box*

5. Click **OK**.
6. The Function Arguments dialog box will appear, as shown in *Figure 4.76*. Select the Number1 field, and enter the cell range such as *B2:E2* to calculate the highest value from a given set of numeric values.

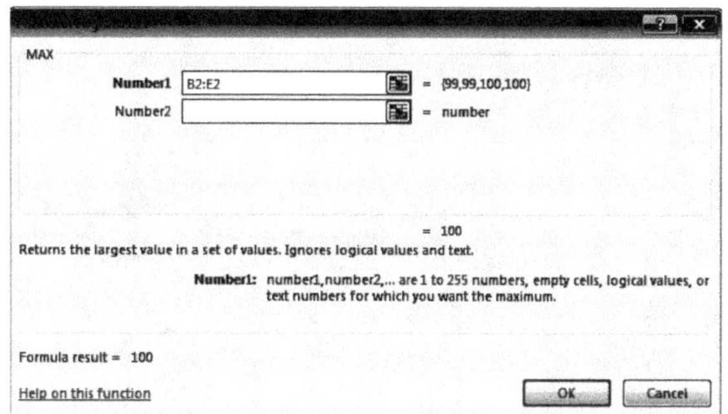

Figure 4.76: *Function Arguments*

7. Click **OK** in the **Function Arguments** dialog box.
8. Now, you can drag the handle of cells G3:G10 to cover each row of the column, and the function is automatically copied in the respective columns, as shown in *Figure 4.77*.

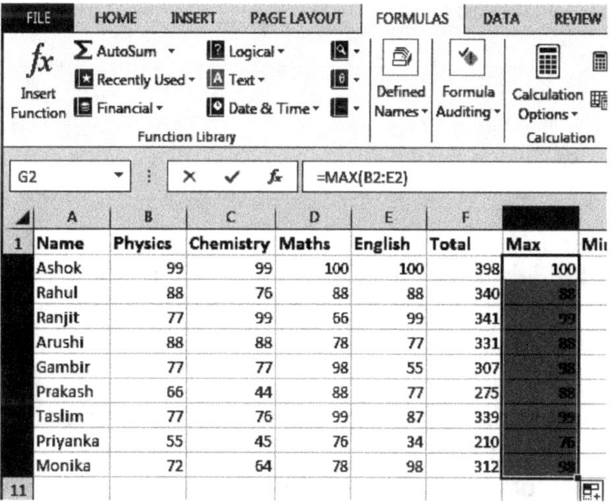

Figure 4.77: *Dragging the handle to copy the formula*

MIN()

Min function returns the smallest value in a set of values stored in a cell. The syntax is MIN(number1,number2,...). Maximum number of arguments can be 255, that is, number1, number2,... number255.

To use the Min function, perform the following steps:

1. Repeat steps 1 to 8 from the previous section.

Another way to find out the minimum value in the cell is as follows:

1. Type the MIN function, that is, =MIN(B2:E2) in the cell *H2*.
2. Press **Enter**. You will get the minimum value in the cell, as shown in *Figure 4.78*:

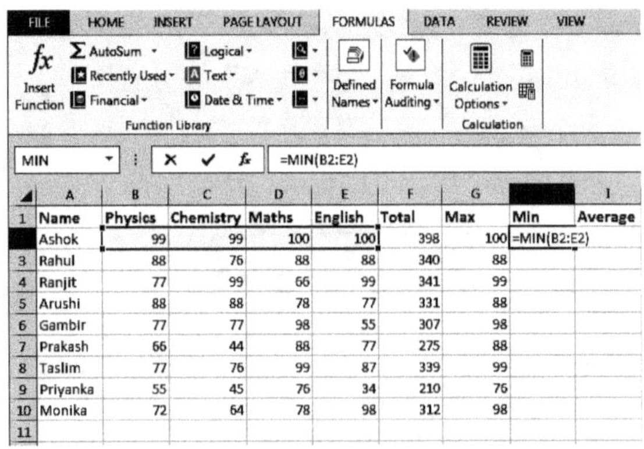

Figure 4.78: *Entering the MIN function in the selected cell*

3. Now, you can drag the handle of cells *H3:H10* to cover each row of the column, and the function is automatically copied in the respective columns.

AVERAGE()

The AVERAGE function returns the average (arithmetic mean) of the arguments which are passed in a function. The syntax is AVERAGE(number1, number2,...).

To use the Average function, perform the following steps:

1. Select the cell you want to insert the average function for. In our example, we have selected cell *I2*.

2. Type the equal sign (=), and type the First letter A; it will show the list of function names. Select the function from the list of suggested functions that appears below the cell as you type. For example, type **=AVERAGE**, as shown in *Figure 4.79*:

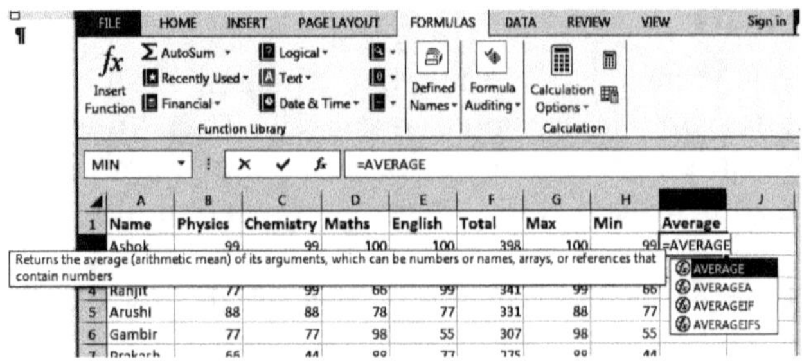

Figure 4.79: *Entering the AVERAGE function in the selected cell*

3. Enter the cell range for the argument inside parentheses, that is, type (B2:E2). This formula will add the values of cells B2:E2, and then divide that value by marks obtained in the

three subjects, as shown in *Figure 4.80*:

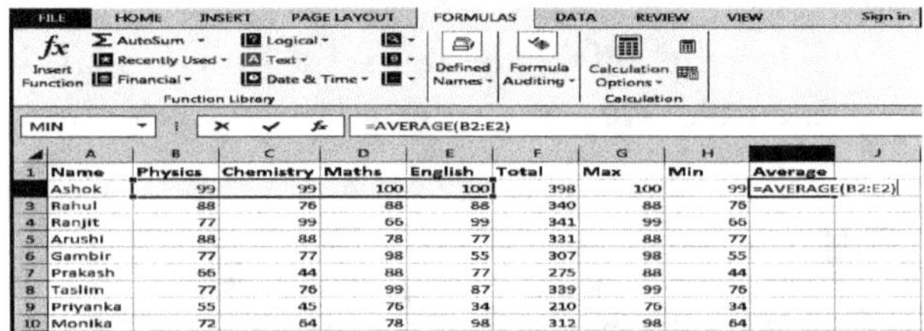

Figure 4.80: *Typing the Average Function Name*

4. Press **Enter**. The function will be calculated, and the result will appear in the cell. Now, you can drag the handle of cells I3:I10 to cover each row of the column, and the function is automatically copied in the respective columns, as shown in *Figure 4.81*:

	A	B	C	D	E	F	G	H		
1	Name	Physics	Chemistry	Maths	English	Total	Max	Min		Average
	Ashok	99	99	100	100	398	100	99		99.5
	Rahul	88	76	88	88	340	88	76		85
	Ranjit	77	99	66	99	341	99	66		85.25
	Arushi	88	88	78	77	331	88	77		82.75
	Gambir	77	77	98	55	307	98	55		76.75
	Prakash	66	44	88	77	275	88	44		68.75
	Taslim	77	76	99	87	339	99	76		84.75
	Priyanka	55	45	76	34	210	76	34		52.5
	Monika	72	64	78	98	312	98	64		78
11										

Figure 4.81: *The AVERAGE function will be performed*

Advanced Filter

The advanced filter is used to filter a data set, depending on user-defined criteria, that can be applied to several columns of data simultaneously. These criteria are specified on the same spreadsheet as the range to be filtered, rather than in a drop-down menu.

In order to perform an Excel advanced filter, you need to specify a list range and a criteria range. These ranges both specify ranges of cells on your working spreadsheet. They are defined as follows:

- **List Range:** The range of cells that you want to filter. This range should include headers at the top of each column.

- **Criteria range:** A range of cells in which the filtering criteria are specified. The criteria range should be headed by headers that match the list range headings. The criteria for the corresponding rows in the list range should be listed under each of these heading.

Suppose you have the following data to filter based on different criteria, as shown in *Figure 4.82*:

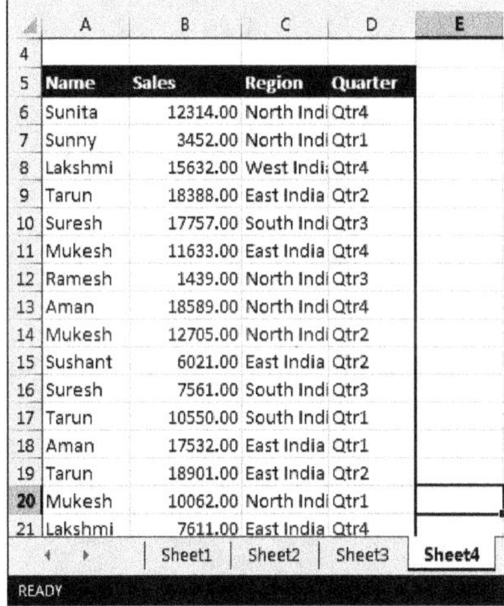

Figure 4.82: *Data to filter based on different criteria*

Now, you need to check sales transaction which was made by North India and South India, then you can use the OR operator which displays the records of the given condition. To get the results, you can apply these filters in Excel.

OR Criteria

To display the Sales Region in North India in *Qtr4* or South India in **Qtr1**, execute the following steps:

1. Copy the column labels you want to use as criteria from the list and paste them into a blank area of the worksheet. Enter the Criteria, shown in *Figure 4.83*, on the worksheet as **G5:J7**.

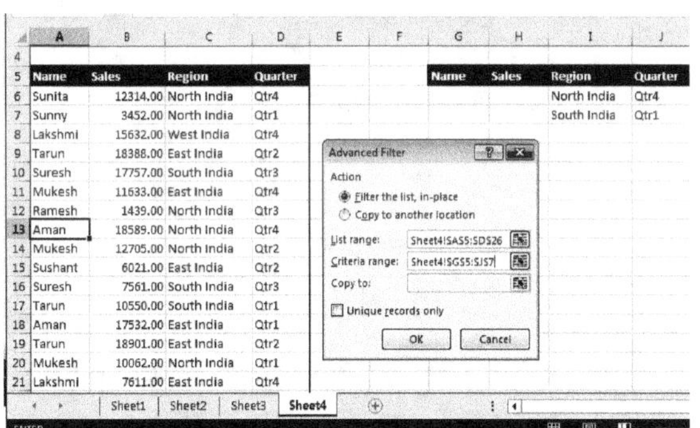

Figure 4.83: *Enter the Criteria range from G5:J7*

2. Click the **Data** tab; in the **Sort & Filter** group, click **Advanced** command.

3. The Advanced Filter dialog box appears as shown in *Figure 4.83*.

4. Click the List range: to specify the list range as Sheet1$A$5:$D$26, and then click Criteria range: as $G$5:$J$7.

5. Click **OK**.

6. You can see all the records having Region as North India or South India filtered out and displayed in a cell range, as shown in *Figure 4.84*:

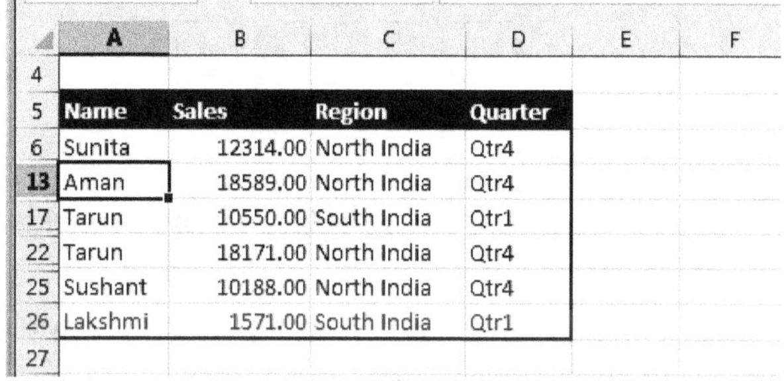

Figure 4.84: *Showing records of North India or South India in the cell range.*

Filter using the AND Criteria

Now you want to get all the sales transaction of **Qtr1** and South India. Criteria Range is as shown below.

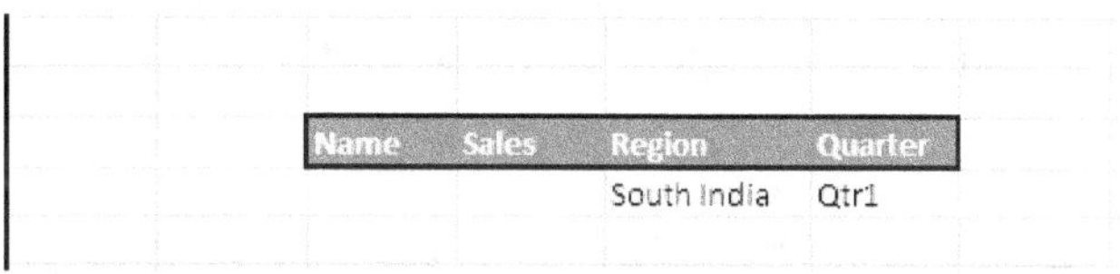

Figure 4.85

As you have here AND condition, i.e., we want to display the records where both the conditions are met, that is why we have mentioned the criteria below both column headings in the same row.

1. Click the **Advanced** command in the **Sort & Filter** group under the **Data** tab.

2. The Advanced Filter dialog box appears as shown in *Figure 4.86*:

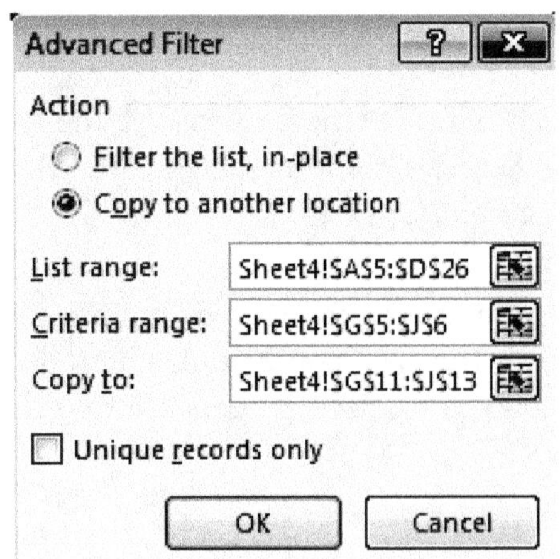

Figure 4.86: *Advanced Filter dialog box*

1. In the Action section, select Copy to another location
2. Click the List range: to specify the list range as Sheet4$A$5:$D$26, and then click Criteria range: as Sheet4!$G$5:$J$6.
3. Click Copy to: to specify the range from Sheet4!$G$11:$J$13, as shown in Figure 4.86.
7. Click OK.
8. You can display the records of Sales transaction in South India in **Qtr1**, that is the conditions are met in the main table data are filtered out in the cell range of column heading,, as shown in *Figure 4.87*:

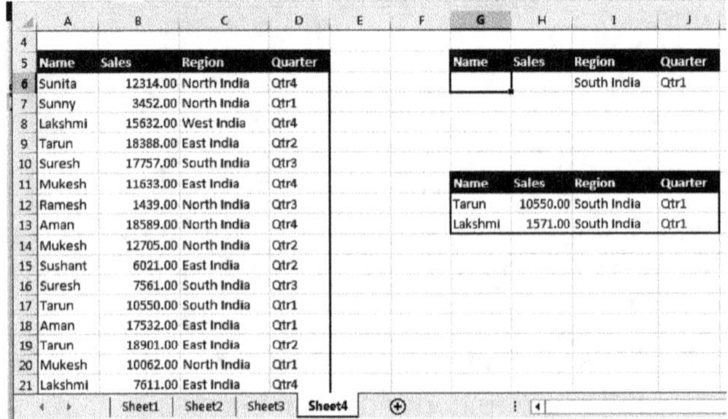

Figure 4.87: *The result of Sales transaction in South India in Qtr1*

Now you want to find all sales of Rs. 2000 -4000 and Rs. 10000-13000.

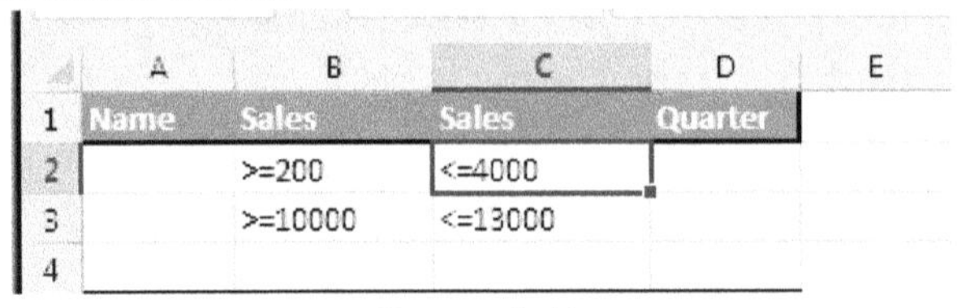

Figure 4.88

As we have four conditions as (Condition 1 AND Condition 2) OR (Condition 3 AND Condition 4).

That is, (>=200 AND <= 4000) OR (>= 10000 AND <=13000)

You have mentioned the condition with "AND" in the same row and Conditions with "OR" in different rows.

1. Click the **Advanced** command in the **Sort & Filter** group under the Data tab.
2. The Advanced Filter dialog box appears as shown in *Figure 4.89*:

Figure 4.89: *Specify list range in the Advanced Filter dialog box.*

3. Click the List range: to specify the list range as Sheet4$A$5:$D$26, as shown in *Figure 4.89*.
4. Then click Criteria range: as Sheet4!$A$1:$D$3, as shown in *Figure 4.90*:

Figure 4.90: Specify the Criteria range in the Advanced filter dialog box

5. Click Copy to: to specify the range from Sheet4!$G$3:$J$13, as shown in *Figure 4.91*:

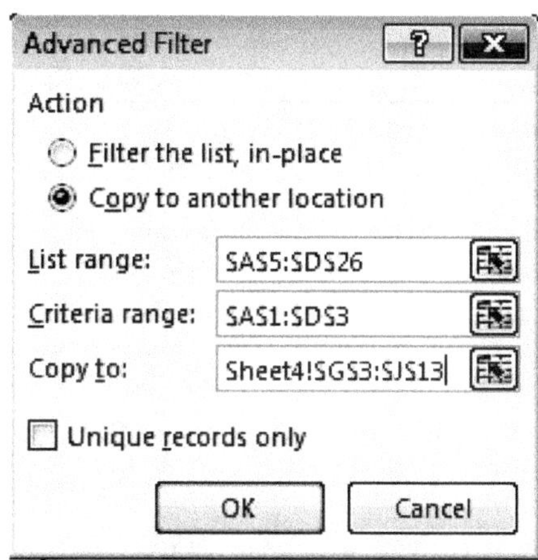

Figure 4.91: *Specify the Copy to: range in the Advanced filter dialog box*

6. Click OK to show the result of Sales Transactions with an amount of Rs 2000 -4000 or 10000-13000, as shown in Figure 4.92:

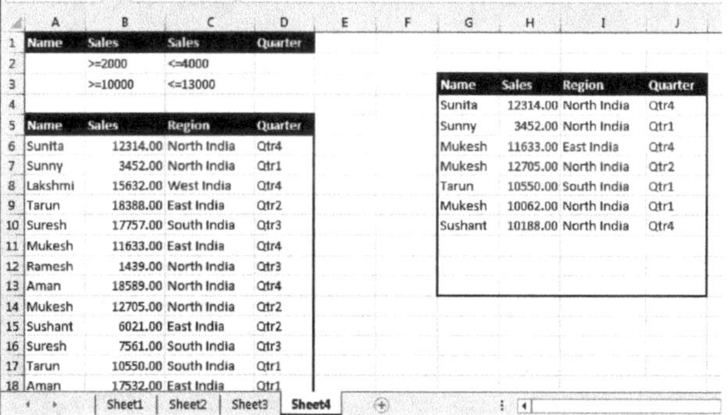

Figure 4.92: *Sales transaction the above given criteria*

Database Functions

The Excel Database functions are designed to assist you when working with an Excel database. It takes the form of a large table of data, where each row in the table stores an individual record. Each column in the table stores a different field for each record.

The database functions perform basic operations such as **Sum, max, min, count**, and so on, but they enable the user to specify criteria so that the operation is performed on selected records only.

DSUM

The DSUM function calculates the sum of a filed (column) in a database for selected records that satisfy user-specified criteria.

The syntax of the DSUM function is:

```
DSUM(database, field, criteria)
```

The function uses the following arguments:

1. Database: This is the range of cells wherein the first row of the database specifies the field names.

2. Field: This is the column within the database that will be summed. Field can be a field name that is the header provided at the top row such as "Area", "Sales", and so on.

3. Criteria: This is a range of cells that contains the conditions specified by us. It specified the record that will be included in the calculation.

How to use the DSUM Function in Excel?

To understand the uses of the DSUM function, let us consider a few examples:

Example 5: Suppose you are given the data as shown in *Figure 4.93*:

Figure 4.93: *Sample database*

You will use the DSUM function to calculate the total values of summer offer in the year 2018 of online payment mode. The Criteria specified are:

Product ID	Year	Discount Type	Payment Mode
RJP25	2018	summer offer	online

As shown below, the formula used are = SUM(A1:F7, "Value", B23:D24) and the solution of DSUM = 144659, as shown in *Figure 4.94*:

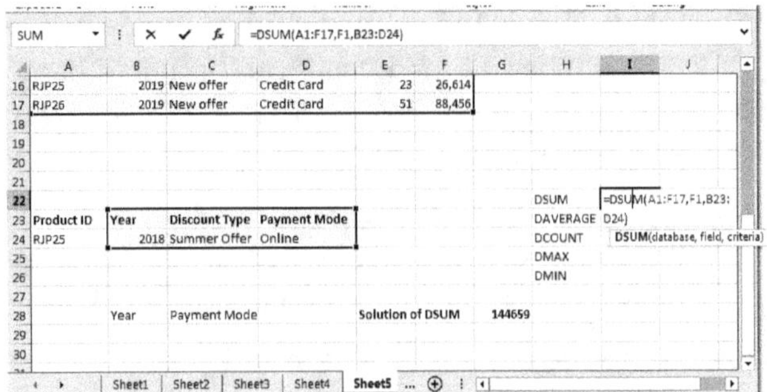

Figure 4.94: *Result of DSUM function in G28*

DAVERAGE

Calculates the average of values in a field of a list or database that satisfy specified conditions.

The syntax of Daverage function is:

DAVERAGE(database, field, criteria)

The following examples are based on the simple database on *Figure 4.86*. The Daverage function is used to calculate the average discount type in the year 2018 and 2019 for the value payment mode.

The figure for Daverage function calculates the average of the values in cells **E2** and **E3** and therefore returns the value 65, as shown in *Figure 4.95*:

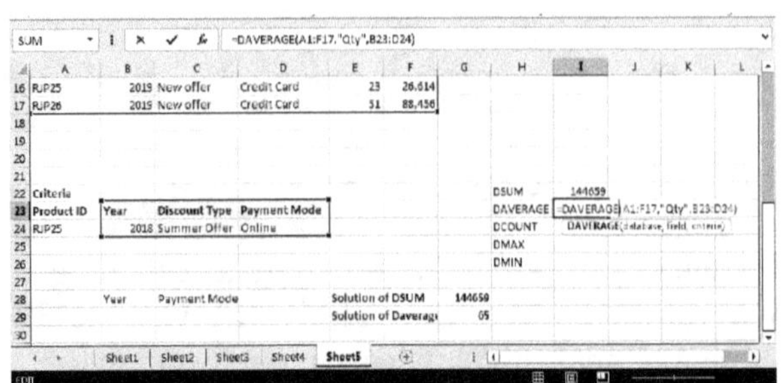

Figure 4.95: *Result of Average function in G28*

DCount

The following examples are based on the sample database in *Figure 4.96*, which stores the examination marks scored by four children in three different subjects.

	A	B	C	D	E
1	Name	Gender	Age	Subject	Percentage
2	Anu	Female	8	Maths	63%
3	Anu	Female	8	English	78%
4	Anu	Female	8	Science	39%
5	Balu	Male	9	Maths	55%
6	Balu	Male	9	English	71%
7	Balu	Male	9	Science	43%
8	Sarika	Female	8	Maths	awaiting
9	Sarika	Female	8	English	52%
10	Sarika	Female	8	Science	48%
11	Tony	Male	9	Maths	78%
12	Tony	Male	9	English	69%
13	Tony	Male	9	Science	65%
14					
15					

Figure 4.96: *Sample database*

The figure uses the Dcount function to count the number of English examination scores recorded for male students. The Criteria are specified in Cells **H3-I4** and the Dcount formula is shown in Cell **H5**, as shown in *Figure 4.97*:

	A	B	C	D	E	F	G	H	I
	H5				=DCOUNT(A1:E13,"Percentage",H3:I4)				
1	Name	Gender	Age	Subject	Percentage				
2	Anu	Female	8	Maths	63%				
3	Anu	Female	8	English	78%			Subject	Gender
4	Anu	Female	8	Science	39%			English	Male
5	Balu	Male	9	Maths	55%			2	
6	Balu	Male	9	English	71%				
7	Balu	Male	9	Science	43%				
8	Sarika	Female	8						
9	Sarika	Female	8	English	52%				
10	Sarika	Female	8	Science	48%				
11	Tony	Male	9	Maths	78%				
12	Tony	Male	9	English	69%				
13	Tony	Male	9	Science	65%				
14									
15									

Figure 4.97: *Result of DCOUNT function in H5*

The above *Figure 4.97* finds that there are two rows for which the Gender is **Male** and the Subject is **English**. However, only two of these rows contain a number in the "Percentage" column. Therefore, the function returns the value 2.

DMAX

The Excel DMAX function finds the maximum value in a field (column) in a database for selected records only. The records to be included in the calculation are defined by a set of one or more user-specified criteria.

The following example based on the simple database, as shown in *Figure 4.86*, is to find the highest value in the Summer offer in the year 2018 are given in the criteria specified in cells **B23 – C24** and the DMAX formula is shown in Cell *I24* and the *Figure 4.98*:

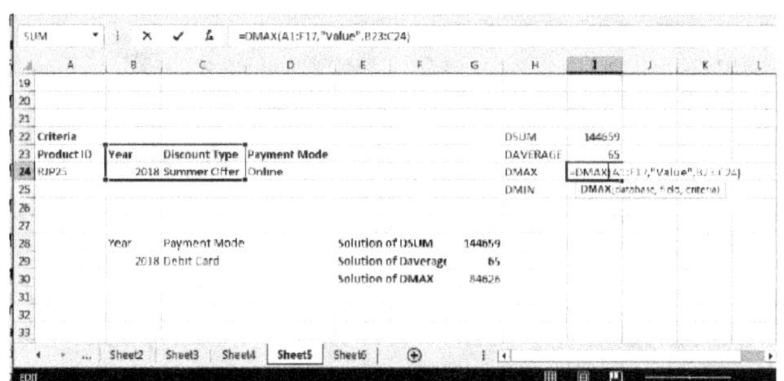

Figure 4.98: *Result of DMAX function in G30*

DMIN

The Excel DMIN function finds the minimum value in a field (column) in a database for selected records only. The records to be included in the calculation are defined by a set of one or more user-specified criteria.

The following example based on the simple database, as shown in *Figure 4.86*, is to find the Minimum value in the Summer offer in the year 2018 are given in the criteria specified in cells **B23 – C24** and the DMIN formula is shown in Cell I25 and the *Figure 4.99*:

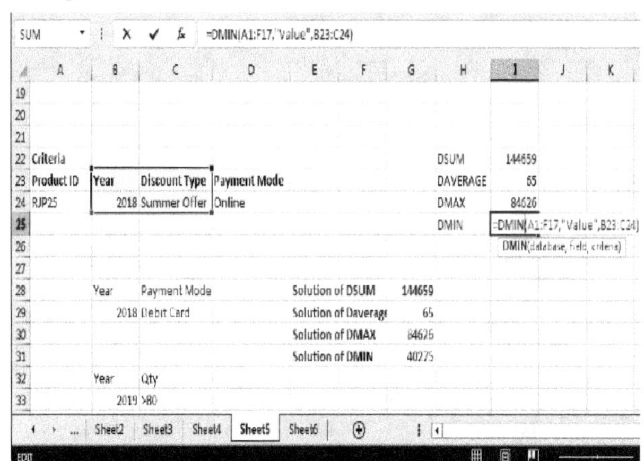

Figure 4.99: *Result of DMAX function in G31*

DCOUNTA

The DCOUNTA function returns the number of non-blank cells, in a field (column) of a database for selected records only. The DCOUNTA function counts all non-blank cells where the DCOUNT function only counts cells containing numeric values.

The following examples are based on the simple database in *Figure 4.89*, which stores the examination marks scored by four children in three different subjects.

The DCOUNTA function is used to count the number of English examination percentage recorded for Female students. The criteria are specified in cells H3-I4 and the DCOUNTA formula is shown in *Figure 4.100*:

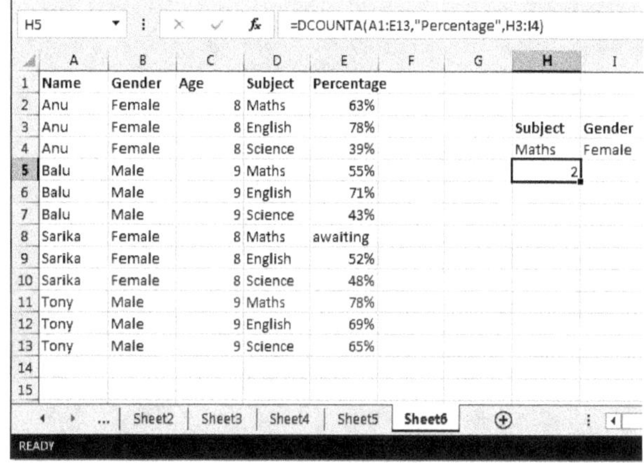

Figure 4.100: *Result of DCOUNTA function*

The above DCOUNTA function finds that there are two rows for which the Gender is **Female** and the Subject is **Maths**. As the Percentage column for the both of these rows is non-blank, the function returns the value 2.

Note that in the above example, the DCOUNTA function has counted cell **E8**, in which the Percentage field contains the text **awaiting**. (This would have been excluded from the count if the DCOUNT function had been used instead of the DCOUNTA function).

What-if Analysis

What-if analysis is the process of changing the values in cells to see how those changes will affect the outcome of formula on the worksheet.

Excel provides you with the following What-if analysis tools that can be used based on your data analysis needs of:

- Data Tables
- Scenario manager
- Goal Seek

Goal Seek in What if Analysis

Let us consider a simple dataset, where the invoice amount is Rs. 10,000, on which there is 9% CGST and 9% SGST, which thus amounts to a total of Rs.

11800, as given below:

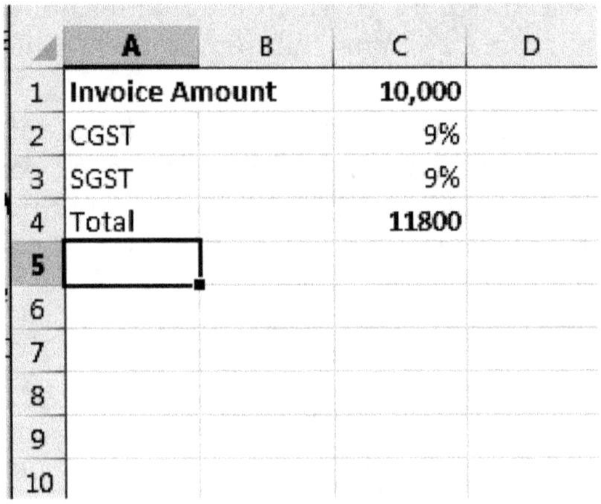

Figure 4.101

The customer asks you for a discount of Rs. 800 and thus the final amount should be Rs. 11,000.

Now, the equation in simple terms is, **X + 18% = 11000**, where *X* is the invoice amount, 18% is the GST.

To find out how much *+ 18% = 11000*, we will use Goal Seek in What-if analysis.

1. Place your cursor on the 'Total' Cell.

2. Click the Data tab. In the Data Tools group, click the What-If-Analysis drop-down arrow and then click on the Goal Seek option, as shown in *Figure 4.102*:

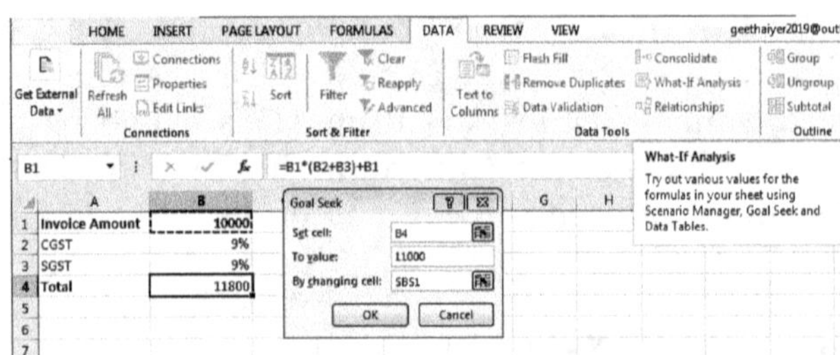

Figure 4.102: *Entering details in Goal Seek dialog box*

3. Set Cell: B4 will automatically be selected as you had kept your cursor on it. In B4, you have entered a formula as =B1(B2+B3)+B1

4. In To Value: Enter the desired value; 11000 in this case

5. In By changing cell: Choose the value that needs to be changed, that is, invoice amount. Thus, cell *B1* is selected.

6. Click OK

7. Excel will reverse Calculate and immediately give you the value as Rs. 9322, which +18%

equals exactly to Rs. 11,000, as shown in *Figure 4.103*:

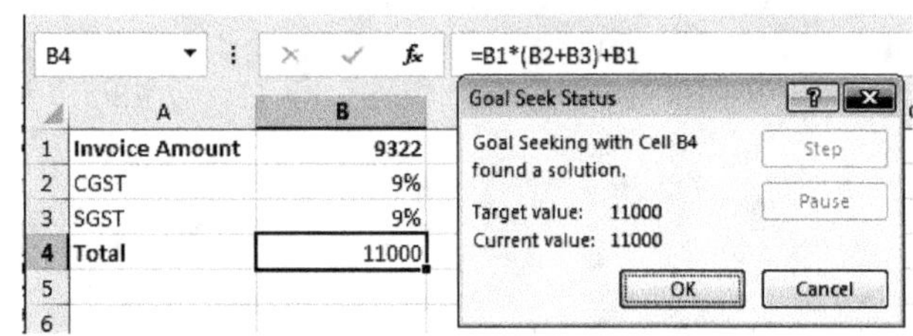

Figure 4.103: *Goal Seek calculate the amount as 9322*

Scenario Manager in What-If Analysis

Let us say you are working in a car showroom in the sales department. You are given the task to plan the sales for the next quarter. You must build multiple scenarios and prepare a comparison of all the scenarios.

1. To create multiple scenarios based on number of cars that you will be able to sell for each of the cars as shown in *Figure 4.104*:

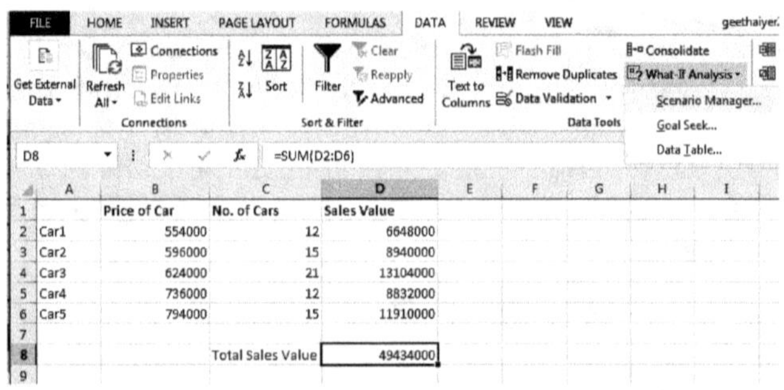

Figure 4.104: *Selecting Scenario Manger*

2. Click the **Data** tab. In the **Data Tools** group, click the What-If-Analysis drop-down arrow and then click on the Scenario manager option, as shown in *Figure 4.104*. The Scenario manager dialog box appears; click the **Add...** button, as shown in *Figure 4.104*:

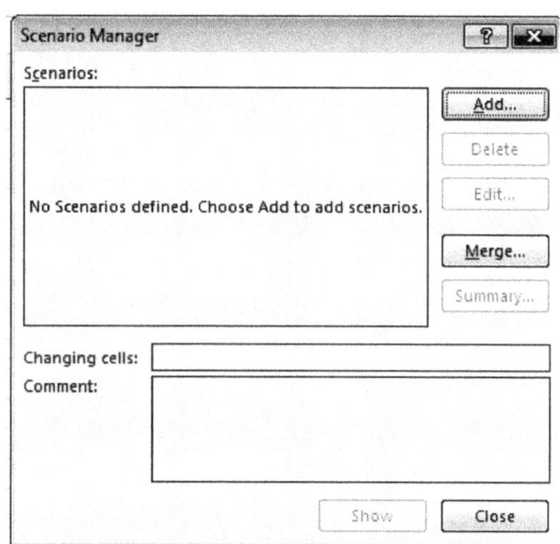

Figure 4.104: *Scenario Manager dialog box*

3. The Add Scenario dialog box appears, as shown in *Figure 4.105*, to create the first scenario.

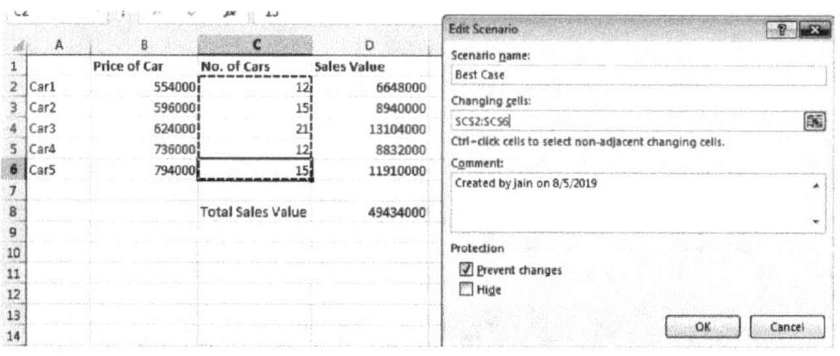

Figure 4.105: *Entering detail in the Edit Scenario dialog box*

4. Enter the name in the Scenario name: as Best case list box.

5. In Changing cells:, select cells *C2:C6* as these are the No. of cars that you will be able to sell, basically the variable cells. The Add Scenario dialog box changes to Edit Scenario, as shown in *Figure 4.105*.

6. Click **OK**.

7. The Scenario values dialog box appears; enter the values for each car and click **OK**, as shown in *Figure 4.106*:

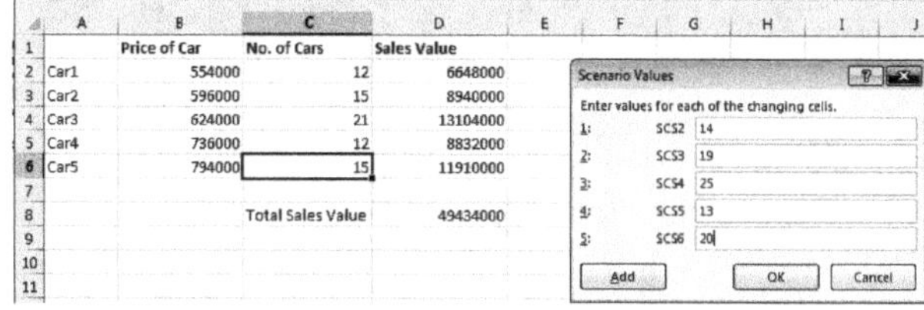

Figure 4.106: *Values entered in Scenario Values dialog box*

8. Similarly, add one more Scenario and name it as **Worst Case**. The changing cells will remain the same.

9. Here, we have entered the values for worst case, as shown in *Figure 4.107*; then click OK.

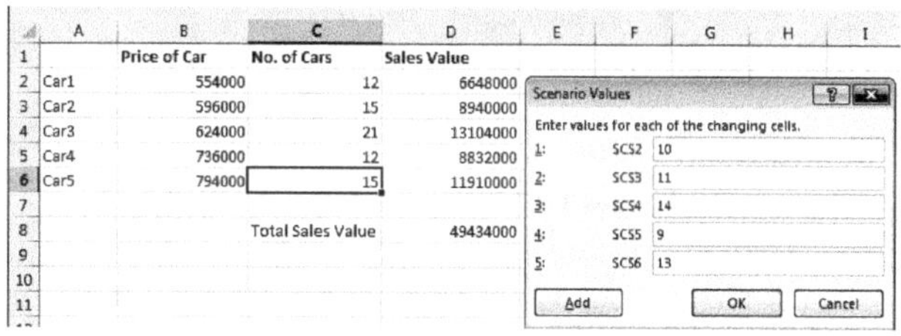

Figure 4.107: *Entering Worst case values in Scenario values dialog box.*

10. Now that you have created two scenarios, let us compare them. In the Scenario Manager Window, click on Summary, as shown in *Figure 4.108*:

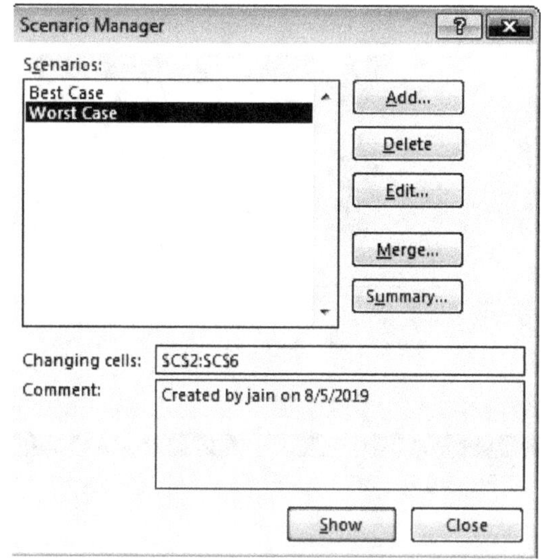

Figure 4.108: *Selecting Summary in the Scenario Manager dialog box*

11. Select Result cells: as Total Sales value, cell **D8** in the Scenario Summary dialog box that you want to compare, as shown in *Figure 4.109*:

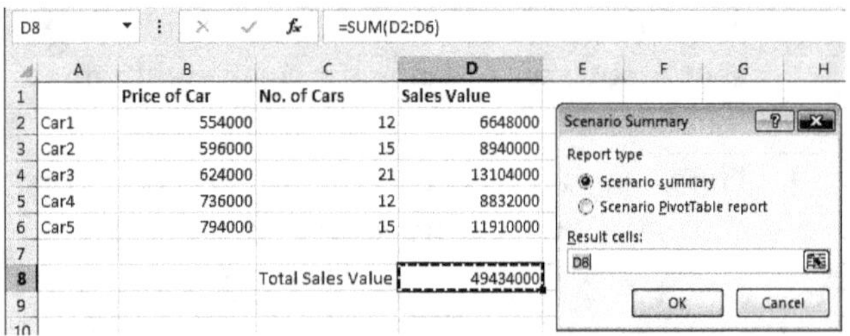

Figure 4.109: *Selecting Sales value in cell D8 in Scenario summary dialog box*

12. Click **OK**. A new sheet will be created automatically, which will give you a comparison of the Current values in the worksheet and two scenarios created, that is, (best case and worst case), as shown in *Figure 4.110*.

Thus, in Best case, the Total Sales is 6 Cr. And Worst case is 3.77 Cr.

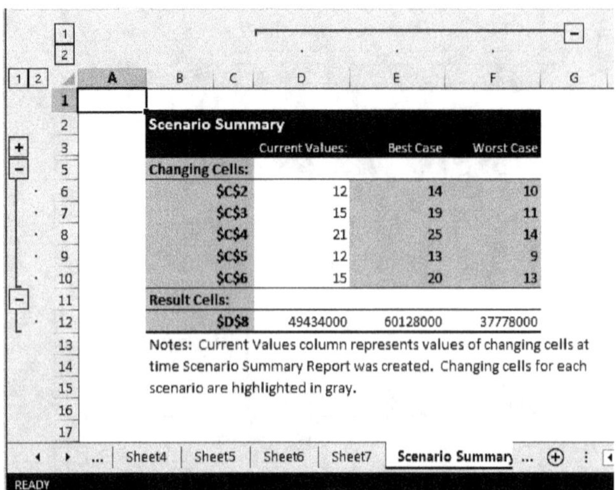

Figure 4.110: *Scenario summary result*

Charts (Bar, Pie, Line)

You can create different types of charts using Excel 2013 that will help you analyze data in a worksheet and give you a visual presentation of results. You can even customize the chart by adding text, arrows, titles, legends, and so on. If you print a chart on a laser printer or plotter, the quality of charts is as good as that of a chart created by a professional artist.

Bar Chart

Bar charts illustrate comparisons among individual items. In a Bar chart, the categories are organized along the vertical axis, and the values are organized along the horizontal axis. The Bar chart has the following sub-types - Clustered Bar Stacked Bar 100%, Stacked Bar 3-D Clustered, Bar 3-D Stacked, Bar 3-D 100%, Stacked Bar.

To create a bar chart, perform the following steps:

1. Select the range of cells to create a chart with the column titles and row labels. The selected cells have the source data for the chart. In our example, we have selected cells *A1:F6*, as shown in *Figure 4.111*:

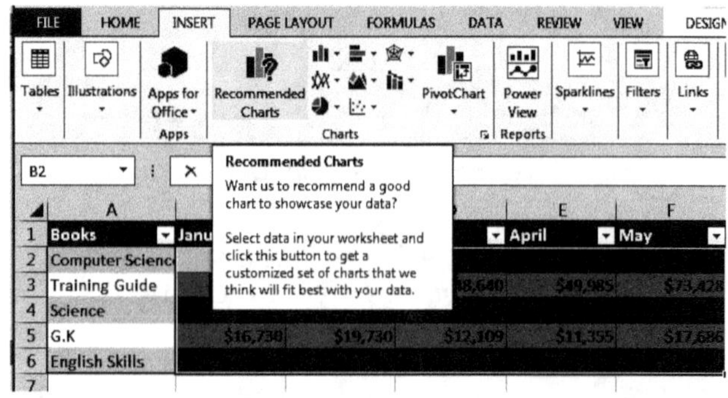

Figure 4.111: *Selecting the data to create a chart*

2. In the Insert tab, click Recommended Charts from the Charts group, as shown in *Figure 4.112*:

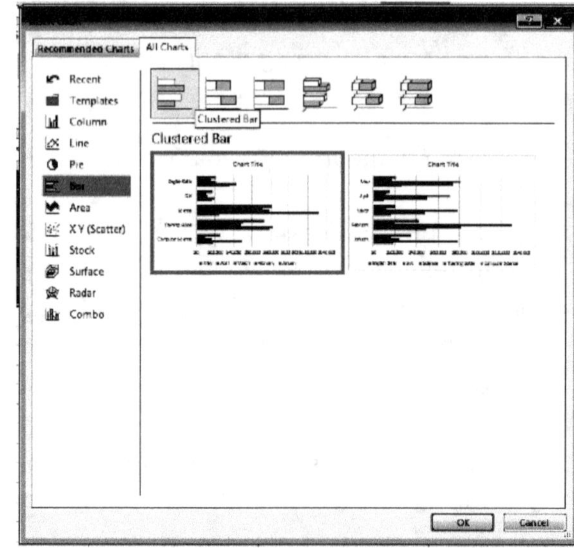

Figure 4.112: *Insert Chart dialog box with All Charts tab*

3. The Insert Chart dialog box appears with Recommended **Charts** tab available. Click the **All Charts** tab. In our example, we have selected the Clustered bar chart type, as shown in *Figure 4.112*.

4. The selected embedded chart is inserted into the worksheet, as shown in *Figure 4.113*:

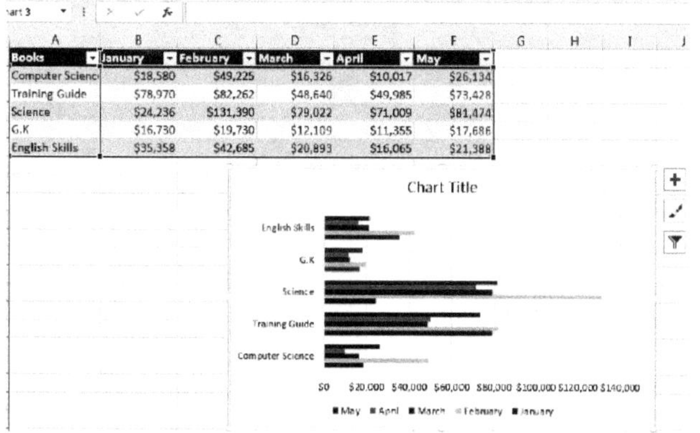

Figure 4.113: *Embedded chart is inserted in the worksheet*

To add Title chart elements, perform the following steps:

1. Activate the chart in which you want to add a title.
2. To edit chart element, simply double-click the chart title placeholder and begin typing.

   Or, click the Add Chart Elements drop-down arrow in the Chart Layouts group. A list of elements appears, highlighting the Chart Title option. A sub-menu appears; select the desired option. Or, select the shortcut button placed near the chart (here, plus sign) option, as shown in *Figure 4.114*:

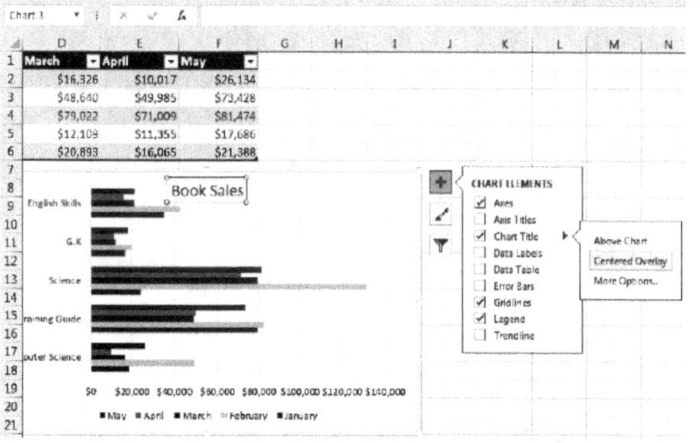

Figure 4.114: *Inserting Chart Title element*

3. Click the Centered Overlay option to position the title in the center and change the title as Book Sales, as shown in *Figure 4.114*.

To add Data Labels, perform the following steps:

1. Click the Add Chart Elements drop-down arrow in the **Chart Layouts** group. A list of elements appears, highlighting the **Data**

Labels option. A sub-menu appears; select the desired option. Or, click the shortcut button placed near the chart, as shown in *Figure 4.115*:

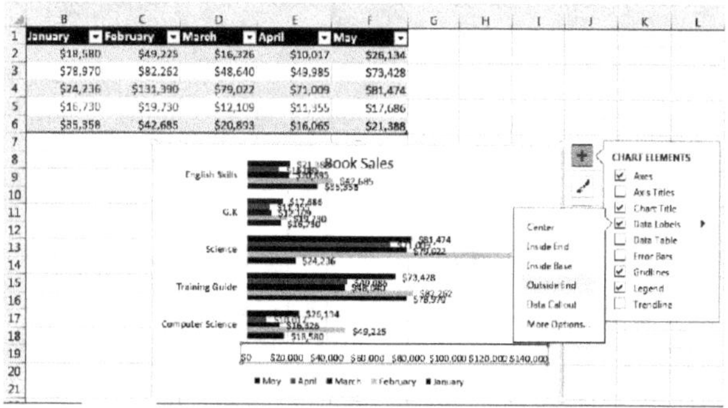

Figure 4.115: *Adding Data Labels*

2. Click the Data Labels checkmark. Highlight Data Labels. A sub menu appears. Select the desired option from the list. In our example, we have selected the Outside end option.
3. Similarly, you can choose other option such as Gridlines and Legends in the chart.

Pie Chart

Pie charts show the size of items in one data series, proportional to the sum of all the items. The data points in the Pie chart are shown as a percentage of the whole pie. To create a Pie chart, arrange the data in one column or row on the worksheet. The Pie Chart has the following sub-types: Pie 3-D Pie, Pie of Pie, and Bar of Pie.

To change the chart type as pie, perform the following steps:

1. Select the chart.
2. Under the **Design** tab, in Type group, click **Change Chart Type** command, as shown in *Figure 4.116*:

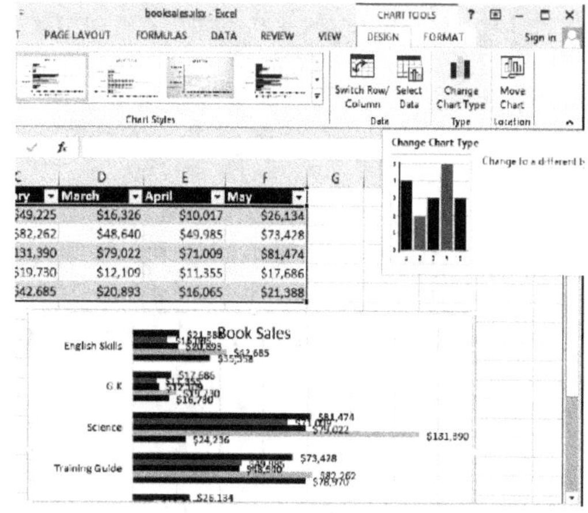

Figure 4.116: *Selecting Change Chart type*

3. A Change Chart Type dialog box, showing different chart types, appears. Click All Charts tab, and select Pie chart from the list, as shown in *Figure 4.117*:

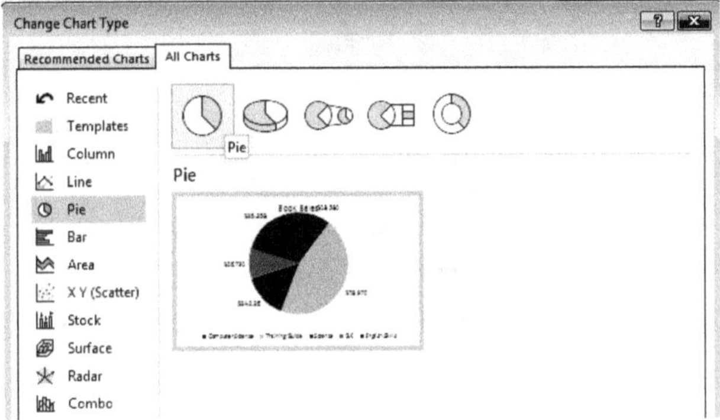

Figure 4.117: *Selecting Pie chart from Change Chart type dialog box*

4. Click the **OK** button. The selected chart type will appear. In our example, the pie chart makes it easier to see data which is shown as a percentage of the whole pie, as shown in *Figure 4.118*:

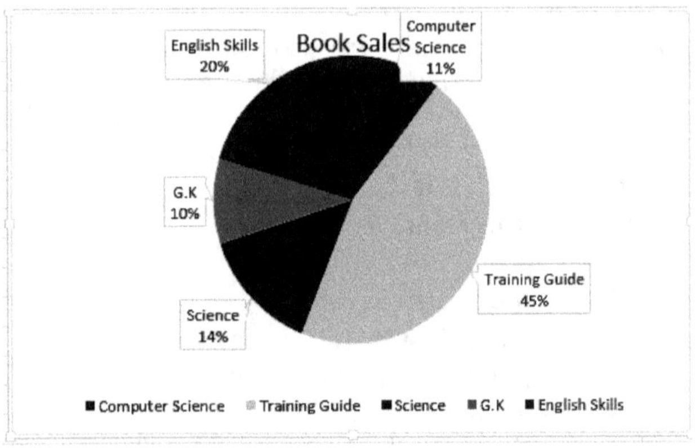

Figure 4.118: *The selected Pie chart type appears on the screen*

Line Chart

A Line chart compares trends over a period of time. Therefore, it is ideal for showing trends in data at equal intervals, such as months, quarters or years.

To change the chart type as Line chart, perform the following steps:

1. Repeat the steps 1 to 4 from the previous section.

2. The selected Line chart appears, as shown in *Figure 4.119*:

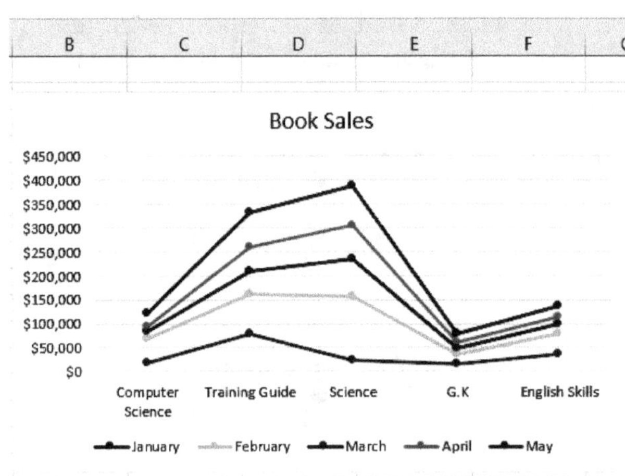

Figure 4.119: *The selected Line chart*

PivotTable

A PivotTable is an interactive table that lets you analyze and view large sizes of data in a list or database form so that it can be easily understood and analyzed. You can rotate its rows and columns to see different summaries, details and views of the source data as per your need. You can use the PivotTable report when you want to do sorting, totaling or to compare related items. In Excel 2013, multithreading helps to speed up data retrieval, sorting, and filtering in PivotTables.

In Excel 2013, it is possible to fill down labels in a PivotTable so that you can more easily use the PivotTable. You can also repeat labels in PivotTables to display item captions of nested fields in all rows and columns.

To create a PivotTable, perform the following steps:

1. Select the table or cells (including column headers) you want to include in the PivotTable, as shown in *Figure 4.120*:

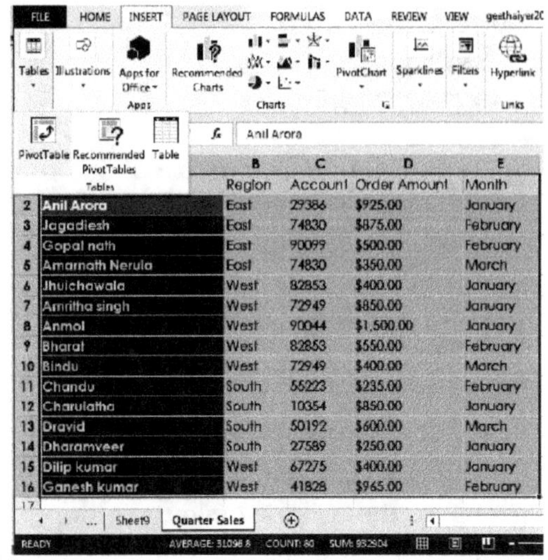

Figure 4.120: *Selecting PivotTable*

2. From the **Insert** tab, click the **PivotTable** command, as shown in *Figure 4.120*.

3. The Create PivotTable dialog box appears, as shown in *Figure 4.121*. Choose your settings, then click **OK**. In our example, we use Table1 as source data and place the PivotTable on a New Worksheet.

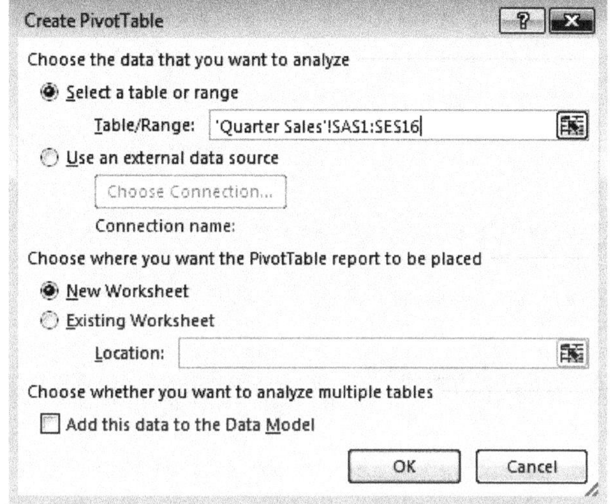

Figure 4.121: *Create PivotTable dialog box*

4. A new blank PivotTable Fields list appears on a new worksheet, as shown in *Figure 4.122*:

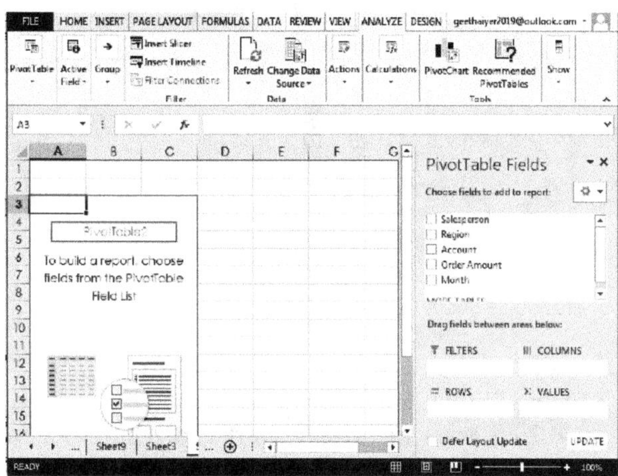

Figure 4.122: *PivotTable Field List*

5. Select the fields you want to add to create a PivotTable. In the PivotTable Field List, click the selected checkbox for each field you want to add. In our example, check the sales person and order Amount fields to know the total amount sold by each salesperson.

The selected fields will be added in the PivotTable areas. The salesperson field has been added to the Rows area, and the order Amount has been added to values.

6. To calculate and summarize the selected fields, the PivotTable shows the amount sold by each salesperson, as shown in *Figure 4.123*:

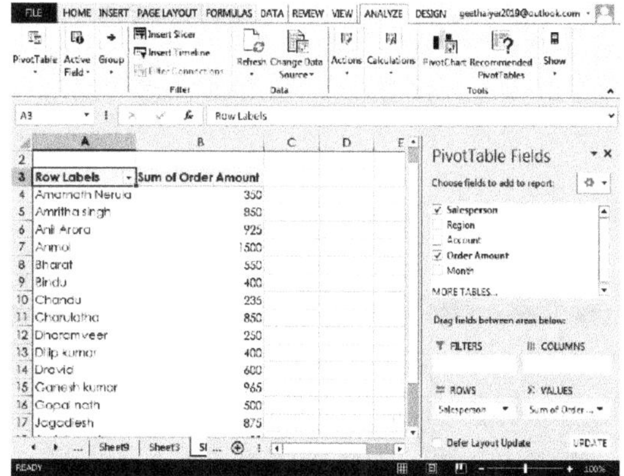

Figure 4.123: *Summarize the selected fields*

To add columns, perform the following steps:

1. To show multiple columns, you need to add a field to the Columns area.

2. To add the Month field, drag a field from the Field List into the Columns area.

3. It will include multiple columns. In our example, there is a column for each person's monthly sales, in addition to the grand total, as shown in *Figure 4.124*:

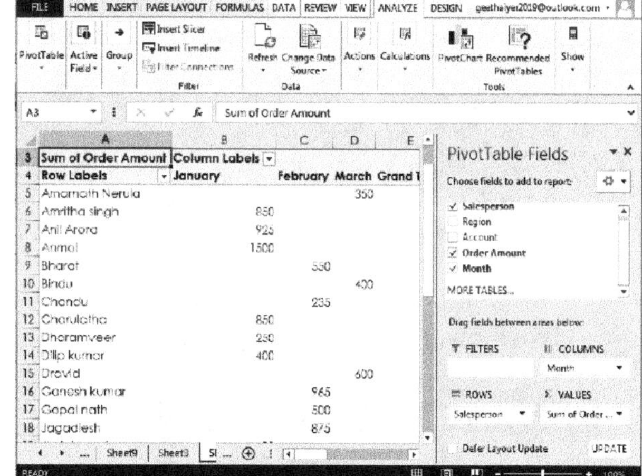

Figure 4.124: *To add columns*

To add a filter, perform the following steps:

1. Drag a field from the Field List to the Filters area. In our example, we select the salesperson field, as shown in *Figure 4.125*:

Module 3: M3–R5

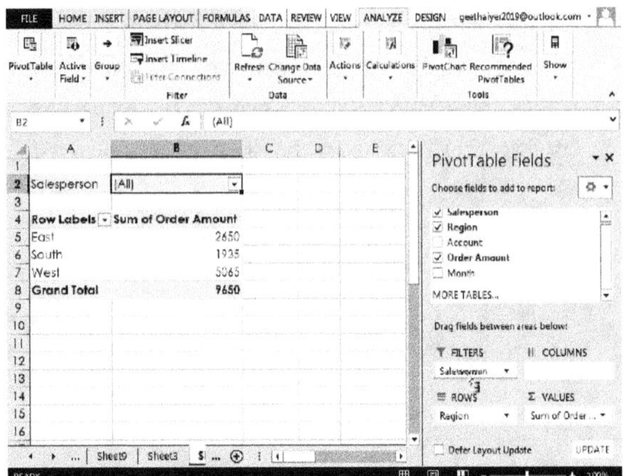

Figure 4.125: *The filter appears in the PivotTable*

2. Click the filter drop-down arrow, then click the check box next to Select Multiple Items, as shown in *Figure 4.125*.

3. If you do not want to include to any items in the PivotTable, click uncheck the box. So, we have to uncheck the boxes for a few salespersons, then click **OK**, as shown in *Figure 4.126*:

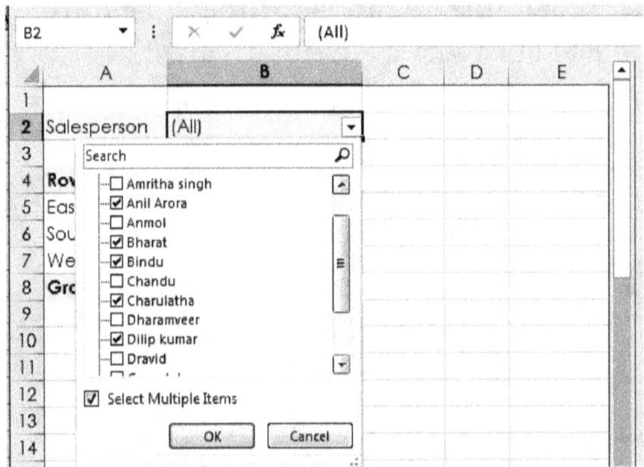

Figure 4.126: *Check and Uncheck the items in the Filter menu*

4. It will adjust to reflect the changes in the PivotTable, as shown in *Figure 4.127*:

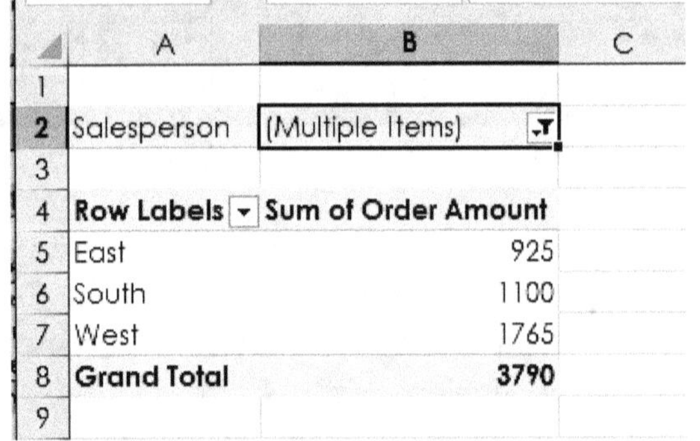

Figure 4.127: *The select items reflect changes in the PivotTable*

Pivot Chart

A pivot chart is the visual representation of a Pivot Table in Excel. Pivot chats and Pivot Tables are connected with each other.

Insert Pivot Chart

To insert a pivot chart, perform the following steps:

1. Click any cell inside the Pivot Table.
2. On the **Analyze** tab, in the **Tools** group, click **PivotChart**, as shown in *Figure 4.128*:

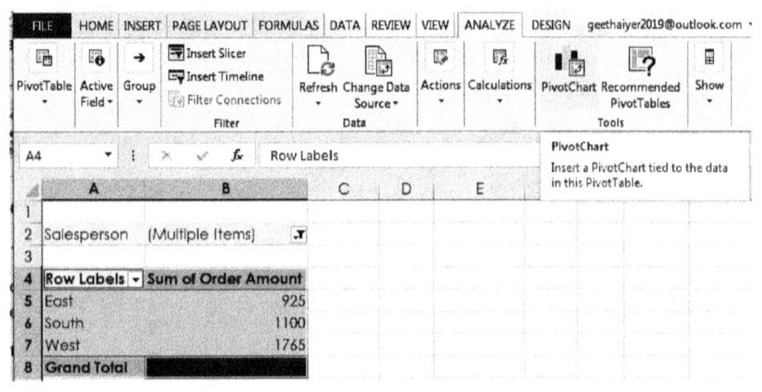

Figure 4.128: *Selecting PivotChart*

3. The Insert Chart dialog box appears; select the chart type. For example, we have selected Column, as shown in *Figure 4.129*:

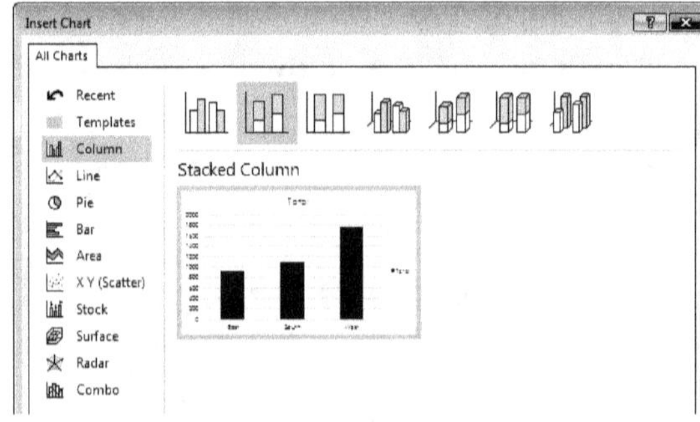

Figure 4.129: *Selecting Chart type in the Insert Chart dialog box*

4. Click **OK**.
5. The Pivot Chart will appear as shown in *Figure 4.130*. You can insert chart types such as bar, line and pie, based on Pivot Table.

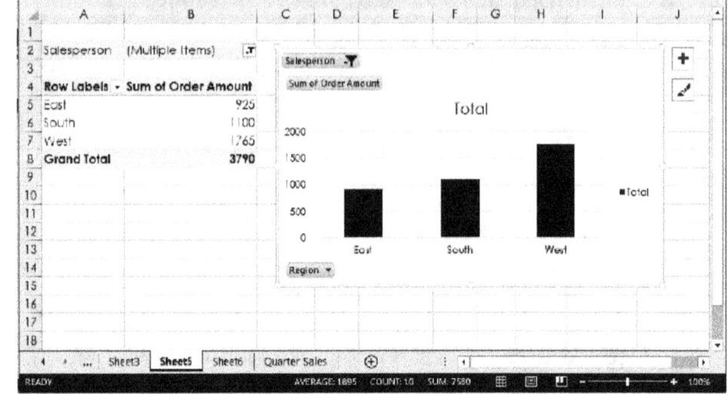

Figure 4.130: *PivotChart chart in the worksheet*

Note: Any changes you make to the pivot chart are immediately reflected in the Pivot Table and vice versa.

Conclusion

Spreadsheet refers to a software package and a worksheet is a work file that is created with the spreadsheet software. You got ourselves introduced to spreadsheet. You learnt about workbook, worksheet and various other elements of spreadsheet. You studied how to create a spreadsheet and opening, closing and saving it. We understood the concept of cell address, selecting a cell, entering a data to it, page setting and printing the worksheet. Next, you studied manipulation of cells and worksheets by editing the cell, moving and copying the cell, dragging and dropping it, moving and filling it, and so on. Then we learnt how to cut, copy and paste the cell and special paste option. The Paste Special is a feature that gives you more control of how the content is displayed when pasted from the clipboard. You learnt about inserting and deleting the rows, columns and cells and changing its height and width. You also learnt about sorting and filtering. Fill is a feature that can be used to quickly copy data from the anchor cell to an adjoining range. The Fill handle is the small bold square in the bottom right corner of a cell which can be used to copy data to adjacent cells in the row or column. Freezing columns/Rows freezing is a technique that can be used in larger spreadsheets to assist in viewing the information on the screen. Sorting is used to arrange information in a particular order. Also, the tables allow you to organize and analyze your data quickly and easily. You saw that the functions and formulas are built into Excel; a formula is an expression or equation that calculates data in the spreadsheet. Functions are predefined formulas in Excel. It is used to perform various mathematical operations such as sum, average and multiplication. Then, we covered a Pivot Table, which is a feature that summarizes and reorganizes selected columns and rows of data in a spreadsheet. In the next chapter, you will be looking into presentations using PowerPoint.

REVIEW QUESTIONS WITH ANSWERS

A. **Multiple Choice Questions.**

1. In Excel, the intersection of a row and column is called:
   a. Square
   b. Cell
   c. Cubicle
   d. Worksheet

2. Which of the following methods cannot be used to enter data in a cell?
   a. Pressing an arrow key
   b. Pressing the Tab key
   c. Pressing the Esc key
   d. Clicking on the Formula bart

3. Extension of Excel file is:
   a. .TMT
   b. .XXL
   c. .xlsx
   d. None of the above

4. How do you delete a column?
   a. Select the column heading you want to delete, and select the Delete Row button on the standard toolbar
   b. Select the column heading you want to delete, and select Insert column from the menu
   c. Select the row heading you want to delete and select Edit > Delete from the menu
   d. Right-click the column heading you want to delete, and select delete from the shortcut menu

5. Which area in an Excel window allows entering values and formulas?
   a. Home tab
   b. Format tab
   c. Formula bar
   d. Design tab

6. Which of the following is not a valid data type in Excel?
   a. Number
   b. Character
   c. Label
   d. Date/time

7. To change the cell reference B2:B9 to an absolute row and column reference, you would enter it as:
   a. B2:B9
   b. $B$2:$B$9
   c. B$2:B$9
   d. none of the above

8. You want to track the progress of the stock market on a daily basis. Which type of chart should you use?
   a. Pie chart
   b. Row chart
   c. Line chart
   d. Column chart

9. Which of the following is not a financial function?
   a. FV()
   b. SUM()
   c. NPV()
   d. PMT()

10. You can use the drag and drop method to:
    a. Copy cell contents
    b. Move cell contents
    c. Add cell contents
    d. Both (a) and (b)

11. What are the tabs that appear at the bottom of each workbook called?
    a. Location tabs
    b. Sheet tabs
    c. Reference tabs
    d. None of the above

12. When a formatted number does not fit within a cell, it displays:
    a. #####
    b. #DIV@
    c. #DIV/0
    d. None of these

13. Which symbol is used to enter number as text?
    a. =
    b. '
    c. "
    d. +

14. Which of the following syntax is correct regarding SUM function in Excel?
    a. = SUM (A1, B1)
    b. = SUM (A1:B9)
    c. = SUM (A1:A9, B1:B9)
    d. All of the above

15. To select multiple non-adjacent cells in a worksheet, you will click the cells while holding:
    a. Alt key
    b. Ctrl + Shift key
    c. Shift Key
    d. Ctrl key

B. State whether the following Statements are True or False.

1. To add a new Excel worksheet, you should insert worksheet tab at the bottom of the screen.

2. To enter a date in a cell, you should use a slash or a hyphen to separate the parts: 7/16/2019 or 16-July-2019. Excel will recognize this as a text.

3. PMT function calculates your monthly mortgage payment.

4. Different cells with in a row can have different height.

5. It is possible to undo the deletion of a sheet.

6. In Excel pressing Ctrl + Spacebar select the entire row.

7. Short cut key to delete the selected column by pressing Ctrl + -.

8. On an excel sheet the active cell in indicated by a dark wide border.

9. Clicking three times with the right mouse button in the spreadsheet to select all the cells in a document.

10. The cell reference for a range of cells that starts in cell C1 and goes over to column H and down to row 10 is C1:H-10.

11. Previewing a worksheet is similar to previewing a chart.

12. To delete a column or row you can select a cell within its range and then choose the Delete command from the cells group in the home tab.

13. Instead of typing in cell references, you can use the mouse click for Excel to enter the cell names into formulas for you.

14. You can only select cells that are adjacent to each other.

15. Dragging the mouse or holding the down Shift key while clicking with the mouse will only select cells that are adjacent to each other.

C. Match the following:

1.	When you start Excel, you can open a file that is called Workbook. Each new workbook comes with:	a.	View tab
2.	Free Panes is option available in which of the Following tab:	b.	Double clicking on column right border on column header
3.	You can auto fit the width of column by:	c.	=now()
4.	Function you use to enter current time in a worksheet cell:	d.	Two or three worksheet(s)
5.	The Autofill feature Painter:	e.	Copy, Paste and Format
6.	Clipboard Group:	f.	Extends a sequential series of data
7.	Worksheet:	g.	Stored in a workbook.
8.	A chart is created on the basis of values in cell	h.	Returns highest value from A1 to A9
9.	Moves to cursor one word left:	i.	Spreadsheet
10.	Automatic recalculation of result of a formula if the data is changed	j.	=currentTime()
		k.	What-if Analysis

D. Fill in the blanks:

Freezing Sheet tabs Legend Insert a row financial Shift + F11 Pie Chart Tabs, groups, Worksheet commands Dollar @symbol Alt + F11

1. The process of identifying specific rows and columns so that certain columns and rows are always visible on the screen in called _________.

2. The box on the chart that contains the name of each individual record is called the _________.

3. If you want to have a blank line after the title in a worksheet, _________ is the best thing for you to do.

4. _________ are the tabs that appear at the bottom of each workbook.

5. A _________ is a grid with labeled columns and rows.

6. _________ function is used to calculate depreciation, rates of return, future values and loan payment amounts.

7. What do you call the _________ that shows the proportions of how one or more data elements relate to another data element?

8. _________ shortcut key to insert a new sheet in the current workbook.

9. The three parts of the Ribbon are _________, _________ and _________.

10. For absolute referencing, _________ sign is used before the parts of formula.

Short Questions with Answers.

1. **Explain Spreadsheet and its Basics.**

   Answers: Spreadsheet can be compared to a paper ledger sheet. It consists of rows and columns and their intersection called cells.

2. **How can you add a new Excel worksheet?**

   Answers: To add a new Excel worksheet, you should insert worksheet tab at the bottom of the screen.

3. **What is the use of NameBox in MS-Excel?**

   Answers: Name Box is used to return to a particular area of the worksheet by typing the range name or cell address in the name box.

4. **How can you resize the column?**

   Answers: To resize the column, you should change the width of one column and then drag the boundary on the right side of the column heading till the width you want. The other way of doing it is to select the Format from the home tab, and in Format you have to select the Autofit column width under cell section.

5. **How many data formats are available in Excel? Name some of them.**

   Answers: Eleven data formats are available in Excel for data storage. Example:

   - Number: Stores data as a number.
   - Currency: Stores data in the form of currency.
   - Date: Data is stored as dates.
   - Percentage: Stores numbers as a percentage.
   - Text formats: Stores data as string of texts.

6. **Differentiate between relative and absolute cell referencing techniques with the help of sample data.**

   Answers: With relative cell addressing, when you copy a formula from one area of the worksheet to another, Excel records the position of the cell relative to the cell that originally contained the formula. This is the default mode of referencing in a spreadsheet. Absolute referencing implies that the coordinates of a cell are not changed when a formula is copied from one cell to another. To make a cell address an absolute cell address, place a dollar sign in front of both the row and column identifiers.

   For example, if the formula =A1+B1 is copied from cell C! to cell C3, then it automatically changes to =A3+B3. But if the formula =$A$1 + $B$1 is copied from cell C1 to cell C3, then it remains unchanged. The dollar sign locks the cell location to a fixed position. Therefore, when it is copied and pasted, it remains exactly the same

7. **How are charts useful in Excel? Compare any three types available in Excel.**

   Answers: Charts are useful as they are an excellent tool to present data in a worksheet in a visually appealing format which aids in analysing and comparing data.

   Three chart types available in Excel are:

   - Column Chart: A column chart shows data changes over a period of time or illustrates comparisons among items.
   - Bar Chart: It illustrates comparisons among individual items. Categories are organized vertically, values horizontally to focus on comparing values and to place less emphasis on time.
   - Pie Chart: It shows the proportional size of data that makes up a data series and is useful when we want to emphasize a significant element.

8. **Difference between Function and Formula in Excel.**

   Answers: Formula is a statement which is written by the user for calculations *Ex: =1+2+3*

   Function is a built-in formula by Excel *Ex =SUM(a1+a2+a3).*

9. **What is COUNT and COUNTA?**

   Answers: COUNT: Counts the number of cells which contains only numbers except for blank cells.

   COUNTA: Counts the number of cells which contains alpha-numeric except blank cells.

10. **What is Freeze Panes in MS-Excel?**

    Answers: To lock any row or column, freeze panes is used. The locked row or column will be visible on the screen even after we scroll the sheet vertically or horizontally.

11. **Write formulas for the operations (a) – (d) based on the spreadsheet given below along with the relevant cell address:**

F16						
	A	B	C	D	E	F	G
1	S.No	Name	Science	Maths	English		
2		1 Swati	70	80	87		
3		2 Shruti	90	98	89		
4		3 Neelu	90	90	98		
5		4 Shreya	60	76	79		
6		5 Rekha	50	45	67		
7	Max						
8	Count						
9							

a. To calculate the Total marks as sum of Science, Maths and English for each student and display them in F.

b. To calculate the average marks for each student and display them in column G.

c. To calculate the highest marks in English and display it in cell E7.

d. To calculate the total number of students appearing for the Science test and display it in cell C8.

Answers: To lock any row or column, freeze panes is used. The locked row or column will be visible on the screen even after we scroll the sheet vertically or horizontally.

a. In cell F2, enter the formula = SUM (c2:e2). Now copy this formula to cells F3, F4, F5, and F6.

b. In cell G2, enter the formula = AVERAGE(c2:e2). Now copy this formula to cells G3, G4, G5, and G6.

c. In cell E7, enter the formula = Max(e2:e6).

d. In cell C8, enter the formula = COUNT(c2:C6) or enter the formula = COUNTA(b2:b6).

	A	B	C	D	E	F	G
1	S.No	Name	Science	Maths	English	Total	Average
2		1 Swati	70	80	87	237	79
3		2 Shruti	90	98	89	277	92
4		3 Neelu	90	90	98	278	93
5		4 Shreya	60	76	79	215	72
6		5 Rekha	50	45	67	162	54
7	Max				98		
8	Count		5	5			

12. Write command for the operations a to c based on the spreadsheet below.

A1					Item Code		
	A	B	C	D	E	F	G
1	Item Code	Item Desc	Type	Unit price	Qty	Amount	Rebate
2	101	Pen	Consumable	150	1500		
3	102	Photo Copier	Non-consumable	240000	24		
4	103	Photo copy machine	Non-consumable	6500	70		
5	104	Eraser	Consumable	110	8400		
6							

a. To calculate the Amount as UnitpriceQty for each item in Column F.

b. To calculate the Rebate as 7% of Amount of Type is consumable, else calculate Rebate as 11% of Amount in Column G.

c. To calculate total Rebate across all itmes in cell G6.

Answers:

a. At cell F2, type =D2E3 and the copy the formula using mouse. Fill handle onto range F3:F5.

b. At cell G2, type = IF(C2="Consumable", F20.07,F20.11) and the copy this formula using mouse Fill handle onto range G3:G5.

c. At cell G6, type = Sum(G2:G5).

13. Suggest the appropriate function for the following situations:

a. Selecting the maximum value out of a range *A1* to *B20*.

b. Calculating average of marks entered in cells *E4, F5, G5, H5,* and *I5*.

c. Determining whether the student has passed (if scored >=40) or not from the marks stored in cell *J10*.

Answers:

a. MAX(A1:B20)

b. =AVG(E5:I5)

c. =IF(J10 >40, "Pass", "Fail")

Descriptive Type Questions.

1. Can you create shortcuts to Excel functions?

2. Write any five advantages about using electronic spreadsheet in place of manual spreadsheet.

3. Define workbook and worksheet. What is the difference between them?

4. Explain active worksheet.

5. What are formulas and how are they created?

6. Define Pivot Table and explain its usage.

7. What is Auto Sum in Excel?

8. What is Excel sort and filter?

9. How will you insert and remove sheets from workbooks?

10. Define function in Spreadsheet Software. Describe any five functions.

Answers

A.	1. b	2. c	3. c	4. d	5. c
	6. b	7. c	8. c	9. b	10. d
	11. b	12. a	13. b	14. c	15. d

B.	1. F	2. F	3. T	4. F	5. F
	6. F	7. T	8. T	9. F	10. F
	11. T	12. T	13. T	14. F	15. T

C.	1. D	2. a	3. b	4. c	5. f
	6. e	7. g	8. i	9. h	10. k

D	1. a	2. c	3. d	4. b	5. i
	6. e	7. g	8. f	9. h	10. j

CHAPTER 5

Presentations Using PowerPoint

Structure

In this chapter, we will discuss the following topics:

- Introduction to PowerPoint
- Creating of presentation
- Manipulating slides
- Presenting of slides
- Slide show
- Providing aesthetics

Objectives

After completing this chapter, the reader will be able to understand the following:

- Basic knowledge of presentations.
- Opening/saving a presentation and printing of slides and handouts.
- Manipulating slides to enhance the look of the slides as well as creating a whole presentation whole presentation by inserting a picture, objects, multimedia formatting, and so on.
- Running a slide show with various transitions.

PowerPoint is a presentation program which helps people present a speech using a collection of slides. Each slide can contain text, graphics, animations, videos and other information. These collections of slides can be used to create an oral presentation.

Introduction to PowerPoint

PowerPoint 2013 is a presentation program developed for the Windows and macOS computer operating systems. It is a part of the Microsoft Office system which is widely used by business people, educators, students, and trainers. It is among the most prevalent forms of persuasion technology. According to its vendor, Microsoft Corporation, some 30 million presentations are made with PowerPoint every day.

In Microsoft PowerPoint, as in most other presentation software, text, graphics, movies, and other objects are positioned on individual pages or "slides". The "slide" is a reference to the slide projector, a device which has become somewhat obsolete due to the use of PowerPoint and other presentation software. Slides can be printed or displayed on-screen and navigated through at the command of the presenter.

Transitions between slides can be animated in a variety of ways, as can the emergence of elements on a slide itself. The overall design of a presentation can be controlled with a master slide. The slide structure, extending to the text on each slide, can be edited using an outliner. Presentations can be saved and run in many types of file formats.

Opening PowerPoint 2013 for Presentation

To start PowerPoint 2013, perform the following steps:

1. Click the **Start** button on the Taskbar.
2. Highlight **All Programs**. The left pane of the start menu displays the programs installed on your computer.
3. Click on Microsoft Office 2013, select **PowerPoint 2013**. The PowerPoint screen appears as shown in *Figure 5.1*:

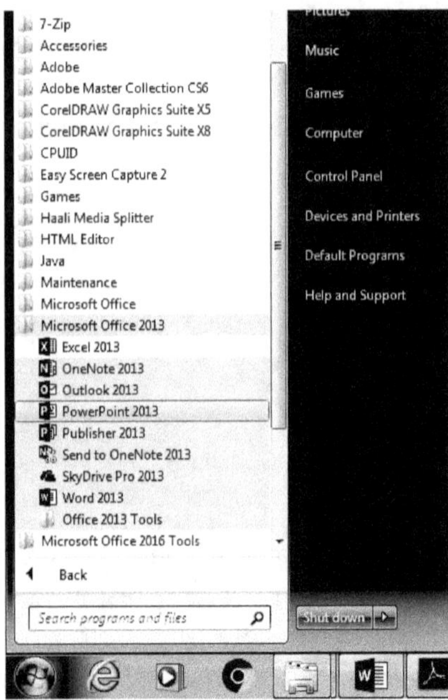

Figure 5.1: *Starting PowerPoint with the Start Button*

4. Other ways to launch a program, click **start** button and type the program's name in the search box the program in the search results to launch it.

When you first start PowerPoint 2013, it displays a blank presentation with a single slide showing. The layout is simple, with a title at the top and a subtitle below (*see Figure 5.2*):

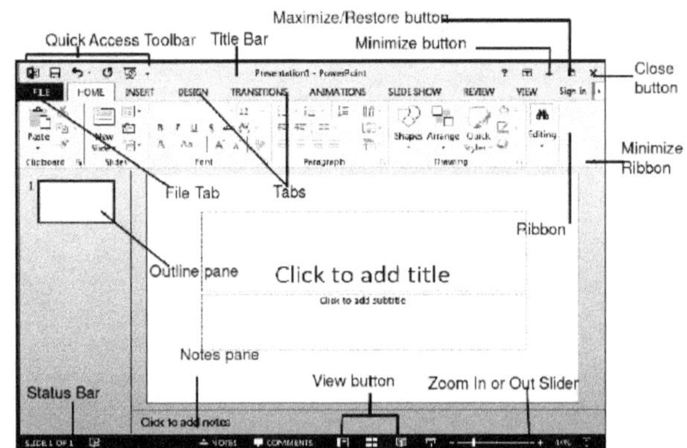

Figure 5.2: *A Blank Presentation displayed by PowerPoint*

Understanding the Screen Elements

You will notice a close resemblance of the PowerPoint 2013 opening screen with the opening screens of Word 2013 and Excel 2013. The main elements of the PowerPoint window are as shown in *Figure 5.2*.

- **Title bar:** The Title bar is at the top of the screen (*see Figure 5.2*). It shows the title PowerPoint and the name of the presentation. If you have not yet saved any presentation, then it displays the default name for the presentation, which is Presentation1.
- **Ribbon:** Ribbon is displayed just below the title bar. In Ribbon, Commands are organized in logical groups, which are collected together under tabs (*Figure 5.2*).
- **Quick Access Toolbar:** This toolbar is located by default at the top of the PowerPoint 2010 window. By default, this toolbar displays the Save, Undo and Repeat buttons.
- **Minimize button:** This shrinks the application window to a bar on the taskbar. You can click its button on the taskbar to reopen it.
- **Restore button:** A double box at the right of a title bar that restores an application or document into a sizable window.
- **Close button:** A box at the right of a title bar (X) that closes the window or dialog box.
- **Work area:** Where active PowerPoint slide(s) appear. It shows it in Normal view, but other views are available that make the work area appear differently.

- **Status bar:** It gives information about the presentation and provides shortcuts for changing the view and the zoom.

Exploring the PowerPoint 2013 Interface

There is a new look for PowerPoint 2013. There is also a new user interface that replaces menus, toolbars, and most of the task panes from the previous versions of PowerPoint.

The new user interface is designed to help you be more productive in PowerPoint, more easily find the right features for various tasks, and also be more efficient.

The PowerPoint 2013 interface consists of various components, which are as follows:

- Minimize/Maximize/Restore and Close buttons. The Minimize, Maximize, and Close buttons are located on the top-right corner of the MS PowerPoint window. The Minimize button is used to minimize the MS PowerPoint window over the Taskbar whereas the Maximize button helps to restore or maximize the MS PowerPoint window. The Close button is used to close the document (*see Figure 5.2*).

- **File Tab:** The File tab is located in the upper-left corner of PowerPoint 2013 and above the Quick Access Toolbar. When you click the File tab, you can see the Backstage view. The File tab contains the basic file management commands such as New, Open, Save, Save As, Print, and so on.

- **Quick Access Toolbar:** The Quick Access Toolbar is a customizable toolbar that contains a set of commands that are independent of the tab that is currently displayed. You can add buttons that represent commands to the Quick Access Toolbar. You can move the Quick Access Toolbar from one of the two possible locations. This toolbar is located by default at the top of the PowerPoint 2013 window. It provides tools that you use frequently, such as Save, Undo and Repeat buttons (*see Figure 5.2*). You can customize the Quick Access Toolbar by adding commands to it.

To add a command to the Quick Access Toolbar, perform the following steps:

1. Right-click the appropriate command that you want to add to the Quick Access Toolbar (*see Figure 5.3*):

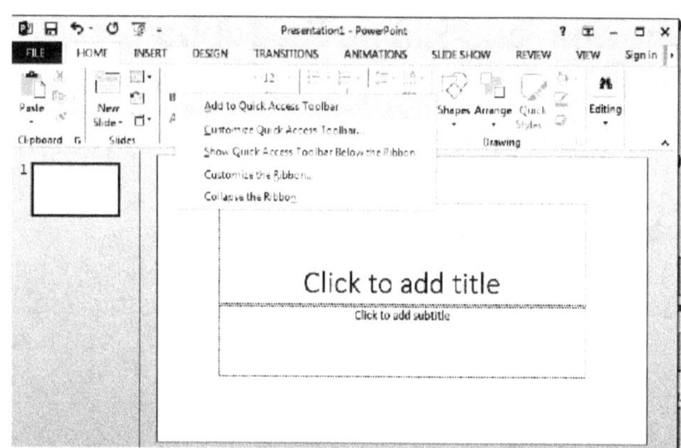

Figure 5.3: *Add command to Quick Access Toolbar*

2. Then click **Add to Quick Access Toolbar** from the context menu, as shown in *Figure 5.3*.

Dialog Box Launchers

The dialog box launchers are small icons that appear in some groups on the Ribbon. Clicking a Dialog Box Launcher opens a related dialog box or task pane, providing more options related to that group.

Ribbon

The primary replacement for menus and toolbars in PowerPoint 2013 is the Ribbon. Designed for easy browsing, the Ribbon consists of tabs that are organized around specific scenarios or objects. The controls on each tab are further organized into several groups. The Ribbon can host richer content than menus and toolbars can, including buttons, galleries, and dialog box contents (*see Figure 5.4*).

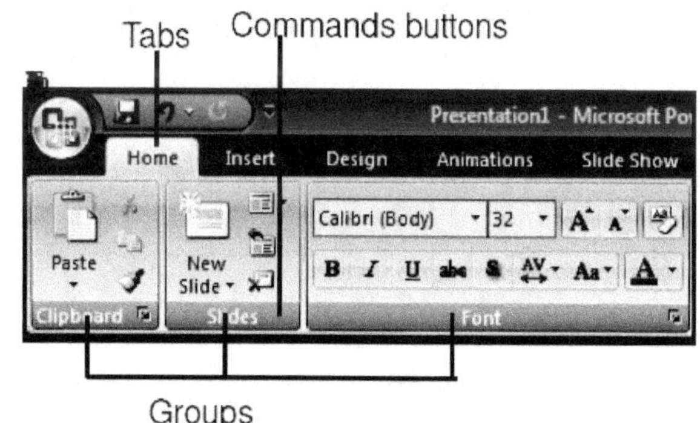

Figure 5.4: *Groups, Command and Tabs on the Ribbon*

1. Tabs are designed to be task-oriented.
2. Groups within each tab breaks a task into sub-tasks.
3. Command buttons in each group carry out a command or display a menu of commands.

Showing and Hiding the Ribbon

The Ribbon is designed to respond to the current task; you can minimize it if you find that it takes up too much screen space. Click the Ribbon Display Options arrow in the upper-right corner of the Ribbon to display the drop-down menu.

- **Auto-hide Ribbon:** Auto-hide displays your workbook in full-screen mode and completely hides the Ribbon. To show the Ribbon, click the Expand Ribbon command at the top of screen.
- **Show Tabs:** This option hides all command groups when they are not in use, but tabs will remain visible. To show the Ribbon, simply click a tab.
- **Show Tabs and Commands:** This option maximizes the Ribbon. All of the tabs and commands will be visible. This option is selected by default when you open PowerPoint for the first time.

Scroll Bar

The Scroll bar appears at the right side of the PowerPoint. You can also scroll between different slides by using the up and down arrow buttons present in the scroll bar.

Work Area

Where active PowerPoint slide(s) appears. It shows it in Normal view, but other views are available that make the work area different.

Status Bar

It gives the information about the presentation of the current slide, such as slide number and theme name. The slide number displays the currently selected slide with the total number of the slides present in the presentations; whereas, the theme name represents the name of the theme applied to the presentation.

Slides Pane

It is located at the upper-right corner of the PowerPoint window. It displays a large view of the current slide. You can use the vertical scroll bar to view other slides in PowerPoint. The thumbnails make it easy for you to navigate through your presentation and to see the effect of any design changes. You can also easily rearrange, add or delete slides.

Notes Pane

It is located below the slide pane and you can type notes for reference. The notes pane lets you add speaker notes or information you want to share with the audience. If you want to have graphic in your notes, you must add the notes in the note's page view. This view helps you prepare the speaker notes used while you are making the presentation to your audience. Notes page view produces a smaller version of the slide on the top part of a page and leaves the lower part free for notes or key points.

Zoom Control

Zoom control appear in the status bar to get a larger or smaller in a presentation or by dragging the Zoom slider right to left. You can also click the Zoom In (+ plus) button to get a larger view and Zoom Out (- minus) button to get a smaller view of the presentation.

Exploring the Tabs

Ribbon in PowerPoint 2013 is a group of tabs. A command tab is a collection of commands of a specific category. Commands in a command tab are placed into different groups. Each command set represents a subcategory of commands. Contextual tabs appear on the Ribbon when you add or select some object, such as image, a table, or a chart on a PowerPoint slide. An example of a contextual tab is the Format tab. Some of the tabs are discussed in the following sections.

Home Tab

When you click it, this tab is active. Buttons related to working with document contents are organized in this tab. It has six groups: Clipboard, Slides, Font, Paragraph, Drawing and Editing. Only the button representing commands that can be performed on the currently selected document element are active. The groups for the **Home** Tab are as follows:

- **Clipboard:** This group contains **Cut, Copy,** and **Paste** commands. It is used to open the clipboard task pane that will display when items are added to the clipboard.
- **Slides:** It allows you to insert new slides. Layout option adjusts or changes the layout of individual slides as well as positions, size and formatting of the slide placeholder and organizes the slide into section.
- **Font:** It adjusts the font type and size and color. You can make it bold, italic, or underline. Change the color or highlighting and also

change the text to uppercase or lowercase.

- **Paragraph:** It creates bullets or numbered lists, and it also changes the alignment of text and changes the spacing between lines.
- **Drawing:** This tab contains options to insert different shapes such as rectangle and circles. You can arrange shapes such as position and rotate on a selected slide. It also applies fill color in the selected shape and adds effect to the shapes.
- **Editing:** This group contains find, edit, select, and replace text in a presentation.

Insert Tab

It has seven groups: Tables, Images, Illustrations, Links, Text, Symbols, and Media. When you need to insert anything into your slide show, this is where you come to do it. The groups available to you are as follows:

- **Tables:** It lets you insert tables into the slide. These can be pre-made or you can make them as you like.
- **Images:** It allows you to insert pictures from a file as well as from the Clip Art in a slide. You can also create a photo album and apply visual effects to pictures. It allows you take a screenshot of all currently opened windows on the computer.
- **Illustrations:** It lets you to insert inbuilt shapes, Smart Arts, and charts in the presentation.
- **Links:** It allows you to insert a hyperlink, which takes you out of your slide show to a Web page. It also applies an action to cause something to happen in the slide show if you hover over to an object to jump to the next slide.
- **Comments:** It lets you insert comments.
- **Text:** It is used to draw a text box when adding text to shapes and objects, and give it an artistic effect. To insert headers and footers along with date, times, slide numbers and other embedded objects.
- **Symbols:** It lets you insert symbols and edit equations in the presentation.
- **Media:** It is used to insert video clips and sounds and to create a truly lively presentation.

Design Tab

This tab contains commands related to the appearance of the slides like Variants, Themes and Customize. It is also used to make changes to a slide's size, background, and other design attributes.

- **Themes:** Click the design to apply it to the presentation
- **Variants:** It is used to change the colors for the selected theme, such as colors, fonts and effects
- **Customize:** This group contains the Slide size and Format Background option. It also changes the slide size from standard to Widescreen and is used to add background pictures to a slide with formatting features.

Transitions

The Transitions tab can be used to set slide transitions effects, add transitions to a slide, and set the timing for the slide show of the presentation. It determines how the slides in the presentations will move from slide to slide. It has three groups: Preview, Transition to this slide and Timing.

- **Preview:** It helps to view the slide after the transition effect is applied.
- **Transition to this slide:** It allows you to apply transition to a slide and set the effect option specific to a transition.
- **Timing:** It allows you to add transition sound and set the time to move to the next slide.

Animations Tab

This tab can be used to set animation for the presentation. It determines how the bullets, pictures, images, and other objects will enter the slide during a presentation. You can add animation effect on individual objects to the slide. They are organized on this tab. It has four groups:

- **Preview:** This option is used to display the transition effect and animation applied on objects and text.
- **Animation:** It allows you to apply animation to a slide and the effect based on the animation type.
- **Advanced Animation:** It allows you to apply advanced animation effect for the selected element in a slide.
- **Timings:** This option is used to set the time duration when an animation should start to

play and also to specify how many seconds to wait before the animation starts to play.

Slide Show

This tab provides options for presenting the slide show to the audience and narration for the show can be recorded. In addition, a custom show can be created. It has **three** groups: Start slide show, Set Up, and Monitors.

- **Start Slide Show:** You can start the slide show at the first slide or start the show at the beginning, even though the insertion point is not in the first slide. You can apply custom slide show displays on only selected slides.
- **Set Up:** It is used to set up advanced options for a presentation, such as viewing the show on a kiosk as well as set to rehearse the timing for a presentation. These timings can be used when a presentation displays on a kiosk. And you have set media controls for audio and video how when the mouse pointer is moved over an object at the time of a slide show presentation.
- **Monitors:** This option is to choose whether to let PowerPoint chose the monitor or to allow the presenter to select the monitor to show the presentation. This option is available when more than one monitor is connected to the computer.

Review Tab

In this tab, you can view and add comments to your presentation, and you might prefer to check the spelling all at once when you finish your document. It has **four** groups: Proofing, Language, Comments and Compare.

- **Proofing:** Check the spelling, open the research task pane to references for more information; find synonyms so you do not use the same word repeatedly, check the grammar, etc.
- **Language:** It allows you to translate the text into other language.
- **Comments:** Add or edit comments about a given slide, or about a specific bit of content on a slide. Helpful when planning narration.
- **Compare:** To compare different presentations, accept or reject the changes, and show the review pane.

View Tab

This tab is used to view the presentation in different formats during presentation. It has seven groups: Presentation Views, Master Views, Show/Hide, Zoom, Color/Grayscale, Window and Macros.

- **Presentation View:** In normal and slide sorter, you can view the slide as slide pane and thumbnails slides view and make it easy to rearrange the slides. Whereas, in notes page view, the slides appear at the top of the page and the speaker notes will show at the bottom of the page. And reading view is used to view the presentation as a side show that fits within the Window.
- **Master Views:** This view is to change the design and layout of the slide masters. These slide master view is a special feature in PowerPoint that allows you to quickly modify the slides and slide layouts in your presentation. From there, you can edit the slide master, which will affect every slide in the presentation.
- **Show/Hide:** This option is to display gridlines, rulers and other tools to help align objects on a slide. And also, to add speaker notes to a presentation.
- **Zoom:** To specify the zoom level of zoom in and zoom out for viewing the slide in the PowerPoint window.
- **Color/Grayscale:** To view the presentation in color, grayscale or even black and white.
- **Window:** This option arranges windows on the screen side-by-side, and you can switch from one window to another window as well.
- **Macros:** Macros are a miniature program used to perform specified tasks within a program.

Creation of Presentation

Microsoft PowerPoint is a presentation program developed by Microsoft. It has become the world's most widely used presentation program. It is a complete presentation program that allows teachers to produce professional-looking presentations in the classroom to give their slide presentations a consistent look. It helps you control the look of your slides - with design-related elements, Visual elements, color schemes, and layouts of slides.

Creating a Presentation Using a Template

A template is a file that contains many types of documents, including resumes, cover letters, business plans and business cards and so on. Microsoft provides templates and presentations that come pre-installed with PowerPoint. These templates offer various layouts, visual elements, and other design-related elements to create presentations.

To create a presentation by using a template, perform the following steps:

1. Click the **File** tab. The Backstage view appears, as shown in *Figure 5.5*.

2. Select the **New** option from the Backstage view. It displays the list of all available templates appearing in the middle pane, as shown in *Figure 5.5*.

Figure 5.5: *Select Sample templates under the Available Templates Themes*

3. In the sample templates, you can see different types of templates, with all formatting, such as background, themes, colors, font, and so on.

4. Select the desired template you want to apply. For example, we have selected Wisp, as shown in *Figure 5.6*:

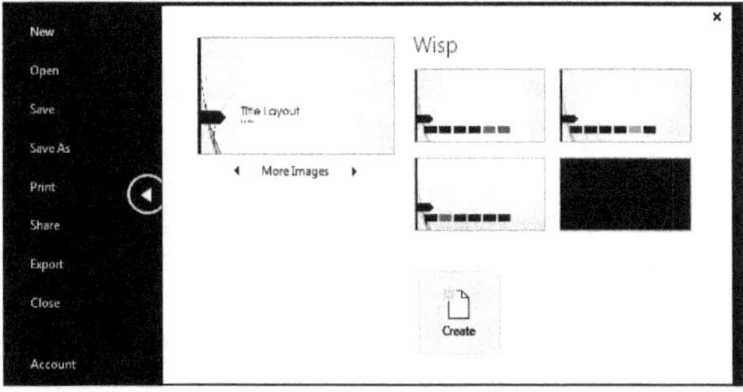

Figure 5.6: *Select desired Template from the sample Templates*

5. Click on the Create button.

6. You can see the selected template as a default name as Presentation4 title name as shown in *Figure 5.7*:

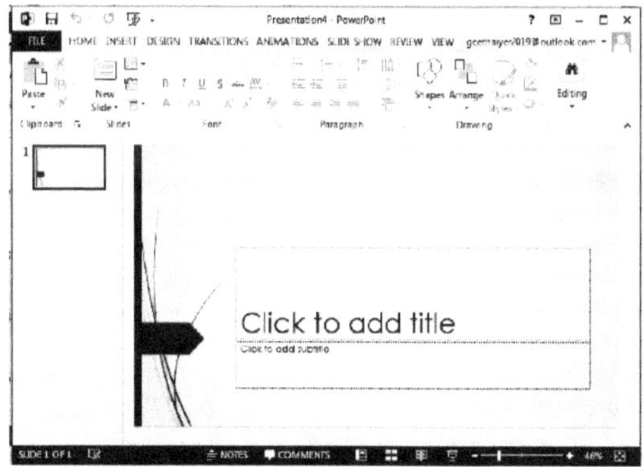

Figure 5.7: *PowerPoint Opens the selected Template*

Creating a Blank Presentation

When you start PowerPoint 2013, the program displays a blank title slide by default. You can begin to add text and pictures on that slide, choose a different slide layout, apply a design, and so on.

If you want to create a PowerPoint presentation on your own, you can use the blank template in PowerPoint 2013. The blank template offers only the basic visual elements of a presentation, such as placeholder to add a title to a slide.

To create a presentation by using the blank template, perform the following steps:

1. Click the **File** tab. The Backstage view appears, displaying various options, as shown in *Figure 5.8*:

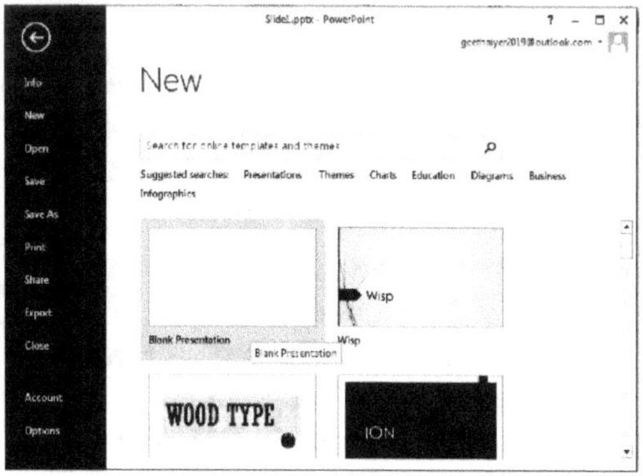

Figure 5.8: *File Backstage View*

2. Select the **New** option from the Backstage view.

3. The list of all available templates appears in the middle pane. Select the Blank presentation option.

4. Click the **Create** button.

5. The new presentation is created with the name Presentation2, as shown in *Figure 5.9*:

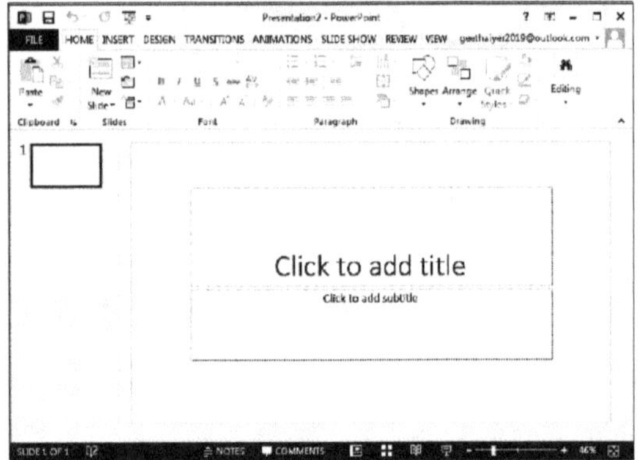

Figure 5.9: *Blank Presentation with the default name Presentation2*

You can see that a blank presentation contains a single slide with text boxes (placeholders) to enter a title and a subtitle. You can also apply different styles and backgrounds to it.

Inserting and Editing Text on a Slide

A PowerPoint slide always contains text of some kind, even if it is just a title. Entering and editing text in PowerPoint is similar to entering and editing text in Word or Excel.

Inserting Text to Slides

You can enter text in a presentation in the following three ways:

- Inserting a new slide with the text place holder.
- Inserting text in an existing slide.
- Inserting a New Slide.

When you insert a new slide, it will usually have placeholders to show you where the content will be placed. Placeholders can contain different types of content, including text, images, and videos. Many placeholders have thumbnail icons you can click on to add specific types of content.

Whenever you start a new presentation, it will contain one slide with the Title Slide layout. You can insert as many slides as you need from a variety of layouts.

To insert a new slide, perform the following steps:

1. Click the **Home** tab, select the **New Slide** drop-down arrow in the Slides group.

2. Choose the desired slide layout from the drop-down menu, as shown in *Figure 5.10*:

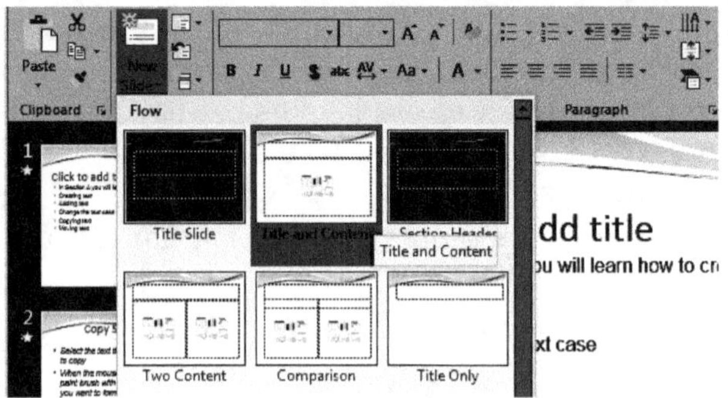

Figure 5.10: *Selecting New Slide*

3. The new slide will appear. Click any placeholder and begin typing to add text. You can also click on an icon to add other types of content, such as a picture or a chart, as shown in *Figure 5.11*:

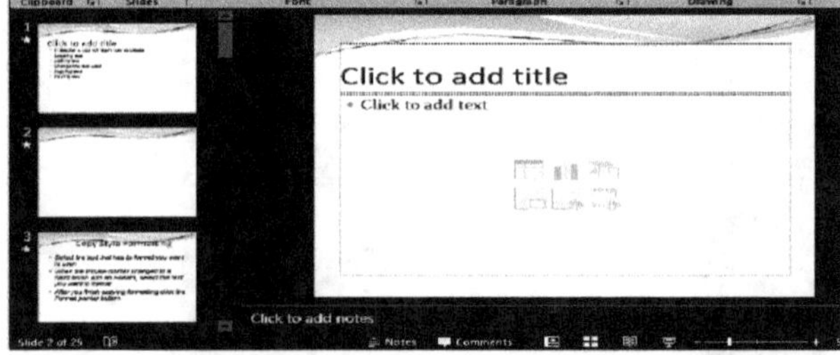

Figure 5.11: *New slide with Title and Content*

4. To change the layout of an existing slide, click the Layout command, then choose the desired layout.

Adding Text in a Placeholder

PowerPoint 2013 comes with pre-defined layouts you want to use, or you can add a blank slide and create a custom layout. Many of these layouts contain text placeholders for title, body and bulleted list.

1. After inserting a new slide, click anywhere within a placeholder to select it. The border indicates that the current placeholder is selected, as shown in *Figure 5.12*:

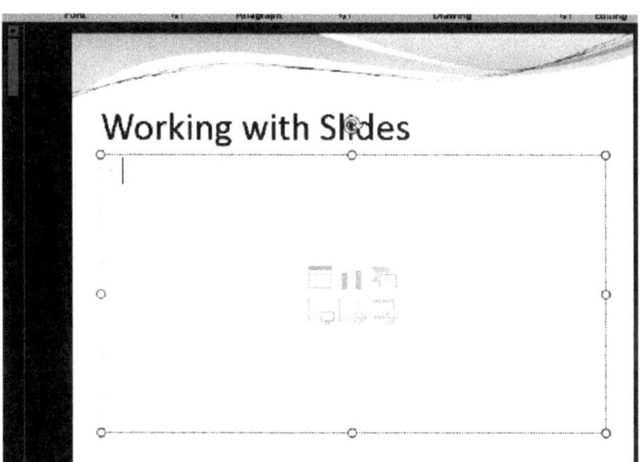

Figure 5.12: *Add text to placeholder*

2. The sample text disappears, and an insertion point appears inside the placeholder, indicating that you can enter or type text.
3. If it is a bulleted-list placeholder, the sample text disappears and the bullet remains with the insertion point positioned where the text will begin.
4. Type the text for the slide inside the selected placeholder and press the **Enter** key.
5. In the case of bullets, press the **Enter** key when you want to begin a new bulleted item. If the bulleted text is too long to fit on one line, PowerPoint automatically wraps the text to the next line and aligns the text.
6. When you finish entering the text, deselect the object by clicking on a blank area of the slide of the gray border around the slide.

Editing Text on a Slide

You can make changes to the text in any text object, simply by clicking on the object. An insertion point appears, indicating that the text is ready for editing. Then, you can start making changes to the text. Before you can change the existing text, you have to select it by using the following techniques:

Select an individual word by double-clicking it. The word and the space following it are selected.

Alternatively, position the insertion point at the beginning of the text you want to select, hold down the **Shift** key, and either press an arrow key to select characters one at a time or click the end of the text you want to select.

Select an entire slide title by clicking its **slide** icon on the **Outline** tab.

Select all the text in a placeholder by clicking inside the placeholder and then clicking select and then **Select All** in the **Editing** group on the **Home** tab.

Copying Text

You can copy the text that appears in one place to another place. Copying of text occurs with the assistance of the Windows Clipboard. The Clipboard is an area of your computer's memory that is used for holding data. As long as the data is on the Clipboard, you can place it anywhere in any Windows software application. The data stays on the Clipboard until you replace it with new data, or until you exit Windows.

To copy text using the ribbon command, perform the following steps:

1. Select the text you want to copy.
2. In the **Home** tab, click on the **copy** icon on the **Clipboard** group or (press the *Ctrl + C* keys together).
3. Move to the place in your presentation where you want to insert this text.
4. Click the **Paste** drop-pointing arrow and choose the **Paste** command on the **Clipboard** group (or press the **Ctrl + V** keys together).

Moving Text

The move operation is similar to the copy operation except that text is moved, that is, it is deleted from the original location and copied to a new place.

To move the text using the Ribbon command, perform the following steps:

1. Click the text to put the text box in edit mode.
2. Select the text you want to move.

   Using Cut and Paste is the way to move text around between slides. Just select and cut the text, move to the appropriate slide, and paste it where you want it.

3. Right-click and choose Cut from the shortcut menu or click the Cut button on the Home tab (or press **Ctrl + X** keys together). Move to the new location, right-click, and choose Paste or click the Paste button on the Home tab (or press **Ctrl +V** keys together).

Deleting Text

You can delete characters, words, or all the text in a text box using one of the following methods:

Method 1 : The **Delete** key erases the character to the right of the cursor.

Method 2 : The **Backspace** key erases the character to the left of the cursor.

Method 3 : If you delete text accidentally, you can undo your action by clicking the Undo button on the Quick Access Toolbar. (You can also press the **Ctrl + Z** keys together).

Inserting and Deleting Slides in a Presentation

To insert slide:

1. In the slide view, display the slide after which you want to insert the slide.
2. In the **Home** tab, click on the **New slide** drop-down arrow and then choose **New slide** with layout. The New slide is inserted.

Deleting Slides

To delete slide:

1. In the Slides pane, select the slide you want to delete.
2. On pressing the **Delete** key, the selected slide gets deleted.

Saving the Presentation

When working on a presentation, it is very important that you save it at regular intervals so that, in case there is system failure, you do not lose much of your work.

PowerPoint has two commands to save your file—the **Save** and **Save As** commands.

- The **Save** command is used to save the presentation.
- The **Save As** command is used when you want to save an existing presentation under a new name or you are saving your presentation for the first time.

To save a presentation, perform the following steps:

1. Click the **File** tab on the Ribbon. The Backstage view will appear. Select the **Save** option from the **File** tab or click the **Save** button on the Quick Access Toolbar or from the keyboard, press **Ctrl + S**.
2. If you have already saved the file, then PowerPoint updates the earlier saved file. If you have not saved the file before, the Save As dialog box, as shown in *Figure 5.13*, appears.

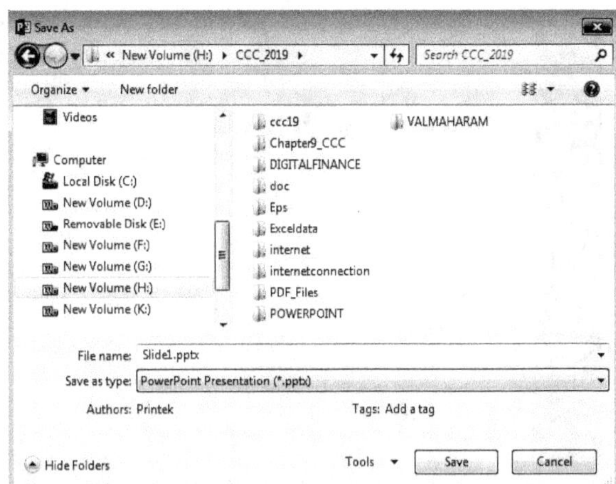

Figure 5.13: *PowerPoint's Save As dialog box*

3. In the Save As, the list box specifies the location where you want to save the file in the Save in: drop-down list. (Choose PowerPoint Template). It adds the template to your list of available templates.
4. Type the desired file name by which you want to save the presentation in the File Name: list box.
5. Click on the **Save** button.

To save a presentation using Save As command:

1. Click the **File** tab and choose **Save As....** The Save As dialog box in *Figure 5.13* appears. Now, follow Step 1 through 5 in the save procedure.

Manipulating Slides

In this section, we will see how to make changes in slides as per the requirement.

Inserting Table

To add some tabulated data, you can do it through many ways such as inserting table from Word file, or you can choose layout options of PowerPoint. You can insert data from the Excel worksheet as well.

You can insert a Table in a slide in two different ways. These are as follows:

1. Create a new slide which is specifically made to contain a table.
2. Insert a table in the existing slide.

To create a new slide with table:

1. Click the Insert tab, click the Table drop-down arrow, as shown in *Figure 5.14*.

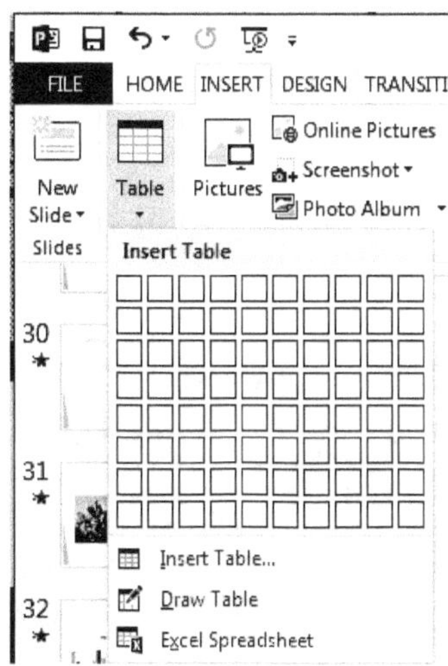

Figure 5.14: *Selecting rows and columns in table command*

2. Hover, the mouse over the grid of squares to select the desired number of columns and rows in the table. In our example, we have to insert a table with four rows and five columns.

   Or, you can also insert a table by clicking the Insert Table command in a placeholder.

3. The table will appear on the current selected side, as shown in *Figure 5.15*:

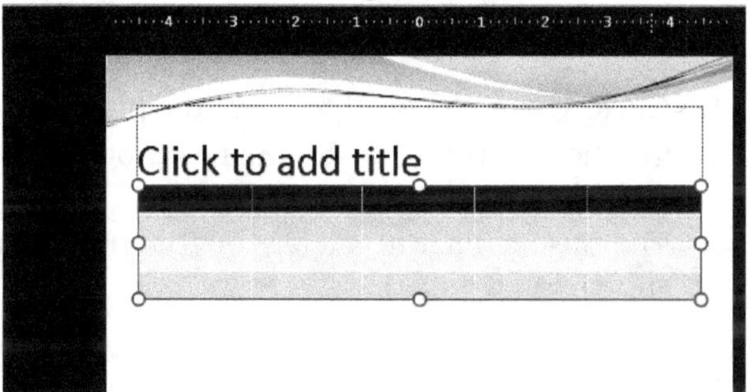

Figure 5.15: *The table is inserted*

Entering Text in a Table

When you create a new table, an empty table appears on the slide, as shown in *Figure 5.16*. When you insert a table, the insertion point flashes in the first cell in the upper-left corner of the table. The text you type appears at the insertion point. After entering the text in the table and to exit the editing mode, click anywhere outside the table. Or

1. Click anywhere in the table and begin typing to add text.

2. You can use the **Tab** key or the arrow keys on the keyboard to navigate through the slide.

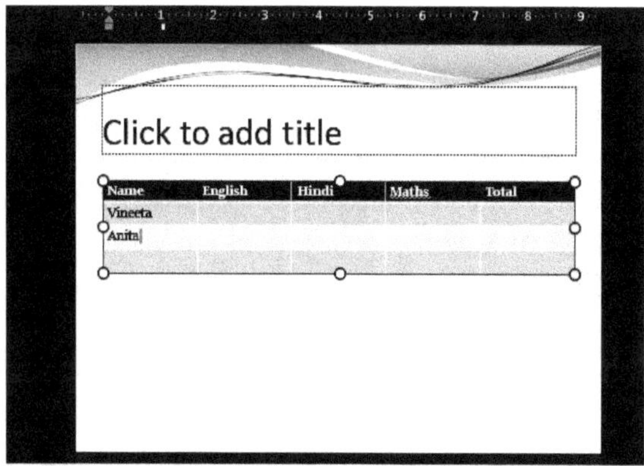

Figure 5.16: *Entering text in a table*

Editing a Table

PowerPoint includes several options for customizing tables, including moving and resizing as well as adding rows and columns.

To move a table, perform the following steps:

1. Click and drag the edge of a table to move it to a new location on a slide as shown below:

Table

Name	English	Hindi	Maths	Physics	Total
Vineta	34	45	56	35	170
Geeta	56	68	35	45	204
Sunita	78	80	47	68	273
Shashi	56	89	89	90	324
Rekha	78	56	90	76	300

Figure 5.17

To resize a table, perform the following steps:

1. Click and drag the sizing handles until the table is the desired size.

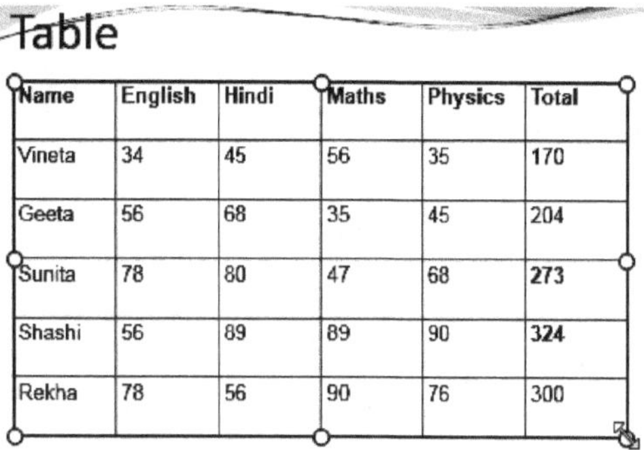

Table

Name	English	Hindi	Maths	Physics	Total
Vineta	34	45	56	35	170
Geeta	56	68	35	45	204
Sunita	78	80	47	68	273
Shashi	56	89	89	90	324
Rekha	78	56	90	76	300

Figure 5.18

Adding Clip Art Pictures

Clip Art gallery is a collection of graphic files in PowerPoint which you can insert in presentations. It has built a gallery of Clip Art images into the Clip Art gallery. But you also have your own collection of artwork available.

PowerPoint can help you select an appropriate piece of art for your slides by looking at keywords in your presentation, and trying to find pictures to match.

1. Select the slide that contain a Clip Art slide.

2. Click the **Insert** tab on the Ribbon, and click the Online Pictures button in the Images group, as shown in *Figure 5.19*. Or

   Click the **New Slide** drop-down arrow in the **Home** tab of **Slides** group. Click the **Picture Layout** option from the list. The Picture placeholder slide appears.

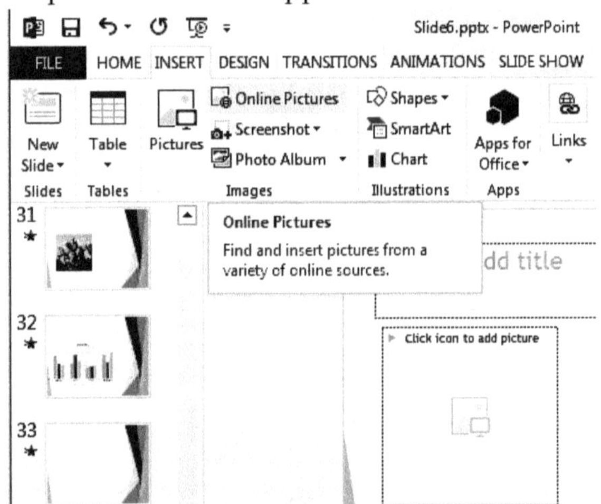

Figure 5.19: *Selecting Online Pictures*

3. The Insert Picture dialog box appears, as shown in *Figure 5.20*:

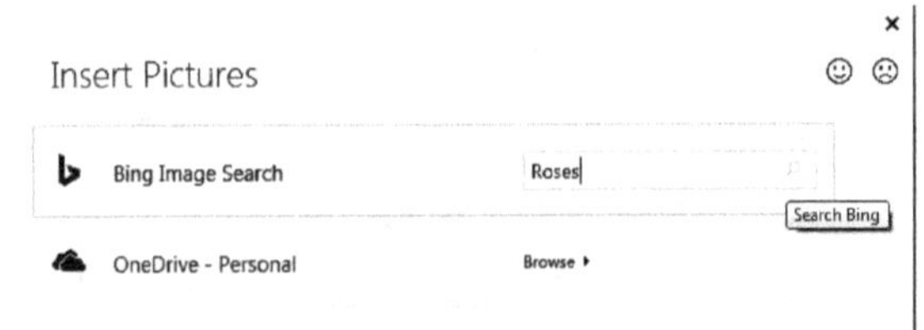

Figure 5.20: *Type the picture in the Insert Pictures dialog box*

4. Type the name of what you are looking for in the Bing Image Search box. For example, type Roses, click magnifying glass icon to search or press the **Enter** key.

5. Select the desired picture you want to insert picture, a small arrow at the right of the side of the picture. Click the arrow and then insert, as shown in *Figure 5.21*:

Figure 5.21: *Bing Search results and select the Picture*

6. The selected picture appears in the slide.

Inserting Other Objects

You may want to add a particular graphic to a presentation but not maintain it in the Clip Gallery. You can insert a picture from another application.

To insert a picture from a file, perform the following steps:

1. Click where you want to insert the picture.

2. On the **Insert** tab, in the **Images** group, click on **Pictures**.

3. The Insert Picture dialog box appears, as shown in *Figure 5.22*.

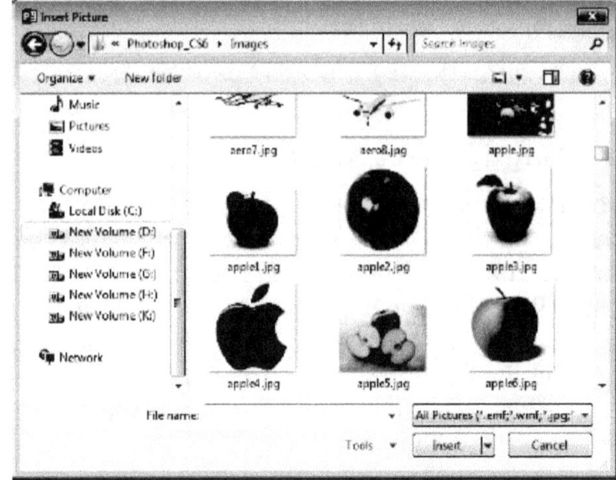

Figure 5.22: *Insert Picture Dialog Box*

4. Search a file in the Address bar.

5. Click the **Insert** button to place the graphic on the current slide.

Resizing and Scaling an Object

Resize an object

To resize or reshape an object, drag one of the object's handles in the direction you want. If you want to maintain the proportions of the object, hold the Shift key while dragging a corner handle. If you want the object to grow out from its current center, hold down while you drag a corner handle.

To resize an object:

1. Select the object you want to resize.
2. Drag a size handle until the object gets the desired shape and size you want (see *Figure 5.23*).

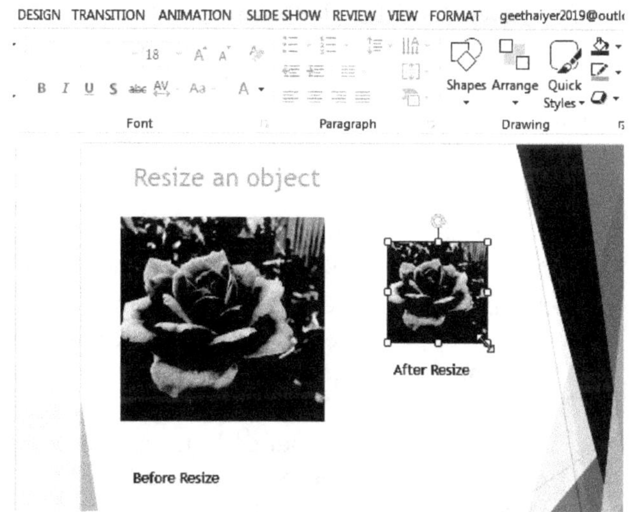

Figure 5.23: *Object has to be Resized*

Scaling an object

Rather than dragging objects into position, you can set object placements and sizing on the size and position tabs of Format Picture.

To scale an object, perform the following steps:

1. Select the object you want to scale.
2. Click the **Picture** Tools Contextual **Format** tab in the **Size** group.
3. Enter the percentage you want to change in the Shape Height: and Width: boxes. Alternatively, click the Size and Position dialog box launcher dialog box.

4. The Format Picture task pane appears at the left side of the window, as shown in *Figure 5.24.*

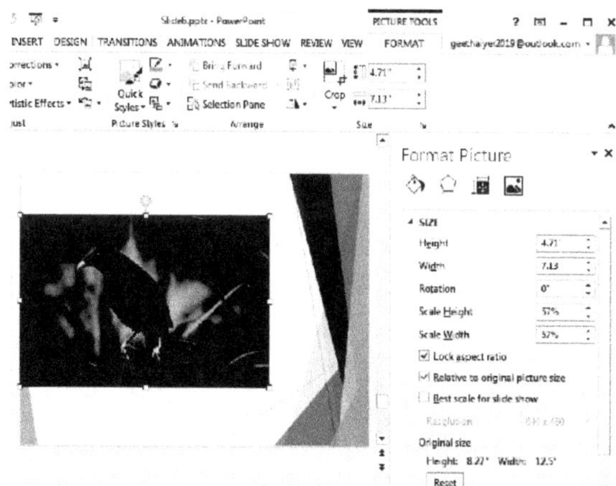

Figure 5.24: *Format Picture task pane*

5. Click the Size & properties tab, enter the percentage you want to change in the Scale Height and Scale Width spinner box.

To maintain the ratio between the object's height and width to resize it, select the Lock aspect ratio check box on the size tab.

Creating and Using Master Slide

Slide Master View is a special feature in PowerPoint that allows you to quickly modify the slides and slide layouts in your presentation. From there, you can edit the slide master, which will affect every slide in the presentation. You can also modify individual slide layouts, which will change any slides using those layouts.

Slide Master View can help you create a consistent, professional presentation without a lot of effort. You could use Slide Master View to change in your presentation, but here are some of its most common uses.

- **Modify backgrounds:** Slide Master View makes it easy to customize the background for all of your slides at the same time.

- **Rearrange placeholders:** If you find that you often rearrange the placeholders on each slide, you can save time by rearranging them in Slide Master View instead. When you adjust one of the layouts in Slide Master View, all of the slides with that layout will change.

- **Customize text formatting:** Instead of changing the text color on each slide individually, you could use the Slide Master to change the text color on all slides at once.

- **Create unique slide layouts:** If you want to create a presentation that looks different from regular PowerPoint themes, you could use Slide Master View to create your own layouts.

To create a master slide, perform the following steps:

1. Click the View tab. In the Master Views groups, click Slide Master.
2. The presentation will switch to Slide Master View, and the Slide Master tab will be selected on the Ribbon.
3. In the left navigation pane, scroll up and select the first slide. This is the slide master, as shown in *Figure 5.25*.

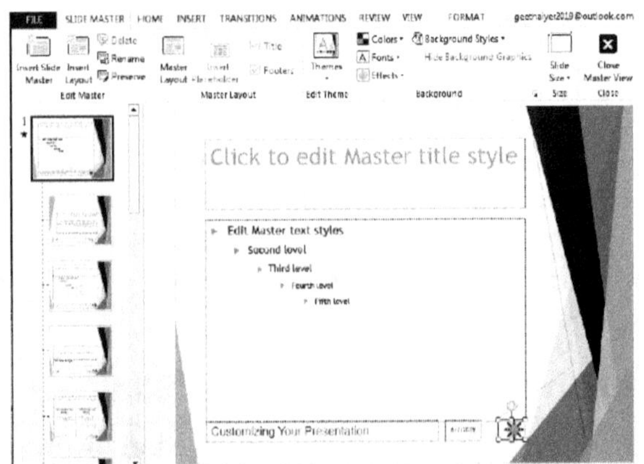

Figure 5.25: *PowerPoint Slide Master*

4. Make the desired changes to the slide master. For example, we insert a picture image.
5. Move, resize or delete slide objects, as needed. For example, we have resized the logo and moved it to the bottom-right corner, as shown in *Figure 5.24*.
6. After you insert the logo, click the Close Master View command on the Slide Master tab, as shown in *Figure 5.26*.

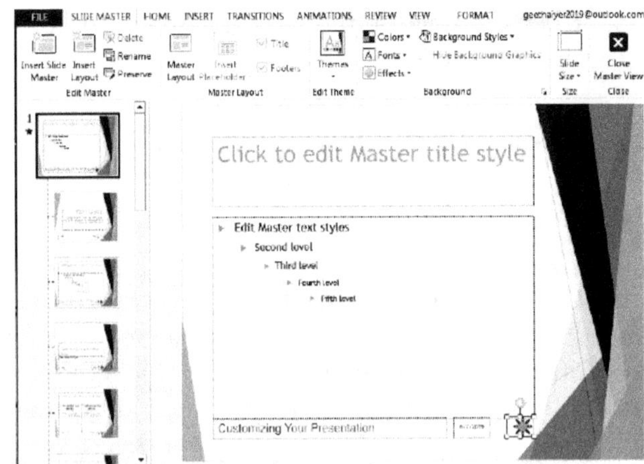

Figure 5.26: *Insert the picture of Logo*

7. The change will appear on all slides of the presentation.

Customizing Text Formatting

To change the text formatting on each slide, you can use the slide master to change the text color, size, and alignment to all slides at once.

To change the text formatting, perform the following steps:

1. Select the master title style on the slide master. For example, to change the font type, right-clicking the mouse button, the mini context toolbar appears select the Arial font option you want to change.
2. The selected Arial font is applied to all slide master and also the changed title font appears in the other slides of the master slide.
3. After you are finished, click the Close Master View command on the slide.

Instead of changing separate placeholders, you might change the theme fonts for a presentation from the Slide Master tab. Select the Fonts option in the Background group, and then click the desired fonts.

Presentation of Slides

Viewing a Presentation

PowerPoint offers **five** ways (views) to look at your presentation. Each view enables you to work on a different aspect of the presentation. The changes made in one view are also reflected in all other views.

To understand the function of views, consider that you are looking at a house. Now, assume you are standing in front of a house. You see one view. Now, you move to one of the sides and you see a different view of the same house. PowerPoint views also allow you to see a presentation in various ways.

The buttons located at the lower-left corner of the PowerPoint window just above the status bar, as shown in *Figure 5.27*, help you switch to different views.

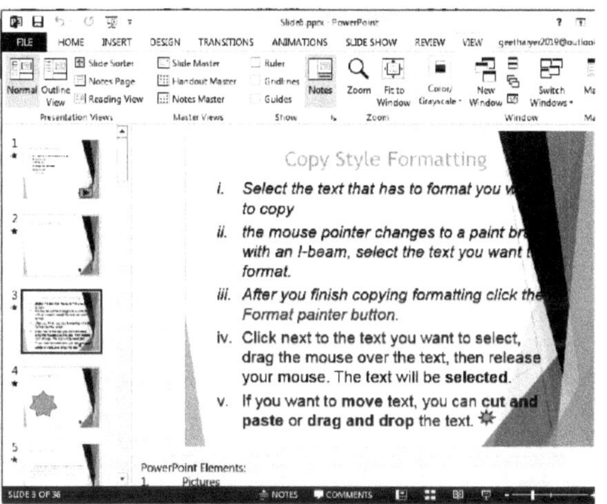

Figure5.27: *Normal View*

In the following section, you will conceptually learn about the view.

Normal View

Normal view is the main editing view, where you write and design your presentation. The view has three working areas:

- **Thumbnails:** This is a great place to view the slides in your presentation as thumbnail-sized images while you edit. The thumbnails make it easy for you to navigate through your presentation and to see the effect of any design changes. You can also easily rearrange, add or delete slides.
- **Slide pane:** In the slide pane, you can see how your text looks on each slide. You can add SmartArt graphics, movies and sounds, create hyperlink and add animations to individual slides.
- **Notes pane:** The Notes pane lets you add speaker notes or information you want to share with the audience. If you want to have graphic in your notes, you must add the notes in Notes page view.

These panes are also shown when you save a presentation as a Web page. The only difference is that the outline pane displays a table of contents so that you can navigate through the complete presentation.

Slide Sorter View

The slide sorter view is a view of your slides in thumbnail form (see *Figure 5.28*).

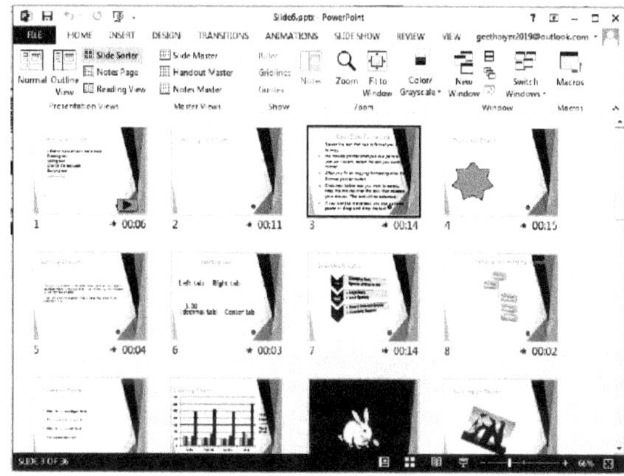

Figure 5.28: *PowerPoint's Slide Sorter View*

Working in this view is like laying out the pages of your presentation or report on the table so that you can see them all at once. In this view, you can see the design consistency and the flow of your presentation, and also you can easily reorder the slides, copy or delete the slides.

Notes Page View

This view helps you prepare the speaker notes used while making the presentation to your audience. Notes page's view produces a smaller version of the slide on the top part of a page and leaves the lower part free for notes or keypoints (see *Figure 5.29*).

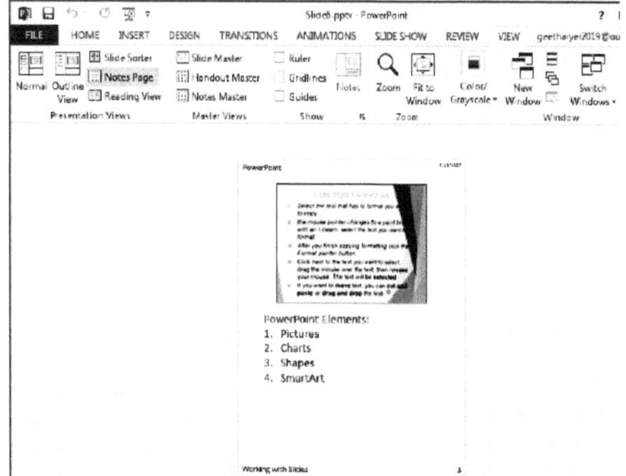

Figure 5.29: *PowerPoint's Notes Pages View*

Slide Show View

Use Slide show view to deliver your presentation to your audience. It occupies the full computer screen, exactly like an actual presentation. You can see how your graphics, timings, movies, animated effects, and transition effects will look during this view. (See *Figure 5.30*).

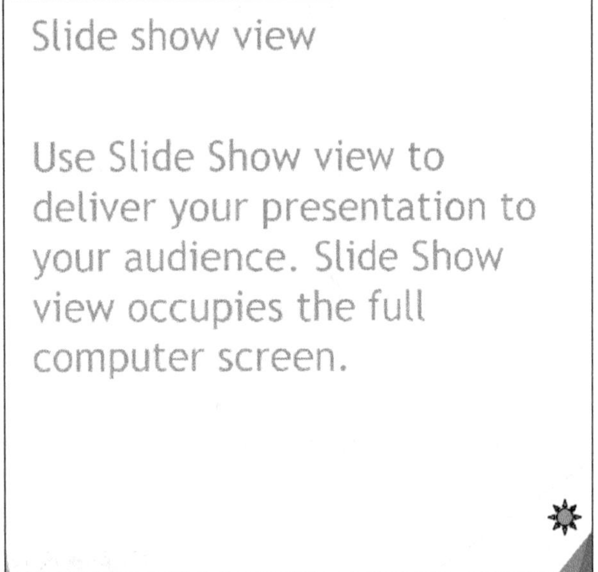

Figure5.30: Slide Show View

Reading View

Reading view is similar to Slide Show view because in both views, the slide is shown in full screen mode. However, in Reading view, you also see the PowerPoint title bar and the Status bar at the top and bottom of the interface.

Choosing a Set Up for Presentation

With the options in the Set Up dialog box, you can choose the type of show to run, and how the show should proceed.

To set a slide show option, perform the following steps:

1. Click the **Slide Show** tab in the **Set Up** group. Choose the Set Up Slide Show icon. The Set Up Show dialog box appears, as shown in *Figure 5.31*.

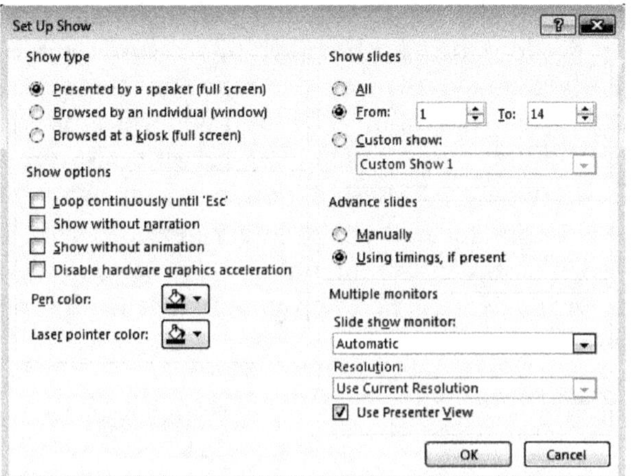

Figure 5.31: *The Set Up Show dialog box*

2. To Show all slides in your presentation, click the All in the Show slides section.
3. To show a specific group of slides from your presentation, enter a starting and ending slide in the From: and To: edit boxes.
4. To start a custom slide presentation that derives from another presentation, click Custom Show: drop-down list, and then click the presentation that you want to view as a custom show.

Header, Footers, and Notes

Header or Footer is the text that appears at the top (header) or bottom (footer) of each page in your presentation. This is a standard text or line of text that might include the company name, copyright or trademark symbols, time and date information or even a page number.

Here are a few things you should know about headers and footers:

1. First, headers and footers can be customized with font color, type, and size.
2. You can also choose to omit the header and footer from the title slide.
3. Only a footer can be added to slides, but both headers and footers can be added to your handouts and your notes pages.
4. Finally, the slide number or footer information can be different for your handouts and notes pages.

To add headers and footers to slides refer Adding Headers and footers.

Printing Slides and Handouts

Handout lets you include two, three, or six small images of the slides in your presentation. You can select the format when you print them.

Handouts can be created in the following two ways:

- Print the Handouts using the standard PowerPoint format, that is, two, three or six slides on a page format.
- The Handout format can be customized to your requirement using the handout master.

If you make Handouts, PowerPoint shrinks the slides you have created and fits them on a page, according to the option you choose in the print Backstage view. To use standard Handout formats, you only have to select the number of slides you want to print on a page when you take the printouts for Handouts.

The header, footer, page numbers and the date on each handout will be printed if you have selected any of these items on your Notes Pages. The same is automatically applied to your Handouts.

In case you want to have different headers, footers, page numbers or dates on your Handouts as compared to the Notes Pages, then you are required to change these in the Headers and Footer dialog box.

The golden rule in presentations is **Say more than you show and handout more than you say**. Therefore, the material that you hand out (either before or after your presentation) should be more than just pictures of your slides.

Printing Slides

In PowerPoint 2013, you can either print all the slides or the current slide of a presentation. In addition, you can decide how many slides you want to print on a single page.

To print a slide, perform the following steps:

1. Open the presentation that you want to print.
2. Click the **File** tab on the ribbon, click the **Print** tab. The Print Backstage view appears, as shown in *Figure 5.32*.

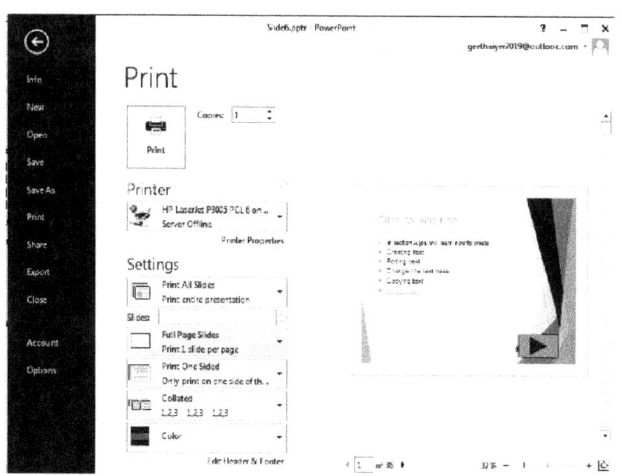

Figure 5.32: *Print Backstage view*

3. The name of the currently selected printer is shown under the Printer drop-down arrow. To print the presentation on a different printer, select the desired printer from the Printer drop-down list.
4. Specify the number of copies you want to print for each slide in the Copies: spinner box.
5. The Setting drop-down list has the option which allows you to select the pages you want to print.

Option	Description
Print All Slides	Choose Print All Slides option to print the entire presentation at one time.
Current slide	Choose the Current slide option to print the slide shown on the monitor.
Custom Range	Choose custom range to print the selected slides, and nter the corresponding slide numbers in the Slides: edit box, e.g., to print slide 3 and 6 through 8, enter 3,6-8 in the Slides edit box.
Custom Show	Prints a certain custom show which has been set up. Each custom show appears on the list.
Print Hidden Slides	If slides are hidden (do not display during a slide show), they can be printed by checking the Print Hidden Slides check box.

Table 5.1

6. **Collate:** Specify if you want to arrange while printing multiple copies. When you choose the collate option, each set is printed completely from the first page to the last page. Then, the next set is printed.

7. Click the Color button and select the color setting for the printouts:

   - **Color:** This is default. When you use this setting with a black-and-white printer, it results in slides with grayscale or black backgrounds.

   - **Grayscale:** To print in grayscale, select the grayscale check box.

   - **Pure black and white option:** Converts all colors in the presentation to either black or white. Prefer this option if you need to print on a printer that cannot print gray shades.

Printing Handouts

You can print your entire presentation—slides, outline, notes and audience handouts. You can also print specific slides, handouts, notes pages, or outline pages.

To print handouts, perform the following steps:

1. Open the presentation you want to print.

2. Click the **File** tab, the Backstage view appears.

3. To click one or multiple slides per page in handout format, under **Handouts**, click the number of slides you want per page, and whether you want them to appear in vertical or horizontal order (see *Figure 5.33*).

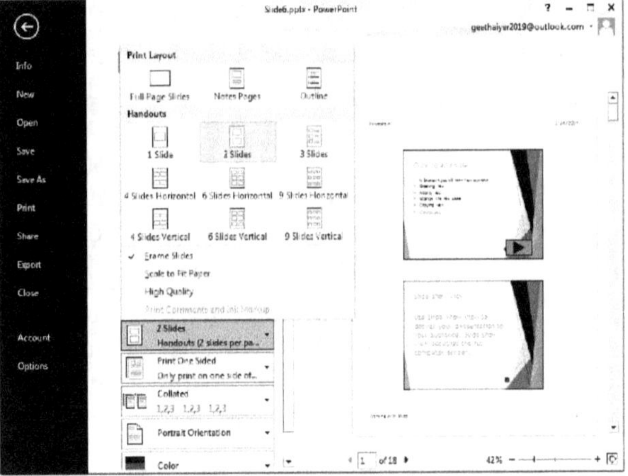

Figure 5.33: *Selecting Slides Per Page in Handout Format in the File Tab*

4. After applying the desired option, click **OK**.

Slide Show
Running a Slide Show

When you develop a slide show in the Slide Sorter view, you can get a preview of transition effects for all slides. But to see the transitions full-screen and to see animated or bulleted text slides, you must select the presentation as a slide show.

Starting the Slide Show

When you view a slide show, you have the following options:

1. Click the **Slide Show** tab in the **Start Slide Show** group, choose **Slide Show From Beginning** or Current Slide press **Shift + F5** keys together.

2. In the slide show, you go to the next slide, press **N** or click the **Backspace key** to go to the previous slide.

Controlling the Slide Show with a Mouse

During a slide Show, you can use the pop-up menu button. A pop-up menu appears as shown in *Figure 5.56*. As mentioned earlier, the button appears in the lower-left corner of the current slide as soon as you move the mouse pointer. You can then click the button to display the slide show pop-up menu.

The Next and Previous commands on the pop-up menu let you move forward or backward through the slides in your slide show.

To move to a specific slide, click on Go to Slide and then choose a slide from the menu (*see Figure 5.34*):

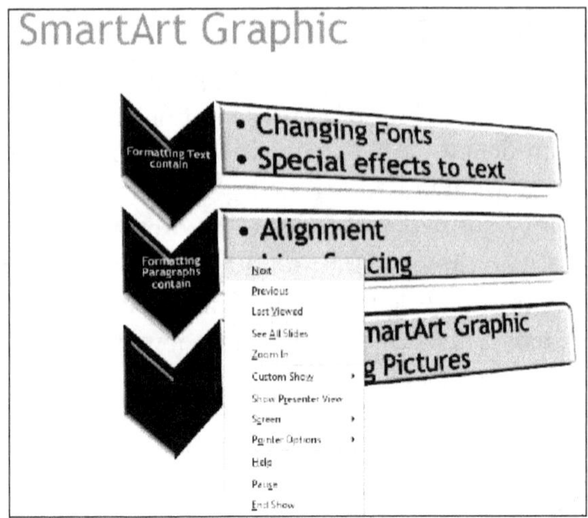

Figure 5.34: *Pop-up menu during Slide Show*

To stop a slide show at any time during a presentation, simply choose End Show from the pop-up menu.

Controlling the Slide Show with a Keyboard

In addition to the slide show pop-up menu, you can use the keys listed in *Table 5.2* to control various aspects of the show.

Press This	To Perform This Action
Spacebar, →, ↓, PgDn, or N	Advance to next slide
Backspace,←, ↑, PgUp, or P	Return to previous slide
Slide number + Enter	Go to slide number
B or period	Blacks/Unblacks the screen
W or comma	Whites/Unwhites the screen
Ctrl +A	Show mouse pointer as rrow
Ctrl + P	Show mouse pointer as pen
S or + (numeric keypad)	Stop/Restart automatic show
H	Go to next slide if hidden
T	Rehearse – use new time
O	Rehearse – use original time
Esc, Ctrl, + break or (-)	End Show

Table 5.2: *Slide Show keyboard controls*

Transitions and Slide Timings

Slide transitions are the effects that take place when one slide gives way to the next one in the presentation, like Roll down from top. Transition time is the actual time that the slide stays active during a slide show before moving on to the next slide. Transition duration is the amount of time it takes to move between slides. A transition can be as simple as fading or flashy as an eye-catching effect. It is easy to apply transitions to some or all of your slides, giving your presentation a professional look. In addition, you can set timings for transitions and also accompanied by transition sounds.

Whatever transition effect you may add, the basic concepts are as follows:

1. Transition effects happen when the slide shows up.
2. Transition speed controls how long it takes to transit from one slide to another.

3. Transition timings indicate how long the slide shows on screen. Most slides that are presented during sessions or conferences do not have fixed transition timings since speakers do not know exactly how long they will end up speaking while a particular slide is shown. In this case, a mouse click takes them to the next slide.

Adding Slide Transitions

Slides transitions are the animation-effects that cause some movement between one slide to the next. You can control the speed of each slide transition effect to set timings for transitions and also accompanied by transition sounds. You can apply a single type of transition to all slides or apply a different transition to any single slide, even having a different transition for every slide in the show.

To add a transition effect perform the following steps:

1. Select the slide or slides(s) which you want apply transition effect to the selected slide during the Slide shows.
2. Select the **TRANSITIONS** tab in the Transition to This slide group, click the down arrow and then select the desired effect which you want applied during the slide show. For example, here, we select Flash under subtle (see *Figure 5.35*).

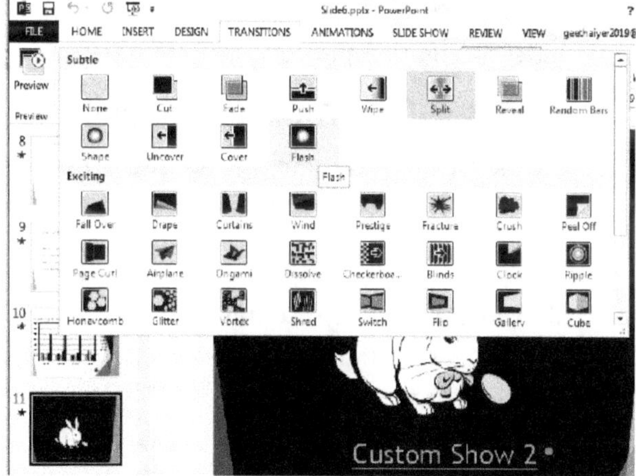

Figure 5.35: *Selecting Transition effect to Slide*

3. If you **Apply** to all slides, click **Apply To All** in the Timings group.
4. Select the Sound option to give sound transitions to your slide show from the Sound: drop-down list in the Timings group.

Slide Transition Timings

1. The Advance slide section has two options for transition:

The Advance Slides settings in the Timing group allows the presentation to advance on its own and displays each slide for a specific amount of time, as shown in *Figure 5.36*.

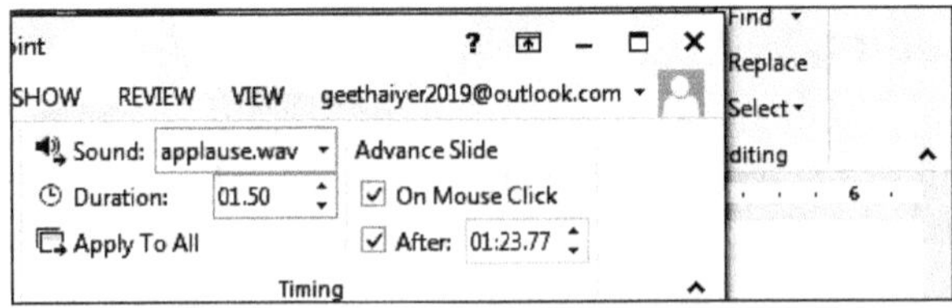

Figure 5.36: *Set Transition Timings*

On Mouse Click check box– if you want the transition to take place on clicking the mouse.

After–To specify the time for the slide to advance automatically, select the After check-box. Enter the amount of time into the associated text box, for which you want the slide to display.

2. After applying all options, you can see the effect in the Slide show, click the Slide Show tab in the Start Slide Show group, click From Beginning icon. Click the next button (i.e. →) to go to the next slide.

3. Click preview command to preview the current transitions effect in the Preview group.

4. Click the Play Animations command in the Slide Navigation pane.

Setting Slide Show Timings Manually

1. On the **Slide Show** tab, in the **Set Up** group, click **Rehearse Timings** to start the show in rehearsal mode.

2. It starts a full-screen slide show in which you can rehearse your presentation.

3. The Rehearsal dialog box appears in the slide show, as seen in *Figure 5.37*. It starts slide timings in the first slide.

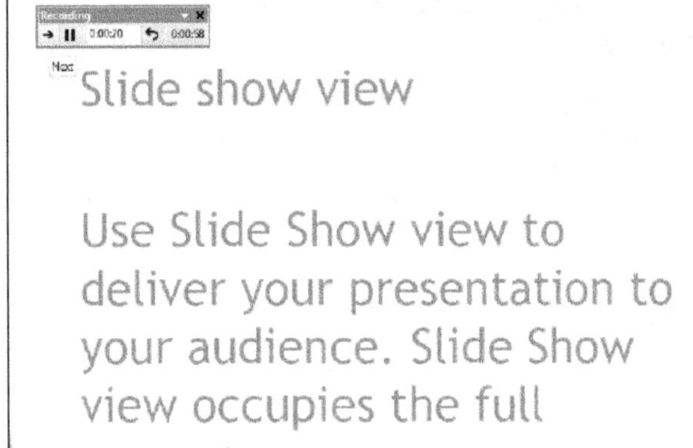

Figure 5.37: *Rehearsal Timings Dialog Box appears in the Slide Show*

4. Click the **Next** button in the Rehearsal dialog box, and fix the time in the second slide.

5. When you reach the end of the slide show, the PowerPoint dialog appears. It asks if the total time for the slide show was 0:00:42. Do you want to keep the new slide timings to use when you view the slide show? Yes or No. Click Yes to accept the timings or No to try again.

6. The amount of time you spend on each slide is recorded, and you can save those timings to run the show automatically in the future.

Automating a Slide Show

One of the most helpful tools found inside PowerPoint is the option to play a presentation automatically. After you finish creating the slides for the PowerPoint presentation, you are ready to configure the autoplay functions. First, confirm that all your slides have the desired content with the appropriate order. After you confirm the arrangement and content, open the **Slide Show** tab and press the **Set Up Slide Show** button. You have the option to configure your presentation for three automatic play modes.

To set up a PowerPoint presentation to run automatically:

1. On the **Slide Show** tab, click **Set Up Slide Show**, as shown in the following screenshot:

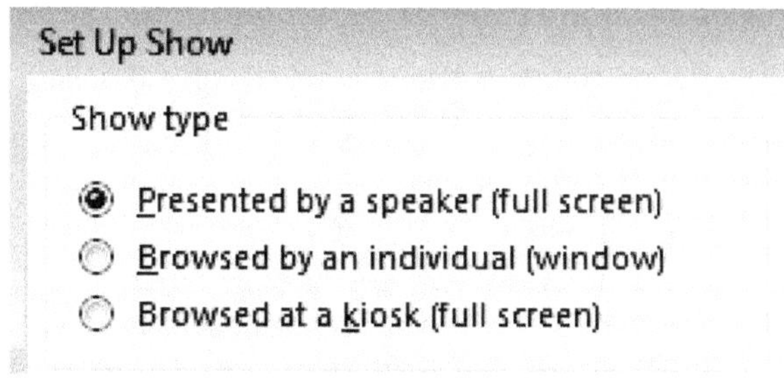

Figure 3.38

2. Under Show type, choose one of the following options:
   - To allow the people watching your slide show to have control over when they advance the slides, select Presented by a speaker (full screen).
   - To present your slide show in a window, where control over advancing the slides is not available to the people watching, select Browsed by an individual (Window).
   - To loop your slide show until the people are watching, press Esc then select Browsed at a kiosk (full screen).

Providing Aesthetics

PowerPoint is designed to give your slide presentations a consistent look. There are four ways that PowerPoint helps you control the look of your slides with design templates, masters, color schemes, and layouts of slides.

Enhancing Text Presentation

Enhancing the text presentation makes your presentation in a more presentable manner by formatting features, such as bold, italic, underline, alignment of text, font size, font style, colors and so on.

Aligning Text in a Slide

Alignment is the way text is placed between the margins of a page or a text box on a slide. The alignment choices are summarized in *Table 5.3*.

Alignment	Effect
Left Align	The left margin of each line is at the same place on the left, while the right edge of each line ends wherever appropriate (called a **ragged right edge**).
Right Align	The right margin of each line is at the same place on the right. The left edge of each line falls in a different place, depending on the contents of the line (called a **ragged left edge**).
Center	Each line is centered. The left and right edges of each line will differ, depending upon the number and size of characters in the line.
Justified	Each line starts at the left margin and ends at the right margin. There are no ragged edges.

Table 5.3: *Aligning Text in a Slide*

To align the text, perform the following steps:
1. Select the text, then click the **Left, Center**, or **Right alignment** button on the **Formatting toolbar**. Alternatively, click the Paragraph Launcher dialog box and select the desired option in the alignment section.

Changing Fonts

Fonts are also called **typefaces** in computer programs. There are groups of characters that share the same style or look.

Fonts are divided into two groups:
- On the basis of the way characters are spaced monospaced or proportionately spaced (see *Figure 5.39*). In monospaced font, all the characters have the same width. In proportionately spaced font, the widths are different, that is, w has more width than i.

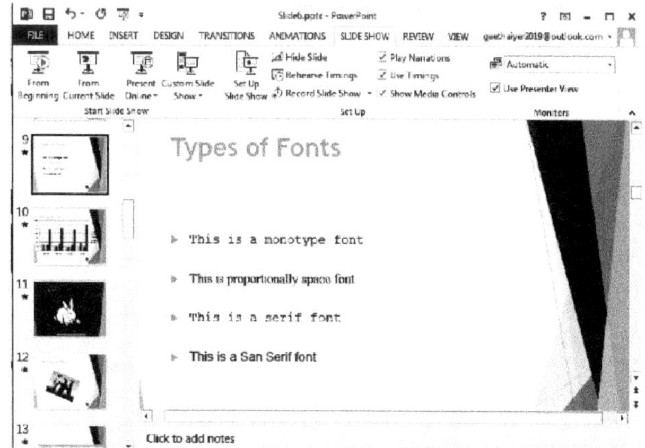

Figure 5.39: *Display of various kind of fonts*

- On the basis of the finishing strokes, that is, Serif and Sans serif. In Sans Serif, the finishing strokes are not there (see *Figure 5.36*). In Serif font, the finishing strokes are there.

While choosing fonts for your presentation, keep in mind the following points:

- Using too many fonts on the same slide looks unprofessional. It is advisable to use one font for the headline and another for the rest of the text or a third font for bulleted items. But do not use too many fonts.
- Fancy fonts do not work well on slides, especially for headlines.
- Sans Serif fonts tend to have a more authoritative and bold look.
- Proportional fonts work extremely well in body text.

To change the font of any text in a slide, perform the following steps:

1. Select the text you want to change.
2. Click the **Home** tab and choose **Font** group or select the text. A mini toolbar appears. Select the desired font themes you want to apply.
3. Or, right-click the mouse button and choose **Font...** from the shortcut menu. The Font dialog box appears as in *Figure 5.37*. Click the Font drop-down list and select the required font. Alternatively, click the down arrow to the right of the Font box on the Ribbon command. A drop-down list of available fonts appears.

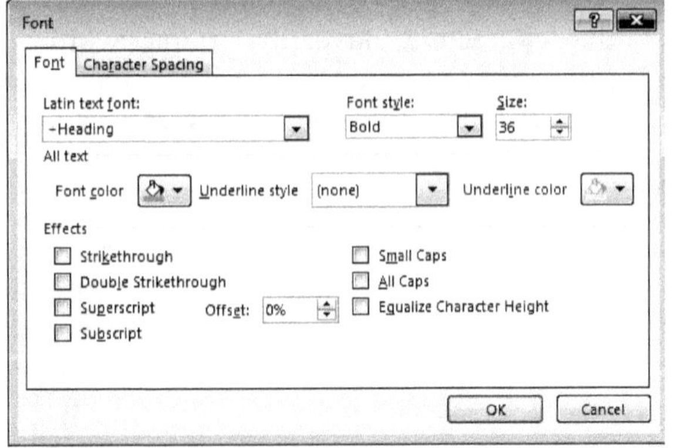

Figure 5.40: *Selecting Font using Dialog Box*

The right type and size of font creates good impression on your audience.

4. Click the font you want to use. The selected text changes to the selected font.

Changing the Text Size

Font size is measured in points, which is a height measurement; each point is **1/72** of an inch.

To change the size of text:

1. Select the text you want to change.
2. Click the **Home** tab and choose **Font** group, or select the text. A mini toolbar appears. Choose the desired font size you want to apply. Or click the right mouse button and choose **Font....** In the Font dialog box that appears, click the size drop-down list and choose the desired size or type the size. Alternatively, click the arrow to the right of the Font Size box on the Ribbon command to see the list of available sizes.
3. Select the new size. Or
   Click the Increase and Decrease font size on the Ribbon command.

Adding Special Effects to Text

One of the easiest ways to make text stand out is to add special formatting effects to characters, sentences, or paragraphs. PowerPoint makes these tasks very easy.

To add special effect, perform the following steps:

1. Select the text which you want to apply special effect to.
2. In the Font dialog box, the options Font style: box has the following:
   - **Regular:** The text appears in a regular way.
   - **Bold:** Text appears bold or highlighted.
   - **Italic:** Text appears italic.
   - **Bold Italic:** Text appears bold and italic.

   The All text has this option:
   - **Font color:** Specifies the color of the selected text. In the box, select the color. You can see the color under the bucket.
   - **Underline style:** Specifies whether selected text is in underlined. Click None to remove underlining.
   - **Underline color:** Specifies the color of the underlined text. This option remains unavailable until you apply an underline style.

   The Effect Areas has the following options:
   - **Strikethrough:** Draws a line through selected text.
   - **Superscript:** Text appears raised like x2y.

- **Subscript:** Text appears lowered like H20.
- **Small caps:** Selected text appears in reduced size. It does not effect numbers, punctuation, or non-alphabetic characters.
- **All caps:** It converts lowercase to capitals.
- **Equalize Character Height:** It reformats the text effects to apply an even character height to text.

The font style and special effects of the above explanation are shown in Figure 5.41:

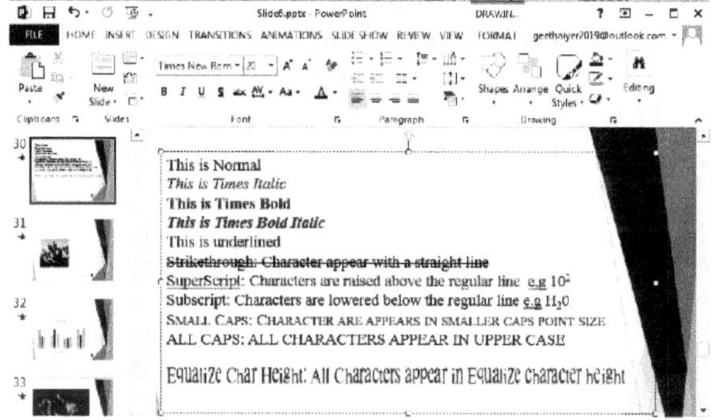

Figure 5.41: *The Font Style Effect*

Changing Text Color

To change the text color, do this:

1. Select the text you want to change.
2. Click the **Home** tab and choose **Font** group or select the text. A mini toolbar appears. Select the desired font themes you want to apply.
3. Move the mouse pointer over the color, you can see the effect changes in the text. Choose the desired color you want to apply to the text.

Applying Character Formatting Using the Keyboard

Most of the character formatting can also be applied using the keyboard shortcut, as discussed in the following sections.

To format using the shortcut keys, perform the following steps:

1. Select the text you want to format and use the shortcut key combinations for the desired formatting effects.

Format	Shortcut
Bold	Ctrl + B
Italic	Ctrl + I

Underline	Ctrl + U
Superscript	Ctrl + Shift + +
Subscript	Ctrl + =
Copy formatting	Ctrl + Shift + C
Paste formatting	Ctrl + Shift + V
Remove formatting	Ctrl + Spacebar
Change case of letters	Shift + F3
Change the font	Ctrl + Shift + F
Change the font size	Ctrl + Shift + P
Increase the font size	Ctrl + Shift + >
Decrease the font size	Ctrl + Shift + <

Working with Color and Line Style

Theme colors determine the default color choices for objects such as text, shapes, captions, outlines, and buttons. In earlier version of PowerPoint, color and line styles, contains a color scheme that provides the various parts of a presentation with a coordinated set of eight default colors. The most distinctive design element of the presentation is the background, so the first color in color scheme is background color. Other seven colors effectively complement the background color and are applied to text, charts, and other objects that appear against the background.

A layout determines where text, graphics, charts and other elements appear on an individual slide. A theme determines the look of an entire presentation's colors, fonts, and overall format. A layout is to a slide what a theme is to an entire presentation. Both specify the way a slide or overall presentation looks. Themes refer to a set of unified design element that provide a look for your document by using colors, fonts, and graphics. You can use predefined themes that come with PowerPoint, or you can define your own.

To select a New slide and apply themes effect, perform the following steps:

1. Click the **Home** tab in the **slides** group. Click the **New** Slide down pointing arrow. PowerPoint opens a layout list from which you can select (see *Figure 5.42*).

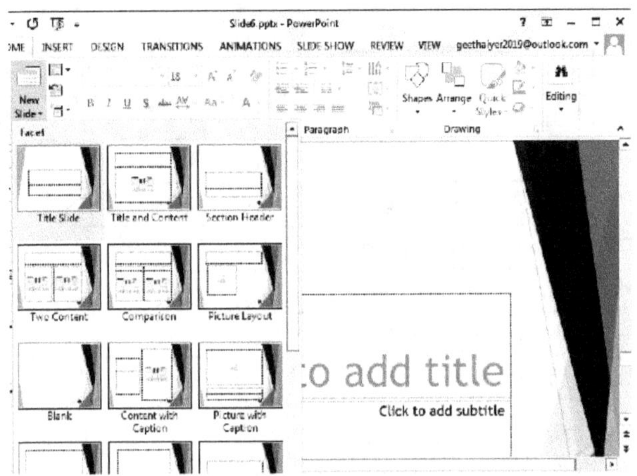

Figure 5.42: *Selecting a New Slide from Home tab*

2. When you click to select a layout, PowerPoint inserts a new slide at that location in your presentation with that layout.

3. Click the **Design** tab in the **Themes** group. In the Themes group click the **More** button at the lower-right corner. A list of themes appears, as seen in *Figure 5.43*.

Figure 5.43: *Selecting a Themes from Design tab*

4. Select a desired style you want to apply to your presentation.

5. If you want to modify the theme, select from the Font, Colors, and Effect buttons to the right of the Themes group.

6. After you have modified a theme to your liking, click the down arrow next to the Ribbon's themes and select **Save** Current Theme.

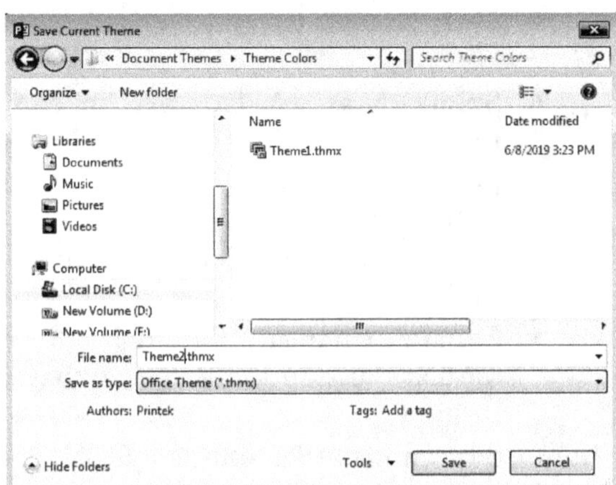

Figure 5.44: *Save Current Theme dialog box*

7. The **Save** Current Theme dialog box appears, as seen in *Figure 5.43*.

8. The Save in: drop-down list contains a default folder (Document Themes).

9. Give the name in the File name: in the drop-down list.

10. Click the **Save** button.

11. After giving a name to the theme, PowerPoint makes that theme available in the Themes list.

Change the Color, Style and Weight of a Line

You can change the look of a line shape by changing its color, line style, or weight.

1. Add a Quick Style to a line.
2. Change the color of a line.
3. Make a line dashed.
4. Change the weight of a line.
5. Add a Quick Style to a line.

Quick Styles for lines include theme colors from the document theme, shadow, line styles, and three-dimensional perspectives.

1. Select the line that you want to change.

   If you want to change multiple lines, select the first line, and then press and hold the **Ctrl** key while you select other lines.

2. Under **Drawing** Tools on the **Format** tab, in the **Shape Styles** group, click the Quick style that you want.

3. To see more Quick Styles, click the More button (see *Figure 5.45*).

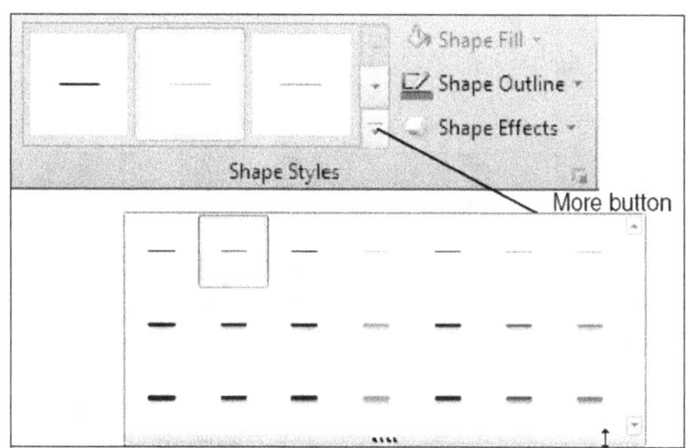

Figure 5.45: *Select the line style from the More button*

Change the Color of a Line

1. Select the line that you want to change.
2. Under the **Drawing** Tools, on the **Format** tab, in the **Shape Styles** group, click the arrow next to Shape Outline, and then click the color that you want (see *Figure 5.46*).

Figure 5.46: *Select the color of a line from the Shape Outline drop-down list*

To change to a color that is not in the theme colors, click More Outline Colors, and then either click the color that you want on the Standard tab, or mix your own color on the Custom tab. Custom colors and colors on the Standard tab are not updated if you later change the document theme.

Make a Line Dashed

You can change thickness, style, and color. To format a line, first select it by clicking it. For selecting multiple lines, press and hold the Shift key while you click the lines. The selected lines appear dimmed and dashed.

1. Select the line that you want to change.
2. Under **Drawing** Tools, on the **Format** tab, in the **Shape Styles** group, click the arrow next to Shape Outline.
3. Point to Dashes, and then click the line style that you want (see *Figure 5.47*).
4. To create a custom style, click More Lines, and then choose the options that you want.

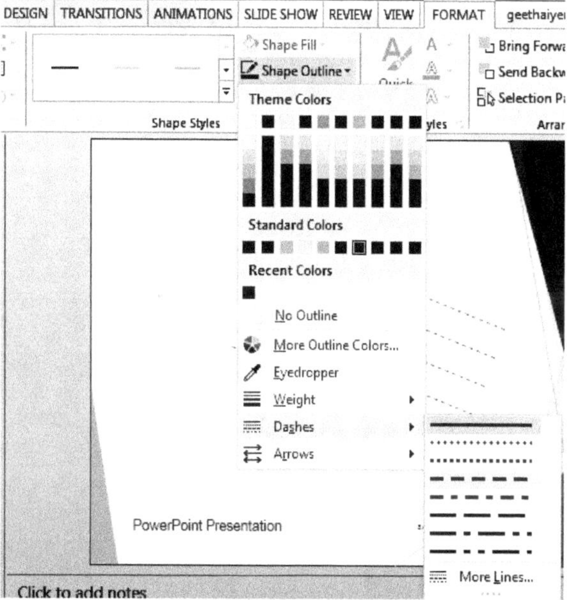

Figure 5.47: *Select the line Dashes from the Shape Outline drop-down list*

Change the Weight of a Line

1. Select the line that you want to change.

   If you want to change multiple lines, select the first line, and then press and hold Ctrl while you select the other lines.
2. Under Drawing Tools, on the Format tab, in the Shape Styles group, click the arrow next to Shape Outline.
3. Point to Weight, and then click the line weight that you want (see *Figure 5.48*).
4. To create a custom style, click More Lines, and then choose the options that you want.

Adding Movie or (Video) and Sound

You insert a music, sound, or video clip on a slide where you want it to play during a slide show. You can choose either to have the sound or video start automatically when you move to the slide, or to have the sound or video start only when you click its icon during a slide show.

One of the exciting new features in PowerPoint 2013 is that you now have the ability to edit and style the video clips you add to your slides. You can insert video files from your computer, download them from the Web, or insert video clips from Microsoft Office Clip Art. This enables you to add life to your slides and share compelling stories in a way that is sure to hold your audience's attention.

PowerPoint supports videos in various formats, such as **Audio Video Interchange (.avi)**, **Motion Pictures Group (.mpg)** and **Movie (.mov)**.

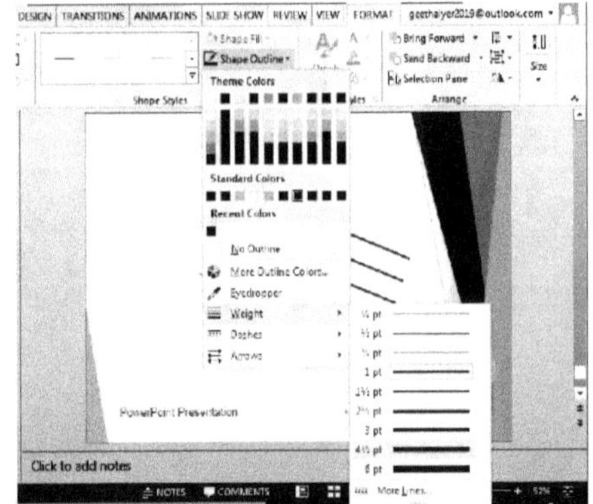

Figure 5.48: *Select the line weight from the Shape Outline dropdown list*

To insert a video from a Clip Art video:

1. Insert the new slide or display the slide that will contain **Media Clip Art**.
2. Click the **Insert** tab.
3. Click **Video** button under the **Media** Group. A drop-down list appears, as seen in *Figure 5.49*:

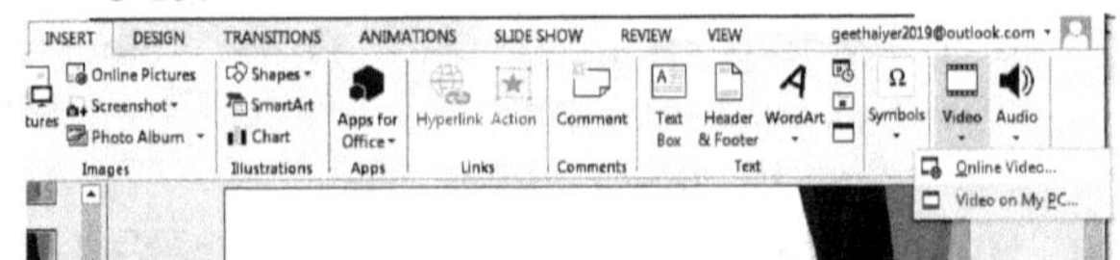

Figure 5.49: *Selecting Video from file from the Insert tab*

4. Select the Video from the File option from the list.
5. The **Insert Video** dialog box appears, as seen in *Figure 5.50*:

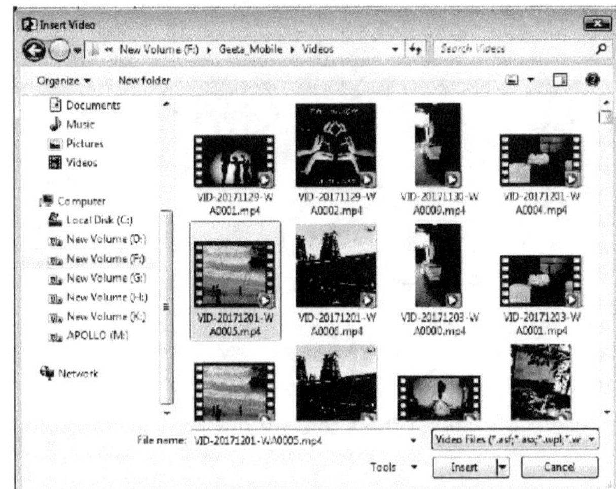

Figure 5.50: *Insert video dialog box*

6. Browse the location where the video is saved on your computer.
7. Select the desired video file. Then click the Insert button.
8. The desired video is inserted in the slide, as seen in *Figure 5.51*:

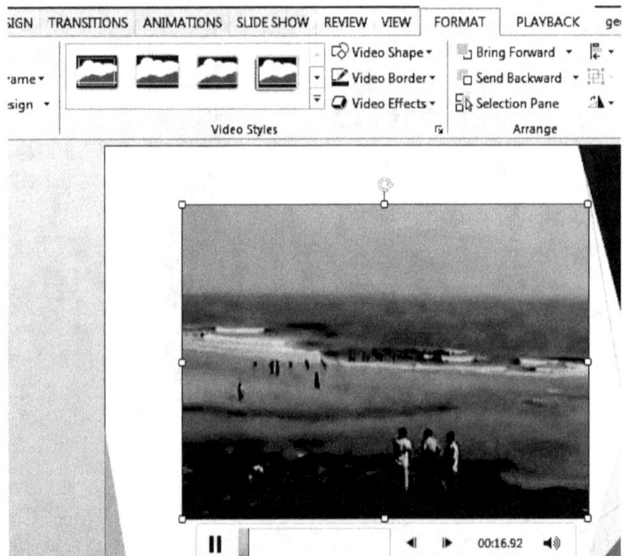

Figure 5.51: *The video file is inserted in the presentation*

9. Drag the sizing handles of the image to set the size of your video, and then drag it to the location you want.
10. Play the video by clicking the **Play** button.

Adding a Sound File

In PowerPoint 2013, you can easily add sound effects, voiceovers and music to individual slides. You can add a soundtrack and narration to the presentation as well. Sound effects, such as music and voice recordings, can add another level of professionalism to slide presentations. Music is an effective way to introduce or end a presentation and it gives your audience something to listen to as they enter and leave the presentation room. You could play a movie theme song as background music for several slides, or play a voice recording that contains advertising slogans to insert on a single slide, for example.

There are many sound file formats. Two common types are wave files (with the .wav filename extension) and Musical Instrument Digital Interface (MIDI) files (with the .mid, .midi, or .rmi filename extension).

To insert a sound into the slide, perform the following steps:

1. Select the slide in which you want to insert the desired sound.
2. Click the Insert tab.
3. Click the Audio button under the Media group, as seen in *Figure 5.51*.
4. A drop-down list appears.
5. Select the Audio from file option from the drop-down list, as seen in *Figure 5.51*.
6. The Insert Audio dialog box appears, as seen in *Figure 5.53*.
7. Browse the location where the sound clip is saved on your computer. For example, we have selected the Sample Music folder, as seen in *Figure 5.53*.
8. Select the desired sound clip and then click the OK button.
9. The audio file is inserted in the slide, as seen in *Figure 5.54*.

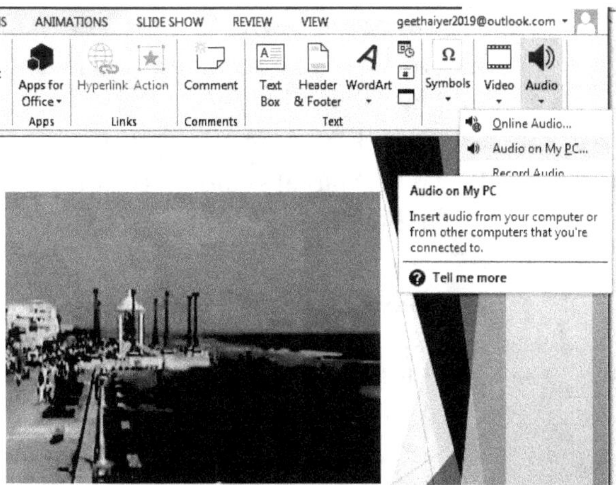

Figure 5.54: *Selecting Audio from file from the Insert Tab*

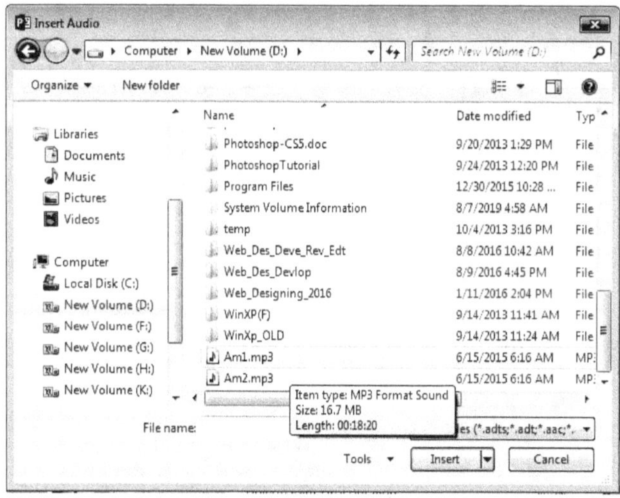

Figure 5.55: *Insert Sound Dialog Box*

Figure 5.56: *The Audio File is inserted in the Presentation*

Adding Headers and Footers

You can add headers, footers, and page numbers to each of the slide or the Note Pages.

To insert header and footer to the slide:

1. In the **Insert** tab, click **Header and Footer** in the **Text** group. Or in the Print Backstage view, click on the **Edit Header** and Footer link option.
2. The **Header and Footer** dialog box appears. Now click the **Notes and Handouts** tab property sheet, as shown in *Figure 5.57*:

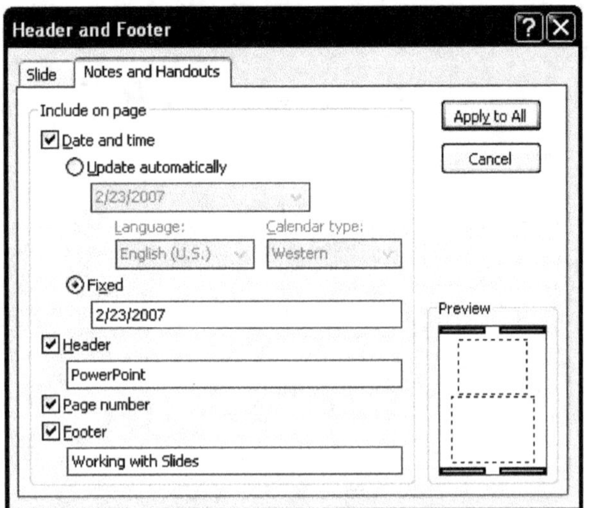

Figure 5.57: *Header and Footer dialog box with Notes and Handouts Tab*

The Notes tab property sheet of Header and Footer dialog box offers the following options:

- **Date and time:** If you select this option, the date and time appears in the upper-right corner of the page.
- **Update automatically:** Select this option to print the actual date and time when printouts are made. Use the list box to select the format you would like the date and time to appear in.
- **Fixed:** Choose this option if you want to specify the specific date to be printed in text box.
- **Header:** The header appears on the top-left corner of the page. Enter the text for the header in the box below the option.
- **Page Number:** The page numbers are shown as numerals only and appear in the lower-right corner of the page. Numbering is automatically increased once this option is on.
- **Footer:** The footer appears in the lower-left corner of the page. Enter the text for the footer in the box below the option.
3. Click **Apply to All** to use the selected settings.

Conclusion

A presentation package can be defined as software that is used for presenting information using PC display in a simple and effective manner. In this chapter, you learnt about what is PowerPoint and took an example of the 2013 version. Then you learnt how to create a presentation by using templates, inserting, deleting and editing texts and slides. Then you saw how to manipulate the slides by inserting tables, adding clip arts and other objects. You saw how to resize and scale them. You also understood how to create and use the master slide. Further, we understood how to view a presentation, choose the set-up, header, footer and printing slides and handouts. One of the most important is slide show. In this, you saw how to run a slide show, set slide timing and automating the slide show. Lastly, you covered how to provide aesthetics by working on enhancing text, working with color and tine style, adding video and sounds and header and footer.

In the next chapter, you will learn Web World and enhance the skills for Web browsers and the use of World Wide Web and Search information on Internet.

Model Questions and Answers

A. Multiple Choice Questions.

1. Which of the following views is not one of PowerPoint views?
   a. Slide Sorter view
   b. Slide view
   c. Slide Show view
   d. Sorter view

2. The Save As dialog box can be used for?
   a. Saving the file for the first time
   b. Save the file by some alternative name
   c. Saving the file in a format other than Word
   d. All of the above

3. In which tab to insert the video from file in PowerPoint 2013?
   a. Insert tab of media group
   b. Insert tab of symbols group
   c. Home tab of editing group
   d. Insert tab of Images group

4. An electronic page in a presentation is called:
   a. Slide
   b. W-slide
   c. E-page
   d. Page

5. Which of the following shortcuts is used to insert a New Slide?
   a. Ctrl + M
   b. Ctrl + N
   c. Ctrl + O
   d. None of the above

6. Which extension is given to the PowerPoint document by default?
   a. .EXT
   b. .COM
   c. .PPT
   d. None

7. Which of the following menus has the Background?
   a. Format
   b. View
   c. Insert
   d. Slide Show

8. Which of the following is true in relation to Clip Art?
   a. PowerPoint displays available pictures in the Clip Art Gallery
   b. You can use a toolbar button or a placeholder to insert Clip Art
   c. You can re-color Clip Art
   d. All of the above

9. In which view does the notes pane appear?
   a. Normal view
   b. Outline vie
   c. Both a. and b.
   d. None of the above

10. In Handout master, the footer area appears at:
    a. Top of the page
    b. Bottom of the page
    c. Center of the page
    d. None of the above

11. You can show the shortcut menu during the slide show by:
    a. Clicking the shortcut button on the ribbon
    b. Right-clicking the current slide
    c. Clicking an icon on the current slide
    d. Both a. and b.

12. Which of the following allows you to select more than one slide in a presentation?
    a. Alt + click each slide
    b. Shift + drag each slide
    c. Shift + click each slide
    d. Ctrl + click each slide

13. The PowerPoint view that displays only text (title and bullets) is:
    a. Slide show
    b. Slide sorter view
    c. Notes page view
    d. Outline view

14. To add a header or footer to your handout, you can use:
    a. Title master
    b. Slide master
    c. Handout master
    d. All of the above

15. What is the easy way to apply varied animations to text on slides?
    a. Apply effects in the custom animation text pane
    b. Apply an animation scheme
    c. Customize bullets with animated clipart
    d. All of above

B. State whether the following Statements are True or False.

1. You can view a presentation using one out of ten views provided by PowerPoint.

2. The Slide Sorter View button automatically sorts the slides alphabetically.

3. Outline view, Slide view, and Slide Show are different ways of viewing the same set of slides.

4. Closing a presentation and exiting PowerPoint are the same thing.

5. You shut down PowerPoint 2010 by using the close button.

6. The first time you save a presentation, you must name it.

7. A textbox can be placed anywhere on the slide.

8. Print settings and print preview appear side by side in Backstage view.

9. A table can be inserted in PowerPoint slide only if MS Word is also installed.

10. Animation effects appear in the Design tab.

11. Both .wav and .mid files are the two kind of sound effects files that can be added to the presentation.

12. Placeholders grow and shrink to accommodate any text that you enter.

13. Rotate is the term used when a clip art image changes the direction of faces.

14. Inserting a new slide is used when you want to add a slide to an existing presentation.

15. Slide sorter view is the best view to use when setting transition effect for all slides in a presentation

C. Match the following.

1.	To use when setting transition effects for all slides in a presentation:	a.	Method of moving items on a side
2.	Rehearsal:	b.	PowerPoint
3.	Color Scheme:	c.	Slide Sorter View
4.	Motion path:	d.	Predefined Ellipse Motion
5.	Program used for presentation:	e.	To set custom timings for slides in a presentation
6.	PowerPoint presentation are given extension:	f.	Slide Show
7.	A set of notes is required to aid the presenter:	g.	Speaker's notes
8.	An electronic presentation, which can be run on the screen of your computer screen:	h.	.pptx
9.	An electronic page that contains information about the presentation topic:	i.	Slide
10.	A set of slide elements that helps in creating a new slide for a presentation:	j.	Slide master
		k.	Slide Layout

D. Fill in the blanks:

> Animation   custom animation   Subtitle   Handout   Slide sorter view   Transition   Templates   Slide Master   Slide Master   Placeholders   Slides

1. A slide contains various elements, namely title, ______ drawing objects, and clipart or pictures.

2. The ______ effects are used to apply movement to the images and objects in slides.

3. A ______ is a special view of the presentation which is suitable to be printed and distributed to the audience.

4. The ______ effects are special types of effects that allow you to specify how you want to navigate from one slide to the other.

5. ____________ to set the timing for each object.

6. Boxes contain objects such as the slide title, bulleted text, charts, tables and pictures are called __________.

7. __________ are the areas on the slide that are enclosed by dotted border.

8. In which view to change the order of slides __________ view option.

9. The pre-defined style that can be used for presentation in PowerPoint is called __________.

10. __________ option is used to make a similar type of formatting in every slide in PowerPoint.

Short Questions with Answers.

1. **What is the difference between Animation and Transition?**

   Answers: Slide transitions are the animation effects that are applied to a whole slide whereas animation effects are applied to objects (text, shape, picture, and so on) on a slide. For a slide, you can have only one transition effect while each object on the slide can have multiple animation effects.

   Transition effects appear in PowerPoint slide show view when slides change from one to the next. Like animation effects, we can control the speed of each slide transition effects, and we can also add music or sound.

   Transition and animation effects provide visual impact and grab the audience's attention but when to use them entirely depends upon your content and target audience. A balanced use of animation and slide transitions can lead to effective presentations which will keep your audience attentive and awake.

2. **How are transition effects helpful in creating an effective PowerPoint?**

   Answers: Transition effects are special effects that play when you view a presentation in slide show. In other words, transition effects appear after vanishing of the current slide and before the appearance of the next slide. These effects are used to enhance the initial appearance of the slides.

3. **What is the difference between a slide and a slide show?**

   Answers: A slide is an electronic page that contains information about the presentation topic. On the other hand, a slide show is defined as an electronic presentation, which can be run on the screen of your computer system or any projection device.

4. **What do you understand by a presentation?**

   Answers: A presentation is a sequential collection of slides in which each slide displays some information in the form of text or graphics.

5. **Define the Slide Sorter view and its significance.**

   Answers: In PowerPoint, the slide Sorter view refers to a view that shows thumbnail versions of all your slides arranged in horizontal rows. This view is useful to make changes to several slides simultaneously. Using the Slide Sorter view, you can easily arrange the order of slides, create duplicate slides, and also delete them.

6. **What do you understand by animation and how does it help in enhancing a presentation?**

   Answers: Animation refers to the visual effects that are added to the text as well as to other objects in the slides in your presentation. In other words, animation effects are used to apply movement in the images and objects in slides. The use of animation enhances your presentation and makes it more attractive.

7. **Explain the following terms and how they help in creating more effective and eye-catching presentations**

   a. **Animation effects**

   b. **Transition effects**

   Answers:

   a. Animation effects refers to the visual effects that are added to the text as well as other objects in the slides in our presentations. Animation effects are used to apply movement in the images and objects in slides. The use of animation enhances your presentation and makes it more attractive.

b. Transition effects refers to the special effects that play when we view a presentation in the slide show. In other words, a transition effect plays after vanishing of the current slide and before the appearance of the next slide.

8. How can you record a slide show in PowerPoint 2013?

Answers: To record a slide show in PowerPoint:

a. Click the slide show tab, then locate the Set Up group.

b. Click the Record Slide Show drop-down arrow. Select either Start recording from current Slide or Start recording from Beginning.

c. A dialog box will appear, select the desired options. 'Select and animation timings' and second option is 'Narration and laser pointer', and then click on the 'Start Recording' option.

d. Soon, we click on 'Start Recording'. Our presentation will open on a full screen.

e. Perform our slide show when you are ready to move to the next slide. Click the 'Next' button represented with an arrow mark on the Recording Toolbar.

9. How can you create a video in PowerPoint 2013?

Answers: To record a slide show in PowerPoint:

a. Select the File tab.

b. Select Export and then click Create a Video. A video export option wil appear on the right.

c. Click the drop-down arrow next

to Computer and HD displays for the size and quality of our video.

d. Select the option according to whether you want to record narration or not.

e. Click Create Video and then save the video.

10. How to use Notes Page view?

Answers: Notes page view can be used in the following ways:

a. Go to the view tab.

b. Click the Notes page command in the presentation views group.

c. Type your notes in the text box, or use the scroll bar to review your slides.

Descriptive Type Questions.

1. What points do you need to keep in mind while creating a presentation?

2. Who uses the presentation software and why?

3. What is the significance of adding header and footer to a presentation?

4. Define slide master and its types in PowerPoint.

5. What do you understand by the slide layout?

6. Hema's teacher asks her to create a presentation in PowerPoint. As Hema has never before worked in PowerPoint, help her perform the following tasks.

    a. She wants that except for the first slide, all the slides should have the same design. For this, what does she need to do?

    b. To easily communicate with her audience, she wants to provide them with a hard copy of the slides of the presentation. What should she create for it?

    c. She wants to insert some pictures in some slides. How can she do that?

7. How to insert a bullet list?

8. How can you copy slide master from one Presentation to another in PowerPoint?

9. How can you rehearse the side show timing in PowerPoint?

10. Identify and explain the view that is suitable for displaying all the sides of a presentation in such a way that you can easily verify the order of slides and whether the presentation has been completed or not.

Answers

A.	1. a	2. d	3. a	4. a	5. a
	6. c	7. a	8. d	9. c	10. b
	11. b	12. c	13. d	14. c	15. b

B.	1. F	2. T	3. T	4. T	5. T
	6. T	7. T	8. T	9. T	10. F
	11. T	12. T	13. T	14. T	15. T

C.	1. c	2. e	3. d	4. a	5. b
	6. h	7. g	8. f	9. i	10. k

D.	1. c	2. a	3. d	4. f	5. b
	6. j	7. i	8. e	9. g	10. h

■■

CHAPTER 6

Introduction to Internet, WWW and Web

Structure

In this chapter, we will discuss the following topics:

- Introduction to internet
- Basics of computer network: LAN, WAN
- Difference between LAN and WAN
- Network topology and protocol
- Internet
- ISP and its role
- Hotspot and Wi-Fi
- IP addresses and classes
- MAC address
- IMEI
- Popular web browsers
- Exploring the internet

Objectives

The reader will be able to understand the following:

- Overview of the Internet, its applications and various browsers available to access the Internet.
- Understanding of various types of networks and topologies.
- Connect to the Internet using various modes of connections/devices available.
- Awareness of device identification on local network as well as on the Internet for both Desktop and Mobile Devices.
- Search Information on the Internet on various topics.
- Download and print web pages.

The Internet, popularly called the **Net**, was created in **1969** for the U.S. defense department. Funding from the **Advanced Research Projects Agency (ARPA)** allowed researchers to experiment with methods for computers to communicate with each other. Their creation, **the Advanced Research Projects Agency Network (ARPANET)**, originally linked only four separate computer sites at U.S. universities and research institutes, where it was used primarily by scientists.

The **National Science Foundation (NSF)** assumed responsibility for linking these users of ARPANET, which was dismantled in **1990**. The NSF Network (NSFNET) now serves as the technical backbone for all Internet communications in the United States.

Internetwork (internet) consists of multiple networks in which LANs are attached to other LANs, other communications networks, remote sites, individual stations and **Wide Area Networks (WANs)**. It permits data to move freely among large numbers of networks and populations. It had made the sharing of data and other information between businesses, the customers and partners extremely easy, even if the users are located across great distances.

Introduction to Internet

Communication is one of the most popular uses of the Internet. The Internet is making it easier for people to communicate with one another using computers. The most popular way of communication on the Internet is the **electronic mail (e-mail)**. With e-mail topping the list of all the technologies used, some types of communication technologies also include e-mail discussion groups, Usenet news, chat groups, and so on. These are unique to networked computer environments and have come into wide popularity because of the Internet. Other technologies, including video and audio conferencing and Internet telephony, are also available on the Internet. They require more multimedia capabilities of computer systems. They are more taxing of network resources than the others. They are also adaptations of other technologies to the Internet.

The Internet provides a capability so powerful that it can be used for almost any purpose that depends on information. It is accessible by every individual who connects to one of its constituent networks. It supports human communication via electronic mail (e-mail), chat rooms, newsgroups, and audio and video transmission. It allows people to work collaboratively at many different locations. It supports access to digital information by many applications, including the **World Wide Web (WWW)**. The Internet has proved to be a spawning ground for a large and growing number of "e-businesses" that carry out most of their sales and services over the Internet. Many experts believe that the Internet will dramatically transform business as well as society.

Basics of Computer Networks

A network is a group of computers connected in some fashion in order to share resources. A group of computers in a network would provide greater storage capacity and processing power than that by stand-alone independent machine. In addition to computers, a network also consists of peripheral devices with carrier and data communication devices used for the purpose of exchanging data and information.

By using computer networks, the cost of data transfer can be made economical because computers can send data at a very fast speed. Thus, computers enable us to reduce both cost and time in transferring data or information. In the network, computers of different make can be connected together and users can work together in a group. Software packages have been developed for groups working in Database Management System (DBMS) as well as in graphical artworks. Also, data from different departments located at distant places can be transferred to and stored on a central computer. This data can then be accessed by the computers located in different departments. The data at the central computer is updated and accessed by all users. This method would prevent any bottlenecks in the smooth functioning of the organization because all the users will get the latest information (for example, inventory) stored in the central computer.

Local Area Network (LAN)

Local Area Network (LAN) is a group of computers located in the same room, on the same floor, or in the same building that are connected to form a single computer network. LANs allow users to share storage devices, printers, applications, data, and other network resources. They are limited to a specific geographical area, usually less than one kilometer in diameter. Example of LAN can be an office, where different departments such as personnel and accounting are located in the same building and connected via bus topology using Ethernet cards.

Figure 6.1 illustrates the basic physical characteristics, information transfer and shared device concepts underlying LAN operation. The line printer and magnetic tape storage are **shared** resources, since any user attached to the network can access these devices through PCs acting as the resource manager, or server, as it is commonly called in LAN terminology. In some networks, the users can directly exchange data or files from Mainframe or mini computers.

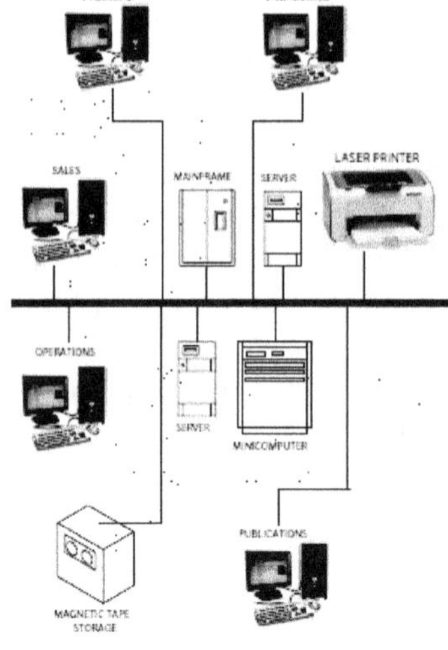

Figure 6.1: *Typical LAN system in an organization with different departments connected with shared storage devices and peripherals, such as printers*

Advantages of LANs are as follows:

- Local area networks allow sharing of expensive resources, such as colored laser printers and high capacity, high-speed mass storage devices among a number of users.
- They allow for high-speed exchange of essential information between key people in an organization. If properly managed, this sharing will promote greater efficiency and productivity, and will lead to more sophisticated applications, such as electronic mail and company's Website.
- Users can access their files from any workstation.
- Files can be stored on the central computer and everyone in the network can see and use data sharing. Further, if due to some problem, data is erased from one computer, then it can be easily recovered from the central computer.

In the case of a business, a LAN should be a visible contributor to increased profitability.

Disadvantages of LANs are as follows:

- The financial cost of local area networking is still high. If one plans to use a network to share a laser printer, he might find it cheaper to purchase another laser printer than to purchase networking hardware and software.
- Local area networking software requires memory space in each of the computers used on the network.
- Local area networking adds another level of complexity to the computer operation. Users may have difficulty in learning the network commands. The installation and management of a LAN requires far more technical and administrative skills than installing and managing several computers that are not networked.
- Some control on the part of the user is lost. You may have to share a printer with other users. You may face a situation like, the entire network is suddenly locking up because one user has made a mistake.
- Some type of security system must be implemented if it is important to protect confidential data.
- Many current application programs will not run in the network environment. The program may require too much memory or have other technical constraints.

Characteristics of LANs

Local area networks are a specialized form of communication systems. However, there are three primary characteristics of LANs that distinguish them from wide area networks such as Telnet, Tymnet, CompuServe and the **Public-Switched Telephone Network (PSTN)**. These are:

- LANs work in a restricted geographical area.
- They operate at relatively high speed when compared to the typical wide area networks currently in use.
- They are private networks, not subject to tariffs or other regulatory controls.
- They use mainly bus, ring and star topology.
- They support a variety of transmission mediums, such as Ethernet, fiber and wireless.

Wide Area Network (WAN)

Wide Area Network (WAN) is a digital communication system which interconnects different sites, computer installations and user terminals. It may also enable LANs to communicate with each other. This type of network may be developed to operate nationwide or worldwide. The transmission media used in WANs are normally public systems, such as telephone lines, microwave links and satellite links.

WAN is used to interconnect LANs which may be at opposite sides of a country or located around the earth's globe.

Wide area networks combine the continuous error detection and correction techniques included in synchronous communications with robust network problem determination and data routing to form powerful backbones that ensure high-quality, reliable service for end users. These networks allow multiple users to access a variety of host computers simultaneously through the same physical medium while separating each user's session so that no user is aware of another on the network. Wide area networks also operate at speeds much higher than the **19,200-bps** limit of normal voice-grade telephone lines.

Figure 6.2 shows a wide area network that a large company might use to connect regional computers. In this example, different Centers, such as manufacturing, distribution, and accounting, are all connected to national headquarters and therefore to each other for communication purposes. Most WANs are complex and serve many users and many functions as compared to LANs.

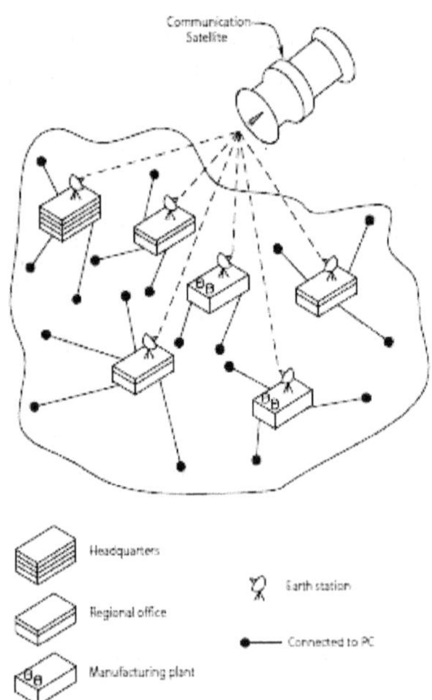

Figure 6.2: *A Wide Area Network Connected to Regional Computers*

WANs are typically created using specially-conditioned telephone lines, microwave communications or satellite data transmission.

Advantages of WAN are as follows:

- WAN covers a larger geographical area. So, computers at longer distances can easily communicate.
- It allows sharing of resources and application software programs among distributed workstations.

Disadvantages of WAN are as follows:

- Investment costs are higher.
- It is difficult to maintain network. It requires technicians and network administrators.
- There are more errors and issues due to wide coverage and use of different technologies.
- It has low security compared to LAN and MAN coverage. It uses more technologies.

Some of the functions that can be performed on WANs are as follows:

Remote Data and Job Entry

It is possible to enter data for sales and transactions at the point-of-sale terminals using WANs. It is also possible to centralize this data in a computer for processing or reporting purposes. For example, Supermarkets in advanced countries connected through WANs can send all sales data from their remote sale Centers. The central purchase Center can monitor all the sale figures on a day-to-day basis. The central distribution Center can thereafter act to supply the grocery items needed in different supermarket branches, based on the data collected from these branches. This helps in controlling all the branches and ensures timely supply of all the items to different branches.

Similarly, Remote Job Entry at colleges and universities enables faculty and students to write and execute their own programs on a central computer. For example, if all Indian Institutes of Technology (IITs) are connected through WANs, then the research projects can be implemented easily because a program developed at one of the IITs can be used online by students of other IITs, and thus, duplication of efforts can be avoided. This not only brings efficiency but also economy of efforts.

Centralizing Information

It is often convenient for a business to centralize regional/national information. For example, auto-part dealers can be helped in locating rare auto parts using a centralized computer file of inventory items. WANs enable such dealers to query centralized databases.

Facilitating Communications

Corporations in advanced countries often use WANs to facilitate employee communications, to save on long-distance phone calls and letter writing, to cut costs on the preparation of written documents, and to overcome the time lags involved in overseas communications. Computer conferencing, in which users communicate with each other through their computer systems, is another possible function of WANs.

Two particularly important types of WANs are:

Hierarchical Networks

Many WANs configure computers in a hierarchy and are therefore called hierarchical networks. The basic idea is that local minicomputers and microcomputers cluster around regional mini and Mainframe computers. This creates a reporting arrangement similar to the hierarchical relationships of an organizational chart. The most powerful computer of a hierarchical network is usually a large Mainframe computer. Often, a front-end processor is used on this Mainframe site to handle input/output, data communications, and computer security tasks of the system, enabling the back-end processor to perform the required data-processing jobs.

Distributed Data-processing Networks

Distributed data-processing networks place computers or terminals at local or regional sites, thereby providing computer power (for example, access to Mainframe computer resources) to these locations. The distributed data-processing system enables the sharing of many hardware and significant software resources among several users who may be located far away from each other.

Using WAN and Network Services

Many wide area network services are emerging these days due to the increasing demand of corporate business houses and public and private sectors.

Users are demanding Wide area network accesses that offer support for transmission of data, video, imaging, fax and voice. The primary driving forces of increased capacity and sophistication for wide area network services are:

Host to Terminal Connection

A terminal is an Input/Output (I/O) device, consisting of a keyboard and a monitor, and the host is a back-end processing computer. Hosts and terminals may be located in different locations. Hosts can be connected to different terminals through local area network connections or through remote dial-up connections. User's commands are typically entered through a terminal. This information is transmitted to a host computer (generally, Mainframe computer) over an Ethernet or Token Ring local area network connection. The mainframe computer processes the input and sends the output over the network to the terminal monitor. Thus, application runs in the host, and the terminal performs user interfacing function. Terminals can be of two types:

- **Local Terminal:** It is directly connected to the host via a serial or LAN connection.
- **Remote Terminal:** It is connected to the host via a phone line with a modem at both the ends.

LAN to LAN Connection

Wide area networking may be used for communicating with devices that reside beyond one's local LAN. For the communication to take place, the two LANs must be in the same WAN. Routers can be used to connect LANs that employ similar protocols. *Figure 6.3* shows the interconnection between two Ethernet LANs:

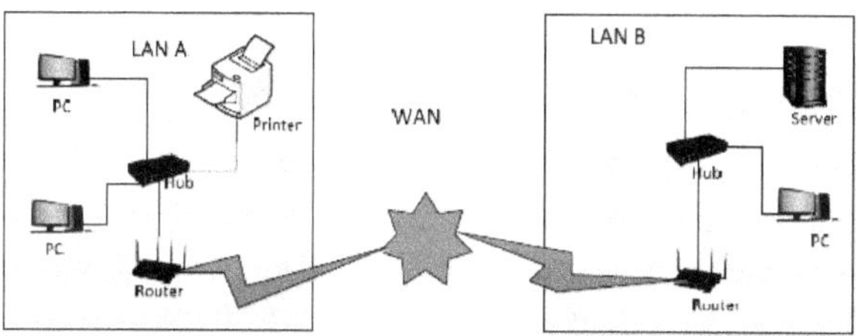

Figure 6.3: *LAN to LAN connection through WAN*

When two dissimilar LANs are to be connected, tunnels and gateways are made use of.

Tunnels are simple constructs that can be used to pass data packets through an otherwise incompatible network region. Data packets are encapsulated with a framing that is recognized by the network that transports it. The original framing and formatting of the data are retained inside the encapsulation.

A **gateway** is a device that is capable of interconnecting networks with dissimilar routing protocols.

A communication link that joins two or more LANs into a WAN is known as **WAN link**.

WAN links can be grouped into the following three main categories:

Circuit-switched Services

A temporary switched circuit is established through the telecommunications system for the duration of the communication session. When the connection is terminated, the carrier switches are freed up for other uses. Examples are modems and dial-up Integrated **Services Digital Network (ISDN)** connections.

Leased Lines

These are dedicated connections that establish a permanent switched circuit that is always ready to carry network traffic.

An example of a leased line is a T1 line or fractional T1 line.

Leased lines are very expensive because they are dedicated to the customer even when they are not in use.

Packet-switched Services

These are dedicated or dial-up connections to a public packet-switching network, such as X.25, a public frame-relay network, or even a Virtual Private Network (VPN). Intermediary switches send data packets along the best route possible by using the logical address of the destination node, which is contained in the packet header.

Remote LAN Connection

Remote access to a LAN can be either through dial-up connection using a modem or through a leased line. The remote access to the office LAN gives the employees and/or customers access to the following services:

- File and print services
- Client/Server applications, such as database applications
- Applications for remote network administration

Programs, such as PC Anywhere, controls the network-access remotely. However, since remote connection is mainly made using a slow modem, network-access control is often slow and jerky. But it provides high security, saves on hardware and licensing costs, and is simple to implement on a network.

Remote LAN connection allows users to access file, print and other services of the company from remote locations.

Difference between LAN and WAN

Difference between LAN and WAN are as follows:

Basics	LAN	WAN
Acronym	Local Area Network	Wide Area Network
Cost	Less costly	Costliest
Speed	Up to 10-100Mbps	256Kbps to 2Mbps
Range	1 Km	Up to 10,000 kms
Topology	Bus and Ring	ATM, Frame Relay, Sonnet
Location of computers connected in the system	Computers are connected within the same buildings.	Computers are distributed all over the country or the Continent. The connection is made via satellite communication link or via Internet.
Examples	LAN example can be an office where different departments such as personnel, accounts, etc. are located in the same building and connected via bus topology using Ethernet cards.	WAN example is the connection of various branches of MNC such as Microsoft or Intel. These branches are linked using microwave satellite communication system or Internet Connection. Each branch has its own LAN circuit. But the different LAN in various branches are communicating with head office using WAN link.

Table 6.1: *Difference between LAN and WAN*

Network Topology and Protocol

Network topology is the schematic description of a network arrangement, connecting various nodes (sender and receiver) through lines of connection.

Bus Topology

Bus topology is a network type in which every computer and network device is connected to a single cable. When it has exactly two endpoints, then it is called **Linear Bus topology**, as shown in *Figure 6.4*:

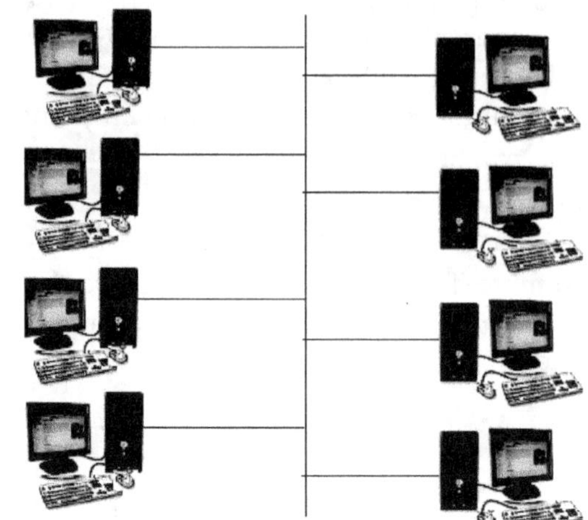

Figure 6.4: *Bus Topology*

Features of Bus Topology:

- The data signal is available to all computers connected to the bus.
- It carries the address of the destination computer.
- Bus topology is good for connecting 15-20 computers.
- Each computer on the network checks the destination address as the data signal travels through the bus.
- Ethernet is a commonly used protocol in networks connected by bus topology.

Advantages of Bus Topology are as follows:

- Bus topology cost is very low.
- Requires less cable length compared to other networks such as start topology.
- Easy to connect computer peripheral to a linear bus.
- It is easy to extend a bus. Two cables can be joined into one longer cable with a connector, making a longer cable and allowing more computers to join the network.
- It works well for small networks.

Disadvantages of Bus Topology are as follows:

- If there is a break in the main cable, the entire network will be shut down.
- If network gets heavy traffic, a node's performance of the network falls.
- The length of cable is limited.
- It is difficult to troubleshoot a bus. A cable break or malfunctioning computer anywhere between two computers can cause them not to be able to communicate with each other. Cable break or loose connector will also cause reflections and bring down the whole network, causing all network activity to stop.

Ring Topology

It is called ring topology because it forms a ring as each computer is connected to the other computer, with the last one connected to the first. Exactly two neighbours are there for each device, as shown in *Figure 6.5*:

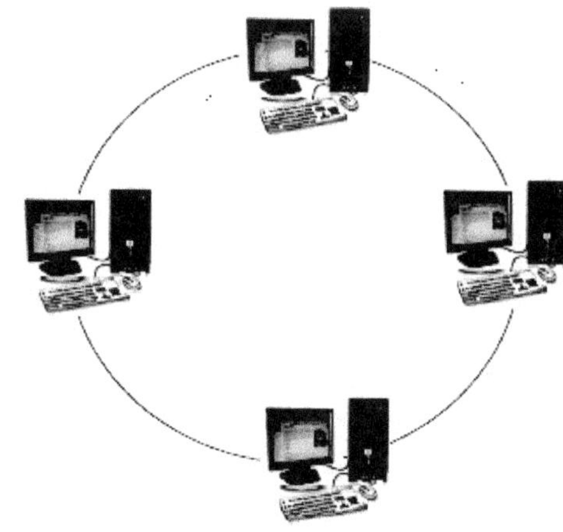

Figure 6.5: *Ring Topology*

Features of Ring Topology are as follows:

- Ring network does not have terminated ends; thus, data signals travel in a circle.
- Ring topology, as shown in Figure 6.5, uses the token passing method to provide access to the devices in the network.
- The computers or devices are connected in the ring using twisted pair cables, coaxial cables or optic fibres.
- The protocols used to implement ring topology are Token Ring and **Fibre Distributed Data Interface (FDDI)**.
- Bit-by-bit data is transferred in a sequential manner. It has to pass through every node of the network till the destination node.

Advantages of Ring Topology are as follows:

- It is a more reliable network, because the communication system is not dependent on the single host computer.
- Easy to install and the maintenance is much easier compared to the bus network.
- Adding components such as nodes will not affect the performance of network.
- Because every computer is given equal access to the token, no one computer can monopolize the network.
- Troubleshoot is easy because cable faults can be easily located.

Disadvantages of Ring Topology are as follows:

- Failure of one computer on the ring affects the whole network.
- Adding or removing devices to the networks would slow down the network activity.

- It is difficult to troubleshooting because it requires special equipment to default the cable faults.
- If any one of the node fails, it disturbs all other networks.

Star Topology

A start network, every host is connected to a central connection point, like a hub or a Switch. The connection between a node and hub device is a point-to-point. The device takes a signal from any node and passes it to all other nodes in the network. It works as a server and it controls the entire function of the network. It is used to connect a computer through Coaxial cable, as shown in *Figure 6.6*:

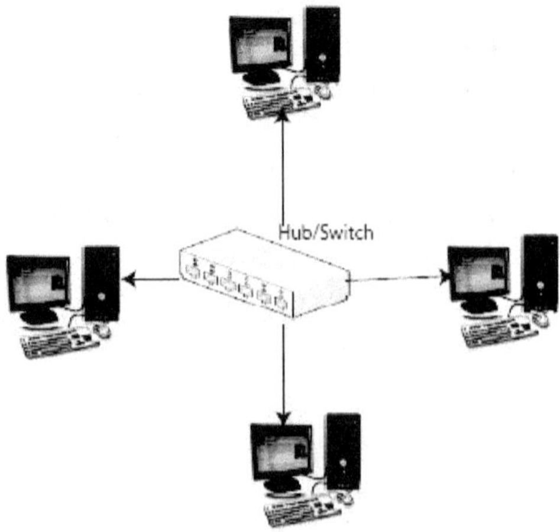

Figure 6.6: *Star Topology*

Features of Star Topology are as follows:
- Every node has its own dedicated connection to the hub.
- Hub acts as a repeater for data flow.
- Can be used with twisted pair, optical fibre or coaxial cable.
- The data signal is transmitted from the source computer to the destination computer via the hub or switch.
- The common protocols used in star topology are Ethernet, Token Ring, and LocalTalk.

Advantages of Star Topology are as follows:
- It is much easier to modify or add new computers to a star network without disturbing the rest of the network. You simply run a new line from the computer to the central location and plug it into the hub. When the capacity of the central hub is exceeded, you can replace it with one that has a larger number of ports to plug lines into it.

- Single computer failures do not necessarily bring down the whole star network. The hub can detect a network fault and isolate the offending computer or network cable and allow the rest of the network to continue its operation.
- Easy to manage and maintain the network because each node has separate cable.
- It supports a high-speed data bandwidth of approximately 100 Mbps.
- Cost effective as it uses inexpensive coaxial cable.

Disadvantages of Star Topology are as follows:
- If the central hub goes down, then all other connected nodes will not be able to communicate with each other.
- It requires more wires compared to the ring and bus topology because it is expensive to use.
- If the hub gets failed then all the connected nodes will not be able to communicate with each other.

Mesh Topology

In a Mesh topology, every node has point-to-point connection to the other node. All the computers are interconnected to each other in a network. This type of mesh topology is very expensive and it is difficult to establish the connections. The connection in mesh topology can be used in wireless network as shown in *Figure 6.7*:

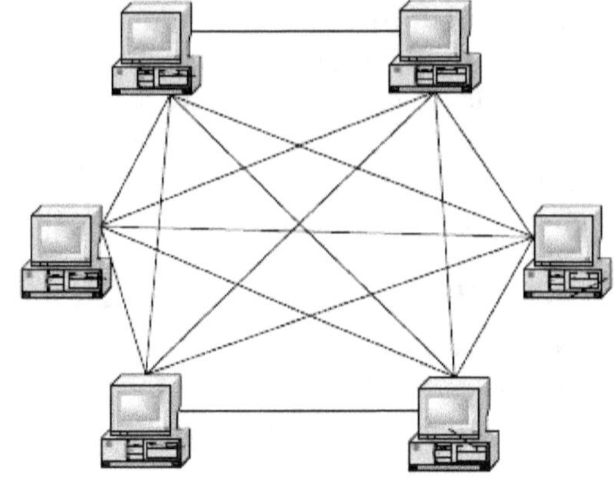

Figure 6.7: *Mesh Topology*

Features of Mesh Topology are as follows:
- In a mesh network topology, each of the network node, computer and other devices, are interconnected with one another.

- Every node not only send its own signals but also relays data from other nodes.
- This type of topology is very expensive as there are many redundant connections.
- The internet is an example of mesh topology.

Advantages of Mesh Topology are as follows:

- The networks are very reliable because if any link breaks, it will not affect the other connected computers.
- There is no link between point-to-points because it is secure.
- Fault is diagnosed easily.
- It is very fast communication between the nodes.

Disadvantages of Mesh Topology are as follows:

- It requires space to run the cables.
- Installation process is difficult, as each node is connected to every node.
- It requires number of cables and Input–output ports for communication.
- The management of mesh network is very large and difficult to maintain and manage. If not monitored carefully, then the communication link in the network fails.

Tree Topology

It has a root node, and all other nodes are connected to it, forming a hierarchy. It is also called hierarchical topology. It should have at least three levels to the hierarchy, as shown in *Figure 6.8*:

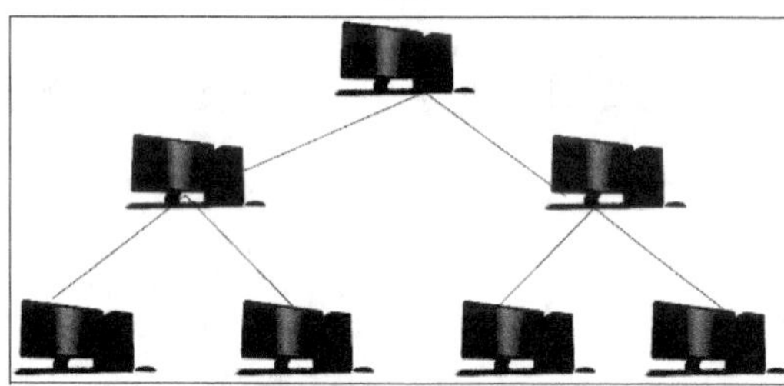

Figure 6.8: *Tree Topology*

Features of Tree Topology are as follows:

- It combines characteristics of linear bus and star topologies.
- It is arranged in a group of star workstations connected to a linear bus backbone cable.
- The top-level node in tree topology is known as a root node, and all other nodes are hierarchy of the root node.

Advantages of Tree Topology are as follows:

- Point-to-point connection of each computer is connected to each part of hub network.
- It is easy to add computer by extending the cables to connect computers.
- Error detection is an easy process.
- Fast expansion of nodes.

Disadvantages of Tree Topology are as follows:

- If any faults occur in the node, it is difficult to maintain.
- Requires high cost devices for broadband transmission.
- If new or more nodes are added, then it becomes difficult to reconfigure.
- Failure in the main bus cable will damage the overall network.

Protocol

Different types of networking operating systems use different languages to control the communication process between the computers. These languages are called **Network protocols**.

A protocol is a set of rules that governs the communications between computers on a network. There are many protocols, each one governing the way a certain technology works. For example, the IP protocol defines a set of rules governing the way computers use IP packets to send data over the Internet. It also defines addressing in IP. Likewise, we have other protocols, such as

- **TCP: Transmission Control Protocol** is used for communication over a network. It is a connection-based protocol. The data is broken down into small packets and then sent to the destination. It is one of the most important protocols that function at the transport layer of the OSI model.
- **HTTP: Hypertext Transfer Protocol** is used for transmitting and displaying information in the form of web pages on browsers. It is basically used for downloading files, media, text and various other forms from the server in a secure way. It makes use of Secure Socket Layer to add an extra feature of security to the network. If data is transferred over the Internet after being encrypted, it makes sure that anyone who intercepts data cannot decipher it easily. It works at the application layer and makes use of TCP protocol for the purpose of transfer of data.

- **FTP: File Transfer Protocol** is used for file transfer (uploading and downloading) over the Internet. It works at the Application layer of the OSI model.
- **POP:** The most common protocol for receiving mail is **Post Office Protocol (POP).** It is now in version 3, so it is called POP3. POP2 is an application layer protocol that allows the client to retrieve and download emails from the server. It is simple to connect to the server to download emails. Once you have downloaded them it is easy to read them offline. This protocol has been used in email applications to serve their purpose.
- **SMTP: Simple Mail Transfer Protocol** is used for email. It is used for the purpose of transmission of emails over the network. Not only can it transfer emails within networks, but it can also transfer them between different networks.
- **Ethernet:** It is the most popular protocol used for LAN communication. It transfers the information in digital packets. If any computer wants to use this protocol, it must contain Ethernet Network Interface Card. This card is a unique address code fixed in the microchip.
- **Wi-Fi:** One of the wireless protocols.
- **IP: Internet Protocol** is also known as **TCP.** It is an addressing protocol. The IP addresses in packets help in routing them through different nodes in a network until they reach their right destination. The IP protocol was developed in 1970.
- **UDP:** It is usually known as **User Datagram Protocol.** It is the transport layer of the OSI model. It is a **connectionless protocol** which enables the transfer of data over the network. However, it does not ensure that the data arrives at its destination perfectly without any error. Moreover, if there is any change or error in the data, it will not be detected ever. Hence, it is used in those situations where the security and perfection of data do not matter, but the speed of transfer is important.
- **Gopher:** Gopher is a collection of rules implemented for searching, retrieving as well as displaying documents from sites. It also works on the client/server principle.
- **Telnet:** It is a set of rules for connecting one system with another. The connecting process is termed as a remote login. The system which

requests for connection is the local computer, and the system which accepts the connection is the remote computer.

Internet

The Internet has been in a state of continuous evolution since the late 1960s. Some simplified descriptions of the Internet are **a large computer network** or **network of networks, an instantaneous and global messaging system**. However, the Internet has become much more than this. It has grown into an important infrastructure supporting widespread, multi-disciplinary community. This community now consists of students, scientists and researchers, large corporations, non-profit organizations, government agencies, and individual consumers.

Internet is an immensely complex combination of thousands of technologies and dozens of services used by tens of millions of people around the world each day. Internet is, thus, a network of networks. *Figure 6.9* shows a Web of computers which is laid around the globe. The Internet is a network of thousands of computer networks. Every network and every computer in these networks exchange information according to certain rules called protocols. These different computers and different networks are united with the common thread of two protocols, that is, **Internet Protocol (IP)** and **Transmission Control Protocol (TCP)**.

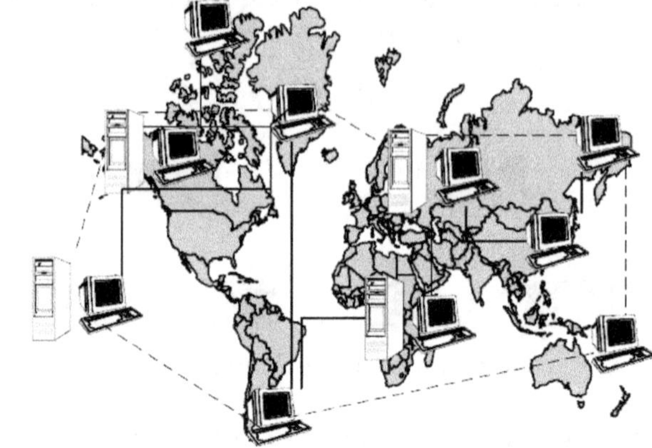

Figure 6.9: *Internet as the network of computers connected with one another all over the world*

Concept of Internet and WWW

Internet is an interconnection of multiple networks. The word internet (lowercase i) is different from Internet (uppercase I). While internet means network of networks, Internet is the term used to refer to a specific worldwide network, World Wide Web (WWW).

The Internet is a global system of interconnected computer networks that uses the standard Internet Protocol Suite (TCP/IP) to serve billions of users worldwide. It is a network of networks that consists of millions of private, public, academic, business, and government networks of local to global scope that are linked by a broad array of electronic and optical networking technologies. The Internet carries a vast array of information resources and services, most notably the inter-linked hypertext documents of the World Wide Web (WWW) and the infrastructure to support electronic mail.

For many Internet users, electronic mail (e-mail) has practically replaced the Postal Service for short written transactions. Electronic mail is the most widely used application on the Net. You can also carry on live **conversations** with other computer users using **Internet Relay Chat (IRC)**. Recently, Internet telephony hardware and software allow real-time voice conversations.

The most widely used part of the Internet is the World Wide Web. Its outstanding feature is hypertext, a method of cross-referencing. In most Websites, certain words or phrases appear in different color than the rest. Often, this text is also underlined. When you select one of these words or phrases, you will be transferred to the site or page that is relevant to this word or phrase. Sometimes, there are buttons, images, or portions of images that are **clickable**. If you move the pointer over a spot on a Website and the pointer changes into a hand, it indicates that you can click and be transferred to another site.

Using the Web, you have access to millions of pages of information. Web browsing is done with a Web browser, the most popular of which are Internet Explorer and Netscape Navigator.

WWW

The World Wide Web is the part of the Internet that contains websites and webpages. It was invented in 1989 by **Tim Berners-Lee** at **CERN, Geneva, Switzerland**. It is basically a system of Internet servers that supports specially formatted documents. The documents are formatted in a markup language called **HyperText Markup Language (HTML)** that supports links to other documents as well as graphics, audio and video files.

The WWW is essentially a huge client-server system with millions of servers distributed worldwide. Each server maintains a collection of documents; each document is stored as a file (although documents can also be generated on request). The server accepts requests for fetching a document and transfers it to the client. In addition, it can also accept requests for storing new documents. The simplest way to refer to a document is by means of a reference called a **Uniform Resource Locator (URL)**.

The Web is the second most popular Internet service next to e-mail, but it accesses a larger quantity and greater variety of data than any other service on the Internet.

How Does It Work?

- The World Wide Web is the fastest growing and most innovative part of the Internet. When you browse the Web, you view multimedia pages composed of text, graphics, sound and video. The Web uses hypertext links that allow you to jump from one place to another on the Web. The language that allows you to use hypertext links and to view Web pages is called Hypertext Markup Language, more commonly known as **HTML**.

- The Web works on client/server model in which client software known as **Web browser** runs on a local computer.

- The server software runs on a Web host. To use the Web, you first make an Internet connection, and then launch your Web browser.

- In the Web browser, you type the **Uniform Resource Locator (URL)** for a location you want to visit or click on a link that will send you to the desired location. The names for Web locations are URLs. Your Web browser sends the URL request using **Hypertext Transfer Protocol (HTTP)**, which defines the way the Web browser and the Web server communicate with one another.

- URLs contain several parts. The first part— the http://—details which Internet protocol to use. The second part–the part that usually has a WWW in it–sometimes tells what kind of Internet resource is being contacted. The third part such as satishibm.com, can vary in length and identifies the Web server to be contacted. The final part identifies a specific directory on the server and a home page, document or other Internet object.

- The request is sent to the Internet. Internet routers examine the request to determine the server to which it is to be sent. The information just to the right of the http://in the URL tells the Internet on which Web server the requested information can be found. Routers send the request to that Web server.

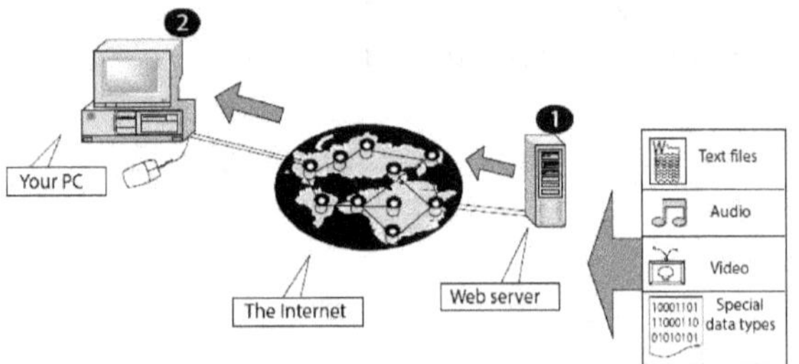

Figure 6.10: *Various types of data available on the Web*

- The Web server receives the request using the **HTTP protocol**. It is told which specific document is being requested.
- When the server finds the requested home page, document, or object, it sends that home page, document, or object back to the Web browser client. The information is then displayed on the computer screen in the Web browser.

Website Address and URL

A **Website** is a collection of Web pages associated with a particular person, business, government, school and organization. Websites are stored on a Web server, a special computer that makes Web pages available for people to browse.

Websites can consist of only a few Web pages or many hundreds of Web pages. For example, Microsoft Website currently offers over **250,000 Web pages**.

Steps for connecting to Website are explained below:

- Type the URL for a Website, say, www.yahoo.com into your Web browser.
- Your browser attempts to make a connection to the Web server.
- The Web server receives the request.
- The Website Home page is downloaded from the Web server to your PC.
- The Web page is displayed by your Web browser, and the connection between the server and your browser is closed.

Website is a collection of information stored as Web pages which may be on one or more computers. A Web page is an electronic document written in computer language called HTML.

Web Page

A web page is an electronic document written in computer language called **Hypertext Markup Language (HTML)**. It contains text, links or tags that will display graphics, video, audio, and downloaded files and other web pages. Each web page has a unique address, called a **Uniform Resource Locator (URL)** that identifies its location on the network.

A website has one or more related web pages. Web pages on a site are linked together through a system of hyperlinks to jump between them by clicking on the link. On the web, you navigate through pages of information according to your interests.

Website Address

A website address is known as a **URL**. It is an Internet name that points to a location where a file, directory or website page is hosted. The first page of the website is called the **Home page**. The home page provides an overview of image, photo, movie or other file made available on the server for viewing, processing or downloading. They can also be embedded into the code of web pages in the form of hyperlinks to direct the user to other locations on the Internet.

Enter a Web Page Address

If you know the address of a specific Web page, you can type the address into the Web browser, and the program will display the page. Internet Explorer Address bar lists the Web page addresses you have entered most recently. By pulling down the list, you can see these recent addresses and select the one to return to that site.

To type a Web page Address, perform the following steps:

1. Select the address bar which you want to type the web page address of.
2. For example, we have typed http://gmail.com and pressed the **Enter** key, as shown in *Figure 6.11*:

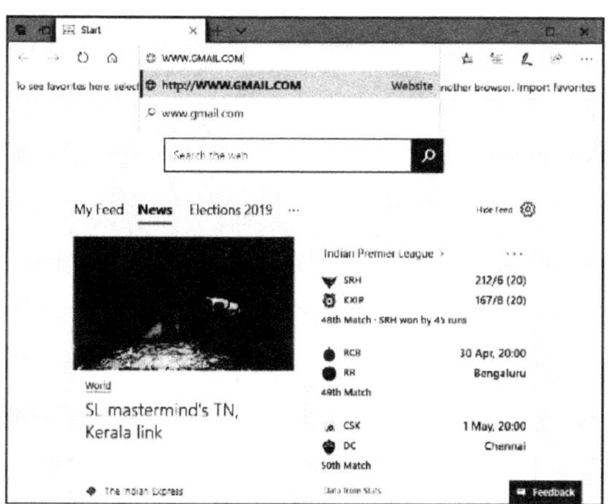

Figure 6.11: *Typing the Address in the Address Bar*

3. The Web page appears in the Microsoft Edge browser, as shown in *Figure 6.12*:

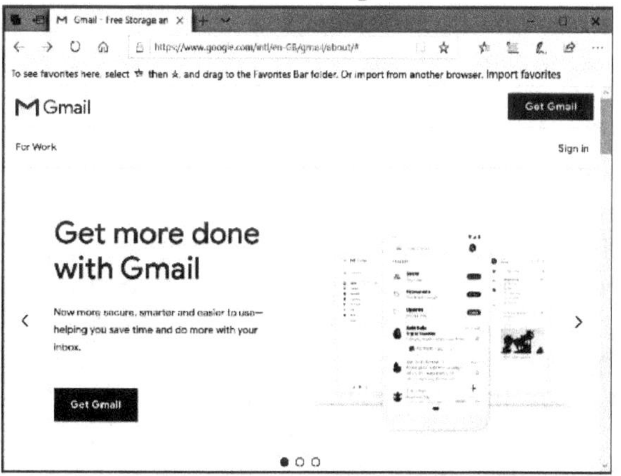

Figure 6.12: *Gmail Web Page Appears*

Internet Addressing Scheme

The Internet has more than a million computers attached to it. In order to communicate, every computer connected to the Internet has a unique address whose format is defined by the IP addressing system. An IP address is a number that represents a single unique computer on the Internet. IP addresses are similar to telephone numbers in that each computer (or telephone) must have its own unique IP address (telephone number). Like telephones, there is a directory system called the **Domain Name System** or **DNS** that can convert a name such as **www.microsoft.com** into a corresponding numeric IP address.

Domain Names

Most organizations use domain names that are easy to remember. Each domain name ends with an identifier that tells you what type of Website it is.

Table 6.1 shows the identifiers commonly used today and the identifiers proposed for use in the future:

Current Domain Identifiers	
.com	Commercial business
.edu	Educational institutions
.gov	Government entities
.net	Internet service providers
.mil	Military sites
.org	Organizations that do not fit any other category
Proposed Domain Identifiers	
.arts	Cultural and entertainment-related organizations
.firm	Businesses
.info	Information services
.nom	Websites of individuals
.rec	Recreation-related organizations
.store	Stores and shops
.web	World Wide Web-related organizations

Table 6.1: *Current and Proposed Domain Name Identifiers*

It is not always necessary to know the full URL of a Web page to locate the page. If you know the domain name, you can start at the home page of the site and click links until you find the Web page you want.

Uniform Resource Locator (URL)

Uniform Resource Locators, or URLs, are the unique addresses of Internet resources. The syntax for specifying a URL is given in *Figure 6.13*. URLs contain information about the access method to use and also about the resource itself. They are used by Web browsers to connect you directly to a specific document or page on the WWW. You do not have to know where that resource is located physically. A sample URL might look like the following:

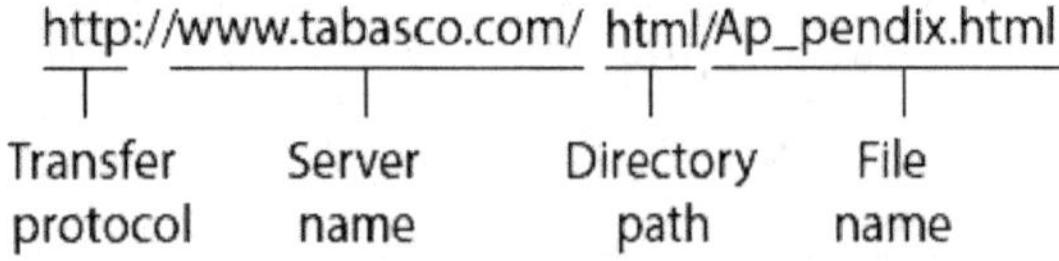

Figure 6.13: *Syntax used for specifying a Uniform Resource Locator (URL)*

First part of the URL is before the colon specifies the access method. On the Web, this is usually http (for Hypertext Transfer Protocol). But ftp or gopher may also be specified. The second part of the URL is after the colon specifies the resource. The text after the two slashes (//) indicates a server name, and the text after the single slash defines the directory or individual file you will be connected to. If you are linking to a document, it will usually have the filename extension .html, the abbreviation for Hypertext Markup Language.

Every page on the Web has a unique address called Uniform Resource Locator (URL). *Figure 6.13* shows the components that make up a URL. The URL used as the example in the figure includes the following:

- **http://:** The first part of the URL indicates the protocol used to transmit Web pages for this URL. Web pages are retrieved using the HTTP protocol or https. The protocol is followed by the ://

- **www.tabasco.com:** This part is your domain name. It is also referred to as the host or server ID. Domain name is followed by the type of category in which the domain is registered. There are many types of categories which were discussed earlier.

- **/html/ (that is, folder-name):** This is the path to the document we want to request. It is a set of characters separated by slashes (/). This is very similar to the paths to folders and files on your computer.

- **Ap_pendix.html:** This part of the URL is the web page filename. The .html at the end indicates that it is a static web page. File names can have different extensions depending on how the web server is set up, and sometimes they end with a /.

Static website and Dynamic website

A static website contains Web pages with fixed content. Each page is coded in HTML and displays the same information to every visitor. Static sites are the most basic type of websites and are the easiest to create. Unlike dynamic websites, they do not require any Web programming or database design. A static site can be built by simply creating a few HTML pages and publishing them to a Web server.

Since static Web pages contain fixed code, the content of each page does not change unless it is manually updated. This works well for small websites, but it makes large sites with hundreds or thousands of pages difficult to maintain. Therefore, larger websites typically use dynamic pages, which can be updated by simply modifying a database record. Static sites that contain a lot of pages are often designed using templates. This makes it possible to update several pages at once, and also helps provide a consistent layout throughout the site.

Dynamic websites contain Web pages that are generated in real-time. These pages include Web scripting code, such as PHP or ASP. When a dynamic page is accessed, the code within the page is parsed on the Web server, and the resulting HTML is sent to the client's Web browser.

Most large websites are dynamic since they are easier to maintain than static websites. This is because each static page contains unique content, that is, they must be manually opened, edited, and published whenever a change is made. Dynamic pages, on the other hand, access information from a database. Therefore, to alter the content of a page, you only need to update a database record. It makes it possible for multiple users to update the content of a website without editing the layout of the pages.

Absolute URL

A fully qualified URL that specifies the location of a resource that resides on the Internet is called an absolute URL. It is the complete path including the domain – filename. For example, http://www.ibdhost.com/images/logo.gif specifies an image file (logo.gif) located in the images directory, for the www.ibdhost.com domain. This type of URL is what you must use when you want to link (or load) a file that is on another server.

Another example is the absolute URL of this page (which is also the address/location of the file) that is, http://www.ibdhost.com/help/path/index.php.

Relative URL

A partially qualified URL is the one that specifies a resource on the Internet whose location is relative to the starting point specified by an absolute URL.

In fact, the concatenated absolute and relative URLs constitute a complete URL.

Once you have viewed a document located somewhere on the network (say, the document http://www.domain.com/default.html), you can use a partial or relative URL to point to another file in the same directory, on the same machine being served by the same server software. For example, if another file exists in the same directory called 'second.html', then second.html is a valid relative URL at that point.

The relative URL points to a file or directory in relation to the present file or directory (folder). Relative URLs help in Website maintenance. It is easy to move a file from one directory (folder) to another, or a website from one domain name to another. We don't have to worry about updating the link(s) or the src(img) path(s).

This provides an easy way to build sets of hypertext documents. If a set of hypertext documents is in a common directory, they can be referred to (that is, by hyperlink) by just their file names. However, if a reader is on one of the documents, a jump can be made to any other document in the same directory by just using the other document filename as the relative URL at that point. The additional information (access method, host name, port number, directory name, and so on.) will be assumed based on the URL used to reach the first document.

Applications of Internet

With the help of Internet, you can:

- Exchange messages using e-mail (Electronic mail).
- Transfer files as well as software.
- Browse through information on any topic on web.
- Communicate in real time (chat) with others connected to the Internet.
- Search databases of government, individuals and organizations.
- Read news available from leading news groups.
- Send or receive animation and picture files from distant places.
- Set up a site with information about your company's products and services.

ISP and Role of ISP

An Internet Service Provider is a company which allows you to connect to the Internet. It provides the gateway to the internet and everything that you do online. You also connect to an ISP by using a PC modem to dial into the ISP modems over a standard telephone line. Your modem connects to a single modem among a bank of modems at your ISP. This is called a dial-up connection. Users within corporations and large organizations mostly connect to an ISP via a high-speed link (typically over fibre optic cabling but not phone lines), and such a connection is called a direct connection.

Regardless of your connection type, an ISP acts as your gateway to the Internet, allowing you to access the various services of the Internet (Web, e-mail, and so on).

The relationship between your computer, your ISP and the Internet is shown pictorially in *Figure 6.14*.

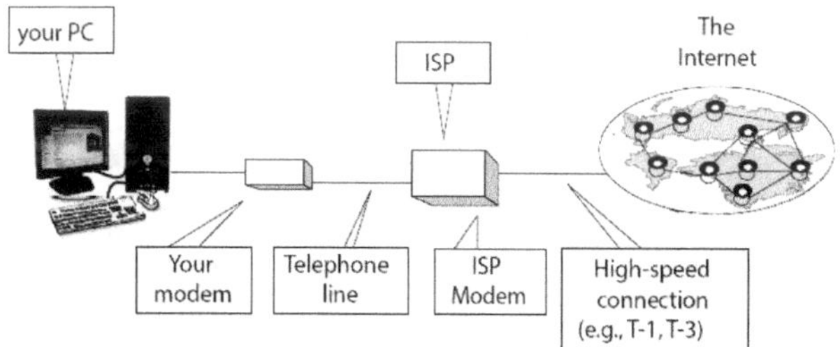

Figure 6.14: *Dial-up connection using an ISP as a gateway to the Internet*

How to Select an ISP?

As with any product or service, the quality and reliability of services provided by ISPs are highly variable. There are many issues which you must consider before selecting a particular ISP. For consumers and businesses alike, it is important to sign up with the ISP that is within local calling distance and does not involve any Standard Trunk Dialing (STD) charges to reach the provider to make a telephonic call.

Some of the popular ISPs in India are:

- **BSNL:** It offers broadband unlimited plans for subscribers for its landline telephone services.
- **MTNL (Mahanagar Telephone Nigam Limited):** It offers wire-line broadband. It is extremely popular in Mumbai, especially among the business sector in the financial hub.

- **Hathway Cable and Datacom:** It offers high speed wire-line broadband internet service through the fibre optic cable network.
- **Bharti Airtel:** It offers broadband wire-line internet service under the brand Vfibre.

Online Service Internet Gateways

Online services provide access to Internet resources (information archived outside the online service network) through Internet gateways.

Internet gateways consist of specific hardware and software that allow the online service to provide its subscribers with access to Internet resources (outside its own network).

Figure 6.15 illustrates the role of an Internet gateway in providing Internet access to an online service user.

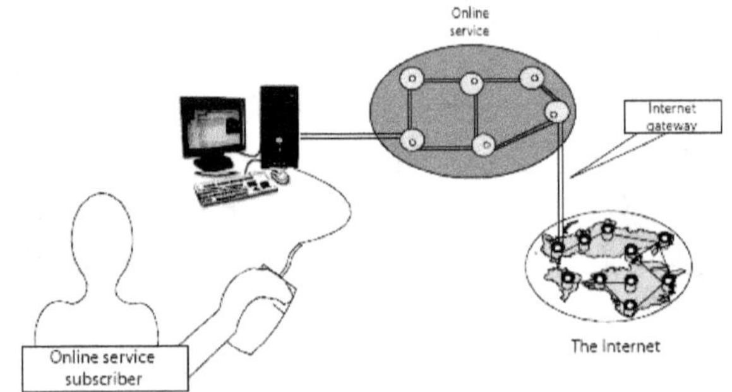

Figure 6.15: *Online Service Gateway to the Internet*

Choosing a Service

The most common way to connect to the Internet is through an Internet Service Provider (ISP). ISPs are essentially a **pass-through** connection. Besides giving basic technical support for the connection itself, the ISP sets up in such a way that you can use Internet mail as well as the World Wide Web.

Most of the major cities have access to Internet via the VSNL and services of other private ISPs. You should expect an ISP to provide you with software and technical support to make you comfortable. Ensure that the dial-up connection uses a local phone number, or your phone bill could end up higher than your Internet connection bill.

Introduction to IP Address

IP stands for Internet Protocols. It is a numerical label or value that is used to uniquely identify a computer on the Internet that uses the Internet protocol for communication. The address is made up of 32-binary bits in an IP address. The numbers are grouped into four octets and are separated by dots. Each octet consists of 8 bits each, that is, 4x8 = 32 bits. In a decimal format, each octet has a minimum value of 0 and maximum value of 255. A binary has a base value of 2, so for 8 bit, 28 = 256. It starts from 0.0.0.0 and the end is 255.255.255.255 in a decimal format.

In IP addressing scheme, a static IP address is permanent address which will never change, whereas a dynamic IP address device changes its IP address every time when accessing internet.

The **32-bit IP** address is grouped into eight bits, each separated by dots, and represented in **decimal** format (known as **dotted decimal notation**). Each bit in the octet has a binary weight (**128, 64, 32, 16, 8, 4, 2, 1**). The minimum value for an octet is 0, and the maximum value for an octet is **255**. *Figure 6.16* illustrates the basic format of an IP address.

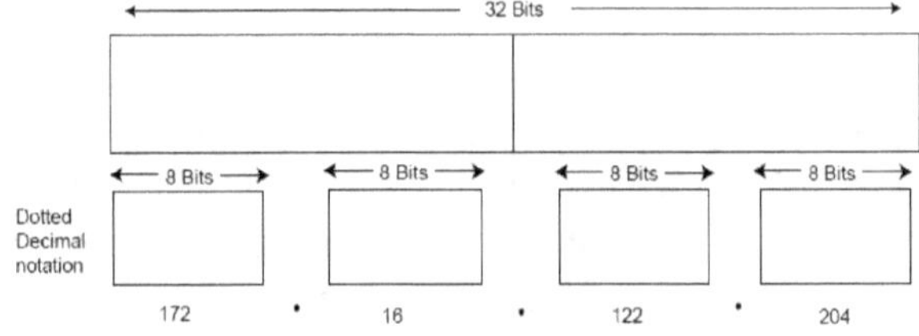

Figure 6.16: *IP Address*

Modes of Connecting Internet

There are different types of Internet Access techniques like **Hotspot, Wireless Fidelity (Wi-Fi), LAN** cable, **BroadBand** and **USB** Tethering. These have been described below.

Hotspot

A hotspot is a physical location where people get Internet access using Wi-Fi technology via a wireless local area network, using a router connected to an internet service provider. Many places offer free Wi-fi hotspots as a public service, including airports, restaurants and hotels to attract customers. Other hotspots require you to pay for using this service.

Using a hotspot can be a security threat to your personal data. Anyone can set up a malicious hotspot that will unencrypt data sent through it. Another way attackers can access your personal information is to eavesdrop on a legitimate Wi-Fi hotspot and watch for unencrypted data being transmitted. Personal information like account passwords, credit card information, messages and photos can all be intercepted if the data is not encrypted.

Today, most smartphones can be configured to create a Wi-Fi hotspot, allowing computers and tablets to connect to the Internet using the Wi-fi signal generated by the smartphone.

Connecting to the Hotspot

Setting up a Hotspot in Windows 10 is easy. To begin, press the [Windows] key and click Settings. When Window Settings appears, click Network and Internet and then select the Mobile Hotspot tab, as shown in *Figure 6.18*. Or, in Windows 10 systems, your hotspot will appear on the wireless network list, as shown in *Figure 6.17*:

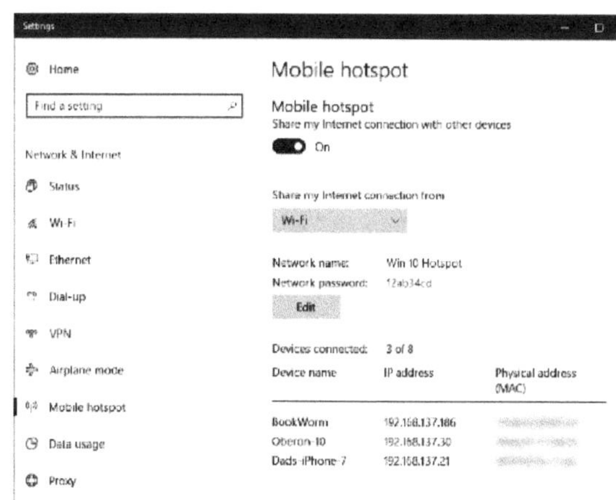

Figure 6.18: *You can see all the Systems that are Currently Connected to the Mobile Hotspot*

In addition to viewing a list of the number of systems connected to the Mobile hotspot, you can also monitor your hotspot on the Mobile Hotspot tile in Action Center, as shown in *Figure 6.19*:

Figure 6.19: *Quick check on your Hotspot on the Mobile Hotspot tile in Action Center*

Figure 6.17: *The Mobile Hotspot as a Wireless Access Point on the Wireless Network List*

From the Mobile Hotspot tab on the system that is sharing its internet connection, you can see the all the systems currently connected to the Mobile hotspot, as shown in *Figure 6.18*:

Turning off the Hotspot

When you are done using your Mobile hotspot, you can disable it. Click the Mobile Hotspot toggle to turn it off. You can see that the mobile hotspot will be disabled.

Or you can connect your smartphone or laptop to the Internet through several Wi-Fi hotspots. Connecting to a wireless hotspot is a simple process.

1. Click the wireless icon on your device to see the names of the nearby wireless networks. Select a wireless network, in some cases, you might also have to click **Connect**.

2. Enter the security key or the password. Most wireless networks are secured and require a password to accept a connection. Some networks are unsecured or open and do not require a password.

3. Select the network type (home, work or public, if you are in Windows device). Choosing the network type will establish a security level for your location. If you select **home** or **work**, your device will be discoverable to other devices. Be sure to select **public** if you are in a public location like a coffee shop, hotel or restaurant.

Connecting Internet LAN Cable

The LAN is used to connect two desktop PCs along with the internet connection method. The LAN internet connection is used to create a local area network for sharing the internet and files/folders.

Steps to Connect Your PC to another PC using LAN Internet Connection:

1. Find the Ethernet port on your PC. You can usually find this on the back of your desktop, or along the side or back of a laptop.

2. Plug one end of an Ethernet cable into your computer. Make sure you are using an Ethernet cable, not a telephone cable.

3. Plug the other end of the cable into an open LAN port. This can be any open LAN port either on the router or the switch, depending on your LAN setup.

4. Test your network. Once all of the computers are connected to a LAN port, they will be assigned IPs automatically and will appear on the network.

5. Also, make sure that you have an Internet connection and account on your PC.

6. Go to the Start menu and search Control Panel. Once you see it, click on it, as shown in *Figure 6.20*:

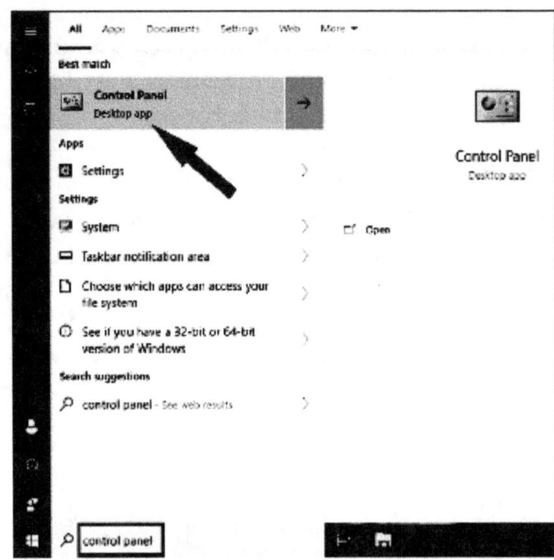

Figure 6.20: *Typing Control Panel in the Search Box*

7. The Control Panel window opens; click on Network and Internet, as shown in *Figure 6.21*:

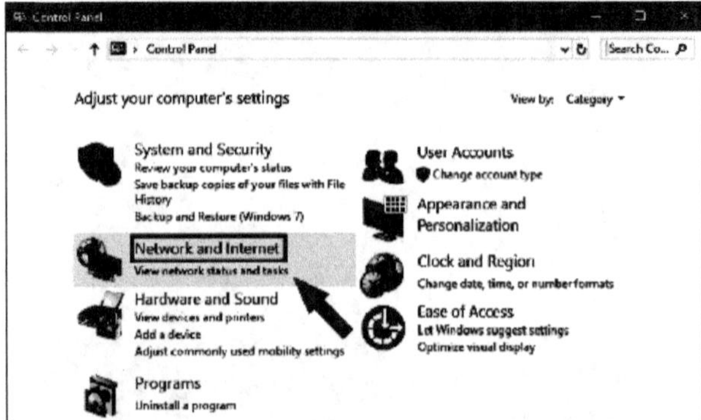

Figure 6.21: *Selecting Network and Internet*

8. A dialog box appears; open Networking and Sharing Center. Alternatively, you can also type Control Panel\Network and Internet\ Network and Sharing Center and press the Enter key. This will redirect you from Control Panel to Network and Sharing Center.

9. On the left-hand side of the Network and Sharing Center Window, click on Change adapter settings, as shown in *Figure 6.22*:

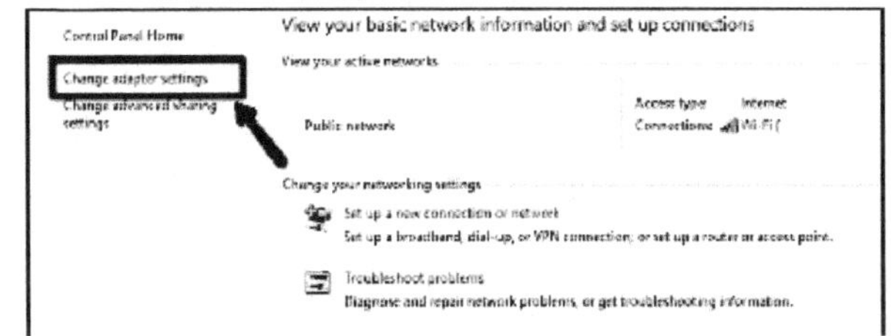

Figure 6.22: *Selecting Change adapter settings*

10. This will display different connections. Select the appropriate connection for your LAN. Select Ethernet and have the description network cable unplugged, as shown in *Figure 6.23.*

11. Right-click on the connection and select Properties. The local area connection properties will appear as shown in *Figure 6.23*:

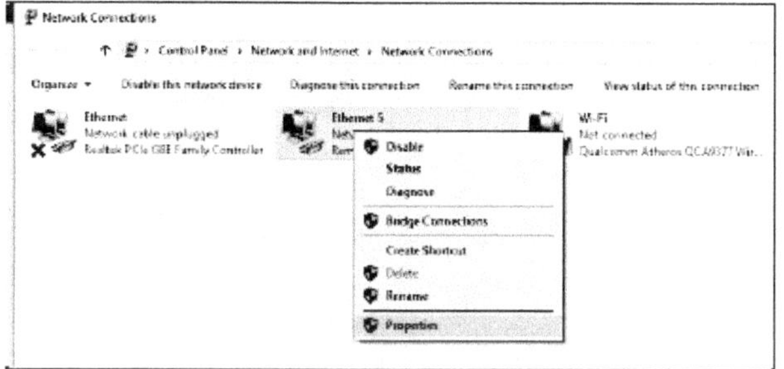

Figure 6.23: *Selecting Properties*

12. Click the Sharing tab, and check Allow other network users to connect through this computer's internet connection under Internet Connection Sharing, as shown in *Figure 6.24*:

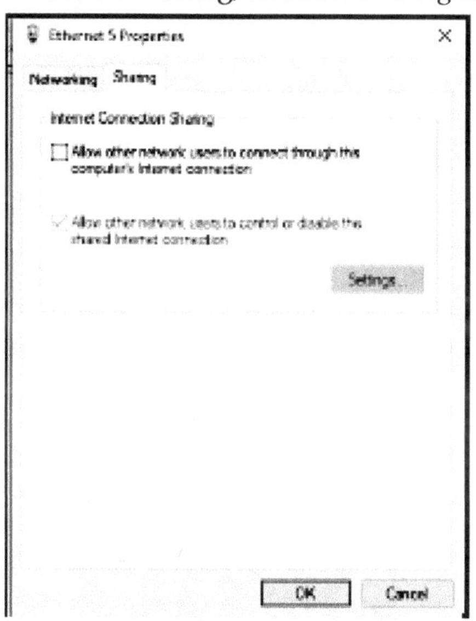

Figure 6.24: *Selecting Sharing Tab*

13. Press **OK**.

14. Now, you have enabled network sharing on both PCs so that both PCs are connected with a physical LAN cable.

15. Click the Networking tab. Select Internet protocol version 4(TCP/IPv4), and then click on the Properties button, as shown in *Figure 6.25*:

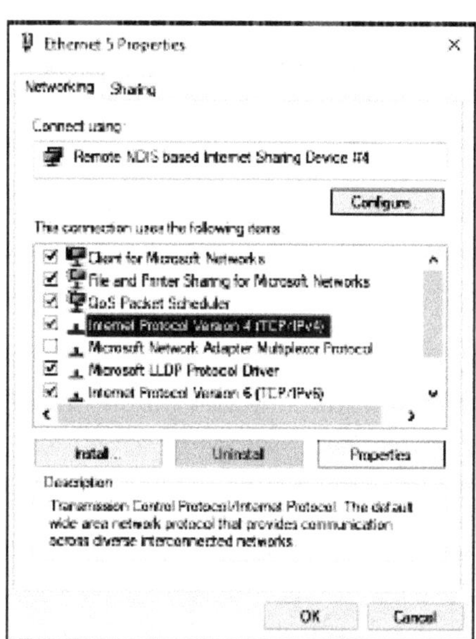

Figure 6.25: *Selecting Networking tab*

16. Here, you need to configure the two PCs with different IP settings, as shown in *Figure 6.26*. In the General tab, set the IP address and subnet mask of the first computer, such as:

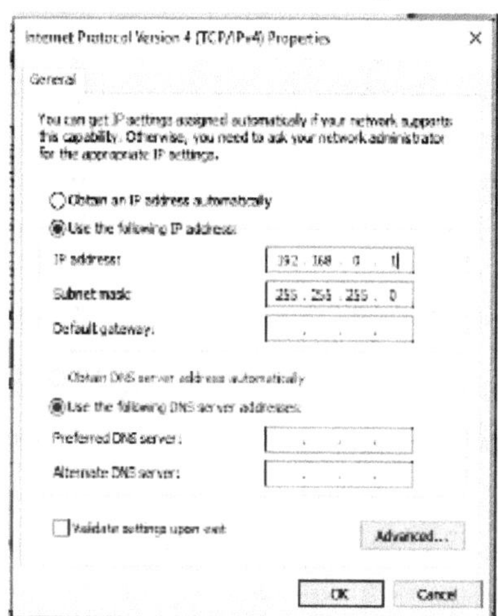

Figure 6.26: *Set the IP Address in the General tab*

For the first computer (say, Computer 1):
```
IP address:       192.168.0.1
Subnet mask:  255.255.255.0
```

For the second computer (say, Computer 2):
```
IP address:       192.168.0.2
Subnet mask:  255.255.255.0
```

It is important to ensure that the last values of the IP addresses for both computers are different.

17. Click the OK button.
18. Connect to the Internet on the server PC (the one actually attached to the Internet) and then try to access the Internet on the other PC(s).

Wireless Fidelity (Wi-Fi) Connections

Wireless Internet access, sometimes referred to as a "hot spot," is a local area network run by radio waves rather than wires. It is broadcast from a central hub, which is a hard-wired device that actually brings in the Internet connection. The hub, located at the main computer system or server, broadcasts Internet connectivity to clients, which includes basically anyone within receiving range equipped with a wireless LAN card.

Wireless Internet access is very convenient in the home; it can be even more so in the workplace. A wired network is not only but very time-consuming to install throughout a building, but also very expensive. Ethernet cables used to connect client machines might need to be routed through walls, ceilings, and floors. In the past, this disadvantage was sometimes overlooked due to the advantages of greater security and faster data transfer speeds provided by Ethernet cables.

The Wireless LANs can be installed in virtually minutes by nearly anyone. They are extremely inexpensive, and can have data transfer rates that rival hard-wired Ethernet LANs. Furthermore, Wi-Fi Protected Access II (WPA2) encrypts all traffic on the LAN, addressing the problem of eavesdropping.

How to connect to a Wi-Fi network using Taskbar?

Using the network flyout in the Taskbar is the way to connect to a new Wi-Fi network.

1. Click on the wireless icon in the bottom-right corner of the taskbar. Alternatively, you can open Action Center (**Windows key + A**), and then click the Network button in the Quick actions section to access the network flyout, as shown in *Figure 6.27*:

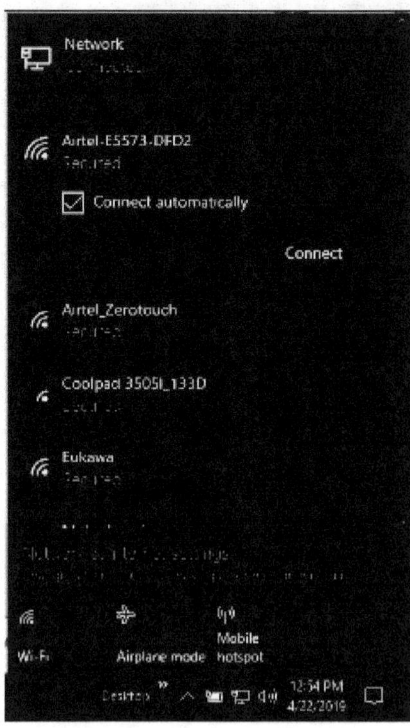

Figure 6.27: *Wireless Icon in the Bottom-right Corner*

2. Select the wireless network you want to connect to.
3. Check the Connect automatically option, as shown in *Figure 6.27*.
4. Click the Connect button, as shown in *Figure 6.27*.
5. Enter the network security key (that is, password).
6. Click the Next button, as shown in *Figure 6.28*:

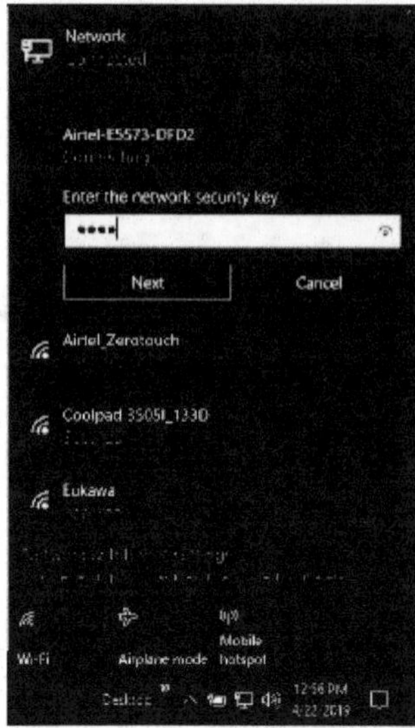

Figure 6.28: *Entering the Network Password*

7. Once you complete these steps, you will be connected to the network using a wireless connection.

8. To disconnect, simply open the Wi-Fi pane, and select the network you are connected to. Press the Disconnect button.

Broadband Connections

A high-speed Internet connection with at least 256 Kbps speed is termed as a Broadband connection. A channel may be broadband if it sends a signal without modulation on a carrier. The signal covers the whole range of frequency that medium can carry. The broadband term is now hijacked by the Internet Service Provider. Hence, the term broadband is used for high-speed Internet access. It gives a high-speed internet access of minimum 512 Kbps and up to a maximum of 100 Mbps.

A customer basically uses landline phone for providing this service. He can use his telephone for a normal telephone call even while he is browsing Internet. There are no separate telephone charges for the connection to the Internet. The access to the Internet will be around 8 times faster than a normal dial up access. The advantages are:

- Cost is Low
- Speed Connection is high (2 Mbps)
- No setup time
- Always On

You can also use mobile broadband technology called wireless wide area network (WWAN) technology to connect to the Internet. To use mobile broadband, you need a data card and a data plan with a mobile broadband provider.

After getting a device and data plan, make sure you activate your subscriber identity module (SIM) and the mobile broadband service for the SIM. Your mobile operator or device retailer will give you the information to do this.

If you have an external data card, ensure that it is correctly inserted into the laptop.

To connect to the Internet using mobile broadband (here, we use Reliance Broadband):

1. Click the Start button on taskbar; highlight All Programs. Click Accessories, and then click Reliance Netconnect-Broadband+, as shown in *Figure 6.29*:

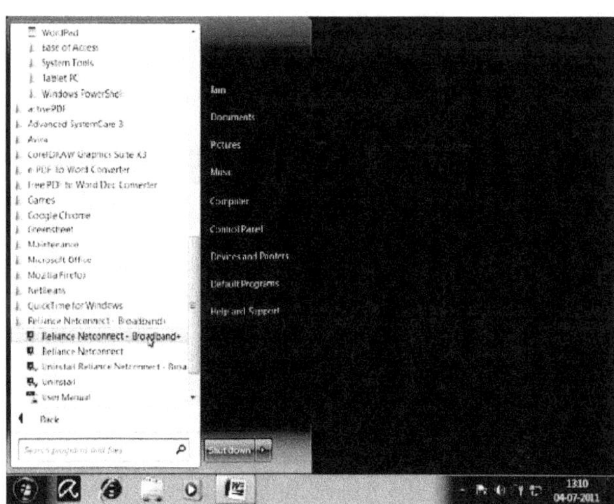

Figure 6.29: *Connecting Internet*

2. In the Reliance Netconnect-Broadband+ window, click on Connect to connect to the Internet, as shown in *Figure 6.30*. If you are connecting to the Internet for the first time, you have to provide the username and the password, and change the settings according to your need.

Figure 6.30: *Connecting Internet using Reliance Netconnect-Broadband+*

To disconnect a mobile broadband Internet connection:

1. In the Reliance Netconnect-Broadband+ window, click Disconnect, as shown in *Figure 6.31*:

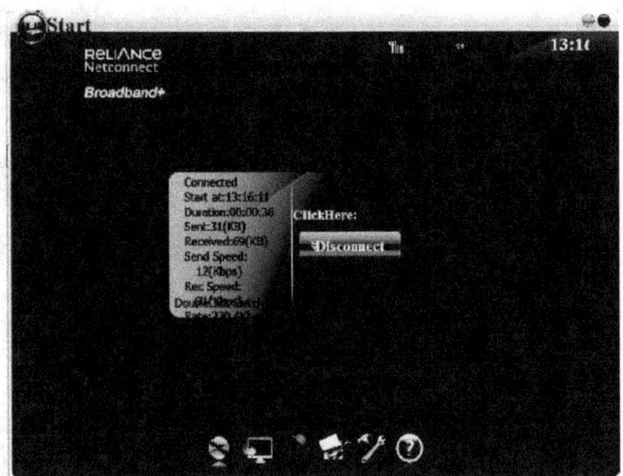

Figure 6.31: *Disconnecting Internet*

Connect to USB Tethering

You can share your phone mobile data to access Internet with other devices, like your laptop, through tethering. You can tether using a Bluetooth or Wi-Fi connection; however, USB Tethering has the fastest speed to share your phone mobile data with other devices.

How to connect to USB Tethering

1. Connect your phone to your PC using USB cable.
2. Select **Settings** on your phone.
3. Click **More networks**, and select **Tethering and portable hotspot**, as shown in *Figure 6.32*:

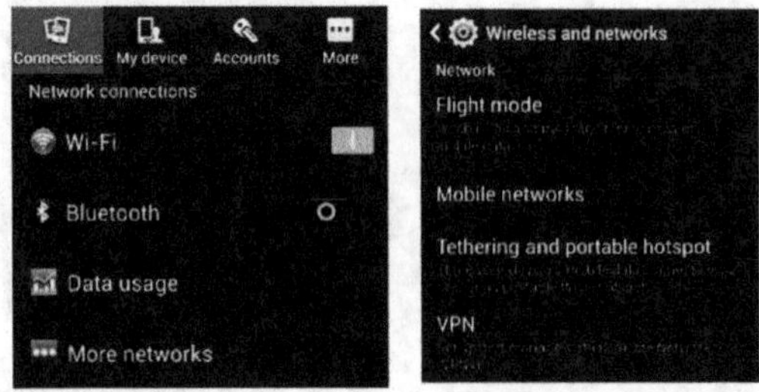

Figure 6.32: *Select Tethering and Portable Hotspot in the Mobile Settings*

4. Click **USB tethering**, as shown in *Figure 6.33*:

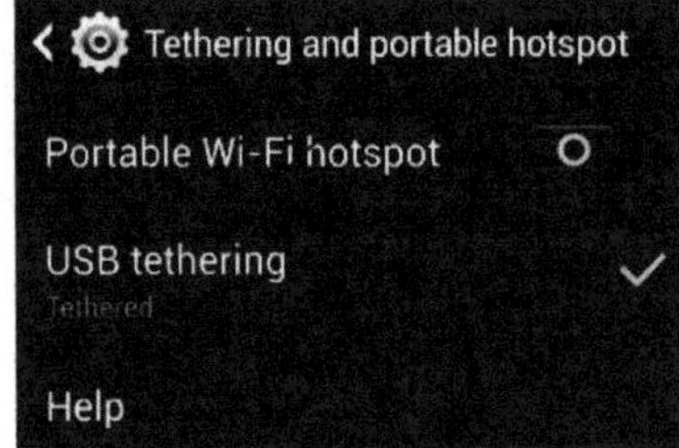

Figure 6.33: *Selecting USB Tethering from mobile*

5. Now, you can access your mobile internet on your laptop or computer.

Identifying IP/MAC/IMEI of various devices and their uses

An Internet Protocol address (IP address) is a numerical label assigned to each device connected to a computer network that uses the Internet Protocol for communication. An IP address serves two principal functions: host or network interface identification and location addressing.

The two versions of IP addresses currently running are IP versions 4 (IPv4) and IP versions 6 (IPv6). There are many features with these two versions.

IPv4

IPv4 defines a 32-bit number space. The maximum number of unique host to **4,294,967,296** or **(2)32**, that is, it provides more than **four billion addresses**.

The IPv4 are further classified into two parts. The network part and the host part.

- **Network part:** The first part of an Internet address identifies if the network number field has been referred to as the network prefix because it is the first portion of each IP address identifies the network number.

- **Host Part:** The second part identifies the particular host on the given network. All hosts on a given network share the same network prefix but must have a unique host number. Similarly, any two hosts on different networks must have different network prefixes but may have the same host number.

IP address and classes

The IPv4 addressing system is divided into five classes of IP address. All the **five classes** are identified by the first octet of the IP address. *Figure 6.34* shows the structure of each IP address class.

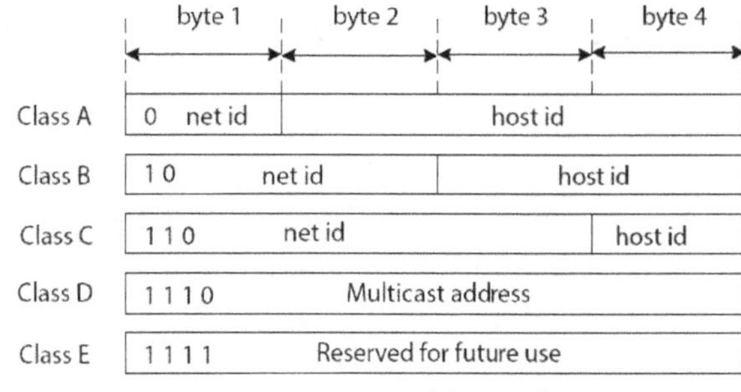

	byte 1	byte 2	byte 3	byte 4
Class A	0 net id		host id	
Class B	1 0 net id		host id	
Class C	1 1 0 net id			host id
Class D	1 1 1 0	Multicast address		
Class E	1 1 1 1	Reserved for future use		

Figure 6.34: *IP address class*

The different classes of the IPv4 address are the following:

Class A address

Class A address is used for very large networks. In class A, the highest order bit of the first octet is always set to 0 and the remaining 7 bits determine network ID. The 24 bits of host ID are used to host in any network. The first octet ranges from 1-127. The Class A address only includes IP starting from 1.x.x.x to 126.x.x.x. The range 127.x.x.x is reserved for loop back IP addresses. Number of network in Network ID is = 27 = 128 and the number of host address ID is 224 – 2 = 16,777,214. The default subnet mask is 255.0.0.0. Class A, IP address format can be written as: 0N.H.H.H.

Class B address

Class B addresses are used for medium-sized networks. In Class B, the highest order bit of the first octet is always set to 10 and the remaining 14 bits determine network ID and other 16 bits of host ID. The IP Addresses range from 128.0.x.x to 191.255.x.x. The default subnet mask for Class B is 255.255.x.x. Number of networks in Network ID is = 214 = 16384 and the number of host address IDs is 216-2 = 65534. Class B IP address format can be written as: 10N.N.H.H.

Class C address

Class C addresses are commonly used for small-sized networks. In Class C, the highest order bit of the first octet is always set to 110 and the remaining 21 bits determine network ID and other 8 bits of host ID. IP addresses range from 192.0.0.x to 223.255.255.x. The default subnet mask for Class C is 255.255.255.x. Number of networks in Network ID is = 221 = 2097152 and the number of host address IDs is 28 – 2 = 254. Class C IP address format can be written as: 110N.N.N.H.

Class D address

Class D addresses are known as **multicast IPv4 addresses**. In class D, the highest order bit of the first octet is always set to 1110 and the remaining bits determine the host ID. Its IP address ranges from 224.0.0.0 to 239.255.255.255. Class D is reserved for Multicasting. Class D does not have any subnet mask.

Class E address

Class E is used for future use and development purposes, and it does not assign any sub net mask. The highest order bits of first octet is always set to 1111. Its IP addresses ranges from 240.0.0.0 to 255.255.255.254.

IPv6

IPv6 is the latest level of the Internet Protocol and is now included as part of the IP support in many products including the major computer operating systems. Formally, IPv6 is a set of specifications from the Internet Engineering Task Force (IETF). IPv6 was designed as an evolutionary set of improvements to the current IP version 4. Network hosts and intermediate nodes with either IPv4 or IPv6 can handle packets formatted for either level of the Internet Protocol. Users and service providers can update to IPv6 independently without having to coordinate with each other.

The most obvious improvement in IPv6 over the IPv4 is that IP addresses are lengthened from **32 bits** to **128 bits**. This extension will take care of future growth of the Internet. This will provide relief for what was perceived as an impending shortage of network addresses. The **128-bit** address is divided in to **16-bits**, and each 16-bit block is converted to a **4-digit** hexadecimal number and separated by colons.

The format of IPv6 address is `xxxx:xxxx:xxxx:xxxx:xxxx:xxxx:xxxx:xxxx` where each x is a hexadecimal digit representing 4 bits or a nibble. IPv6 addresses range from `0000:0000:0000:0000:0000:0000:0000:0000` to `ffff:ffff:ffff:ffff:ffff:ffff:ffff:ffff`.

An IPv6 address can be simplified by two methods:

- **Omit leading zeroes:** Omit the leading zeroes in any 16-bits. For example, IPv6 address 2001:0DB8:0000:0000:0022:F376:FF3B:AC99 may be written as 2001:DB8:0:0:22:F376:FF3B:AC99.
- **Double colon:** Use double colons (::) in place of a series of zeroes. For example, the above address can further be simplified as 2001:DB8::22:F376:FF3B:AC99.

To identify IP address using command prompt:

1. Open the **command prompt**.
2. Type **ipconfig** and press **Enter**.
3. This will display a list of your network connection information. All of the network connections on your computer will display IPv4 addresses, as shown in *Figure 6.34*.

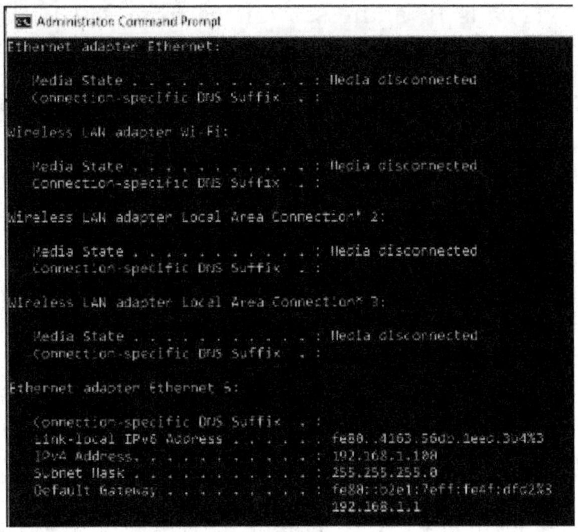

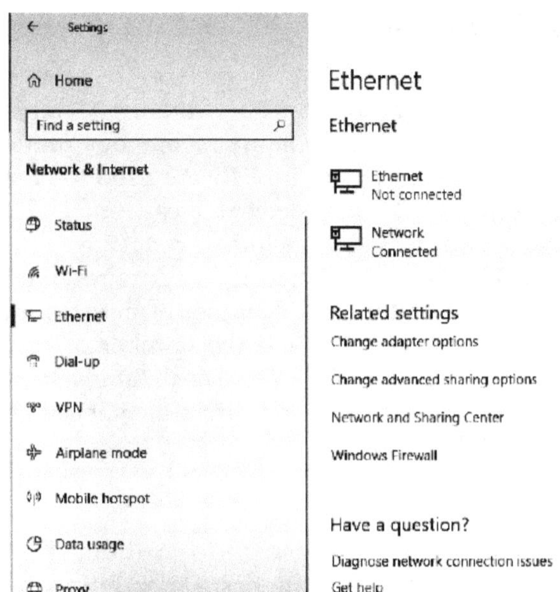

Figure 6.34: *List of Network Connection Information*

MAC Address

MAC stands for Media Access Control. It is a unique identifier assigned to a network interface card (NIC) by the manufacturer. It is used to connect to the Ethernet network, and it has its own unique MAC address. The MAC addresses are assigned permanently to adapters and cannot be changed as they are a unique identification of the hardware interface of network. They are the physical addresses. This address is sent to your local network, i.e., to your router or ISP, where it is used to route information to your computer and serves as identification print on your network.

MAC address is a **48-bit hexadecimal** address. The format of a MAC address is MM:MM:MM:SS:SS:SS, where MM:MM:MM. The first 3-bytes include address of the manufacturer, and the second half is the serial number of NIC card (that is, SS:SS:SS). MAC Address of each computer on a network is unique. When you change or replace the NIC card of your computer, your MAC address also gets changed. MAC address is used at the data link layer of OSI/TCP/IP model. **Address Resolution Protocol (ARP)** is a protocol used to receive MAC address of a device. The MAC address may look like: 00 12 0E A6 B0 68.

To identify MAC address in Windows 10:

1. Click the **Start** menu, and select **Settings**. The Windows Settings page appears.

2. Click **Network & Internet**. Click the Ethernet option from the left-hand side. On the right, you will see the connections listed; click the one you want, as shown in *Figure 6.35*:

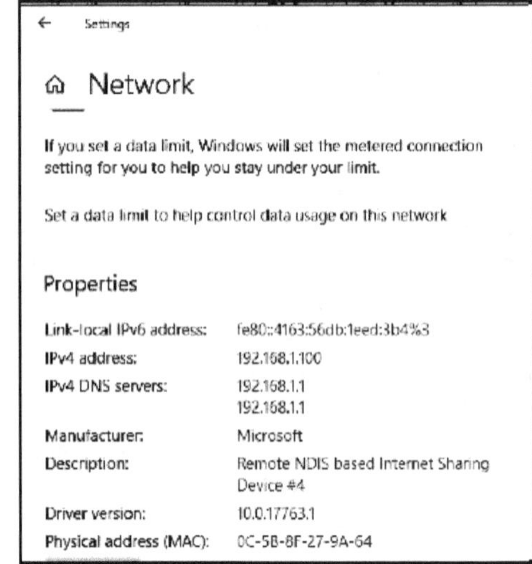

Figure 6.35: *Selecting Ethernet*

3. Scroll down to the Properties section, and you will find the information, as shown in *Figure 6.36*:

Figure 6.36: *MAC Address shown in Properties Section*

To find MAC/IP address through Control Panel:

1. In the search box, type **Control Panel**. The Control Panel window appears.

2. Click **Network and Sharing**, and then click **Change adapter settings**.

3. Right-click the connection for which you want information, and then choose Status from the context menu, as shown in *Figure 6.37*:

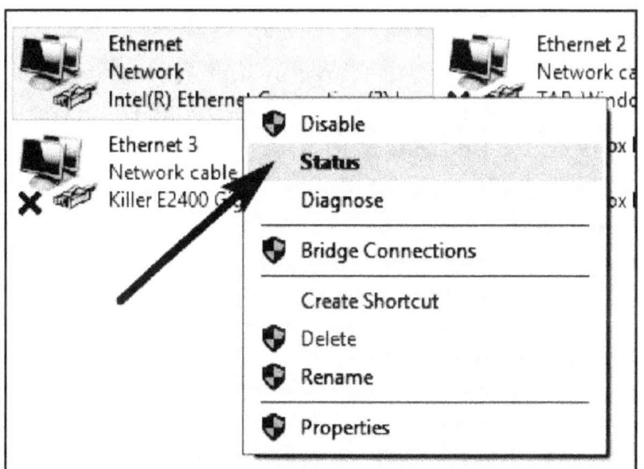

Figure 6.37: *Selecting Status from the Context Menu*

4. In the Ethernet Status window, click the Details button, as shown in *Figure 6.38*:

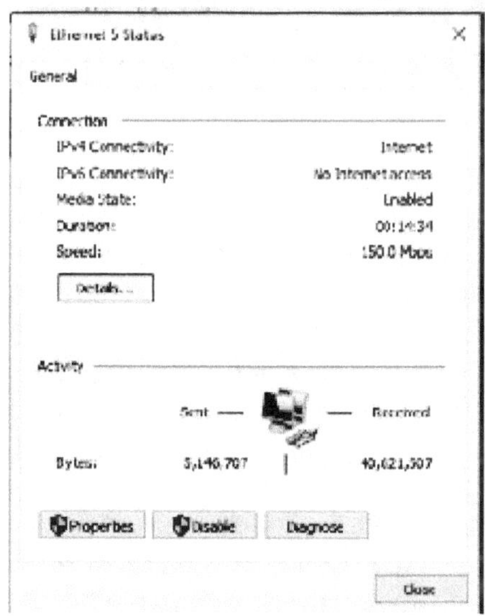

Figure 6.38: *Selecting Details from Ethernet status*

5. The Network Connection Details window will have the information you want. Note that the MAC address is listed as Physical Address, as shown in *Figure 6.39*:

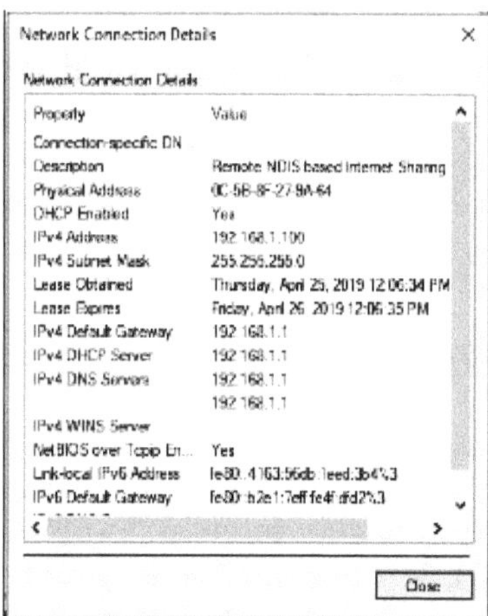

Figure 6.39: *Details window showing MAC address as Physical address*

IMEI

An **International Mobile Equipment Identity (IMEI)** number is a globally unique identification or serial number that is given to all mobile phones and smart phones. It is a **15-digit number** assigned to all cellular devices, which identifies your device within the mobile network, as shown in *Figure 6.40*. We can use this number to present a mobile phone from being used by another person or phone company if it has been lost or stolen.

Figure 6.40: *IMEI Number*

The IMEI can be displayed on the screen of the phone by entering **#06#** into the keypad on most phones. It can also be printed behind the battery of the phone.

Popular Web Browsers

A web browser is a software application which enables a user to display and view Web pages such as images, videos, music and other information. Text and images on a web page can contain hyperlinks which allow a user to quickly and easily access information provided on many web pages at many websites. Some popular Web browsers are briefly described below.

Microsoft Internet Explorer

This browser was made by **Microsoft Corporation** and bundled together into Windows operating system. The latest operating system, Windows, comes with Microsoft's latest web browser named Internet Explorer 11. Internet Explorer supports **HTML 4.01, CSS Level 1, XML 1.0**, and **DOM Level**. Microsoft Edge replaced IE as Windows' default browser beginning with Windows 10, but IE is still a popular browser for users running older versions of Windows.

Microsoft Edge

Microsoft Edge is the new browser built into Windows 10. Internet Explorer 11 remains available alongside Edge on Windows 10 for compatibility. The browser includes an integrated Adobe Flash player and a PDF reader. It also integrates with online platforms in order to provide voice control, search functionality, and dynamic information related to searches within the address bar. Users can make annotations to web pages that can be stored with OneDrive but cannot save HTML pages and does not support ActiveX.

Mozilla Firefox

Mozilla Firefox has become popular because it is a fast and full-featured Web browser and makes browsing very efficient. It is a free and open source web browser which is made by the Mozilla Foundation. Some of Firefox's features include pop-up blocking, tab-browsing, live bookmarking, a download manager, and an integrated search system that uses the user's search engine.

Opera

Opera, created by the Opera Software Company, is another popular web browser. It includes features such as tab-browsing, page zooming, mouse gestures and an integrated download manager. Its security features are phishing and malware protection, strong encryption while browsing secure websites, and the ability to easily delete private data such as cookies and browsing history. It runs on Windows, OS X, and Linux.

Google Chrome

Google built Google Chrome just for speed to be used by any type of user to browse the Web. It has become popular due to its fast loading speed. Google Chrome is designed with minimalistic user interface. It is built with a fast browsing engine.

To open Microsoft Edge:

1. Click on the Microsoft Edge icon on the taskbar, as shown in *Figure 6.41*:

Figure 6.41: *Selecting Microsoft Edge*

The parts of Microsoft Edge are explained below:

- **Title Bar:** On the left, the title bar displays the name of the currently open Web page and on the right side, there are maximize/minimize, restore and close buttons.

- **Address bar:** It displays the address of the page you are currently viewing. You can also use the Address bar for navigation. Type the address of a page you want to go to in the Address bar, and press the *Enter* key. Address Bar contains the following buttons:

  o **Back:** Displays a page from the list of previously viewed pages.

  o **Forward:** Displays a page from the list of next viewed pages.

  o **Stop:** Stops downloading the current page.

  o **Refresh:** Displays the latest version of the current Web page.

- **Reading view:** Click the book icon to go into reading mode which removes the distractions of the page and opens a clean view of just the main content of the page.

- **Reading List:** It allows us to save web pages for later viewing. Like the Favorites folder, you can also add webpages to Reading List. If there is a website that you want to read later, you can either drag the favicon on Edge browser address bar to Reading List, or you can click on the star and from the drop-down menu, select Reading List instead of Favorites.

- **Pin the Sites to Start menu:** Open your favourite website. Click on the settings button. Once the settings menu appears, simply click the Pin to Start option. Your favourite website will now appear in your Start Menu.
- **Sharing:** Regular web pages can be shared by sending a link. For pages with Web notes, an image of the page is sent to the recipient.
- **Web notes:** Windows 10 users can keep track of what is useful for them and what is not within each webpage or document. They can underline, highlight and circle specific parts directly on webpages and save them in the local hard disk or to the cloud.
- **Advanced Tab management options in Edge Browser:** Edge has focused on tab browsing in tab management options. Simply right-click on any browser tab, and you should see a context menu options. These can be used to Reopen closed ta bs, Refresh tabs, Close all tabs or Move a tab to a new window.

Exploring the Internet

The Internet is a vast network connecting smaller networks of computer and overseas. It is a major tool for sharing computer resources, research, and communication with groups or individuals.

Surfing the Web

Surfing the web includes the act of browsing the Internet from one web page to another web page using hyperlinks in an Internet browser. The term surfing was first defined by **Mark McCahill**. When someone is surfing the Internet, they can be referred to as a surfer or a net surfer. Surfing is also defined as going through information on different subjects on the different websites.

To access Web browser, perform the following steps:

1. Open Microsoft Edge browser in the taskbar.
2. The starting page is called the **browser home page**, and you can set it can be set to any page on the Internet.

To type a Web page Address, perform the following steps:

1. Type the address of the Web page in the Address bar. For example, we have typed http://gmail.com, as shown in *Figure 6.11*.
2. Click the **Go** button or press **Enter** to open the Web page, as shown in *Figure 6.12*.

Most Web addresses starts with http://. When you type your address; Internet Explorer adds them automatically.

To redisplay a Web page:

1. Click drop-down arrow in the Address bar.
2. A list of visiting web addresses you have typed appears, as shown in *Figure 6.12*. Select the desired site address you want to display. That Web page appears.

Set Tabs Aside and Share a Tab Group.

Edge feature browser have a tab groups. This feature lets you set aside a group of tabs, which you can restore later or you can add the tab group of favorite.

Set Tabs aside in Edge

Open a set of tabs in edge browser. For instance, you can open different websites such as new sites which you want to group them aside. Click the Set these tabs aside icon in the top-left corner of the title bar, shown as follows:

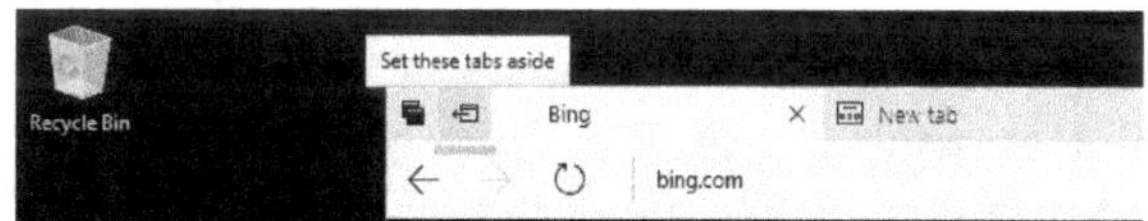

Figure 4.42: *Set these tabs aside icon*

By creating a new tab group, you can keep all the open tabs aside, as shown in Figure 6.43. You can create as many groups as you can and restore later. To restore the tabs which you have set aside, click **tabs you have set aside** in the top-left corner of the title bar. To restore tabs, select the tab group you want to restore and click **restore tabs**.

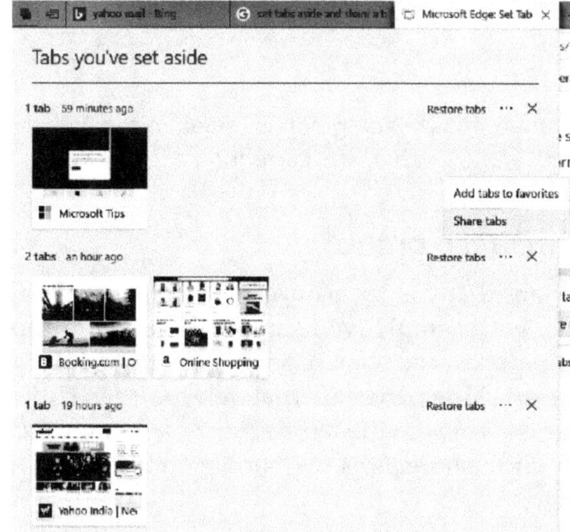

Figure 6.43: *Showing all tabs Set a side group*

Add a tab group to favorites

To add group of favorites website by clicking the more button (that is, three dots) and clicking "add tabs to favorites" as shown in *Figure 6.44*:

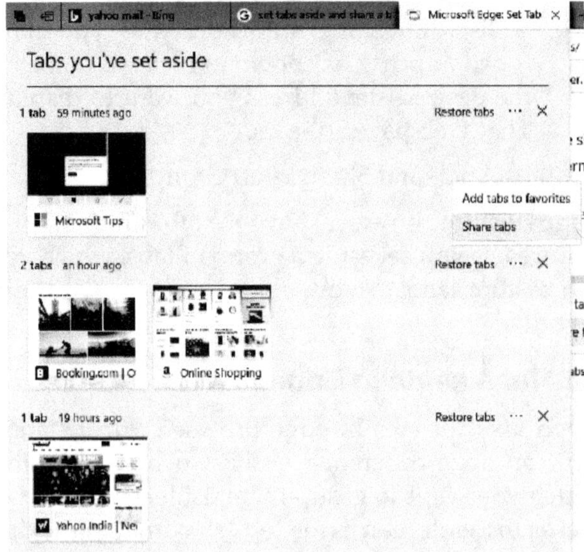

Figure 6.44: *Add tabs to favorites*

The tab group is added to favorites in a new folder under favorites. The newly created folder uses the Tabs from current data name, given as follows:

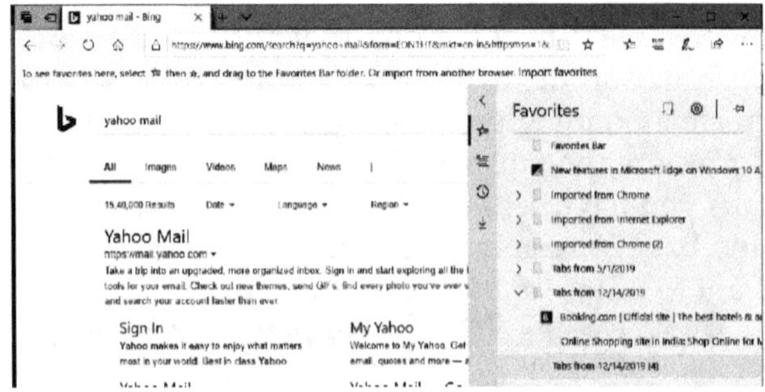

Figure 6.45: *The tab group is added to the Favorites bar with current date*

Share a tab group

The tabs that you set aside can be shared with other apps. For example, you can send the tab group to Mail app via the share option. Open the **Tabs you have set aside** panel; alternatively, you can click the three dots next to the tab session you want to share, and click **share tabs**, as shown in the following image:

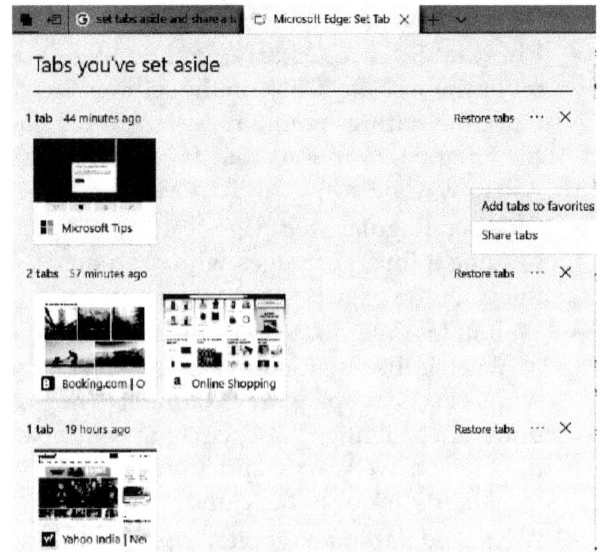

Figure 6.46: *Share tabs*

Select the app with which you want to share the list of website address in that tab group with the thumbnail image, such as **OneNote** or **Mail**.

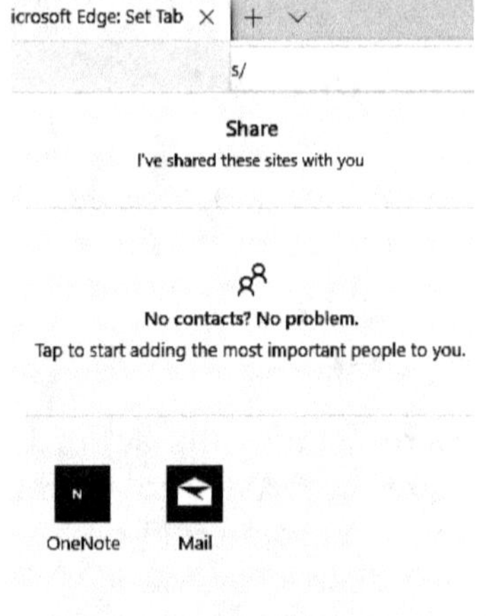

Figure 6.47: *OneNote or Mail*

Open a Web page in a Tab

When you open a new tab by clicking a link in the current tab, Internet Explorer displays the original tab and the newcomer in the same color, showing you at a glance that the two tabs hold related content.

1. Select the topic link which you want to open.
2. A list of options appears; select Open in **New Tab**, as shown in See *Figure 6.48*:

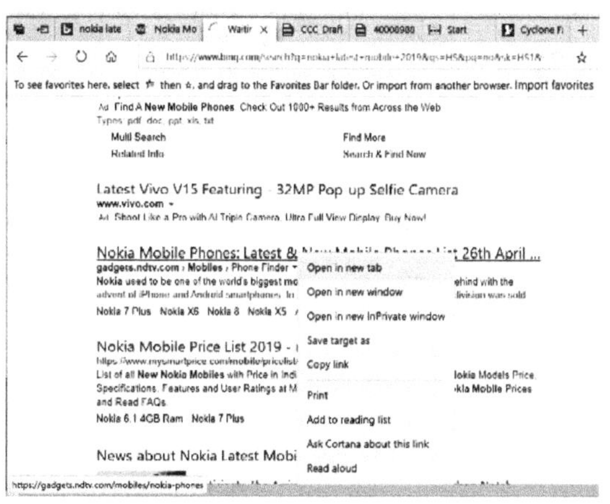

Figure 6.48: *Open in New Tab*

3. A new tab appears with the selected page title, as shown in *Figure 6.49*:

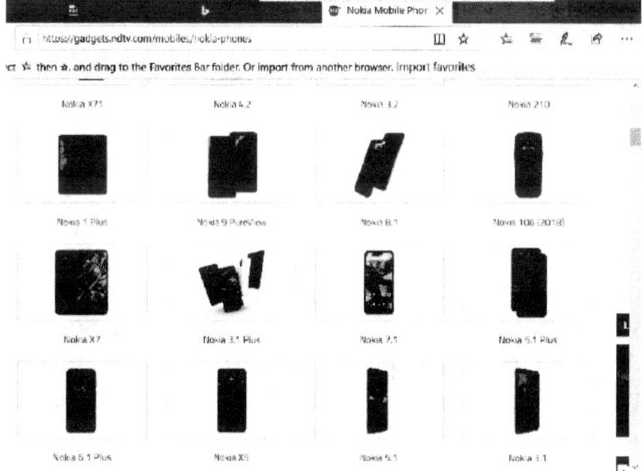

Figure 6.49: *A New tab with the Page Title*

4. Click the tab to display the page.

You can also open a page in a tab by holding Ctrl while clicking the link. If you press **Ctrl + Shift** while clicking a link, the tab displays automatically. If you type an address, press **Alt + Enter** to open the page in new tab.

Navigate Tabs

1. To Navigate Tabs, perform the following steps:
2. 1. Use the scroll tab back and Forwarded button to allow you to move navigate websites pages you have recently visited, as shown in *Figure 6.50*:

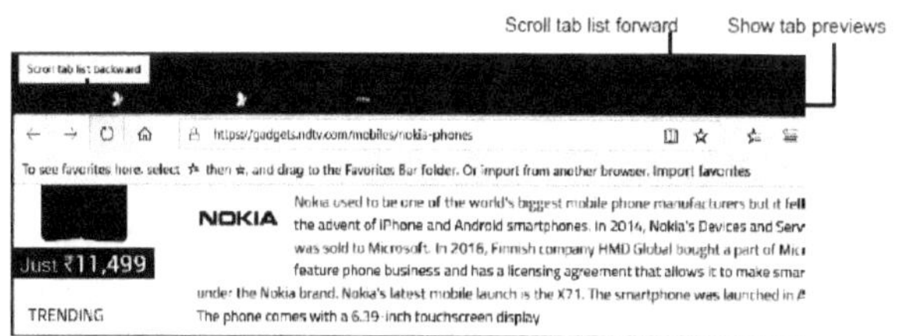

Figure 6.50: *Navigating Tabs through Scroll Tab List*

3. Click the tab. The Web page loaded in the tab appears.
4. Click the Back (**Alt + Left arrow**) button to go the previous page you visited.
5. Click the Forward (**Alt + Right arrow**) button to go back one page you previously visited.

If you are at the last page of the selected link, the Forward button is not active.

Setting the Home Page

While browsing, it is easy to get puzzled wandering around the Web. Therefore, you should designate one page or multiple pages as your home page. Home page is the first page which appears after opening a Web browser. It is also known by different names like **front page start page** or **Web page**.

To set the home page:

1. Open Setting and more (that is, ...) (*Alt + X*) at the right corner of the browser window.
2. Click the **Settings** option. The General pane appears, as shown in *Figure 6.51*:

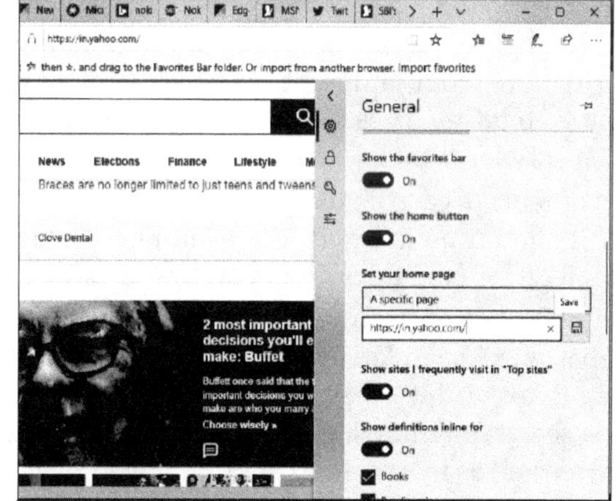

Figure 6.51: *Set the Home Tab in the General Pane*

3. Drag the slider on to the Show the home button.
4. Under the Set your home page button, click the drop-down arrow to select the desired option.

5. Type the website address to save the website to set the home page.

Popular Search Engines

A Web search engine is used to search for information on the Internet. The search results are generally presented in a list and are often called hits. The information may consist of Web pages, images, text and other types of files.

You can consider that the Web Search is an Information Retrieval Problem. As compared to searching a database, the search for a document contents are more terrifying since it is not structured. Documents should be indexed for making search easier and less time consuming.

Each document has object terms, namely, the author's name, document URL, and the date of publication. It may also have non-objective terms intended to reflect the information known as content terms.

How Search Engine Works?

Search Engine is the software program that helps users find information stored on a personal computer, or a network of computers, such as the Internet. A user enters a keyword or a phrase. The search engine retrieves a list of Web sites.

A search engine makes search in the following order:

Web crawling

Search engine works by matching the required information from different websites and storing many web pages. These pages are then retrieved by a Web crawler (also known as a **spider**).

The contents of each page are then analysed to check how it should be indexed. For example, words are extracted from the titles and headings are shown.

Data collected on web pages is stored in an index database for use in later queries. The purpose of an index is to get information as quickly as possible. Some search engines store all or part of the source page as well as information about the web pages.

Indexing

The indexing software collects the document as well as URLs from the agent. The software then extracts information from the documents and indexes it. Each search engine extracts and indexes different types of information.

When a user enters a query into a search engine by using key words, the engine examines its index and provides a listing of best-matching web pages according to its criteria. The index is thus built from the information stored with the data and the method by which the information was indexed.

Search Algorithm

Search using Boolean operators allow you to combine words and phrases using the words AND, OR and NOT to specify the search more accurately. When we perform the search by entering keywords, the search engine searches its database using search algorithm.

Some of the popular search engine include Yahoo, **Bing, Ask** and **Google**.

Yahoo!

Yahoo is widely known for its great search engine services. The web portal search engine of yahoo is accessible to all its users where you can discover anything over the web. You can search anything even if you are not signed up for the Yahoo! Account. This is then one of the most important feature is that you can save your search preferences over it and you can get access to all Yahoo services. Yahoo Search sent queries to a searchable index of pages with its directory of websites. In **1995**, they introduced a search engine function, called Yahoo! Search, which allows users to search the Yahoo! Directory. It was the first search engine on the web. Yahoo search indexed and cached the common HTML page formats, as well as several files types such as PDF, Excel and word documents and plain text files. These cached links on their search results allow these file-types in standard html.

Bing

Bing is a search engine from **Microsoft** that was launched on **May 28, 2009**. It is designed to return search results in a format that organizes answers to address your needs. When you search on Bing, in addition to providing relevant search results, the search engine also shows a list of related searches on the left-hand side of the **search engine results page (SERP)**. You can also access a quick link to see recent search history.

Bing was launched with several features that are unique in the search market. For example, when you hover your mouse over a Bing result, a small pop-up provides additional information for that result, including an e-mail address if available.

Opera

Open PLC European Research Alliance (OPERA) is a web browser developed by Opera Software. The latest version is available for Microsoft Windows, OS X, and Linux operating system.

It is the first browser with tabs, RSS support, and built-in BitTorrent client and tab thumbnails. It allows for duplication of tabs, Goto URL feature for web address that is not hyperlinked, fitting to window size, rewinding, crash recovery, page zoom, instant back, tab closing, and so on.

MSN

It is an acronym for the Microsoft Network. The network includes web-based programs and services offered by Microsoft Corporation. It offers a range of services including news, search engines, user-driven forums, instant messaging, e-mail, and services to connect to the internet. Microsoft Windows users are able to synchronize their computer system with online services offered as a method of centrally organizing and managing tasks.

In **1996, MSN 2.0** offered a version of Internet Explorer for Web access titled MSN Program Viewer. In addition to dial-up, MSN also partnered with Verizon and other carriers to offer DSL connections. Later, the MSN brand was retained for Internet access and the general portal, while Web-based services such as e-mail and messaging migrated to the Windows Live platform.

Ask.com

Ask.com (originally known as **Ask Jeeves**) is a question answering-focused e-business and web search engine founded in **1996** by **Garrett Gruener** and **David Warthen** in Berkeley, California. The Ask browser toolbar is an extension that can appear as an extra bar added to the browser window. It was often unintentionally installed during the installation of partner software, including Oracle Java that is, taking advantage of a user's lack of technical experience.

Google

Google is an interesting search engine having many unique features. For example, you want to search company information. It is useful for company searches because of the unusual way it ranks

Websites. Type **http://www.google.com** in the Address bar, and press **Enter** to go to the Google homepage. When you are there, type the company name in the search box and click the Google Search button. Google is pretty good at finding the best matching Websites in a search; it offers a feature to automatically look for the best possible match and load it. To use this feature, type a company's name in the search box and click the I'm Feeling Lucky button. It gives the related company information.

Searching Information on Google Website:

1. Open **www.google.com**.
2. Type one or more search terms into the search box that best describe the information you want, as shown in *Figure 6.52*:

Figure 6.52: *Google Search*

3. Then, press the **Enter** key or click on Google Search button.
4. Google produces a list of web pages related to your search terms.

A search engine continuously sends out the so-called spiders, which start at the homepage of a website and pursue all links step-by-step to collect all its information.

Basics of Google Search

1. Choosing the right search terms is the key to finding the information you need. It is advisable to use multiple search terms. Choose your search terms carefully because Google looks for the search terms you select.
2. Google searches are **not case-sensitive**. All letters, regardless of how you type them, will be understood as if written in lower case.
3. By default, Google only returns pages that include all of your search terms. There is no need to include **and** between the terms. Keep in mind that the order in which the terms are typed will affect the search results. To restrict the further search, just include more terms.

4. Google ignores common words and characters, such as **where** and **how**, as well as certain single digits and single letters, since they tend to slow down your search without improving the results.

5. When you want results for the terms that include an exact phrase, simply put quotation marks around such phrases. For example, **Mother Teresa**.

6. If your search term has more than one meaning, you can focus your search by putting a minus sign ("-") in front of the words related to the meaning you want to avoid.

Searching on Internet

There are many search engines available on the Web. The searching process is the same for such search engines. We describe the information searching process for Yahoo!

To search for web pages pertaining to a specific information:

1. Go to the Yahoo! home page by logging on to **www.yahoo.com**.

2. Type the information to be searched for in the box. For example, we have typed money control and then clicked the **Search web** button, as shown in *Figure 6.53*:

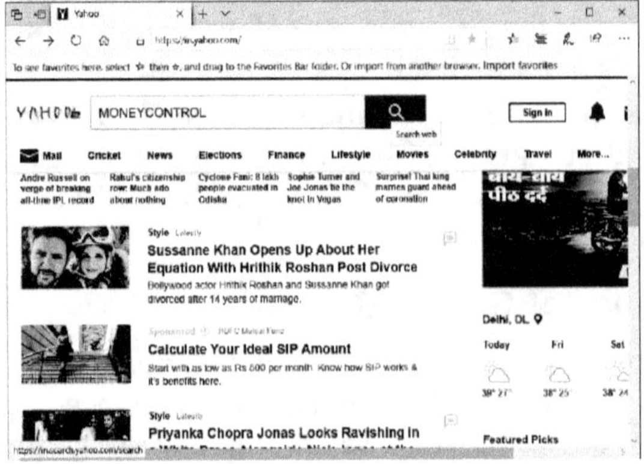

Figure 6.53: *Type the Query in the Search Box*

3. It will display different website links, as shown in *Figure 6.54*. Select the link and right-click on it to open it in a new tab:

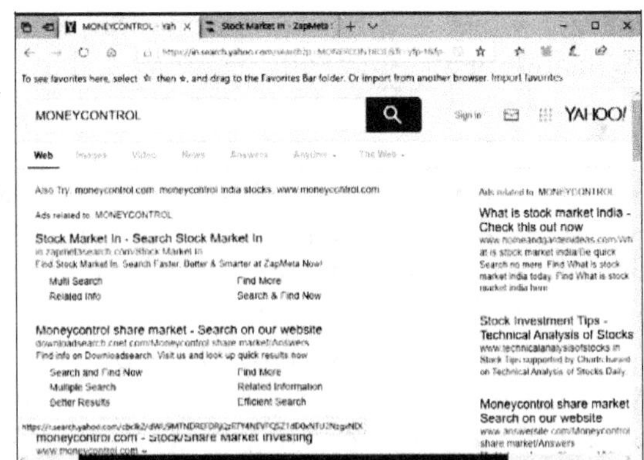

Figure 6.54: *Result of the Query*

4. If you type advanced query in the search box, it will open advanced search links such as Google and Yahoo, as shown in *Figure 6.55*. For example, we have selected yahoo advanced search link.

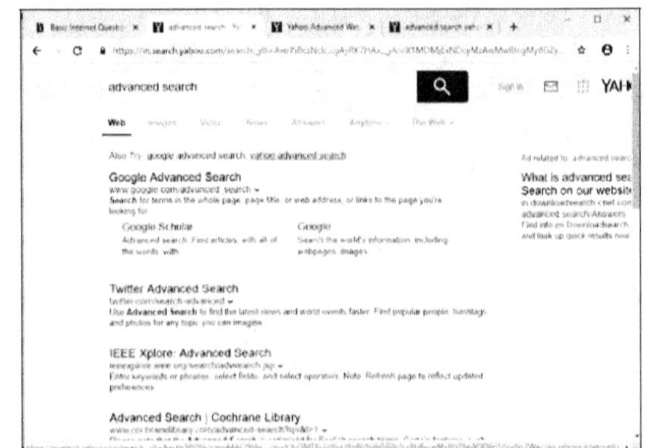

Figure 6.55: *Select Advanced Search Link*

5. The Advanced Web Search page opens with query form, as shown in *Figure 6.56*:

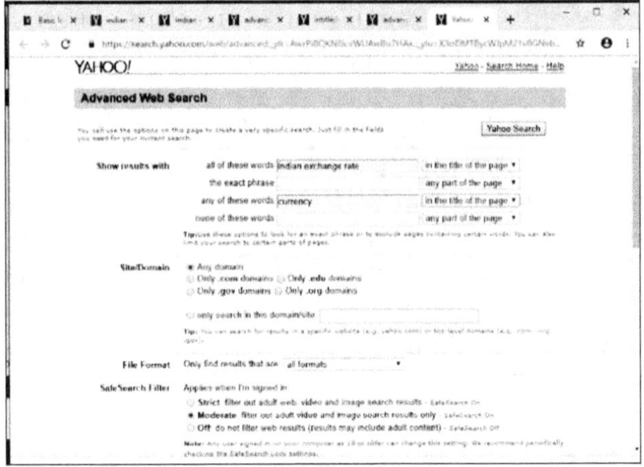

Figure 6.56: *Query Form for Yahoo Advanced Web Search*

6. Within a few seconds, the search engine will search for that information and display the links to the web pages, which are associated with your desired information in some way, as shown in *Figure 6.57*:

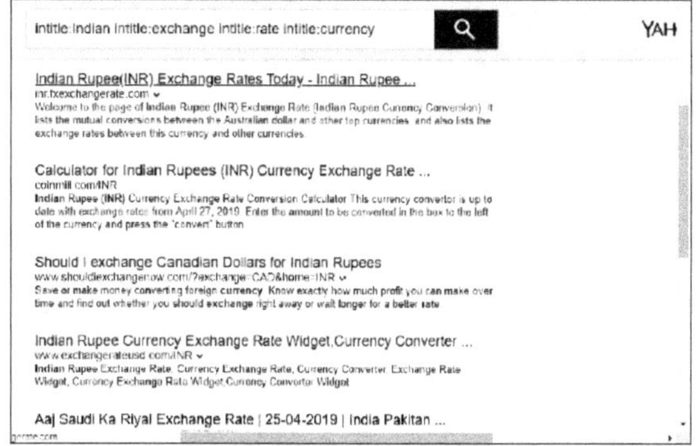

Figure 6.57: *Result of Advanced Search*

Downloading Web Pages

Uploading is the transmission of a file from one computer system to another, usually a larger computer system. From a network user's point-of-view, to upload a file is to send it to another computer that is set up to receive it. People who share images with others on **Bulletin Board Services (BBS)** upload files to the BBS.

Transmission in the other direction is downloading, i.e., from a usually larger computer to a usually smaller computer. From an Internet user's point-of-view, downloading is receiving a file from another computer.

The FTP is the Internet facility for downloading and uploading files. (If you are uploading a file to another site, you must usually have permission in advance to access the site and the directory where the file is to be placed.)

When you send or receive an attached file with an e-mail note, this is just an attachment, not a download or an upload. However, in practice, many people use **upload** to mean **send** and **download** to mean receive.

In short, from the ordinary workstation or small computer user's point-of-view, to upload is to send a file and to download is to receive a file.

The Web is one of the most popular components of the Internet. It is made up of hypertext documents stored on many servers around the world.

Hypertext documents contain links which you can click to move to another section of the page, to different documents, or to another type of

Internet resource, such as electronic mail (e-mail) or newsgroups.

Web pages include text, graphics, animation, sound, and sometimes movies also. The rich content, along with the ability to jump from one page to other page using links, has contributed to the explosive growth of the Web.

For example, you are researching an art course paper. You have found a file that you want to save.

To download a web page, perform the following steps:

1. Click the File menu and choose Save. Save As dialog box appears, as shown in *Figure 6.58*:

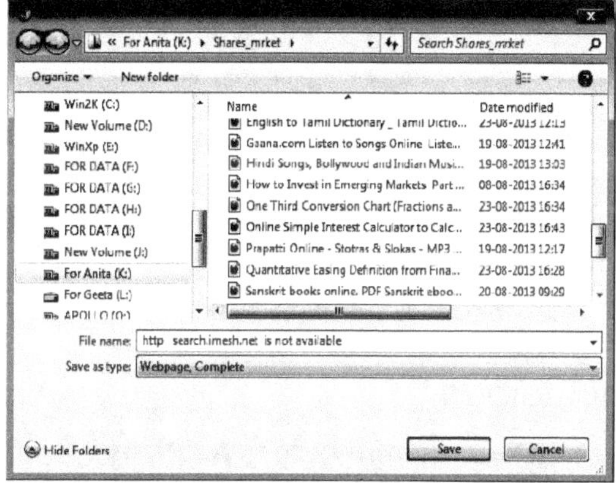

Figure 6.58: *Save Web Page Dialog Box*

2. Notice that there is a default value in the File name: text box. Either accept this name or change it to something appropriate.
3. Choose the drive location folder where you want to save the file in the Address bar.
4. Then, click the **Save** button to save the file.

Printing Web Pages

As you browse, you may come across pages containing information that you want to keep as hard copy. Internet Explorer provides many print options. These are as follows:

- Printing all documents linked to the current page.
- Printing a list of links contained on the current page.
- Printing selected portions of a page that has been constructed using frames. This option is available only if the current page has frames.

To print a Web page using the Print dialog box, perform the following steps:

1. Click on the **File** menu and choose **Print**.

Or click on the arrow next to the Print button on the Command bar.

2. Then choose the Print option.

3. A Print dialog box appears, as shown in *Figure 6.59*. In this dialog box, select the printer, pages, and number of copies you want.

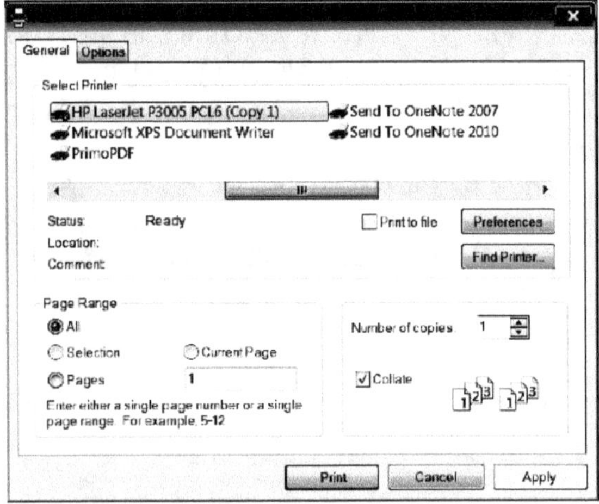

Figure 6.59: *Print Dialog Box*

Conclusions

The Internet is a world-wide network by computers that are connecting network and are using the communication method called TCP/IP. You started the chapter with an introduction to internet. Then we took a deep dive into various computer networks such as LAN and WAN along with its characteristics, advantages and disadvantages. Then you saw their difference. You then covered different types of topologies such as bus, ring, star, nest, and tree and the protocols. Further, you saw what is internet by understanding the concept of internet and WWW. WWW is the part of the Internet that contains websites and webpages. It is a search tool that helps you find and retrieve information from a web URL. Static website and dynamic website was another concept that we introduced. Then, you covered various applications of internet and ISP and its role. You understood various modes of connectivity such as hotspot, Wi-Fi connection and so on. Then you studied various IP address and classes. You looked at MAC address and IMEI. You saw various popular web browsers such as Google Chrome, Mozilla Firefox, and so on. At last, you learnt how to explore the internet by surfing web, searching on the internet, and downloading and printing web pages.

In the next chapter, you will learn about e-mail, social networking and e-governance services.

Model Questions and Answers

A. Multiple Choice Questions.

1. What is NIC?
   a. Network Interface Card
   b. Network Information Card
   c. Network Interface Computer
   d. Network Information Computer

2. What are the uses of the Internet?
   a. Communication
   b. Information Retrieval
   c. Presentation of Information
   d. All of the above

3. Which among the following is not an internet browser?
   a. Netscape Navigator
   b. Edge
   c. Drupal
   d. Opera

4. A modem is not needed while accessing the internet through:
   a. LAN
   b. Cable
   c. Wi-Fi
   d. None of these

5. What is IMEI?
   a. Identity Mobile Equipment International
   b. International Mobile Equipment Identity
   c. International Method Equipment Identity
   d. International Mobile Elight Identiy

6. In order to use cable for browsing web, you will need:
   a. A cable modem
   b. Network Interface Card
   c. Both a. and b.
   d. None of these

7. What is the minimum bandwidth required for broadband connection?
   a. 128 kbps
   b. 256 kbps
   c. 512 kbps
   d. None of these
8. Web pages are uniquely identified using:
   a. IP address
   b. Domain
   c. URL
   d. File name
9. Which of the following networking solution is suitable for networking in a building?
   a. WAN
   b. MAN
   c. LAN
   d. All of the above
10. Internet protocol recognizes only:
    a. An IP address
    b. A location of the host
    c. A postal mail address
    d. None of the above

B. State whether the following Statements are True or False.

1. From an e-mail address, one can find out the domain name where this e-mail address is hosted.
2. Web browser lets you download only while surfing the Internet.
3. You can configure most e-mail applications to check for mail as frequently as you desire.
4. E-mail can be used to send broadcast messages, but only within your own company.
5. Internet is not a commercial information service.
6. Any computer on the Internet can connect to any other computer on the Internet.
7. Internet is a single, very large network.
8. Hypertext is also known as hyperlink.

9. A set of rules is known as protocol.
10. Internet is a network of networks.

C. Match the following:

1.	A Vast collection of different networks:	a.	Packet switching
2.	IPv6 addressed have a size of:	b.	LAN
3.	Internet works on:	c.	Internet
4.	To transmit information on the WWW:	d.	The advantage of LAN
5.	Standard protocol of the Internet is:	e.	Start
6.	A computer on Internet are identified by:	f.	128 bits
7.	Ethernet is a family of protocol used in:	g.	IP address
8.	Hub is associated with:	h.	megabits per second
9.	Sharing peripherals:	i.	HTTP
10.	Typical data transfer rate in LAN are of the order of:	j.	bits per second
		k.	TCP/IP

D. Fill in the blanks:

> Internet Protocol   WAN   Medium   Star
> Downloading   Digital subscriber line
> Network station   Mesh   FTP
> BUS   Network server

1. Internet access by transmitting digital data over the wires of a local telephone network is provided by ___________.
2. The ___________ is the physical path over which a message travels.
3. In Internet terminology IP means ___________.
4. The process of transferring files from a computer on the Internet to your computer is called ___________.
5. A communication network which is used by large organizations over regional, national or global area is called ___________.

Module 3: M3–R5

6. _________ topology of LAN uses circuit switching.

7. In a network with 25 computers, _________ topology would require the most extensive cabling?

8. For transferring files from one host to another host over a TCP network _________ protocol we use.

9. _________ is the most important/ powerful computer in a typical network.

10. Network components are connected to the same cable in the _________ topology.

Short Questions with Answers.

1. **What is a web browser?**

   Answers: A browser is a software program to present and explore content on the World Wide Web. It includes pictures, videos, and web pages that are connected using hyperlinks and classified with URLs.

2. **What is the Internet?**

   Answers: The Internet is the largest computer network in the world, connecting millions of computers. A network is a group of two or more computer systems linked together.

3. **How to find information on the Internet?**

   Answers: Most information is found on the Internet by using search engines. It is a web service that uses web robots to query millions of pages on the Internet and creates an index of those web pages. Internet users can then use these services to find information on the Internet.

4. **Explain Web Server.**

   Answers: A Web server is a server on the Internet that holds web documents and makes them available for viewing by remote browsers.

5. **What is a Web Page?**

   Answers: A web page is a rich document that can contain richly formatted text, graphics, animation, sound, etc. Every web page on the Internet has a unique address which starts with the name of the computer that holds that page. Within a web page, words and pictures can be linked to other pages. When we activate a link, yo u will be taken to the other page automatically.

6. **What is Local area network?**

   Answers: Local area network allows users to share files between computers, send e-mails and access the Internet. Most companies use LAN so that users can access information within or outside the LAN.

7. **What is Encryption?**

   Answers: Encryption is a procedure used in cryptography to convert plain text into cipher text to prevent anyone but the intended recipient from reading that data.

8. **What is IP address?**

   Answers: Each computer is assigned an IP address. These are similar to phone numbers. When we attempt to connect to an IP address, we will connect to the computer with that IP address.

9. **What are the requirements to build the wide area networks?**

   Answers: For this, the requirements are: Same type, high bandwidth communication source link, high speed processor.

10. **What is a Modem? What is its function?**

    Answers: A modem is a computer peripheral that connects a workstation to other workstation via telephones lines and facilitates communications. It is short form for modulation/ demodulation.

    Modem converts digital signals to Audio Frequency tones which are in the frequency range that the telephone lines can transmit. It can also convert transmitted tones back to digital information.

11. **Write two advantages and disadvantages of Star topology.**

    Answers: Advantages of Star topology:

    a. One device per connection.

b.   Easy to access.

Disadvantages of Start topology:

a.   Central node dependency.

b.   Long cable length.

12.   **What is client-server technology?**

Answers: IT is a network where one computer acts as the server and another is called client. The server is the most important part of the network system providing access to resources and security.

13.   **How to identify MAC address in Windows 10?**

Answers:

a.   Click the Start menu and select Settings. The Windows Settings page appears.

b.   Click **Network & Internet**. Click **Ethernet** option from the left-hand side. On the right, you will see the connections listed; click the one we want, as shown in *Figure 6.35*.

c.   Scroll down to the **Properties** section, and we will find the information as shown in *Figure 6.36*.

14.   **What are the main functions of TCP?**

Answers: The TCP does the following activities:

It breaks the data into packets of the network.

Verifies that all the packets arrived at the destination.

Reassembles the data.

15.   **What is protocol? How many types of protocols are there?**

Answers: When computers communicate each other, there needs to be a common set of rules and instructions that each computer follows. A specific set of communication rules is called a protocol. Some protocols are HTTP, PPP, SLIP, FTP and TCP/IP.

16.   **What is a URL? Explain the structure of a URL.**

Answers: Uniform Resource Locators, or URLs, are the unique addresses of Internet resources. The syntax for specifying a URL is given in Figure 1. URLs contain information about both the access method to use and also about the resource itself. They are used by Web browsers to connect us directly to a specific document or page on the WWW. We do not have to know where that resource is located physically. A sample URL might look like the following:

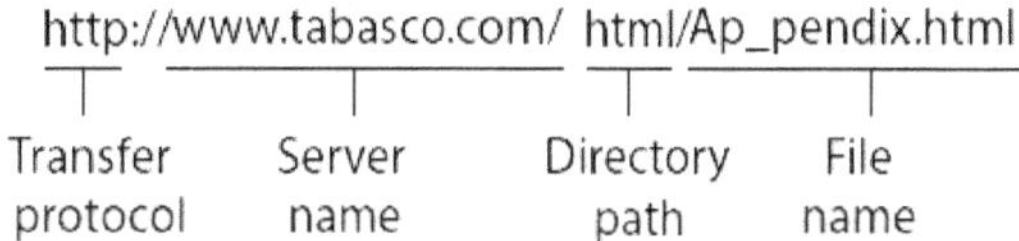

Figure 1: *Syntax used in specifying a Uniform Resource Locator (URL)*

First part of the URL is before the colon specifies the access method. On the Web this is usually http (for Hypertext Transfer Protocol). But ftp or gopher also may be specified. The second part of the URL is after the colon, specifies the resource. The text after the two slashes (//) indicates a server name, and the text after the single slash defines the directory or individual file you will be connected to. If we are linking to a document, it will usually have the file name extension .html, the abbreviation for Hypertext Markup Language.

17.   **What are IP Classes and how can you identify the IP class of a given IP address?**

Answers: IP classes are differentiated based on the number of hosts it supports on a single network. If IP classes support more networks, then very few IP addresses are available for each network.

There are three types of IP classes and these are based on the first octet of IP addresses, which are classified as Class A, B or C. If the first octet begins with 0 bit, then it is of type Class A.

Class A type has a range up to 127.x.x.x (except 127.0.0.1). If it starts with bits 10, then it belongs to Class B. Class B having a range from 128.x to 191.x and it begins with bits 10. Class C has a range from 192.x to 223.x.

18. **Define the various types of Internet connections.**

    Answers: There are three types of Internet connections. They are:

    a. Broadband connection: This type of connection gives continuous high-speed Internet. Suppose, if we log off from the Internet for any reason then there is no need to log in again.

       For example, Modems of cables, Fibres, wireless connection, satellite connection, and so on.

    b. Wi-Fi: It is a wireless internet connection between the devices. It uses radio waves to connect to the devices or gadgets.

    c. WIMAX: It is the most advanced type of internet connection which is more featured than Wi-Fi. It is nothing but the high-speed and advanced type of broadband connection.

19. **Define Static IP and Dynamic IP.**

    Answers: When a device or computer is assigned a specified IP address, then it is named as Static IP. It is assigned by the Internet Service Provider as a permanent address.

    Dynamic IP is the temporary IP address assigned by the network to a computing device. It is automatically assigned by the server to the network device.

20. **Explain DNS.**

    Answers: DNS stand for Domain Naming Server. DMS acts as a translator between domain name and IP address. As humans remember names, the computer understands only numbers. Generally, we assign names to websites and computers like gmail.com, Hotmail, etc. When we type such names, the DNS translates it into numbers and executes our requests. Translating the name into numbers or IP address is named as a Forward lookup. Translating the IP address to names is named as a Reverse lookup.

Descriptive Type Questions.

1. Explain different types of computer networks.
2. Mention the disadvantages of client-server technology.
3. What do you mean by topology? What are the most popular topologies?
4. Differentiate between tree and bus topologies of a network.
5. Differentiate between Internet and Intranet.
6. What are the major differences between LAN and WAN?
7. Explain various types of networks based on their sizes.

--------------- **Answers** ---------------

A.	1. a	2. d	3. c	4. a	5. b
	6. c	7. b	8. c	9. c	10. a

B.	1. T	2. T	3. T	4. F	5. T
	6. T	7. F	8. F	9. T	10. T

C.	1. c	2. f	3. a	4. i	5. k
	6. g	7. b	8. e	9. d	10. h

D.	1. f	2. c	3. a	4. e	5. b
	6. d	7. h	8. i	9. k	10. j

CHAPTER 7

Email, Social Networking and e-Governance Services

Structure

In this chapter, we will discuss the following topics:

- Introduction to email
- Structure of email
- Bounced email
- Outlook 2013
- Using email
- Mailbox: inbox and outbox
- Creating, sending, replying, forwarding an email
- Sorting and searching an email
- Attaching files to email
- Email signature
- Social networking and e-commerce
- Blogs and netiquette
- Overview of e-governance services
- UMANG app
- Digital locker

Objectives

The reader will be able to understand the following after reading this chapter:

- Create an email account, compose an email, reply to an email and send the email along with attachments
- Introduction to Social Networking, Instant Messaging and Blogs
- Introduction to e-Governance Services, e-Commerce and Mobile Apps
- Download and print web pages.

In Information and communication technologies have become a part of people's life but also the growing use of technology such as Internet has significant impact on the way individuals interact, communicate and connect with each other. The development of social media like blogs and other social networking services like **Facebook** and **Twitter** makes governments around the world join these sites to benefit from a new way of communication. In addition, e-government can be defined as government use of information and communication technologies to offer for citizen and businesses to give chance and conduct business with government by using different electronic media such as smart cards, e-mail and Internet.

Introduction to E-mail

The most popular way of communication on the Internet is the electronic mail (e-mail). E-mail is a method of sending messages, voice, video and graphics over digital communication links, such as the Internet, anywhere in the world at a very cost-effective rate. Technically, it is a type of client/server application that provides a routed, stored message service between any two e-mail accounts.

Since all modern computers can be connected to the Internet, users can send e-mail over the Internet to any location that has telephone or wireless digital service.

Structure of E-mail Message

An e-mail message is made up of binary data, usually in the **American Standard Code for Information Interchange (ASCII)** text format. ASCII is a standard that enables any computer, regardless of its system or hardware, to read the text. ASCII code describes the characters you see on your computer screen.

Figure 7.1 shows the similarity between an e-mail message and the postal mail message. In the To line, you type the e-mail address of the person to whom you are sending a message. The address must be typed according to a set of very strict rules. If you type a single letter or the syntax is wrong, your message will not get to the intended recipient. Your e-mail address will appear on the From line. Using this address, the recipient of your message will be able to respond to you.

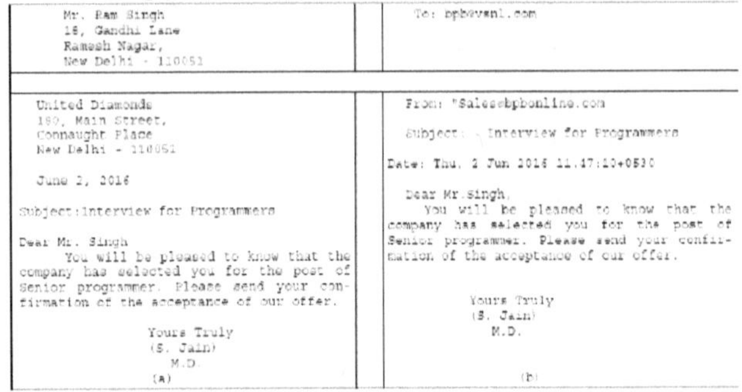

Figure 7.1: *(a) Postal Mail Format (b) E-mail format*

On the Subject line, you may type the subject of your message or a very brief summary. At the bottom of the message is a **signature** area that can contain personalized information about you. Some mail programs will automatically append this signature to the bottom of every message you send. Signature areas are not required and are used at the discretion of the person who creates the e-mail message. Signature portion should not exceed five lines.

There are five sections of an e-mail message:

- E-mail address
- Header
- Body
- Signature (optional)
- Attachment(s) (optional)

Figure 7.2 shows the major sections of an e-mail message. Note that signatures and attachments are optional. Many messages do not show them, and some e-mail applications do not support them.

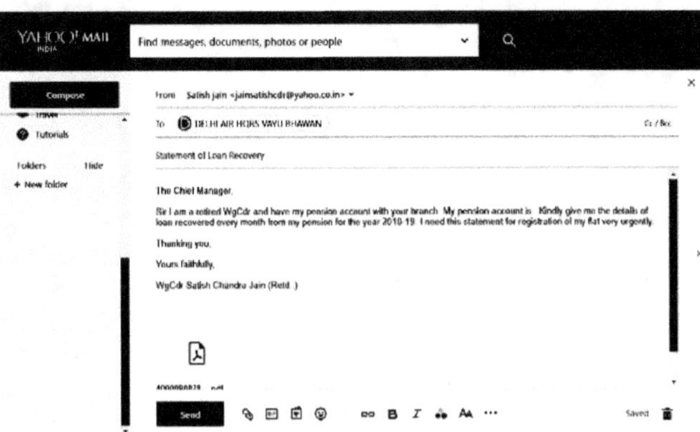

Figure 7.2: *Major Sections of an E-mail Message*

E-mail Address

An e-mail address is composed of two separate parts:

- The domain name of the mail server computer on which you have an e-mail account.
- Your personal identity or account name (username) on that mail server.

For example, 100 people have e-mail accounts with the same **Internet Service Provider (ISP)** or organizations. All 100 users will share the same domain name (say hotmail.com), but each person will possess a unique user name, such as **rakesh** or **aparna**. The username and domain name are separated by an @ (**at**) symbol. Together, they form a complete e-mail address. The components of a typical e-mail address are shown in *Figure 7.3*.

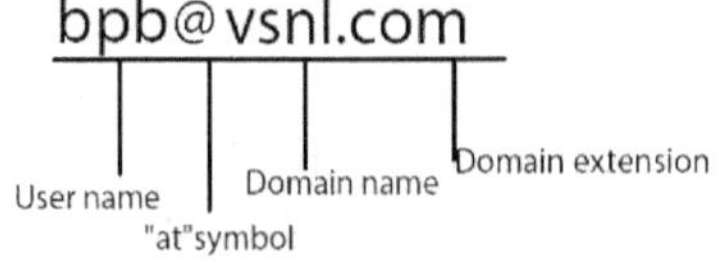

Figure 7.3: *Syntax for E-mail Address*

Users with multiple e-mail accounts—perhaps with different ISPs or organizations—will have a different e-mail address for each account.

Header

The header of the e-mail message is the upper-most section. It displays information regarding the status of the message. It records message information and provides it to the recipient(s) of the message.

Headers are present in both outgoing (sent) and incoming (received) messages.

The principal header fields related to message transported are listed in *Table 7.1*. These are mandatory to be used by all the people using e-mail facilities on the Internet.

Name	Function
To:	E-mail address/addresses of primary recipient (s).
Cc:	E-mail address/addresses of secondary recipient (s) to whom copy needs to be sent.
Bcc:	E-mail address/addresses of secondary recipient (s) to whom copy needs to be sent, but the primary recipient does not know about the dispatch of mail to these addressees.
From:	The originator or creator of the e-mail.
Sender:	E-mail address of the actual sender.
Received:	Line added by each transfer agent along the route containing the agent's identity, the date and time the message was received.
Return Path:	May be used to identify the path back to the sender.

Table 7.1: Header Fields in an E-mail

Note that there are no spaces in the above address; e-mail software and server computers will not accept spaces in an address. Messages will not reach their destination if spaces are included.

In addition to the header fields given in *Table 7.1*, there are additional headers which are not mandatory but may be used if required, as shown in *Table 7.2*.

Name	Function
Date:	Date and time the message was sent.
Reply-to:	E-mail address to which replies should be sent.
In-Reply-to:	Message-identification number of the message to which this is a reply.

Name	Function
Message-ID:	A unique number identifying the message that may be used to refer to the message.
References:	Other relevant message identification numbers.
Keywords:	Keywords that are selected by the user.
Subject:	A summary of the message for the one-line display.

Table 7.2: Additional Header Fields in an E-mail

The header shows the following information:

- Time and date of a message.
- Subject of a message (as typed by the sender).
- Whether carbon copies were sent.
- Whether files are attached to the message.
- The e-mail address of the sender.

Body

The body of e-mail message is the primary focus because it contains the actual message. Although there is no limit to the size (number of characters) of an e-mail message, many ISPs do limit the size of an e-mail message.

Attachments

E-mail has become all the more attractive to businesses because now it allows users to attach a file to any e-mail message. Any file format such as word processing documents, spreadsheets, images, or video files can be attached to an e-mail message. E-mail allows complex data as attachments but not in the body.

E-mail messages cannot contain viruses, but they can still be sent through attachments. Therefore, you should scan all e-mail attachments with a virus detection and eradication software program, such as McAfee VirusScan or Norton Anti-Virus, before opening or forwarding them.

Most e-mail applications alert you if an incoming message contains an attachment. Such e-mail applications show an icon within the body of the messages to represent an attached file. The icon indicates the type of file that is attached and allows the recipient to double-click the icon to automatically launch the attachment on their computer.

Signature

The signature for an e-mail message is the personal information which automatically appears at the bottom of the outgoing message.

Carbon Copy (Cc)

This feature lets you send a copy, that is, carbon copy of the mail to another recipient. In this case, the main recipient is informed about the other people who receive the same message.

Blind Carbon Copy (Bcc)

In this option, the recipient of the first e-mail copy does not know the name of the other recipients who receive the carbon copies of the same message.

Bounced Mail

Bounced mail is an e-mail message that has failed to reach its destination and therefore such e-mail messages are returned to the sender. The message "bounces" back to its sender from the mail server after the server fails to locate the message recipient address (or the recipient's Internet Service Provider).

Bounced mail messages typically feature a text clip near the top of the message and/or in the subject field, such as **Returned Mail** or **Mail Undeliverable**. The bounced message alerts you that your e-mail has gone undelivered and that you must again send the message with the correct address in order to ensure that your message reaches its recipient.

Configuring E-mail Client

When an e-mail software is executed, the user may ask for a summary of this e-mail. The mailbox may contain a number of messages. In a simple e-mail message system, the choice of fields displayed is built into the program, which may be one of the following types:

- Sl. No. Flags
- Size in bytes
- Sender
- Address
- Subject

In the above format, the first field is the message number. The second field is the Flags, which can contain various words, such as the new message. The third field shows the size of the message, and the next field indicates the sender and its address. The final column indicates the subject of the e-mail message. Once the messages are listed by the e-mail

package, the user can process his e-mail box and can lay priority to the different messages received from various senders. E-mail has come a long way from the earlier days when it was just file transfer to very sophisticated software, such as Lotus Notes and Microsoft Outlook Express. The user agents make it possible to manage a large volume of e-mail messages.

The RFC 822 gives the format of the e-mail messages and multimedia extensions.

Outlook 2013

Outlook 2013 is the Microsoft e-mail program that is included with Windows and with Internet Explorer. It puts the world of online communication on your computer desktop. If you want to exchange e-mail with colleagues and friends or join newsgroups to trade ideas and information, then you have to use the different tools of Outlook 2013. You can perform the following functions with the help of Outlook 2013.

- **Manage Multiple Mails:** If you have several mail or news accounts, you can use them all from one window with the help of Outlook 2013. You can also create multiple users, or identities, for the same computer.

- **Browse Messages quickly:** Using the message list, you can view a list of messages and read individual messages at the same time. The Folders list contains mail folders, news servers, and newsgroups, and you can easily switch among them.

- **Keep Mail on a Server:** If your ISP uses an IMAP mail server for incoming mail, you can place your messages in folders on the server without downloading the messages to your computer so that you can view messages from any other computers.

- **Address Book:** You can save names and addresses in your Address Book automatically by simply replying to a message or by importing them from other programs.

- **Send and Receive Secure Messages:** You can digitally sign and encrypt messages by using digital IDs so that you can send and receive secure messages.

- **Download Newsgroup Messages for Offline Reading:** You can also use Outlook 2013 to use your online time efficiently by downloading messages or entire newsgroups so that you can read newsgroup messages for offline reading.

Web-based E-mail

Each e-mail service, whether it is an online service or a commercial e-mail service, has its own way to handle mail. Most of the e-mail services use the Internet as their gateway, that is, describes the path of how messages are passed from one service to another service. Internet connects the computers around the world so that people can share information with each other. When you send the message using e-mail service to someone's system, the message will travel across the Internet to reach its destination. Youshould write address of the message properly so that the Internet knows where to deliver the message. Here are some Web-based free E-mail accounts, such as Yahoo! Mail, Gmail, Hotmail and AOL that offer Web-based e-mail access.

Using E-mail

E-mail or electronic mail can be sent over the Internet to anybody who has an e-mail address. To use e-mail, you need both an e-mail address and a program to handle it. To create a free e-mail account by Internet or Outlook Express, consider the following sections.

Opening E-mail Account

Before you actually settle down to send a mail, you will first need to create an e-mail account. There are various sites in the Internet by which you can create free e-mail account. Some of the sites are given below:

- www.yahoo.com
- www.rediffmail.com
- www.msn.com
- www.hotmail.com

Here, you create an e-mail account with the Gmail. com.

To open an e-mail account:

1. Log on to www.gmail.com. Type **www.gmail. com** in the **address bar**, as shown in *Figure 7.4*:

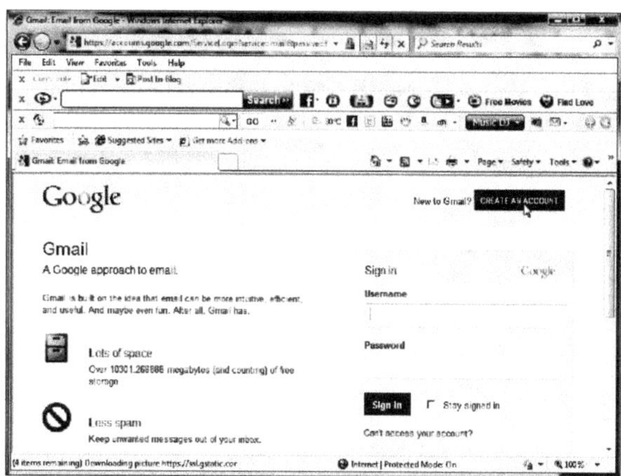

Figure 7.4: Gmail Google Window

2. Click the Create an account button in the Gmail from Google window, as shown in *Figure 7.4*.

3. The Gmail Accounts window appears, as shown in *Figure 7.5*:

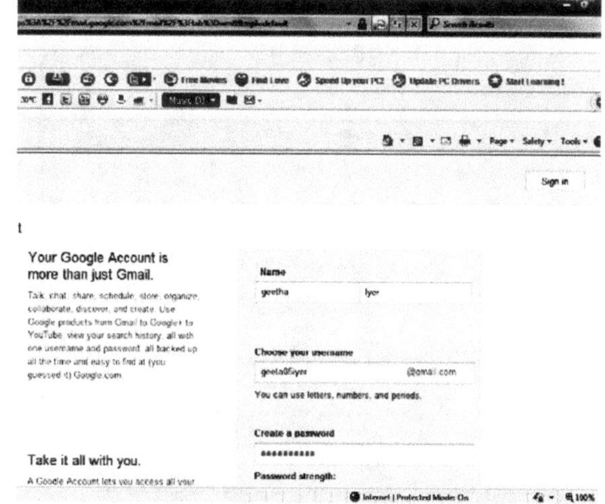

Figure 7.5: *Type the Information in the Google Account Textbox*

4. Type the **first** and **last** name in the **Name box**, as shown in *Figure 7.5*.

5. Type a desired **login ID** which you want to create in the **Choose your username** textbox.

6. Type the password in the **Create a password** textbox, as shown in *Figure 7.5*.

7. Again, type the password in the Confirm your password textbox, as shown in *Figure 7.6*:

Figure 7.6: *Type the Password in Confirm your Password Textbox*

8. Type the date of birth in the Birthday textbox, as shown in *Figure 7.6*.

9. Select the type of gender in the Gender drop-down list, as shown in *Figure 7.7*:

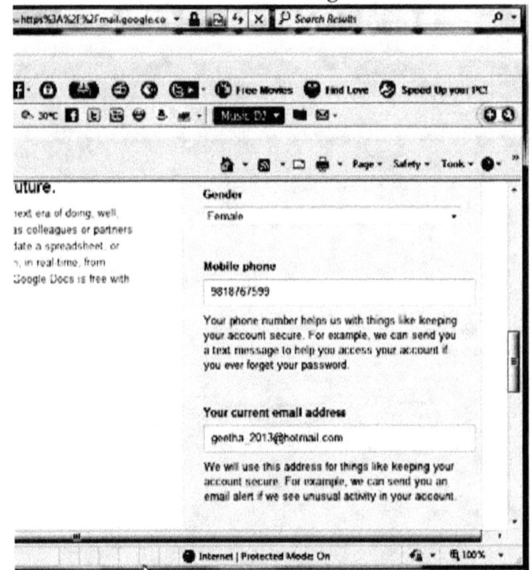

Figure 7.7: *Type Mobile Number in the Mobile Phone Textbox*

10. Type the mobile number in the Mobile phone textbox, as shown in *Figure 7.7*.

11. Type an e-mail address in Your current e-mail address textbox to keep your account secure.

12. Type the character you see in the picture in the textbox below the Type the two pieces of text: box, as shown in *Figure 7.8*:

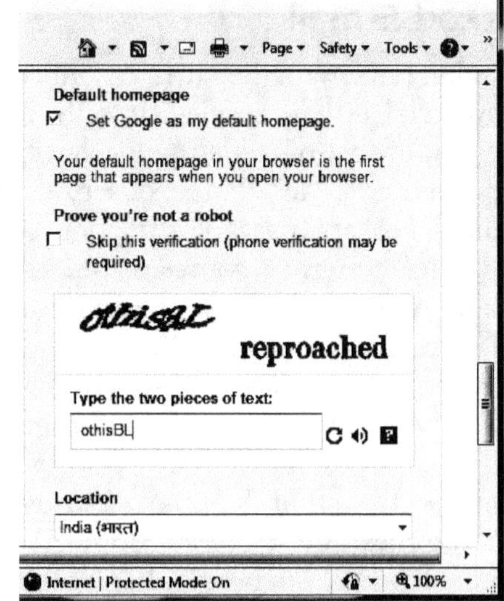

Figure 7.8: *Character*

13. Select the place in the Location drop-down list.

14. Click the Next Step button to continue to the next page.

15. The Verify your account page appears, as shown in *Figure 7.9*.

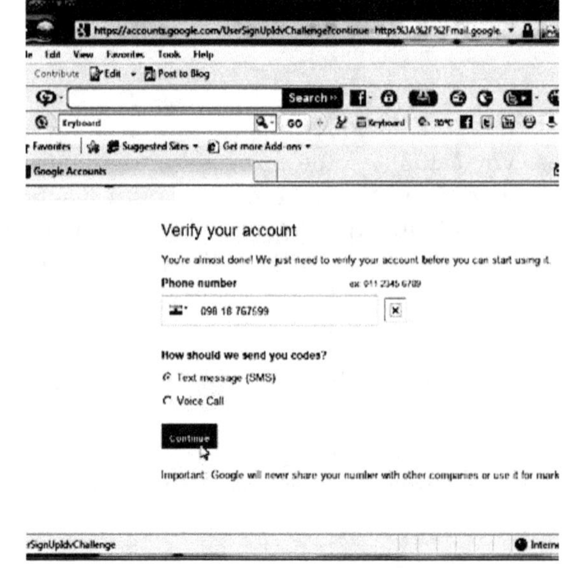

Figure 7.9: *Google Accounts shows Verify your account*

16. Select the desired option from Verify your account page, that is, How should we send your codes? Click on Text message (SMS) or Voice call. For instance, if you select Text message (SMS), you will receive a verification code from Google to your mobile number, which you have entered in the Verify your account page.

17. Click the Continue button, as shown in *Figure 7.9*.

18. Type the code that you have received in your mobile number in the Enter verification code textbox on the Verify your account page, as shown in *Figure 7.10*:

Figure 7.10: *Mobile Verification*

19. Click the **Continue** button.

20. The Google Welcome! page appears and shows that you have created a new e-mail address. Click the Continue to Gmail button which is ready to use, as shown in *Figure 7.11*:

Figure 7.11: *Google Welcome Page Screen*

The Gmail inbox shows the e-mail messages that you have received. You can click the e-mail to view the message, as shown in *Figure 7.12*:

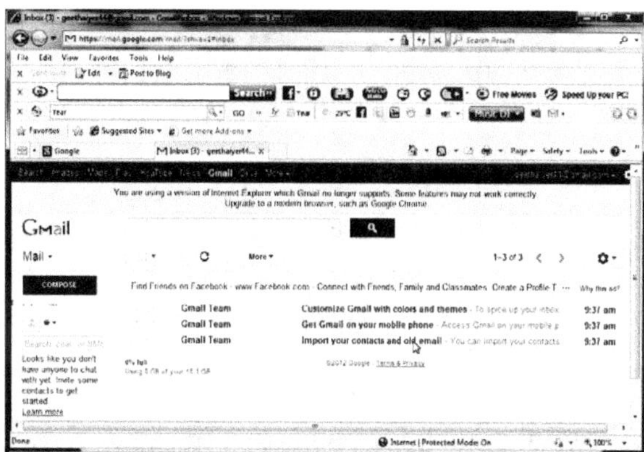

Figure 7.12: *Gmail Mail Box Window*

21. Click the e-mail that you have received from the Gmail Team, as shown in *Figure 7.12*. You will see the e-mail message on the Gmail window, as shown in *Figure 7.12*.

22. To write an e-mail message, click the Compose mail button at the left side of the Gmail window. The Compose Mail window appears, as shown in *Figure 7.13*:

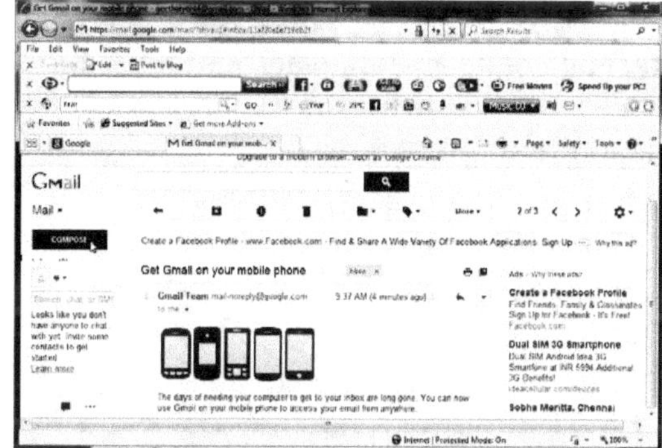

Figure 7.13: *Selecting Compose Mail*

23. In the Compose Message window, you will see various fields, which are to be filled as shown in *Figure 7.14*:

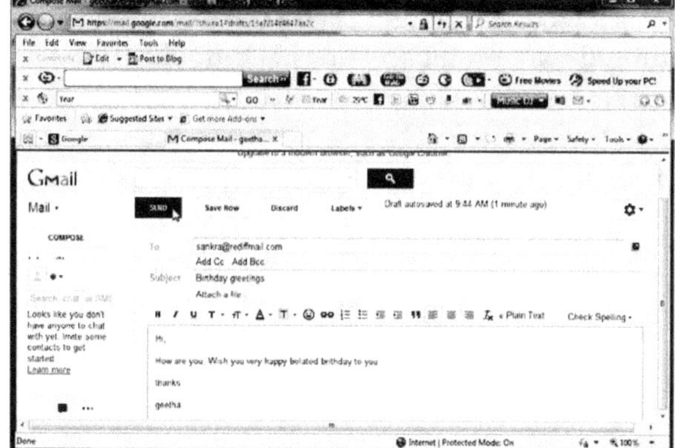

Figure 7.14: *Showing Various Fields of Compose Mail Window*

The fields are as follows:

    a. Type the e-mail address in the To: textbox, to which you want to send the message.

    b. Type the Title of the message in the Subject: textbox.

    c. Type the body of the e-mail message in the message area, as shown in *Figure 7.14*.

24. Click the Send button to send the message.

    The Gmail Inbox window appears, showing the message that your message has been sent.

25. Click your e-mail address drop-down arrow, and then select the Sign out button to sign out from the Google account.

Adding an E-mail Account in MS Outlook 2013

Outlook is one of those e-mail management programs that you can send and receive e-mail from different accounts. You will need to go through each step for every e-mail account you have set up.

Before, you create an e-mail account in outlook, you may need the following information to setup the e-mail account.

About the e-mail server information:

- The type of Incoming e-mail servers: **POP3** or **IMAP** protocols receive messages and are used to process incoming mail.
- The name of the incoming e-mail server: **SMTP** protocol sends messages and handles outgoing mail requests.

Second, information about your account:

- Your account name and password.
- Find out if your **ISP** mail servers requires secure port for both **POP3** and **SMTP** servers.

Let us look at the steps which you need to follow for setting up an e-mail account in Outlook 2013.

To set up an e-mail account in Outlook 2013, perform the following steps:

1. Click the **File** tab, and then choose the **Info tab**.

2. Under Account Information, click the **Add Account** or **Account Settings drop-down** arrow, as shown in *Figure 7.15*:

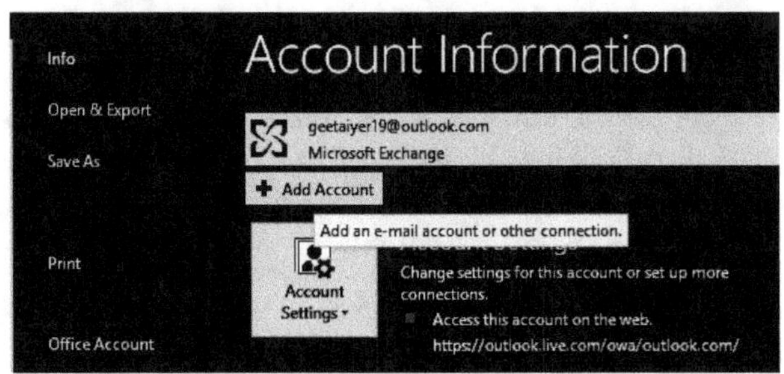

Figure 7.15: *Setting E-mail Account*

3. The Account Settings dialog box appears, as shown in *Figure 7.16*. In this dialog box, click the **New... button**.

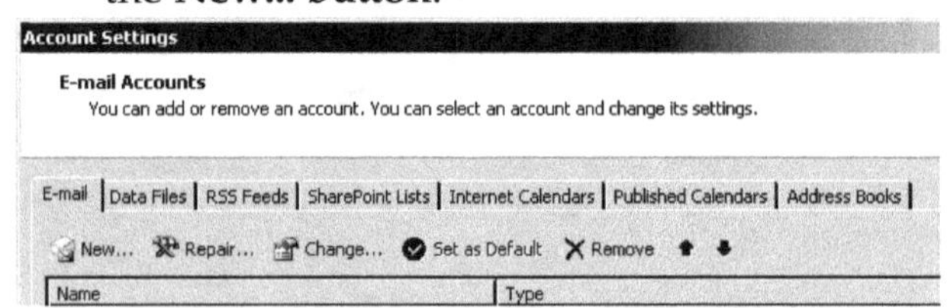

Figure 7.16: *Account Settings Dialog Box*

It will display the Add Account dialog box, as shown in *Figure 7.17*:

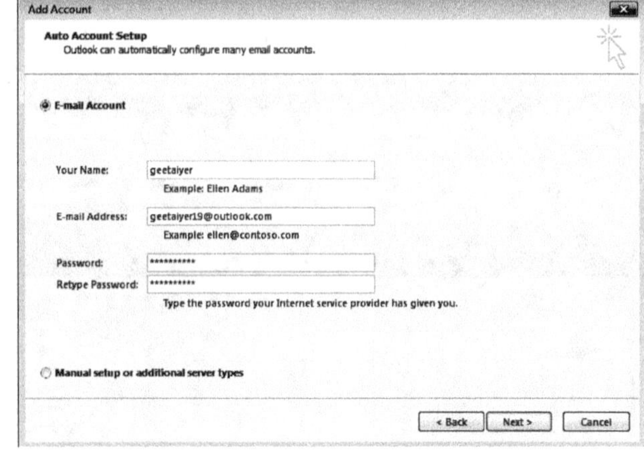

Figure 7.17: *Add Account Dialog Box*

4. In this dialog box, type the name in the Your Name: text box and type e-mail address in the E-mail Address: text box. After that, type password in the Password: textbox and in the Retype Password: textbox, confirm the password. Then, click the **Next > button**.

5. As soon as you click the Next > button, it will display another dialog box showing the progress indicator as your account is being configured. It may take several minutes, as shown in *Figure 7.18*:

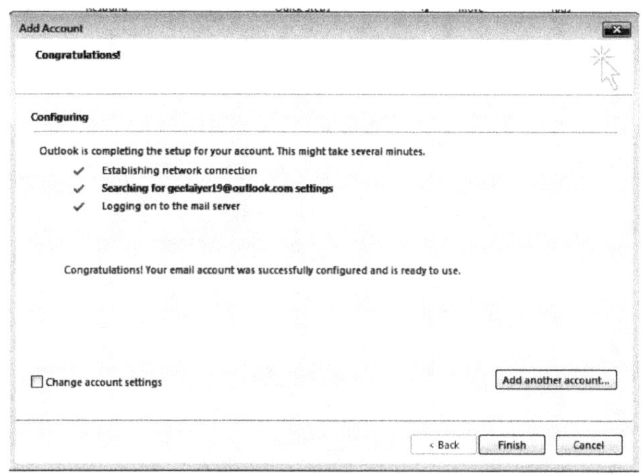

Figure 7.18: *Add Account Showing Configuring E-mail Server Settings*

6. After the account is successfully added, you can add more accounts by clicking the Add another **account...** button, as shown in *Figure 7.18*.

7. To exit the Add Account dialog box, click the Finish button to configure your e-mail account which is ready to use, as shown in *Figure 7.18*.

If Outlook 2013 fails to set up the e-mail account automatically, there is one more thing you can try. If you get this message: An encrypted connection to your server is not available, click Next to attempt using an unencrypted connection.

Mailbox – Inbox and Outbox

To receive electronic mail, a user must have a mailbox, a storage area that holds incoming e-mail messages until the user has time to read them. When a message arrives, e-mail software automatically stores it in the user's mailbox.

Inbox

In Outlook 2013 Inbox, messages are sorted by the date and time received in descending order, which means the most recent message is at the top of the Inbox and the oldest at the bottom. You can click on any of the Field headers (From, Subject, Received, and so on) to sort the message list by that field. Clicking a second time alternates the list between ascending and descending order.

Outbox

The New Message window closes, and your message is now in the Outbox. It has not actually been sent yet. You are still offline. You can write messages to several people and store them in the Outbox. When

you are ready, you can send them all at once. This uses only a few seconds of online time and saves on the phone bill. You can look at the contents of the Outbox and edit a message before you send it.

To edit a message in the Outbox:

1. Click Outbox in the Folders pane to select it.
2. Double-click the message header in the Message List pane.
3. An Edit window appears, and you can edit the message.
4. Click Send to put it back in the Outbox.
5. If prompted to Connect, click Cancel.

To send a message from the Outbox:

1. Click the Send/Receive tab. Select the message you want to edit.
   a. If you are offline, you will be prompted to go online. Click Yes, and then Connect at the next prompt.
2. After clicking the **Connect** button, the message will be sent to the recipient address.
3. Edit the message, and then click the **Send** button.

Logging In of an E-mail Account

Each time you wish to view your e-mail, you must do the following:

1. Use a computer with Internet access.
2. Open the website that hosts your e-mail account.
3. For example, here we open **www.gmail.com** for Google.
4. Enter your credentials (e-mail address and password) to log in. For Google, click Sign In, as shown in *Figure 7.19*:

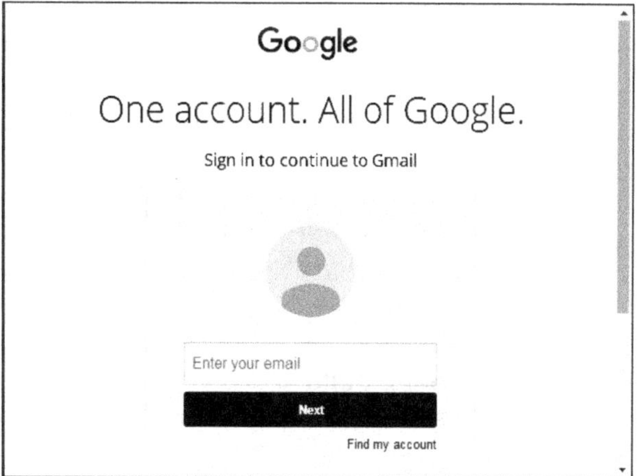

Figure 7.19: *Log in Gmail account*

Creating and Sending a New E-mail

To create a new e-mail message to be sent to your friends and relatives, you need to first log in to your e-mail account and then follow these steps:

1. After logging in to your e-mail account, click the Compose button in the upper-left side of your Gmail inbox. It opens a **New Message** window in the lower-right corner of the page, as shown in *Figure 7.20*:

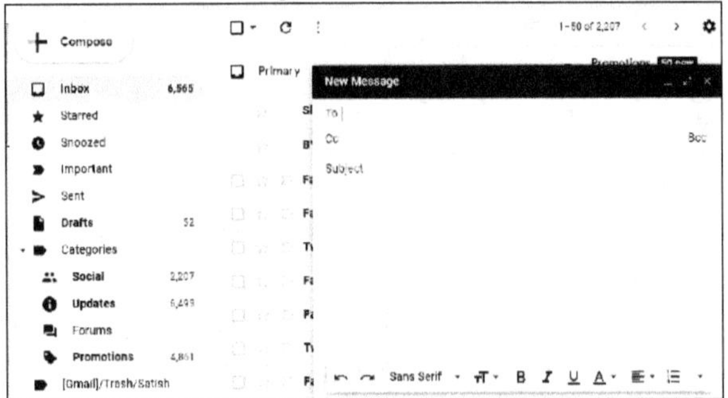

Figure 7.20: *Selecting Compose Mail to opens New Message Window*

2. Enter the other person's e-mail address in various fields such as:
    (a) Type the e-mail address in the To: textbox, that is, the Mail-ID address of recipient.
    (b) Select Cc: textbox, enter mail-IDs of recipients to whom copy needs to be sent. This field allows you to send the same mail message to multiple recipients at the same time.
    (c) Select Bcc: textbox, enter mail-IDs of recipients of **Blind Carbon Copy**. This field allows the sender to send same mail message to multiple recipients without letting them know that some other person has also received the same message.
    (d) Click the Subject text field. Then type in whatever you want the subject of the e-mail to be. This field is a brief description of the message.
    (e) Type the body of the e-mail message in the message area, as shown in *Figure 7.21*.

3. Click the **Send** button to send the message to the address of the recipient's Inbox, as shown in *Figure 7.21*.

Figure 7.21: *Enter the E-mail Address and Click Send Button*

The Gmail Inbox Window appears, showing the information that your message has been sent.

Replying to an E-mail Message

While you are reading an e-mail message, you receive messages from anyone who knows your e-mail address. You can reply to the sender of this message immediately by clicking the **Reply** button, as shown in *Figure 7.22*:

Figure 7.22: *Reply an E-mail Message*

1. When you click the **Reply** button, it takes you to the small Window. The recipient's e-mail address will automatically appear in the To: field, as shown in *Figure 7.22*. If the message was sent to multiple recipients, you will also have the option to Reply to all.

2. Now, you can write the reply mail message and then click the **Send** button.

Forwarding an E-mail Message

If you have received some important information, and you want to send the same information to someone else, you can do so by clicking the Forward button. After clicking the forward button, you need to specify the e-mail addresses of the recipients in the To field or choose a recipient from your contacts to whom you intend to forward it to, as shown in *Figure 7.23*:

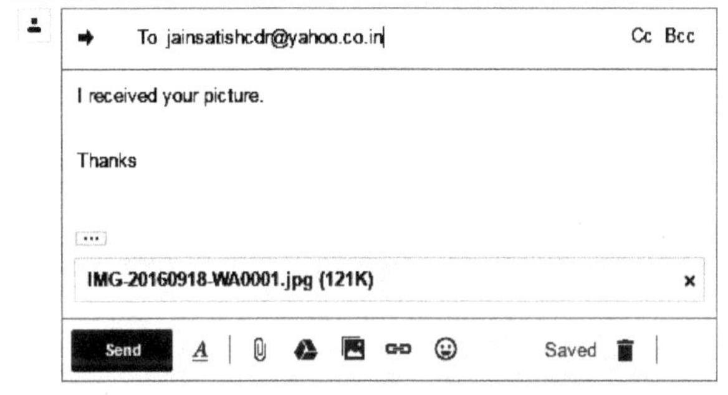

Figure 7.23: *Forward an E-mail Message*

Type your message in the Body field and then click Send.

Sorting and Searching e-mails

Gmail has a better search feature compared to other E-mail services, and it also allows you to filter and sort e-mail messages. You will find below a number of ways to filter and sort Gmail, that is, by Sender Name or E-mail Address by using inbox search techniques.

Sorting Gmail by Sender Name

By default, E-mails in Gmail are arranged by the date they land into the Inbox, which results in e-mails from multiple senders being dumped into the Inbox.

Sorting Gmail Using Search Function

Perform the following steps:

1. Login to your Gmail Account.
2. Enter your e-mail address and password before proceeding.
3. Type from: Name (or e-mail address) into the search bar, and click on the Search button.

This will immediately list all the e-mails received from and sent to this particular contact of yours.

Sorting Gmail By Hovering Mouse Over Sender Name

Take a look at the following steps:

1. Login to your Gmail Account.
2. Open an e-mail from the sender whose messages you want to sort. Place your mouse cursor over their name in the upper-left side of the e-mail, and then look for the e-mail address at the bottom of the pop-up window that appears, as shown in *Figure 7.24*:

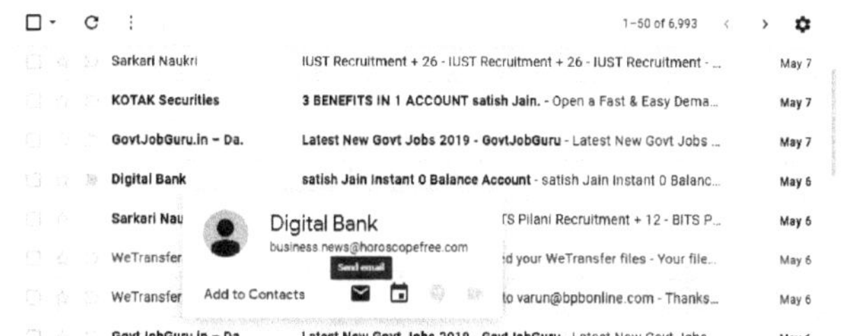

Figure 7.24: *Click Send E-mail in the Pop-up Window*

3. Click and drag your mouse across the entire e-mail address. Right-click the mouse, and then copy the e-mail address from the context menu, as shown in *Figure 7.25*:

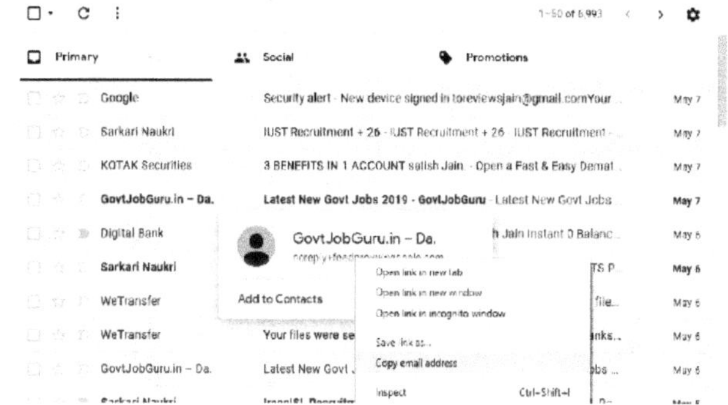

Figure 7.25: *Copy E-mail Address from the Context Menu*

4. Click the Gmail search bar at the top of the inbox. Paste the copied e-mail address in the textbox, as shown in *Figure 7.26*:

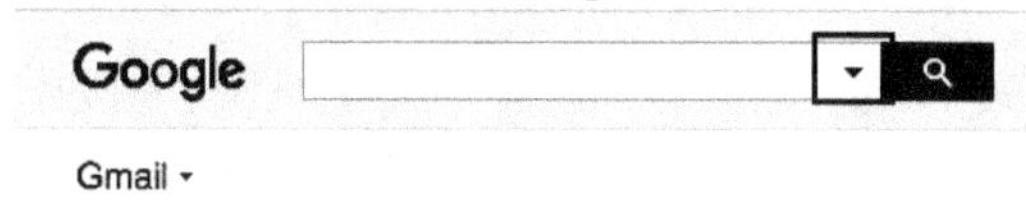

Figure 7.26: *Paste the Copied E-mail Address in the Search Box*

5. Press Enter to search your inbox for the e-mail address. You should see a list of e-mails from your selected sender list, as shown in *Figure 7.27*.

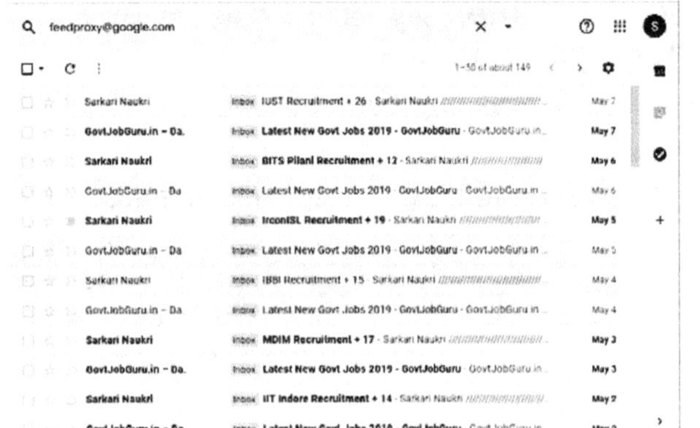

Figure 7.27: *Selected Sender List of E-mail Address*

Sort Your Messages by Subject or using Filters

Using Labels and Filters is also a way of sorting Gmail messages. This method allows you to sort Gmail based on sender name, e-mail address, date and other criteria.

1. Login to your Gmail Account.
2. Click on the drop-down icon located at the right end of the search bar to bring up Gmail Search Form.
3. Type the name or e-mail address of the sender in the From field, and click on the Create Filter option, as shown in *Figure 7.28*:

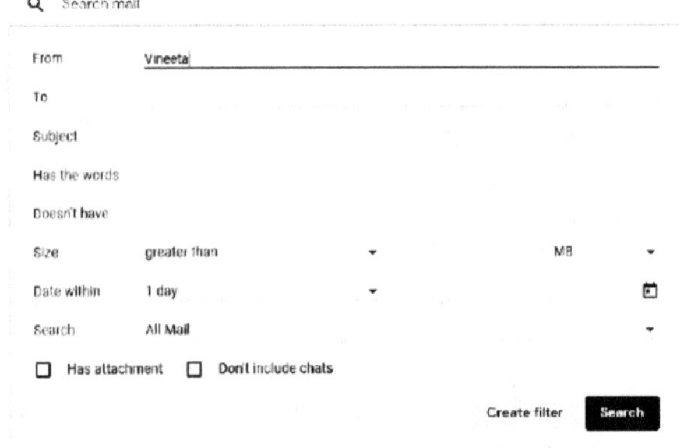

Figure 7.28: *Select Gmail Search form*

4. On the next screen, select the Apply the Label: option. Click on Choose **Label**, and select the **New Label** option in the drop-down list, as shown in *Figure 7.29*:

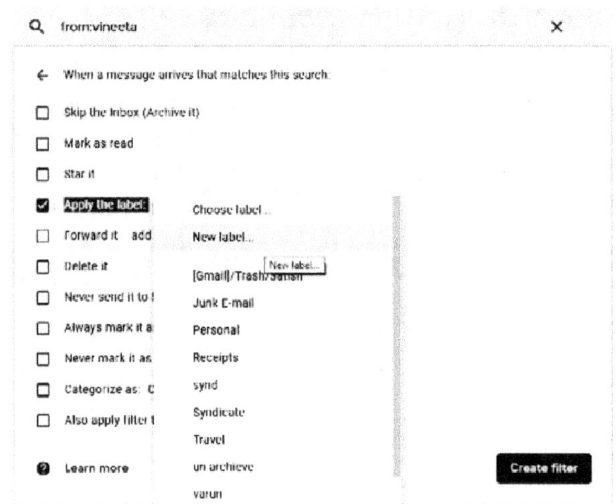

Figure 7.29: *Select New Label from Apply the Label option*

5. The **New** Label dialog box appears. Type a Name for the **New** Label, and click on **Create**, as shown in *Figure 7.30*:

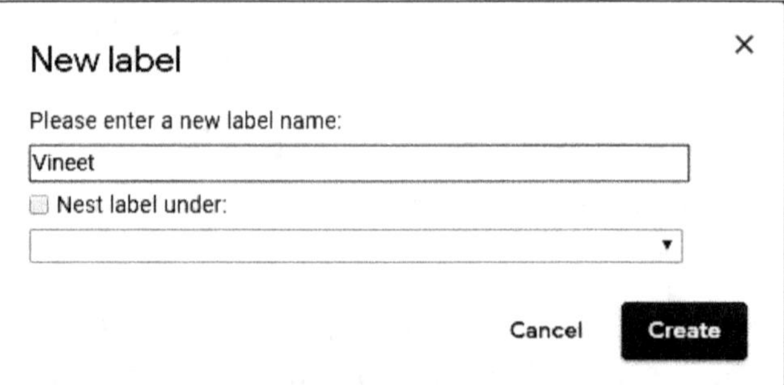

Figure 7.30: *New Label Dialog Box*

6. Once the Label is created, select the Apply filter to matching messages option and click on the **Create Filter** button, as shown in *Figure 7.31*:

Figure 7.31: *Select Apply Filter to Matching Conversations*

7. The **New Label** that you just created will appear in the side menu under Categories, as shown in *Figure 7.32*:

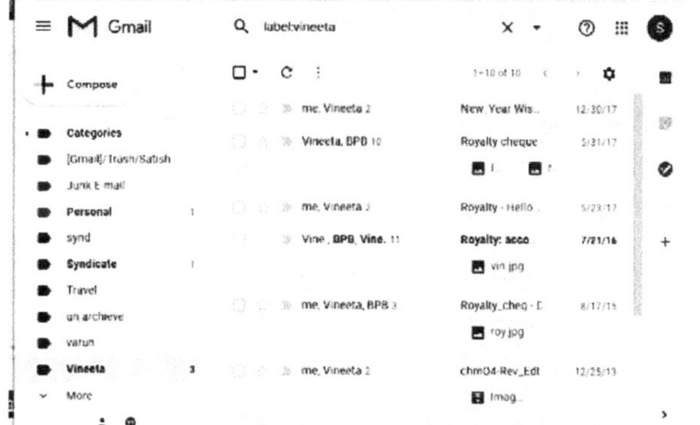

Figure 7.32: *The New Label appears Under Categories*

8. Click on New Label, and you will be able to see all the messages from this particular contact.

Attaching Files with E-mail

Attaching a file to an e-mail is an easy way to send important documents or pictures.

1. Go to Gmail.
2. Click **Compose**.
3. Click the **Attach** button (that is, paper clip icon), as shown in *Figure 7.33*:

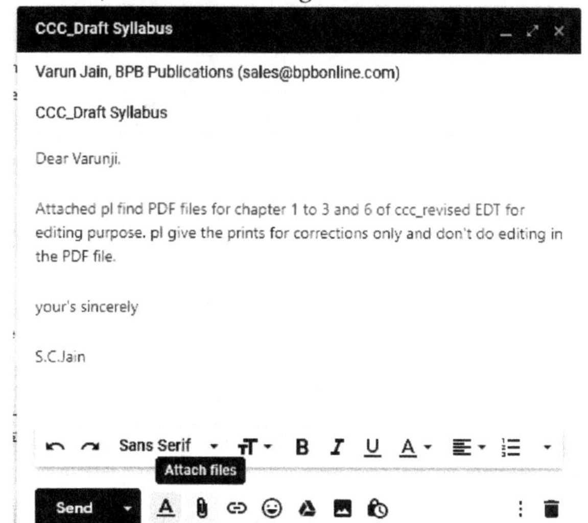

Figure 7.33: *Select the Attach Icon*

4. Once you click the attach button, the Open dialog box appears. Choose the files you want to upload, as shown in *Figure 7.34*:

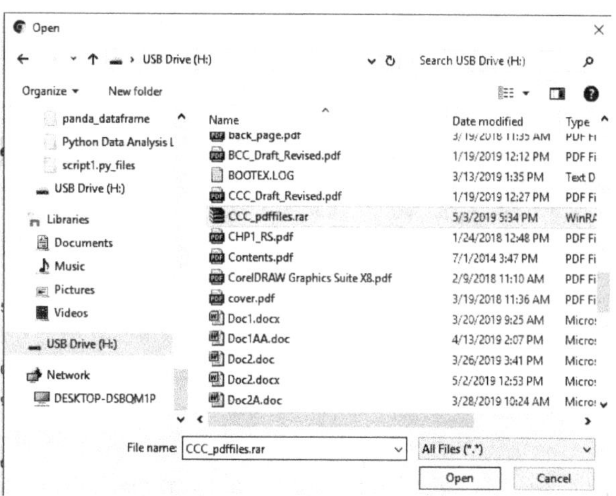

Figure 7.34: *Open Dialog Box*

5. Select the file, and click the **Open** button. It will start the process of attaching the file to your outgoing e-mail message, as shown in *Figure 7.35*:

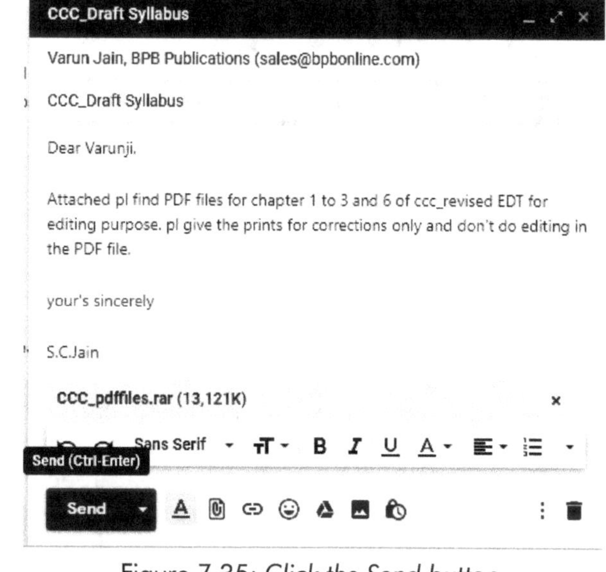

Figure 7.35: *Click the Send button*

6. Click the **Send** button.

Create and Send an E-mail Message in Outlook 2013

To create a new e-mail message in Outlook:

1. In the **Home** tab, under the **New** group, click New E-mail, as shown in *Figure 7.36*:

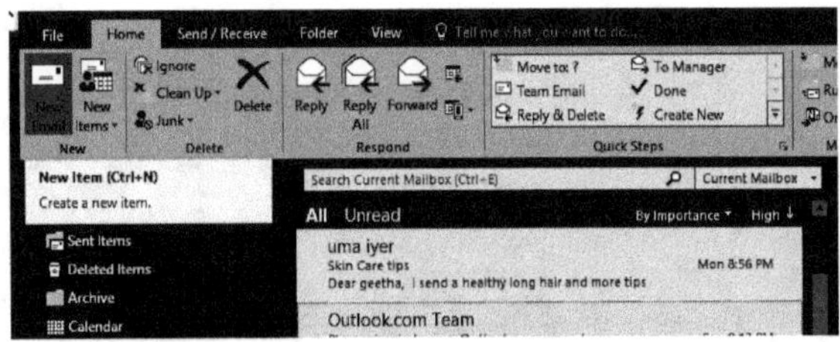

Figure 7.36: *Creating new e-mail message*

Shortcut key to open New mail message is **Ctrl + N or Ctrl + Shift + M** keys pressed together.

2. Outlook 2013 opens an Untitled Message window.

3. In this window, enter the recipient addresses in the To... textbox, as shown in *Figure 7.37*. If you want to enter multiple recipient addresses, you can separate them by a semi-colon and one space.

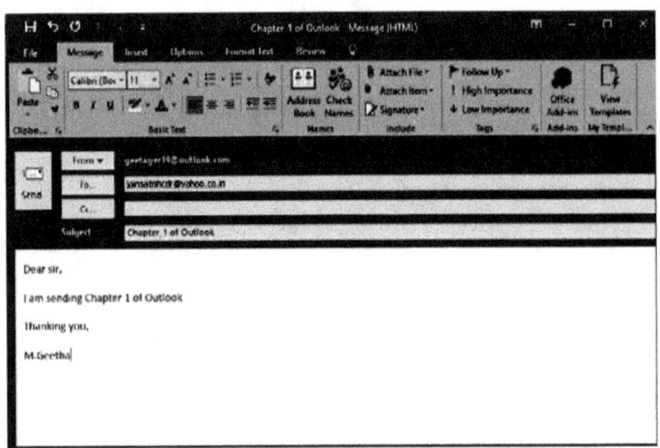

Figure 7.37: *Message Window*

4. If you want to send a copy of the message to someone besides the recipient, enter the address in the Cc... text box.

5. The new message window Title Bar appears. It displays Untitled - Message (Plain Text) until you enter text on the Subject line. The subject line then appears in the Title Bar of the message Window.

6. Type the body of the message in the message window below the subject line.

7. Then, click the **Send** icon to send the message.

Reply to an e-mail Message

To reply to an e-mail message, perform the following steps:

1. In your message list, choose the message that you want to reply to.

2. In the **Home** tab, under the **Respond** group, click the **Reply** or **Reply All** icon, as shown in *Figure 7.38*:

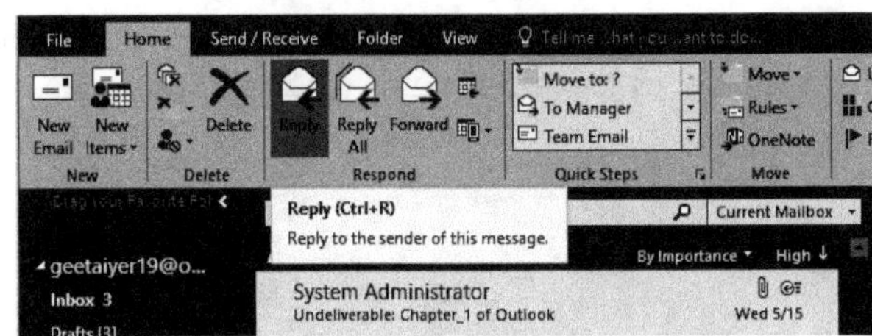

Figure 7.38: *Select the Message List to Reply*

3. When you reply to a message, you will see RE: added to the subject line. The original message is added below the new message, as shown in *Figure 7.39*.

4. Outlook displays a message window with the recipient's e-mail address and subject line already typed, along with a copy of the original message, as shown in *Figure 7.39*:

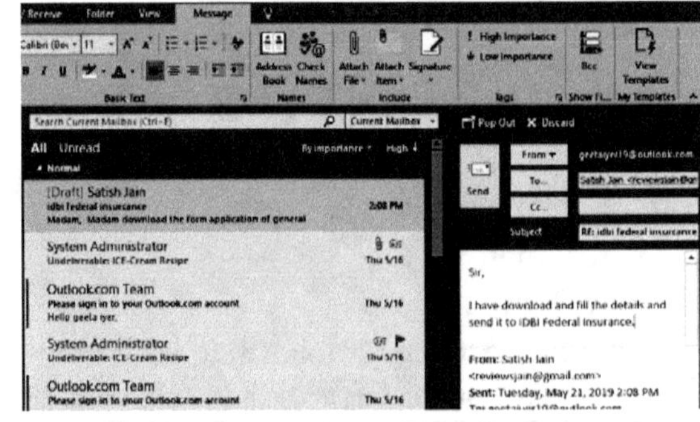

Figure 7.39: *Reply to the Selected Recipient E-mail Address*

5. To add a recipient, click on the **To, Cc** or **Bcc** box. **Compose** the message, and then click the Send icon.

By default, the original e-mail and its history will not be displayed when you are replying to a message. To show the original mail or change the e-mail subject, select .... at the bottom of the message pane.

Forward an E-mail Message

To forward an e-mail message, perform the following steps:

1. In the **Home** tab, under the **Respond** group, click the **Forward** icon, or double-click the message that you want to forward, as shown in *Figure 7.40*:

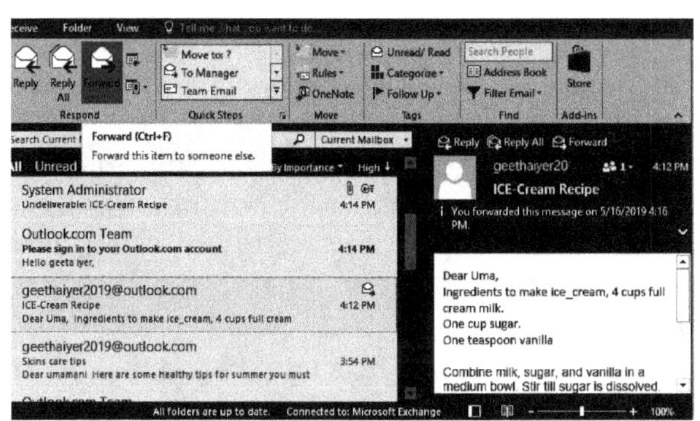

Figure 7.40: Forward an e-mail

2. A message Window appears that contains your chosen message.
3. Click on the To: textbox and type an e-mail address.
4. Click on the message window and type any additional text you want to send, along with the forwarded message.
5. Click the **Send** button.

You can forward only one message at a time. If you want to forward two or more messages, select the first message, hold **Ctrl** key and then select each additional message. Each message will be forwarded as an attachment in a new message.

Sorting and Searching E-mails in Outlook 2013

The e-mails in the list can be arranged in the order of date, sender, size and other properties.

To sort e-mail:

1. Get into the e-mail folder in which you want to sort e-mails by date.
2. Click the **View** tab on the Ribbon. In the **Arrangement** group, click the **Arrange By** drop-down arrow, select the date option from the list. Then, you can see the e-mails are arranged by date series.
3. Or, you can select **View Settings**..., as shown in *Figure 7.41*:

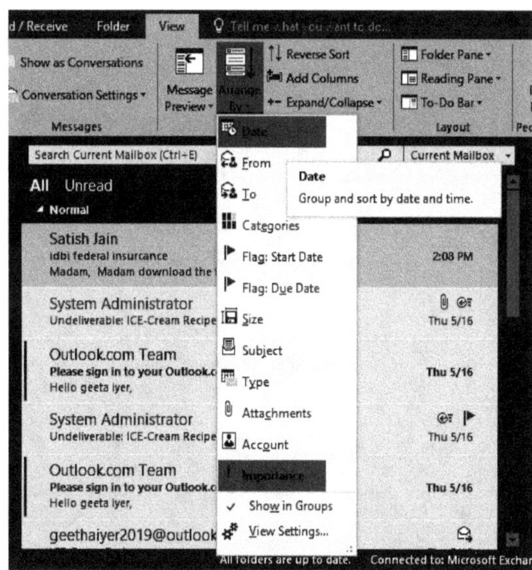

Figure 7.4: Selecting View Settings in the Arrangement group

4. The Advanced View Settings dialog box appears, as shown in *Figure 7.42*:

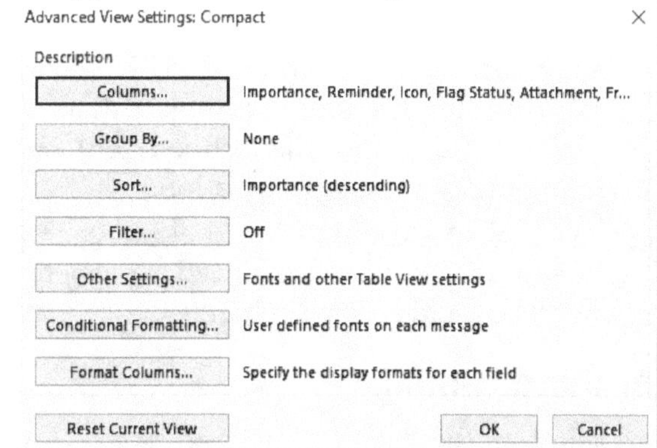

Figure 7.42: Advanced View Settings Dialog Box

5. In the **Advanced View** Settings dialog box, click the **Sort**... button. The Sort dialog box appears, as shown in *Figure 7.43*.

Figure 7.43: Sort Dialog Box

6. In the Select available fields from: drop-down list at the bottom of the dialog box, select the field set containing the fields that you want to use for sorting.
7. In the Sort Items by drop-down list, select an item from the list, such as Subject, Received, Sent and Size, and then choose either the Ascending or Descending option.
8. Click OK to close the Sort dialog box. Click OK again to close the Advanced View Settings dialog box and see your changes.

Searching E-mail

Several sites on the World Wide Web (WWW) offer huge directories of e-mail addresses. If you want to contact a person, company, or other organization but don't know the contact's e-mail address, you can use Outlook 2013 to search through each of these directories.

To search someone's e-mail address:

1. To look for the e-mail address of a person in Outlook 2013, type a word to search for in the Search box and press **Enter**. You can see the highlighted yellow items in the middle of the Window.

Search Address Book

To search through your personal address book in Outlook 2013, choose **Address Book** in the Find group of the **Home** tab. The Address Book dialog box appears. Type the name you are looking for in the Search box Name, E-mail Address, Display Name. Click the Go button to start the search.

E-mail Signature

A signature block is a personalized information or text automatically added at the bottom of an e-mail message. It includes a signature which is used to provide the recipient with a name, e-mail address and information.

The purpose of a signature (also called a **signature block signature file**) is to provide a message recipient with personal contact information.

Information in a signature block may include the following:

*   Full name
*   Job title/position
*   Organization name and division
*   Phone and fax numbers
*   Physical (snail mail) address
*   E-mail address
*   Website address Uniform Resource Locator (URL)

A signature allows information in this part to be included with each outgoing message in an automated and time-saving manner for the message sender.

Here are some of the basic rules you might want to follow for e-mail signature etiquette:

1. Your signature should be easy to scan.
2. It should quickly identify you and your business.
3. Your company logo or symbol must be readily identifiable and quick to load.
4. Need not include your signature when you reply to an existing e-mail. However, you may desire to include your signature when you forward a message.

Social Networking and E-commerce

A social networking service is an online service, platform, or site that focuses on building and reflecting of social networks or social relations among people, e.g., who share common interests and/or activities. A social network service essentially consists of a representation of each user (often a profile), his/her social links, and a variety of additional services. Most social network services are Web based and provide means for users to interact over the Internet, such as e-mail and instant messaging, video calling, chat, file sharing, discussion groups, voice chats, e-mails, blogging and so on. Online community services are sometimes considered as a social network service. Social networking sites allow users to share ideas, activities, events, and interests within their individual networks.

Social networking is all about communication. People with common interests are able to share information with each other through a huge variety of social networking sites. Sites are created specifically to make sharing, communicating, and creating information as simple and efficient as possible. Examples of social networking sites:

- Facebook
- LinkedIn
- Twitter

Electronic commerce or e-commerce refers to a wide range of online business activities for products and services. It also pertains to any form of business transaction in which the parties interact electronically rather than by physical exchanges or direct physical contact.

E-commerce is usually associated with buying and selling over the Internet, or conducting any transaction involving the transfer of ownership or rights to use goods or services through a computer-mediated network. A more complete definition is— E-commerce is the use of electronic communications and digital information processing technology in business transactions to create, transform, and redefine relationships for value creation between or among organizations, and between organizations and individuals.

Some common applications related to electronic commerce are as follows:

- Enterprise content management
- E-mail
- Automated online assistants
- Instant messaging
- Newsgroups
- Online shopping and order tracking
- Electronic tickets
- Teleconferencing

Facebook, Twitter, LinkedIn, Instagram

Facebook

Facebook is a social networking Website intended to connect friends, family, and business associates. It is the largest networking site. By creating a Facebook profile, the user can fill different information about himself and share content such as text, pictures, music, video, and so on with others.

Creating an Account

To create a Facebook account:

1. Go to **www.facebook.com**
2. Enter your name (first name and last initial), **e-mail address**, and a **password** in the textboxes provided for them, as shown in *Figure 7.44*:

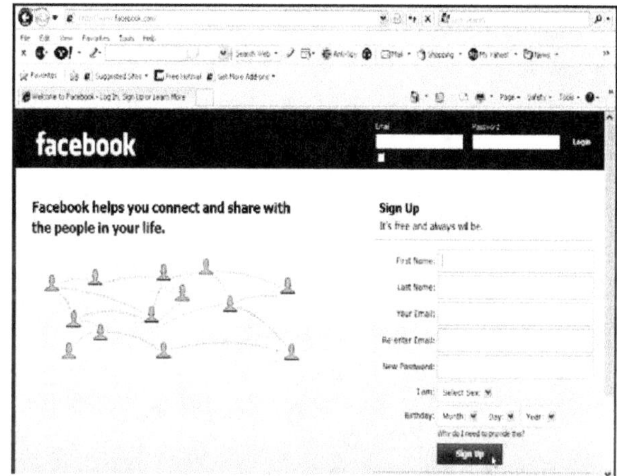

Figure 7.44: *Facebook Sign in Window*

3. Then, click on **Sign Up**.
4. After that, a **security code** appears, and you have to enter that code.
5. A confirmation link would be sent to your e-mail address. You need to click on that link and once you do that, you will be directed to the **Getting Started** page of Facebook. If anyone has been on the lookout for you, their names would appear, and you can opt to add them in your friends list.

Twitter

Twitter is a free social networking and micro-blogging service that has changed the way people communicate with each other. It is a message service that allows people to send and receive short messages (called **tweets**) within their Twitter community. Twitter community consists of:

1. **People You Follow:** You define your community by following other Twitter users. You see the tweets created by everyone you follow. Following someone means that you subscribe to their tweets.
2. **People Who Follow You:** Other people read your tweets and decide to follow you. Your followers see the tweets you send out.

Twitter was created by a software development team to solve their own communication challenges. They took features from other communication tools like e-mail, chat, and instant messaging and mashed them together to create Twitter.

How to Find People on Twitter

There are several ways to find people to follow on Twitter. These are as under:
- Name Search
- E-mail Search
- Keyword Search

Types of Tweets

There are three types of tweets:
- **General Tweets:** A public tweet is sent to everyone who follows you.
- **@Replies:** A public tweet is sent to a specific person on Twitter. You may send @reply in response to a tweet sent out by a person, or you can use @reply to send a message to anyone on Twitter.
- **Direct Message:** A private tweet is sent to a person who follows you. You cannot send a direct message to someone who does not follow you.

While creating an account, use your real name if you want people to find you using the Twitter search feature.

How to Tweet?

In order to tweet, you will have to go to the Home page of Twitter and sign in, as shown in the *Figure 7.45*:

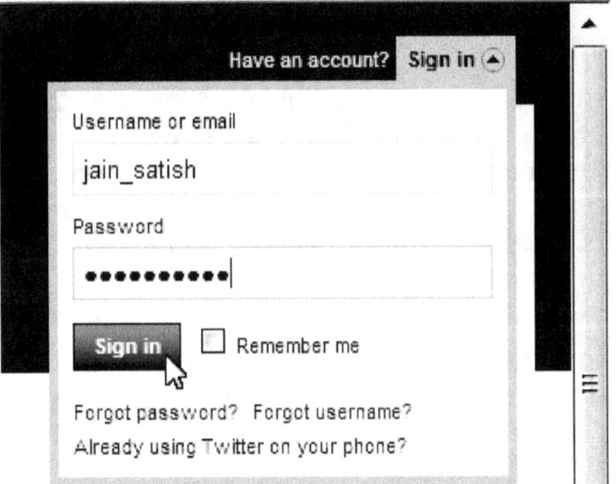

Figure 7.45: *Sign in Screen Twitter Dialog Box*

After sign-in in, you will be able to type your 'tweet'—a **280-character message**. (This limit was set to make the service compatible to text messages). While you type your tweet, the interface itself will show you how many characters are left, as shown in *Figure 7.46*:

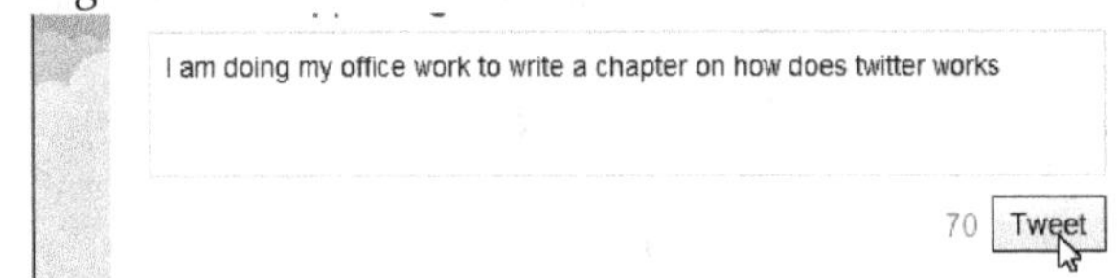

Figure 7.46: *Message Box*

How to Send a Tweet on Twitter?

Twitter is an extremely interesting and versatile application that you can use to talk with friends, conduct business and even promote a blog or other type of Website. Each update you enter into Twitter is known as a **tweet**. A tweet can be no longer than **280 characters**, and you can send a general tweet to everyone, reply to a specific person or direct a tweet to only one person.

To send a tweet on twitter:

1. Log in to Twitter through the Twitter Home Page, or through a Twitter **API application** such as **Twhirl**. You can also update Twitter through Facebook and several other applications that use the Twitter **Application Programming Interface (API)**.

2. Enter your message in the box with the label **What are you doing?** Keep in mind that your tweet can be no longer than **140 characters** at the most. This limitation exists because Twitter uses the **Short Message Service (SMS)** network to send notifications through cell phone to those who desire it.

3. Click **Update** to send the Tweet to everyone on Twitter.

4. Type **d USERNAME** before your tweet to send a direct message to a particular user. Only that user will see the message.

5. Put **@USERNAME** at the beginning of your tweet to send a reply to a particular user. That user, your followers, and that user's followers will all be able to see the tweet, but it will not appear on the public timeline.

How to Find People by Name?

1. Type the person's name into the search box at

the top of your Twitter Home Page.

2. Results for your search will show up under the People tab on the search page. Or,

You can also search by typing the person's name into the search box on the Connect page.

The list of People results for Sachin Tendulkar appears, as shown in *Figure 7.47*:

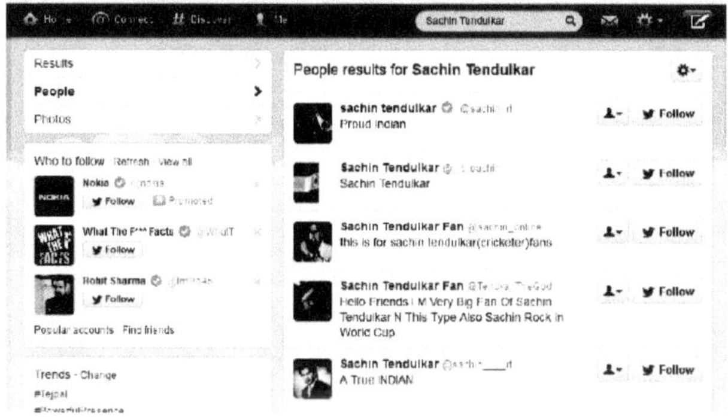

Figure 7.47: *People Search Results*

To send a direct message via the Web:

1. **Sign** in to **Twitter** account.

2. Click on the envelope icon in the top-right navigation bar.

3. You will see a pop up showing your direct message history. Click the **New** message button.

4. In the address box, type the name or username of the person you wish to **send** a message to.

5. Enter your message and click Send message.

Make sure that user follows you. You can only send a direct message to your followers.

To delete a direct message via the web:

1. Click on the envelope icon in the top-right Navigation bar.

2. You will see a pop up showing your direct message history. Click the conversation containing the message you would like to delete.

3. Locate the desired message and hover your mouse over it. A **trash** icon will appear, as shown in *Figure 7.48*. Click it.

Figure 7.48: *Delete Message*

4. A message will be displayed at the bottom of the DM inbox asking **Are you sure you want to delete this message?** Click **Delete** message.

LinkedIn

LinkedIn is a social network within the larger world of social media that is geared toward business. It is very popular with those who are seeking work and trying to build their network of contacts so they can reach out to employers. It is also popular as a way of marketing a business, because business owners can interact with those who are interested in their services by answering questions, participating in discussions and more.

How to Use LinkedIn?

LinkedIn is a popular Website for professionals to network, and college students also use it to meet someone in a company that they want to work for. It is advantageous to have a LinkedIn account, and here are some ways to make the most out of the online networking experience.

- **Network with those you already know:** If you are new to LinkedIn, the best and easiest way to increase your connections is to add those you already know in person. LinkedIn allows you to import friends from your e-mail accounts, such as **Gmail, Yahoo, American Online (AOL)** and **Windows Live**.

- **Online Identity:** LinkedIn helps you build an online profile or recreate a professional identity. It usually gets **top** ranking on **Google**; when someone plugs your name in the search engine, your professional profile comes up first. This is beneficial when you want to establish your professional identity because what they see on LinkedIn is a mini resume.

- **Jobs:** Although LinkedIn is more popular as a networking tool that allows you to contact people and companies, there is also a jobs section on the page. You can not only apply for these jobs through the jobs page, but also utilize your knowledge of the contact person by being more assertive and contact them directly regarding the position.

- Find People: LinkedIn is also useful when you want to look for someone in a particular company or to find out what positions people hold in a particular organization. LinkedIn has a feature that helps you approach someone and send them a message or e-mail.

- **Recommendations:** LinkedIn has a built-in page for recommendations. You can receive recommendations from colleagues, and you can also give recommendations to those who work for you. These recommendations are helpful since you can showcase your achievements and gain credibility.

How to Create a LinkedIn Login?

You can use LinkedIn to find jobs, promote yourself or your business and much more. But first, you will need to create a LinkedIn login (account) in order to start using LinkedIn.

How to Create a LinkedIn Account?

In order to get started with LinkedIn, you will need to create an account. Once your account is set up, you can then start adding others to your network and building a powerful tool.

Start Creating Your LinkedIn Login:

1. Open your Web browser and go to **LinkedIn. com.**
2. Complete the information in the Join Linked (right) area of the page.
   a. Type your First Name in the First Name: box.
   b. Type your Last Name in the Last Name: box.
   c. Type a valid e-mail address for receiving e-mails in the E-mail: box.

Type a Password for your account in the Password: box. The password needs to be at least **six** letters. It's a good practise to use both **lowercase** and **capital letters**, along with at least **one number** or **special character** (, !, and so on) to create a strong password. Don't leave any blank spaces.

Click the **Join Now** button as shown in *Figure 7.49*:

Figure 7.49: *Joined Now*

This will take you to the next LinkedIn screen, as shown in *Figure 7.50*:

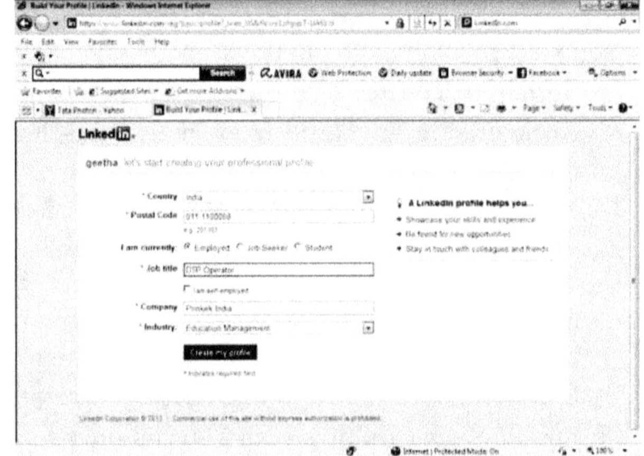

Figure 7.50: *Creating Profile*

3. The next step in creating a LinkedIn login is to provide your employment status and location information.
4. Select one of the following options in the I am currently: drop-down list. These are: Employed Job Seeker and Student.
5. For example, if you select Employed, the remaining fields you will need to complete will be Company, Job Title, Industry, as shown in *Figure 7.52*.

Importing Your E-mail Contacts (Optional)

You have the option to import e-mail addresses through LinkedIn login setup process, as shown in *Figure 7.51*. If you select this optional step, LinkedIn will check to see if any of the e-mail addresses in your address book belong to existing LinkedIn members:

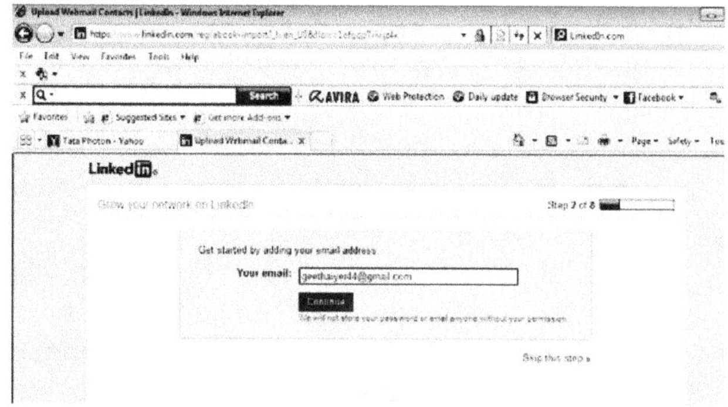

Figure 7.51: *Import E-mail Addresses*

Keep in mind:

If you do not want to use this feature, you can Skip this step at the bottom of the screen.

Once you have either passed through the e-mail address or skipped over it, a confirmation screen shows confirmation message send to account you just registered with LinkedIn. If LinkedIn recognized your e-mail provider, you can go directly to your (Webmail) e-mail provider when you click a button available there, you can log in and receive the confirmation message sent by LinkedIn as shown in *Figure 7.52*:

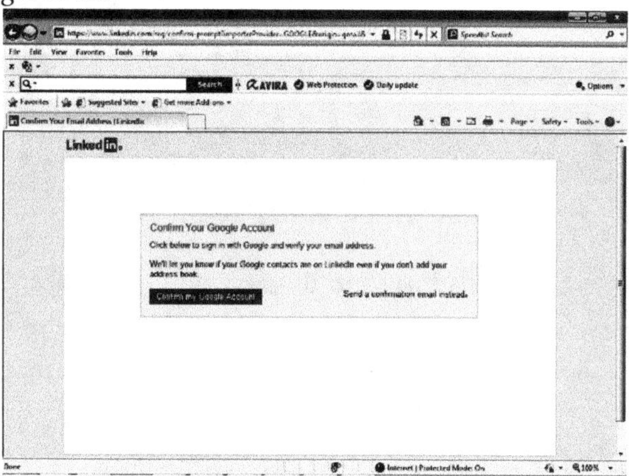

Figure 7.52: *Confirm message*

You may receive the confirmation message immediately from LinkedIn, or it could take several minutes. Once you receive the message, you need to do the following:

1. Select the link in LinkedIn confirmation message.
2. Press **Log in** to LinkedIn you just created.
3. You can start using **LinkedIn!**

Instagram

Instagram is an online photo sharing social Web service that lets you share your life and experiences with friends and others through a series of pictures captured with a mobile device. It also supports video uploads and lets the users instantly share photos on several social sites, including Twitter and Facebook.

It was created by **Kevin Systrom** and **Mike Krieger**, and launched in **October 2010** on iOS. A version for Android devices was released in **April 2012**, and apps for Windows 10 Mobile and Windows 10 in **April 2016** and **October 2016**, respectively. Instagram is available for free on iOS, Android and Windows phone devices. It can also be accessed on the web from a computer, but the users can only upload and share photos or videos from their devices. It also permits the users to add some captions, hashtags using the # symbol for describing the pictures and videos, and tag or mention other users by using the @ symbol before posting them.

Instagram social network is asymmetric, implying that if user **A** follows **B** then **B** need not follow *A*. Users can choose their privacy settings according to their own preferences such that their posted photos and videos are available only to their followers; others need approval from the user to be his/her followers. By default, their images and videos are public, which implies that they are visible to anyone using Instagram app or Instagram Website.

Instant Messaging (WhatsApp, Facebook Messenger and Telegram)

Instant Messaging (IM) is a form of real-time direct text-based communication between two or more people using personal computers or other devices, along with shared clients. The user's text is conveyed over a network, such as the Internet. More advanced instant messaging software clients also allow enhanced modes of communication, such as **live voice** or **video calling**.

It is a type of online chat that offers video calling features such as Voice over Internet Protocol (VoIP) and Web conferencing services over the Internet. Instant messaging works independent of your computer browser which allows the users to communicate with each other without interrupting other applications. It also allows two people to communicate via networks, or talk directly over the internet using a microphone and head phone or just as if they were having a face-to-face conversation.

Most of the Instant Messaging Providers give you the following facilities:

- **Instant messages:** You can send notes to your friend when he/she is online.
- **Chat:** In a chat room, you can chat with friends or co-workers.
- **Web links:** You can share links with favourite Websites.
- **Video:** Send and view video messages, and face-to-face conversation.
- **Files:** You can share files by sending them directly to your friends.
- **Talk:** Use the Internet instead of a phone to talk with friends.
- **Streaming content:** Real-time stock quotes and news.
- **Mobile capabilities:** Sending instant messages from your cell phone.

WhatsApp

WhatsApp is the most popular instant messaging app which allows you to communicate with friends using text, phone call, video, sharing of files, in group or personal and other media. It is basically an alternative way to send free SMS text messages using internet connection.

More than **50 billion people use WhatsApp** to stay in touch with friends and family, and it is the biggest online messenger transfer a day. WhatsApp was founded by **Jan Koum** and **Brian Acton**. It is one of the best and fastest growing freeware cross-platform messaging and **Voice over IP (VoIP)** service. It provides services for text and audio messaging, free voice calls and exchanging photos or videos and even for sharing of limited types of documents.

WhatsApp makes use of extensible messaging and presence protocol server. This facilitates that can transfer messages between two or more users at any point of time. The main purpose is the data processing of the message file length which is associated with a node which is being monitored. Suppose the contents of multimedia messages are uploaded into a HTTP server, then the receiving node can accept or block; it depends on its choice.

The desktop app works in exactly the same way as WhatsApp web. The new desktop app is available for **Window 8** and above and is synced with WhatsApp on your mobile device. Additionally, it can also be used with Chrome, a web-based browser.

You can send messages from your contacts screen with WhatsApp for mobile phone:

1. Start WhatsApp from your Home screen. It is an icon that looks like a white telephone inside a green speech bubble.
2. Click the **Contacts** tab that you will find at the top or bottom of the screen.
3. Click the contact to whom you would like to send a message. You can tell whether or not they have WhatsApp on their phone, depending on a greeting under their name. For example, the default message is **Hey there! I am using WhatsApp**, or say something like **Available**.
4. Click **send** message.
5. Click the text field and compose your message.
6. Click **Send** to send your message.

How to send a text message in WhatsApp?

1. Sending a text in WhatsApp is just as easy as sending a text through messages.
2. Click the text field in the chat window to bring up the keyboard.
3. Type your message, as shown in *Figure 7.53*:

Figure 7.53: *Send Text Message in WhatsApp*

4. Click **Send** to send the text.
5. Click the Emoji icon near the bottom-left corner.
6. Swipe through the emoji screens until you find the suitable emoji.
7. Click to add an emoji to the text field, and click Send to send your message.

How to forward messages and media using WhatsApp?

1. Click and hold the message or media you want to forward. It will turn blue. You can click other messages or media to send.
2. Click the **forward** icon on the top-right of your screen. It is a white arrow, as shown below:

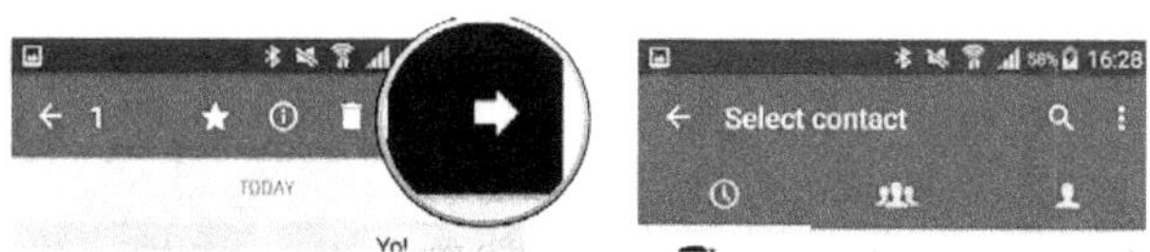

Figure 7.54: *White arrow to forward message*

3. You can choose the desired recipient option to forward a message.
4. Click the recent chats clock icon on the top-left to forward a message to someone you were chatting with recently.
5. Click the **group** icon, that is, three heads in the middle of your screen, to send to a group chat.
6. Click the **Contact** icon single head on the top-right of the screen to send to a specific contact.

How to Use WhatsApp from a Computer?

WhatsApp has provided a web client to access the WhatsApp interface from your computer in your browser window. It is available for **Mac OS** x 10.9 and higher version, and for **Windows 8** to new versions of Windows. You can use WhatsApp from a phone through the Website, or via the WhatsApp Desktop app.

If you do not have the mobile app, you will need to download it before setting up WhatsApp to use on your computer. Visit WhatsApp Web for a browser version, or download the desktop program through the Download WhatsApp page.

If you are using the desktop version, select the download link that corresponds with your computer's operating system such as **Windows** or **Mac**. Once you have opened, the desktop program and web client will show a large QR code, as shown in *Figure 7.55*:

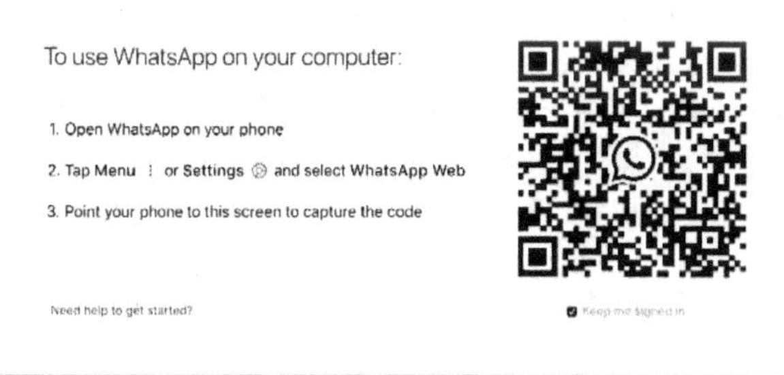

Figure 7.55: *WhatsApp on your Phone to Scan the Code*

1. Open WhatsApp from your phone.
2. Navigate to Settings. Then click **WhatsApp Web/Desktop.**
3. Scroll down and choose Scan **QR Code.** Your

phone might ask for permission to use the camera. Allow it as shown in *Figure 7.56*:

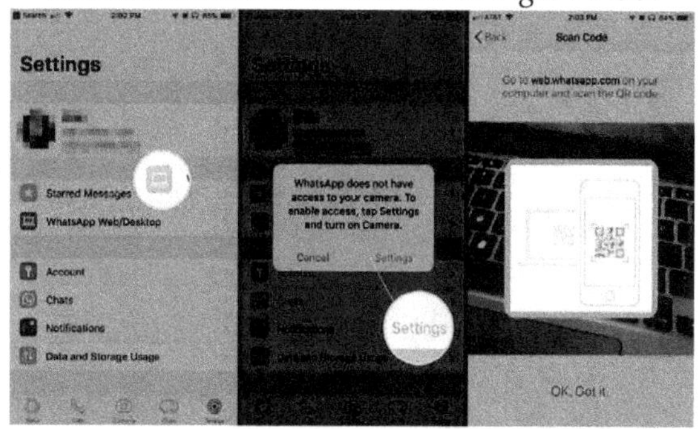

Figure 7.56: *Go to Settings and choose WhatsApp Web/Desktop and Scan OR code*

4. Hold your phone up to the computer screen to scan the **QR code**. It will do everything automatically; you just have to point the camera in that direction, as shown in *Figure 7.56*:
5. That WhatsApp client will open immediately and show you any messages you already have on your phone. Now, you will be able to send and receive WhatsApp on your computer, as shown in *Figure 7.57*:

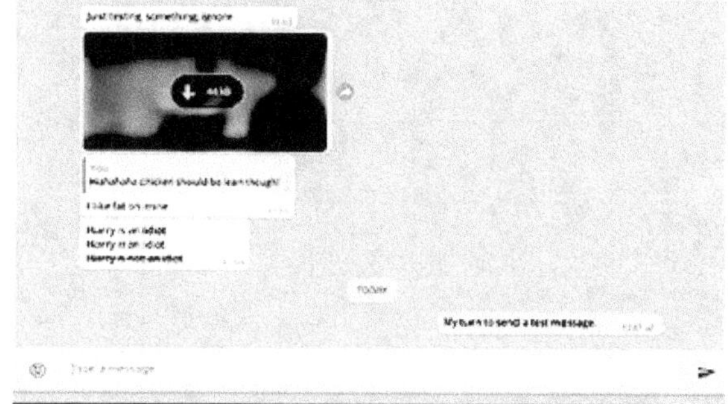

Figure 7.57: *Open Messages on your Computer*

6. Once you have set it up, WhatsApp will automatically connect any time you have desktop or web app open. If you want to log out, click on the menu settings drop-down icon and select Log Out, as shown in Figure 7.58:

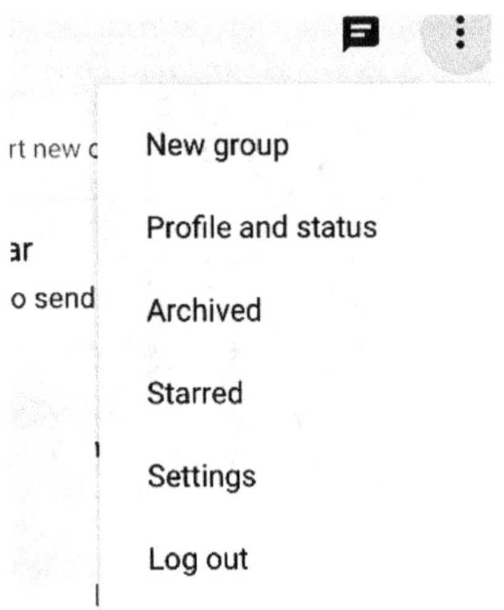

Figure 7.58: *Select Settings from menu and Choose Log Out from your Phone*

7. You can also log out of all your computers from the mobile app by going to the WhatsApp Web screen and tapping **Log out from all computers**, as shown in *Figure 7.59*:

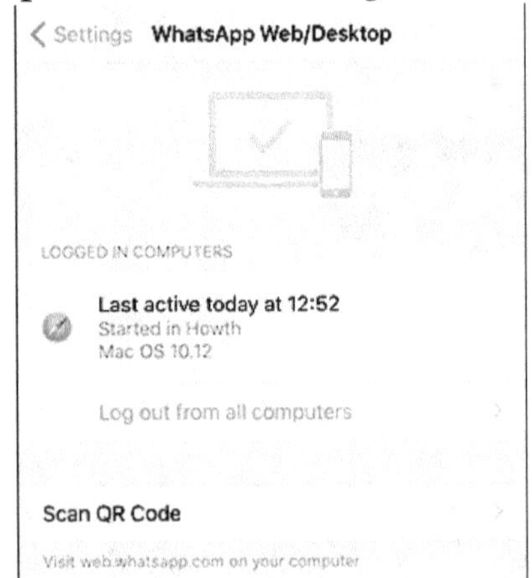

Figure 7.58: *Logout from Computers*

Facebook Messenger

Facebook Messenger is known as **Messenger**. It is a messaging app that enables chat, voice and video communications between the social media site's web-based messaging and smartphones. It is also available for iOS, Android, Windows 10 devices and can connect through Wi-Fi or a mobile data plan.

Users can send messages and exchange photos, videos, stickers, audio, and files, as well as react to other users' messages and interact with bots. The service also supports voice and video calling. The standalone apps support using multiple accounts, conversations with optional end-to-end encryption.

1. Open **Facebook** in your computer web browser. This will open your **News Feed** page, as shown in *Figure 7.60*:

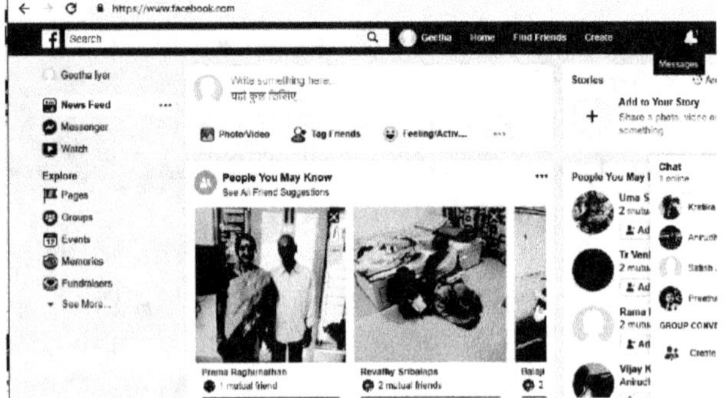

Figure 7.60: *Select Message from News Feed page*

2. Click the **Message** icon with a lightning bolt icon in the upper-right corner of the page. A drop-down menu will appear.
3. Click **New** Message; it opens a new chat Window at the bottom of the page, as shown in *Figure 7.61*:

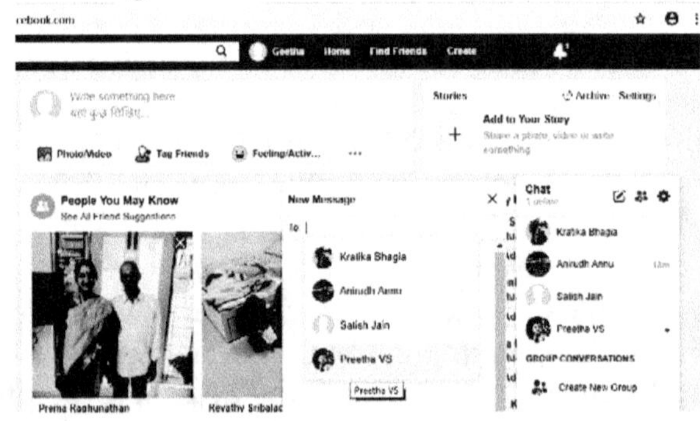

Figure 7.61: *New Message Chat Window Appears*

Or, if you want to create a group message, click **New Group** at the top of the drop-down menu.

4. Type the first few letters of a friend's name, it quickly appears a list of matching names to appear in a drop-down menu, as shown in *Figure 7.61*.
5. Select the name of the friend with whom you want to talk. The name will be added to the chat, as shown in *Figure 7.62*:

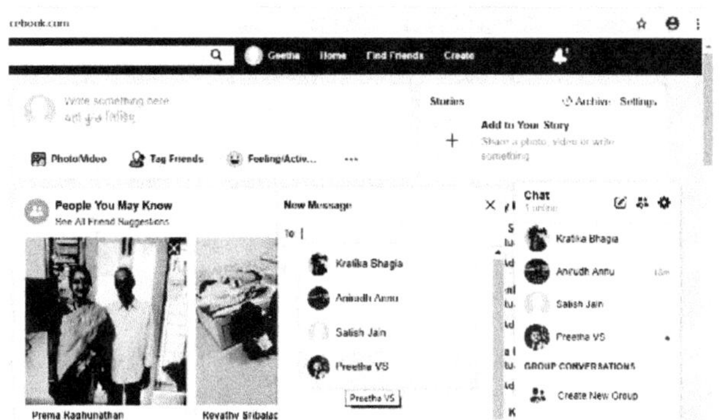

Figure 7.62: *Type Message in Text Field and Press Enter*

6. Click the **Type a message** text field. It is located at the bottom of the chat Window, as shown in *Figure 7.62*.
7. Pressing **Enter** by itself will send your message.
8. Add items to your messages if you like, such as photos, stickers, or other content through Facebook, as shown in *Figure 7.63*:

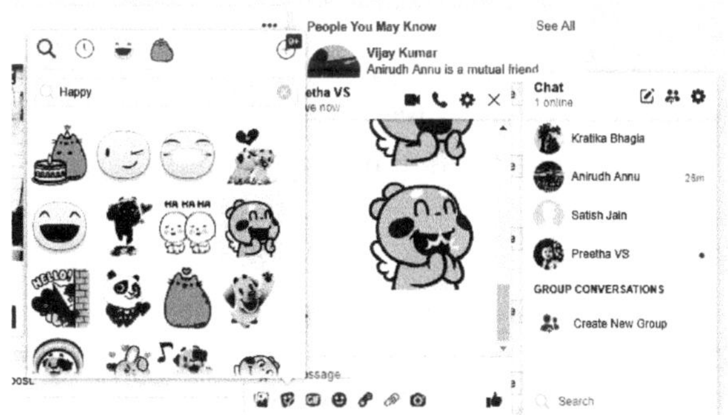

Figure 7.63: *Select sticker category*

- **Photos:** To send a photo, click the Photos icon in the bottom-left corner of the chat Window.
- **Sticker:** To send a sticker icon, select a sticker category from the list.
- **GIFs:** To send a GIF image, click the GIF button at the bottom of the chat Window.
- **Emoji:** To want to use emoji to send, click the smiley face icon at the bottom of the chat window.
- **Files:** Click the paperclip icon at the bottom of the chat Window. Select a file from your computer, and press **Enter** to send the file.

Telegram

Telegram is a cloud-based instant messaging and voice over IP service developed by the **Russian entrepreneur Pavel Durov** and his brother Nikolai.

It can be used on smartphones, tablets, laptops and desktop computers. It is also available for Android, iOS, Windows Phone, Windows NT, macOS and Linux. Users can send messages and exchange photos, videos, stickers, audio and other types of files up to 1.5 GB.

Telegram is client-server encrypted and it is stored on the servers by default. This service provides end-to-end encryption for voice calls and optional end-to-end encrypted **secret** chats between two online users.

There are various ways to use Telegram on your computer:

- Using Windows/Mac OSX/Linux application
- Using app from the Chrome web store
- Using a web client
- Using Telegram Windows Application:
  1. If you do not have the app, download it free from **https://desktop.telegram.org/**.
  2. Open the **Telegram app**.
  3. Click the **Start Messaging** icon. It is the blue button at the bottom of the Window.
  4. Type your mobile number so that you can set up Telegram.
  5. Click **Next**. Telegram will send you an SMS message that contains a **5-digit** code.
  6. Enter the code from the SMS message. It will take several minutes to get access.
  7. Click **Next**. You are now signed into Telegram.
- Using Web Store:
  1. Go to **https://web.telegram.org** in a browser. This will access the version of Telegram from any web browser such as **Chrome**, **Safari** or **Edge**.
  2. Type your mobile phone number to set up Telegram.
  3. Click **Next**. It will now send a **5-digit confirmation** code to the phone number.
  4. Enter the confirmation code you received through the SMS message.
  5. Click **Next**. You are now signed into Telegram.

Introduction to Blogs

A blog is a type of website that is updated regularly with new content. It is an online journal or informational website displaying information in the reverse chronological order with latest posts appearing first. The content of a blog typically includes text, pictures, videos, animated GIFs and journals of hard copy documents. Since a blog can exist for personal use, sharing information with an exclusive group or to engage the public, a blog owner can set her/his blog for private or public access.

Why are many people blogging?

Some people today are creating a blog for various reasons. Every human being has its own story to tell. Hence, through the internet, bloggers can communicate to a larger group of people. Why is it so popular? Because you need to rely on the topics that you love and strive to make your blog as one of the best blogs on the web. For instance, you can refine your writing skills; the more you write, the better you become it. Professional bloggers write on a regular basis and therefore analyse and proof read their writing constantly. You may get feedback from readers to help you become a better writer. However, being a good writer is not a requirement for a successful blog. Many high-profile bloggers are self-asserted writers, and part of their success could be attributed to their message.

There are many reasons why people blog. Here are some of the most common reasons:

- To share their experiences and expertise.
- To speak up about an issue they care about
- To become more involved with hobbies and passions.
- To be a part of a community.
- To keep family and friends updated about their life.

No matter what their main reason for blogging is, they are passionate enough about a topic to write about it over and over again. If there is a topic you care deeply about, you might enjoy blogging about it. When you have your own blog, you have unlimited space and freedom to express your opinions and discuss the things you care about with others. There is another reason for blogging for many. Some people earn money from their blogs by hosting advertisements, selling products, or publishing their blog posts in the form of a book or printed articles.

Basics of E-Commerce

E-commerce allows consumers to electronically exchange goods and services with no barriers of time or distance. It has expanded rapidly over the past five years and is predicted to continue at this rate, or even accelerate. In the near future, the boundaries between **conventional** and **electronic** commerce will become increasingly blurred as more and more businesses move sections of their operations onto the Internet.

Electronic commerce draws on such technologies as electronic funds transfer, supply chain management, Internet marketing, online transaction processing, **Electronic Data Interchange (EDI)**, inventory management systems, and automated data collection systems. Modern electronic commerce typically uses the **World Wide Web (WWW)** at least at one point in the transaction life cycle, although it may encompass a wider range of technologies such as e-mail, mobile devices and telephones as well.

The *Information Technology Act, 2000*, governs the activities of e-commerce in India.

Some common applications related to electronic commerce are as follows:

- Enterprise content management
- E-mail
- Automated online assistants
- Instant messaging
- Newsgroups
- Online shopping and order tracking
- Electronic tickets
- Teleconferencing

Netiquette

Netiquettes are the rules for correct behaviour on the Internet. They distinguish the Internet from traditional forms of communications, such as telephonic conversation, face-to-face meetings, and paper-based letters. It helps you avoid misunderstandings that may arise during communication accomplished through any Internet services, especially e-mail, chat and mailing lists, and so on.

Nature of Poor Netiquette

Poor Netiquette includes the following:

- Poor grammar and spelling errors
- Junk mails
- Harsh language

Rules for Internet Etiquettes

- Be concise; use appropriate language.
- No Spam, and include a subject line.

Characteristics of Good Netiquette

Communications that do not waste the user's time are considered as good netiquette.

Overview of E-Governance Services like Railway Reservation, Passport and e-hospital (Ors)

E-Governance refers to the utilization of the Internet and the World Wide Web for delivering government information and services to the citizen. In the past, all the services provided by government of India, such as postal services, railway ticket booking, applying for passport, etc. were on offline platform and were done manually with no support of information technology. Now, the government has taken many services on information technology platform, better known as **e-governance**.

The use of internet not only delivers the services faster but also brings more transparency between the government and the citizens. e-Governance is also playing a very important role in the railway reservation system. It facilitates the passengers to enquire about the trains available on the basis of source and destination, booking and cancellation of tickets and the status of the booked ticket, etc.

The various advantages of using the online Reservation system are as follows:

- Convenient
- Saves Times and Effort
- Towards a green planet

Reservation and cancellation of train tickets can be done using the official website of **Indian Railways Catering and Tourism Corporation Limited (IRCTC)**, which is **www.irctc.co.in.**

Passport

The government of India has taken many initiatives to lead in the era of e-Governance, and to improve the delivery of public services. The National **e-Governance Plan (NeGP)** includes many high impact e-Governance projects that focus on reforming Passport services in India.

The Ministry of External Affairs is responsible for issuance of Passport to Indian Citizens through a network of 37 Passport offices and 180 Indian **Embassies and Consulates abroad.**

A Passport is essential for those who are traveling abroad for education, tourism, pilgrimage, medical attendance, business purposes and family visits.

The **Passport Seva Project (PSP)** is transforming passport and related services in India to deliver passport services in a reliable, convenient and transparent manner, within defined service levels. Key aspects of the service transformation achieved by PSP are as follows:

- **Anywhere Anytime Access:** Citizens can submit passport application and seek an appointment on payment of passport fees online through the PSP portal (www. passportindia.gov.in) at their convenience. It also provides latest information on all passport related services.
- **Increased Network:** It has extended 37 Passport Offices.
- **State-of-the-Art Technology Infrastructure:** It is also supported by state-of-the-art technology infrastructure which enables end-to-end passport services to be delivered with enhanced security.
- **Call Centre and Helpdesk:** National call centre operating Indian languages enable citizens to obtain passport service related information and receive updates about their passport application on all seven working days.

e-Hospital (ORS)

Information Technology has been playing an important role in improving facilities provided to patients in hospitals. Even today, in major Government hospitals, patients have to stand in long queues to get registered and obtain an **Out-Patient Department (OPD)** Slip before being able to consult a doctor and wait for long hours to consult doctors.

Under Digital India initiative, National Informatics Centre (NIC) has developed an Online Registration System (ORS) to book online OPD appointment for various departments in the government hospital. The patient portal is available over the internet at http://ors.gov.in.

Portal facilitates online appointments with various departments of different Hospitals. The appointment can be taken in the following ways:

- Using **e-Know Your Customer (eKYC)** data of Aadhaar number, if patient's mobile number is registered with Unique Identification Authority of India (UIDAI).

- In case mobile number is not registered with UIDAI, it uses patient's name.

- New Patient will get appointment as well as **Unique Health Identification (UHID)** number. If Aadhaar number is already linked with UHID number, then appointment number will be given and UHID will remain same.

Features

Simple Appointment Process–For first visit to hospital, registration and appointment with doctor, all you have to do is verify yourself using Aadhaar Number, select Hospital, Department, and Date of Appointment, and receive SMS for Appointment.

- **Dashboard Reports:** All the hospitals for which appointment can be taken through web, along with their departments for which online appointment can be taken, are shown in reports. You can see detailed reports showing information about new and old patients taking appointment through this portal.

- **Hospital on Boarding:** Hospitals can come on board this platform and provide their appointment slots for online booking by patients. The system facilitates hospitals to easily manage their registration and appointment process and monitor them.

Process to take appointment for a new patient:

1. Visit the portal http://ors.gov.in/copp/appointment.jsp.

2. If you have Aadhaar number of the patient and mobile number is registered with UIDAI, then **One Time PIN (OTP)** will be sent by UIDAI through SMS. Aadhaar holder would need to give consent to share his/her KYC data as stored in UIDAI with the hospital for the purpose of taking OPD appointment.

3. If patient does not have mobile number and is not registered with UIDAI, then patient's name as in Aadhaar needs to be given. After doing demographic authentication with UIDAI, patient will be requested to give a mobile number and other details like address, age, and so on.

4. In case the user does not have an Aadhaar number, he can take an online appointment but would have to collect the OPD card from the hospital after providing the identity of the patient.

5. User can select the Department in a Government hospital where patient needs to visit for check-up.

6. Thereafter, user will be sent a confirmation through SMS, giving details of OPD appointment.

Accessing E-Governance Services on Mobile Using "UMANG App"

The full form of UMANG is **Unified Mobile Application for New-age Governance**. This App has been developed by **National e-Governance Division (NeGD)** and the **Ministry of Electronics and Information Technology (MeitY)** with the aim of driving mobile governance in India. It is also designed to provide individuals with access to a range of central, state and local government services using only a single platform.

The Government of India is providing all-in-one single unified secure multi-channel freeware mobile app for accessing over **1,200 central** and **state government services** in different Indian languages over Android, iOS, Windows. It supports services such as AADHAR, DigiLocker, Bharat Bill Payment System, PAN, EPFO services, PMKVY services, AICTE, CBSE, tax and fee or utilities bills payments, education, job search, tax, business, health, agriculture, travel, birth certificates, e-District, passport, etc.

This e-Governance service can be accessed through multiple channels, such as mobile app, IVR, website, and so on. You can register on UMANG through the following sites for Web https://web.umang.gov.in/web/#/ and Mobile App https://web.umang.gov.in/uaw/appdown.html.

How to download the UMANG App on your Mobile phone?

1. Scan the **QR Code** provided on the Official **UMANG** App website.

2. Receive the UMANG App link on your phone by making a missed call to **97183-97183**.

3. Get a download link for the App by SMS to phone number provided by you on the

UMANG website.

Ho w to Register on UMANG App?

The following steps guide you to a new user registration on UMANG App:

1. Launch the UMANG App and click on the Register option, as shown in *Figure 7.64*:

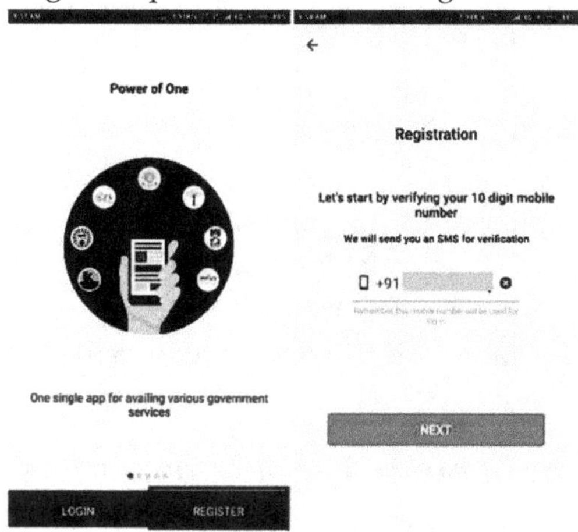

Figure 7.64: *Registration on UMANG*

2. Once you click the registration option, you will be redirected to the mobile number verification page. On this page, you need to provide your mobile number in order to generate an OTP to complete the UMANG App registration process, as shown in *Figure 7.63*.

3. Once you have generated and input the **OTP**, you will be asked to create an **MPIN** and once you have set an **MPIN**, the registration is complete and you can view the UMANG App Home Page. This page shows a short list of recently opened services available through the UMANG App, as shown in *Figure 7.65*:

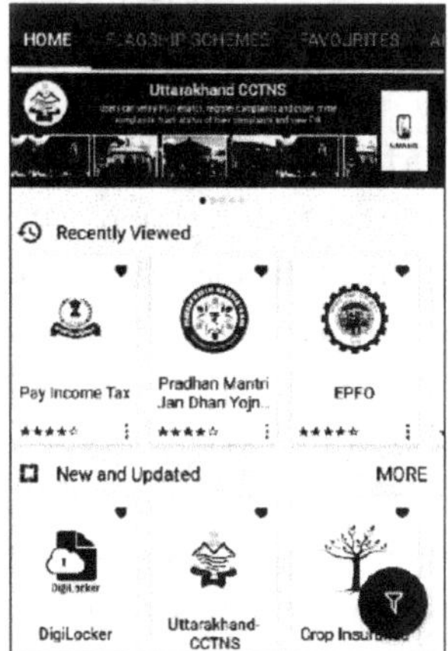

Figure 7.65: *UMANG App Home page*

UMANG App Login

You can log into the UMANG App using various methods as follows:

1. Mobile number registered with **UMANG App** and **MPIN**.

2. Mobile number registered with **UMANG App** and **OTP**.

3. In case you have updated your social media account details with the app, you can login using your **Facebook**, **Google+**, or **Twitter** credentials.

Key Features and Benefits of UMANG App

The following are some key features of this Government scheme app:

*   Helps in searching for a specific State or Central Government service using the in-app filter.
*   Available in multiple regional languages as well as English.
*   You can avail over 150 different Central and State government services using the App.
*   Option of easy online payment of various utility bills, gas, water, electricity, and so on.
*   Key integration services on offer through UMANG App include Digilocker and Aadhaar.

The services available through the UMANG Application for Mobile are as follows:

*   **Digilocker:** A secure cloud-based platform for storing, sharing and verifying documents/ certificates.
*   **Aadhaar Card:** It allows you to view as well as download your Aadhaar Card from Digilocker Account.
*   **EPFO:** It allows you to monitor your **Employee Provident Fund (EPF)** Account Balance, EPF Pension Account Balance, and so on using UAN and OTP to registered mobile number.
*   **NPS: National Pension System (NPS)** Login through UMANG App allows you to check your Tier 1 and Tier 2 Account balances, etc. through PRAN and password.
*   **Pay Income Tax:** UMANG application allows tax payers to pay their Advance Tax, Self-Assessment Tax using Challan 280. After tax

payment, the tax payment challan can also be tracked using the Track Challan Status service.

- **e-RaktKosh:** It is designed to provide access to blood banks through greater digitisation and connectivity of blood banks across the country.
- **Jeevan Pramaan:** This service is available only to pensioners. It allows pensioners to generate a Life Certificate using a mobile handset connected to an external biometric device.
- **CBSE:** You can view exam results and locate the exam centre for all your CBSE Board and competitive exams.
- **Passport Seva:** It is an initiative by Ministry of External affairs. Govt. of India. It enables simple processes for delivery of passport and related services.

Digital Locker

DigiLocker is a **digital locker** service operated by the **Department of Electronics and Information Technology (DeitY)** Govt. of India. It enables Indian citizens to store certain official documents on the cloud, as shown in *Figure 7.66*. The service is aimed towards reducing the need to carry physical documents. You can store data up to 1 GB like store identification card issued by government agencies, education certificates, PAN cards, driving license, vehicle document, and so on.

Figure 7.66: *Digital Locker*

Digital Locker portal

To use this portal, visit **digitallocker.gov.in**. Sign up for Digital locker using Aadhaar card number. The one-time password sent to the Aadhaar associated mobile number needs to be entered.

Digital Locker system has the following objectives:

- It enables digital empowerment of residents by providing them with Digital Locker on the cloud.
- It enables e-Signing of documents and makes them available electronically and online. It minimizes the use of physical documents.
- Ensures authenticity of the e-documents, thereby eliminating usage of fake documents.
- Provides secure access to Government issued documents through a web portal and mobile application for residents.
- Anytime, anywhere access to the documents by the resident.
- Open and interoperable standards based architecture to support a well-structured standard document format and easy sharing of documents across departments and agencies.
- Ensures privacy and authorized access to residents' data.

Components of Digital Locker System

Repository is a collection of e-Documents which are uploaded by issuers in a standard format. It exposes a set of standard APIs for secure real-time search and access.

Access Gateway provides a secure online mechanism for requesters to access e-documents from various repositories in real-time using **e-Document Uniform Resource Indicator (URI)**. The URI is a link to the e-Document uploaded by an issuer in the repository. The gateway will identify the address of the repository where the e-Document is stored based on the URI and will fetch the e-Document from that repository.

Conclusion

E-mail is a method of sending message over digital communication such as Internet, anywhere in the world at a very cost-effective rate. So, the structure of e-mail includes e-mail address, header, body, signature and attachment. Then we learnt what is bounced e-mail, how to configure e-mail client and web-based e-mail. The most common and highly used is Outlook 2013. Thus, we saw how to use e-mail by adding an e-mail account in MS Outlook 2013, and opening an e-mail account. Further, you learnt what is a mailbox, that is, inbox and outbox; how to create an e-mail; and how to reply to it and forward it. Next, you covered sorting and searching e-mails. Then we covered attaching files in an e-mail and how to create an e-mail signature. The e-mail signature normally includes full name, job title, organization name and division, phone and fax number, physical address, e-mail address and URL. Then you jumped into social networking and E-commerce. Social network refers to a group or individual and organization together via network, to share thoughts and interests. There are many web-based social network services available such as Facebook, Twitter and LinkedIn. WhatsApp, Facebook Messenger and Telegram are Instant Messaging services, offers online chatting, video calling and sharing text message using Internet connection. Electronic commerce refers to the buying and selling goods or services using the internet and also exchange of currency for goods or services online. The government of India has taken many initiatives to lead in the era of e-Governance to improve the delivery of public services such as rail reservation, passport seva and e-hospital. The new topic discussed with mobile apps, that is, UMANG APPs. It is a unified mobile application for new-age governance. This app has been developed by National e-governance division and the ministry of electronics and information technology.

Lastly, you covered DigiLocker, which is a digital locker service operated by the department of electronics and information technology, Government of India.

In the next chapter, you will learn about digital financial tools and applications.

Model Questions and Answers

A. Multiple Choice Questions.

1. Which of the following symbols separates the two parts of an e-mail address?

   a. _   b. &
   c. @   d. None of these

2. Usually, the e-mail address is in __________.

   a. Lowercase   b. Proper case
   c. Uppercase   d. All of these

3. Which of these is the easiest way of communication?

   a. E-mail   b. Telephone
   c. Fax   d. Letter

4. What do you need to do before you delete a message from your inbox?

   a. Erase the message
   b. Select the message
   c. Deselect the message
   d. Backspace the message

5. To move a message, point to the message and then:

   a. Point to the folder you want to move
   b. Click the mouse and drag it
   c. Double-click the message
   d. None of the above

6. Mail access starts with client when user needs to download e-mail from the:

   a. Mailbox
   b. Mail Server
   c. Mail host
   d. Internet

7. Under the Digital India initiative, __________ had developed online registration system.

   a. Nationality Information centre
   b. Nation information centre
   c. National Informatics centre
   d. Nationalism informatics centre

8. Which of the following is the most popular social networking site on the internet?

   a. MySpace   b. Orkut
   c. Facebook   d. Friendset

9. What services are available on UMANG?

   a. EPFO   b. Pension Portal
   c. CBSE   d. All of the above

10. __________ is the exchange of computer-stored messages by telecommunication.

   a. E-Web   b. E-mail
   c. E-net   d. E-chart

B. State whether the following Statements are True or False.

1. E-mail is information stored on a computer that is exchanged between two users over telecommunications.
2. When referring to e-mail, an attachment is a file sent with an e-mail message.
3. In addition to text message being sent over e-mail, it is not possible to attach a file or other data in an e-mail.
4. Your e-mail address must be unique.
5. You cannot delete e-mails from a web-based e-mail account.
6. You cannot store web-based e-mail messages in online folders.
7. You can only send one attachment per e-mail message.
8. When you reply to a message, you need to enter the text in the Subject: field.
9. If you want to respond to the sender of a message, click the Respond button.
10. You cannot format text in an e-mail message.

C. Match the following:

1.	POP3:	a.	FTP
2.	FTP:	b.	MIME
3.	Format of e-mail attachments:	c.	UPI
4.	Standard for Transfer of Electronic Mail:	d.	Mail
5.	Unified Payments Interface:	e.	Twitter
6.	Shares his or her opinion on different topics for a target audience:	f.	Ray Tomlinson
7.	It is also called micro blogging:	g.	SMTP
8.	Father of E-mail:	h.	Blogger
9.	Full of UMANG:	i.	Encryption
10.	E-mail message can be protected by Governance:	j.	Unified Mobile application for New-age
		k.	Unique Payments Interface

D. Fill in the blanks:

Digital Signature   POP   Less cash more digital
Mail Box   Flame   X.509   Spam   B2C
VoIP   Uploading   Forwarding

1. ________ is a protocol that is used to retrieve e-mail from a mail server.
2. An inflammatory remark or a message usually associated with e-mail or an article posted to a newsgroup is referred to as ________.
3. ________ is for authenticating a document in Electronix Universe.
4. Mail access starts with client when user needs to download e-mail from the ________.
5. ________ is the Slogan f UPI.
6. Unsolicited commercial e-mail is known as ________.
7. ________ is a digital certificate standard.
8. Many instant messaging services offer video calling features such as ________ and Web conferencing services.
9. The exchange of information, products or services between a ________ as opposed to between two businesses.
10. The process of transferring files from a computer on the Internet to your computer is called ________.

Short Questions with Answers.

1. **What is E-mail?**

   Answers: E-mail is short for electronic mail. It is similar to a letter, sent through the Internet to a recipient. An e-mail address is required to receive e-mail and that address is unique to the user.

2. **What are the benefits and features of using e-mail?**

   Answers:
   a. It is quick—recipient receives the e-mail as soon as they go online and check their mail.
   b. It is secure.
   c. It is low cost.
   d. Photos, documents and other files can be attached to an e-mail, so that more information can be shared.
   e. One e-mail can be sent to more than one recipient at a time.

3. **How to forward an e-mail message?**

   Answers: When you receive an e-mail message, you can read, delete, or reply to that e-mail. You can also send that e-mail to another person, known as forwarding an e-mail.
   a. Access your e-mail account or client program.
   b. Open the e-mail message you want to forward.
   c. At the top of the e-mail message, click the Forward icon.
   d. A new e-mail message window will open. In the To: field, enter the e-mail address of the person you want to forward the message.
   e. In the subject field, modify the e-mail subject.
   f. In the body of the e-mail message, type a message explaining the reason for forwarding the e-mail.
   g. When you are ready to forward the e-mail, click the Send button.

4. **How to create an e-mail account?**

   Answers: E-mail is a way to send and receive information over the internet. However, as there are many different e-mail and webmail clients, the steps used to start an account differ.

   To create a new e-mail account with Google Gmail, do the following:
   a. Go to the Gmail website.
   b. At the bottom of the sign in screen, click the create account link.
   c. On the account creation screen, fill out all the fields and then click next.
   d. On the next screen, fill out your birth date and gender as well as any optional information that you are comfortable with, then click Next.
   e. Read Google's Privacy and Terms, then click the I Agree button.
   f. Click the Next button until you have moved through the features menu.
   g. Click the Go to Gmail button and you will be able to access your new account.

5. **What is an Attachment?**

   Answers: An attachment is a file sent with an e-mail message. An attachment can be a picture, document, a movie, a sound file or any other file that requires another program to open it.

6. **What is social networking?**

   Answers: Group of individuals and organizations together using a medium for sharing thoughts, interest and activities is called social networking. There are many web-based social network services in market such as Twitter, Facebook, LinkedIn, and so on, which are easy to use and more interactive. Many users are connected within the country and with people overseas as well. There are apps created for these network services to use it in mobile, such as WhatsApp and so on.

7. **What is E-mail Address?**

   Answers: It is a unique name for every user e-mail account. Users can send and receive messages according to the e-mail address. E-mail is in the form of username@domainname. Consider webcreative@futurejobs.com is an e-mail address where the username is webcreative and the domain name is futurejobs.com. An @ (at) symbol divides the username and the domain name.

E-mail addresses are not case-sensitive and the address should not have spaces.

8. What is the UMANG App?

Answers: UMANG, Unified Mobile Application for New-age Governance, is all about e-governance. It is developed by Ministry of Electronics and Information Technology and National e-Governance Division. It is an evolving platform designed for citizens of India to offer them access to the pan India e-Gov services from the Central, State and Agencies of government on app, web, SMS and IVR channels.

9. What services are available on UMANG?

Answers:

a. myPAN: New PAN Card application form 49A for Individual, firm, etc. We can change PAN card details using the CSF form. We can track PAN card status and make payment online.

b. EPFO: EPFO assists the Central board in monitoring the PF for the workforce engaged in the organized sector in India. The services offered in the app are generic search services and employee services.

c. CBSE: We can view exam results and locate the exam center for all your CBSE Board and competitive exams.

d. GST: Goods and Services Tax Network provides GST related IT infrastructure and services. It plays a crucial role in registration and search of GST taxpayers, GST payment and filing of returns.

10. How to register for UMANG App?

Answers: UMANG app is available for Windows, iOS, and Android platform. Download the UMANG app from our respective app store such as Google Play Store for Android users. During the UMANG Installation, we have to choose the desired language and verify the mobile number through the OTP. It also asks permission for call and SMS.

a. Launch the UMANG app.

b. Click New user. The Select Registration Mode screen appears.

c. Select the Mobile Number option. The Registration screen appears.

d. Enter the mobile number and click the proceed icon to continue. The Mobile Number Verification screen appears.

e. Enter the OTP received on the mobile number. If the entered OTP is correct, then the Set MPIN screen appears.

f. In Enter your MPIN, enter the MPIN to be set.

g. In Confirm MPIN, enter the same MPIN for confirmation.

h. Choose Proceed and answer the security question and continue.

i. Now, enter Aadhar number if we want to link it or click Skip to move on to the Profile Information screen, where we will have to enter profile details and click Save & Proceed.

j. This completes the registration process and you will be redirected to the home screen.

Descriptive Type Questions.

1. Explain an e-mail message and its components.

2. What are E-mail Etiquettes?

3. Write down the advantages and Disadvantages of E-mail.

4. What are key benefits for citizens for using the UMANG App?

5. What is an E-mail Provider? Explain the prominent e-mail service providers?

6. What is E-commerce? Which act governs the activities of e-commerce in India? Give some application of E-Commerce.

7. What is Outlook Express? How is it used?

8. What are the different types of e-Commerce available on the Internet?

9. How can the contents of an e-mail be protected?

10. How is an e-mail is delivered using Internet?

Answers

A.	1. c	2. a	3. a	4. b	5. b
	6. a	7. c	8. c	9. d	10. b

B.	1. T	2. T	3. F	4. T	5. F
	6. F	7. F	8. F	9. F	10. F

C.	1. d	2. a	3. b	4. g	5. c
	6. h	7. e	8. f	9. j	10. i

D.	1. b	2. e	3. a	4. d	5. c
	6. g	7. f	8. i	9. h	10. j

■■

CHAPTER 8

Digital Financial Tools and Applications

Structure

In this chapter, we will learn the following topics:

- Introducing digital financial tools
- OTP and QR codes
- UPI
- Aadhaar-enabled payment system
- Unstructured supplementary service data
- Cards
- e-Wallet
- Point of sale
- POS software and hardware
- NEFT
- RTGS
- Immediate payment service
- Online bill payment

Objectives

After completing this chapter, the readers will be able to:

- To know about Digital Financial Tools.
- Understanding the Knowledge of the InterNet banking Modes.
- Use the Digital Locker and will be able to store documents in Digital Locker.

Digital financial services are accessed and delivered through digital channels, including payments, credit and saving, and so on. M-banking is the use of a mobile phone to access banking services and execute financial transaction. The Government of India introduced new services to move toward cashless economy; all transactions are carried out using different payment methods such as Aadhaar-enabled payment system, unified payment interface, immediate payment service and taking several measures to promote and encourage digital payments in India.

Introducing Digital Financial Tools

Digital financial tools expand the delivery of basic financial services to the people through new technologies like Internet, mobile phones and transfer of money through new digital channels. These channels have significantly driven down the costs for customers and service providers, opening the door to provide 24 hour service for 365 days, as shown in *Figure 8.1*.

Figure 8.1: *Digital Financial Service*

Digital Financial Tools

You define digital finance as financial services delivered over digital infrastructure, including mobile and Internet. Mobile phones, computers, or cards used over **Point-Of-Sale (POS)** devices connect individuals and businesses to a digitized national payments infrastructure, enabling seamless transactions across all parties.

It includes:

- All types of financial services, such as payments, savings accounts, credit, insurance, and other financial products.
- All types of users, including individuals at all income levels, businesses of all sizes, and government entities at all levels.
- All types of providers of financial services, including banks, payment providers, other financial institutions, telecom companies, **financial technology (FinTech)** start-ups, retailers, and other businesses.

Understanding OTP (One Time Password) and QR (Quick Response) Code

One-Time Password (OTP) is also known as **One-Time Pin**. It is a string of characters or numbers automatically generated that is valid for only one login session or transaction, on a computer system or other digital device. This prevents some forms of identity theft by making sure that a captured username/password pair cannot be used for the second time.

One-time passwords can be sent to the user's phone through SMS or Push messaging and are used to protect web-based services, private credentials and data. OTPs will minimize the risk of fraudulent login attempts and thus, the risk of stolen data.

When users create a digital asset or an account, they are prompted to enable the two-factor authentication system such as username and password. Next time, when the user tries to login, the system sends the temporary password (either four or six digits) to the registered mobile handset, and the user punches the code into the system. The code is a random series of numeric and alphanumeric characters. These OTPs are usually valid for a certain number of minutes. The information flow works like this:

- User enters the username and password.
  - Request is sent to backend.
- Username and password is matched.
- User receives OTP through SMS.
- User enters OTP and logs into the site.

OTP works through random algorithms that generate a new and random password each time they are used. The algorithm always uses random characters and symbols to create a password so that a hacker/cracker cannot guess the future password. It uses several techniques to create a password, including:

- **Time-Synchronization:** OTP is valid only for a short period of time.
- **Mathematical Algorithm:** The password is generated using random numbers processed within an algorithm.

Why is a one-time password safe?

This prevents some forms of identity theft by making sure that a captured username/password pair cannot be used a second time. Typically, the user's login name stays the same, and the one-time password changes with each login. One-time passwords are a form of strong authentication, providing much better protection to e-Banking, corporate networks and other systems containing sensitive data.

Features of OTP

There are three characteristics of OTP which makes it a viable option to implement and ensure data safety. These features are secured access, simple infrastructure, and swift delivery. The cycle of OTP begins and ends in a couple of seconds. Through OTP SMS, the users receive four or six digit codes. Apart from the SMS system, users also receive the OTP through IVR, or it can be generated by the consumers and delivered through SMS.

Quick Response Code (QR)

The QR code system was invented in 1994 by the Japanese company **Denso Wave**. It is a two-dimensional barcode used for adding web links to a printed page. When you scan such a QR barcode using a webcam or mobile phone camera, the QR application takes you to a Website, a YouTube video or some other web content. It is an easy way of sending people to a site without having to type a URL.

The code contains information in both the horizontal and vertical axis. Compared to regular barcodes, it allows much larger amounts of raw data to be embedded. These can be numeric, alphanumeric or binary data of which up to **2953 bytes** can be stored.

The smallest element (black or white square grid) of the QR code is called a **module**. A QR code is composed of a combination of black and white modules, position detection patterns, timing patterns, format information that contains error correction level, which includes **Reed-Solomon error correction**.

Figure 8.2 shows the structure of a QR code's elements:

Figure 8.2: *Structure of QR Code*

- **Position detection patterns:** The position detection patterns are arranged at three corners of the QR codes (Micro QR has one.) The position of QR code is detected with the position detection patterns that allow high-speed reading. It can be read from any direction, which significantly improves work efficiency. From any position of *A, B, C*, the rate of black and white modules is 1:1:3:1:1 to specify the rotation of the code.

- **Alignment pattern:** The alignment pattern is used for position detection when there is displacement of modules due to distortion.

- **Margin:** The margin is a blank area around the QR code. Model 1 and 2 require a margin of four modules and Micro QR code requires that of two modules.

- **Timing pattern:** White and black modules are alternately arranged to determine the coordinate.

- **Format information:** It contains the error correction rate and mask pattern of the code. The format information is read first when the code is decoded.

- **Error-correction code (Reed-Solomon code):** Reed-Solomon code is applied to restore the data when a part of QR code is missing or damaged. The restoration rate varies on 4 different error correction levels.

QR codes contain other types of information

- Business card can contain an electronic version of the contact information. Scan the code, and the reader application adds the contact to your address list.

- It can contain an e-mail message with a subject and message text. That message can be a request for information so that in return you might get a reply email with additional information and attached files.

- It can contain a geographical location. Scan the code on a poster advertising for a restaurant, and its location becomes available to your navigation software, informing you how to get to that place.

- Now, let us look at some business-related scenarios where you would use QR codes.

- Use a QR Code to direct a customer to the URL of your website, Facebook, Twitter or other social media pages.

- Use it on your business card with your contact details embedded inside the code.

- Use it to link to a Google Maps location for your new store location.

Unified Payment Interface (UPI)

A **Unified Payment Interface (UPI)** is an instant real-time payment system which allows users to transfer money between two bank accounts on a mobile. It was developed by **National Payments Corporation** of India facilitating inter-bank transactions. To carry out any transaction, a user will only have to use a virtual address, known as a **Virtual Payment Address (VPA)**. UPI has been developed by the **National Payments Corporation of India (NPCI)** and is regulated by the **Reserve Bank of India (RBI)**.

UPI has now become the most preferred form of digital payment. The UPI payment application is compatible with most banks and digital wallets. Some of the apps include Google Tez, Bank, PhonePe, Paytm, and Airtel Payments

Features of UPI

Some of the features of UPI allows users to benefit from a number of services. The transactions that can be carried out using UPI:

- It offers instant money transfer via mobile device 24x7 for all 365 days.
- Sending and receiving funds from/to bank account using VPA.
- Making requests for funds from/to the bank account using mobile number.

Transaction Limit

Per day transaction limit is up to **Rs. 1 lakh**. The transaction limit may be revised from time to time.

The following are the types of the transactions which can be conducted through UPI:

- **Remittances:** By using this app, you can send or transfer money quickly to your friends and family.
- **Bill payments:** Pay utility bills such as mobile bills, electricity bills and shopping bills.
- **Merchant transactions:** Booking movie tickets online and buying groceries on an online app.

Register with UPI

Here are the steps you need to follow for registering on your bank's UPI app:

1. Download the UPI application from the Google Play App Store or the Bank's website.
2. Once you have finished downloading the app, create a profile by entering your details for the registration, such as your name, a virtual ID and password. The virtual ID you create will be your payment address.
3. There is an option, such as Add or Link or Manage Bank Account which allows you to link your bank account number with the newly created virtual ID.
4. When you make payment through UPI, it is required to enter the M-PIN which has to be set at the time of registration. To generate M-PIN, perform the following steps:
5. Choose the bank account from which you want to pay using UPI and Mobile Banking Registration/Generate MPIN.
6. If you click Generate MPIN, you will receive a One-Time Password (OTP) from the bank on your registered mobile number.
7. Now you will enter the last 6 digits of debit card number and the expiry date of your card.
8. Enter the 6 digits of OTP and MPIN and click submit button and your MPIN will be generated.

How to Make Payments Using UPI?

1. Log on to your bank's UPI mobile application.
2. Select the option make payment/send or Pay
3. Enter the beneficiary's virtual ID and amount to be transferred followed by the account number.
4. You get a confirmation message, once again check the payment details to confirm the payment.
5. Enter the MPIN to authenticate your payment. Click the Submit button, the amount will be transferred in seconds.

How to Receive Payment Using UPI?

To receive money from a person, it will help you understand how to accept or decline if someone sends you a UPI payment.

1. Login to your UPI app. Go the UPI payment option.
2. Click the collect or request money option.
3. Enter the payer's virtual ID, and the amount that needs to be credited.
4. Check to review the payment details and then click to Confirm.
5. The request money will be sent to the payer in the form of a notification.
6. Now, the payer accepts the request to send notification. He/she will be prompted to enter the UPI MPIN to complete the money transfer transaction.
7. If the payer is the correct UPI MPIN, the requested amounted will be debited from the payee's account.
8. Once you know the transaction is complete, both the payer and payee will get verification about the transactions, the fund will be transferred immediately to the payee.

Aadhaar-Enabled Payment System

Aadhaar-Enabled Payment System (AePS) is a secure payment platform for financial transactions based on Unique Identification Number that enables a user for the cashless transactions. This system developed by the National Payments Corporation of India allows the user to perform necessary banking transactions like balance enquiry, cash deposit, cash withdrawal and remittances through a Business Correspondent.

RBI has set no limit for transactions made through **AePS**. Some banks have set a daily limit of maximum Rs. 50,000 on transactions.

The following services offered by AePS are available in both inter-bank and intra-bank modes:

- Cash Withdrawal
- Cash Deposit
- Balance Enquiry
- Aadhaar to Aadhaar Fund Transfer
- Mini Statement

Features of Aadhaar-Enabled Payment System are as follows

- Supports debit cards, magnetic stripe cards, virtual cards and card less transactions.
- Aadhaar biometric-based transactions.
- Supports various network protocols (CDMA/GPRS/PSTN/IP).
- Manages multiple Technology Service Providers (TSP) on-boarded by the Bank.
- Auto locks Micro ATMs when idle.

There are a number of benefits of AePS. Some of those are mentioned below:

- One can pay money, deposit amount, get a mini statement and check the balance.
- A banking correspondent of any bank can do the specified transaction of any bank.
- There is no requirement for a debit card.
- It is fast and secure.
- Banking correspondent can reach to the distant rural place with the micro POS.
- Shopkeepers can also use AePS to take payments.

How to use AePS?

Aeps is a payment method using a unique identification number. This feature is available in the forms of payment systems that is credit money into the beneficiary's account and enable account holders to withdraw cash. If you want to start using Aeps to withdraw or deposit cash, you need to link your bank account with your Aadhaar number. Approach the business correspondent; he/she will guide you to a basic banking service using a micro-ATM. This is done by entering the customer's UID number, fingerprints and financial transaction through micro-ATM.

The process of using AePS is quite easy:

1. Go to a micro-ATM or banking correspondent.
2. Enter your 12-digit Aadhaar number in the PoS Machine.
3. Choose the type of transaction, such as cash deposit, withdrawal, mini statement, fund transfer, balance enquiry.
4. Select the bank name.
5. Enter the amount for the transaction.
6. Confirm the transaction using your biometric (fingerprint or iris scan).
7. The transaction gets completed in a second. A bank correspondent gives the receipt details.

Unstructured Supplementary Service Data

Unstructured Supplementary Service Data (USSD) is also referred to as **Quick Codes** or "Feature codes". It is a communications protocol used by GSM cellular telephones to communicate with the mobile network operator's computers, as shown in *Figure 8.3:*

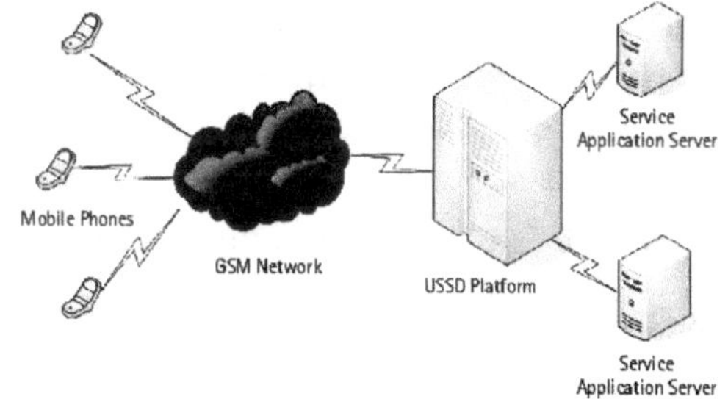

Figure 8.3: *USSD Platform*

It is a technology platform through which information can be transmitted through a GSM network on a basic phone and will be available on all mobile phones with SMS facility. To use USSD, users will have to dial **99#** to get the mobile balance. You must have noticed that this code starts with *** (asterisk)** and ends with **# (hash)**. These are the USSD codes. These codes directly communicate with the server of Telecom Company known as

USSD.

How to Send Money Using USSD 99#, Using IFSC Code & Bank Account Number?

1. Dial 99# from your registered mobile number.
2. Proceed to key in 3 letters of your bank short name, first 4 letters of bank IFSC, or 2-digit bank numeric code.
3. Choose the option to transfer funds using IFSC code and mobile number.
4. Enter beneficiary/payee account number, IFSC code and transaction amount.
5. Enter key in MPIN and last 4 digits of your bank account number. A confirmation message will be displayed on screen.

Card (Credit/Debit)

It is a piece of plastic card that contains personal data in a machine-readable form and is used to obtain cash.

Credit Card

A Credit card allows you to use money from a bank to make purchase. The card issuer pays for the purchase, and the cardholder pays the issuer at a later date. It is a convenient way of buying things, especially if you do not have cash handy. The card issuer creates a revolving account and provides the cardholder with a line of credit. The customer can borrow money from this line of credit to buy things.

Credit card makes money in three ways:

- Transaction fees charged to the merchant every time you use your credit card.
- Interest payments when you do not pay off your debt.
- Fees, like late payment or annual fees.

Debit Card

A debit card is a plastic card or checking card or bank card that can be used instead of cash while making purchases. Debit cards are like digitized versions of cheque books; they are linked to your bank account. Any time you use the debit card to buy something, money is deducted from your account as soon as the transaction occurs. With the debit card, you can only spend the money you have available to you. It is also used to conveniently withdraw cash from ATMs.

Difference between Credit and Debit cards is as follows:

Credit Card	Debit Card
• The payment is made by the bank on the customer's behalf	• The payment is made directly through the customer's account linked to the card.
• Pay later.	• Pay now
• The bank account is not pre-requisite for issuing a credit card.	• The bank account is a must for issuing a debit card.
• The maximum limit of withdrawing money is determined according to the credit rating of the holder.	• The maximum limit of withdrawing money will be less than the money lying in the saving bank account.
• The card holder has to pay the credit card bill within 30 days of every month.	• The is no bill; the amount is directly deducted from the customer's account.
• Interest is charged when payment is not made to the bank within a specified time period.	• No interest is charged.

Figure 8.4: *Difference between Credit and Debit*

e-Wallet

An e-Wallet is a digital system which stores a person's payment information. This is the short form for electronic wallet, i.e., the **e** of e-Wallet stands for electronic. You also call it a digital wallet. The e-Wallet stores users' cards digitally so that they can buy things electronically. It is a system that securely stores users' payment information and passwords for payment methods, and users can complete purchases easily and quickly with near-field communications technology. It is used for transactions made online through a computer or smartphone. It needs to be linked with the individual's bank account to make payments. The main objective of e-Wallet is to make paperless money transaction.

e-Wallet has mainly **two components – software** and **information**. Software components store personal information and provide security and encryption of the data, whereas information component is a database of details provided by the user, which includes their name, shipping address, payment method, amount to be paid, credit, debit card details, and so on.

Benefits of e-Wallet are as follows:

- Send and receive payments anywhere in the world.
- Unlimited transfers.
- Ease of use without having to enter your debit/credit card details for every online transaction.
- Manage your account from your mobile phone.

- Security for your bank account and credit card numbers.
- Access your communications faster.
- Receive wired funds/transfer directly into your e-Wallet.

Why use e-Wallet?

e-Wallet saves you time because you do not have to look for your credit card or bank account information every time you make a payment. You can use e-Wallet for the following payments:

- Utility payments
- Buying online
- Recharging mobile phones

How does e-Wallet work?

e-Wallet provides the ability to store multiple credit cards, debit cards and bank account information for making faster payments. You can create two separate profiles for both credit and debit cards.

PoS (Point of Sale)

Point of sale is a stage at which a customer makes a payment to the merchant in exchange of goods or service. In this, the merchant prepares an invoice for the customer, calculates the amount owed by the customer and after that, provides options to customer for making payment (either by Credit or Debit card).

> **Activity:** A group of 2-3 students can discuss the importance of opening a bank account and then proceed to the branch to open an account. One student can come to withdraw the scholarship amount received in his account by filling the withdrawal slip available with the cashier and then inquiring about Education Loan for further studies.

Understanding Point of Sale Terminology

Understanding what a POS system is—it is software and hardware components—will enable you to make an educated buying decision. Point of sales refers to where consumers take their purchased goods and pay for the items. Supermarkets, stores and other business firms make use of a POS system; it also refers to the way of transactions through the

use of a machine or computer system. The electronic cash register is the basic of POS system. The items purchased and passed through a cash register detect the item's code and print a receipt.

Components of a POS System

POS system consists of software and hardware components which makes your daily business operations for billing in a retail store. The dealer calculates the total amount owed by the customer and takes print for that bill and also gives options for customers to make the payment.

POS Software

Point of sale software is installed on POS hardware and it is either a local server or internet connection. It is a software on calculating sales through cash registers. It is a system that software program helps the whole system and is responsible on sending and receiving information in the system.

POS Hardware

POS hardware is the component of the POS system. It includes a display screen, you can see the full product line, create order, view customer information and sale reports. It is also synced with your backend site. It helps you manage database easily and save time to again enter the products being purchased. Barcode is used in retail stores, and the scanner is linked with an inventory system to update the product accordingly. Printer to print receipts. And the card machine to process payments by debit or credit cards through POS terminal.

Some other components are considered as:

- **Power Backup:** Take backup, install UPS to prevent data losses during a power cut.
- **Connecting the components:** If you use a cloud-based POS, you need to connect to the internet for accessing hardware components.
- **Using an iPad POS:** If you use an iPad in the store as the POS hardware, it helps if you use the product for scanning for payments.
- **Printing receipts:** Connect the iPad or POS system to a printer for taking receipts.

Benefits of a Point of Sale Software

There are several benefits of using a Point of Sale software in the store. We discuss some of them below:

1. **Billing and Order Processing:** The system has the basic functionality of billing and order

processing by scanning items and capturing, adding discount, generating order invoice and different payments modes.

2. **Sales Monitoring and Reporting:** POS systems must be able to report hourly, daily, weekly, and monthly to generate report on sales result so that the sellers can easily understand the overall success of their business.

    Some of the features of an advanced POS sales trends, such as seasonal demand in products, prediction on the basis of sales trends, and information relating to stock management, are reporting on your store's sales performance.

3. **Inventory and Stock Management:** The most important function of POS system is inventory management; it keeps track of all products so you know when it is time to order/or not order specific products. The POS system should enable you to:

    a. Scan and count product digitally.

    b. Manage your stock by creating product variations such as size and color.

    c. Identify pieces of inventory with a unique serial number.

    d. Track inventory levels across multiple locations.

    e. Enable seamless ordering such as automatically setting custom reorders of best-sellers.

4. **Cross Channel Returns Management:** Some of the functionalities of a POS returns management is returns for one sales order at different time intervals. It should enter details, like the reason for return, salesperson's name, and remarks.

5. **Customer Management:** It creates strong relationships with the customers. A POS should have customer relationship management to track all customer data.

    The POS system should enable you to:

    a. Attach a sale/transaction to a customer.

    b. Keep track of your customer's purchase history.

    c. Capture customer information such as name, age, birthday, phone number and email address.

6. **Employee Reporting and Management:** The performance of the employees can make or break the success of a store having the ability to set sales target as well as know who your top performance.

    The POS system should enable you to:

    a. Add employees to your system.

    b. Create and modify schedules for employees based on forecasted activity.

    c. E-mail schedules to employees.

    d. Track employees' hours weekly and overtime.

7. **Loyalty Programs and Gift Cards:** As the sales of gift cards is increasing every year, your POS system must have the capability to manage and track your customer loyalty incentives using the POS system.

InterNet banking

InterNet banking is an electronic system which enables the customers to conduct transactions on a bank's website and perform activities such as maintaining account, transferring money, and paying bills. It is safe and secure, but the only thing required is that the customer must have the Internet connection on computer or mobile, as shown in *Figure 8.5:*

Figure 8.5: *InterNet banking*

To access InterNet banking

1. Open the bank's secure website.

2. Login to the InterNet banking facility by using the Customer ID and password, as shown in *Figure 8.6:*

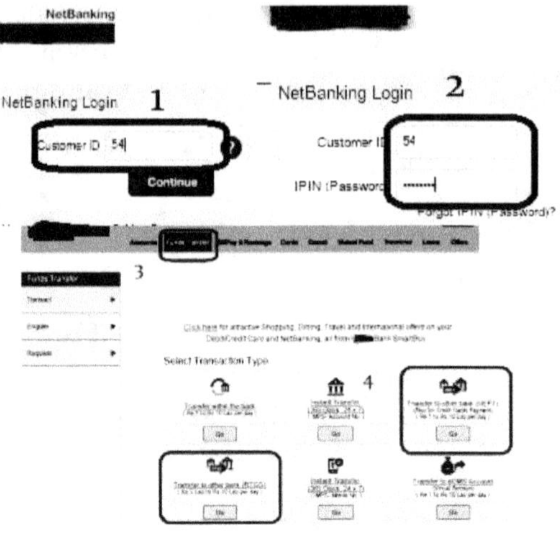

Figure 8.6: *Accessing InterNet banking*

Features

By using InterNet banking, the user can:

- View account balances, statement history, recent transactions and transfer the fund between the customer's linked accounts.
- Pay credit card bills.
- View the records of paid cheques, order and cheque books.
- Pay income tax, online tax remittance and other tax.
- Apply online for loan and top up of existing loan.
- Invest in mutual funds and buy insurance.
- Pay utility bills (electricity, telephone, gas, and mobile).
- Get the Demand Draft in favour of anybody.

> **Note:** Do not give password to anybody else under any circumstances.

National Electronic Fund Transfer (NEFT)

National Electronic Funds Transfer is the most prominent inter-bank electronic funds transfer system of India, which provides a facility to bank customers to transfer the funds easily and securely on a one-to-one basis, which saves the time and is done via electronic messages. It is a **net** transfer facility, executed in hourly batches, as shown *Figure 8.7*:

Figure 8.7: *NEFT/RTGS Procedure*

How NEFT works?

Figure 8.8 shows an example. Consider the customer as a person who transfers the money and the recipient as a person who will get the money.

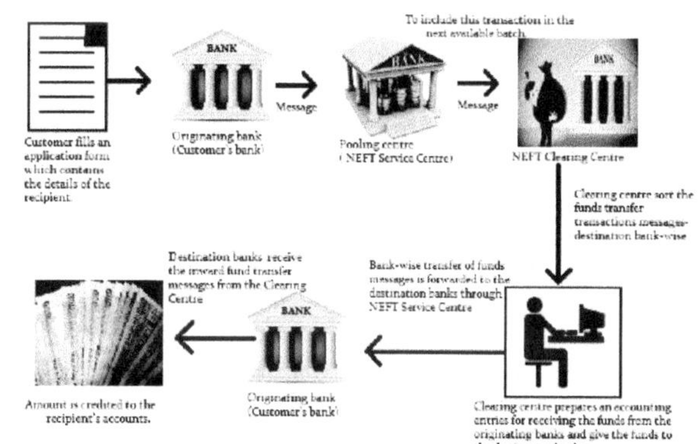

Figure 8.8: *Working of NEFT*

Real Time Gross Settlement (RTGS)

Real time gross settlement (RTGS) is an inter-bank transfer system, which transfers money from one bank to another on a **real time** and on **gross** basis. It is used for high-value transactions which require an immediate clearing and is used to transfer of Rs. 2 Lakhs and above.

> **Note:** Once the payment is processed, it is final and is irrevocable.

Figure 8.9 summarizes the differences between NEFT and RTGS:

BASIS	NEFT	RTGS
Full Form	National Electronic Fund Transfer	Real Time Gross Settlement
Speed	Slow	Fast
Time to credit the amount	Transactions are completed in batches at specific times.	Transaction is completed on a one-to-one basis.
Used for	Small Money Transfer	Large Money Transfer
*Minimum amount to be transferred	Rs. 10,000 - Rs. 2 lakh	Above Rs. 2 Lakh
*Maximum amount to be transferred	Rs. 2 Lakh	No limit

Figure 8.9: *Differences between NEFT and RTGS*

Maximum and minimum amount to be transferred through RTGS and NEFT may vary from one bank to the other.

Immediate Payment Service

Immediate Payment service is an instant payment inter-bank electronic funds transfer system in India. It offers the inter-bank electronic fund transfer service through mobile phone. It is managed by the National Payments Corporation of India and is built upon the existing National Financial Switch network.

The main feature of IMPS is that it transfers funds immediately and is a great banking platform. The transaction's charges transfer limit is Rs. 2 Lakhs per day.

How to transfer funds using IMPS?

IMPS using bank account and IFSC details are used to transfer funds. You can use this method to transfer funds to anyone holding a bank account with any bank. You need an internet connection, netbanking or mobile banking.

1. Log on to your Net banking account.
2. Add a new beneficiary. If you have the receiver as a beneficiary, then you can select the correct details from the beneficiary account. Make sure you have the correct bank account and IFSC code details. You might receive an OTP on your mobile number to complete the beneficiary addition process.
3. Once the beneficiary is added, you can select the details and mention the amount you want to transfer.
4. Verify the details.
5. Click Confirm.
6. The money will be debited from your account and credited to the receiver's account immediately in a few seconds.
7. You will receive an SMS from your bank with transaction details. Keep the reference number with yourself in case of confusion or error in money transfer.

Advantages of IMPS

1. Real-time money transfer.
2. You can transfer funds through IMPS anytime during 24x7, 365 days in a year.
3. Transaction limit of IMPS is from Rs. 1 lakh to Rs. 2 lakhs.
4. Available through multiple channels like Net banking, ATM, SMS and Mobile application.

Online Bill Payment

The use of online payment system began in the 1960s. It was used mainly among financial and banking institutions. It is a service that allows you to manage and pay bills electronically on a monthly basis such as power bills, car payments or credit card payment, or they can be one-time payments to companies or even individuals.

Online payment systems enable various forms of financial transactions. Examples of such transaction categories include Business-to-Business (B2B), Business-to-Consumer (B2C), Consumer-to-Business (C2C), and Consumer-to-Consumer (C2C).

Tips for safe use of online bill payment

When selecting and using an online bill paying service:

1. Do not respond to any bill paying service that asks for personal information directly through e-mail.
2. Do not pay bills from a link in an e-mail.
3. Avoid clicking on any e-mail links that appear to be from your bill paying service.
4. Read the privacy or security policy that should mention strong data encryption of the bill paying service.
5. After you pay bills online, log out of your account to prevent anyone from accessing when you leave your computer.
6. While using online bill services, enable a password lock on your computer.
7. Always use firewall software and antivirus software.

Conclusions

In this chapter, you discussed the broad range of financial services accessed and delivered through digital channels, such as payments. The new topic discussed OTP, Quick Response Code, Unified Payment Interface, Aadhaar-Enabled Payment System, etc. One-Time password is also known as one-time pin and is valid for transaction on a digital device. Quick Response code is a scannable barcode that is used to provide easy access to information through a smartphone. The Unified Payment Interface is a real-time payment system introduced by National Payment Corporation of India. The value of transaction limit through UPI is Rs. 1 lakh. The National Electronic Fund transfer is an electronic funds transfer system maintained by the Reserve Bank of India. Real time gross settlement system is a continuous real-time settlement of funds transfer, individually on a transaction basis. It is used to transfer money from one bank to another on a real time and a gross basis. RTGS and NEFT both are used for electronic fund transfer, which you understood in detail in this chapter. Then you saw IMPS, which is an instant payment inter-bank electronic funds transfer service through mobile phone. Though there are various systems for online transfer of funds schemes, such as digital wallets, UPI, and NEFT, RTGS and IMPS are the most common and highly used methods. Then we saw the AePS, which is a secure payment platform for financial transactions based on a unique identification number that enables a user for cashless transactions. Further, you covered Unstructured Supplementary Service Data which is a communications protocol used by GSM cellular telephone to communicate with mobile network operators. It is a piece of plastic card that contains personal data in a machine readable. Lastly, an e-Wallet is a digital system which stores a person's payment information.

In the next chapter, you will learn IT Technology and Cyber Security.

Model Questions and Answers

A. Multiple Choice Questions.:

1. What does USSD stand for?
   a. Unstructured Supplementary Service data
   b. Unstructured supply service date
   c. Unstructured supplement service data
   d. None of the above

2. Abbreviation of UPI is:
   a. Unique Payment Interface
   b. Unified Payment Interface
   c. Union Pay Interface
   d. Unified Pay Interface

3. A person can make payments __________ option.
   a. Using Mobile number and MMID (P2P)
   b. Using Account number and IFS code (P2A)
   c. Using Aadhaar number (ABRS)
   d. All of the above

4. What are the facilities offered under 99# service?
   a. Interbank account to account fund transfer
   b. Balance enquiry
   c. Mini statement besides host of other services
   d. All of the above

5. UPI is an __________ payment service.
   a. Offline
   b. Online
   c. Mobile Net
   d. All of the above

6. By whom was UPI launched?
   a. Urjit Patel
   b. R.Gandhi
   c. Raghuram Rajan
   d. Narendra Modi

7. Which of the following is not true about the National Electronic Funds Transfer (NEFT) system?
   a. There is no limit on transaction through NEFT
   b. NEFT operates on an hourly basis
   c. NEFT is a payment system which facilitates one-to-one fund transfer
   d. All of the above

8. Which of the following is not true about Unified Payments Interface (UPI)?
   a. UPI is an instant payment system developed by the National Payments Corporation of India (NPCI)
   b. All payments are instant and take place during banking hours through UPI
   c. Under UPI, a person will have a single identity and password for using multiple bank accounts
   d. All of the above

9. AePS allows banking transactions.
   a. Balance enquiry
   b. Cash withdrawal
   c. Cash deposit
   d. All of the above

10. Which of the following is not true about Aadhaar-enabled payment system?
    a. AePS enables bank customers to access their Aadhaar-linked bank accounts through the Aadhaar authentication
    b. In transactions through AePS, only Aadhaar number and fingerprint

captured during the enrolment are required

   c. AEPS allows inter-operability among different systems adopted by different banks in a safe and secured manner

   d. Customers can find out their account balance, deposit cash, withdraw money and transfer funds to other Aadhaar-linked bank accounts with the help of business correspondents of the bank they have an account in

B. State whether the following Statements are True or False.

1. RTGS is the fastest possible money transfer system through banking channel.
2. Virtual card creation feature is currently present in AePS.
3. PoS stands for Point of Service.
4. Banks act as a medium for the transfer of money.
5. QR stands for Quick Reasons.
6. One-time password is safe because it is different for every access.
7. InterNet banking is used to pay utility bills.
8. Special characters mixed with case characters should be used in a password to make it strong.
9. If you want to make a bank payment online, you have to enter their account number, type, bank name and IFSC code.
10. The beneficiary can expect to get credit for the NEFT transactions within two business hours.

C. Match the following.

1.	Minimum amount for RTGS transactions:	a.	Rs. 1 Lakh
2.	UPI developed by	b.	POS
3.	It is used for requesting money in UPI:	c.	Rs. 2 Lakhs
4.	Limit of fund transfer using UPI:	d.	PULL
5.	Stored data using patterns of black dots and white space in a square grid:	e.	To transfer funds directly from one account to another.
6.	It is place where a customer executes the payment for goods and services:	f.	NPCI
7.	E-Banking:	g.	QR codes
8.	____ type of e-commerce, consumer sells consumer directly:	h.	RTGS
9.	Real Time Gross Settlement:	i.	MPIN
10.	Details required for USSD fund transfer:	j.	C2C
		k.	NEFT

D. Fill in the blanks:

Biometric   USSD   PoS   Mobile   Enabled   MMID   B2B   e-wallet   IFSC   NPCI   Aadhaar

1. What does E stand for in AEPS?
2. AEPS is a bank-led model which allows online interoperable financial inclusion transactions at _________.
3. In AEPS, Unique ID and ______ is used for authentication purpose.
4. MMID is used for fund transfer in IMPS. What does the first M in MMID stand for _________?
5. _________ is a technology platform through which information can be transmitted through GSM network on a basic phone.
6. _________ is the largest community in classification of e-commerce.
7. _________ provides the ability to store multiple credit cards, debit cards and bank account information for making faster payment.

8. _______ is a 7-digit code that is issued to bank customers. This code is used during to fund transfer process.

9. _______ is an 11-digit alphanumeric doe that is designed by the RBI to identify each bank's branch.

10. _______ is a unified organization for all systems for retail payments across India.

Short Questions with Answers.

1. **What is the RTGS system?**

   Answers: RTGS stands for Real Time Gross Settlement. It is a funds transfer mechanism where transfer of money takes place from one bank to another on a real time and on a gross basis. This is the fastest possible money transfer system through the banking channel. The minimum amount to be remitted through RTGS is Rs. 2 lakhs. There is no top limit for RTGS transactions.

2. **What is a credit card and a debit card?**

   Answers: Credit Card is a payment method that financial institutions or banks provide to customers so that they can use it to pay for goods and services without actual payment at the time of purchase. There will be a credit limit set for each customer based on their financial history. Customers can use credit cards to buy goods and plan to repay to the bank at a later time. Interest is not taken from customers if repayment is done before the due date. High interest rates if we miss to repay the amount before the due date.

   On contrary, debit cards usually help people to access only the balance available in their accounts. Debit cards draw money directly from your account when we make the purchase.

3. **What is the difference between NEFT and RTGS?**

   Answers: Fund transfer transactions are settled in batches for NEFT, while individual settlements are done in RTGS. Hence, RTGS is a faster method compared to NEFT.

4. **What is online banking?**

   Answers: Nothing but anywhere banking. A customer can operate his account from any branch of a particular bank.

5. **What is IFSC?**

   Answers: IFSC (Indian Financial System Code) is an alpha-numeric code that uniquely identifies a bank branch participating in the NEFT system. This is an 11-digit code. IFSC is used by the NEFT system to identify the originating/ destination banks/branches and also to route the messages appropriately to the concerned banks/branches.

6. **What is the time taken for effecting funds transfer from one account to another under RTGS?**

   Answers: Under normal circumstances, the beneficiary branches are expected to receive the funds in real time as soon as funds are transferred by the remitting bank. The beneficiary bank has to credit the beneficiary's account within two hours of receiving the funds transfer message.

7. **How is RTS different from Electronic Fund Transfer System or National Electronics Funds Transfer System?**

   Answers: EFT and NEFT are electronic fund transfer modes that operate on a deferred net settlement (DNS) basis which settles transactions in batches. In DNS, the settlement takes place at a particular point of time. All transactions are held up till that time. For example, NEFT settlement takes place 6 times a day during the weekdays (9.30 am, 10.30 am and 12.00 noon).

8. **Define IMPS.**

   Answers: IMPS stands for Immediate Payment Service.

   National Payments Corporation of India introduced the IMPS facility in November 2010 under the National Financial Switch (NFS) Network.

   Under IMPS, funds can be transferred instantly, and unlike NEFT and RTGS, transactions through IMPS are available 24x7 (even on holidays).

The Mobile banking service of the bank should be approved by RBI in order for them to be eligible for IMPS.

9. What is UPI?

Answers: The Unified Payment Interface can be thought of like an e-mail ID for your money. It will be a unique identifier that your bank uses to transfer money and make payments using the IMPS. IMPS is faster than NEFT and lets you transfer money immediately. This means that the online payments will become much easier without requiring a digital wallet or credit or debit card.

10. Who is behind UPI?

Answers: Unified Payment Interface is an initiative by National Payments Corporation of India, with the support of the Reserve Bank of India and Indian Bank Association. The NPCI operates the Rupay payments infrastructure that—like Visa and Master Card—allows different banks to interconnect and transfer funds.

11. What is Aadhaar-Enabled Payment System?

Answers: AePS is a banking system that motivates a customer to use Aadhaar as his/her identity to access his/her respective Aadhaar-enabled bank account and can perform basic banking transactions like cash deposit, balance enquiry, cash withdrawal and remittance at a low-cost access devices called Micro-ATMS.

12. What is a QR Code?

Answers: QR is short for Quick Response. They can be ready quickly by a cell phone. The data contained by a QR code can be anything from a simple text to email addresses, phone numbers and so on.

QR codes store data using patterns of black dots and white spaces, arranged in a square grid. These patterns can be scanned and translated into human-readable information with the help of an imaging device, like a camera or a scanner.

13. What are QR codes used for?

Answers: As they can store different types of information, QR codes are used for many purposes. QR codes are used for holding data such as:

- Simple text: Welcome messages at conferences.
- URLs: Addresses of websites or specific web pages.
- Online accounts authentication: Websites can display a QR code which a registered user can scan with his or her smartphone and automatically login.
- Payments: QR codes can store information about our bank account or credit card.

14. What is USSD and how does it work?

Answers: USSD is short for Unstructured Supplementary Service Data. It is a protocol used by GSM (Global system for Mobile) communication with their service provider's computers. USSD can be used for WAP browsing, prepaid call-back service, mobile money service, location-based content services, and menu-based information services on the network. USSD messages can be up to 182 characters long, and they create a real-time communication between the phone and another device.

Your USSD gateway sends the request to your USSD application, then responds to the request, and USSD gateway goes ahead and displays our content to the user.

a. User enters a predetermined short code into phone (for example, 1097233#).

b. Phone sends it to the MNO.

c. Received by a MNO computer dedicated to USSD.

d. Answer from computer is sent back to the phone (displayed on screen).

e. The entire process takes a few seconds.

15. What is Point of Sale?

Answers: Point of Sale, a piece of a pint of purchase, refers to the place where a customer executes the payment for goods or services and where sales taxes may become payable. It can be in a physical store, where POS terminals and systems are used to process card payments or a virtual sales pint such as a computer or mobile electronic device.

For example, department stores often have PoS for individual product groups, such as appliances, electronics and apparel. The designated staff can actively promote products and guide consumers through purchase decisions rather than simply processing transactions.

Descriptive Type Questions.

1. What is NEFT?
2. What is Debit cum ATM card?
3. Is there any minimum/maximum amount stipulation for RTGS transactions?
4. What is the maximum amount that can be transferred through UPI?
5. How different is UPI from Mobile banking?
6. What is Virtual Payment Address?
7. What does one-time password mean?
8. What are the services of the Aadhaar-Enabled payment system?
9. Why are QR Codes useful?
10. Define e-Wallet?

Answers

A.	1. a	2. b	3. c	4. d	5. b
	6. c	7. b	8. b	9. d	10. d

B.	1. T	2. F	3. F	4. T	5. F
	6. T	7. T	8. T	9. T	10. T

C.	1. c	2. f	3. d	4. a	5. g
	6. b	7. e	8. j	9. h	10. i

D.	1. e	2. c	3. a	4. d	5. b
	6. g	7. h	8. f	9. i	10. j

■■

CHAPTER 9

Overview on Futuristic IT Technology and Cyber Security

Structure

In this chapter, we will learn the following topics:

- Internet of Things (IoT)
- Major components
- Hardware and software of IoT
- Big Data analytics
- IaaS, PaaS, SaaS
- Virtual reality
- Artificial Intelligence
- Blockchain
- Bitcoin
- Public key cryptography
- 3D printing/additive manufacturing
- Robotics process automation
- Cyber security

Objectives

The reader will be able to understand the following:

- Latest trends and technologies in upcoming fields in IECT.
- Need of Cyber Security and how to secure their PC and Mobile devices by using basic security features.

The future of Information technology and cyber security is the concept involving the development, maintenance and use of computer systems, software and networks of the processing and distribution of data. It is important to understand that the digital transformation involves using digital technologies to remake a process to become more efficient or effective such as Internet of Things, Big data analytics, Artificial Intelligence, and others instead of doing existing processes to adapt to digital technologies.

Internet of Things (IoT)

IoT stands for **Internet of Things**. It was developed by **Kevin Ashton**. It is a concept that refers to connections between physical devices like vehicles, home appliances, and other items embedded in electronics, such as sensors and software which enables these things to connect, collect and exchange data.

The Internet of Things has evolved due to convergence of multiple technologies, real-time analytics, machine learning, commodity sensors and embedded systems. The field of embedded systems, wireless sensor networks, control systems, automation (including home and building automation) and others all contribute to enabling the Internet of Things.

The term Internet of Things refers to everything in day-to-day life which is accessed or connected through the Internet. The following image shows various examples where IoT is used:

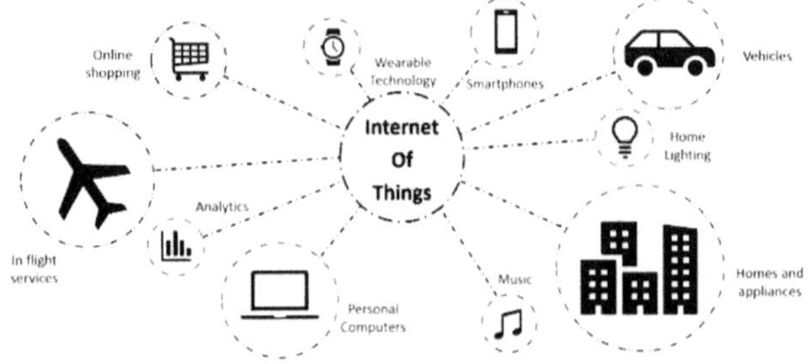

Figure 9.1: *Internet of Things*

IoT is an advanced automation and analytics system which deals with artificial intelligence, sensor, networking, electronic, cloud messaging, etc. to deliver complete systems for the product or services. The system created by IoT has greater transparency, control and performance.

How Does Internet of Things Work?

The entire IoT process starts with the devices themselves like smartphone, smartwatches, electronic appliances like TV and Washing Machine, which helps you communicate with the IoT platform.

IoT applications are used in everyday objects with connectivity and intelligence in various domains, such as:

- Nest Smart Thermostat
- Wearable Technology
- Smart Home Applications
- Healthcare
- Agriculture
- Industrial Automation

Features of IoT

The important features of IoT work on connectivity, analyzing, integrating, and many more. These are listed below:

- **Connectivity:** It refers to establishing a proper connection between all the things of IoT platform such as server or cloud.
- **Analyzing:** It comes to real-time analyzing the data collected and uses them to build effective business intelligence.

- **Integrating:** IoT integrating the various models to improve the user experience.
- **Artificial Intelligence:** IoT makes things smart and enhances life through the use of data.
- **Sensing:** The sensor devices used in IoT technologies detect and measure any changes in the environment and report on their status. Without sensors, they could not hold an effective or true IoT environment.
- **Active Engagement:** IoT makes the connected technology, product, or services to active engagement between each other.

Major Components of IoT

IoT is a transformation process of connecting our smart devices and objects to network to perform:

- Smart devices and Sensors
- Networks
- Standards
- Intelligent Analysis
- Intelligent Actions

Smart Devices and Sensors

Devices and sensors are the components of the device connectivity layer. These smart sensors are continuously collecting data from the environment and transmitting the information to the next layer.

Latest techniques in the semiconductor technology is capable of producing micro smart sensors for various applications. The common sensors are:

- Temperature sensors and thermostats
- Pressure sensors
- Humidity/Moisture level
- Moisture sensors

How the devices are connected?

The smart devices and sensors can be connected to lower power wireless networks like Wi-Fi, ZigBee, Bluetooth, Z-wave, and so on. Each of these wireless technologies has its own pros and cons in terms of power, data transfer and overall efficiency.

In the developments in the low power, low cost wireless transmitting devices are in the area of IoT due to its long battery life and efficiency. Latest protocols like 6LoWPAN-IPv6 over Lower Power Wireless Personal Area Networks have been adapted by many companies to implement energy-efficient data transmission for IoT networks. 6LoWPAN uses reduced transmission time and thus saves energy.

Networks

The second field is to transmit the signals collected by sensors over networks with all the different components of a typical network, including routers, and bridges in different topologies, including LAN, WAN and MAN. Connecting the different parts of networks to the sensors can be done by different technologies including Wi-Fi, Bluetooth, Low Power Wi-Fi, Wi-Max, regular Ethernet, Long Term Evolutoin (LTE).

The driving forces for wide spread network in IoT can be summarized as follows:

- High Data
- Low prices of data usage
- Virtualization
- XaaS concept (SaaS, PaaS, and IaaS)
- IPv6 deployment
- Challenges facing network implementation in IoT
- The enormous growth in number of connected devices
- Availability of networks coverage
- Security
- Power Consumption

Standards

The third field is to process the sum of all activities of handling processing and storing the data collected from the sensors. This aggregation increases the value of data by increasing the scale, scope and frequency of data available for analysis, but aggregation is only achieved through the use of various standards depending on the IoT application used.

Types of Standards

Two types of standards are relevant for the aggregation process; technology standards (including network protocols, communication protocols, and data–aggregation standards) and regulatory standards (related to security and privacy of data).

Challenges facing the adoptions of standards within IoT:

- **Standard for handling unstructured data:** Structured data is stored in relational databases and queried through SQL. Unstructured data is stored in different types of SQL database without a standard querying approach.

- **Security and privacy issues:** There is a need for clear guidelines on the retention, use, and security of the data as well as metadata.
- **Technical skills to leverage newer aggregation tools:** Companies that are keen on leveraging big-data tools often face a shortage of talent to plan, execute and maintain systems.

Intelligent Analysis

The fourth stage in IoT implementation is extracting insight from data for analysis. It is driven by cognitive technologies and the accompanying models that facilitate the use of cognitive technologies.

With advances in cognitive technology's ability to process varied forms of information, vision and voice have also become usable. The list of selected cognitive technologies that are experiencing adoption and being deployed for predictive and prescriptive analytics:

- Computer vision refers to a computer's ability to identify objects, scenes, and activities in images.
- Natural-language processing refers to computer's ability to work with text the way humans do, extracting meaning from text or even generating text that is readable.
- Speech recognition focuses on accurately transcribing human speech.
- Challenges facing the adoptions of intelligent analytics within IoT.
- Inaccurate analysis due to flaws in the data model.
- Legacy system's ability to analyze unstructured data.
- Legacy system's ability to manage real-time data.

Intelligent Actions

Intelligent actions can be expressed as Machine to Machine and Machine to Human interfaces.

Factors driving adoption of intelligent actions within the IoT are:

- Lower machine prices
- Improved machine functionality
- Machine influencing human actions through behavioural science rationale
- Deep learning tools
- Challenges facing the adoption of intelligent actions within IoT

- Machine's action in unpredictable situations
- Information security and privacy
- Machine interoperability
- Slow adoption of new technologies

The Internet of Things has been evolving ever since it started its journey few year back. New technologies and protocols joined the IoT ecosystem to make it more accessible, cost-effective, energy-efficient and most importantly secure. You will witness a continuous development in IoT due to a huge demand in different sectors.

The advantages and disadvantages of Internet of Things:

Advantages

Some advantages of IoT are:

- **Communication:** IoT encourages the communication between devices, also known as Machine-to-Machine (M2M) communication. Because of this, the physical devices are able to stay connected and hence the total transparency is available with lesser inefficiencies and greater quality.
- **Automation and Control:** Due to physical objects getting connected and controlled digitally and centrally with wireless infrastructure, there is a large amount of automation and control in the workings. Without human intervention, the machines are able to communicate with each other, leading to faster and timely output.
- **Information:** The more the information, the easier it is to make the right decision. Knowing what to get from the grocery while you are out, without having to check on your own, not only saves time but is convenient as well.
- **Tracking:** The computer keeps a track both on the quality and the viability of things at home. Knowing the expiration date of products before one consumes them improves safety and quality of life. Also, you will never run out of anything when you need it at the last moment.
- **Money:** The biggest advantage of IoT is saving money. If the price of the tagging and monitoring equipment is less than the amount of money saved, then the Internet of Things will be very widely adopted. IoT fundamentally proves to be very helpful to people in their daily routines by making

the appliances communicate to each other in an effective manner, thereby saving and conserving energy and cost.

- **Efficient and Saves Time:** The machine-to-machine interaction provides better efficiency; hence, accurate results can be obtained fast. This results in saving valuable time. Instead of repeating the same tasks every day, it enables people to do other creative jobs.
- **Saves Money:** Optimum utilization of energy and resources can be achieved by adopting this technology and keeping the devices under surveillance. You can be alerted in case of possible bottlenecks, breakdown, and damages to the system.

Disadvantages of IoT

- **Compatibility:** There is no standard for tagging and monitoring with sensors. A uniform concept like the USB or Bluetooth is required, which should not be that difficult to do.
- **Complexity:** There are several opportunities for failure with complex systems. For example, both you and your spouse may receive messages that the milk is over and both of you may end up buying the same. That leaves you with double the quantity required. Or there is a software bug causing the printer to order ink multiple times when it requires a single cartridge.
- **Privacy/Security:** Privacy is a big issue with IoT. All the data must be encrypted so that data about your financial status or how much milk you consume is not common knowledge at the work place or with your friends.
- **Safety:** There is a chance that the software can be hacked and your personal information misused. The possibilities are endless. Your prescription being changed or your account details being hacked could put you at risk. Hence, all the safety risk become the consumer's responsibility.

Hardware and Software of IoT

Hardware of IoT devices, server, routers, and so on. This device handles tasks and functions, like:

- System activation
- Security
- Action specification

- communication
- Detection of goals and actions

Sensors

Sensors are the important hardware part of IoT. It comprises of:

- Power Management Modules
- Energy Modules
- **Sensing Modules:** Manage sensing through active and passive measurement devices.
- **RF Modules:** Manage communication through Bluetooth, Wi-Fi, Signal Processing, ZigBee and BAW.

Wearable Electronics

Wearable Devices are the small electronic devices that can be worn on arms, neck, head, feet, etc. These devices are not only the part of IoT system, but they enable access for improved productivity.

Standard Devices

- Desktop, Tablet, Cellphone, Routers, and Switches are the integral part of IoT.
- Desktop provides the highest level of control over the system settings.
- Ta blet has access to key features of system, and in a way, it acts like a remote.
- Cellphone has essential setting modification and provides an essential set of functionalities.

IoT Software

IoT addresses key areas of networking, embedded systems, partner systems, and middleware. These applications are responsible for collaboration with business systems.

The following points explain the IoT software applications that are responsible for data collection, device integration and real-time analytics and application and process extension within the IoT network.

- **Application and process extension:** Applications extend the reach of present software and system towards a wider effective network.
- **Data Collection:** It manages sensing, filtering, measuring, security and aggregation of data. It works specific protocols to connect sensors with real-time, machine-to-machine networks. It collects data from multiple devices and

distributes it accordingly, over the devices.

- **Device Integration:** Software integration relates system devices to create an IoT system. It ensures stable networking among the devices. They define the software technology of IoT network.
- **Real-Time Analytics:** These applications take input data from several devices and convert it into viable actions and patterns for analysis. They analyse data based on settings so as to execute automation-related tasks.

The following image shows an application of IoT hardware and software:

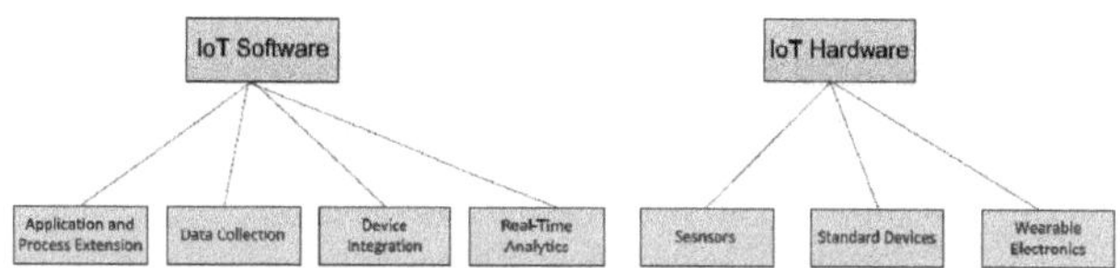

Figure 9.2: *IoT Software and Hardware*

Big Data Analytics

Big data analytics refers to the method of analysing huge volumes of big data. It is the process of collecting, organizing and analysing a large amount of data to uncover hidden patterns, correlations, market trends and other meaningful information. It helps an organization understand the information contained in their data and use it to provide new opportunities to improve their business, which in turn leads to more efficient operations, higher profits and happier customers.

To analyse such a large volume of data, Big Data analytics applications enable big data analyst, data scientists, predictive modellers, statisticians, and other analytical performers to analyse the growing volume of structured and unstructured data. It is performed using specialized software tools and applications. Using these tools, various data operations can be performed like data mining, text mining, predictive analysis, forecasting, etc. All these processes are performed separately and are a part of high-performance analytics. Big Data analytic tools and software enable an organization to process a large amount of data and provide meaningful insights that provide better business decisions in the future.

Benefits of Big Data Analytics

Big Data Analytics has been popular among various organizations like e-commerce industry, social media, healthcare, Banking, Entertainment industries, and so on.

E-commerce industries like Amazon, Flipkart, Myntra and many other online shopping sites make use of big data.

What is Data?

The quantities, characters, or symbols on which operations are performed by a computer, which may be stored and transmitted in the form of electrical signals and recorded on magnetic, optical or mechanical recording media.

What is Big Data?

Big Data is also data but with large size. It is a term used to describe a collection of data that is large in size and yet growing with time.

Examples of Big Data

Some of the examples of Big Data:

The BSE stock exchange generates large data per day.

Social media statistic shows the 500+terabytes of new data get ingested into the databases of social media site, that is, Facebook, every day. The data generated in terms of photo and video uploads, message exchanges, putting comments, and so on.

A single jet engine can generate 10+terabytes of data in 30 minutes of flight time.

Types of Big Data

Big Data are in three forms:

- Structured
- Unstructured
- Semi-structured

Structured: Any data that can be stored, accessed and processed in the form of fixed format is termed as structured data. It refers to highly organized information that can be readily and seamlessly stored and accessed from a database by simple search engine. For example, the employee table in a company database will be structured as the employee details, their jobs positions, their salaries, etc. will be in organized manner.

Unstructured: Any data with no order (unknown from) or the structure is classified as unstructured data. For example, e-mail is an example of unstructured data.

Semi-structured: Semi-structured data is information that does not reside in a relational database but that does have some organizational properties that make it easier to analyze Examples of semi-structured data is a data represented in an XML file.

Characteristics of Big Data

- **Volume:** The name Big Data itself is related to a size which is enormous. The size of data plays a very crucial role in determining value out of data. Also, whether a particular data can actually be considered as a Big Data or not, is dependent upon the volume of data. Hence, "volume" is one characteristic which needs to be considered while dealing with Big Data.

- **Variety:** It refers to heterogeneous sources and the nature of data, both structured and unstructured. Data in the form of e-mail, photos, videos, monitoring devices, PDFs, audio, etc. are also being considered in the analysis applications. This variety of unstructured data has certain issues for storage, mining and analysing, and so on.

- **Velocity:** The term velocity refers to the speed of generation of data. How fast the data is generated and processed to meet the demands. Big Data Velocity deals with the speed at which data flows in from sources like business processes, application logs, networks and social media sites, sensors, mobile devices, etc. The flow of data is massive and continuous.

- **Variability:** This refers to the inconsistency which can be shown by the data at times; thus, hampering the process of being able to handle and manage the data effectively.

What is Big Data Analytics?

Big Data refers to data that exceeds the typical storage, processing and computing capacity of conventional databases and data analysis techniques. As resources, Big Data requires tools and methods that can be applied to analyse and extract patterns from large-scale data.

Big Data Analytics refers to the process of collecting, organizing, analysing large data sets to discover different patterns and other useful information.

Types of Big Data Analytics

There are five types of big data analytics:

- **Descriptive Analytics:** The simple way to define descriptive analytics is that it answers the question "What has happened?". This type of analytics analyses the data coming in real-time for insights on how to approach the future. The main objective of descriptive analytics is to find out the reasons behind success or failure in the past. A business learns from past behaviours to understand how they will impact future outcomes. It is leverage to understand the overall performance of the company at an aggregate level and describe the various aspects.

  The example to explain descriptive analytics are the results that a business gets from the web server through the Google Analytics tools to help understand what actually happened in the past and validate if a promotional campaign was successful or not based on basic parameters like page view.

- **Diagnostic Analytics:** It consists of asking the questions: Why did it happen? Diagnostic analytics looks for the root cause of a problem. It is used to determine why something happened. This type attempts to find and understand the causes of events and behaviours.

- **Prescriptive Analytics:** Prescriptive analytics adds the spice of manipulating the future. It advises on possible outcomes and results in actions that are likely to maximize key business metrics. It basically uses simulation and optimization to ask **What should a business do**?

  It is an advanced analytics concept based on:

  - o Optimization that helps achieve the best outcomes.

  - o It helps understand how to achieve the best outcome and identify data uncertainties to make better decisions.

  Prescriptive analysis explores several possible actions and suggests actions depending on the results of descriptive tend predictive analytics of a given dataset. It is a combination of data and various business rules. The data for prescriptive analytics can be both internal (within the organization) and external (like social media data). If implemented properly, it can have a major impact on business grown. As increasing number of organizations realize the big data is a competitive advantage, they should ensure that they choose the right kind of data analytics solutions to reduce operational costs and enhance service quality.

- **Predictive Analytics:** It consists of asking the question: What is likely to happen? It uses past data in order to predict the future. It is all about forecasting. Predictive analytics uses many techniques like data mining and artificial intelligence to analyse current data and make scenarios of what might happen.

  Organizations like Walmart, Amazon and other retailers leverage predictive analytics to identify trends in sales based on purchase patterns of customers, forecasting customer behaviour, forecasting inventory level, predicting what products customers are likely to purchase together so that they can offer personalized recommendations, predicting the amount of sales at the end of the quarter or the year.

- **Advantages of Big Data**

  - o One of the biggest advantages of Big Data is predictive analysis. Big Data analytics tools can predict outcomes accurately, thereby, allowing businesses and organizations to make better decisions, while simultaneously optimizing their operational efficiencies and reducing risks.

  - o By harnessing data from social media platforms using Big Data analytics tools, businesses around the world are streamlining their digital marketing strategies to enhance the overall consumer experience. It provides insights into the customer pain points and allows companies to improve upon their products and services.

  - o Keeping irrelevant data is a curse for the database since it will make the filtering process complicated. But the statistics say, around 43% of companies are having tools which are unable to filter the junk data. A simple thing like filtering the customers from web analytics will be able to provide an insight for the efforts of your acquisition.

o Big Data analytics could help companies generate more sale lead which would naturally mean a boost in revenue. Businesses are using Big Data analytics tools to understand how well their product/services are doing in the market and how the customers are responding to them. Thus, they can understand better ways to invest their time and money.

o With Big Data insights, you can always stay a step ahead of your competitors. You can screen the market to know what kind of promotions and offers your rivals are providing, and then you can come up with better offers for your customers. Also, Big Data insights allow you to learn customer behaviour to understand the customer trends and provide a highly personalized experience to them.

- **Using Big Data Applications**

  The people who are using Big Data know better what Big Data is. Let us look some such industries:

  o **Healthcare:** Big Data has already started to create a huge difference in the healthcare sector. With the help of predictive analytics, medical professionals are now able to provide personalized healthcare services to individual patients. Apart from that, fitness, wearable, telemedicine, remote monitoring—all powered by Big Data and AI—are helping change lives for the better.

  o **Academia:** Bid Data is also helping enhance education today. There are numerous online educational courses to learn from. Academic institutions are investing in digital courses powered by Big Data technologies to aid the all-around development of growing learners.

  o **Banking:** The banking sector relies on Big Data for fraud detection. Big Data tools can efficiently detect fraudulent acts in real-time such as misuse of credit/ debit cards.

o **Manufacturing:** According to Global Trend Study, the most significant benefit of Big Data in manufacturing is improving the supply strategies and product quality. In this sector, Big data helps create a transparent infrastructure, thereby, predicting uncertainties and in competencies that can affect the business adversely.

o **IT:** One of the largest uses of Big Data, IT companies around the world, are using Big Data to optimize their functioning, enhance employee productivity, and minimize risk in business operations. By combining Big Data technologies with ML and AI, the IT sector is continually powering innovation to find solutions even for the most complex of problems.

Social and Mobile

Today, social and mobile are the fastest growing forms of online marketing. For example, mobile devices are useful for accessing Facebook and other social sites. They allow for the sharing and creation of knowledge over social networks, which enhances collaboration and information distribution across a business. They are a platform for effective social networking and new ways to work.

Cloud Computing

The term **Cloud** came from a network of engineers to represent the location of various network devices. In simple terms, cloud computing means storing and accessing data and programs over the Internet instead of your computer hard drive. The cloud is just a metaphor for the Internet. An example of a Cloud computing provider is Google's Gmail. Gmail users can access files and applications via the Internet from any device.

With increase in computer and Mobile users, data storage has become a priority in all fields. Many large and small businessmen today thrive on their data and they spend a huge amount of money to maintain this data. It requires a strong IT support and a storage hub. The user can access the data from anywhere with the help of an Internet connection. To access cloud computing, the user should register and provide ID and password for security reasons. The speed of transfer depends on Internet speed and the capacity of the server.

Features of Cloud Computing

Following are the characteristics of Cloud Computing:

- **Resource Pooling:** The provider's computing resources are pooled to serve multiple consumers using a multi-tenant model, with different physical and virtual resources dynamically assigned and reassigned according to consumer demand. There is a sense of location independence in that the customer generally has no control or knowledge over the exact location of the provided resources, but may be able to specify location at a higher level of abstraction. Examples of resources include storage, processing, memory and network bandwidth

- **On-demand Self-Service:** A consumer can separately provision computing capabilities, such as server time and network storage, as needed automatically without requiring human interaction with each service provider.

- **Easy Maintenance:** The servers are easily maintained and the downtime is very low in some cases, there is no downtime. The cloud computing comes up with an update every time making it better. The updates are more compatible with the devices and perform faster than older ones along with the bugs which are fixed.

- **Large Network Access:** Capabilities are available over the network and accessed through standard mechanisms that promote use by heterogeneous thin or thick client platforms (for example, mobile phones, tablets, laptops, and workstations).

- **Availability:** The Cloud capabilities can be modified as per the use and extended a lot. It analyses the storage usage and allows the user to buy extra cloud storage, if needed, for a very small amount.

- **Automatic System:** Cloud computing mechanically analyses the data needed support a metering capability at some level of services.

- **Economical:** It is the one-time investment as the company (host) has to buy the storage and a small part of it can be provided to the many companies which save the host from monthly or yearly cost.

- **Security:** It is one of the features of cloud computing. It creates a snapshot of the data stored so that the data may not get lost even if one of the servers gets damaged.

- **Pay as you go:** They use to pay only for the service or the space they have utilized. The service is economical and most of the time some space is allotted for free.

- **Measured Service:** The resources usage is metered and manufacturing organizations pay accordingly for what they have used. This resource utilization is analyzed by supporting charge per use capabilities. It means that the cloud resources usages-whether virtual server instances that are running in the cloud getting monitored measured and reported by the service provider.

Advantages of Cloud Computing:

- **Low cost:** To run cloud technology, users do not require high power computer and technology because the application will run on the cloud and not on users' PC.

- **Storage capacity:** The cloud storage capacity is unlimited and generally offers a huge storage capacity based on the requirement.

- **Low cost of IT infrastructure:** The investment will be less if an organization uses cloud technology.

- **Increase computing power:** Cloud servers have a very high capacity of running and processing tasks as well as processing applications.

- **Reduce software costs:** It minimizes the software costs as users do not need to purchase software for organizations or every computer.

- **Security:** The service vendors select the highest level of security of the data, for which a user can set proper passwords and encryption.

Disadvantages of Cloud Computing:

- **Internet Connectivity:** It needs internet connectivity; if there will be no internet connection, you would not be able to access the cloud.

- **Lower Bandwidth:** It reduces the benefits of the clouds such that it cannot be used properly. A satellite connection can lead to quality disruption due to higher latency or higher bandwidth.

- **Internet Speed:** If a client is using an internet which is used by multiple users to download files such as music, documents, etc., it will reduce the speed to use the Cloud.

- **Security:** Data storage might not be secure. With Cloud computing, all the data gets stored in the cloud and hence unauthorized use may gain access to user's data in the cloud.

How Does Cloud Computing Work?

To understand the workings of a cloud system, it is easier to divide it into two sections: the front end and the back end. They are connected to each other through a network, usually the Internet. The front end is the side of the computer user or client. The back end is the cloud section of the system.

The front end consists of the client's computer or computer network. Also, the application is essential to access the cloud computing system. It is not necessary that all cloud computing systems have the same user interface.

On the back end of the cloud technology system, there are various computers, servers and data storage systems that make the cloud. All these features and functions are managed by the central server. The central server ensures that everything runs smoothly and in a perfect manner. It pursues a set of rules called protocols and uses a special kind of software known as Middleware. It permits the networked computer to communicate with each other.

Platforms of Cloud Computing

There are three categories of Cloud computing, such as Infrastructure as a service (IaaS), Platform as service (PaaS), and Software as a service (Saas).

- **Infrastructure as a service (IaaS):** Infrastructure as a service is a cloud model in which the company or organization outsources the necessary hardware, storage device, networking related equipment and services, which are used to support the business operations of any organization. Cloud service provider is responsible for maintaining the running applications and services for the organization. IaaS cloud model company will pay only for what the service company used for their business. It works as utility bills how much you consumed that which you have to pay. A cloud computing service provider, such as Azure, manages the infrastructure, while you purchase, install, configure, and manage your own software—operating systems, middleware, and applications.

- **Platform as a service (PaaS):** Platform as a service is a set of software and product development tools hosted on the provider's infrastructure. It is a cloud technique which is hire the hardware, operating systems, storages and network capacity over the internet. The PaaS are service delivery model that allows the clients to rent the server and associated service for running existing applications or developing developers can create the applications on the provider's platform over the internet.

- **Software as a service (SaaS):** In software as a service, the cloud services are provided by the third party over the internet. The software in Software as a Service license is on a subscription basis and centrally host. It is one of the common delivery models for many business applications such as business applications, including office software, messaging software, payroll processing software, and so on. The applications of SaaS are also known as hosted software, on-demand software and web-based software.

Types of Data Clouds for the Clients

- **Public Clouds:** A public cloud sells computer service to anyone on the Internet. It is a data centre that delivers the hosted services to a limited number of the clients. The main purpose of the public clouds is to provide easy service to computing resources and IT services for their clients.

  Few public clouds which present in the information technology sector are:

  - o Amazon elastic compute cloud
  - o IBM's Blue cloud
  - o Sun cloud

- **Community Clouds:** Community cloud may establish where many organizations have the same information technology applications and requirements for their business operations. These organizations can share the infrastructure jointly and take the benefit by sharing the cost of the community cloud which is hosted and managed by the third party. The high level of data privacy, data security and strong policies are required for the clients.

- **Hybrid clouds:** A hybrid is a cloud computing in which an organization provides and manages some services in-house and some services are provided externally in the place of the clients. In hybrid clouding, a company may use the public cloud service but continue to maintain their in-house data storage for their operation. The hybrid cloud may be very cost effective for the clients and public clouding may save the company's personal data from third parties.

- **Private Cloud:** Private cloud will provide the infrastructure to only one organization or company, whether managed internally or by a third party, and hosted either internally or externally. Private cloud Provider Company will help and manage only one company data and their business operation's applications. This cloud is used by that company which is ready to share their business data with third parties.

- **Cloud Service Providers**
  - **Amazon Web Service:** It is a cloud computing platform that provides services such as computer power, database storage, content delivery and other functions to integrate a business. The Amazon Web Services is flexible, scalable and reliable are implementing it in their work.
  - **Google Cloud Platform:** It is one of the leading cloud computing services which are affected by Google, and it runs on the same infrastructure that Google uses for tis end-user products. The Google cloud platform is basically used for Google search and YouTube. There are various services offered by Google Cloud such as data analysis, machine learning, and data storage.
  - **Adobe Creative Cloud:** Adobe creative cloud provides the best experience of app services, design photography and web. It provides many facilities to the beginner as well as professionals for easy access to the cloud. It consists of many applications and services that provide access to a collection of software which is used for video editing, web

development, photography and graphic design. There are mobile applications as well as computer applications which can be used by the customers.

Uses of Cloud Computing

- **Working Freedom:** With help from cloud computing, any employee of a company can work from anywhere in the world with the help of Internet, which is very useful for company operations.

- **Cost Control of Software:** By embracing the cloud computing technology by any companies, they can reduce their information technology budget by using the cloud computing for their organization. They use all these software by paying the monthly subscription from the cloud data provider companies.

- **Hardware Cost saver by using cloud computing:** By using the cloud computing technology, every company can save the cost of their computer network. When any company uses cloud computing, these companies do not require the network server and computer networking for their organization. The company only requires Internet connection for using the cloud computing service.

- **Work Efficiency Increases:** By using cloud computing, the work efficiency will increase. When you are working on the company's network connection, that connection may get very slow some time. In slow network, it is very difficult to work on the network. To detect the fault and rectification of that fault, it will take 2-3 days. These types of problem may affect the business. With the help of cloud computing, every company can solve all these problems because cloud computing is a web-based service and is managed by the e-remote companies.

- **Low Maintenance:** The company which will embrace cloud computing has low maintenance cost from their information department.

Virtual Reality

Virtual means 'Near or Implied' and Reality means the state of things as they actually exist. Thus, virtual reality is nothing but 'Near Reality'. Virtual Reality is a simulation of a physical entity into a virtual or imaginary environment that is created using software or programs that defy beliefs of a user compelling she/he to accept it as actual reality. Today, the Virtual Reality (VR) technology is applied to advanced fields of medicine, engineering, education, design, training, and entertainment. VR is a computer interface which tries to mimic real world beyond the flat monitor to give an immersive Three Dimension (3D) visual experience.

We experience the world through our five senses, such as touch, taste, sight, smell and hearing; all this is done with the help of our brain. In simple words, our entire sense of reality is due to the combination of sense-making mechanism of the brain and sensory information that we perceive. Virtual Reality actually exploits and plays with the sensations and perceptions of our brain by simulating an artificial environment which actually does not really exist, but our brain thinks that it does just like make believe. There are several applications of virtual technology used in entertainment, marketing, education and medicine.

- Virtual Reality (VR): it is typically made of equipment such as Head Mounted Displays (HMDs) and input devices.
- Head-Mounted Display: It is a device which contains a display mounted in front of the user's eyes.
- Input Devices: Data Gloves, Trackpads, and Joysticks.

There are three main types of VR:

- Non-immersive simulation: Only some of the user sensors are stimulated (the user is still aware of the reality outside the virtual simulation).
- Semi-immersive simulations: The user is partly but not fully immersed in the virtual environment (for example, flight simulation).
- Fully immersive simulations: Use of accessories such as Head Mounted Display and input devices stimulate all the senses of the user.

What is Augmented Reality?

Augmented reality is a technology that takes the world around you and adds virtual content on top such that it looks like it is actually there in the real world. The main reason behind AR is to superimpose virtual objects and information over a real-world environment in real-time to make the user experience more immersive.

The use of AR is projected to increase in the next few years and companies such as Google and Apple already developed tools such as ARCore and ARKit to make it easier for developers to create AR apps respectively for the Play Store and App Store.

Artificial Intelligence is nowadays being commonly integrated into both AR and VR applications in order to optimize the customer experience.

There are different types of Augmented Reality applications, these are:

- **Marker Based AR:** It makes use of a comer and a virtual marker (for example, QR Coder), to activate some AR components just when the marker is identified by the camera.
- **Markerless AR:** It uses GPS, accelerometers and digital compasses embedded in a device (for example, smartphone) to offer AR content on the user location. This can be used to make mapping systems more interactive.
- **Projection based AR:** This is one of the simplest types of AR which is the projection of light on a surface. It is appealing and interactive where light is blown onto a surface and the interaction is done by touching the projected surface with hand. The widespread uses of projection-based AR techniques can be used to create deception about the position, orientation, and depth of an object.
- **Superposition based AR:** This AR provides a replacement view of the object in focus. This is done by replacing the entire or partial view with an augmented view of the object. Here object recognition plays a vital role where replacing a view of an object with an augmented view is done.

How Does Virtual Reality Work?

VR technology works with several devices interconnected with each other. Each component like headsets, game controller and smartphone/computer together let you experience virtual reality. After wearing Head-Mounted Display that resembles a helmet and consists of two small screens, a 3-D images is created which takes the user into a completely different world. This activity is known as head-tracking, in which direction you move your head or walk, the visuals in front of you will shift accordingly.

Using headsets which have a small screen attached to it, the user gets completely immersed into the virtual reality environment. Now, you can jump from the mountains while sitting in the office in real time.

Concepts in Virtual Reality and How VR is Different from Other Media

The key elements of Virtual reality and differentiate it from other media. These are virtual world, immersion, sensory feedback and interactivity.

- **Virtual word:** A virtual world is a three-dimensional environment generated by a computer in which one can interact with others and create objects as part of that interaction.
- **Immersion:** The term immersion refers to both physical and mental sensation of being in an environment. "Being immersed" generally refers to an emotional or mental state – a feeling of being involved in the experience. In the medium of VR, however, physical immersion is also the property of a VR system because participants physically interact with the virtual environment.
- **Sensory feedback:** In VR, participants are provided with direct sensory feedback based on their physical positions and activities in the virtual world. A virtual display, for example, responds to a participant moving his or her head by updating the displayed image accordingly.

  In other words, VR is a medium that allows us to have a simulated experience of the physical reality. Because of this, VR allows us to purposefully reduce the danger of physical reality and to more safely scenarios that are not possible in the real world.
- **Interactivity:** For VR to seem authentic, it should be interactive in responding to a users' action in the virtual world. If the virtual environment responds to a user's action in a natural manner, the sense of immersion will remain. If the virtual environment cannot respond quickly enough, the human brain will readily notice and the sense of immersion will diminish.

Applications of Virtual Reality

With the advancement in display, sensing and computer technology, it gives the user a new VR experience which is more realistic and immersive for different VR applications. VR can lead to new

and exciting discoveries in different fields. There are a wide range of applications for VR which includes: Military, Sport, and Education.

Where is virtual reality used?

- **Military:** Virtual reality has been adopted by the military. It includes all three services (army, navy and air force). It is used for training purposes. This is particularly useful for training soldiers for combat situations to learn how to react in an appropriate manner.
- VR can put a trainee in a number of different situations, places and environments so the military are using it for flight simulations, battlefield simulations, medic training, vehicle simulation and virtual boot camp, among other things. A key benefit for the use of VR in the military is the reduction in costs for training.
- **Sport:** VR is revolutionizing the sports industry for both players and viewers. It is used as a training aid in many sports and to help measure athletic performance and analyze technique. It has also been used to enhance the viewer's experience of a sporting event. Broadcasters are now streaming live games in virtual reality and preparing to one day sell virtual tickets to live games.
- **Mental Health:** VR has become a primary method for treating post-traumatic stress. Using VR exposure therapy, a person enters a re-enactment of a traumatic event. It has also been used to treat anxiety and depression. This technology can provide a safe environment for patients to come into contact with things they fear, whilst remaining in a controlled and safe environment.
- **Education:** Virtual reality has been adopted in education for teaching and learning situations. The advantage of this is it enables large groups of students to interact with each other as well as within a three-dimensional environment. For example, astronomy students can learn about the solar system and how it works by physical engagement with the objects within. They can move planets, see around stars and track the progress of a comet. It also enables them to see how abstract concepts work in a three-dimensional environment which makes them easier to understand and retain.

Artificial Intelligence

John McCarthy defined the term Artificial Intelligence in the year 1950. It is a concept that refers to a computer's ability to perform tasks and make decisions that require some level of human intelligence. AI is a part of our daily life. This technology is used in a wide range of day-to-day services. It reduces human effort. Now, in many industries, people are using this technology to develop machine slaves to perform the different activities. The machine is used to speed up the process of doing work and give you an accurate result.

There are several sectors that have already started the use of AI, like healthcare, automobiles, heavy industries, etc. Many companies like Amazon, Facebook and Apple have identified the value of this technology and are planning to invest more to advance their machine learning technologies.

AI is a vast subject and its field of study includes many theories, methods and technology. There are many major subfields under it:

- Machine learning
- Neural networks
- Deep learning
- Cognitive computing
- Computer vision
- Natural language processing

What is AI Technique?

In the real world:

- Its volume is huge, next to unimaginable
- It is not well-organized
- It keeps changing constantly

AI technique is a manner to organize and use the knowledge efficiently in such a way that:

- It should be perceivable by the people who provide it
- It should be easily modifiable to correct errors
- It should be useful in many situations though it is incomplete or inaccurate

Applications of AI

AI is used in applicable in many aspects such as Finance, Medical, Entertainment, Pattern recognition, and Data mining. Some important applications of AI are listed below:

- **Gaming:** It plays an important role in designing strategic games such as chess, tic-tac-toe, etc. These are the logical games in which the system can determine the various available options based on the information fed.
- **Natural Language Processing:** It is possible to interact with the computer that understands human language.
- **Expert System:** Expert systems are developed to solve complex problems by the knowledge of reasoning, which is represented primarily using if-then rules rather than conventional procedural code.
- **Vision System:** Computer vision system is a technology of obtaining models to control information from visual data. For example, a spying aeroplane takes photographs which are used to figure out spatial information or map of the areas.
- **Speech Recognition:** Some intelligent systems are capable of hearing and comprehending the language in terms of sentences and their meanings while a human talks to it. It can handle different accents, noise in the background, change in human's noise due to cold, and so on.
- **Handwriting Recognition:** The software reads the text written on paper by a pen or on screen by a stylus. It can recognize the shapes of the letters and convert it into editable text.
- **Intelligent Robotics:** It is able to perform the tasks by a human. They have sensors to detect physical data from the real world such as light, heat, temperature, movement, sound. In addition, they are capable of learning from their mistakes and they can adapt to the new environment.

Types of Artificial Intelligence

Artificial Intelligence can be divided in various types. There are mainly two types, which are based on capabilities and functionally of AI.

- Based on Capabilities
- Based on Functionality

Type 1 Based on Capabilities

- **Weak or Narrow AI:** Narrow AI is a type of AI which is able to perform a dedicated task with intelligence. The currently available AI is Narrow AI in the world of Artificial

Intelligence. It cannot perform beyond its field or limitations, as it is only trained for specific tasks. Hence, it is also known as weak AI. Apple's Siri is a good example of Narrow AI, but it operates with a limited pre-defined range of functions. IBM's Watson supercomputer also comes under Narrow AI, as it uses an Expert system approach combined with Machine learning and natural language processing. Some examples of Narrow AI are playing chess e-commerce site, speech recognition and image recognition.

- **General AI:** General AI is a type of intelligence which could perform any intellectual task with efficiency like a human. The general AI systems could be smarter and think like a human by its own. Currently, no such system exists which could come under general AI and can perform any task as human. As systems with general AI are still under research, it will take lots of efforts to develop such systems.

- **Super AI:** Super AI is a level of Intelligence of systems at which machines could surpass human intelligence, and can perform any task better than human. The key characteristics of strong AI includes the ability to think, solve the puzzle, learn and communicate by its own. It is still a hypothetical concept of Artificial Intelligence. Development of such system in real is still a world-changing task.

Type 2 Based on Functionality

- **Reactive Machines:** These forms of AI systems have extremely limited capability. They emulate the human mind's ability to respond to different kinds of incitements. They do not have memory-based functionality. Such machines cannot use previously gained experiences to inform their present actions, i.e., these are machined to have the ability to learn. These could only be used to automatically respond to a limited set of inputs. For example, a reactive AI machine is IBM's Deep Blue, a machine that beat chess **Grandmaster, Garry Kasparov in 1997**.

- **Limited Memory:** Limited memory is comprised of machine learning models that derive knowledge from previously-learned information, stored data or events. Although limited memory builds on observational data in conjunction with pre-programmed data,

the machines already contain these pieces of information which are fleeting. For example, autonomous vehicles, or self-driving cars, use the principle of limited memory, in that, they depend on a combination of observation and pre-programmed knowledge. Driverless cars without limited memory AI took as long as seconds to react and make judgments on external factors.

- **Theory of Mind:** This type of AI should be able to understand people's emotions, beliefs, thoughts, and expectations and be able to interact socially even though a lot of improvements are there in this field. Theory of mind is a highly-advanced form of proposed artificial intelligence that would require machines to thoroughly acknowledge rapid shifts in emotional and behavioural patterns in humans, and also understand human behaviour. Thus, theory of mind machines would have to be able to learn rapidly. Some elements of theory of mind AI currently exist or have existed in the recent past. Two examples are the robots Kismet and Sophia, created in **2000** and **2016**. **Kismet**, developed by **Professor Cynthia Breazeal**, was capable of recognizing human facial signals (emotions) and could replicate said emotions with its face, which was structured with human facial features: yes, lips, ears, and eyelids and eyebrows.

- **Self-awareness:** Self-aware AI involves machines that have human-level consciousness. This form of AI is not currently in existence, but would be considered the most advanced form of artificial intelligence. Facets of self-aware AI include the ability to not only recognize and replicate humanlike actions, but also to think for itself, have desires, and understand its feelings. Self-aware AI, in essence, is an advancement and extension of theory of mind AI, where theory of mind only focuses on the aspects of comprehension and replication of human practices.

There are many ways AI can be achieved, some of them are as follows:

- **Machine Learning:** It is a method where the target is defined and the steps to reach that target is learned by the machine itself by training. For example, to identify a simple object such as an apple or orange. The target is achieved not by clearly specifying the details about it but it is just as we teach a child by showing multiple different pictures of it and therefore allowing the machine to define the steps to identify it like an apple or orange.

- **Natural Language Processing:** It is broadly defined as the automatic manipulation of natural language, like speech and text, by software. One of the well-known examples of this is e-mail spam detection as we can see how it has improved in our mail system.

- **Vision:** Machine vision captures and analyses visual information using a camera, analog-to-digital conversion and digital signal processing. It can be compared to human eyesight but it is not bound by the human limitation which can enable it to see through walls. It is usually achieved through machine learning to get the best possible results so we could say that these two fields are interlinked.

- **Robotics:** It is a field of engineering focused on the design and manufacturing of robots. They are often used to perform tasks that are difficult for humans to perform or perform consistently. Examples include car assembly lines, in hospitals, office cleaner, serving foods, patrolling farm areas and even as police officers.

- **Autonomous Vehicles:** This area of AI has gathered a lot of attention. The list of vehicles includes cars, buses, trucks, trains, ships, and so on.

Blockchain Technology

Blockchain is the technology of Digital CryptoCurrency Bitcoin. It is a distributed database of records of all transactions that have been executed and shared among participating parties. Each transaction is verified by the majority of participants of the system. It contains every single record of each transaction. BitCoin is the most popular cryptocurrency example of the blockchain. Blockchain was invented by a person (or group of people) using the name 'Satoshi Nakamoto' in 2008 to serve as the public transaction ledger of the cryptocurrency bitcoin.

The Three Pillars of Blockchain Technology

The three main properties of Blockchain Technology which have gained widespread acclaim are as follows:

- **Decentralization:** Bitcoin and BitTorrent are used to centralize services. You have a centralized entity which stores all the data and interacts solely with this entity to get whatever information you require. For example, in Google, when you search for something, you send a query to the server and then it gets back to you with the relevant information.

  Centralized systems have treated us well over the years, but they have several flaws:

  o Because all the data is stored in one spot, it makes them easy target spots for hackers.

  o If the system shuts down, no one would be able to access the information.

  o If the system needed to be upgraded, the whole system needs to be halted.

  o If the entity gets corrupted, then all the data in the blockchain would be compromised.

- **Immutability:** Immutability, in the context of the blockchain, means that once something has been entered into the blockchain, it cannot be tampered with. In simple terms, hashing is when data is converted into a unique string of text. This means that any type/piece of data can be hashed. In terms of cyptocurrency, the transactions are turn through a hashing algorithm, which gives an output of specific length. In the same way, there are different types of data, and different types of hashing (for example, MD5, SHA-2, SHA-256, CRC32).

- **Transparency:** One of the most interesting and misunderstood concepts in blockchain technology is transparency. Some people say that it gives you privacy while some say that it is transparent. A person's identity is hidden through complex cryptography and represented only by their public address. So, if you were to look up a person's transaction history, you will not see "bot sent 1 BTC" instead you will see

"1MF1bhsFLKBzzz9vpFYEmvw TwTbyCt7NZJ sent 1 BTC".

So, even though the person's identity is a secret, all their transaction that were done by their public address are transparent. Therefore, if you know the public address of a big company, you can simply enter it into your browser and look at all the transactions they have engaged in.

How Does Blockchain Work?

1. Blockchain keeps a record of all data exchanges. This record is referred to as a **ledger** in the cryptocurrency world, and each data exchange is a **transaction**. Every verified transaction is added to the ledger as a **block**.

2. It utilizes a distributed system to verify each transaction. It is a peer-to-peer network of nodes.

3. Once signed and verified, the new transaction is added to the blockchain and cannot be altered.

   For example, imagine two entities (for example, banks) need to update their own user account balances when there is a request to transfer money from one customer to another. They need to spend a tremendous amount of time and effort for coordination, synchronization, messaging and checking to ensure that each transaction happens exactly as it should. Typically, the money being transferred is held by the originator until it can be confirmed that it was received by the recipient. With the blockchain, a single ledger of transaction entries that both parties have access to can simplify the coordination and validation efforts because there is always a single version of records, not two disperse databases.

Benefits of Blockchain Technology

- **Secure data:** Blockchain network is way better than the traditional methods of saving records on papers. The details of every transaction are stored across the network, which makes it difficult for hackers to hinder with the security. This is the reason why industries such as finance, banking, and so on. where the data shared is sensitive, are turning to blockchain technology for a solution.

- **Transparency:** A piece of data that is shared via blockchain technology is complete in itself, accurate and consistent with all the members. The distributed structure of blockchain makes it possible for users to control and access details about the transactions.

- **Easy to trace:** The company deals with products that are complex in nature and pass through various computer networks. It is quite possible that you might never know where the product originated and where it was finally delivered. But with blockchain, you can easily trace the entire journey that the product made throughout the network. This helps prevent any fraud or manipulation.

  It is not impossible for hackers to hack data on a blockchain network, but it is way too difficult to understand every single block.

- **Faster transactions:** Interbank transactions can potentially take days for clearing and final settlement, especially outside of working hours. Blockchain transactions can reduce transaction times to minutes and are processed 24*7.

Disadvantages of Blockchain Technology

- **Effects the entire process:** If a single data in blockchain network is to be altered, then the complete set of related data also needs to be changes. Thus, if at a certain time, you need to alter a single data entry, then you need to go through the entire process of changing every related data.

- **Large energy consumption:** The Bitcoin blockchain network's miners are attempting 450 thousand trillion solutions per second in efforts to validate transactions, using substantial amounts of computer power.

- **Integration concerns:** Blockchain applications offer solutions that require significant changes to existing systems. In order to make the switch, companies must strategize the transition.

- **Cultural adoption:** Blockchain represents a complete shift to a decentralized network which requires the buy-in of its users and operators.

- **Cost:** Blockchain offers tremendous savings in transaction costs and time but the high initial capital costs could be a deterrent.

Who Uses the Blockchain?

Blockchain technology can be integrated into multiple areas. The primary use of blockchains is as a distributed ledger for cryptocurrencies. It shows great across a wide range of business applications like banking, finance, government, healthcare, Insurance, Media and Entertainment, retail, and so on.

Need of Blockchain

Blockchain Technology has become popular because of the following reasons:

- **Time reduction:** In the financial industry, blockchain allows the quicker settlement of trades. It does not take a lengthy process for verification, settlement, and clearance. It is because of a single version data available between all stakeholders.
- **Unchangeable transactions:** Blockchain registers transactions in a chronological order which certifies the inalterability of all operations; it means when a new block is added to the chain of ledgers, it cannot be removed or modified.
- **Realibility:** It certifies and verifies the identities of each interested parties. This removes double records, reducing rates and accelerates transactions.
- **Security:** It uses advanced cryptography to make sure that the information is locked inside the blockchain. It uses distributed ledger technology where each party holds a copy of the original chain, so the system remains operative, even the large number of other nodes fall.
- **Collaboration:** It allows each party to transact directly with each other without requiring a third-party intermediary.
- **Decentralized:** It is decentralized because there is no central authority. There are standard rules on how every node exchanges the blockchain information. This method ensures that all transactions are validated, and all valid transactions are added one by one.

What is Bitcoin?

It is important that you understand what bitcoin is. It is a crypto-currency and digital payment system invented by Satoshi Nakamoto. It means they can be used like a currency which can be used to buy things online. These are similar to digital cash that exist as bits on people's computers. Bitcoins exist only in the cloud, like Paypal or Paytm. Even though they are virtual, rather than physical, they are used like cash when transferred between people through the web.

The bitcoin system is peer-to-peer network based and transactions take place between users directly, without an intermediary. These transactions are verified by network nodes and recorded in a public-distributed leger called a Blockchain. The system works without a central repository or single administrator. Bitcoin is called the first decentralized digital currency. Bitcoins get created whenever a block containing valid transactions is added to the Blockchain. This is the only means for creating Bitcoins and through various mathematical and encryption algorithms and no fake bitcoins are created or circulated.

Features of Blockchain

The important features of Blockchain technology that has made it a revolutionary technology are:

- **Hash Function:** The core algorithm used in blockchain technology is the SHA256. The purpose of using a hash in the output is not 'encryption' i.e., it cannot be decrypted back to the original text. It is a one-way cryptographic function, and is a fixed size for any size of source text. For example, let's look at an example below:

Figure 9.3: *Hash function*

If you look at the first example, we are feeding the input as **Hello World** and getting an output as

"a591a6d40bf420404a011733cf b7b190d62c65bf0bcda32b57b277d9 ad9f146e".

However, by just adding an "!" at the end, the output completely changes to "7f83b1657ff1fc53b92dc18148a1d65dfc2d4b1 fa3d677284addd200126 d9069".

If you change "H" to "h" and "W" to "w", then the output value changes to "7509e5bda0c762d2bac7f90d758b5b2263fa01ccb c542ab5e3df163be08e6ca9".

In the above example, you understood how complex the algorithm is as even the slightest change in the input can cause a massive change in the output.

- **Public Key Cryptography:** Cryptography helps the user by creating a set of keys referred as Public key and Private key. The public key is shared with others whereas the private key is kept a secret by the user. Let us look at the example below for better understanding.

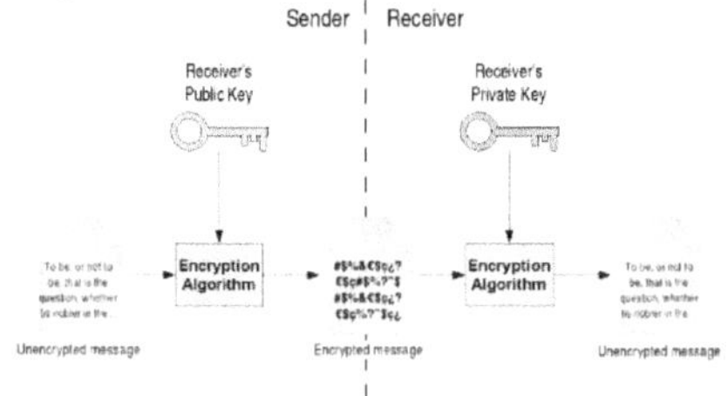

Figure 9.4: *Public key cryptography*

If Chandu sends some bitcoins to Joe, that transaction will have three pieces of information:

- Joe's bitcoin address. (Joe's Public key)
- The mount of bitcoins that Chandu is sending to Joe.
- Chandu's bitcoin address. (Chandu's Public key)

Now, all this data, along with an encrypted digital signature, is sent through the network for verification. The Digital signature is again a hash value achieved by the combination of the Chandu's bitcoin address and the amount he is sending to Joe. This digital signature is encrypted by the private key. Once this data is received by a miner who has to verify this transaction, there are two process he does simultaneously:

He takes all the un-encrypted data like transaction amount and public key of both Joe and Chandu, and feed it to a hash algorithm to get a hash value which you shall call Hash 1.

He takes the digital signature and decrypts it using Chandu's public key to get a hash value which you will call as Hash2.

If both Hash1 and Hash2 are the same, then it means that this a valid transaction.

Distributed Ledger or P2P Network

Every single person on the network has a copy of the ledger and there is no single centralized copy. There are no accounts and balances in the Bitcoin Blockchain ledger. Every transaction from the first one is stored on a continuous growing database called **Blockchain**. This ledger is distributed across all users of Bitcoin Blockchain, that is, the ledger has no central location where it is stored. Everyone on the network owns a copy of the ledger and the true cop is the collection of all the distributed ledgers.

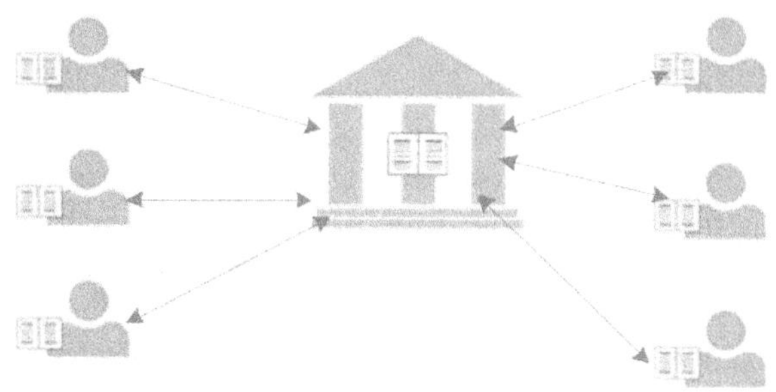

Figure 9.5: *Distributed ledger*

Proof of Work

If everyone equally owns the ledger, who adds blocks to the Blockchain? How can people trust this person? This work is done by people in the Bitcoin network you call miners. The work of these miners is to verify the transactions and solve a complex mathematical puzzle associated with the block being created. In the above figure, each block has a hash value which is the combination of the previous block's final hash, transaction data's hash value and the value. The final resulting hash for the block must start with a specified number of zeroes. It is this computation to find the value which satisfies the condition that makes mining so computationally.

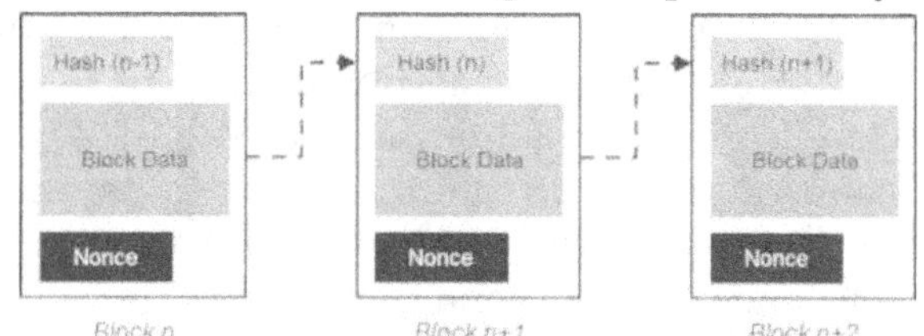

Figure 9.6: *Proof of work*

So, the person who finds this value is the successful miner and he/she can add their block to the blockchain. Through our P2P-distributed network, he/she broadcasts their block and everyone verifies if hashes match, updates their blockchain and moves on to solving the next block immediately.

Incentives for Validation

Bitcoin transaction is to giving a reward to the miner who has created the latest block. This reward is provided by the blockchain system for validating the transactions and maintain the blockchain.

3D Printing/Additive Manufacturing

3D printing is a form of additive manufacturing technology where a three-dimensional object is created by laying down successive layers of material. It is also known as **rapid prototyping**, which is a mechanized method whereby 3D objects are quickly made on a reasonably-sized machine connected to a computer containing blueprints for the object. This method for creating 3D models with the use of inkjet technology saves time and cost by eliminating the need to design, print and glue together separate model parts. Now, you can create a complete model in a single process using 3D printing. The basic principles include material cartridges, flexibility of output, and translation of code into a visible pattern.

3D Printers are machines that produce physical 3D models from digital data by printing layer-by-layer. They can make physical models of objects either designed with a CAD program or scanned with a 3D Scanner. They are used in a variety of industries, including jewellery, footwear, industrial design, architecture, engineering and construction, automotive, aerospace, dental and medical industries, education and consumer products.

Robotics Process Automation

Robotic process automation (RPA) is the use of software with **artificial intelligence (AI)** and machine learning capabilities to handle high-volume, repeatable tasks that require humans to perform. These tasks can include queries, calculations and maintenance of records and transactions.

Robotic process automation (RPA) is the application of technology that allows employees in a company to configure computer software or a **robot** to capture and interpret existing applications for processing a transaction, manipulating data, triggering responses and communicating with other digital systems.

Any company that uses labour on a large scale for general knowledge process work, where people are performing high-volume, high transactional process functions, will boost their capabilities and save money and time with robotic process automatic software.

Applications of RPA

Some of the applications of RPA include:

- **Customer service:** It can help companies offer better customer service by verifying e-signatures and uploading scanned documents.
- **Accounting service:** It is used for general accounting, operational accounting, transactional reporting and budgeting.
- **Financial Services:** It can be used for foreign exchange payments.
- **Health care:** It can be used for handling patient records.
- **Banking:** Automation of credit card applications in bank loan processing.

Cyber Security

Cyber security deals with the security of information technology. It also refers to protecting computers, networks, programs and data from unauthorized users.

The information stored in the cyber environment and user's assets is connected to computer devices, applications, services and telecommunications systems. Cyber Security is also used to protect your Internet and network-based digital equipment and information from unauthorized access. Its purpose is to defend the assets against all threat actors throughout the entire life cycle of a cyber-attack.

Why Cyber Security is Important?

You all live in a digital era world which is networked together, from internet banking to government infrastructure, where data is stored on computers and other devices. A portion of that data can be sensitive information, whether that be intellectual property, financial data, personal information, or other types of data for which unauthorized access could have negative concerns that hacks and other security attacks could endanger the global economy.

Organizations transmit sensitive data across network and other devices, cyber security to protect that information and the systems used to process or store it.

Cyber Security Goals

The main objective of Cyber security is to protect information from being stolen, compromised or attacked. It can be measured by three goals:

- Protect the confidentially of data.
- Preserve the integrity of data.
- Promote the availability of data for authorized users.

These three goals form the Confidentially, Integrity, Availability (CIA) triad, the basis of all security programs. This is also referred to as the Availability, Integrity, and Confidentiality (AIC) triad to avoid the confusion with the Central intelligence Agency. The elements are considered the three most crucial components of security.

- **Confidentiality:** It is equivalent to privacy and avoids the unauthorized disclosure of information. It involves the protection of data, providing access for those who are allowed to see it while disallowing others from learning about its content. Data encryption is a good example to ensure confidentiality.

- **Integrity:** It refers to the methods for ensuring that data is real, accurate and safeguard from unauthorized user modification. The information has not been altered in an unauthorized way, and that source of the information is genuine.

- **Availability:** It is the guarantee of reliable and constant access to our sensitive data by authorized people.

Types of Cyber Attacks

A cyber-attack is an exploitation of computer systems and networks. It uses malicious code to alter computer code, logic or data and leads to cybercrime, such as information and identity theft. Cyber-attacks can be classified into the following categories:

- **Web-based attacks:** These are the attacks which occur on a websites or web applications. Some of the important web-based attacks are:
  - o Injection attacks
  - o DNS Spoofing
  - o Session Hijacking
  - o Phishing
  - o Brute force

- System-based attacks: These are the attacks which are intended to compromise a computer or a computer network. Some of the important system-based attacks are:
  - o Virus
  - o Worm
  - o Trojan horse
  - o Backdoors
  - o Bots

Cyber Security Challenges

In India, there are many challenges related to cyber security. With the increase of cyber-attack, every organization needs a security analyst who makes sure that their system is secured. These security analysts face many challenges related to cyber security such as securing confidential data of government organizations, securing the private organization servers, and so on.

The important cyber security challenges are as follows:

- Blockchain Revolution
- Ransomware Evolution
- IoT Threats
- AI Expansion
- Serverless Apps Vulnerability

Need for Cyber Security

Cyber security is an important part of individuals, as well as organizations, governments, educational institutions and our business. It is essential for families and parents to protect the children and family members from online fraud. In terms of financial security, it is crucial to secure our financial information that can affect our personal financial status. Internet is very important for students, staff and educational institutions and has provided lots of learning opportunities with a number of online risks.

There is a need for Internet users to understand how to protect themselves from online fraud and identity theft. Small and medium-sized organizations also experience various security-related challenges because of limited resources and inadequate cyber security skills. The rapid expansion of technologies is also creating and making the cyber security more challenging and presenting various frameworks or technologies to protect our network and information, but all of these provide protection for short term only. However, better security understanding and appropriate strategies can help us to protect intellectual property and trade secrets and reduce financial and reputation loss.

Most of the time, governments face difficulties due to inappropriate infrastructure, lack of awareness and sufficient funding. It is important for the government bodies to provide reliable services to society, maintain healthy citizen-to-government communications and protect confidential information.

Securing Your PC

No doubt, computer has become an essential part of your daily lives. You get almost everything done online via PC or laptop. You can secure your PC from virus and spyware in the following ways:

- **Creating Strong Password:** Passwords give the first line of protection against any unauthorized access to your computer. The stronger your password, the more protected your computer is from hackers and malicious software.
- **Keep Windows up-to-date:** Choose an operating system based on its security and vulnerability. Make sure you update your operating system with security updates.
- **Turn on the Windows firewall:** Windows has a built-in firewall that protects your PC from unwanted attention via the Internet.
- **Install, update and use anti-virus software:** Installing antivirus software may sound like an obvious first step to protect against malware.
- **Encrypt your Connection to the Internet:** One of the best encryption tools is none other than VPN. A VPN encrypts your Internet connection and keeps your online activities safe; by using a VPN, you ensure that your computer or laptop is safe while connected to the Internet.

Securing Your Mob]ile

Smart phones, tablets, and other mobile devices have become a necessary part of many people's lives. Here are some simple steps to keep you and your devices safe and secure.

- Protect your device physically by choosing a strong password using the auto-lock feature, and by not sharing your device with others.
- Keep your data secure by regularly backing up and syncing, staying up-to-date with patches and doing operating system updates, and not overriding any software or security features.
- Safeguard your personally identifiable information (PII) like Social Security numbers, passwords, and account numbers. Do not share this information via text; make sure any mobile shopping or banking is done over a secure connection, and disable geo tagging.
- Protect your device from malware by being cautious about installing apps.

- Try to use private data connection and switch off Wi-Fi on your mobile phone whenever you are in public place.

Conclusion

The Internet of Things is a system of interrelated computing devices, such as physical objects that are embedded with sensors, software technologies for the purpose of connect and exchange data with other devices and system over the internet. IoT devices are implemented using both hardware and software components. Big Data Analytics is the process of large data sets containing a variety of data types. For example, industries that use big data analytics such as hospitality industry, healthcare companies, etc. Storing and accessing data and programs over the internet instead of a computer's hard drive is known as cloud computing. There are three categories of Cloud computing such as Infrastructure as a service (IaaS), Platform as service (PaaS), and Software as a service (Saas). Virtual reality is the creation of a virtual environment presented to our senses in a such a way that you experience it as if we are really there. The main types of virtual reality are non, semi and fully immersive. AI is a part of our daily life; it refers to a computer's ability to perform tasks and make decisions that require some level of human intelligence. Some important applications of AI are used in applicable in many aspects such as Finance, Medical, Entertainment, Pattern recognition, and Data mining. Blockchain is the technology of Digital CryptoCurrency Bitcoin. Cryptography helps the user by creating asset of key referred as Public key and Private key. 3D printing is a process of making three-dimensional sold objects from a digital file. The term Robotic process automation is a software tool that replicates the actions of an actual human interacting with one or more software applications to perform task such as responding to simple customer service queries. Cyber security deals with the security of information technology. It also refers to protecting computers, networks, programs and data from unauthorized users. These were all the concepts you studied in this chapter.

Model Questions and Answers

A. Multiple Choice Questions.

1. Which role do Internet technologies and the 'IoT' play in the context of Industry 4.0?

a. They form the base to connect everyday items

b. They form the base for an environmental-friendly production

c. They form among others the base for corporate communication

d. None of the above

2. What is Artificial Intelligence?

a. Putting your intelligence into Computer

b. Programming with your own intelligence

c. Making a machine intelligent

d. Putting more memory into computer

3. Who created Bitcoin?

a. Satoshi Nakamoto

b. Samsung

c. John Mcafee

d. China

4. When will the Industry 4.0 reach the market?

a. To reach a production environment

b. First implementations will be released by 2020

c. Industry 4.0 is already being used in several production lines

d. All of the above

5. Which of these is not a type of cloud computing usage?

a. Platform as a service

b. Hardware as a service

c. Software as a service

d. Infrastructure as a service

6. What is a private key?

a. A key on your key chain

b. A key given to the public

c. A key NOT to be given to the public

d. A key that opens a secret door

7. Cloud Services have a __________ relationship with their customers.

a. Many-to -Many

b. One-to-Many

c. One-to-One

d. None of these

8. Which one is not an element of IoT?

a. Security

b. Process

c. People

d. Things

9. The device connected to the Internet of Things have to communicate automatically, not via humans. What is this called?

a. Bot-to-Bot (B2B)

b. Machine-to-Machine (M2M)

c. InterCloud

d. Skynet

10. What is a blockchain?

a. A distributed ledger on a peer-to-peer network

b. A type of Cryptocurrency

c. An exchange

d. A centralized ledger

B. State whether the following Statements are True or False.

1. Bitcoin is the first distributed blockchain implementation.

2. A node is a computer on a blockchain network.

3. Cloud computing networks are designed to support only private or hybrid clouds.

4. You cannot access your data from any computer in the world, as long as you have an Internet connection.

5. A block in the blockchain can never have more than one parent block.

6. Cloud computing refers to applications and services that run on a distributed network using virtualized resources.

7. Trojan horses are very similar to virus in that they are computer programs that replicate copies of themselves.

8. 3D printing technology is expanding and is now able to print metal parts.

9. In blockchain, each block is linked backward to the previous block.

10. VR is used for medical, piloting, and military training purposes.

C. Match the following:

1.	Making a machine intelligent:	a.	Private Cloud
2.	It is a realistic three-dimensional image:	b.	Blockchain
3.	A service that can be accessed by a limited amount of people:	c.	Artificial Intelligence
4.	HMD stands for:	d.	Miner
5.	A distributed ledger on a P2P network:	e.	Limited memory
6.	Computer that validate and process blockchain transaction:	f.	Virtual Reality
7.	Computer that validate and process blockchain transaction:	g.	Hadoop
8.	Bid Data processing and analysis can be done by:	h.	Head mounted display
9.	It is the protection of Internetconnected system including hardware, software and data:	i.	Security
10.	Passwords are used to improve the _____ of a network:	j.	Cybersecurity

D. Fill in the blanks:

> SHA256   Immersive   Hash algorithm
> M2M   Public   Software-as a Service
> Predictive analytics   Blockchain
> Radio identification   technology
> Theory of mind   Publick key

1. Bitcoin is based on _______ blockchain?
2. __________ hash identifying each block in the Blockchain is generated using cryptographic algorithm.
3. The entire blockchain is protected by a strong cryptographic _________.
4. _________ describes a distribution model in which applications are hosted by a service provider and made available to users.
5. In __________ VR, subjects are visually isolated from the real environment.
6. The huge numbers of devices connected to the Internet of Things have to communicate automatically is called ___________.
7. ___________ is being used by Internet of Things.
8. __________ uses many techniques like data mining and artificial intelligence to analyze current data and make scenarios of that might happen.
9. Bitcoin transactions are verified by network nodes and recorded in a public distribute ledger called a ___________.
10. ___________ understand the human emotions, people, beliefs, and be able to interact social like humans.

Short Questions with Answers

1. **What is IoT?**

   Answers: IoT stands for an Internet of Things. It is largely a network which can talk to each other the use of the internet as an approach to communicate between them. It includes a wide variety of "smart" devices, from industrial machines that transmit data about the production process to sensors that track information about the human body.

2. **How does the Internet of Things work?**

   Answers: Since the mechanism of IoT devices is highly technical, so for many it is quite confusing how an IoT system actually works. A complete IoT system is made up of four distinct components that work together to deliver the desired output.

   - Sensors/devices
   - Connectivity
   - Data Processing
   - User Interface

3. **What are the benefits of IoT?**

   a. **Access to High-Quality Data:** Especially marketers and entrepreneurs, data and with the invention of IoT devices.

   b. **Better Tracking and Management:** IoT makes tracking and management a breeze for organization.

   c. **Efficient Resource Utilization:** Be it home, office, hotel or car, IoT facilitates an efficient utilization of assets for improved productivity.

   d. **Automation and Control:** Automation is the need of the hour and IoT is renowned for the same. For instance, home appliances such as air conditioner, washing machines, ovens, and refrigerators can be automatically get operated.

   e. **Comport and Convenience:** The interconnectivity of devices and aggregation of data provides you full control over all devices that are connected with each other through the IoT system.

   f. **Saves Time and Money:** IoT not only saves your precious time but also your hard-earned money. For example, if your kitchen electronic appliance has the ability to turn off itself after the task is done, this saves your time and efforts as well as extra expenditure caused by the unnecessary use of electricity.

4. **What are the important components of Internet of Things?**

   Answers: The important components that exist in the Internet of Things are as follows:

   a. **Hardware:** This will make physical items responsive and give them functionality to store records and respond to instructions.

   b. **Software:** It allows the facts collection such as storing, processing, manipulating and instructing.

   c. **Infrastructure:** Infrastructure which consists of protocols and technologies which allow two bodily gadgets to exchange information.

5. **What does Big Data Analytics mean?**

   Answers: The term Big data analytics refers to the strategy of analysing large volumes of data, or big data. The large amount of data which grouped a wide variety of sources, including social network, videos, digital images, sensors and sales transactions record is called Big Data. The main purpose in analysing all this data is to uncover patterns and connections that might otherwise be invisible, and that might provide valuable insights about the users who created it.

6. **Why is big data analytics important?**

   Answers: The most important advantages of Big Data analysis is that it helps organizations harness their data and use it to identify new opportunities. With the help of this, companies lead to smarter business, more efficient operations, higher profits and happier customers.

7. **List some tools used for Big Data?**

   Answers: There are various tools in Big Data technology which are deployed for importing, sorting, and analysing data.

Some tools are as follows:

   a. Apache Hive

   b. MongoDB

   c. MapReduce

   d. Apache Sqoop

   e. Apache Pig

   f. Apache Hadoop

8. What are the sources of unstructured data in Big Data?

Answers: The sources of unstructured data are as follows:

   a. Text files and documents

   b. Server website and application log

   c. E-mails

   d. Social media Data

   e. Images, videos and audio files

9. What is Cloud Computing?

Answers: Cloud computing is a new age computer technology that is internet base. It is the next generation technology that utilized the web-based clouds to provide the services whenever the user need it.

10. What is Cloud?

Answers: A cloud is an amalgamation of hardware, network, services, storage and interfaces that aid in delivering computing as a service. It has three users:

   a. End users

   b. Business management users

   c. Cloud service provider

The end users are the one who use the services provided by the cloud. The business management user in the cloud takes the responsibility of the data and the services provided by the cloud. The cloud service provider is the one who takes care or is responsible for the maintenance of the IT assets of the cloud. It acts as a common center for its users to fulfil their computing needs.

11. What are the basic characteristic of cloud computing?

Answers: The four basic characteristics of cloud computing are given as follows:

   a. Elasticity and scalability

   b. Self-Service provisioning and automatic de-provisioning

   c. Standardized interfaces

   d. Billing self-service based usage model.

12. How can a company benefit from cloud computing?

Answers:

   a. More secure data backup and data storage

   b. Software as a service

   c. Take advantage of powerful server capabilities without hardware investment

   d. Better positioning for growth and scale

   e. Increased productivity

   f. Cost-effectiveness

13. What is a Virtual Reality?

Answers: VR is a realistic three-dimensional image (3D image) or artificial environment. It is created with a mixture of interactive hardware and software and presented to the user in such a way that the any doubts are suspended. It is accepted as a real environment in which it is interacted with in a seemingly real or physical way.

14. What are the different types of VR?

Answers:

   a. Immersive virtual reality

   b. Non-Immersive systems

   c. Semi-Immersive projection systems

   d. Fully immersive head-mounted display systems

   e. Enhanced Reality

   f. Desktop virtual reality

   g. Projection virtual reality

   h. Simulation virtual reality

15. **What is the difference between strong and weak artificial Intelligence?**

    Answers:

Weak AI	Strong AI
Narrow application, with very limited scope.	Widely applied, with vast scope.
Good at specific tasks.	Incredible human-level intelligence.
Uses supervised and unsupervised.	Uses clustering and association to.
Learning to process data.	Process data.
For example: Siri, Alexa, and so on.	For example: Advanced Robotics.

16. List some applications of AI.

    Answers:

    - Natural language processing
    - Chatbots
    - Sales prediction
    - Self-driving card
    - Facial expression recognition
    - Image tagging

17. What is Blockchain?

    Answers:

    It is an incorruptible digital ledger of economic transactions that can be programmed to record not only financial transactions but virtually everything of value. In simple terms, it is a decentralized distributed database of immutable records that are managed by a group of computers but not owned by any single entity. It is stored as a database or a flat-file.

18. How does blockchain work?

    Answers:

    It consists of immutable records of data called blocks with are linked using cryptography. It is nothing but a process to encrypt and secure data communication from third parties in reading private messages. Once the data has been recorded, it will not be changed. It works like a digital notary with timestamps to avoid tampering of information.

19. Define Encryption and why it is used?

    Answers:

    It is a process of converting the data of file into an unreadable format to protect the data from attack. It is being widely used in an organization to secure their data.

20. What are the key terms of Security?

    Answers:

    The key terms for security are Confidentiality, Integrity and Availability. It is also known as CIA. These three things are considered to be the most important components of the security. Confidentiality means protecting the information and the information remains between the client and organization, and not sharing the information with other people. Integrity means the reliability and trusted data, which refers to real and accurate data. Availability refers to access information from the specified location.

Descriptive Type Questions.

1. What are the different sectors where the Internet of Things can actually add value to the Current process?
2. What role does the network play in the Internet of Everything?
3. What is the difference between IoT devices and embedded devices?
4. What is Big Data analytics?
5. Explain any two types of big Data analytics.
6. What is Big Data?
7. What are Advantages and Dis advantage of Cloud computing?
8. What are main features of Cloud Service?
9. How many types of deployment model are used in Cloud?
10. What it the difference between AR and VR?

11. What is Artificial Intelligence?
12. What are types of blockchain? Explain the types in short.
13. What is the difference between private and public blockchain?
14. What are the principals to identify cyber attacks?
15. Explain Cyber Attack?

Answers

A.	1. a	2. c	3. a	4. c	5. b
	6. c	7. b	8. a	9. b	10. a

B.	1. T	2. T	3. F	4. F	5. T
	6. T	7. F	8. T	9. F	10. T

C.	1. c	2. f	3. a	4. h	5. b
	6. d	7. e	8. g	9. j	10. i

D.	1. e	2. a	3. c	4. f	5. b
	6. d	7. i	8. g	9. h	10. j

■■

Solved Sample Question Paper

A. Multiple Choice Questions:

1. Which of the following retains the information it's storing when the power of the system is turned off?
   a. CPU
   b. ROM
   c. RAM
   d. DIMM

2. In a digital computer, data is represented in:
   a. Octal form
   b. Hexadecimal form
   c. Binary form
   d. Numerical form

3. Which protocol sends electronic mail?
   a. Outlook Express
   b. POP3
   c. FTP
   d. SMTP

4. What is the name of new built-in browser included in Windows 10?
   a. Cortana
   b. Edge
   c. Opera
   d. Internet Explorer Pro

5. Which of the following features allow Windows 10 to adopt to different device types?
   a. Flexi
   b. Continuum
   c. Hub
   d. Unifi

6. Cookies are:
   a. A product made in berkley
   b. Mechanism for storing an information on the net
   c. Mechanism for storing persistent data on clients in the file called cookies
   d. None of these

7. Blog is a:
   a. Present article in reverse chronological order
   b. Title of a book
   c. Special partition in web server
   d. Name of a search engine

8. In MS-Word, to delete the selected item permanently without placing the item in the Recycle bin:
   a. Shift + Delete
   b. Ctrl while dragging an item
   c. Ctrl + Shift
   d. None of these

9. In PowerPoint, the Header & Footer button can be found on the Insert tab in what group?
   a. Illustrations group
   b. Tables group
   c. Text group
   d. None of these

10. In order to access Internet banking, customer needs:
    a. Customer ID and Password
    b. Customer name and Password
    c. Customer ID and Date of Birth
    d. Customer ID and Phone number

B. State whether the following Statements are True or False.

1. Worms and Trojan horses are easily detected and eliminated by antivirus software.
2. CPU controls only input data of computer.
3. IPv6 Internet Protocol address is represented as eight groups of four octal digits.
4. An SD card is an output device.
5. Firmware is software that is embedded in hardware device.
6. A folder cannot contain files as well as sub-folders.
7. A Passport is essential for those who are traveling abroad for education, tourism and family visits.
8. Social networking involves communication between a computer and a router.
9. In Excel, you can indicate absolute references by a hash sign (#).
10. Different elements in a chart cannot have different transitions.

C. Match the following.

1.	Memories must be refreshed many times per sec:	a.	Bharat Interface for Money
2.	Device is used to connect two systems using different protocols:	b.	Dynamic RAM
3.	Abbreviation of BHIM:	c.	Executing
4.	Is the process of carrying out commands:	d.	Gateway
5.	A file is often referred to as:	e.	Web page
6.	HTML is used to create:	f.	Document

7.	One has to made advance payment:	g.	Personal identification number
8.	PIN stands for :	h.	Credit card
9.	Special effects used to introduce slides in:	i.	One
10.	=MOD(-3,2) entered in a cell displays:	j.	Three
		k.	Transitions

D. Fill in the blanks

> Switch   Ping   E-banking   Hacking   File   RAM   IP address   web browser   Rehearsal   Social networking

1. To identify TCP/IP errors such as connection problems, _________ command can be used.
2. The information stored in ___________ is erased when the computer is turned off.
3. A ___________ is a computer program that continuously and rapidly explores the World Wide Web.
4. Twitter is a ___________ website.
5. A _________ is a collection of information saved as unit.
6. A computer on Internet is identified by _______.
7. Knowing someone else's password by certain illegal means is _________.
8. A computer which converts data transmission protocol between networks is ___________.
9. _________ is simply the use of electronic means to transfer funds directly form one account to another, rather than by cheque or cash.
10. ______ option can be used to set custom timings for slides in a presentation.

Descriptive type Questions.

1. Distinguish between
   a. What are the different functions of a computer?

Answer: A computer carries out the following functions:

    i. Accepting data

    ii. Processing data

    iii. Storing data

    iv. Displaying data

b. What is a Storage Device? What is the common classification?

Answer: Storage devices are used to store data in the computer. The different types of storage devices are:

- Magnetic devices
- Optical devices
- Solid-state storage devices

c. State the basic units of a computer. Name the sub-units that make up the CPU and give the functions of each of the units.

Answer: The five basic units of a computer are:

- Input unit
- Output unit
- Storage unit
- Central Processing Unit
- Arithmetic and Logic Unit
- Control Unit

The CPU has two sub-units: the control unit and the arithmetic logic unit. The control unit controls the entire operation being carried out. The ALU performs the arithmetic and logical operations.

d. What is the difference between IoT devices and embedded devices?

Answer: Internet of Things is a type of embedded system that connects to the Internet. Embedded systems tend to be small software programs that implement a few functions. Internet of Things may be updated constantly according to the environment and learn by itself.

e. What is the RTGS System?

Answer: RTGS system is a funds transfer mechanism where transfer of money takes place from one bank to another on a real-time and gross basis. This the fastest money transfer system through the banking channel. Settlement in real time means payment transactions are settled as soon as they are processed. Gross settlement means the transaction is settled on a one-to-one basis without gathering any other transaction.

f. How do you check spellings and grammar in a MS-Word document?

Answer: Place the cursor at the beginning of the document or at the beginning of the section that you want to check. Click the Review tab on the toolbar. Click Spelling & Grammar on the proofing group.

g. What are the features and significance of electronic spreadsheets?

Answer: There are many features of an electronic spreadsheet that makes it really significant. It helps to organize and assess different types of information with ease. It can be used to generate various kinds of reports for communication within departments. The sheet can calculate mathematical formulae based on content entered in other cells. It also enhances productivity by reducing time spent on everyday accounting tasks.

h. How can you play music for the duration of your slide show in PowerPoint?

Answer:

    i. Download or store music to your PC hard drive and from there upload it to PowerPoint.

    ii. In the Insert tab, click Audio and then click on Audio on my PC.

    iii. Locate and double-click the music file.

    iv. Click on Play in Background under the Playback tab.

i. What is e-mail? What are the steps required for sending an e-mail?

Answer

Electronic mail lets you send and receive messages in electronic form. The steps required for sending an e-mail are:

    i. Start an e-mail program.

    ii. Type the address where to send the e-mail.

    iii. Compose a message.

    iv. Click the Send button.

    2. Explain the following terms:

    a. Define e-Wallet. What are the two components of e-Wallet?

    b. Virtual Payment Address

    c. What are QR Codes are used for?

d. Explain USSD features and benefits of USSD

Answer: a. e-wallet is a type of electronic card which is used for transactions made online through a computer or a smartphone. Its utility is the same as a credit or debit card. An E-wallet needs to be linked with the individual's bank account to make payments.

The two components are software and information. The software component stores personal information and provides security and encryption of the data. The information component is a database of details provided by the user, which includes their name, shipping address, payment methods, amount to be paid, credit or debit card details, and so on.

b. A virtual payment address, also referred to as VPA, is something like an email ID, which is given to an individual using the Unified Payment Interface service to send or receive money. With UPI, fund transfers can be initiated without IFSC code or bank account number. So, VPA is essentially the only piece of information required or all transactions. The UPI interface gives users the privilege to send money to any bank account holder with UPI on a 24 by 7 basis instantaneously.

c. QR codes are easy to generate and use. They are a convenient way to store all kinds of data in a small space. They can store different types of information. QR codes are used for many purposes; they are used for holding data such as:

i. Simple text
ii. Addresses
iii. Phone numbers
iv. E-mail addresses
v. URLs
vi. Payments
vii. Online accounts authentication
viii. Wi-Fi authentication

d. USSD stands for unstructured supplementary service data. It is a Global system for Mobile communication technology that is used to send text between a mobile phone and an application program in the network. USSD is similar to short messaging service. The payment service *99# works on USSD channel. This service allows mobile banking transactions using a basic mobile phone feature; there is no need to have mobile internet data facility for using USSD-based mobile banking. Key services offered under *99# service include interbank account to account fund transfer, balance enquiry and mini statement.

Features and benefits of USSD:

i. Works on a basic phone
ii. Round-the-clock service
iii. Easy and accessible
iv. Secure interface with a limited credential requirement
v. Multilingual service
vi. Faster transactions
vii. Service anytime anywhere

Answers.

A.	1. a	2. c	3. d	4. b	5. b
	6. c	7. a	8. a	9. c	10. a

B.	1. T	2. F	3. F	4. F	5. T
	6. F	7. T	8. F	9. F	10. T

C.	1. b	2. d	3. a	4. c	5. f
	6. e	7. h	8. g	9. k	10. i

D.	1. b	2. f	3. h	4. j	5. e
	6. g	7. d	8. a	9. c	10. i

Solved Sample Question Paper

A. Multiple Choice Questions:

1. Which of the following statements is correct?
   a. 1 KB = 1024 bytes
   b. 1 MB = 2048 bytes
   c. 1 MB = 1000 kilobytes
   d. 1 KB = 1000 bytes

2. In which year was Windows 10 launched?
   a. 2014
   b. 2014
   c. 2013
   d. 2015

3. What is the official name of the Twitter bird?
   a. Chip
   b. Birdy
   c. Larry
   d. None of these

4. What is the maximum amount of characters allowed in a single Tweet?
   a. 100
   b. 140
   c. 120
   d. 200

5. In this type of VR environment, the three-dimensional scene is considered as a part of the physical environment.
   a. Immersive
   b. Semi immersive
   c. None immersive
   d. Augmented

6. In Excel, which one is a denoted a range from B1 through E5?
   a. B1 –E5
   b. B1:E5
   c. B1toE5
   d. B1$E5

7. Virus infection via email attachments can be minimized using which of the following?
   a. Opening attachments from external hard drives
   b. Copying attachments
   c. Right clicking attachments
   d. Deleting mail containing attachments from unknown senders

8. The characteristics of a QR code are:
   a. Large volume data
   b. High-speed reading
   c. High density recording
   d. All of the above

9. Artificial intelligence has its expansion in the following application:
   a. Planning and scheduling
   b. Game playing
   c. Robotics
   d. All of the above

10. The process of arranging the items of a column in some sequence or order is known as __________.
   a. Arranging
   b. Autofill
   c. Sorting
   d. Filtering

B. State whether the following Statements are True or False.

1. Twitter is an online social networking and blogging service.
2. A microphone is used an input device.
3. Primary memory has a higher storage capacity than secondary memory.
4. OCR is a device that scans written or typed text and transforms it into computer readable form.

5. The Windows control panel gives you access to all of your computer settings and enables you to install and remove programs.
6. National Payments Corporation of India is an independent organization set up to administer all retail payment systems in India.
7. DigiLocker is an online documents platform that facilitates sharing of documents between government agencies and DigiLocker users.
8. You can say Credit card is also known as an ATM card.
9. UPI has been developed by the NPCI organization.
10. VR is used for medical, piloting, and military training purposes.

C.   Match the following.   [1×5=5]

1. CD-ROM is:	a. Physical structure of computer is
2. Hardware:	b. Four digits
3. Keyboard converts types in designing a model of a:	c. Secondary memory
4. Payment Service used by BHIM app:	d. ASCII
5. len():	e. Notes page
6. In PowerPoint, it can be used used to enter speaker comments:	f. Finds related records
7. Function in Excel tells how many numeric entries are there:	g. IMPS
8. Vital information resources under siege:	h. Source and destination address
9. VLookup function do:	i. COUNT
10. Each IP packet must contain:	j. Four alphabets
	k. Virus

	1. Source or destination address

D.   Fill in the blanks

> Line spacing   Line chart   SMTP   E-commerce
> Transpose   World Wide Web   Slide sorter view
> Firewall   Public key technique   Binding side
> Add space to the footer side

1. __________ is one of which is a safety measure in banking network.
2. Asymmetric key cryptography is also known as ____________.
3. __________ PowerPoint view works best for adding slide transitions.
4. The amount of vertical space between lines of text in a document is called ________.
5. ________ type of chart will you use to compare performance of two employees in the year 2019?
6. The __________ function displays row data in a column or column data in a row.
7. ________ is the encompassing term that involves the use of electronic platforms, intranets, extranets and the Internet to conduct a company's business.
8. Use ________ to send and receive electronic mail.
9. The collection of links throughout the Internet creates an interconnected network called __________.
10. Gutter margin is __________ used to add space.

Descriptive type Questions

1. Answer the following questions
   a. Differentiate between CPU and ALU.
   b. What are the different e-commerce business models?
   c. Explain CD-ROM.
2. Answer the following questions
   a. What impact will the Internet of Things have on infrastructure and smart cities sector?
   b. How is RTGS different from the Electronic fund transfer system?
   c. What are the different data formats in Excel?

d. What is the difference between a function and a formula in Excel?

3. Explain the following terms:
   a. What is an Interface?
   b. Explain Taskbar.
   c. What is Client/Server?
   d. Describe Various Network Types.

4. Answer the following questions.
   a. How to create cross-referencing in Word 2013?
   b. What are the types of data used in Cloud computing?
   c. What is the difference between cloud computing and mobile computing?

5. Answer the following questions.
   a. Write the comparison between Dot matrix printers and Laser printers with respect to print quality, speed, Noise and cost parameters.
   b. Explain ISP and its role.
   c. Explain Wireless Fidelity and how to connect the Wi-Fi network using Taskbar.

6. Answer the following questions.
   a. Define Digital locker and the components of a digital locker system.

   b. Write about the safe use of online bill payment.
   c. Write a short note on any one storage devices of computer.

7. Answer the following questions.
   a. Explain following with examples in Word:
      i.   Mail Merge
      ii. Header & Footer
   b. What is an information kiosk? What is a handout PowerPoint presentation? What is the purpose of handouts?
   c. Write a short note on applications of IT in Railways reservation.

8. Answer the following questions.
   a. Explain the example cell referencing. What are the different types of referencing?
   b. What is the difference between private and public blockchain?
   c. Explain any two types of big Data analytics.

9. Explain the following terms:
   a. LAN and WAN
   b. Domain Name system
   c. Website and Web server
   d. E-mail address

Linux Operating System

Linux is an open-source operating system. We are all familiar with other operating systems like Windows, Apple macOS, iOS, Android, and so on. An OS is a software that enables communication between computer hardware and software. It conveys input to get processed by the processor and brings output to the hardware to display it.

Overview of LINUX

Linux is a multi-user, multi-tasking operating system first developed by Linus Benedict Torvalds in the year 1991. Linux is a 32-bit operating system. It runs on a wide variety of platforms, such as Intel, Sparc, Alpha, and so on. It can be considered in every sense as a full-blown implementation of UNIX. But it cannot be called as UNIX because UNIX is a registered trademark product owned by AT&T. Linux is distributed as a free software under a free software license called the GNU General Public License (GPL).

Structure of Linux Operating System

It is a collection of software, each designed for a specific function.

Linux OS has the following components:

- Kernel
- System Libraries
- System Tools
- Development Tools
- End User Tools

Kernel

Kernel is the core of the operating system. It determines communication between devices and software. It has four responsibilities:

- **Device management:** A system has many devices connected to CPU, such as a memory device, sound cards, a graphic card, and so on. A kernel stores all the data related to all the devices in the device driver. It knows what a device can do and how to manipulate it to being outperformance. It has certain rules that have to be followed by all the devices.
- **Memory management:** This function manages the memory management. It keeps a track of used and unused memory and makes sure that processes do not manipulate data of each other using virtual memory address.
- **Process management:** The process management kernel assigns enough time and gives priorities to processes before handling CPU to other processes.
- **Handling system calls:** It means a programmer can write a query or ask the kernel to perform a task.

System Libraries

It has special programs that help in accessing the kernel's features. It has to be triggered to perform a task and this triggering is done by the application. But applications know how to place a system call because each kernel has a different set of system calls. Programmers have developed a standard library of procedures to communicate with kernel.

System Tools

It has a set of utility tools which are usually simple commands. With the help of a command, you can access your files, edit and manipulate data in your directories or files, also change location of files.

Development Tools

To update your system, you have additional tools and libraries. These additional tools and libraries are written by the programmers and are called tool chain. It is a vital development tool used by the developers to produce a working application.

End User Tools

These end tools make a system unique for a user. End tools are not required for the OS but are necessary for a user. Examples of end tools are graphic design, office suites, browsers, multimedia players, and so on.

Linux Features

- **Multiuser capability:** It can access the same system resources like memory, hard disk, and so on. But they have to use different terminals to operate.
- **Multitasking:** More than one function can be performed simultaneously by dividing the CPU time intelligently.
- Portability: It means that it supports different types of hardware.
- **Security:** It provides security in three ways, namely, authenticating, authorization and encryption.
- **GUI:** Linux is command line-based OS but it can be converted to GUI based by installing packages.
- **Support customized keyboard:** It supports different language keyboards.
- **File System:** It provides a hierarchical file system in which files and directories are arranged.
- **Open Source:** Linux code is freely available to all and is a community-based development project.

Why Use Linux?

Linux is completely different from other OS in many ways:

- It is an open source OS which gives a great advantage to the programmers, so they can design their own custom operating system.
- It gives you a lot of option of programs and features so you can choose according to your need.
- Companies like Google, Amazon and Facebook use Linux in order to protect their servers as it is highly reliable and stable.
- You do not have to pay for software and server licensing to install Linux; it's free and you can install it on as many computers as you want.
- It's a completely free operating system and does not have an issue with viruses, malware and slowing down your computer.

Advantages of Linux over Windows

The advantages of Linux operating system are:

- **Low cost:** The majority of Linux variants are available for free at a much lower price than Microsoft Windows.
- **Stability:** Linux does not need to be rebooted periodically to maintain performance levels. It does not freeze up or slow down over time due to memory leaks.
- **Performance:** Linux provides persistent high performance on workstations and on networks. It can handle unusually large numbers of users simultaneously.
- **Network friendliness:** Linux was developed by a group of programmers over the Internet and has therefore strong support for network functionality; client and server systems can be easily set up on any computer running Linux. It can perform tasks such as network backups faster and more reliably than alternative systems.
- **Flexibility:** Linux can be used for high performance server applications, desktop applications, and embedded systems. You can save disk space by installing the components needed for a particular use.
- **Compatibility:** It runs all common UNIX software packages and can process all common file formats.
- **Fast and easy installation:** Most Linux distributions come with user-friendly installation and setup programs. Popular Linux distributions come with tools that make installation of additional software very user-friendly as well.
- **Full use of hard disk:** Linux continues work well even when the hard disk is almost full.
- **Multitasking:** Linux is designed to do many things at the same time; for example, a large printing job in the background would not slow down other work.

Disadvantages of Linux over Windows

- Linux has more than 300 versions and all versions cannot be installed on a single computer system.
- There are so many distributions of Linux that new users may get confused.
- Some hardware devices and software may not be compatible with a particular version of Linux.

Linux Principles

The five Linux principles are discussed in the following sub-sections.

Everything is a File

UNIX and Linux systems treat everything as a file, including hardware. UNIX systems have many powerful utilities designed to create and manipulate files. The UNIX security model is based around the security of files. By treating everything as a file, a consistency emerges. We can secure access to hardware in the same way as we secure access to a document.

Small, Single-Purpose Programs

UNIX provides many small utilities that perform one task very well. When new functionality is required, the general philosophy is to create a separate program rather than to extend an existing utility with new features.

Ability to Chain Programs

A core design feature of UNIX is that the output of one program can be the input for another. This gives the user the flexibility to combine many small programs together to perform a larger, more complex task.

Avoid Captive User Interfaces

Interactive commands are rare in UNIX. Most commands expect their options and arguments to be typed on the command line when the command is launched. The command completes normally, possibly producing output, or generates an error message and quits. Interactivity is reserved for programs where it makes sense, for example, text editors.

Configuration Data Stored in Text

Text is a universal interface, and many UNIX utilities exist to manipulate text. Storing configuration in text allows an administrator to move a configuration from one machine to another easily. There are several revision control applications that enable an administrator to track which change was made on a particular day, and provide the ability to rollback a system configuration to a particular date and time.

Basic Linux Elements

The basic elements of LINUX are discussed in the following sub-sections:

Kernel

The kernel is at the core of LINUX system and is loaded into the memory as soon as the system starts up. It manages main memory, files and peripheral devices. Maintaining the time and date, launching applications, and allocating system resources are also functions of this part of the operating system.

Shell

Shell is a program which interprets commands given by the user. The command can be either typed in through the command line or contained in a file called 'shell script'. Commands in 'shell script' files are interpreted by the shell.

File System

Linux treats everything as a file. Even a directory is treated as a file that contains entries for several other files. All the hardware devices, such as I/O devices, storage devices, etc., are treated as files.

The Linux file system is organized in a hierarchy which starts with the root directory. The root is represented by a forward slash (/). Under the root directory are several system directories and the home directory. Figure A.1 lists the standard system directories in Linux.

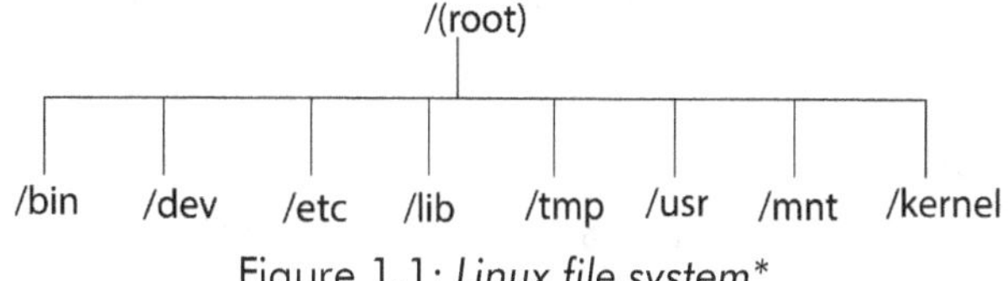

Figure 1.1: *Linux file system**

Linux uses the forward slash (/) as a separator (Windows or DOS use backslash (\) as a separator). For example, a subdirectory mydir of the directory usr, will be shown as /usr/mydir. The slash (/) before the usr represents the root directory.

/bin

This directory contains executable program files (binary files). In this directory, one can find the files for the Linux commands. (Similar to the command. com file in DOS).

/dev

This directory contains the special device files. For example, the printer may be a file known as prn in this directory, the hard disk may be an hda file and its first partition would be had().

/etc

This directory contains all the system-wide configuration information as text files.

/lib

This directory contains the library files. Library files contain the reusable functions and routines for the programmer to use.

/tmp

This directory contains all the temporary files, which will eventually be deleted from the system. This is similar to the "C:\windows\temp directory" file in Windows 98.

/usr

This directory contains the home directories of the users, source text for the online manual (man) pages, games and other directories. There is one home directory for each user. For example, for a user called mini, there will be a directory with the same name in the usr directory. The directory mini will contain all the files and sub-directories created by the user `mini'.

/kernel

This directory contains all the kernel specific code. Kernel is the heart of the Linux system. It is responsible for resource allocation, security and low-level hardware interfaces.

/mnt

This is the directory where the storage devices other than hard disks (floppy disks and CD disks) are mounted. This directory contains the sub-directories `floppy' and `cdrom', which, when these devices are mounted, show the contents of the CD-ROM or floppy disk respectively.

Linux transparently supports many different file systems, such as MSDOS, MINIX, VFAT, PROC, ISO9660, EXT2, and so on. Transparently, it means all of the mounted file systems and files appear as a single hierarchical virtual file system to the user. Users need not know what type of file or file system they are using. The files in floppy disks, compact disks, and so on all form part of this virtual file system.

Commands

A Linux command is a series of characters that you type. These characters consist of words which are separated by white spaces. The first word is the command itself and the rest are the command's arguments. These arguments provide information that the command may need for its execution. Linux commands are case-sensitive. That is, cp is different from CP and cP.

You must type all Linux commands in lowercase letters.

Commands are issued to the shell at the command line. A command line comprises of commands, the line of instructions, options and any command-line arguments that you may provide. For example, the following is a command line:

```
$ man cp
```

Commands are entered at the shell prompt ($, #). Prompt is merely a symbol that appears at the start of a command line. This lets the operator know that Linux is ready and waiting for your command.

Device Drivers

Device drivers are software packages that form a major part of the kernel. They control the interaction between the hardware devices and the operating system.

Utilities

Utilities are software tools that are included with the Linux operating system and lets you do miscellaneous jobs such as text editing, programming and communications.

File Handling in Linux

Each directory or file in Linux is referred to by using its pathname, beginning from the root directory. For example, the usr directory is referred to as /usr (/ or root is its parent directory); mini is referred to as /usr/mini, where usr is the parent directory of mini directory.

There are two types of pathnames. These are:

- Absolute Pathname
- Relative Pathname

An absolute pathname tells you the complete path of a directory starting from the root, as explained above. Root is represented by a forward slash (/). For example, absolute pathname of the "Delhi" directory is /usr/mini/sales/north/Delhi.

Relative pathname gives location of a directory, relative to the current working directory. For example, suppose your current working directory is /usr/mini/sales/north. Then the relative pathname to the `Delhi' directory is Delhi. Relative pathnames do not start with a `/'.

If you do not start a pathname with `/', Linux assumes that you are using a relative pathname.

Identifying the Current Working Directory

To find out which directory you are currently working in, type the following command:

`$ pwd Enter`

The **pwd** command prints the absolute pathname of your current working directory. It takes no arguments. For example, in *Figure A.1*, the user "mini" got the result as /usr/mini.

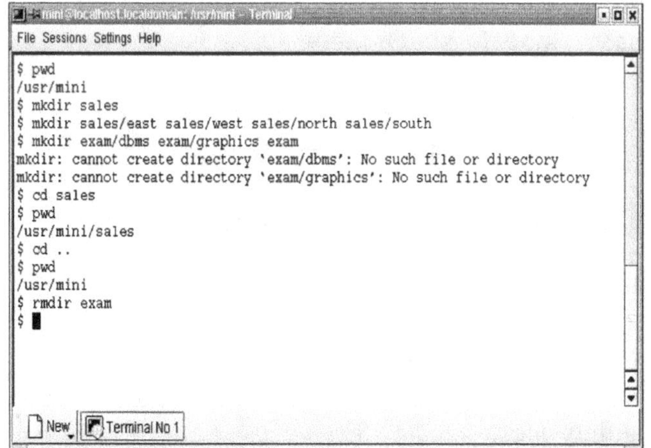

Figure 1.2: *Sample Linux session using commands*

Change Directory

The 'Cd' stands for change directory and this command is used to change the current directory, that is, the directory in which the user is currently working. With the help of this command, you can move all your directories in your system. You can go to your previous directory or previous to previous directory.

Syntax:

`Cd<dirname>`

Cd options

Option	Description
cd ~	Brings you to your home directory.
cd -	Brings you to your previous directory of the current directory.
cd..	Brings you to parent directory of current directory.
cd /	It takes you to the entire system's root directory.
Cd ../ ../dir1/dir2	It will take you two directories up, then move to dir1 and then to dir2.

Making New Directories (mkdir)

To create a new directory, use the **mkdir** command followed by the directory name. For example, suppose user mini (who is currently in the home directory /usr/mini) wants to create a directory named `sales', she should give the following command (see *Figure A.1*):

`$ mkdir sales Enter`

The `sales' sub-directory is created under the current directory (that is, /usr/mini).

To create a number of directories with one **mkdir** command, separate the directory names with spaces. For example, the following command creates various directories (see *Figure 3.40*):

$ mkdir sales/east sales/west sales/north sales/south Enter

The above command will create four directories under the sales directory.

The order of specifying the arguments is important.

Note that we cannot create a sub-directory before creating its parent directory.

If we enter the command as:

$ mkdir exam/dbms exam/graphics exam Enter

Then, in this case, the system will fail to create the two sub-directories dbms and graphics, but it will create the exam directory.

Moving to a Different Directory (cd)

You can change your working directory using the cd command followed by the pathname (absolute or relative) to which you want to move.

For example, to move to the sales directory, type the following command:

$ cd sales Enter

Note that in the above command, we have made use of the relative pathname. After giving the above command, if you give the pwd command, you will see the result as **/usr/mini/sales** (See *Figure A.1*).

The cd command without any following pathname always takes the user back to the user's HOME directory.

Linux uses a single dot (.) to represent the current working directory and double dots (..) to represent the parent directory of the current working directory. For example, typing cd.. will take user `mini' to her HOME directory (/usr/mini), since that is the parent directory of sales.

Removing a Directory (rmdir)

The **rmdir** command is used for deleting a directory. The directory to be deleted must be empty for this command to work. For example, to remove the "exam" directory, type the following command (see Figure 1.2):

```
$ rmdir exam Enter
```

We can also delete more than one directory by separating the multiple directory names with spaces:

You cannot remove a directory if you are placed in one of its sub-directories.

Listing the Contents of Directories (ls)

To list the files and sub-directories of the current directory, ls command is used. Its function is equivalent to the DIR command of DOS. For example, to list the contents of her current directory, user `mini' should type the following:

```
$ ls
```

She will get the following result:

```
east
north
south
west
```

The order of display is numerals uppercase characters lowercase characters. That is, the list is displayed with numerals having precedence over alphabets and in alphabets, uppercase has precedence over lowercase.

If the names of files and directories under a specified directory (say north) are to be listed out, then we need to specify the directory name with the ls command, as follows:

```
$ ls north
```

The above command will give the result as shown in *Figure 3.41*.

Usually, a directory contains many files, and a user may be interested in knowing whether a particular file is available or not. In that case, he/she just has to use ls with the filename, as follows:

```
$ ls March
```

The above command will prompt- **File Not Found** error, since there is no file called `March' in our current directory. Had the file existed, **ls** would have displayed the filename.

The ls command can be used along with a number of options. Options are nothing but predetermined arguments used along with a minus sign (-). The different options forces the command to work differently.

For example, the following command will display file and directory names in multiple columns.

```
$ ls -x
east   north south west
$ ls -1
```

The purpose of -1 is that along with file and directory names, it will display names of hidden files also.

```
$ ps
```

It will display information about a selection of active process.

```
$ kill all
```

It sends a signal to all processes running any of the specified commands.

Table 3.1 given below lists the different options of ls and its uses.

Ls option	Description
Ls –a	Hidden files start with . (dot) symbols and they are not visible in the directory
Ls –l	It will show the list in a long list format
Ls –d */	It is used to display only sub-directories
Ls –p	It is used to identify the directory easily by making the directories with a slash (/) line sign
Ls ~	It gives the contents of home directory
Ls ../	It gives the content of parent directory
Ls –R	It will display the content of the sub-directories
Ls –r	Lists files and sub-directories in reverse order
Ls –t	Lists files and sub-directories in time order
Ls –A	List all files excluding , and ..

Table 3.1 Options of the command ls

Creating Files (using cat)

To create a file, type the command cat at the shell prompt, followed by > character and the filename. For example, to create a file called January, enter the following command:

```
$ cat > January Enter
```

After you press the Enter key, you will be prompted to enter the contents of the file. Type the data and press the *Ctrl + D* keys together to terminate the command line (see *Figure 1.3*).

Listing the Contents of Files (cat)

To list the contents of a file, use the cat command followed by the filename. DOS has the TYPE command for this.

For example, to list the contents of file January, type the following:

```
$ cat January Enter
```

Absolute pathname can be given to display a file in another directory. The cat command can also display more than one file by separating different filenames with spaces, as shown in the following command:

```
$ cat January February Enter
```

The above command will display the contents of the two files in different rows. Use of the cat method to create and display the contents of files is shown in *Figure A.2*.

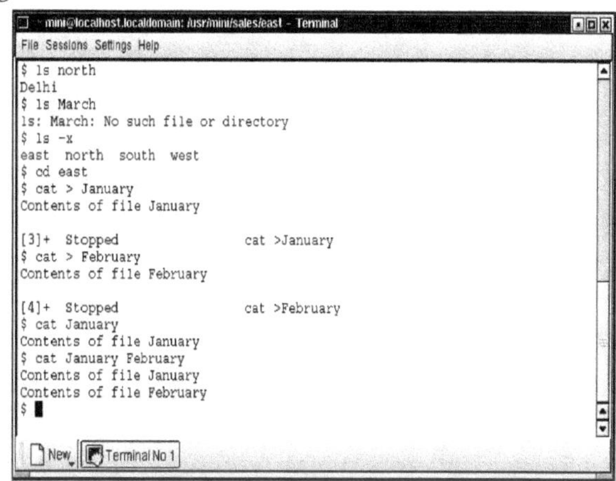

Figure A.2: *A sample Linux using ls and cat commands*

Copying Files (cp)

The cp command is used to copy a file into another. DOS equivalent for cp is the COPY command. Like in DOS, the cp command requires two arguments: a source filename, the contents of which are to be copied, and a target filename, to which the contents are to be copied.

For example, to copy the February file into another file, say March, type the following (see *Figure A.3*):

```
$ cp January March Enter
```

Note that the **ls** command will now show three files, namely January, February and March.

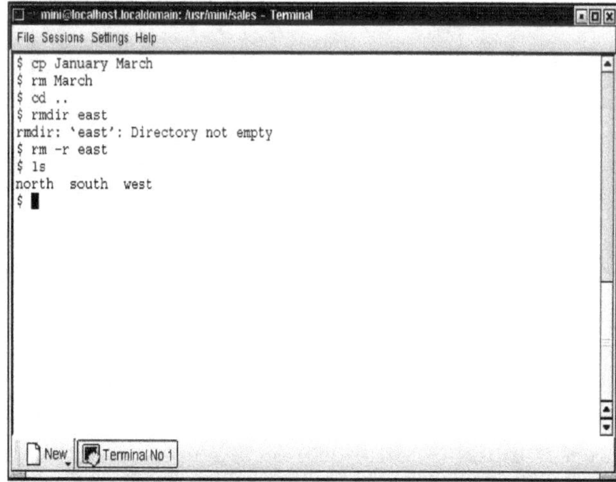

Figure 1.3 *A sample Linux session using cp and rm commands*

Use cp with the -i option if you want the system to ask for confirmation before copying the files.

Here, the January file is copied to a new file called March.

If the March file already exists, its contents will be destroyed and replaced by contents of the January file.

If you want to give more than one option along with a command, you can use either of the following:

```
$ ls -l -a -t
$ ls -lat
```

Both the above commands will work.

Deleting Files (rm)

To delete or remove a file, the rm command is used. This is equivalent to the DEL command in DOS.

For example, to remove the March file, type the following command:

$ rm March*

This is shown in *Figure 1.4.*

Use rm with the -i option if you want the system to ask for confirmation, like in cp.

To remove a directory, use **rm** with the **-r** option. Here **-r** stands for recursive deletion. For example, the following command will remove the directory accounts:

```
$ rm -r accounts*
```

Unlike **rmdir, rm -r** will remove directories even if they are not empty.

In *Figure A.3*, the system did not delete the `east' directory when the **rmdir** command was given, but did so with the rm -r command.

Moving Files (mv)

A file can be moved using the mv command. Equivalent command in DOS is MOVE. The following command will displace the north directory from the `sales' directory to the `/usr/mini' directory:

```
$ mv north /usr/mini/north Enter
```

The above command does not create a copy of `north' but displaces it.

Now, if you type the **ls** command, you will only see two directories, south and west (see *Figure A.4)*. The **east** directory was removed using the **rm -r** command and `north' is moved to a different directory. The `/usr/mini' directory now contains the north directory and all its sub-directories and files, as shown by the **ls** command in *Figure 1.5.*

Perform the mv operation again to bring back the directory.

```
$ mv /usr/mini/north .
```

Note that the dot (.) represents the current directory.

Files and directory can also be renamed using the mv command. For example, the following command will rename the `west' directory as `bombay' (see *Figure A.4*):

```
$ mv west Bombay Enter
```

Files can also be renamed in the same way. If the destination exists, it will be overwritten and if it does not exist, it will be created.

mv also has the -i option like the **cp** and **rm** commands and works in the same way.

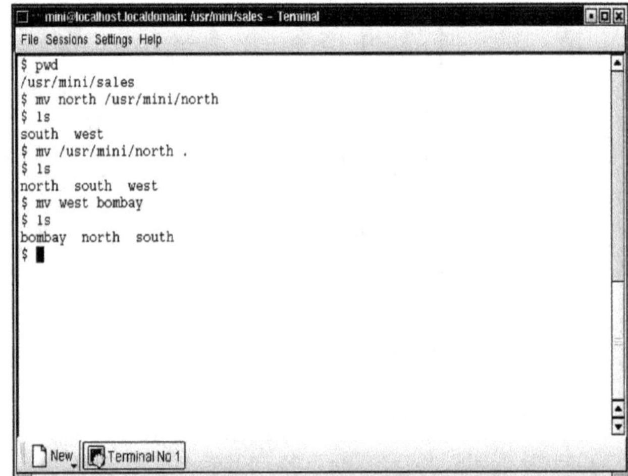

Figure 1.5 *A sample Linux session using commands all discussed till now*

Using Wildcards (* and ?)

The characters * and ? function in exactly the same way in Linux as they do in DOS. The * character matches any number of characters (that is, 0 to *). The ? character matches a single character. Often, you may be required to enter a number of filenames in the command line. If the files follow some common pattern, you can make use of these wildcards. For example, look at the following command:

$ rm uni

When the * character is appended to the "uni" string, it matches all files whose names start with "uni" followed by any number of characters (including the file named just "uni"). That is, all such files will get removed by a single command.

Now, look at the following command:

```
$ ls -x uni??
```

The above command will list all those files that contain five characters in their filename, the first three characters being "uni".

Security Permissions in Linux

Typically, users on a Linux system are open with the files. The usual set of permissions given to files is **rw-r--r--**, which lets other users read the file but not change it in any way. The usual set of permissions given to directories is **rwxr-xr-x,** which lets other users look through your directories, but not create or delete files within them.

However, many users wish to keep other users out of their files. Setting the permissions of a file to rw------ will prevent any other user from accessing the file. Likewise, setting the permissions of a directory to **rwx------** will keep other users out of the directory in question.

In order to change the default permissions and set your own, the **chmod** command is used. Only the owner of a file can change the permission on that file. That is, only the user who owns the file can execute the **chmod** command. The syntax of **chmod** is:

chmod category operation permission filename(s)

The argument category specifies the user's class. The argument operation specifies whether the permission is to be granted or denied. The argument permission specifies the type of permission.

In the first argument, you supply one or more of **a** (all), **u** (owner), **g** (group) and **o** (others). Then, you specify whether you are adding rights (+) or taking them away (-). Finally, you specify one or more of **r** (read), **w** (write) and **x** (execute) permissions.

Installation of Linux

We will be discussing the installation of the popular Red Hat Linux 7.2 in this section. Before listing the procedures to follow for installing the Linux operating system, let us see what the hardware and software requirements of Linux are:

Hardware Requirements

Red Hat Linux can be installed if the following basic hardware requirements are met:

- x86 platform namely 80386, 80486, and so on

- Intel, Sparc, Alpha or AMD processor
- x386 CPU family or above
- Minimum 128 MB RAM
- Minimum 2 GB free hard disk space
- Input devices such as keyboard, mouse, and so on
- Controller cards such as SCSI, IDE, Firewire, and so on
- A Network card such as ISA, PCI or USB, and so on
- Sound card compatible to LINUX

Software Requirements

Software requirements for Linux installation are listed as follows:

- A partitioning program such as fdisk or disk druid supplied by Red Hat.
- Linux Software package.

Preliminary Steps before Installation

The first step is to create an installation disk.

To create the installation disk, do this:

1. Copy the `**boot.img**' file from the Red Hat CD-ROM disk into a floppy disk. This file can be found in the **/images** directory of the CD. The file can be created using either the DOS rewrite command (in a DOS/WINDOWS system) or the Linux **dd** command (in an existing Linux or UNIX system). For example, to create an installation diskette using the **dd** command, follow the below-mentioned steps.

   a. Insert and mount the CD-ROM and then insert a blank floppy into the floppy drive of your computer.

   b. Now, give the following commands:

   ```
   # dd  if=mnt/cdrom/images/boot.
   img
   of=/dev/fd0 bs=1440k Enter
   ```

The above command will copy from the input file ("if") mnt/cdrom/boot.img onto the output file ("of") /dev/fd0. It is assumed that the floppy drive is accessible from /dev/fd0.

To create an installation diskette using the rawrite program, give the following command (it is assumed that CD-ROM is accessible as drive D):

```
D:>cd images dosutils\rawrite Enter
```

For the source file, enter "D:\boot.img", and for destination, enter "A:".

The bootable installation disk is now ready and you can use it to install your Linux system.

Red Hat Linux can also be installed by booting, using any of the following methods:

- Booting using a floppy diskette (created as explained above)
- Booting directly from the CD-ROM (your BIOS should support this)
- Using a hard drive partition to hold the installation software
- Booting from a DOS command line
- Booting from across a network using HTTP or FTP protocols
- Booting from an NFS (Network File System) mounted hard drive

2. The next step is to plan a partitioning strategy. This step is based on the knowledge of existing hardware. The planning process should also take into consideration the future expansion of the system. Knowing how to allocate the hard disk space for each of the Linux software is a real big challenge every Linux system administrator has to take. He should find answers to the following questions:

   a. How much of the disk is required presently and in future?

   b. Is any other operating system also required?

   c. How many application software packages are expected to be installed in the future?

   d. How much data needs to be backed up?

   e. How many users will the system have?

3. If you require that the system should boot any other operating system also along with Linux, the next step is to choose a boot loader. Boot loader is a software that is responsible for booting Linux along with any other operating systems. Examples include **Linux Loader (LILO)** and **Grand Unified Boot loader (GRUB)**.

4. Now, insert the floppy disk (the installation diskette you have created if you are using floppy to boot your system) into a floppy drive and turn on your system. After a few moments, the Red Hat installation program screen will appear.

Hard Drive Partitioning

A hard disk must be partitioned taking into consideration the present and future requirements. For example, let us consider that we have a given hard disk of 40 GB capacity. The different partitions can be as follows:

- **/swap directory:** About double the main memory size. For example, a system having 128 MB memory should get 256 MB swap space.
- **/ directory (root):** About 60% of the available space.
- **/bin directory:** About 20% of the available space.
- **/usr directory:** Remaining space.

The size of /usr should be the largest one. This is because all the users' directories and files, installed application software, web pages, log files, and so on, will be stored here.

Booting a LINUX system

The general booting procedure involves checking of the basic sub-systems of your computer, such as amount and validity of RAM, CPU time and speed, presence of floppy, CD-ROM or hard drive and keyboard and other attributes. The Linux may fail to boot if it detects a hardware failure, missing hardware or hardware misconfiguration.

Next, the BIOS will look for the bootable disk in the order given in the settings (such as search floppy first, then CD-ROM and then the hard drive). Following this, it will look for the boot code in the **Master Boot Record (MBR)** of the first hard disk. This area of the disk (MBR) contains the boot sector, which loads the boot loader (that is, LILO, GRUB or BootMagic).

When the LINUX kernel is loaded, the kernel will carry out the following:

1. Initialize and load a RAM disk image.
2. Perform timing tests.
3. Parse for any boot time kernel arguments.
4. Recognize, setup and initialize the CPU.
5. Set up kernel memory and process handling.
6. Open a console for displaying kernel boot messages.
7. Initialize configured system devices.
8. Start memory handling (paging, and so on)
9. Set up and mount the file system.
10. Start the **init** command.

The entire sequence of events that takes place when the Linux kernel is loaded can be found in the `usr/src/linux/init/main.c` file.

If all goes well, you will see a **login** prompt. You can now login using your username and password.